D0555292

HISTORY OF THE ISLAMIC PEOPLES

History of the Islamic Peoples

BY CARL BROCKELMANN

Translated by Joel Carmichael and Moshe Perlmann

ILLUSTRATED WITH 8 MAPS

ROUTLEDGE & KEGAN PAUL
London and Henley

First published in Great Britain in 1948
by Routledge & Kegan Paul Ltd
39 Store Street, London WC1E 7DD and
Broadway House, Newtown Road
Henley-on-Thames, Oxon RG9 1EN
Printed in Great Britain by
The Thetford Press Ltd
Thetford, Norfolk
Reprinted in 1949, 1951, 1955, 1957, 1963, 1979 and 1982

ISBN 0 7100 1118 0

From the Preface to the German Edition

IT IS still a very risky undertaking to write a history of the Islamic peoples and states from the beginnings down to the present, since the sources for such an account are far from having been made accessible, to say nothing of having been subjected to critical analysis. No individual can dare to solve this problem. But it appears desirable to offer to those interested in questions of world politics a bird's-eye view of the fortunes of the believers in Islam, which today are interwoven more intimately than ever with world events in general, and can only be presented in a fragmentary form in works of reference and general world histories.

In addition to a political history I have also attempted to give a sketch of culture and intellectual life in so far as permitted by the narrow framework at my disposal.

The map-sketches cannot, of course, replace a historical atlas for Islamic history, of which we are still in need; they are intended to give the reader only the outlines of the terrain on which this history unfolded. The bibliography indicates only the most important new accounts; here and there individual studies are mentioned directly at the foot of the page. I scarcely need tell my professional colleagues that in this book they need not expect an exhaustive bibliography of Islamic history. They will in any case perceive without difficulty to what scholars I am indebted in detail; nevertheless I should not wish to omit special mention of the works of J. Wellhausen and L. Caetani for the history of the Arabs, those of W. Barthold and V. Minorsky for Central Asia, and those of P. Wittek for the Ottoman Empire.

Translators' Note

THE author's preface to the German original of this book is dated March 1939. The translation offered here was prepared during the war and the author could not supervise it. Certain corrections were made, sometimes on the basis of reviews of the book. Just before the final proofreading, the author was reached, and a few changes forwarded by him have been incorporated.

In the transliteration of oriental words and names an effort was made to be as exact as possible without the use of special marks. Inconsistencies, though, could hardly be avoided in the mass of Arabic, Persian, Berber, and Turkish nomenclature thrown together in these pages. In some cases elucidation will be found in the indexes with their numerous cross references.

A brief sketch of events since 1939 has been added and the bibliography was enlarged, especially with reference to works available in English.

There are a few notes by us, in brackets.

J. C.
M. P.

March, 1947

Contents

Maps

1. The Arabs and the Arab Empire

1. *Arabia before Islam*

ARABIA, the "island of the Arabs" as it is called by its own inhabitants, is a primary geological formation of southwest Asia about a million square miles in extent. As early as the Jurassic epoch the deep Indian Ocean and the Persian Gulf cut it off from India and Persia, whose mountainous conformation is still retained in the coastal region of 'Uman. In the Tertiary period, Arabia was divided from North Africa by the irruption of the Red Sea, which elevated the western mountain chain of the Sarat, in which Jabal Nabi Shu'ayb, west of the Yemenite capital of San'a in the south, rises to a height of more than 12,300 feet. Stretched out before this range lies the coastal plain of the Tihamah, about 30 miles wide; its northern part together with the mountain country is called the Hijaz. The mountain chain around the coast is partially crisscrossed by volcanoes now extinct, the source of the broad lava layers of the Harrah. Toward the east the chain casts out two spurs into the plains north of Medina, the mountain ranges Aja and Salma, now called Jabal Shammar. They divide the Syrian desert, which stretches as far as the swamplands of the Tigris and Euphrates in the east and the Syro-Palestinian limestone tableland in the west, together with its southern offshoot, the Nufud, from the central plateau of the Najd, the great desert tableland of primordial rock overlain by sandstone which slopes down into the Persian Gulf in the east. This is separated from the mountainous ridges of the southeastern coastal territory of 'Uman by a great sandy waste, the Rub' al-Khali, or "Empty Quarter," as it is called, which was crossed for the first time in February 1931 by Bertram Thomas and in January-March 1932 by St. John Philby.

Only a few watered valleys, wadis, of which Wadi Sirhan in the north and Wadi Rummah and Wadi Dawasir in the south are the most important, cut across the steppe; in the rainy season these fill with water, which, though occasionally swelling for a short time into a tearing river, generally dries up quickly, giving at least a certain fertility, however, to its immediate surroundings. In a few cases (Tayma and Khaybar on the rim of the northwest lava regions are the best-known), a few subterranean pools of water are formed and emerge as deep wells on which palm plantations can subsist. In the Aflaj oasis Philby even found a lake 400 meters wide and 1¼ kilometers long. But these bodies of water may also prove harmful; the Yamamah region in the southern Najd, which was still flourishing in the time of the prophet Muhammad, was probably destroyed by a catastrophic flood.

Only in the south, where the monsoons empty their rain clouds on the slopes of the mountain range, is any profitable agriculture or horticulture possible, by painstaking husbanding of the water. The northern steppes, outside of the oases, can offer only a meager living to the nomads and their herds who follow after the sparse plant growth called forth by the rain. It is impossible to determine whether the climate of Arabia, as some have surmised, was any more favorable in historic times and has later succumbed to a progressive desiccation.

The inhabitants of the peninsula, the Arabs, are the principal representatives of what Eugen Fischer called the Oriental race, distinguished by a long head with narrow face, curved nose, and extreme protrusion of the occiput, as well as by a medium and invariably slender build. It is a variety of the Mediterranean race dominant in North Africa. In the north the Arabs intermingled with the Near Eastern race, which once prevailed in Asia Minor and in the west of the Iranian uplands as well and has been preserved in its purest form among the present-day Armenians, characterized by a steep occiput and a large curved nose. At one time this type must have been spread out farther toward the south, since from antiquity on, its distinguishing features are also to be met with among the Yemenite Arabs. From the third millennium B.C. on, swarms of peoples from the Arabian peninsula, under the pressure of particularly acute periods of drought, pushed into the north; in Mesopotamia, as Babylonians, they took over the culture of the Sumerians; as Canaanites, Hebrews, and Arameans in Syria, Palestine, and Phoenicia they borrowed that of the Near Eastern race, which also passed on to them some of its physical traits. Only their language, because of which we call them Semites, preserved its basic characteristics, akin to Arabic, though considerably modified.

In southern Arabia, where the climate was more favorable for agriculture, an advanced civilization based on agriculture and trade flourished as early as the second millennium B.C. Dams to secure the watercourses, fortified cities, castles and temples still bear witness today to the industry, public spirit, and piety of the builders. But so far as we can learn from the inscriptions, their intellectual life seems to have exhausted itself in a legal code which carefully regulated all property relationships. By the second millennium B.C. the Minaeans, one of the South Arabian tribes, had already extended their trading colonies far into the north. After them the Sabaeans created a kingdom which, based on powerful aristocratic families, prevented the emergence of any strong central power. Their successors, the Himyarites, lost the chief source of prosperity when part of their Indian trade was diverted to Egypt during the Hellenistic era, but in 24 B.C. they were still able to escape from the political influence of the Roman Empire, after Aelius Gallus's attempt to subject them to the dominion of Augustus had misfired. For a time Judaism gained such influence in their empire that the rulers themselves were converted and, like Dhu Nuwas (d. 525), persecuted Christianity, which was, however, able to hold its ground, particularly in Najran, until the beginnings of Islam. But it was through Abyssinia, once colonized by the ancestors of the Himyarites themselves, that their final decline was brought about. There Christianity had been victorious since the fourth century. In 530 A.D., no doubt upon the prodding of Byzantium, which desired to come to grips with its ancient adversary Persia also in the south, the Abyssinian governor Abraha conquered South Arabia and even pressed forward for an attack on Persia in the north, but failed to advance beyond Mecca. Forty years later, however, his son and second successor lost the country to a marshal of the Sassanid king Chosroes I (Nushirwan), and so South Arabia remained a Persian province until the incursion of the Muslims.

Social conditions in northern Arabia are determined by the desert, which makes up the bulk of the land.* Its sparse plant growth sup-

* See J. Wellhausen, *Ein Gemeinwesen ohne Obrigkeit,* Rede zur Feier des Geburtstages S. Majestät am 27. Januar 1900, Göttingen.

ports only small cattle and the camel, whose needs are satisfied with unusual ease and which provides the Arab with the basis of his food and clothing. Since this breed can only be cared for by migrations through widely extended regions, any political organization based on fixed dwelling places is impossible for the Bedouins. Blood relationship alone traces the orbit of their lives; it binds families into clans, and clans into tribes. Even the great tribal federations still trace their descent through an ostensible blood relationship, grouping the whole people together into a genealogical system like that of the ancient Hebrews. But this community feeling does not comprise the whole of the people; it extends from the clan of the most closely related families, who always set up their tents together, to take in the single tribe, a few thousand strong, which wanders and grazes together. Anyone venturing into the territory of a strange tribe does so at the risk of being killed and robbed by these strangers, who merely as such are his enemies. He is protected against this only if he succeeds in touching the clothing or the tent of an enemy, or in entering his dwelling place. This protection is also given to a traveler voluntarily; a member of the tribe may even adopt a stranger into his clan for good. In this way the tribe may assimilate whole communities, which at first are only tolerated as squatters, but after a few generations are granted all the rights of blood relationship.

The Bedouin is above all a purely egotistic individualist. "God have mercy on me and Muhammad, and on no one else besides," one tradition still permits an Arab convert to Islam to say in prayer. Within the tribe, however, all members have the same rights and duties, which flow out of the blood relationship. The Bedouin is obligated to stand by his brother in distress, and may not ask whether he is right or wrong. At first, to be sure, this duty falls on the clan involved, and only if its strength is inadequate does the entire tribe stand behind it. But this community, founded on general freedom and equality, nevertheless displays a number of tendencies toward the centralization of authority. The clans and tribes tolerate as leaders men who on the basis of their personal qualities and ability are voluntarily recognized as such. Even though this position may often be passed on from father to son, still the latter must always win it for himself again by independently proving his mettle. These leaders (sayyids) have no real *rights* at all, even though in the general councils there may be a greater inclination to listen to them than to the others. In contrast their duties are all the greater. In war they are expected to be ready at all times to sacrifice their lives, and in peace their possessions, on behalf of the tribe and of fellow tribesmen in need of help. But their chief concern is the maintenance of tribal unity, often imperiled by the self-seeking of the individual.

Property conflicts between members of the same tribe are settled in daily assemblies. In cases of dissension between members of different tribes a wise man or woman is turned to, often a priest or seer. Compliance with their decision, however, depends only on the good will of the disputants or on the superior strength of one of them. Since the leaders of the tribe themselves possess no executive power either, there is no criminal law, and each individual must have recourse to private justice against a thief or murderer of a kinsman. If someone murdered by an unknown hand is found in a clan's territory and if suspicion falls on one of its members, then the clan takes the oath of purification on his behalf, but the effect of this may be neutralized by the victim's clan by means of a new oath. The duty of avenging the murder falls on the victim's next of kin. But since the culprit's clan generally takes his side, the blood vengeance gives rise to the blood feud, which often drags on for generations in renewed assassinations. It is true that blood guilt can be atoned for by payment in camels also, and it is up to the leaders within the tribe to see to it that a compromise is reached, which, to be sure, they can only hand down, not enjoin. But for the most part the clans come to this decision only after having exhausted themselves in protracted feuding. The blood feud is avoided whenever the murderer is voluntarily delivered up to the injured parties for vengeance to be executed, but this passes as something so dishonorable that the clan is more likely to decide to kill him itself first. The high sense of honor which determines all the actions of the Bedouin is the basis of his morality.

It was substantially this desert law that was still in force also in the cities of the Hijaz: Taif, Mecca, and Medina. Like the Bedouins in their tents, the individual clans here also were free and independent in their quarters, submitting to orders from no one. In Mecca,* to be sure, the feeling of honor, sometimes exaggeratedly sensitive in the desert, was softened a little by a common interest in the holy

* See H. Lammens, *La République marchandise de la Mecque vers l'an 600 de notre ère, Bull. de l'Inst. Egypt.* 5 série, t. 4, p. 23-54; *La Mecque à la veille de l'Hégire, Mélanges de la Faculté Orientale de Beyrouth,* 1924; *La cité arabe de Taif à la veille de l'hégire,* 1922.

Ka'bah and the trade dependent on its prosperity; since everyone participated in this, economic relationships were more complex and the preponderance of the prosperous clans over the poor ones was greater than in the desert. But in Medina, where agriculture and palm growing were the chief sources of livelihood, conditions were even more primitive. It is precisely at the beginning of the Islamic era that blood feuds had become so numerous that hardly anyone could leave his fortified grounds without risk.*

In the north, in the Syrian desert, the Arabs were involved in world politics very much earlier.† Even under the Assyrian king Tiglath-Pileser III (745-728 B.C.) there was an Aribi kingdom there with its capital in the Jawf, which was ruled by queens and remained one of the vassal states of Assyria until the time of Esarhaddon (681-669 B.C.). The Babylonian king Nabunaid (556-539 B.C.) had his residence for some time in the oasis of Tayma, which was the base of his expeditions against the west. An Aramaic inscription from the Persian era found there indicates the organization of the city cult, with its priests and temple gods. As early as the period of the last Achaemenians the Nabatean state sprang up; during the Hellenistic period it controlled the caravan trade from South Arabia to Medina. It remained independent, since Alexander the Great's last project, of conquering Arabia by sea from the east and west simultaneously, was not resumed by his successors. The Nabatean capital was Petra, a mountain fortress lying about halfway between the Dead Sea and the tip of the Arabian Gulf; today important ruins and numerous inscriptions on its rock-cut tombs still bear witness to its flourishing civilization. For these inscriptions the Nabateans used Aramaic, which even under the Achaemenians had been made an official language; they took the titles of their officials and military leaders from the neighboring Hellenistic states. The Romans allowed them their independence as allies until the time of Trajan; but since they had already displayed an ambiguous attitude during the Jewish insurrection under Titus, their kingdom was absorbed in 106 and made into Provincia Arabia. The civilized areas were marked off from the desert by a chain of fortifications, which were, however, far from being as strong as the Limes on the

* See J. Wellhausen, *Medina vor dem Islam, Skizzen und Vorarbeiten, 4. Heft, I*, Berlin, 1889.

† See H. Dussaud, *Les Arabes en Syrie avant l'islamisme*, Paris, 1907.

Rhine and on the Danube frontier.* At first Petra's commerce was drawn to Bostra, whence caravans proceeded to Chalcis, below the Lebanon, and Emesa, Edessa, and Hatra toward the north and east.

The Nabateans found a more fortunate heir in Palmyra, which was also ruled by Arabs, though the strongly Hellenized Arameans constituted the majority of its inhabitants. In the wars between Rome and the Parthians it was strengthened by a prudent neutrality, and by the time of Augustus was able to extend its trade connections as far as Rome, Dacia, Gaul, and Spain. It was shown special favor at this time by the Severian dynasty, half Semitic itself. Under the emperor Alexander Severus the dynasty of the Julii Aurelii Septimii grew powerful there. From 260 on, successful wars against the Persians had enabled King Odenat to extend his rule over the whole of Syria; he was even acknowledged by the weak Roman emperor Gallienus as co-emperor for the Orient. After his death in 268 his wife, Zenobia, maintained his power for a time, until Aurelianus destroyed Palmyra in 273. Her tragic fate must have made a deep impression on the desert Arabs. In the first centuries of Islam the saga of Queen Zaynab, by this time retaining only a very loose connection with historical events, was still being related.

After this there were no more independent Arab states in the north. The Romans and their successors, the Byzantines, were always able to gain Arabs as vassals on the border of the wilderness and with their help ward off the incursions of the nomads into the settled regions. In the sixth century we find the Ghassanid dynasty at Damascus in this position, as rulers of the country east of the Jordan. The most famous prince of this house, al-Harith V, was designated by Justinian in 529 as *patricius* and phylarch and entrusted with supreme authority over all the Arabs in northern Syria. After his death the power which had been united in his hands once again dissolved into fragmentary principalities, and after their victory over the Persians the East Roman emperors allowed the country to be ruled by its own officials. It is not until the Muslim onslaught that another Ghassanid is encountered as supreme ruler of the Syrian Arabs.†

The same policy toward the Arabs as that of the Romans was

* Significantly, the few Latin loan words in Arabic all stem from the military: *strata* (our "street") is *sirat; castra* is *qasr* (whence Sp. Alcazar), and *palatium* (G. *Pfalz*) is *balad*, i.e., locality.

† Th. Nöldeke, *Die Ghassanischen Fürsten aus dem Hause Gafnas, Abh. der Akademie der Wissenschaften*, Berlin, 1887.

practiced by their hereditary enemies, the Persians. Shapur I (241-272) himself is supposed to have designated 'Amr ibn-'Adi from the Lakhmid house as king of the Babylonian Arabs. But around 328 Imru'u-l-Qays, 'Amr's son, is apparently indicated as vassal of the Romans in the inscription on his tombstone, found at Nemarah, southeast of Damascus. His successors, as Persian satraps, had their seat at Hirah, about ten miles south of the ruins of Babylon. They were generally at war with the Ghassanids, whose king Mundhir conquered Hirah around 575 and destroyed it. Their subjects had already professed Nestorian Christianity for some time, whereas they themselves clung strongly to their pagan beliefs. Only the last ruler of this house, Nu'man III (580-602), went over to Christianity, at least outwardly. Since on several occasions the Persians had found him refractory, Chosroes II lured him to his residence at Ctesiphon and had him removed. The consequences were not long in appearing. In 610 three thousand Arabs attacked the Euphrates area and decisively defeated the Persians at Dhu Qar. The absence of a strong border watch also facilitated the Muslim conquest of the country later on.

The religion of the Arabs, as well as their political life, was on a thoroughly primitive level.* Like so many other peoples of low culture, the Arabs also believed that their natural surroundings were charged with forces superior to those of man, but which appropriate means could compel to serve him. On a somewhat higher plane these forces were represented as being like the human soul, but gifted with dangerous power; they became demons. In particular the Semites regarded trees, caves, springs, and large stones as being inhabited by spirits; like the Black Stone of Islam in a corner of the Ka'bah at Mecca, in Petra and other places in Arabia stones were venerated also. But these demons were accorded reverence only after they revealed their names to mankind, as Yahweh did to Jacob in his dream at Beth-El. It was only after the name of a demon was known that it was possible to appeal to him effectively. Through the ritual, at the core of which there lay the sacrifice, the gods entered into a blood tie with the worshiping tribe; they became its patron and often its ancestral lord, so that their original nature becomes very indistinct. Every tribe worshiped its own god, but also recognized the power of other tribal gods in their own sphere. Among the Arabs, in any case, the bond between a tribe and its god

* See J. Wellhausen, *Reste arabsichen Heidentums*, 2. ed., Berlin, 1897.

was not so intimate as that in Israel, for instance, between Yahweh and his people. Individual clans sometimes named themselves after other gods than those of the tribe, and the same divinity was worshiped by various tribes. The gods had fixed abodes, in which, after the tribe departed, they enjoyed the worship of its successors; the tribe returned to them once or twice a year on holidays.

Certain holy places exercised a special attraction. Various tribes would make a pilgrimage to ‘Ukaz, for instance, and to Mecca, often from a great distance. On festival days the Lord's Truce reigned in the wilderness. Fairs and market days became associated with the religious ceremony, and led to an exchange not only of wares but of spiritual goods as well. It was to a large extent to these fairs, and so indirectly to religion, that the Arabs owed the possession of a common world outlook, common customs and obligatory notions of honor, as well as their poetic expression in the established forms of a language transcending all dialects.

Three goddesses in particular had elevated themselves above the circle of the inferior demons. The goddess of fate, al-Manat, corresponding to the Tyche Soteira of the Greeks, though known in Mecca, was worshiped chiefly among the neighboring Bedouin tribes of the Hudhayl. Allat—"the Goddess," who in Taif was called ar-Rabbah, "the Lady," and whom Herodotus equates with Urania —corresponded to the great mother of the gods, Astarte of the northern Semites; al-‘Uzza, "the Mightiest," worshiped in the planet Venus, was merely a variant form.

In addition to all these gods and goddesses the Arabs, like many other primitive peoples, believed in a God who was creator of the world, Allah, whom the Arabs did not, as has often been thought, owe to the Jews and Christians. At first, to be sure, the ritual bond applied only to those gods who were closer to the Arabs than Allah, the great god of the worlds, but on the eve of Islamic times this cult no longer filled, as it did among primitive men, the entire religious consciousness of the Arabs. The more the significance of the cult declined, the greater became the value of a general religious temper associated with Allah. Among the Meccans he was already coming to take the place of the old moon-god Hubal as the lord of the Ka‘bah; because of this a Christian poet in Hirah, ‘Adi ibn-Zayd, could unhesitatingly call on him next to the Messiah as witness to an oath. Allah was actually the guardian of contracts, though at first these were still settled at a special ritual locality and so subordinate to the supervision of an idol. In particular he was regarded as the guardian of the alien guest, though consideration for him still lagged behind duty to one's kinsmen. Immutably ordained fate was regarded as his will. This belief in fate did not have an enfeebling effect on the Arab, but merely spurred him on to attain his goal without help from above. But together with this there was often manifested a recognition of the triviality of all earthly endeavor, as in the famous verses of the poet-king Imru'u-l-Qays (who exhausted himself in an endless series of adventures subsidized by Byzantium in a vain attempt to revive the rule of his house, the Kindah, established by his grandfather for a short time among the tribes of northern Arabia): "Are we not subject to a blind Fate and allow ourselves to be deceived by food and drink? We are birds, flies and worms, and yet bolder than ravening wolves. The roots of my nobility reach deep into the earth, but Death robs me of my youth, my body and my life and soon brings me to dust. How can I hope for compassion from Fate, which spares not the solid mountains, since I know it will shortly clutch me in its talons, as it dealt with my father Hujr and my grandfather?"

This inner disintegration of paganism was still further accelerated by the influence of the monotheistic religions which for a long time had been finding adherents in Arabia. In South Arabia, as mentioned above, the influence of Judaism became so powerful for a time that native rulers were converted to it and persecuted the Christians engaged in struggling against it. In the oases in the northwest, in Tayma, Khaybar, Yathrib, and Fadak, Jews had been immigrating since the first century A.D. and had become rich; they dwelt in isolated communities, but had undoubtedly already converted some Arabs and assimilated them. Their language conformed entirely to that of the population. Although indispensable as farmers, traders, and goldsmiths, they were nevertheless mistrusted by the Bedouins and could scarcely have exerted a more profound religious influence on them.

Christianity approached the Arabs, extremely sensitive to external impressions, in quite a different way. All the Bedouins in the north were in intimate contact with the indigenous Aramean population, whose civilization had long since been swallowed up by Christianity. In the Roman Empire Christianity exercised a great power of attraction simply as the state religion, but even the Lakhmid dynasty in Hirah in the service of the Persians had finally gone over to the Christian faith of their urban subjects. Inner Arabia also, especially the trading cities of the Hijaz, must have been permeated by a knowledge of Christian teachings and customs, however superficial, as a result of the steady traffic with related tribes in the north. The anchorites, whose cells must have spread from Palestine and the Sinai peninsula far into the desert, no doubt also made a great many contributions. In addition, the desert was an asylum for some sects persecuted by the established church, and precisely these may often have spread their doctrines with more success than the orthodox state church.

As mentioned above, the Arabs owed their awareness of constituting a people, in spite of all tribal contradictions, principally to their most important common spiritual possession, their poetry, which to a certain extent evolved and expanded under the auspices of religion. Poetry had probably already been associated with religion since its earliest beginnings. No doubt its primary impulse lay in the play instinct, in the pleasure in sound and rhythm, which helped primitive man endure the burdens of life; among the nomads the first little melodies may have arisen on the march. But at the same time the word, solemnly spoken, gave primitive man a guarantee of attaining any desired effect by nothing more than his own powers; in this way the ancient art of speech simultaneously served magic, which on this cultural level was not yet hostilely counterposed to religion. In war particularly, the duty of cursing the enemy fell to whoever had power over the right word, as Balak demanded of Balaam. The malediction, when faith in its magical power waned, evolved into the satirical poem, passing from relations between the tribes into the sphere of personalities, where as a feared weapon it finally degenerated into a source of income for the poet unafraid of blackmail. Sexual love in Arab poetry, as among most primitive peoples, also played only a subordinate role. In the only artistic poetry known to us it served the poet merely as an overture to his real theme, the glorification of his own person or of his tribe, and among professional bards the eulogy of a patron. The form of these tendentious poems (*qasidah*s, as they were called) had been established for a long time. The qasidah began with the expression of a yearning for vanished happiness in love; but before the poet touched on his real object, he first had to regale his audience with descriptions of nature. In the description of the desert and its characteristic animals, such as the camel, with which their lives were bound up, the Arabs produced remarkable work. But these portrayals were not based on personal observation either, but expressed in forms handed down from of old. Accordingly, this art did not afford the singer much occasion to display his own personality. Only the sharpest contrasts are set off against each other: the wandering poet-king Imru'u-l-Qays, whose ancestors, of the princely South Arab Kindah clan, had united the most powerful Bedouin tribes in the north at the turn of the sixth century for devastating raids into the Roman and Persian empires, and who wore himself out in the attempt to regain this position for his house until he was finally poisoned as guest of the Byzantine emperor at Ancyra in Asia Minor; Zuhayr, the poet of distilled worldly wisdom; the professional bard al-A'sha, whose begging excursions led him as far as South Arabia. Not only the artistic poets, but the goatherds of the Hudhayl, who pitched their tents near Mecca, also made poetical use of a common language, which, though fed by all dialects and understood everywhere, was still sharply distinguished from daily speech. This song language, which we find among many primitive peoples, seems to have prevailed not only throughout Najd and the Hijaz but as far as the interior of Babylonia. It became the mother of classical Arabic, which Islam made into a world language in the Near East and along the entire southern coast of the Mediterranean.

2. *The Prophet Muhammad*

Mecca, the Arab prophet's birthplace (which Ptolemy calls Macoraba, probably after the South Arabian *miqrab*, "temple") lies in the Hijaz, in a stony, barren valley stretching from north to south between the mountains of Abu Qubays in the east and Jabal Hindi in the west. In the center of its stands the Ka'bah, a four-cornered structure, (now 16½ yards high, after many reconstructions), in the corner of which the Black Stone, probably the oldest idol worshiped there, is imbedded in the wall 58½ inches off the floor. The Ka'bah contained an image of the moon-god Hubal, in addition to which the three goddesses Allat, al-'Uzza, and al-Manat were worshiped. The famous spring Zamzam, around which the city no doubt sprang up, gushes out in the temple court. Even before Muhammad its area was regarded as *harim*, that is, holy and inviolable. Mecca was subject to the Quraysh tribe; among them the families of Makhzum and Umayyah were the most looked up to. The wealth of the city rested on the commerce bound up with the ceremonial pilgrimage to the Ka'bah and the near-by mountain of 'Arafat. Mecca was the transfer point for the caravan trade between South Arabia and Syria. Twice a year, during the seventh month, the Rajab, and from the eleventh to the first of the New Year, in Dhu-l-Qa'dah, Dhu-l-Hijjah, and Muharram, a general truce prevailed in the country, not only in the cities, but throughout North Arabia, so that the caravans which had been fitted out in Mecca could arrive at their destinations in safety.

The birth year of the Prophet has not been handed down; it is generally reckoned at about 570, but no doubt must be assumed to be somewhat later.* His clan, the *banu* Hashim, does not seem to have played a role of any distinction in the city. No matter how energetically tradition attempts to glorify the Prophet from the very beginning on, it cannot conceal the fact that at the time he was born his family was in quite wretched circumstances. His father 'Abdallah, the son of 'Abd-al-Muttalib, is supposed to have been a petty merchant and to have died two months after the boy's birth on a business trip to Medina. A few years later he was followed by his wife, Aminah, of the Zuhrah clan, and so the orphan grew up under the guardianship first of his grandfather, 'Abd-al-Muttalib, then of his uncle, Abu Talib. The only credible testimony as to the Prophet's youth in our possession are the verses in the Qur'an, Surah 93: 6-11:

Did He not find thee an orphan and gave thee a home?
And found thee erring and guided thee,
And found thee needy and enriched thee.
As to the orphan therefore wrong him not;
And as to him that asketh of thee, chide him not away;
And as for the favors of thy Lord, tell them abroad.

When Muhammad had grown up, he entered the service of Khadijah, a rich merchant's widow. The latter was independently carrying on the business inherited from her first two husbands, since women in pre-Islamic Arabia generally, especially if they were economically independent, enjoyed far greater freedom than later. In her service Muhammad seems to have accompanied some Meccan caravans to the south, perhaps also to Bostra, which as the principal Byzantine fortress east of the Jordan was a central resort for the

* H. Lammens, *L'âge de Mahomet et la chronologie de la Sira, Journal asiatique*, série XI, t. 171, p. 209-250.

grain trade. Even at that time he seems to have displayed particular talent; at any rate his employer, though she was about fifteen years older, conceived a lively attachment for him. She herself proposed marriage to him, and this marriage not only raised him above material needs but apparently satisfied him in other ways as well. Four daughters seem to have sprung from their connection, and two sons as well, who, however, died in childhood. As husband he no doubt at first devoted himself to his wife's enterprises with zeal; nor in later life did he deny his being a merchant; in his metaphorical speech he had a fondness for allusions to trade.

Muhammad's interest must have turned to religious questions very early. This was far from unusual for the more profound spirits among his contemporaries, whom pagan worship no longer satisfied. According to tradition, he met Jews and Christians on his travels, but in Mecca itself he probably associated with Christians, whose biblical knowledge, to be sure, was extremely meager. The belief in Allah filled him more and more and made him perceive the emptiness of the other gods. But in the first few years of his activity as preacher he also must have acknowledged the three goddesses of the Ka'bah, whom his countrymen regarded as daughters of Allah. In one of his revelations he called them superior beings (*gharaniq*),* whose intercession might be hoped for. Later on he recognized only the angels as intercessors with the Lord. As his monotheistic awareness became more acute, he must have withdrawn this concession; in the Surah 53 he contested the belief that these goddesses were the daughters of Allah. Later tradition could regard this concession only as an aberration Satan had seduced him into, and consequently postponed it to the time of his deepest need in Mecca, as an act of desperation he disavowed the very next day.

But whereas some of his contemporaries, such as the poet Umayyah ibn-abi-as-Salt in Taif, a town next to Mecca, were content with a general monotheism, Muhammad seems to have flung himself into the arms of asceticism and succumbed to broodings about his soul's salvation for whole nights through on Mt. Hira, near Mecca. His insight into the emptiness of his countrymen's polytheism posed for him the problem: how long was God going to leave

* Actually white herons. Perhaps some obscure notion reached the Prophet about the divine bird of the Egyptians, the phoenix, the gray heron? Cf. S. Hess in *Zeitschrift der Deutschen Morgenländischen Gesellschaft*, 69 (1915) pp. 385-8.

them in disbelief, since He had, after all, revealed Himself to other peoples through His prophets? Thus the thought ripened within him that he himself had been called to this mission of a prophet. But for a long time a native shyness prevented him from appearing as prophet in public, and it was not until he underwent an extraordinary experience on Mt. Hira that his doubts were dissipated. A figure once appeared before him there, which he later represented to be the angel Gabriel, and to which Muhammad ascribed the voice within which told him he had been sent by God. His wife at once believed in his divine mission, and he himself was rid of his last doubts when the attacks during which the divine voice called him were repeated more and more often. As soon as these were over he proclaimed as a revelation what he thought he had heard. At first he aroused no particular sensation among his countrymen. They were accustomed to the emergence in almost every tribe of a soothsayer, or *kahin*, as well as a poet, who would ascribe his decisions concerning the conflicts and the doubtful questions (of murder, theft, strayed camels, etc.) which were laid before him to his supernatural familiar (*sahib*) and announce them in the same rhymed prose as the prophet his revelations. Again and again Muhammad had to take precautions against being placed on the same level as such people.

At the core of Muhammad's oldest revelations there was the expectation of a judgment day for each individual; he himself stood in fear of it, like the earliest Christians, and as the Christian sectarians of his own time might still have done. It was only later that he spoke of a great judgment on his entire people which would wipe Allah's enemies and his own from off the face of the earth. In contrast to these visions of terror he then portrayed the joys of paradise in glowing colors. Iranian concepts persisted with him, as they did with Aramean Christians; by the way, a sculptured work in Palmyra shows the deceased dining in festive clothing.

The exaltation experienced by the Prophet during these first years found expression in the very form of his discourses, the bold images and rhetorical diction which are full of rhythmic movement and are marked by genuine poetic feeling. Like the sayings of the pagan kahins, they are usually quite brief and often introduced by odd formulae of oaths.

His wife and daughters were followed by his cousin 'Ali, his slave and freedman Zayd, and his friends Abu Bakr and Sa'd ibn-abi-

Waqqas in being converted to a belief in his preaching; the sequence of these first faithful believers is not certain and has often been inverted later out of dynastic considerations.* Muhammad's other followers at first were only slaves and paupers, though in the beginning he seems to have been on good terms with the ruling classes as well, whose pride in the famous sanctuary of his native city was shared by him. It was only after he attacked the belief in the gods of their fathers that they felt themselves affected and imperiled. What they thought particularly offensive in his preaching of the last judgment was the doctrine of the resurrection of the body. Moreover, they were averse to seeing him, a man from an inferior clan, at the head of a community, however small, like a state within a state. He defended himself against the attacks of these opponents in discourses which became more and more violent, rising to the point of malediction; among them he even named his own uncle Abu Lahab.

Muhammad demanded of his followers profession of belief in the One God and the surrender to God's will, *islam,* after which his religion took its name. Probably very early he also levied a poor-tax for the maintenance of needy members of the community, but it was only later in Medina that it assumed greater significance. The chief duty of the faithful, by virtue of which they professed membership in the community, was praying at first twice, then three times, and only later five times a day. Other religious exercises, such as the calling on God, particularly in nocturnal vigils, which Muhammad himself, after the example of Christian ascetics, practiced zealously, were regarded as private matters. But no doubt from the very beginning these prayers were preceded by ablutions, such as were also customary in some Christian sects.

In the unsuccessful and exhausting struggle against the disbelief of his aristocratic fellow citizens, Muhammad consoled himself by the example of earlier prophets who had had no better a time of it. In his earlier revelations, accordingly, he showed a preference for referring to their histories, particularly that of Moses. His acquaintanceship with biblical material was, to be sure, extremely superficial and rich in errors. He may have owed some of its characteristics to the Jewish legends of the Haggadah, but more to Christian teachers who in addition acquainted him with the Gospel of the Infancy,

* See Th. Nöldeke, *Zur tendenziösen Gestaltung der Urgeschichte des Islams, Zeitschrift der Deutschen Morgenländischen Gesellschaft,* 52 (1898), pp. 16-38.

the legend of the Seven Sleepers, the saga of Alexander, and the other recurrent themes of medieval world literature. In addition there were some Arab tales, such as the one about the destruction of the tribe of Thamud, for which he probably invented the trifling story of the prophet Salih as a necessary supplement. In these tales his style became more and more diffuse and less fiery; he was fond of garnishing them with long rhetorical discussions concerning the apprehension of God by means of the portents scattered throughout nature.

But his adversaries soon became dissatisfied with a simple rejection of his sermons. Scenting a danger to their general welfare in the spread of the new faith, they tortured the slaves and freedmen who professed adherence to him. The Prophet himself remained secure in the protection of his clan. Indeed, Muhammad's friend Abu Bakr is said to have expended a substantial portion of his possessions in buying martyrs freedom; but of course his own means were far from adequate to protect all his fellow believers from insult. Accordingly, the Prophet made up his mind to withdraw at least a part of his community beyond the reach of their persecutors through flight. Since at that time he did not consider his religion to be very different from Christianity, he referred his followers to the Abyssinian negus, the nearest political representative of Christianity within range. Muhammad's pagan countrymen had connections with South Arabia, which at this time belonged to the Persian Empire. But Persia was an ancient enemy of the Christian powers; the victory the Persians had won in 614 against the Byzantines in Syria had been hailed by Muhammad's fellow citizens with joy, while he warned them, in Surah 30 of the Qur'an, of an imminent counter-blow. So he was making no miscalculation in assuming that the Christian negus would accord a refuge to his followers, persecuted by the pagans. This emigration is said to have taken place in the fifth year of his prophetic mission. We are told that the emigrants, eighty-two men and a few women, included the Prophet's daughter Ruqayyah and her husband 'Uthman, the future third caliph.

Meanwhile the community remaining behind in Mecca gained a valuable new member through the conversion of 'Umar ibn-al-Khattab, who on his mother's side was related to the wealthy and powerful Makhzum clan and by virtue of his personal qualities enjoyed great prestige in the city. The impression this conversion made was all the greater because up to then 'Umar had particularly distinguished himself as one of Muhammad's opponents, who consequently sought to make up for this defection by stronger measures; they proclaimed a boycott against Muhammad and all his followers and shut them up in their quarter in the ravine of Abu Talib. Although the latter, his uncle and foster father, was persistently indifferent to his mission, he nevertheless indignantly rejected the suggestion of the Meccans that he withdraw his protecting hand. As a matter of fact, in a little while the Meccans had to lift the boycott, which could not be made effective. But soon afterward the Prophet was smitten by two heavy blows; in the same year, 619, both his wife and his uncle Abu Talib died. The latter's place was taken by his brother Abu Lahab, a fanatical opponent of the new religion, whom the Prophet himself had cursed in a surah, but who, as head of the clan, was honor-bound to assume his protection. However, this unnatural relationship could not last long.

This desperate situation gave the Prophet the idea of seeking his salvation outside Mecca. After making a vain attempt to recruit followers at the great fairs in the neighborhood, he tried his luck at Taif, a more southerly city whose inhabitants, the Thaqif, had active trade relationships with the Meccans. But he found just as little understanding for his preaching there as among his fellow citizens; he was not only sneered at, but driven away by stoning and had to seek asylum in the orchard of a pagan fellow tribesman. He did not dare return to Mecca before receiving a solemn assurance of protection from a respected kinsman in his clan.

In March 620 at the next pilgrimage festival, Muhammad attempted to win followers for his teachings among the numerous strangers streaming in and out of the whole of Arabia. While engaged in this, he met some members of the Khazraj tribe resident in Medina. This city harbored a large community of Jews, who in the endless feuds must often have threatened the pagans with the awaited Messiah as the avenger of the injuries inflicted on them. This had familiarized these Medinese with the concept of a divine messenger, and they accepted Islam, primarily because as a result of the fortunes of their community they were quite differently prepared for religious ideas than the sated, worldly Meccans.

Their city, which at that time was still called Yathrib and not Medina (Medinat Rasul-Allah, "the city of the Apostle of God") till later, lies in a well-watered plain of the northern Hijaz, near the mountain ridge separating the Najd from the Tihamah. Like other civilized cities in the oases of northwestern Arabia, Yathrib consisted of individual cultivated plots of ground and permanent houses, which lay strewn about between palm plantations, gardens, and sowed fields. The rulers of this oasis were the tribes of Aus and Khazraj, later included under the Muslim honorary name of *Ansar*, that is, "the Helpers" (of the Prophet). They considered themselves South Arabs. Before they immigrated into Medina, the city is supposed to have been in the hands of the Jews. But the latter's economic power was apparently broken as a result of the abovementioned South Arabian campaign of the Abyssinian satrap Abraha; from then on the Jews had lived dispersed among the Aus and Khazraj, who had begun by being squatters on their land. Only the Qaynuqa' tribe had kept its enclosed quarter, but had likewise lost its land. Land was held only by the tribes of Nadir and Qurayzah, who lived among the Aus and had just recently attained an equal footing in their political relations with them.

The Medinese Arabs had become peasants, living in hedged-in courtyards, but they had not yet given up the free customs of nomadic life. They were not subject to any central authority, but because of their sedentary life were no longer able as before to avoid the new conflicts continually arising. As a result there were continuous internal struggles and finally a civil war between the two tribes of the Aus and Khazraj, which divided the sympathies of the entire city. The Aus had succumbed to the Khazraj; some of them had accepted a humiliating peace and by losing their land had almost sunk to the level of squatters; the others, through an excess of pride, had preferred being driven off all their land. But in alliance with the Jewish tribes Nadir and Qurayzah, the Aus had rallied once again and had beaten the Khazraj in a great and decisive battle at Bu'ath after a lengthy struggle; but there was no honorable peace as a result. The internecine strife continued, and insecurity finally became so great that a man could no longer go about his affairs without constant fear of death. Both tribes must have found this condition all the more insupportable inasmuch as they had not yet lost consciousness of their unity. But no one among them had enough prestige to quell the dissension; an arbiter, long since indispensable, could only come from outside. The office might have fallen to some heathen kahin. Instead, the murderous fratricidal strife had smoothed the way for the Prophet.

The six Khazrajites whom Muhammad had met during the 620

pilgrimage returned home and became active on behalf of the new faith, aided by one of the Muslims who had previously emigrated to Abyssinia. The next year five of them came back again to Mecca with seven newly won believers and met Muhammad at the 'Aqabah, the pass between Mina and Mecca. Here he enjoined upon them the basic laws of Islam and dismissed them again in the company of an able reader of the Qur'an.

At this time, according to tradition, the mother community in Mecca was undergoing another crisis. Muhammad's account of a supernatural, nocturnal journey, in Gabriel's company, to Jerusalem and then into Heaven, is supposed to have aroused a shocked incredulity among some of the believers; but by his example of unshakable faith Abu Bakr had succeeded in silencing the skeptics. This heavenly ascension of the Prophet, however, which was later given frequent treatment in the poetic legends of all Islamic literature, possibly belongs to the very beginning of his mission; such visions during the seer's vigil are testified to among some primitive peoples. In 622 quite a substantial number of new believers from Medina were already coming to the pilgrimage, members of both the Aus and Khazraj tribes, and now Muhammad formally had his uncle 'Abbas take him out of the society of his clan into the protection of the new believers, at another meeting on the 'Aqabah.

Very quietly, in the summer of 622, Muhammad's followers left Mecca and proceeded to Yathrib. The Prophet himself, accompanied by Abu Bakr, did not follow them until autumn, since he first had to settle some of his followers' business affairs. On September 20, 622, he arrived in Qubah, a suburb about three-fourths of a mile south of Medina. He waited five days before moving into the city. In order not to arouse any jealousy, he gave his she-camel a free rein; she set herself down in the quarter of the Khazraj, and the Prophet first took up his sojourn at the house of one of them. This Hijrah of the Prophet—that is, not a flight, but a migration which constituted a break with an untenable past and the beginning of a new life—with justice seemed so important to the Muslims that under the rule of the second caliph, their new calendar opened with it. As a natural result, they had to accept the beginning of the year as being that of the era, also.

Shortly afterward the Prophet apparently set up his own household. Like that of his new fellow citizens, it consisted of a number of living and working quarters in the center of a court surrounded by brick walls. These were made out of palm stems and roofed over with palm leaves overlaid by a covering of lime. Later the Prophet's courtyard acquired a reception tent with expensive materials and carpets, for accepting the submission of the tribal delegations in a dignified way. During the lifetime of the Prophet, this was the courtyard the believers assembled in for daily prayers.

Muhammad's principal support in his new home were those countrymen of his who had migrated from Mecca, the *Muhajirun* (emigrés). Whereas the Meccans with some means dispersed throughout the quarters of the city, the fairly large number without money or homes among them remained in the Prophet's neighborhood, with no fixed dwelling place, and stayed overnight in the *suffah*, a covered gallery in his courtyard. They formed his bodyguard and contributed a good deal toward raising his prestige among his new fellow citizens.

The task of peacemaker, which fell to him as a matter of course, was performed by him in the second year after his arrival, when war with Mecca was looming up, in a very detailed treaty between the inhabitants of the city, the text of which has come down to us. The various clans agreed to form one community under Allah's protection. But since the believers were the moving spirit of the community, and since according to ancient Arab views their actions were binding on everyone, they automatically achieved the ascendancy. The general feuding code was eliminated. The murderer was subject to blood vengeance, but no one was permitted to take his side. The community was to stand together against external enemies, but the Jews, when it was not a question of an attack on the city itself, were obligated only to contribute to the costs of the war, not to participate actively.

The Prophet's religious interests in the early days of his stay in Medina were governed by his relationship to the Jews.* On his arrival he must have hoped that they would be converted to his doctrines, and so he attempted to win them over by adapting the ritual of his community to theirs in some points. After the example of the Jewish fast on the Day of Atonement, the tenth of Tishri, he established a fast for the day of the 'Ashura, the tenth of Muharram. Whereas his believers in Mecca had prayed only twice a day, now, after the example of the Jews, he introduced a third prayer at

* See A. J. Wensinck, *Mohammed en de Joden te Medina*, Leiden, 1908. [H. Z. (J. W.) Hirshberg, *Israel in Arabia*, Tel Aviv, 1945 (Hebrew).]

midday. Since in Medina he and his community were able from the very beginning to hold divine service in public undisturbed, he now appointed a prayer caller, the *mu'adhdhin.* In this, to be sure, he was already setting himself in opposition to both monotheistic religions. While in Oriental synagogues blasts of the trumpet were the summons to prayer, the Christians made use of great wooden clappers (semanteries) in place of church bells. In contradistinction to both customs, Muhammad chose the human voice for calling his believers to prayer. As the day of public prayer he settled on Friday, corresponding to the Jewish Sabbath, and in contrast to the Jews allowed the rest of the day to be free for worldly affairs.

But Muhammad soon got into all sorts of disputes with the Jewish scholars. However meager their knowledge in such a remote community might have been, they were nevertheless very superior in positive information and acuteness of perception to the completely untrained Prophet; the gaps of various kinds in his knowledge of the Old Testament, which he had left unguarded in the Meccan surahs, could not remain concealed from them. But their sneering allusions to this were unable to shake his faith in the truth of his revelations. The opposition of the Jews to his doctrines could only lead him to conclude that they had fallen away from the true faith and falsified the Holy Scriptures which he himself had recognized as emanating from God.

This struggle with the Jews soon had practical consequences as well. He laid continually greater emphasis on the national Arab character of his religion. He did not, to be sure, abolish the 'Ashura fast, which he had borrowed from the Jews, and which even today still survives in custom as a voluntary exercise, but in addition he introduced a fast, still practiced today, throughout Ramadan, the ninth month of the lunar year. While the Christians merely abstained from eating meat during their quadragesimal fast, during this month Muhammad demanded that his believers abstain throughout the day from every form of nourishment, allowing them in return the liberty of making amends for it after sundown. It is not yet clear whether he borrowed this prescription from some gnostic sect or the Manicheans, whose missionaries penetrated Arabia too. He can scarcely have known anything of the Harranians in Mesopotamia, who likewise had a March fast in honor of the moon.

After the Prophet had abandoned hope of converting the Jews, the lore of his native Mecca came to the fore in his religious concepts. To enhance the value of this lore, he traced it back to Abraham: who now was regarded by him not merely as one of the numerous prophets of old but as the very founder of the true faith of Islam. It was Abraham, he decided, who had founded the sanctuary in Mecca for his son Ishmael and established the pilgrimage festival. This only needed to be purified of the pagan abuses of a later time for a direct connection with the divine tradition of Abraham to be re-established.

In this way he also laid down the first and most important goal of his foreign policy, the subjugation of his pagan countrymen. Because of circumstances he was unable to begin an immediate and systematic campaign against them. The emigrants (Muhajirun) were held back from a war against their kinfolk by the ancient Arab conception of honor, and the Medinese were scarcely inclined to break the peace with their powerful neighbors. But the Meccan caravans which passed by Medina very soon aroused a lust for booty among the impoverished believers, who as emigrés in the thickly settled city at first had to struggle with great need, and whom the Prophet kept reminding of the injustices inflicted on them. Even in the first year and the beginning of the second, Muhammad is supposed to have made several vain attempts to intercept these caravans. Not until the beginning of the holy month of Rajab did a raiding party sent out by him under sealed orders succeed in surprising * a very richly laden Meccan caravan—whose military escort was proceeding with unconcerned confidence in God's Truce—and bringing home a heavy booty. But when this breach of the tribal moral code aroused a storm of indignation in Medina itself, Muhammad denied the deed, which had incontestably been done in accordance with his desires, as resting on a misinterpretation of his orders. It was only in a later revelation, when the sight of the rich booty had sufficiently aroused his greed, that he dared declare war against unbelievers, and the division of the spoils, justified, even in the holy month.

Two months later another occasion for a sortie presented itself. The Syrian caravan from Gaza, in which nearly every Meccan firm had some capital involved, was imminently expected in Mecca. Its leader was Abu Sufyan, the head of the Umayyah house. At Muhammad's summons three hundred volunteers were found from among the Muhajirun as well as the Medinese, ready for a raid on the caravan. But Abu Sufyan was already prepared for an attack

* (In the valley of Nakhlah to the east of Mecca.)

and led his men along the coast by a detour. By a special messenger he warned the Meccans of the danger threatening, and they set out on the road northward, reportedly three times as strong as the Muslims. Muhammad intended to lie in wait for Abu Sufyan at Badr, a spot on the caravan highway with good drinking water, but instead of a feeble escort, a powerful army came out to meet him. The Prophet had to summon up all his powers of inspiration to induce his followers to take up the unequal struggle. But once he was successful in this, the obedience and discipline they had acquired in their daily communal religious exercises won a victory over the numerically superior yet undisciplined Meccans.

The moral effect of this first success was very great. Almost every Meccan family had the death of a kinsman to mourn or the freedom of a prisoner to buy back. In Medina the victory strengthened the influence of the Prophet enormously and enabled him to take energetic steps against his opponents, whom he had hitherto had to endure in silence. The Medinese who had still remained pagans now had to accept Islam. Many of them, to be sure, did this only against inner opposition, and for some time the "doubters" were to remain a source of concern for the Prophet.

It was worse for the Jews. The Qaynuqa' tribe of goldsmiths were the first to feel his power. Only a month after the battle of Badr, Muhammad summoned his warriors against them—ostensibly because of their having summarily killed a Muslim who had killed a Jew in a quarrel—and forced them to surrender, after besieging them in their quarter for several weeks. At the intercession of the Khazraj chieftain he changed the sentence of death originally decreed against them to loss of all their possessions and banishment from the country.

Since Muhammad continued disturbing the caravan trade of the Meccans, the latter, together with their neighbors the Thaqif in Taif, and a few Bedouin tribes, made up their minds to avenge their defeat at Badr. They assembled an army which for Arabian circumstances was very powerful—reportedly three thousand men, among them seven hundred in armor, as well as two hundred horses and three thousand camels. Since they took with them a great baggage train with many women, they could only move very slowly. At the beginning of 624 they arrived at the plain stretching from north of Medina to Mt. Uhud, a good half hour's distance from the city. Although at first Muhammad, on the advice of the Khazraj chieftain, intended to await their attack in the city, he allowed himself to be persuaded by the warlike spirit of his men into making a sortie. But when the believers' courage evaporated nevertheless at seeing the mighty army, he insisted on waging the battle in the open field, nor did he allow himself to be dissuaded even when the head of the Khazraj took three hundred men and withdrew into the city. In spite of this bad beginning the Muslims had an advantage at first, and even pressed into the enemy camp. But at seeing this, the archers, who were supposed to be covering Muhammad's left flank, feared they might be done out of some of the loot and left their posts. Khalid ibn-al-Walid, giving the first proof of a military acumen he was later to demonstrate frequently in the service of Islam, took advantage of this to overrun the exposed Muslim flank at the head of the Meccan cavalry. This was how the Muslims lost the day. Muhammad himself was wounded slightly, and the false rumor of his death robbed his men of their last remaining powers of resistance. Luckily for them the Meccans were unable to exploit their victory, but simply returned home happy in their success.

This defeat could scarcely injure the Prophet seriously in the eyes of his followers, whose disobedience made them conscious of their own culpability. Nevertheless, his prestige had suffered a blow among the local Bedouins; this was shown, for instance, by the murder of forty of his apostles in the territory of the Hawazin tribe. Muhammad had to recoup this loss in martial glory by a new enterprise; once again the Jews were his first and principal victims. On some flimsy pretext he attacked the Nadir and shut them up in their quarter. Since even their coreligionists, the Qurayzah, did not dare help them, they were compelled to surrender after a siege lasting a few weeks. They emigrated to the Khaybar oasis, twenty miles north of Medina, which was already the seat of a large Jewish community. Muhammad gave their landholdings to his Muhajirun.

Shortly after this Muhammad's believers were forbidden wine, which in Surah 16:69 he had still praised as a magnificent bounty of God's, as well as the *maysir* game, a raffling off of camel's meat which had already involved many Bedouins in material ruin. The interdiction on wine (2:216 and 5:92), which was later broken often enough, was aimed at the unrestrained carousing the poets had often glorified but which might easily have impaired the rigid military discipline Muhammad sought for his believers.

But in the meanwhile the Meccans had succeeded in founding a great alliance against Muhammad. Sometime in March 627 about ten thousand men, among them four thousand Qurayshites under the command of Abu Sufyan, moved against Medina. This time they drew up with such unusual swiftness that Muhammad had only a week to arm for their reception. In view of the superiority of the enemy an open struggle in the field was out of the question. He had to make a stand in Medina itself, especially since it was only under such circumstances that all the inhabitants were obligated to military service. On three of its sides the city was quite well covered by connecting rows of houses; it was open only toward the north. Reputedly on the advice of a former Persian slave, Salman, Muhammad laid out a broad trench here to secure himself against cavalry attacks. This means of defense had hitherto been unknown in Arabia and caused such a sensation that the battle was named the Campaign of the Trench, after it. In fact, it achieved Muhammad's aim completely; the enemy saw a siege imposed on him and soon tired of it, since the work of supply in the still barren fields was difficult. When negotiations with the Jewish tribe of the Qurayzah who lived at the edge of the town misfired as a result of the latter's indecisiveness, and when the besiegers saw their most valuable possession, their riding animals, succumbing by droves to the inclemency of the weather, they soon made up their minds to withdraw. That same day Muhammad attacked the Qurayzah, who had displayed an ambiguous attitude in any case. After a fortnight's siege they had to surrender; to set an example, Muhammad had the men (six hundred in number) killed and the women and children sold into slavery.

In the course of 627 the Prophet also undertook a number of raiding expeditions against a few Bedouin tribes, one of which took him as far as the neighborhood of Mecca. These expeditions were safe enough for him to take along two of his wives. On one occasion his favorite wife, ʻAishah, the then fourteen-year-old daughter of Abu Bakr, strayed away from the army one evening while looking for a lost necklace and did not return to the camp until the following day, accompanied by a young man whom she had once known before. This put her under suspicion of infidelity, and the Prophet sent her back to her parents' house. But in a revelation to him a month later Allah confirmed her innocence, adding at the same time that any accusation of a married woman which could not be sustained by four eyewitnesses was to be punished as slander by one hundred strokes of the lash. The Prophet's son-in-law ʻAli was one of the enemies of ʻAishah who urged him to divorce her; the hatred with which ʻAishah persecuted him during his caliphate no doubt stemmed from this time. This necklace escapade, however, never had any effect on the social position of women in Islam, as may have been thought: the wearing of the veil by married women was an ancient Arab custom and had already been enjoined by the Prophet for other reasons. The veil did not prevent women, before Islam as well as up to the time of the Umayyads, from moving around in public with a good deal of freedom and sometimes exercising quite considerable influence. It was only the institution of the harem, introduced by the 'Abbasids on the Christian-Byzantine pattern, that finally degraded the women of the Orient.

Since Muhammad's recognition, while in Medina, of the sanctity of the Ka'bah, its possession had become his ultimate political goal. At first, to be sure, he made only one attempt to participate with his followers in the Little Pilgrimage (*'Umrah*) of 627. Although his Bedouin allies disappointed his hopes of their accompanying him on it, he set out in pilgrim's garb on the road to Mecca with fifteen hundred men bearing a sword as their only weapon. When he had come within ten miles of the city, he learned that the Meccans and their allies had set up a camp in front of the north gate and sent out their cavalry ahead on the highway to Medina. Consequently Muhammad wheeled off westward, circumvented the cavalry outposts, and by out-of-the-way paths came up to Hudaybiyah, at the boundary of the holy area. There he encamped and began negotiations with the Meccans, dispatching to the city his son-in-law 'Uthman, who as an Umayyad had great influence. Upon his not returning for three days the rumor spread that he had been murdered. Although unprepared for battle, Muhammad could not leave such a breach of the intertribal code unavenged; he assembled his followers and, standing under a large tree, once again assured himself of their loyalty. To have participated in this "God-pleasing homage" was later regarded as an exalted title of honor. But the rumor proved unfounded and the Meccans displayed every inclination toward a peaceful agreement. They dispatched a mediator to the Prophet's camp, and the latter concluded a ten-year truce. Muhammad was to agree to abandon his objective this time and turn back; in return the Meccans would clear the city for three days a year so that he and his followers could make the pilgrimage undisturbed. Muhammad bound himself to send back youthful Qurayshites who should come over to him during the period of the truce against the will of their guardians, whereas turncoats from his side would be able to remain in Mecca unmolested. This concession made the Prophet's entourage all the more indignant since in the treaty document he waived reference to himself as the Apostle of God. But the future justified him. On the basis of the treaty he did, to be sure, turn over to the banu Zuhrah a client of theirs, but while on the road to Mecca the latter killed one of the two men escorting him and fled to the coast. Numerous refugees from Mecca who were in the same position soon assembled there and under his leadership attacked passing Meccan caravans. The Meccans themselves now had to ask the Prophet to strike out the calamitous paragraph and take charge of these highwaymen himself.

In May 628, as compensation for his apparent failure at Hudaybiyah, Muhammad led his followers against the wealthy Jewish colony in Khaybar. The latter brought over four thousand Bedouins from the Ghatafan tribe for their protection, but when they failed to advance against the Prophet in open combat, shutting themselves up in their fortresses instead, their allies withdrew once again. Since the Muslims were not armed for a siege, their efforts were at first of no avail. Treachery finally enabled them to penetrate one of the quarters. When they turned the weapons they found there against the other fortresses, the Jews surrendered; they were granted free passage with their women and children, but had to abandon all their possessions. However, since it seemed inadvisable at that time to settle believers far from Medina, which would enfeeble the strength of the youthful community, the Prophet allowed the Jews their land in return for their binding themselves to turn over half their harvests. The Jewish colonies in Fadak, Wadi al-Qura, and Tayma also submitted soon afterward under the same conditions, partly voluntarily, partly after a short struggle; but the Prophet laid claim to Fadak as his private property.

On the basis of the treaty Muhammad was then able to make his entry into Mecca during the next pilgrimage festival. Although the pagans had left the city, his kinsmen, headed by his uncle 'Abbas, remained. This pilgrimage made so strong an impression even on his adversaries that a few of their leaders, like Khalid ibn-al-Walid, the victor of Uhud, later called "the Sword of Islam," and the Umayyad 'Amr ibn-al-'As, later the first governor of Egypt, came to Medina by 629 to make their profession of faith.

This newly emerging Arabian power had already attracted the attention of the governors of the bordering Byzantine provinces. Egypt had just been wrested from the Persians, who had conquered

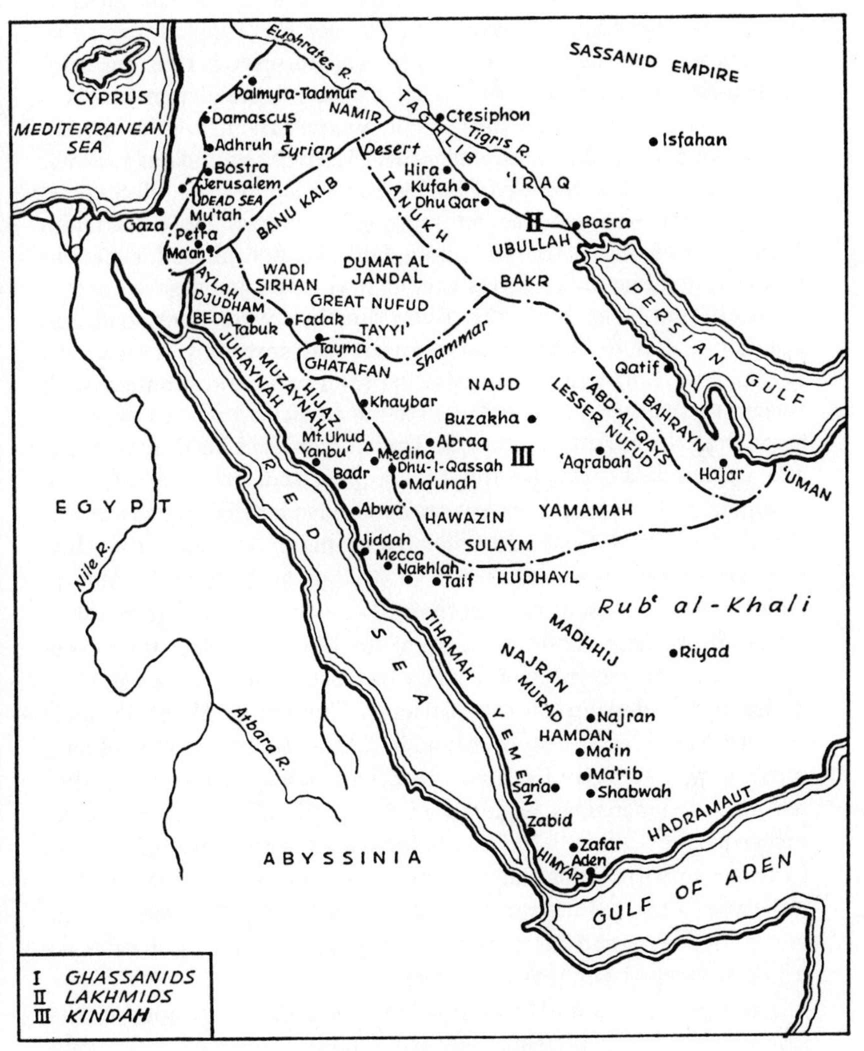

ARABIA BEFORE ISLAM

it under the emperor Heraclius. Cyrus, the new Byzantine governor (whom the Arabs of Alexandria called Muqawqis, mistaking as a title a sneer at the patriarch, who at the time of the Muslim conquest exercised temporal powers too), sent the Prophet, concerning whose tastes he must have been well informed, two beautiful slave girls among other gifts. Muhammad presented one of them to his court poet Hassan ibn-Thabit, whose task it was to glorify the exploits of the Muslims. The other, Mariyah, he took as his own concubine, and had the joy of having her bear him a son, all his legal wives except Khadijah having remained childless. He named him Ibrahim after the patriarch whose faith he felt himself called to revive; but this son died in his very first year, on January 27, 632.

Muslim relations with the Byzantines in Syria developed less peacefully. Since Muhammad's power was spreading among the Bedouins of northern Arabia also, he soon came into contact with Byzantine frontier posts. In 629 a messenger he had sent to the commander of the fortress of Bostra, Transjordan, had been intercepted and executed. To avenge this the Prophet sent an army of three thousand men under his foster son Zayd ibn-Harithah northward in September. The Ghassanid border troops marched against the Muslims, and only a few miles north of Medina a battle took place in which the believers were victorious. They then pushed forward as far as Mu'tah near the southern tip of the Dead Sea. Here they came up against a Byzantine army which had been assembled meanwhile under the leadership of the patricius Theodorus. With all their bravery the Muslims were unequal to the latter's overwhelming superiority. After Zayd and two successors whom Muhammad himself had designated as leaders had fallen, Khalid, with difficulty, succeeded in leading back to Medina the badly weakened troops. In order to soften the bad impression of this setback the Prophet soon afterward sent 'Amr ibn-al-'As against the Bedouins in the northern desert, and his energetic measures induced most of these tribes to accept Islam that same year.

The Qurayshites in Mecca had long since given up hope of defeating the Prophet again, and were now concerned only with maintaining the Hudaybiyah truce and not conjuring up new dangers to their trade, badly afflicted as it was in any case. Muhammad, on the contrary, was simply waiting for a pretext to settle accounts with them once and for all. A brawl between a Bedouin tribe converted to Islam and some partisans of the Quraysh, in which some townsmen from Mecca itself are supposed to have taken part, presented a pretext for declaring the peace broken.

In Ramadan of the year 8, the beginning of 630, he set out against his native city with a great levy of Medinese and Bedouins, totaling ten thousand men. When he was halfway there a number of Meccans, among them his uncle 'Abbas, came out and joined him. Only a very small party in the city was still considering serious resistance. When the Prophet set up camp in Marr az-Zahran, northwest of Mecca, even Abu Sufyan, once the heart of the opposition, turned up and made his profession of faith. He obtained a promise of complete safety for his family and all those who might seek refuge in his house, and returned to the city. His counsel not to oppose the entry of the Prophet found willing ears among his fellow citizens. Only a small band of diehards held out ready for battle. Muhammad had his troops advance on Mecca from two sides simultaneously. It was only at the south gate, occupied by the war party, perhaps in the hope of fighting their way into Yemen, that Khalid met with brief opposition. Without any serious struggle the city prostrated herself at the feet of the great son she had driven into exile eight years before.

When he arrived at the Ka'bah, Muhammad rode around the sanctuary seven times, touching the Black Stone with his staff each time. He thus absorbed this pagan ritual into the religion. He ordered the images of the temple idols destroyed and also demanded that the idols still to be found in private dwellings be handed over, though he did not take for granted an immediate acceptance of Islam on the part of his fellow citizens. He made only a few of his former opponents atone for particularly grievous misdeeds by death; among them were two women singers who had sung some songs in mockery of him. He showed such indulgence to the others that he aroused the jealousy of the Medinese, although their fear that he would remain in Mecca soon proved unfounded.

The Prophet could only enjoy this success in his birthplace for a fortnight. During this time a menacing cloud had been gathering against him. The Thaqif of Taif, the city just south of Mecca, had united with the Hawazin, a related tribe widely scattered in the Najd. An allied army of thirty thousand men—for Arabian circumstances, prodigious—was encamped at Autas. When Muhammad moved against them, they attacked him at Hunayn. The Bedouins in the vanguard of his troops at first let themselves be overrun, but the unyielding calm of his picked Medinese troops could not be shaken by the numerical superiority of the allies. However, most of the Hawazin succeeded in escaping to Taif, since Muhammad's Bedouins inopportunely recollected their blood ties and pursued sluggishly. But the rich booty in their camp fell into the hands of the victors, which later gave the Prophet an opportunity to fortify his newly converted countrymen in their faith by "heart-winning" gifts.

Muhammad was less fortunate in his plans against Taif itself. Without delaying for the division of the booty he advanced beneath its walls directly from the battlefield of Hunayn. But the Thaqif met him with a stubborn resistance he was unable to break, since his primitive machines of siege were continually being destroyed by flames. Only three weeks later he gave up the tedious enterprise and returned to the booty, which was stacked up in a camp near the battlefield. A number of Bedouins who had originally fled to Taif had now assembled here in order to regain their kinsmen and their belongings in return for their conversion. Accordingly, he could unconcernedly leave the pagans shut up in Taif, held in check by their former allies.

After the Prophet's return to Medina delegations from nearly all the Bedouin tribes arrived in the course of the following two years to announce their voluntary submission. Only seldom was he now compelled to avenge an attack on his religious emissaries or tax collectors by punitive expedition. In 630 Taif also surrendered, after the Thaqif had been reduced almost to beggary by the Bedouins constantly patrolling beneath their walls. In vain did the emissaries announcing their submission beg for a brief respite for their goddess, Allat. The Prophet was implacable. One of their people, Mughirah ibn-Shu'bah, who had already come to Medina and whom we shall encounter later as an unscrupulous careerist, was charged with the destruction of the image of the city goddess. Spiritually, paganism offered no further opposition to the Prophet. It was as individual tribes that the Arabs submitted to his political authority. Even some of the Christians in northern Arabia surrendered their religion without more ado, although the South Arabian church of Najran, which had already given proof of its faith throughout a violent persecution under a Jewish king of Yemen, now too held fast to its Christianity. The Prophet exhausted all his powers of persuasion on its bishop, Abu-l-Harith, and the prince, 'Abd-al-Masih, who had come to Medina for negotiations face to face; they remained inflexible, and so Muhammad had to be content with a treaty granting them freedom of worship in return for a substantial tribute.

The firmness of Muhammad's grip on great stretches of Arabia by this time was shown in the recognition accorded his authority by the most important poets of the period. Under paganism poets had not only been the pride of their tribes but had also wielded an important political influence through their rhetorical power. Two of the most celebrated poets of the time, Labid and al-A'sha, accepted Islam. The former had acquired great renown even in his youth as spokesman for his tribe, the Kilab, a member of the Hawazin group; he belonged to the tribal delegation which had come to Medina in 631 to negotiate on the question of joining the new political body, and at that time accepted Islam. His poems, which for a long time had carried a religious undertone, from then on gave it more and more emphasis, and became a model for Islamic religious poetry. The second, who had traveled across all of Arabia as a wandering troubadour in the service of various rulers, sang the Prophet's praises in a great panegyric, though the genuineness of this in the version now extant may be contested. At bottom the Prophet was not particularly well disposed to their poetry, it being one of the most beautiful flowers of the ancient pagan way of life. It is true he himself maintained a court poet, the above-mentioned Hassan ibn-Thabit, in order to answer the Bedouin rhetoricians in their own style; but if one of these dared misuse his skill against the faith itself, the Prophet was implacable. At that time Ka'b, the son of one of the most important poets of the days of paganism, Zuhayr, lived among the Muzaynah tribe. Heir to his father's art, he observed with repugnance the spread of the new faith, which penetrated the habits of life so deeply with its troublesome exigencies. On top of that he now had to experience the conversion of his own brother Bujayr to the new doctrines, and he gave vent to his feelings in bitterly scornful verse. The Prophet could not let this pass unpunished. Ka'b was declared outlawed, and consequently went in peril of his life until he could secure the Prophet's pardon. He then concentrated all his artistic skill into a resounding eulogy of the new ruler of the Arab world. He got to Medina safely and contrived to secure permission for a performance in Muhammad's presence. His verses, which were composed entirely in the style of the ancient poetry, and completely devoid of any religious note, nevertheless made such a deep impression on Muhammad that he threw him his own mantle as a gift; in ancient Arabia generally, as in medieval France, the mantle often served as a fee for poets and singers. The gift was so valued by Ka'b that he refused to give it up even when the caliph Mu'awiyah later offered him ten thousand dirhams for it. It was only after his death that the Prince was able to secure the revered garment from the heirs. After that it was preserved in the treasury of the Commander of the Believers as one of its most precious possessions, first in Damascus and then in Baghdad, until 1258, when flames destroyed it during the Mongol conquest of the city.

Muhammad himself took the field only once again. The defeat his troops had suffered at the hands of the Byzantines at Mu'tah had, after all, gone unavenged. At the height of the summer heat of 630 he summoned his followers to a campaign against the Byzantines. It is not clear what made him do this precisely at this time; he may have thought he had to give some further employment to the Medinese, still in a state of discontent after the division of the Hunayn booty. But he was probably considering the subjugation of the remaining Christian Arabs, who were supported by Byzantium. He set out northward with thirty thousand men, but got only as far as Tabuk, an oasis with grain fields and palm plantations, near the Byzantine frontier. Here, already infirm through advancing age, he made a halt; he may have convinced himself of the impracticability of his plans. He accepted the oath of allegiance of the Christian prince of Aylah (now 'Aqabah) at the northeastern tip of the eastern arm of the Red Sea; the Christians there also were granted freedom of worship in return for an obligation to pay tribute.

But paganism in Arabia was soon to lose its last foothold. After the taking of Mecca, the Prophet at first had endured in silence the celebration of the pilgrimage festival in the old pagan manner. In 630 he sent Abu Bakr from Medina to Mecca as the leader of the pilgrimage, presumably in order not to sanction the abuses prevailing there by his own presence. At the conclusion of the festival, however, his son-in-law 'Ali read out at Mina on his orders a decree which has been retained in the beginning of the ninth surah of the

Qur'an. In it the Prophet finally broke with the idol-worshipers: in the future no unbeliever was to perform the pilgrimage within the holy area; treaties the Prophet had concluded with the unbelievers were to remain in force till the expiration of the interludes agreed upon, provided the latter continued their punctilious observance, but anyone unable to point to such a treaty had only the choice of accepting Islam or of a war to the death; the pagans had time to return to their homes unmolested until the end of the holy month, later they would be attacked wherever found. This renunciation was effective; in only a few cases were the Muslims to be compelled to resort to force within Arabia itself.

Toward the end of the year 10 of the Hijrah, in the spring of 632, Muhammad could regard his mission in Arabia as fulfilled. In demonstration of this he undertook a solemn pilgrimage to Mecca, with all his wives and a great company of believers, a farewell pilgrimage, as it is called in biographical tradition. Every single action he took during those days has been handed down to us with painful exactitude; this pilgrimage is regarded by Muslims down to this day as the model of the correct performance of the sacred rites. On the second or third day the Prophet is supposed to have made an address in which, particularly, he established a lunar calendar of twelve months and enjoined the basic duties of Islam upon the believers.

After the Prophet returned from the pilgrimage all sorts of threatening news began to come into Medina. In central Arabia, Musaylimah, a chieftain of the banu Hanifah, had arisen and in an impudent letter called upon the Prophet to recognize him as having equal rights. In the far east also, among the banu Asad, a suspicious ferment had broken out. Nevertheless the Prophet decided on a new campaign against the Byzantines. In March 632 he delegated the command of the troops being sent out against the Christians to Usamah, the son of the Zayd who had fallen at Mu'tah. In the midst of these preparations the Prophet fell ill, probably of malaria, which in Medina was endemic. Although he was not more than sixty years at the most, his strength had waned considerably during the hardships of the past years and through an excess of pleasure-taking in the harem. He soon had to give up his custom of staying overnight in the huts of each one of his wives in turn, and to settle down permanently with his favorite wife 'Aishah. After exhorting to obedience the believers who were grumbling against the selection of the youthful Usamah, he had to give up leading the daily prayers. He transferred this office to his old friend and father-in-law Abu Bakr. His powers were dwindling away more and more, and while conscious he was disturbed by delirium. On Sunday, July 7, when he tried to dictate his last will, 'Umar already thought it advisable to refuse him this last request, so that no ill-considered commands might endanger the cause of the believers. The next night the fever fell away somewhat, and in the morning an improvement seemed to have taken place. When the believers had gathered for prayer, the Prophet stepped out of the door of 'Aishah's hut in order to see his faithful followers once more. But he had scarcely returned to his couch when he began to turn feverish again. The death throes began. Toward noon 'Aishah felt his hand go limp in her own. One more soft outcry: "God forgive me, have compassion on me, and take me into the highest heaven," and Muhammad was dead.

3. *Muhammad and His Teachings*

The religious enthusiast Muhammad, who felt he was a prophet and "warner" sent to his people in Mecca, developed, in Medina, into a leader of a political body, into a gifted statesman not to be deflected from his final goal, rule over Arabia, and not deterred by temporary rebuffs, such as the treaty of Hudaybiyah. His political decrees in Medina were also made public as "Qur'an" and laid claim to divine inspiration. But the form had to be adjusted for the sake of content, and only the rhyme, often poorly treated, remained as a sign of the revelation style.

Muhammad's religion must not, of course, be judged only by the Qur'an. There is really no question of his having system; acuteness and intellectual consistency were never his strong points. His intellectual world was his own only to the smallest degree; it stemmed mostly from Judaism and Christianity, and was skillfully adapted by him to the religious needs of his people. In doing this he raised them to a higher level of intuitive belief and moral sensitivity.

Muhammad's God is the Lord, first and foremost. From the Babylonian period on, the Semite has seen in his God a self-willed, capricious, and cruel peremptory commander, whose will is unfathomable only because it is as fickle as an Oriental despot's. Allah does not ordain his decrees because they are holy and just, but because it pleases him to do it; consequently he can alter them as he sees fit or rescind them at any time. But Muhammad's God is also kindly and compassionate. His kindliness was felt by the Prophet himself; he knew God had no desire of making the performance of their religious duties needlessly difficult for his believers, since he was aware of their weakness (Surah 4:32). In this, however, there was no question of any consistency. Sometimes Muhammad had God lay down for all eternity who among mankind could attain grace through faith, who had to languish in unbelief and who fall prey to eternal damnation; sometimes he tried not to eliminate human free will. It is no wonder that the most savage conflicts in later dogmatic speculation flared up precisely over this point. Eventually the doctrine of absolute predestination prevailed, and with it that fatalism which has been one of the most basic elements of the Muslim *Weltanschauung* ever since.

Moreover, the abstract monotheism which to a considerable extent was the basis of the proselytizing power of Islam developed only gradually. The Prophet's initial inclination to recognize the principal Meccan goddesses as intercessors with Allah has been mentioned before. As the concept of the deity solidified, a crass anthropomorphism kept pace with it. This also gave rise later on to violent dogmatic conflicts from which the orthodox party, with its strict literal interpretation of all relevant passages in the Qur'an, emerged victorious, clearly in the spirit of the founder of the religion himself.

The second basic dogma of Islam is: Muhammad is the Apostle of God. The Prophet had taken from the Old Testament the doctrine of the fall, and he taught that in order to warn mankind of sin, particularly of idol worship, God had sent prophets to every people at given times to whom he revealed his will through the angel Gabriel. These revelations–not, to be sure, without falsifications–were present in the Holy Scriptures of the Jews and the Christians. Jesus ('Isa) was next-to-the-last prophet; like his predecessors he had predicted the coming of Muhammad, who, however, was the last of the prophets. Muhammad had been sent to the Arabs first of all, but his religion, Islam, was to restore throughout the world the pure doctrine of Abraham which had been falsified by the Jews and Christians. Whether and from what point onward the Prophet himself had felt himself called to such a universal mission cannot, to be sure, be determined with certainty. God's word to Muhammad is the Qur'an. At first this was the name of each individual revelation; it was not until later that this word ("reading") was applied to all the collected revelations. As the norm and touchstone of life the Qur'an was supplemented for the Muslim by the Prophet's Sunnah, his words and deeds as handed down to posterity by his companions. But the tradition concerning this did not arise for the most part until after two centuries of Islam, and so may be used as a source for the doctrine of the Prophet himself only with the greatest of caution.

In Mecca, Muhammad's religious ideas at first revolved around his eschatology. His conceptions of the hereafter go back to Jewish, and so, indirectly, to Persian and ancient Babylonian sources. At first he believed that the hour of judgment was imminent; later on he found himself compelled to keep postponing the date, knowledge of which God had reserved for himself. He expected a mighty blow or peal as proclamation of the hour of judgment; later on he spoke of a blast of trumpets or an angel's summons: the earth was to begin trembling at once, the mountains to quiver like a mirage or fly away like clouds and be ground to dust; the sea to overflow its shores; the sun to turn on its axis, the moon darken and split in two, the stars hurtle to earth, and the heavens to open and reveal the future world before the eyes of mankind.

At the judgment, as depicted in the early surahs, the Divine Book is opened in which all human deeds are recorded, and judgment apportioned accordingly. Every man receives a list of his deeds, to read aloud himself; if placed in his right hand it also contains his reward, but whoever receives it in his left hand knows himself to be damned. The blessed stand at God's right hand, the damned at his left; nearest the throne stand the most pious in three groups. Later on the Prophet paints this procedure in more and more lively colors. Then God weighs the deeds in a scale; the damned try to excuse themselves, but the prophets of their time testify against them. Judgment is followed by immediate reward or punishment. The upright are removed to the Garden of Eden or to Paradise, which Muhammad, a city Arab grown up in the burning heat of the valley, conceived of as being on a cool mountaintop. A live spring bubbles up here, with easy chairs and gaily colored carpets around it. Here the blessed loll about radiating joy in green satin garments with silver buckles, and drink the spring water mingled with costly spices, or magnificent wine out of jugs sealed with musk. The open square is surrounded by trees which give them shade as well as fruit and grapes to sate their hunger. In addition they enjoy the company of dark-eyed virgins (*hur*) whom God has granted eternal youth. As can be seen, these paradisiacal joys are calculated exclusively for a masculine imagination. Women, to whom the Prophet also held out the prospect of entry into this garden, were promised freedom from hatred and envy, as well as joy in pious discourses and in God's greeting.

While Paradise is opened for the blessed, the damned go down to the Jahannam, an abyss filled with fiery flames. Muhammad threatens the wicked with other terrors besides the torments of the heat, but with no systematic gradation of the punishments as encountered in Jewish and Christian fantasies of hell. The spring of Paradise is paralleled here by a hot, stinking salt well, whose moisture lacerates the entrails of the thirsty. Instead of fruit they are offered a malodorous plant which does not allay the pangs of hunger. Later Muhammad names the tree Zaqqum, "which cometh up from the bottom of hell and its fruit is as it were the heads of Satans" (Surah 37: 62, 63). In other places he traditionally portrays hell as a torture chamber with neck irons and chains manipulated by nineteen infernal guards under the command of a superior. To the afflictions of the body are added torments of the spirit, self-accusations, maledictions, and vain pleas for redemption. The infernal punishments are just as eternal as the joys of Paradise, and Jewish hopes for a merely temporal punishment of sinners from among the people of Israel were combated by Muhammad in Medina with the utmost rigor.

The religious obligations of the Qur'an have no inherent connection with the faith of the believer; as in later-day Judaism, they have a character of external legalism. Purely ceremonial prescriptions, such as ablutions before prayer, are put on exactly the same level as commandments of an elevated moral value, such as that of honesty. Ablutions are, as a matter of fact, the primary canonical duty of believers; if water cannot be obtained, sand may be used as an abrasive. The second duty is prayer itself. This consists of a series of quite fixed formulae and Qur'anic verses which are to be repeated in equally fixed and regularly alternating bodily postures. The totality of these formulae and postures is called a *rak'ah*, which must be repeated at least twice for each prayer. While Muhammad and his followers prayed twice a day in Mecca, and according to Jewish example three times a day in Medina, subsequent ritual, under Persian influence, makes five prayer periods obligatory: before dawn, at noon, in the afternoon until just before sunset, in the evening, and at nightfall. The hours of prayer are announced by a crier, a mu'adhdhin, from the tower of the mosque. The Arabs became acquainted with these towers (minarets, from *manarah*—"lighthouse") only in the conquered lands, whose achitectural style they borrowed; in the Mediterranean countries the models were lighthouses, in Syria watch- and church towers, in Persia and India signal towers and stambhas as tokens of divinity; these minarets were first closely attached to the mosque in Asia Minor, especially under the Osmanlis. On Friday the noonday prayer is held in a public service. It is accompanied by the khutbah, a pulpit address by the leader of the prayers, later by an official preacher, which, after a silent prayer, runs into the profession of faith and an intercession for Muhammad and his house, for the particularly meritorious among the first adherents of Islam as well as for all believers in general, for the victory of Muslim arms, and later also for the reigning prince, in particular, whom the community recognizes as such by this prayer. The pulpit in the mosque, the *minbar*, simply developed out of the prince's seat, which according to the ancient Oriental example the Prophet was accustomed to ascend on ceremonial occasions; this was taken over first of all by the provincial governors, who in the chief settlements conducted Friday worship themselves, and it was not until the second century of the Hijrah that the custom of ascending the pulpit became general. In contradistinction to the Jews, as already mentioned, the Prophet forbore to enjoin on his believers freedom from labor on Fridays.

The third chief religious duty is fasting, the renunciation of food and drink and all other enjoyments such as, for instance, sweet smells, from dawn till sunset throughout the month of Ramadan. Since because of the lunar year this cuts across all seasons, the performance of this duty, particularly in tropical countries, often means a severe sacrifice for the believers. The night before the twenty-seventh of Ramadan is considered especially holy; it is the Laylat al-Qadr, the "Night of Determination," in which the Prophet was called to his office by the revelation of the 96th surah. Only invalids, travelers, and soldiers on the march are relieved of the duty of fasting, but they must make up for any days missed.

The fourth canonical duty, the performance of which is demanded of every believer at least once during his lifetime, is the pilgrimage to Mecca; * only poverty, illness, or bondage can excuse its omission. When the pilgrim arrives at the boundary line of the holy area he changes his clothing for the pilgrim's garments, consisting of two pieces of any material, one of which is wrapped around the shoulders and the other around the waist. Only sandals are permitted in addition; the head must remain uncovered even during the hottest summer. This is the garb of a long vanished stage of civilization, a ritual survival here as in other religions. In Mecca itself the pilgrim first of all visits the Ka'bah. This is a somewhat irregular cube-shaped structure about forty feet long, thirty feet wide, and thirty-five to forty feet in height. It is covered with cloth on all four sides. The Ka'bah stands in the approximate center of an open square about two hundred paces long and a hundred and fifty paces wide; on which today only a few small outbuildings are still to be found, and which is enclosed within a double row of columns. Before Muhammad's return the Ka'bah contained images of idols; now it probably holds only candelabra and besoms. The corners point approximately to the four points of the compass. Plastered into the wall in the east corner, five feet above the ground, there is the famous Black Stone, an ovoid about eleven inches in diameter, which now consists of a number of small stones and three larger ones, and consequently is held together by a silver band. This stone is probably the oldest idol of pagan Mecca, similar to other sacred stones often encountered among the Semites; Muhammad took over the custom of kissing it in the pilgrimage ceremonial without giving it any more explicit foundation. At the inception of Islam there was no lack of opposition to the cult of stones, which was consciously felt as pagan. Next to the Ka'bah there is the Zamzam spring, which according to legend saved Ishmael, the ancestor of the North Arabs, and his mother Hagar from dying of thirst. Its water is drunk by the believers with reverence, after the Ka'bah is circumambulated as prescribed. Then there is the run between Safa and Marwah. These are the names of two hills, which today show only a slight projection above the ground. The first one, about fifty paces distant from the southeast side of the Mosque, is distinguished by three small open arches led up to by three stone steps; the second is about six hundred feet farther on and carries a platform which is also to be ascended by steps. The distance between the two

* See Snouck Hurgronje, *Het mekkaansche Feest,* Leiden, 1880.

hills must be traversed seven times at a trot, so that one finishes at Marwah. This completes the ceremonies of the Little Pilgrimage, the 'Umrah. This Ka'bah festival in the month of Rajab was manifestly united long before Muhammad with the Hajj in the month of Dhu-l-Hijjah (the last month of the year) which originally was to be made only to Mt. 'Arafat.

At the great annual pilgrimage on the eighth of Dhu-l-Hijjah, after the first circumambulation of the Ka'bah, the pilgrims pass by Mina, where if possible the preceding night was to have been spent, to the broad plain at the foot of Mt. 'Arafat, a granite hill about two hundred feet high, lying about four hours by camel east of Mecca. According to Islamic legend Gabriel is supposed to have first instructed Adam in prayer on its peak. In remembrance of this the pilgrims linger there in meditation from noon of the ninth of Dhu-l-Hijjah till sunset. In the evening they return and spend the night in Muzdalifah, between 'Arafat and Mina. The next morning they go as far as Mina. There, after a short rest, they assemble before a rock heap on which each pilgrim must throw seven small stones. This is supposed to take place in memory of Abraham who, in this way, once drove through here the Devil, barring his passage. Here the festival is brought to a close with a ceremonial sacrifice. For this purpose the Bedouins drive up great flocks of sheep, and with his face turned toward Mecca, each pilgrim cuts the throat of one animal with the words: "In the name of God, the Compassionate, the Merciful, God is great." Then the pilgrims cast off their pilgrim's garments, and their hair, which no knife was permitted to come in contact with during the holy period, is cut. They then return to Mecca, circle the Ka'bah another seven times, and run the distance between Safa and Marwah if this was not done immediately upon arrival in Mecca after kissing the Ka'bah. The days from the eleventh to the thirteenth of Dhu-l-Hijjah are passed at Mina in festive spirit at luxuriant banquets; fasting, which otherwise is always meritorious, is flatly prohibited during these days. The pilgrim's only remaining duty is to throw every day seven small stones on the above-mentioned rock heap and on two similar ones each in its neighborhood.

These three days are also a holiday for those Muslims who do not participate in the pilgrimage. It is the great festival which the Turks call *Qurban Bayram*, or sacrificial festival, at which a sheep must be slaughtered in every house.

The Muslim's fifth canonical obligation, the poor-tax, has grown more and more into a state tax during the evolution of Muslim society, as will be shown later. Almsgiving does not arise only from the desire of the pious man to help his needy fellows but serves as a means of alienating a part of his goods, possession of which binds him to the world and estranges him from the hereafter.

Besides these five canonical duties, which are regarded as inviolable, the Muslim's entire private and public life is encompassed by a multiple chain of prescriptions, the observation of which is likewise part of the religion. Only the most important of these can be touched on briefly here.

The Muslim may show only hostility to infidels when encountered: war against them is a religious duty. Idol-worshipers must always be attacked without more ado, Jews and Christians, however, only after they have ignored a summons, made three times, to accept Islam. After defeat the men are to be killed, women and children to be sold into slavery. Whoever is killed in the Holy War is sure of paradise, as a martyr. In addition, it is permitted to conclude treaties with Jews and Christians, following the example of the Prophet; later on the Parsee Zoroastrians were placed on the same level as these "People of the Book." But the obligation of the Holy War is merely postponed by such contracts, not annulled.

In daily life food and drink in particular are regulated, to a certain extent in accordance with the Old Testament. All animals not slaughtered or killed in hunting are excluded from consumption as unclean, as well as blood and meat touched by anything unclean, such as, for instance, an infidel. Beasts of prey, dogs, cats, and swine are altogether prohibited. All intoxicating liquors are forbidden; though the Qur'an names only wine, later teachers of law have extended the interdiction by analogy to alcohol in every form, though without invariable success. Together with wine the Qur'an condemns gambling, which particularly as a raffle for camel's flesh was very popular in ancient Arabia and ruined many fortunes. A superstition common to many peoples of the earth is the basis of the interdiction on images, which is recorded only by tradition, and which, although transgressed often enough during the efflorescence of Islamic civilization, nevertheless inhibited on the whole the development of the plastic arts.

Though the Islamic marriage code put an end to the freedom between the sexes which prevailed in ancient Arabia, it did not abolish polygamy but limited it to four wives, in addition to which a man was to have his slaves at his disposal. The Prophet authorized an unlimited number of wives only for himself. But the law prescribes that each wife is to be supported in keeping with her station; consequently the great mass of the people must content themselves with monogamy if only for economic reasons. Divorce, to be sure, is very easy, but this is merely a necessary compensation for the separation of the sexes enjoined by custom, which almost excludes marriages of affection. Since every Muslim may have as many slaves as he likes for concubines, besides his four legitimate wives, the temptation for the well-to-do classes to disregard an orderly family life was very great. A child's legitimacy does not depend on the position of the mother, but only on its recognition by the father, which also equalizes the property rights of the children of the slave women and of the wives. Nevertheless, during the first centuries of Islam nobility of descent was valued in the maternal line also, at least in the circles of the Arab aristocracy, and it was only the harem system which first emerged during the 'Abbasid period that led to unchecked miscegenation.

Muhammad did not do away with slavery any more than the old Christian church touched this foundation of ancient economy, but he softened its rigors in many ways. In any case the slave, whether taken captive in war, or purchased, or born in the household, is legally an object that may be bequeathed in inheritance or given away. The owner has free control over the slave's person and labor but is obligated to treat him well. If the master intends to have any progeny by a slave woman, he may no longer send her out of his household, and at his death she becomes free. In general it is considered a good work to free a slave; the slave may also purchase his own freedom if he has gathered the requisite means by his own efforts, although the freedman retains a certain dependent relation to his master as his client.

The penal code of Islam has remained on a rather primitive level and only marks a slight advance over the ancient pagan concepts of law. The murderer is subject to death through blood vengeance; manslaughter through negligence is recompensed by an indemnity to the survivors. Bodily injuries may be atoned for by the culprit according to the principles of *lex talionis*—"an eye for an eye, a tooth for a tooth"—but the culprit may also redeem himself by paying damages. Theft is punished by amputation of the right hand, in case of relapse by additional maiming. Adultery is punished by a hundred strokes of the lash; but if an infidel seduces a Muslim woman, he is subject to the death penalty. Blasphemy with respect to God, the Prophet, and his predecessors is punished by death, as is defection from Islam, if the culprit persists in his disbelief.

4. *The First Four Caliphs*

At first the Prophet's death seemed to imperil his life's work, the religious and political unification of Arabia. In Medina itself the unexpected news aroused such indescribable confusion that for a whole day no one bothered about the dead body, and not until the following day was it buried in 'Aishah's hut. All the political passions suppressed by his prestige flared up. The number of "doubters" in the city was still very large. The old-established Ansar would gladly have rid themselves of the preponderance of the Muhajirun to become the sole masters in their own house once again. As the Prophet's closest relative, his cousin and son-in-law 'Ali laid claim to the succession as head of the state. But neither he nor the leader of the Ansar, Sa'd ibn-'Ubadah, had enough energy or influence to assert his claim of authority. Consequently the circle of Muhammad's old companions soon succeeded in securing the recognition of his father-in-law Abu Bakr, who with 'Umar and Abu 'Ubaydah ibn-al-Jarrah had previously exercised a decisive influence on the Prophet's politics, as his successor, or *khalifah*, and the Ansar then had no choice but to recognize the new ruler.

But a spirit of defection soon came to life throughout Arabia. In this religious motives played scarcely any role at all; there was simply a desire to be rid of the troublesome rule of the Muslims in Medina. The prophets who assumed command of the rebels acted, like Muhammad, in the name of Allah, not in the name of any of the old gods. Some rebels declared that they still wanted to worship God, but not to pay any more taxes. They were embittered principally at the religious emissaries Muhammad had been sending to many tribes in preceding years to instruct them in the new usages and collect the taxes; as agents for the Medina government they were troublesome and odious to the tribes, who had hitherto been free and independent on their own grazing grounds.

During his very last days the Prophet had busied himself with the equipment of the troops that were to avenge the Byzantine victory at Mu'tah. Abu Bakr felt himself in duty bound to execute this last plan of his, although menacing news of the tumult in Arabia was already coming in from all quarters. Accordingly, the best combat forces of Islam set out northward under Usamah's command; however, we have no information about what they accomplished or whether they even crossed the Byzantine frontier. In any case they were away from Medina for two months. This plight of the capital, denuded of its protection, was first taken advantage of for an attack by the Asad and Ghatafan tribes living in the immediate neighborhood. But Abu Bakr succeeded in holding out till the army's return, when he transferred the command to the tested "Sword of God," Khalid ibn-al-Walid, who defeated both tribes at the Well of Buzakha so decisively that they submitted at once.

The insurrection of the banu Hanifah in Yamamah proved more dangerous. While Muhammad was still alive a man there by the name of Maslamah, whom the Muslims contemptuously called by the diminutive Musaylimah, had emerged as prophet and demanded recognition by Medina as entitled to equal rights. Muslim tradition has naturally handed down only fragments of his religious thought. Maslamah appears to have laid special emphasis on asceticism: he recommended fasting, prohibited wine, and exhorted his followers to chastity, permitting conjugal intercourse only until the birth of a male heir. In his discourses there are even more echoes of Christian ideas than in Muhammad's. They were clothed in the language of a tribesman tilling the soil; he spoke "of the black sheep and the white milk, of milling and baking, of the frog living on the watered and cultivated land, but also of the kingdom of Heaven and of him who will come from Heaven." In spite of a plain appearance he filled his followers with such enthusiasm that for years after his fall many of them refused to abandon faith in him.

A movement similar to Maslamah's among the Hanifah was kindled by a woman called Sajah in the north of the peninsula among the Tamim tribe, tenting in the neighborhood of the Persian border. She had begun her career among her maternal kinfolk, the Taghlib in Mesopotamia, among whom Christianity was widespread; on the report of Muhammad's death she set out with quite a substantial following to her tribal kinsmen, the Tamim, who as pure Bedouins stood on a lower cultural level and worshiped the sun in particular as a deity. At first only her closest relatives, the Hanzalah, supported her, but she soon won over the entire tribe. Then she is supposed to have gone on farther south and allied herself with Maslamah. But the two did not succeed in unifying their followers for a common struggle against Medina. In consequence they soon separated again, and Sajah returned to Mesopotamia, where her career soon came to an end; she is reported to have died a Muslim. When Khalid ibn-al-Walid appeared in the territory of the Tamim, he found obedience almost everywhere. Only Malik ibn-Nuwayrah, chief of the Yarbu', a subtribe of the Hanzalah, who had fallen away from Medina directly upon Muhammad's death, was still faithful to Sajah. But when Khalid had him surrounded together with his troops, he surrendered also. Nevertheless Khalid had him cut down, along with his followers, because, as the story has it, of his lust for Malik's beautiful wife.

After subjugating the Tamim, Khalid marched against Maslamah's supporters in Yamamah, who meanwhile had already defeated a Muslim force under 'Ikrimah. After this initial success Maslamah pressed forward as far as the northern boundary of the Yamamah, where at 'Aqrabah a decisive battle took place, the most violent ever waged in Arabia itself. In order to inflame his men's ambition Khalid had Muhajirun, Ansar, and Bedouins fight separately. The Hanifah were in the majority, and the believers fell back under the impact of their first violent charge. But the mockery of their enemies spurred on the Medinese above all to do their utmost, and they succeeded in bringing the battle to a halt, then gradually pressing the enemy back. When the latter saw defeat before their eyes they retreated into a large orchard buttressing their position, in the hope of finding some protection behind its strong walls against the Muslims' frontal assault. But precisely this brought about their undoing. After the Muslims had once pressed into the Garden of Death, as it is traditionally called, they instituted a frightful blood bath from which no one escaped and in which Maslamah himself was killed. But the Muslims also had heavy losses to mourn; of the Muhajirun and Ansar alone about seven hundred had fallen, among them many of the oldest companions of the Prophet and the greatest connoisseurs of the revelations.

This dearly bought victory determined the fate not only of the Hanifah but of the Arabs in general. The scattered remnants of Maslamah's supporters cast themselves into their fortresses and saved their lives by capitulating. All opposition had been broken here for good.

In Bahrayn, the coastal region along the Persian Gulf which was subjugated only shortly before Muhammad's death, an attempt had also been made to shake off the Medinese yoke. In Hajar, the capital, a scion of the ancient Hirah dynasty which had extended its power into these regions assumed command of the movement. But 'Ala, the governor appointed by Muhammad himself, held out in a fortress north of Hajar until relieved after Maslamah's fall by Khalid. Then the latter set out for Hajar in person and very soon had the rebellion under control. The coastal population, the bulk of whom consisted of Persians, offered more prolonged resistance. Their leader Firoz held out in the harbor city of Sara (probably the modern Qatif) until the beginning of 'Umar's reign. It was only then, after cutting off his water, that the governor 'Ala was able to force him to surrender.

In 'Uman the population, consisting mostly of fishermen and pirates, was able to maintain its independence throughout almost the whole of the Middle Ages down to the present-day sultans of Masqat. At that time a rebellion against the old-established dynasty of the Julandah, who ruled there until the time of the 'Abbasids, gave the Muslims an occasion for interference. King 'Amr had accepted Islam, but the Bedouins in the interior rose against the tax collectors sent out by him on the orders of the central government. 'Ikrimah, who had exerted himself in vain against Maslamah, received an order from Abu Bakr to help the king, and the Bedouins were compelled to yield to the combined forces of the Muslims.

From 'Uman, 'Ikrimah moved on Hadramaut and Yemen, where the insurrection had broken out earliest, and where it took the Muslims longest to crush it. By the time Islam came into the country the Bedouins living in the northern portion of the country, the Tihamah, had almost entirely smothered the old Sabaean population of the fertile south, which was under Persian rule. As the Persian Empire rapidly declined after the assassination of the Sassanid Chosroes II (Parvez) in 628, the Arabian provinces, particularly remote Yemen, had been left to themselves. In the general anarchy which now broke out numerous tribes after the fall of Mecca had announced their allegiance through delegations to Medina. Shortly before his death Muhammad had introduced order into the country, and the tax assessments laid down by him were later considered exemplary. Yet his emissaries did not supplant the numerous petty indigenous rulers but stood at their side like the residents of modern colonial powers at the side of native princes. They established a general supervision, regulated jurisdiction and worship, and above all collected taxes. Since this most unpopular aspect of their official power often drove them to ruthless measures, they had in the Prophet's own lifetime aroused an insurrection in Hadramaut, which was, however, put down with savage rigor. Even before this a prophet had appeared among the Aus tribe, Ayhabah Dhu-l-Himar, "the Donkey Rider." (In the Orient generally the donkey was regarded from of old [Zechariah 9:9] as the riding beast of the awaited Saviour. This was why Jesus made his entry into Jerusalem on a she-donkey, and the founder of a fanatical North African sect in the tenth century was called Dhu-l-Himar, and even at the beginning of this century the leader of an insurrection against the sultan of Morocco was known as Bu Hamarah.) Monotheism had already been widely spread by Jews and Christians in South Arabia, and so this prophet also did not act in the name of some idol or other but in that of God, Allah the Compassionate. The news that Muhammad had fallen ill on his return from the last pilgrimage encouraged him to come out into the open. From Najran he attacked the Persian governor still resident in San'a; after defeating him all of Yemen lay at his feet. But in spite of his illness Muhammad had been able to exert an influence there through emissaries and letters, so that those loyal to him acted in concert against the false prophet. Incited by one of these emissaries, the aristocratic Persians in San'a conspired to bring about the assassination of Ayhabah, supposedly one day before Muhammad's death. But a new defection soon followed this brief victory for Islam. Ayhabah's most important partisan, Qays, supported by the Arabs, rose against the Persians. Abu Bakr, however, then sent out an army under a governor formerly installed by Muhammad himself over a section of Hadramaut, who soon pacified the country.

In this way, now that all of Arabia in this relatively short space of time had submitted to the authority of Islam, Abu Bakr was able to take up the Prophet's final plan, that of spreading the faith beyond the boundaries of his homeland. For he had to create an opportunity of external development for those forces which in the past had always been ready to exhaust each other in endless bickerings. But whereas the Prophet, overestimating his own power and falsely evaluating the international situation, particularly with respect to Byzantium, had first attempted to attack Byzantium, his successor directed his gaze eastward first of all, toward the Persian Empire, whose weakness he must long since have observed.

For centuries Persia and Rome had been wrestling for hegemony in the Near East. Like the Parthians under the Arsacids, their followers the Sassanids had beaten back the advances of the East Roman empire on Mesopotamia. Under Chosroes II (590-628) the Persians had pushed far ahead to the attack, conquering Jerusalem and even Egypt.* But the emperor Heraclius had wrested his conquests away from him again and pursued him into his own residency itself. Here the Persian king was assassinated by his own son Kawad II, and the latter had to sue the Emperor for peace. Thereafter the Sassanid empire was heading toward its inexorable doom. It had never possessed the firm foundation of a homogeneous race. The Aryans who had migrated into the country during the prehistoric period were much inferior in numbers to the original Near Eastern population that soon absorbed them, even though a Zoroastrian religious decree had gone as far as recommending marriage between relatives in order to maintain racial purity. The physical type of the Near East had prevailed completely, and the language the immigrants had imposed on their subjects was strongly influenced by the latter. Ever since the Sassanids had removed the center of gravity of their empire to Babylon, with the capital at Ctesiphon-Seleucia, the Aramean Christians had given them a great deal of trouble. It was not until the Nestorians in their empire had founded a church in 484 independent of the Byzantine church that they acquired greater influence among the Iranians as well, for the latter also suffered severely from time to time under the fanaticism of the Zoroastrian fire priests.

Twice in their history the Persians had vainly attempted to revolt against them. Under Shapur I (241-72), Mani had emerged as founder of a new gnostic religion influenced by Christianity as much as by Babylon and Iran, and apparently had won over the great king himself; but under the latter's successor, Bahram I, he died in prison, and under Shapur II (309-79) his followers were persecuted throughout the empire. All the greater were the successes destined to Manicheanism in the Roman Empire, and more particularly among the Persians' eastern neighbors, the Turks, among whom it vied with Buddhism in spreading the blessings of a peace-loving civilization. But it also continued having an effect in its land of origin, Babylonia;

* The Meccans hailed these Persian victories; but Muhammad, who then still felt attached to the Christians, dared to foretell (Surah 30: 1-4) the early defeat of the Persians.

here its influence on Islam will still be met with. Two centuries later, during the chaos which followed the defeat and fall of King Peroz in the battle against the White Huns in 484, there arose a new religious teacher, Mazdak, who, like Mani, continued the gnostic tendency in Iran, but whose teachings in practice led to the communization of wives and goods. The new king Kawad I joined this sect in 488, no doubt in the hope of being able to break the preponderance of the clergy and the nobility, which imperiled the monarchy. But both in alliance were still powerful enough to overthrow him. His son and successor Chosroes I restored orthodox Zoroastrianism, and was distinguished by its grateful priests with the name of Nushirwan, "of immortal soul." The nobility had in part arisen from among the territorial princes, who under the Arsacids had been practically independent and although limited by the Sassanids, had not been suppressed. They were indispensable to the empire, for their tenants constituted the core of the army, the heavily armed armored cavalry. Consequently high military commands, just like some court offices, were hereditary in certain families. Just as they had meddled with the state power often before, to the country's ruin, so they rose up, after Kawad II died of the plague in 628, and overthrew a series of new rulers, including two daughters of Chosroes II. Even the power of the imperial marshal, which for a time overshadowed all other forces, was no longer capable of propping up the state structure, shaken to its foundations. When the last Sassanid, Yezdegerd, mounted the throne in 632, the Arabs had already poised themselves for the decisive blow against Iran's independence.

One of Abu Bakr's generals, Muthanna ibn-al-Harith, who had taken part in the subjugation of Bahrayn, was already making raiding forays from there across the Persian border. On the Caliph's orders Khalid ibn-al-Walid joined forces with him, after putting down Maslamah's insurrection in Yamamah. They turned to Hirah first of all. At this time Hirah had long since lost its earlier importance as border outpost against the Bedouins, since the last Lakhmid, Mundhir V, had been eliminated in 602 by Chosroes II. The Persian commandant of the Hirah garrison was beaten at Ullays, the ancient Vologesias, and in 633 Hirah itself fell into the hands of the Muslims without further resistance.

After the conquest of South Babylonia had succeeded with such unexpected ease, the goal already set by the Prophet, the occupation of the Holy Land, was energetically recalled in Medina.* Arabs were, after all, living in the Byzantine Empire, just as in the Persian, to whom it was necessary to bring the blessings of Islam and who had to be integrated into the newly arisen national state. The Arab vassal of the Byzantines in Damascus was no longer to be feared, since the Melkite church which had subsidized the payment of Emperor Heraclius's troops had, because of the monstrous burden of debts resulting from the Persian war, denied any further credit. In accordance with the difficulty of the enterprise, which had already vainly been embarked on twice in the time of the Prophet, the campaign against Syria was given careful preparation in Medina from the outset. In the spring of 634 Abu Bakr sent out two armies against Syria, one of them, under 'Amr ibn-al-'As, attacking southeastern Palestine, the second, under Yazid ibn-Shurahbil and Abu 'Ubaydah, the territory of ancient Moab. Only after 'Amr had made quite an extended advance did the Byzantines dispatch a larger army against him. At the news of these successes in the west Khalid had hurried forward with a picked troop of horsemen from Babylonia and assumed supreme command of the army in the Transjordan. With this he now came to 'Amr's help. In July or August a great battle took place, reputedly at Ajnadayn,† in Palestine between Ramlah and Bayt Jibrin, in which the united Muslim armies conquered the Byzantines under Aretion. While the latter sought refuge in Jerusalem, his commanders were only able to bring their fleeing ranks to a halt and gather them together on the other side of the Jordan. They had pierced the dams at Baysan, making the fords across the Jordan impassable, but Khalid got across nevertheless. In January 635 he attacked the enemy again at Fahl (the Greek Pella) on the western slopes of Transjordan where they had gathered southeast of Baysan, forced them to retreat, and pursued them as far as Damascus. Meanwhile a smaller Muslim detachment had pressed north through the unprotected countryside and taken the city of Hims (ancient Emesa). The emperor Heraclius, who had led the campaign from there the year before, had meanwhile retired to Antioch. Khalid gave the Byzantines another battle before the walls of Damascus, and then shut them up in the city. After a half-year siege Damascus surrendered, in September 635. For reasons unknown to us the supreme command now went from Khalid to

* M. J. de Goeje, *Mémoire sur la conquête de la Syrie*, 2 éd., *Mém. d'hist. et de géog. arabe* II, Leiden, 1901.

† See note on page 53.

Abu 'Ubaydah, but the former continued to be the real driving force of the campaign. Meanwhile the Emperor had sent out a new army from Antioch into Syria, probably with orders to relieve Damascus. Although it was too late for that, it was at least able to retake Hims. During the autumn and winter a truce appears to have prevailed.

In the summer of 636 the Byzantines reopened the campaign with a mighty army under the command of Sacellarius * Theodorus. The Muslims awaited them on the Yarmuk, a Jordan tributary rising in the Hawran and discharging below the Sea of Galilee,† and there on August 20 inflicted an annihilating defeat on them, for the Armenians forming almost half of their army had a grudge against Byzantium and were unwilling to fight. The Muslims then pressed northward in triumph and occupied Hims a second time.

Meanwhile the battles against the Persians were also going on farther eastward. After Khalid's expedition in the spring of 634, Muthanna, of the Bakr tribe, had assumed supreme command in Hirah. In July of the same year the caliph Abu Bakr had died in Medina, and 'Umar, the most powerful and respected of the Muhajirun, had assumed authority. In the same way as he had expedited the Syrian campaign before, he now sent reinforcements to Babylonia under Abu 'Ubayd of the Thaqif tribe. But the Persians were also making preparations to defend themselves against the invaders. At Quss an-Natif near Hirah a Persian army came up against the Muslims. Abu 'Ubayd crossed the Euphrates on a bridge of ships at this point and accepted battle, but was defeated and killed. Since the bridge of ships had already been partially disrupted by an overzealous Muslim, Muthanna had a great deal of difficulty in securing the retreat of the fleeing troops. The extremely involved internal politics of the Persian Empire prevented the victors from exploiting their success. But as a result of this first failure 'Umar also lost all interest in this Babylonian theater of war.

It was not until the following year that the Persians advanced

* [Comptroller general of the army.]

† The reports sometimes confuse this battle with that of Ajnadayn. It has been surmised in consequence that this battle took place at the biblical Yarmuth, the present-day Khirbat Yarmuk on the Judean plain. Since the name Ajnadayn has not been handed down anywhere else, the Russian scholar Myednikov has conjectured, no doubt correctly, that it is a corruption of Jannabatayn, since there are two places in the neighborhood, Jannabah West and Jannabah East, which may be lumped together in this dual form, as happens elsewhere.

again to the attack. Muthanna was awaiting them at Buwayb, on the other side of one of the western Euphrates canals. Here, in spite of valiant resistance, the Persians were defeated, whereupon the Muslims began venturing a considerable distance into the country on their raids. In the beginning of the summer of 635 the Persians armed for a last decisive blow. Muthanna had died in the meantime, and in his place Sa'd ibn-abi-Waqqas, one of the oldest and most faithful of the Prophet's companions, had assumed supreme command. At the head of the Persian army there stood the imperial field marshal Rustam himself. Shortly before, after a protracted period of women's rule, the youthful Yezdegerd had mounted the Sassanid throne and was openly making earnest efforts to clear out the endangered border province. At Qadisiyah, south of the present-day Najaf and eighteen and a half miles from the army encampment of Kufah (which was erected after the battle and later developed into a city), a decisive battle took place, after the adversaries had been expectantly confronting each other for a number of weeks. Although a quantity of romantic details of this engagement has been handed down, we lack a clear picture of its course. Since, on the Persian side a unified strategic command can scarcely be assumed, and since the Arabs fought separately by tribe, the battle must have been resolved by a series of individual engagements. In any case the Persians were seriously defeated; but the Muslims, who had been assured of victory only by reinforcements arriving from Syria during the battle, had also suffered such losses that at first they were compelled to let the enemy withdraw unmolested. But then they advanced across the Euphrates toward Ctesiphon and Seleucia, the capital of the empire. After two inconsequential rear-guard actions the Persians had to abandon Babylonia, and the Arabs entered their capital city. The booty which fell into their hands there, and of which tradition has all sorts of marvels to relate, naturally acted as a powerful incentive in Arabia also when it came to recruiting replacements for the losses suffered. The Persians had at first withdrawn to Hulwan, at the foot of the passes of the Zagros; here Yezdegerd gathered together the ruins of the imperial army, augmenting them by new levies. Then, when the Persians began gradually venturing down again into the valley of the Diyala River, which pours into the Tigris above Ctesiphon, Sa'd sent his nephew out against them with twelve thousand men. Toward the end of 637 the latter defeated them at Jalula, on the right bank of the Diyala, at the east end of the pass leading through Jabal Hamrin along the old caravan highway between Babylonia and Iran. Although the Persian court managed to hold out for a short while in the fortifications of Hulwan, the flatland as far as the Median border was in the hands of the Muslims, who had already indicated the permanent character of their occupation by building their mosque in the capital.

The conquest of Syria was also completed in the same year. The Muslim headquarters were at Jabiyah in the Jawlan, a day's journey south of Damascus, where the Ghassanid princes had formerly resided, and which retained its military importance until the time of the Umayyads. In 637 the caliph 'Umar, escorted by the most revered of the Prophet's companions with the exception of 'Ali, set out there to introduce order into the conquered lands. By the "Day of Jabiyah," in which all leaders of the Syrian army participated, the foundations had probably already been laid of the pension system, which assured participants in the war and their descendants of a fixed income from the revenues of the conquered territories. From there 'Umar dispatched Khalid ibn-Thabit to conquer Jerusalem, which soon surrendered; 'Umar himself approved the rather mild terms. The Christians were granted security of life and property, the maintenance of their churches, and religious freedom in return for the customary payment of tribute, while the Jews were forbidden to live among them. Then 'Umar himself came to Jerusalem, and in the desolate temple square had the sacred rock—which Jews, Christians, and Muslims alike regarded as the navel of the earth—cleaned and divine worship established.

When the Muslims had once become masters of Syria and Babylonia, Mesopotamia, lying in between, had to fall to them of itself. Byzantine troops were still there only in a few fortified places. The indigenous Aramean population had always been oppressed for its Monophysite faith by the dominant Greek orthodoxy, and so had no interest in maintaining the imperial power. For centuries previous Arabian nomads had overrun the country and even ruled from time to time in Edessa and Hatra, and so Mesopotamia was quite prepared for the Arab conquest.

The Muslims' attack started from Syria. After the death of Abu 'Ubaydah in 639, whom plague had snatched in Amwas (Emmaus),*

* His memory still lives today as that of a saint among the Palestinian Muslims; in 1933 the emir of Transjordan, 'Abdallah, made a pilgrimage to his grave in atonement for having rented a large estate in Ghor al-Kabid to the Jews; see *Revue des études islamiques*, 1933, 547.

'Umar had installed 'Iyad ibn-Ghanim there as governor of Hims and Qinnasrin with orders to extend his power throughout Mesopotamia. In the second half of the year he advanced into the country, and in a year and a half forced nearly every city to capitulate; only Reshayna had to be taken by a hard struggle. Having undertaken a raid into Armenia itself in 641, 'Iyad died soon after returning to his residence.

The conquest of Mesopotamia was simultaneously accompanied by that of Egypt,* which as a granary of ancient repute must have seemed particularly desirable to the Medina government, and whose confused conditions had already been known even to the Prophet. In 628, after Emperor Heraclius had wrested the country away again from its Persian conquerors, he attempted to unite the Monophysite Copts with the imperial church. In 631 he had installed Cyrus (the Muqawqis of the Arabs), who up to then had been bishop of Phasis in the Caucasus, both as patriarch of Alexandria and head of the civil administration at the same time. His ecclesiastical policy and his tax demands weighed so heavily on the Copts that they necessarily greeted the Arabs as emancipators, just as their Syrian fellow believers had done. In December 639 the Umayyad 'Amr ibn-al-'As, the initial commander of the army sent to Palestine, made an attack from there on the fertile Fayyum plain, apparently without orders from the caliph 'Umar and with insufficient troops, and conquered Pelusium in January 640. At first 'Amr dared not go any further, since the *augustalis* Theodorus had gathered together a powerful body of troops in Babylon, the old Memphis. Now 'Umar sent Zubayr, a revered companion of the Prophet, to Egypt with five thousand reinforcements; he was also to keep watch over 'Amr, who had an inclination toward independent action. In June 640, 'Amr lured the Byzantines out of their fortress into an open battle and conquered them at Heliopolis. Meanwhile the fortress in Babylon was still holding. From there Cyrus himself entered into negotiations with 'Amr and then went to Byzantium to secure the Emperor's approval of the concessions he had made the Arabs. Heraclius, who treated him as a traitor, died on February 11, 641. Meanwhile, Arab raiding bands were ranging up and down the country plundering and ravaging. Theodorus pleaded urgently but in vain for reinforcements. The regents of the new emperor Con-

* See A. J. Butler, *The Arab Conquest of Egypt and the Last Thirty Years of the Roman Dominion*, Oxford, 1902.

stans II, at this time only eleven years old,* were compelled to allow events in the Orient to take their gloomy course: they needed their troops in the capital itself against the threat of a revolution, and were also tied down in Italy by the wars with the Lombards. On the Monday after Easter, April 9, 641, Babylon surrendered, and 'Amr moved slowly across the Nile on Alexandria. The Byzantine government consequently sent Cyrus to Egypt again to negotiate with 'Amr. In return for the promise of a fixed payment of tribute the Muslims bound themselves to leave the Christians in possession of their churches and not to interfere in the administration of their communal affairs. In fulfillment of this treaty Alexandria was evacuated by the Byzantines on September 17, 642, and occupied by the Arabs. As first token of the possession of the Nile valley by Islam, 'Amr ibn-al-'As erected the mosque which still bears his name in Fustat, the military encampment at Babylon, later Old Cairo. At its renovation under Mu'awiyah this mosque, as the seat of the prayer callers, had small watch huts with steps set up on the corners, the oldest form of the minaret, which subsequently developed in a variety of styles, and which has been preserved down to the present day in a few village mosques of Egypt and Asia Minor.†

Only once more, in 645, did a Byzantine fleet appear before Alexandria for its reconquest. The inhabitants of the city opened the gates to them, and it was not until 646 that 'Amr could drive them out again. He had previously been removed from governorship by 'Umar, but 'Uthman, who succeeded 'Umar, had to reinstall him, since his successor proved no match for the situation.

In Egypt, as in the other provinces, the Muslims took over the substance of their predecessors' administrative system; they even left all their functionaries at their posts, which were generally administered by Copts later also. As the caliph's governor an emir exercised military and police power; but for the latter not to grow too powerful, an *'amil* was associated with him as director of finances. It is to the dry Egyptian climate that we owe the preservation of the numerous papyri which allow a quite precise view of the course of affairs. The Romans, for the support of their garrisons, and the Byzantines for the provisioning of their capital as well, had deducted in advance the duty on the wheat harvest of every village while it still lay on the threshing floor; the Arabs made the same claim for

* A grandson of Heraclius. He ascended the throne on the death of his father, who reigned for four months.

† See J. Schacht in *Ars Islamica* V (1938), p. 46 ff.

their warriors and their families. Every community received an annual notice from the governor, generally toward the end of the year, shortly before the new sowing period, concerning the wheat quota it was supposed to raise. The head of the district was responsible for directing the collection of this tax in kind. There were tax collectors under him who got five per cent of the produce as a fee for their services and as replacement for any shortages. They gave the state a guarantee for the grain delivered by the peasants until it was placed in the state depot in the individual communities and more particularly in the district capitals. From there the wheat was usually taken by water to the capital and from there distributed among the troops and their families. In addition to these payments in kind the communities had to collect a money tax, primarily for the protection and freedom of worship accorded them by the state. The money, of course, could only be derived by the peasants from the grain trade. But this was always carefully supervised by the state: all grain had to be brought to a state threshing floor, on which presumably the sales also took place. Again, the government may also have not infrequently accepted grain instead of the formally prescribed taxes in cash.*

Meanwhile the fate of the Persian Empire had also been consummated. In 640 King Yezdegerd abandoned Hulwan, where he no longer felt secure now that the country round about had fallen into the hands of the Arabs, and withdrew to Persis. There he armed for final resistance. But before he could imperil the newly won Arab settlements, 'Umar had him attacked by an army under the command of Nu'man ibn-Muqarrin, drawn from all the troops available at the border. In 642, at the very beginning of the campaign, the Muslims were able to occupy Qarmasin, northeast of Hulwan, and so had the passes into the mountain country within their grasp. At Nihawend, south of Hamadan (the old Ecbatana), they came into contact with the enemy under the command of the tried general, Firozan. The Persians were in the majority; the battle lasted a couple of days, and for some time the outcome was dubious. Nu'man himself was killed, but his successor, Hudhayfah ibn-al-Yaman, who had already been designated by 'Umar in advance, was finally victorious.

* See C. H. Becker, *Grundlagen der wirtschaftlichen Entwicklung Agyptens in den ersten Jahrhunderten des Islams*, *Islamstudien* I, Leipzig, 1924, 201-17; H. Bell, *The Administration of Egypt under the Umayyad Khalifate*, in *Byzant. Zeitschrift* XXVII (1928), 278 ff.; H. Lammens, *Etudes sur le siècle des Omayyades*, Beyrouth, 1930, 303-23.

After this defeat there could be no further thought of any unified resistance in the center of the empire. The shattered army fell back on the fortified cities and defended these individually against the steadily advancing Muslims. By 643 the important city of Isfahan fell, where Yezdegerd himself had taken refuge after the battle. Now he had to fall back before the pursuing Muslims to Istakhr, which had supplanted Persepolis, the old capital of the Persian ancestral homeland. Here he was besieged for a time without success, since throughout the provinces and particularly in the mountains the native population was carrying on a final struggle of desperation. When the King could no longer hold out even in Istakhr, he accepted an invitation to visit the *ispahbadh* of Tabaristan, the mountainous region on the southern rim of the Caspian Sea, in the hope of still finding effective assistance among the satraps of the eastern provinces. Although on this flight through Khorasan, the old border country of Iran and the Turkish steppes, he was hospitably received everywhere, no one heeded his demands for means to carry on the war. In him the fate savored a thousand years ago in these same countries by Darius, the last of the Achaemenians, was repeated. Indeed, his vassal in Khorasan even incited the neighboring Turkish prince into a struggle against the sovereign. In this way Yezdegerd lost his remaining followers. He himself escaped to Merv, but the city shut its gates in his face. A miller gave him asylum, and in 651 the treacherous satrap had him assassinated in this last hiding place of his. Such was the end of the last Sassanid; his memory has survived to the present day among the last adherents of the national Iranian religion, the Parsees in India, who date their era from the day of his ascension to the throne.

The grandiose external expansion of the Arab state had not been kept pace with by its development in the interior. In concept it had been founded as a theocracy, but the very question of whom the temporal leadership devolved upon had really remained open. As long as Muhammad was alive, he was certainly, as the Apostle of God, a ruler whose authority no one questioned. But he died without having provided for a successor. During his lifetime the believers may have expected that he himself would guide the community till Judgment Day itself, but after his death partisan strife in Medina seemed to threaten the body politic with total dissolution. A personal leader of public worship and of the regime was absolutely indispensable. There were no hereditary rights, still less a procedure of election, and the Qur'an, by which the Prophet had ruled the community, did not give any guidance as to who after him should be called upon as leader. In the midst of this dissension only a bold decision could salvage the state. Even during his lifetime the oldest and most intimate Meccan supporters of the Prophet had constantly counseled him in the affairs of the regime; the most restricted circle among them consisted of his two fathers-in-law, Abu Bakr and 'Umar ibn-al-Khattab, and Abu 'Ubaydah 'Amir ibn-'Abdallah ibn-al-Jarrah, distinguished for his military talent.* These at once took up the reins fallen from the Prophet's hand. The most important among them was 'Umar; as a rule this tall man traditionally appears with a lash in his hand, with which he held in check not only his daughter Hafsah but also the Prophet's other wives more ably than the latter himself. He did not, however, take over the regime directly but gave precedence to Muhammad's oldest friend, Abu Bakr. It was not until after the latter had died two years later that he formally assumed authority. Abu Bakr and 'Umar were always perfectly conscious of the fact that they occupied their office only as representatives of the sole rightful prince of the theocracy, the Prophet. Hence Abu Bakr called himself the khalifah, i.e. vicar, of the Apostle of God, and 'Umar, in the beginning, khalifah of the khalifah of the Apostle of God; it was only after this title proved too cumbersome for daily life that he simply had himself called Khalifah and Commander of the Believers.

However, it was not only the Prophet's Muhajirun who helped influence the affairs of the regime, but in addition certain of their fellow tribesmen, the Quraysh, who had joined Islam last of all and only after its incontestable triumph. But this favored position of theirs was contested by the Ansar; even during the Prophet's lifetime they had protested against his unduly favoring his own people in the division of spoils and particularly of land. But the old hostility between the Aus and the Khazraj had not yet died down as a result of the interests they had in common as against the Meccans, so that Muhammad had always been able to pacify the Ansar again and again. In Medina, finally, they were scarcely in the majority now, and after the Prophet's death their final attempt to win their independence once again had been shattered by 'Umar's

* H. Lammens in his *Etudes sur le siècle des Omayyades* and earlier in the *Mélanges de la Faculté Orientale de Beyrouth* IV, 113 ff., suggested that this "triumvirate" had attempted even during the Prophet's lifetime to counteract his autocratic tendency.

resolution. The revolt of the other Arabs then united Ansar and Muhajirun against the common danger; the former also took a prominent part in the wars of conquest, though not in dominating positions. 'Umar had a difficult task in the midst of this community, so frequently agitated by intrigues and petty jealousies, particularly since the oldest companions of the Prophet supervised his actions as a kind of senate. Since he was presented with new problems almost daily during the twelve years of his rule he was as yet unable to think of a more rigid organization of the state.

The Arab tribes who had fallen away after the Prophet's death and only laboriously been subjected again to Islam became now attached to Islam in the course of the wars of conquest, and the advantages they derived reconciled them to the sacrifice of their unfettered independence. Only one religion, Islam, was henceforth to be tolerated within the Arabian peninsula itself; consequently 'Umar transplanted the Jews, whom Muhammad had still tolerated in Khaybar, to Syria.* Whoever accepted Islam became an Arab by virtue of it, and joined one of the tribes as a client. But at first no one at all expected the non-Arabs to be converted; the object of the Holy War was rather that of subjecting them to the rule of the born citizens of the theocracy.

Thus the theocratic empire which developed after the Prophet's death out of the national state founded by him contained two religiously and hence politically distinct classes. The Muslims as rulers also constituted the warrior caste. The exercise of piety receded for a time entirely into the background, military demands taking precedence. The Muslims were organized as an army. All men of military age were entered on army rolls by tribe and by clan. They settled in the conquered cities and so were also called *muhajirs*, or emigrants (which is also what the Turks who settled among the Christians on the Balkan peninsula centuries later called themselves). But very often new military colonies were established for them, like Fustat (Old Cairo) in Egypt, Qayrawan in Roman Africa later on, and particularly Kufah and Basra in 'Iraq.

Muslim rule in the conquered countries retained its military organization for a very long time afterward. The commanders of the garrison troops were at the same time the caliph's first governors, but also, since the army and the religious community were coextensive, the prayer leaders and Friday preachers. In the beginning they

* Only in South Arabia did Jewish Communities survive.

were also in charge of the administration of law, for which special officials were not appointed until under the founder of the Umayyad dynasty. Only the administration of the taxes was subject from the beginning to an official directly responsible to the caliph.

As previously in the desert, many powers which in a state based on law would have been under the cognizance of the authorities were now also left to the autonomy of the tribes. But whereas in the desert the smaller clans had attended to discipline and order among themselves, in the military colonies the larger tribal groups assumed an active role as a result of their encompassing the members of the small confederations which had been atomized by the campaigns.

The non-Arabs were counterposed to the Arab warrior caste as subjects—the *ra'iyah*, in the plural *ra'aya*, or herd, as they were called by an ancient Semitic metaphor current even among the Assyrians. While the Muslims only paid the poor-tax, the ra'aya had to produce the tribute and so provide for the support of the Muslims. But the regime was even less concerned about their internal affairs than about those of the tribes. In formerly Christian countries the administration of community affairs was taken over by the bishops; in Persia the gentry, the *dihqan*s, or the village magistrature, retained a dominant position.

The cities and rural areas which had submitted to the Muslims without a struggle retained their freedom and their property; the tribute which was to be paid by them in return was settled directly as part of the terms of capitulation. Localities which had had to be taken by force of arms fell to the victors as booty. A fifth part of this, and in addition former crown lands and estates abandoned by their owners, was taken by the state. Everything else, including property in land and its inhabitants, was to be divided up among the warriors who had taken part in the conquest. However, since the Muslims could not leave their military confederations in order to settle on the land and cultivate it, the former owners had to be left in their places. In practice, accordingly, the position of the conquered territories was not distinguished substantially from that of areas which had voluntarily capitulated, except that their tribute could arbitrarily be increased at any time. However, the state also reserved the collection returns from this tribute for itself, and simply fixed pensions out of it for the combatants and their descendants. As mentioned before, this system had already been established in outline by 'Umar at the Jabiyah convocation.

In 644, in the midst of the great work of spreading Islam, the caliph 'Umar, just past the vigor of middle age, was violently killed upon returning from the pilgrimage he used to make annually. A Persian slave, Abu Lu'lu'ah Firoz, who was working in Medina for the governor of Kufah, Mughirah ibn-Shu'bah, had complained to the Caliph about the extent of the duties he was supposed to collect for his master, but had been dismissed. On the following morning, when the Caliph appeared in the mosque to lead early morning prayers, the Persian, out of revenge, inflicted two dagger wounds on him, one of which was fatal. Surprised by death, 'Umar had been unable to make any provision for the succession. Abu 'Ubaydah, with whom after Abu Bakr he was most intimate, had died before him. It cannot be determined with certainty whether 'Umar himself on his deathbed appointed the electoral conclave which determined the question after his death. He died on November 23, 644.

Both of the Prophet's sons-in-law, 'Ali and 'Uthman, as well as three of his most intimate companions—'Abd-ar-Rahman ibn-'Awf, Zubayr, and Sa'd ibn-abi-Waqqas—met as a board of election; Talhah, who would have taken part as the sixth, was absent and did not arrive in Medina in time. The choice of this board of election fell on its most insignificant member, 'Uthman ibn-'Affan of the house of Umayyah. This aristocratic origin of his, which even in the Prophet's eyes had made up for his lack of personal ability, may have been decisive; no doubt it was also hoped he would be easier to deal with. But this hope was disappointed, though not so much by the Caliph himself, to be sure, as by his clan, to whose influence he surrendered completely. The Umayyah were related to the Hashimids, the Prophet's clan, but in the pagan period they had been far superior in power and prestige. For years their able leader, Abu Sufyan, had been the heart of the opposition of the Quraysh to the Prophet. After the fall of Mecca most of them settled in Medina, where the Prophet made very great concessions to them. Under Abu Bakr and 'Umar, Yazid, the son of Abu Sufyan, and after his death his brother Mu'awiyah, had already achieved frequent distinction. With 'Uthman the Umayyads arrived at the helm; for his reign was that of his house. He left the management of affairs to his cousin Marwan in Medina, and appointed his kinsmen to all the important governors' posts. The old companions of the

Prophet, who had become extraordinarily wealthy personally during the conquests, and in addition to their real property in Mecca had acquired the same in Taif and extensive landholdings besides, saw their old position menaced by the newly rising dynasty. After trying in vain to extricate the Caliph from the influence of his clan, they turned against him personally. 'Uthman soon had very few friends left in Medina, especially since the youthful and intriguing widow of the Prophet, 'Aishah, "Mother of the Believers," took sides against him also. And in the provinces, too, the Arabs let themselves be incited against the Caliph.

After the tumult of the first few years of war had died down, the warriors of the faith gradually perceived that they had acted against their interests in leaving the government the plunder in all the real property. This had enabled the state to make itself independent of the army, to which, after all, it owed everything, since it independently settled the size of the stipends to be paid and was able to evade troublemakers entirely. The dissatisfaction aired itself occasionally in the plundering of a provincial money chest and especially in protests against the dispatching of any surplus to the capital.

It is true that this system had been introduced by 'Umar before this, but whereas no one had dared rise up against him, 'Uthman lacked his predecessor's authority, particularly since the caprices of the governors, generally his kinsmen, were also blamed on him. Even quite sensible measures he took soon encountered derogatory criticism everywhere. In 653, during a campaign in Armenia participated in by troops from Syria and 'Iraq, discrepancies in the versions of their Qur'ans became evident. Since the tension between the inhabitants of these provinces was far from trivial at that time anyhow, this falling out concerning the various readings considered proper did not pass off without outbursts of violence. To make a repetition of this impossible, the Caliph decided to establish an official version of the Qur'an. Even during the Prophet's lifetime many revelations had been written down individually. 'Umar had had all available copies gathered together by Zayd ibn-Thabit, a young Medinese who had already served as the Prophet's scribe. But this had given rise to nothing more than a private work with no claim to general authority, which passed after 'Umar's death into the possession of his daughter Hafsah. 'Uthman had recourse to this first collection. He charged Zayd, together with three respected Qurayshites, with revising it once again. The care 'Uthman's commission took in discharging their office is indicated by their subsequently achieving canonical veneration everywhere without opposition. But at the time it offered the Kufans welcome material for incitement against the Caliph. One of them was 'Abdallah ibn-Mas'ud, among the oldest of the Prophet's companions, who regarded himself as one of the greatest experts on the Qur'an. He raised the monstrous accusation that the revised edition was falsified and incomplete, revelations in which the Umayyads had also been damned among Muhammad's enemies having been suppressed.

The Caliph's opponents in Medina, headed by 'Ali, Talhah, and Zubayr, were able to take advantage of the general dissatisfaction. Although they considered their mission the defense of the true theocracy against the secularized regime of 'Uthman, nevertheless they did not dare begin a struggle against him in the open; this odious task they left to the provincials, in whose hands, moreover, the material power of Islam was concentrated in any case. In 655 the leaders intimated to the provincials that Medina would now afford them a greater opportunity for active struggle on behalf of the faith than the frontier territories. The storm broke in Kufah. In June 655, when the local governor Sa'id returned from the pilgrimage, one thousand men under the command of the Yemenite Malik al-Ashtar, who was devoted to 'Ali personally, prevented his entry into the city. 'Uthman thought he could conjure away the catastrophe once again and substituted a man agreeable to the Kufans for Sa'id.

In Egypt, 'Uthman had not shrunk from deposing the conqueror of the land, 'Amr ibn-al-'As, and supplanting him as governor with his cousin ibn-abi-Sarh, though the Prophet had once outlawed the latter. Agitation against 'Uthman was now being carried on in Egypt not only by 'Amr but by Muhammad ibn-abi-Hudhayfah, a foster son of Abu Bakr and an enthusiastic supporter of 'Ali's. In the very midst of a great sea battle on the Lycian coast which the Egyptian fleet had offered the Byzantines under Emperor Constans II, the malcontents had withdrawn with one ship under the pretense that the true Holy War was now being neglected. The following year five hundred Arabs from Egypt set out for Medina to start the war desired by God against the enemy within. In April 656 they appeared before the city. Most of the Medinese took their side. 'Uthman, at that time ruler of the mightiest empire on earth, had no arms whatever available in his residence; accordingly, he had to enter on negotiations with the five hundred rebels. He persuaded them to withdraw by promising to redress their grievances. But then the Umayyads raised their heads again and induced the Caliph to assert, in his next Friday sermon, that the Egyptians had left because they had seen themselves to be in the wrong. At this the Medinese grew so indignant that they reviled the Caliph and stoned him. He had to be borne unconscious out of the mosque, which he was not to set foot in again.

The Medinese assembled in front of his house and refused to budge from the place. The Egyptians returned also; they claimed to have intercepted a letter of 'Uthman's to his governor ibn-abi-Sarh ordering the latter to remove the ringleaders after their return, although the Caliph denied any knowledge of the letter which was laid before him. It was then demanded that he abdicate, if something like this could take place behind his back. He rejected this presumptuous suggestion with dignity, whereupon he was besieged in his house, which was defended only by a few of his relatives with some slaves and clients. The actual instigators of the insurrection, 'Ali, Talhah, and Zubayr, held back to save appearances. The astute 'Aishah had even left the city, under the pretext of a pilgrimage to Mecca, in order not to be present later on.

The final struggle was opened by one of 'Uthman's defenders who hurled a stone and killed one of the Egyptians. When his extradition was refused the rebels stormed the house from the adjoining grounds, killed the Caliph, who had been praying quietly without taking part in the battle, and plundered his house. This was on Friday, June 17, 656. His blood flowed over the copy of the Qur'an in which he had just been reading; this was hidden, presumably as a relic, but a number of libraries later contended for the honor of possessing the genuine copy. 'Uthman's wife, the Kalbite Na'ilah, who was wounded herself, and a few friends, interred the Caliph's dead body in the still of night. Several severed fingers of Na'ilah were sent to 'Uthman's cousin Mu'awiyah, the governor of Syria, who had them exhibited from the pulpit to inspire the believers to vengeance for the Caliph. On the news of the murder the troops Mu'awiyah had sent to help hurriedly turned back midway.

Even during the siege 'Ali, the Prophet's son-in-law and now incontestably first among the Muslims, had conducted prayers and also designated a leader for the pilgrims to Mecca. On the same day 'Uthman was murdered he accepted the public oath of allegiance in the mosque as caliph. But Talhah and Zubayr, who up to then seem to have been working on his behalf, broke with him and blamed him for the murder. They followed 'Aishah to Mecca. The Mother of the Believers still retained her old hatred of 'Ali; when she learned he had accepted the oath of allegiance, she summoned the believers to avenge the murdered man. She was joined not only by the Umayyads but also by a number of other people who shared only her dislike for 'Ali. On the advice of ibn-'Amir they decided to proceed to Basra, where he had for a long time, and still had, a great many connections. Four months after 'Uthman's death the conspirators, after assembling in a camp on the highway to 'Iraq, set out.

Once in Basra they treacherously removed the governor, who had preferred to wait for orders from 'Ali instead of joining them. Directly after the seizure of the city a quarrel developed between Talhah and Zubayr as to who was to lead the public prayers; 'Aishah settled it for the time being by designating her nephew 'Abdallah, Zubayr's son, for this function.

But 'Ali, having no troops in Medina, could not remain there either. In October 656 he set out for 'Iraq with about a hundred men, hoping to find supporters in Kufah, the second military colony of 'Iraq, whose inhabitants had felt a certain jealousy of Basra from the very beginning. He sent his son Hasan there in advance, and Hasan did in fact succeed in winning over the city's fighting men for his father. But 'Ali was still in his camp at Dhu Qar, and with twelve thousand Kufans gathered around him he set out against Basra from there. After the collapse of negotiations with Talhah and Zubayr, the battle took place. The former was mortally wounded; the latter was driven from the battlefield by pangs of conscience and was killed while in flight. But at the camel which 'Aishah was mounted on, encouraging the warriors after the ancient Arab custom, the battle came to a halt. It was not until the camel, after which this Battle of the Camel received its name, was killed that victory fell to 'Ali, on December 4, 656. 'Aishah offered the victor her support, but it was rejected; she died on July 13, 678, at the age of sixty-four.* 'Ali was recognized as caliph throughout 'Iraq, where he remained, establishing his residence in Kufah.

In consequence, the role of leadership left Arabia, and Medina in particular, to move to the provinces, where the material power had already been concentrated for a long time. The Prophet's com-

* [N. Abbott, *Aishah,* Chicago, 1942.]

panions who remained in Medina lost all political influence; they merely continued cultivating the study of tradition. The Prophet's example, according to which the individual and the community were supposed to shape their lives, was zealously discussed in their milieu and laid down as a standard. But even religious practice, as we may see by the number of the daily prayers, could not escape the influence of the new environment. The political theories of the Medinese concerning the character of the caliphate were never fully realized.

For civil life an attempt was made in each individual case to adapt the functioning common law, which may have already been influenced by provincial Roman legal statutes, to the principles of Islam; the decision as to whether an action was admissible or inadmissible was determined by considerations of ethics more than of law. The oral character of the tradition was maintained for a long time: anything written down remained in private hands; a century went by before the tradition and the legal code acquired written form. The city which for a time had ruled the Near East now became the seat of learning for the pious, while the more worldly-minded aristocracy, which saw itself being squeezed out of control of the state by the provincials, devoted itself to a frivolous enjoyment of life. In Mecca a wealthy private citizen built the first playing and reading room, in which chess and other board games, as well as books, were available to the guests. In Medina the poet al-Ahwas cultivated the poetry of love, and the Persian Yunus adapted music to the greater refinements of sensual living through new foreign melodies. But Medinese pastimes were not always so innocuous. The City of the Prophet soon won the reputation of harboring not only the best but also the most compliant singing girls.

The duty of avenging 'Uthman's death devolved on the head of the Umayyad house, the governor of Syria, Mu'awiyah ibn-abi-Sufyan. But before he could fulfill this duty he had to secure his province, which was still being menaced by the Byzantines. For this he needed Egypt above all. He succeeded in taking captive the governor sent out there by 'Ali, but before he could overpower the country itself he had to settle accounts with 'Ali, who as caliph had to compel recognition throughout the empire. In the spring of 657 'Ali set out northwest, and Mu'awiyah came out to meet him along the Syrian frontier at Siffin, on the right bank of the Euphrates, between Raqqah and Balis, on a narrow piece of swampland full of pools and thickly overgrown by willows and Euphrates poplars, which only a single paved road penetrated to the Euphrates.

At least a month went by in futile negotiations, since 'Ali could not comply with Mu'awiyah's demand that the murderers of 'Uthman be handed over. In May they came to grips, and 'Ali succeeded in wresting access to the river for his troops. On June 19 the traditionally peaceful month of Muharram began, for which a truce was agreed upon. But negotiations were unsuccessful in this month also. After the holy month elapsed the battle began again. For some time it wavered indecisively back and forth; enthusiasm was small on both sides, since to a great extent members of the same tribes were facing each other. Although the Syrians had better military training than the disorderly 'Iraqis, the latter, under the command of Malik al-Ashtar, an enthusiastic supporter of 'Ali's, nevertheless succeeded in forcing their opponents into such straits that Mu'awiyah was already considering flight. The pious Qur'an reciters had been energetically working for peace on both sides. At this critical moment the cunning 'Amr ibn-al-'As, conqueror and former governor of Egypt, is supposed to have advised Mu'awiyah to send out new troops with Qur'ans fixed to the points of their lances, as a sign that they were appealing to God's Word over the decision of the weapons as to who should be ruler. Though this incident may be fictitious, at any rate the 'Iraqis forced 'Ali, who considered victory already in his hand, to cut short the battle and start negotiations with Mu'awiyah again. Agreement was reached on the choice of two arbiters, 'Amr ibn-al-'As for Mu'awiyah, and Abu Musa al-Ash'ari for 'Ali, to decide between the two parties on the basis of the Qur'an. They were supposed to meet in the month of Ramadan, at a place situated between Syria and 'Iraq.

This court of arbitration met in Adhruh, between Ma'an and Petra in ancient Edom. Both arbiters appeared with an escort of four hundred men, and a number of eminent companions of the Prophet attended the negotiations as witnesses. Since no precise objective had been laid down in advance, both parties spoke at cross purposes. The 'Iraqis thought they were waiting for nothing more than a formal confirmation of 'Ali's caliphate, whereas what Mu'awiyah wanted to have examined was whether 'Ali's culpability in the assassination of 'Uthman did not make him unfit to rule. But his representative treated both rivals as claimants for the throne and by successive suggestions persuaded his adversary to declare them both ineligible. 'Ali could not submit to this decision and saw himself compelled to break his oath. Since by doing this he put himself in the wrong, from now on Mu'awiyah's troops themselves saluted the latter as caliph.

'Ali's position in 'Iraq soon deteriorated considerably. Even on the road back from Siffin a group of his army, mostly from the Tamim tribe, had reproached him violently for having been ready to submit to a man-made court of arbitration. They thought the decision should have been reserved to God alone, and broke with 'Ali, to withdraw to the village of Harura, not far from Kufah, and elect one of their own people, 'Abdallah ar-Rasibi, to the caliphate. When the judgment of the court of arbitration became known in Kufah, many more of 'Ali's supporters left the city as emigrés (*khawarij*) * and joined those in Harura. Their chief had set up a camp on the road to Persia not far from the future site of Baghdad, along the Nahrawan canal, which discharges into the Tigris at its bridgehead. Here 'Ali attacked the rebels on July 17, 658, and inflicted a terrible defeat on them, which did not, however, eradicate the sect.

Meanwhile Mu'awiyah had set about the conquest of Egypt again, from which he had been diverted by 'Ali's attack. The latter's newly appointed governor came forward to oppose him as he was advancing into the Nile valley, and in July 658 was beaten. Mu'awiyah was then able to leave the further subjugation of the country to 'Amr ibn-al-'As, and secured himself against a Byzantine attack by concluding a truce that same year with Emperor Constans II in return for the payment of an annual tribute. Then at the end of May 660, in Jerusalem, he accepted a formal oath of allegiance as caliph. Since his troops constantly kept at the attack in 'Iraq, 'Ali prepared for a campaign in Syria. But before he could even start the battle, he was assassinated in the mosque of Kufah on January 24, 661. This was an act of vengeance for Nahrawan, the execution of which a woman by the name of Qatam had imposed on her lover, ibn-Muljam, as a bride price.

* This name was later applied to other rebels against the established government and to different sects that had only the extremist point of view on the caliphate in common (that the caliph is the one elected by the community even if he be a black slave). Their last remnants survive at present in 'Uman and in Tripoli in North Africa. Cf. J. Wellhausen, *Die religiös-politischen Oppositionsparteien im alten Islam, Abhandlungen d. Ges. d. Wiss. zu Göttingen*, N.F., V 2, Berlin, 1901.

5. *The Umayyads*

Mu'awiyah * had already set out on the road through Mesopotamia to 'Iraq before 'Ali's assassination. At first 'Ali's incompetent son Hasan had assumed the succession, but he could not be induced to lead his troops into attack. He consented to negotiations with Mu'awiyah and waived his claims in return for his being left the five million dirhams in the state treasury at Kufah. 'Abdallah ibn-'Abbas, the ancestor of the 'Abbasid dynasty later to come into power, had already made off with the public treasure chest of Basra and joined forces with Mu'awiyah.

Mu'awiyah left his governors in Kufah and Basra the difficult task of making his power effective among the persistently turbulent 'Iraqis. In Kufah he installed Mughirah ibn-Shu'bah, an unscrupulous careerist who as a young man had had to leave his native Taif because of a common murder and by 629 had already come to Muhammad in Medina. Acting on his orders, he had then destroyed the image of his city's goddess and through piety secured a place in the new aristocracy of the faith. In the wars against the Sassanid empire he had performed a number of diplomatic services through his knowledge of Persian. For this he was rewarded by 'Umar with the governorship of Bahrayn and then transferred by him to the much more important post at Basra. In 638 he had been removed because of adultery, but as a result of the civil war, in which he displayed a prudent reserve, he came to the surface again. As governor of Kufah, by a shrewd policy of playing Kharijites and supporters of 'Ali (*Shi'ah*) off against each other, he was able to restrain his subjects from open opposition to the Syrians, although they made no secret of their dislike for the Syrians.

The governor of Basra was also a native of Taif, but of obscure origin; only the name of the slave woman Sumayyah, his mother, was known, and consequently he was called Ziyad "ibn-Abihi" ("the son of his father"). Ziyad † had begun his career as a scribe in the Basra army; 'Ali had sent him to Persia, and in this province, the devotion of whose inhabitants he won without the use of vio-

* H. Lammens, *Etude sur le règne du calife Omaijade Moawiya I*, *Mélanges de la Faculté Orientale de Beyrouth*, 1906.

† See H. Lammens, *Ziyad ibn Abihi, viceroi de l'Iraq, lieutenant de Moawiya*, *Rivista degli studi orientali IV*, 1-45, 199-236, 632-693; *Etudes sur le siècle des Omayyades*, Beyrouth, 1930, 27-162.

lence by virtue of nothing more than the wisdom of his conduct, he retained his independence of Mu'awiyah until 662. His countryman Mughirah then negotiated a peace with the new regime on his behalf. Mu'awiyah summoned him to Damascus and tied the highly useful man to the service of his house by acknowledging him as the extramarital son of his own father Abu Sufyan. Then he sent him to Basra as governor; he began his rule there with an impromptu pulpit speech, since become famous in Arabic literature, in which he proclaimed the severest measures against the lack of restraint hitherto prevalent among his subjects. His iron energy restored the authority of the regime, which had been totally undermined by the dissension between the tribes. In his province, and into the heart of the desert itself, there soon prevailed a security previously quite unknown. Upon Mughirah's death in 670 he took over his province as well.

An armed uprising among the followers of 'Ali, who had been spoiled by the laxness of his predecessor, soon gave Ziyad an opportunity to settle accounts with them once and for all. After suppressing the insurrection without much effort, he dissolved the former tribal confederations of fighting men and formed them into four groups with a reliable man of the regime at the head of each. He settled the most seriously infected Kufans and their families, as well as fifty thousand Bedouins, in the eastern Persian province of Khorasan. From Basra he well-nigh independently governed the entire eastern half of the empire which had been conquered from there, while Mu'awiyah's interest lay in the west. He entirely justified the great confidence placed in him by Mu'awiyah.

Through Mu'awiyah, Syria had become the seat of the regime. While in 'Iraq the principal mass of the Arab population had only come into the land from the desert as a result of the wars of conquest, the Syrian Arabs for the most part had already been living in their homeland for centuries, and long contact with the Christian church and the Roman Empire had accustomed them to complying with a state order. Mu'awiyah, who ruled from Damascus, was regarded by them as the legitimate successor of their old Ghassanid princely house. His wife was an elegant aristocrat of the South Arab tribe of the Kalb, the most powerful in Syria, which assured their son Yazid, the heir to the throne, of the support of kinsmen. He won over his former opponents of the families of 'Ali and Hashim by abundant gifts. He treated his Umayyad relatives with prudent caution, to prevent their becoming a danger to himself or his son. He was always able to utilize the great influence still exercised on public opinion by the poets of his time on behalf of his dynastic interests. The Arabs were on good terms with the Christian population of Aramean descent that had known them from of old. They did not live here, as in 'Iraq, in newly founded colonies, but in the great cities, in the midst of the Christians, with whom they even held divine services here and there under the same roof. At Mu'awiyah's court the Christian Sarjun ibn-Mansur played the role of an influential financial counselor. The Christians repaid Mu'awiyah and his house for this tolerance with a faithful devotion that in Christian tradition we still encounter even in the Spanish chronicles. Mu'awiyah did not rule his Arabs like an Oriental despot but like an old-time tribal *sayyid.* During Friday services in the mosque, from the minbar, which was more of a magistrate's seat than a pulpit for him, he used to discuss his political measures with the heads of the nobility, with whom he generally kept regular counsel in his palace also. He frequently received delegations from the provinces, too, in order to accept complaints and smooth over differences between the tribes. All such dealings displayed the chief trait of his character, the mild composure and self-control which was accounted the principal virtue of a sayyid because it was otherwise so rare among the Arabs. He erected the Islamic state anew on the foundations laid by 'Umar and shattered during the civil war, by going back, like his great predecessor, to Hellenistic-Roman administrative practice tested over the course of centuries. In financial matters he re-established the taxes hitherto paid into the central treasury by the provinces only with reluctance, and saw to it that they were collected regularly, while at the same time he freed them from a part of the gigantic pensions previous rulers had allowed their followers. In the Hijaz, greatly neglected since the civil wars, he aided agriculture by vast projects for improving methods of cultivation.

Mu'awiyah always regarded the war against the Byzantines as one of his most important tasks.* He had taken up the struggle even as governor under 'Umar's caliphate. He had still found the Phoenician coastal cities in the possession of the Byzantines and could wrest them decisively from them only by a second advance during 'Uth-

* J. Wellhausen, *Die Kämpfe der Araber mit den Rhomäern in der Zeit der Umaijaden, Nachr. d. Ges. d. Wiss.*, Göttingen, 1901, p. 91 ff.

man's reign. In order to insure their possession he had to meet his opponents on the sea as well. 'Umar had still withheld his approval, and it was not until 'Uthman's rule that approval was secured for this step into a field hitherto unknown to the Arabs, to which, however, they soon became acclimated. In the summer of 649 Mu'awiyah attacked Cyprus, and only six years later he was arming a fleet against Constantinople itself. The emperor Constans II, grandson of Heraclius, came to meet it on the Lycian coast, but suffered a crushing defeat. In spite of this success the Arabs were still unable to attain their goal, since Mu'awiyah, who was simultaneously advancing on land, did not get past Caesarea in Cappadocia. Mu'awiyah then had to bargain for peace with Byzantium, to face the conflict with 'Ali, but as soon as he had united the empire, he resumed the struggle through annual summer forays into Asia Minor. Twice his troops arrived before the gates of the capital of the Byzantine Empire, but again the latter, by virtue of its cultural superiority, was able to ward off the barbarians' onslaught. In 667 an insurgent general in Armenia, Saborius, had called the Arabs into the country. But by the time they arrived in Melitene, the uprising had already been put down by the Emperor; nevertheless, they pushed on as far as Chalcedon. Now Mu'awiyah sent his own son Yazid, who up to then had lived only for pleasure, into the army. After the Arabs had held out in Chalcedon over the winter, they advanced as far as Byzantium itself in the spring, but had to give up the siege as soon as summer came and return to Syria. In 674 Mu'awiyah made one more energetic attempt to penetrate to the heart of the Christian power. He dispatched a mighty fleet, which in fact succeeded in establishing itself in Cyzicus, on the south bank of the Propontis. From there he harassed the capital for seven years, but nothing was of any avail against its powerful fortifications and against the Greek fire. Finally Mu'awiyah gave up the hopeless struggle and concluded peace with Byzantium.

The Arabs won lasting successes in the second theater of war, against the Christians in Africa.* Soon after 647 'Uthman's governor in Egypt, ibn-abi-Sarh, had already conquered Tripolis, but had

* M. Caudel, *Les premières invasions des Arabes dans l'Afrique du Nord*, *Journal asiatique*, 1900, série IX, t. 13, 14; Ch. Torrey, *The Muhammedan Conquest of Egypt and North Africa*, publications in Semitic philology of the University of Yale, 1901, 279-300; C. H. Becker, "The Expansion of the Saracens" in *Cambridge Medieval History*, II, 329-390 (1912).

then contented himself with the payment of a tribute. In 667 Mu'awiyah's governor ibn-Hudayj resumed the war against the Christians in the west, and on his very first marauding excursion got as far as Sicily. But the real founder of Arab rule in North Africa was 'Uqbah ibn-Nafi', a nephew of 'Amr, the conqueror of Egypt. 'Uqbah had already conquered Barqah from out of Egypt, and in 670, in alliance with the Berbers, he succeeded in destroying Christian rule in North Africa altogether; he was recalled after founding a military colony in Qayrawan. But in 682 Mu'awiyah's successor reinstalled him as governor, and he undertook one more campaign westward, which apparently brought him as far as the sea. The Berber tribes, however, whose territory he crossed as far as the middle Atlas, were not decisively subjugated as a result of this. Their leader, Kusaylah, whom he had taken along with him as captive, escaped, and in alliance with the Byzantine garrisons still remaining in the country organized the opposition against the Arabs. 'Uqbah then incautiously also divided his army and struck out along the road to the Aures mountains with a small detachment. In 683, at Tahudah on the edge of the Sahara, he was fallen on by the Berbers and killed with his entire company. His tomb-mosque in the region named after him, Sidi 'Uqbah, south of Biskra, is the oldest, and still quite primitive, monument of Muslim architecture in Africa.

Mu'awiyah died on April 18, 680. He was followed by his son Yazid,* to whom he had already had allegiance sworn during his lifetime. The heads of the Islamic aristocracy—Husayn, the second son of 'Ali; 'Abdallah, the son of 'Umar; 'Abdallah, the son of Zubayr—had refused to take this oath of allegiance, and when it was demanded of them again after Mu'awiyah's death, only 'Umar's son complied, both the others escaping the power of the Medinese governor in charge by flight to Mecca. The Kufans urgently pressed Husayn to join them and take up his reign among them. He succumbed to this temptation but then failed to find in 'Iraq the support he expected. His cousin Muslim ibn-'Aqil, who had wanted to prepare the ground for him there beforehand, had been captured by Yazid's governor 'Ubaydallah ibn-Ziyad and executed. While on his way there Husayn was intercepted by the latter's advance patrols, and since he refused to turn back they escorted him as far as Ker-

* See H. Lammens, *Le califat de Jésid I, Mélanges de la Faculté Orientale de Beyrouth,* IV, 233-312.

bela, west of the Euphrates, about sixty-two miles south southwest of Baghdad on the rim of the desert. They hemmed him in here in the hope that thirst would force him to surrender. On the tenth of Muharram of the Hijrah year 61, i.e. October 10, 680, an ultimatum was given him by the commander of Yazid's troops, 'Umar, the son of the distinguished companion of the Prophet and military leader Sa'd ibn-abi-Waqqas. Although Husayn could expect no further aid from his supporters in Kufah, who were disconcerted by Muslim's execution, he again refused to surrender; as the Prophet's grandson he was presuming on his inviolability. He fell a short while after the battle was joined. His head was sent to the Caliph, who deeply regretted this unforeseen outcome and had the 'Alids who had escaped the massacre brought back to Medina and there generously provided for. This martyr's death of Husayn, of no political effect whatever, nevertheless furthered the religious development of the Shi'ah, the party of the 'Alids, which later became the focal point for all Arabophobe tendencies; today Husayn's grave in Kerbela is still the most sacred goal of pilgrimage for all Shi'ites, particularly the Persians, whose most ardent desire has remained that of finding their last resting place at his side.

A much more dangerous adversary for the Umayyads proved to be 'Abdallah ibn-az-Zubayr, who defied the Caliph in the sacred asylum of Mecca. From there he stirred up the Medinese, who had every reason to find fault with the regime which had robbed their city of its ancient splendor. In vain did Yazid make another attempt in 683 to win them over. Soon afterward the Umayyads established there, about a thousand men, were set upon and had to seek refuge in the quarter of their chieftain, Marwan ibn-al-Hakam ibn-al-'As, who under Mu'awiyah had been governor in Hijaz for a time. The Caliph sent an army of twelve thousand Syrians to help them under the command of Muslim ibn-'Uqbah, who had already proved his mettle in the service of his father. The Umayyads besieged in Medina had capitulated in return for freedom of withdrawal, and joined forces with him on the road to Syria. In August 683 Muslim encamped on the Harrah, the lava field north of the city. After the expiration of a short respite accorded them, the rebels advanced against him for a battle which ended with an annihilating defeat for the flower of the Quraysh and Ansar nobility. On the following day Muslim accepted the allegiance of the Medinese on behalf of Yazid, after ordering the execution of the surviving ringleaders.

From Medina, Muslim went on to Mecca, but he died on the road and the command was taken over by Husayn ibn-Numayr. After besieging the city for two months the latter heard of the death of the caliph Yazid, whereupon he entered into negotiations with 'Abdallah ibn-az-Zubayr and offered him allegiance as caliph if he would not only waive vengeance for the preceding warfare but also come to Syria so that the seat of the regime would remain there. 'Abdallah refused to agree to this second condition, but Husayn lifted the siege nevertheless and returned to Syria.

Yazid had died on November 11, 683. It is true that even as caliph he had devoted himself to wine, music, and sport more than to state affairs and had put an end to the war with the Byzantines, in which as prince he had taken part only with reluctance. Christian tradition praises his extraordinary conviviality. But during his short reign he had also embarked, not without skill, on a reform of the financial administration and had turned his attention to the irrigation of the Ghutah, the oasis of Damascus. His son Mu'awiyah II, still very young, was recognized in Damascus immediately but died after a very brief reign.

Even during the latter's lifetime, warfare in Syria had begun between the Arab tribes, and it never really subsided under the Umayyad regime from then on. The North Arab tribal group of the Qays, various branches of which, such as the Ghatafan, Mudar, and so on, were settled in northern Syria, Mesopotamia, and 'Iraq, was dissatisfied with the way in which Mu'awiyah I himself had already begun to favor the South Arab Kalb, the principal tribe of the Quda'ah, settled between Palmyra and ancient Moab.* Now, after 'Abdallah ibn-az-Zubayr obtained recognition in 'Iraq, the Qays rose up under the leadership of Zufar ibn-al-Harith and drove out the governor of Qinnasrin, a Kalbite. After Mu'awiyah's death the governor of Hims also recognized ibn-az-Zubayr as caliph. Finally Dahhaq ibn-Qays, who was in power in Damascus, went over to the latter's party. Marwan, the head of the Umayyad house, who had settled in Damascus after Yazid's death, showed an inclina-

* Goldziher was inclined to regard the opposition between the North Arabs and South Arabs as a secondary consequence of the rivalry between the Quraysh and the Ansar, who counted as South Arabs; but from the very outset it seems to have consisted of an opposition based on race between the pure Oriental North Arabs and the South Arabs with an admixture of alien blood; the enmity between the two groups continued to have aftereffects for a long time, and will be encountered again in the history of Spain.

tion at first to waive his claims in favor of the caliph residing in Mecca, but then allowed himself to be induced to accept the oath of allegiance in Jabiyah on June 22, 684. Here he was joined by Yazid's maternal uncle Hassan ibn-Bahdal, the one Umayyad partisan who, as governor of Transjordan, had any real power at his disposal. Together with him, Marwan set out for Damascus; the Qaysites came out to meet him on the plain north of Damascus at Marj Rahit, and were defeated. In August 684 Marwan was also able to accept the oath of allegiance in Damascus, after having seized the state treasury in advance. But although this victory at Marj Rahit restored the rule of the Umayyads, at the same time it was only afterward that the hatred between the Qays and the Kalb really became inflamed, as a result of the attendant blood feuds, and consequently shattered the foundations of Umayyad power.

Marwan was also denied a lengthy reign, and it was filled with continuous strife. He succeeded in taking possession of Egypt, by means of a surprise march while his governors in Palestine covered his rear and warded off an attack by Mus'ab, brother of 'Abdallah ibn-az-Zubayr. At first he had to recognize a son of Yazid I as successor, but in a series of long-drawn-out negotiations he succeeded in persuading the latter to decline in favor of his own sons 'Abd-al-Malik and the younger 'Abd-al-'Aziz, whom he had made governor in Egypt.

The Caliph, who as a young man had been severely wounded in 'Uthman's defense and again in the Battle of the Camel, was nearing his seventieth year when the plague, carried into Syria again from 'Iraq, snatched him on May 7, 685, as it had Mu'awiyah II before him. That his wife, Yazid's widow, had him strangled in order to avenge her son's exclusion from the succession is a piece of fiction.

His son 'Abd-al-Malik now had to begin a tenacious struggle for his inheritance. He was still being defied in Syria by Zufar, the head of the Euphrates Qays; the other provinces all stood with ibn-az-Zubayr. He was occupied for another two years in protecting northern Syria against the incursions of the Byzantines, and it was only after this that he could turn to 'Iraq, which was being ruled by 'Abdallah ibn-az-Zubayr's brother Mus'ab as governor. The latter had had to struggle against great difficulties before. Lacking leaders of any talent, the 'Alids had lain low after Husayn's defeat at Kerbela, but now one such emerged in the person of the Thaqifite al-Mukhtar, an orphan brought up by his uncle, 'Ali's governor in al-Mada'in.* He had already taken part in the uprising of Muslim ibn-'Aqil and after his release from prison joined ibn-Zubayr in Mecca. Three years later he turned up again in 'Iraq, apparently as messenger for one of 'Ali's younger sons, Muhammad, named ibn-al-Hanafiyah after his mother. Since this son had not inherited any of the Prophet's blood through Fatimah and accordingly could really have laid no claims to the succession, Mukhtar then quickly chose a different course: ostensibly inspired by the angel Gabriel, he preached, in an obscure rhymed prose modeled on the Qur'an, the imminent appearance of a Mahdi who at the end of creation would eliminate all injustice on earth and fill the world with righteousness. He attracted clients of Aramaic and Iranian origin converted to Islam, who were treated by the Arabs as second-class citizens, and gave military command over them to Ibrahim ibn-Malik al-Ashtar, the son of a famous general of 'Ali's. The latter conquered the Arabs in Kufah, and from there Mukhtar won over the whole of 'Iraq and the eastern provinces, where the subject population enthusiastically followed his banner. But he failed to win over the Arabs of Kufah, who utilized an absence of ibn-al-Ashtar, who had advanced with his troops against 'Abd-al-Malik, as an occasion to attack Mukhtar. The latter was in great danger by the time the army, hearing of it, turned back and freed him. Thereupon he decreed a savage punitive judgment on all his opponents on the pretext of their having been fellow culprits in Husayn's martyrdom. Two days later ibn-al-Ashtar defeated the Syrian army under 'Ubaydallah ibn-Ziyad, the same leader who had the Kerbela massacre on his conscience, at the Khazir, where ibn-Ziyad himself was killed. This greatest of Mukhtar's triumphs, which he celebrated in a strange ceremony before an empty throne revered as the seat of divinity, was soon followed by his overthrow. Mus'ab, who had hitherto remained steadfastly in Basra during the wars with the Kharijites, advanced against him and after two bloody battles shut him up in the fortress of Kufah. After a defense lasting four months Mukhtar was killed in a sortie on April 4, 687. His teachings sur-

* See H. G. van Gelder, *Mochtar, de valsche Propet*, Leiden, 1888; G. van Vloten, *Recherches sur la domination arabe, le chitisme et les croyances messianiques sous le califat des Omaiyades*, *Verh. d. Akad.*, Amsterdam, 1894, Nr. 3; J. Wellhausen, *Die religiös-politischen Oppositionsparteien im alten Islam*, 74-89.

vived in Shi'ite eschatology, although Mus'ab extirpated his supporters with savage cruelty.

Mus'ab had still been able to suppress a few minor Umayyad movements in 'Iraq, but in 691 'Abd-al-Malik himself appeared in 'Iraq with an army, at a time when Mus'ab's best troops were tied down by the struggle with the Kharijites. He advanced against the Caliph above Baghdad, at the cloister of the Catholicus on the west bank of the Tigris. But his officers proved unreliable, going so far as to enter into negotiations with the Caliph, who did not, however, accept their treachery and even offered Mus'ab the governorship of 'Iraq if he would join him. Mus'ab, however, was faithful to his brother and in the middle of October was killed in battle.

Now 'Abd-al-Malik only had to deal with 'Abdallah ibn-az-Zubayr, who asserted his rule throughout the Hijaz from his Meccan residence. Against him he sent Hajjaj ibn-Yusuf, a Thaqifite from Taif, who had won his favor in the campaign against Mus'ab. He took his native city as base of operations and from there advanced on Mecca. Indifferent to the sanctity of the city, he began to bombard it from Mt. Abu Qubays. But the rival caliph held out another seven months in the Ka'bah quarter and was killed in a sortie in October 692 after being abandoned even by his own sons. In this way the unity of the empire was restored. As a reward the victorious general received the governorship of Hijaz, in addition to Yemen and Yamamah. In December 694, after restoring order there within the space of two years, he was summoned by the Caliph to the most important post in the empire, the governship of 'Iraq, as successor to the Caliph's deceased brother Bishr. He assumed control in Kufah with a pulpit address which has become just as famous as that of his predecessor Ziyad.

After finishing off his rival, 'Abd-al-Malik at once resumed the war against Byzantium, which had been quiescent for about fifteen years, after having been at first compelled to purchase peace himself by the payment of a tribute. The resumption of hostilities is supposed to have been connected with the coinage reform introduced by 'Abd-al-Malik. Up to then, according to the legendary tradition, only Byzantine money had been current in the Arab Empire, the coins stamped in the interior also bearing Greek inscriptions. The Byzantines for their part procured their paper in Egypt, where it was made for them in state factories with Christian inscriptions and the cross as a watermark. The Caliph is said to have

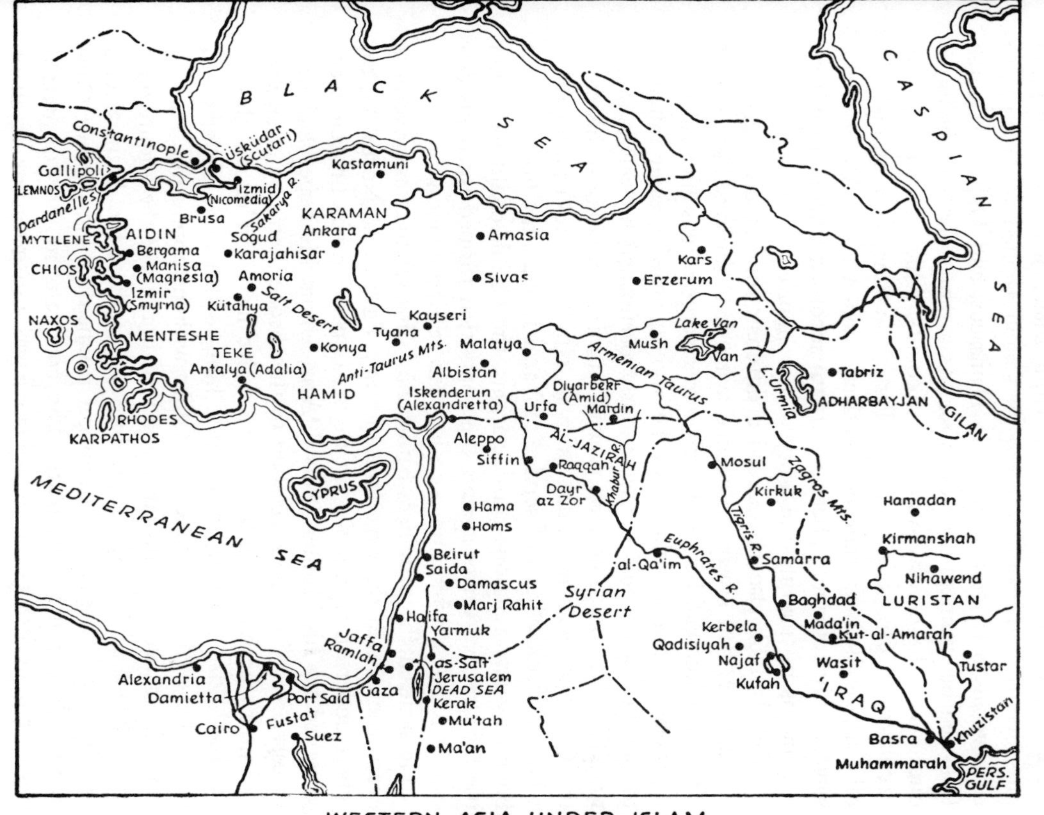

WESTERN ASIA UNDER ISLAM

replaced this by the Islamic profession of faith. Thereupon the Byzantines threatened to provide the gold dinar, which the Arabs were still procuring exclusively from them, with an inscription offensive to their Prophet. In 693 the Caliph decided in consequence to have his own coins minted in Damascus, and Hajjaj in Kufah followed his example the year after. As a result, Arabic was introduced into the official system of accounts, which up to then had been kept in Greek in Syria and Persian in 'Iraq, even though the officials, as before, remained entirely non-Arab.* 'Abd-al-Malik substantially restricted liberties hitherto accorded Christian subjects, as a means of insuring the unity of the empire.

'Abd-al-Malik also introduced a different tone at his court. His predecessors had always associated with their subjects like ancient Arab tribal chiefs; he was the first to emerge as absolute ruler. As representative of the theocracy he also accorded greater influence to the theologians and conscientiously performed his religious duties. This did not, to be sure, prevent him from inviting to his court the Christian poet al-Akhtal, born in Hirah, of the Taghlib tribe, who had already been of service to Yazid I. Since the poet was not bound by any religious considerations, the Caliph could have him use his effective verses against the opposition formed by pious circles in Medina, which on occasion was still troublesome.†

He secured the provinces by installing his relatives as governors everywhere with the exception of 'Iraq. Egypt and North Africa, where under his regime the last Berber opposition was broken, were governed by his brother 'Abd-al-'Aziz, whom his father had previously assured of the succession to the throne. Later he attempted in vain to persuade his brother to waive his claim to the throne. 'Abd-al-'Aziz, however, died before him, so that in 705 Walid, son of 'Abd-al-Malik, succeeded his father without opposition.

Walid carried his arms far beyond the borders of the empire once again. Tyana in Asia Minor fell into the hands of the Arabs after a lengthy siege, though the campaign planned by him against Constantinople did not materialize. The conquests in the east started from 'Iraq, whose governor al-Hajjaj was also governor of all of

* Directly after his assumption of the government Athanasius Bar Gummaya from Edessa had been sent to the Caliph's brother 'Abd-al-'Aziz in Egypt, in order to reconstruct the administration; in this Athanasius grew so wealthy that he was able to construct two great churches with his own means.

† H. Lammens, *Un poète royal a la cour de Damas*, *Etudes sur le siècle des Omayyades*, 210-62.

Iran.* In 704, on his advice, 'Abd-al-Malik had already installed Qutaybah ibn-Muslim as governor of the eastern province of Khorasan, which reached from the river Oxus-Jayhun (the modern Amu-Darya) as far as the Hindu Kush. For centuries Iranian and Turkish peoples had been coming into contact here. At this time the Turks, about whose prehistory there will be a more detailed account in the discussion of their decisive entry into the Islamic world, had, under Kapghan Kaghan † (called Metchuo by the Chinese), extended westward their northern domain, freed from Chinese sovereignty in 682. One of their vassals resided as *tarkan* in Samarqand, the capital city of Soghdiana, Transoxania (in Arabic, Ma wara an-nahr), on the southern bank of the Zarafshan. On the lower reaches of this river lies Bukhara, where a Turkish dynasty ruled a mixed Iranian-Turkish population. Dissensions under this last dynasty were taken advantage of by Qutaybah to install a young man there as prince. The latter himself embraced Islam, which thereafter was firmly rooted in Bukhara. The tarkan of Samarqand also submitted to Qutaybah, but was then deposed by his embittered subjects. His successor, Ghurak, was forced by Qutaybah to surrender after a protracted siege. Although he retained his throne, he had to accept an Arab garrison. Thenceforth, in spite of some disturbances, Islam maintained itself in both these cities, which later became its most important bulwark in central Asia. From there Qutaybah pushed forward farther eastward against Ferghana. In the summer of 714 he was overtaken there by the news of Hajjaj's death, and in consequence withdrew to his base in Merv. The following year, when Walid also died, he feared the vengeance of Sulayman, the heir to the throne, whom he had declared himself against and refused allegiance; but Qutaybah was killed in a soldier's mutiny. In 711 Hajjaj's governor in Basra, his son-in-law Muhammad ibn-Qasim, began the conquest of Sind from southern Persia and Baluchistan, which opened another vast sphere of power for Islam in India.‡

In the west the Arabs, during Walid's reign, crossed the Straits of Gibraltar and on July 25-26, 711, at the Battle of Wadi Bakkah, at one time incorrectly named after Xeres de la Frontera, dealt a

* More detail in H. A. R. Gibb, *The Arab Conquests in Central Asia.*

† See page 164 on the tribal organization of the Turks.

‡ For a history of Indian Islam see Sir George Dunbar's *A History of India*, 2 vols., London, 1936, 3d ed. 1943. This is not gone into in the following pages.

mortal blow to the Visigothic kingdom, enfeebled by internal disorders. Roderick, the last Gothic king, was killed here. The victorious army consisted almost entirely of Berbers, whom Musa ibn-Nusayr, governor in North Africa appointed by 'Abd-al-'Aziz and confirmed in his office by Walid, had initially sent out across the straits only as a reconnoitering party under his client Tariq ibn-Ziyad. The mountain on which the latter assembled his troops after the landing is still called Gibraltar after him (Jabal Tariq). This unexpected success of Tariq's aroused the jealousy of his superior, who followed him at once with predominantly Arab troops and pushed still farther into the country. After his initial successes at Medina Sidonia and Carmona he was held up for a year by the siege of Seville and Merida, during which time other troops were fighting against the Gothic prince Theodomir in Orihuela. He then joined forces again with his client Tariq before Toledo, and together with him subjugated all of northern Spain from Saragossa to Navarre. In 714 he returned to Africa with vast booty and in a stately triumphal procession set out on the road to Syria, where Walid was waiting impatiently; soon after he arrived in Damascus the Caliph, barely forty years old, died, in February 715.

In the interior of his empire Walid enjoyed the fruits of his father's activity and was recognized everywhere as absolute sovereign. He kept eliminating more and more Christians from the administrative apparatus, and even dispensed with the services of the family of Sarjun ibn-Mansur, which since the time of Mu'awiyah himself had been in control of financial affairs. Like so many ancient Oriental princes, Walid was addicted to public works, not only, however, out of pleasure of display, but to increase the revenues of his estates. The Syrians regarded him as an ideal ruler.

The principal work that established Walid's fame as a builder is the great mosque in Damascus, usually called the Mosque of the Umayyads. The simple form of the area set aside for prayer, a court with roofed portico, as in the Prophet's dwelling in Medina, had soon become outmoded. The first army camps of the conquerors, in Kufah and Basra in 'Iraq as well as Fustat in Egypt, were content with imitations of the old mosque of the Prophet. 'Umar and 'Uthman had already had the mosques in Medina and Mecca extended by the purchase of surrounding houses and had replaced the simple bowers by columned porticoes in stone. This example was also followed in the provinces; Sa'd ibn-abi-Waqqas fitted out

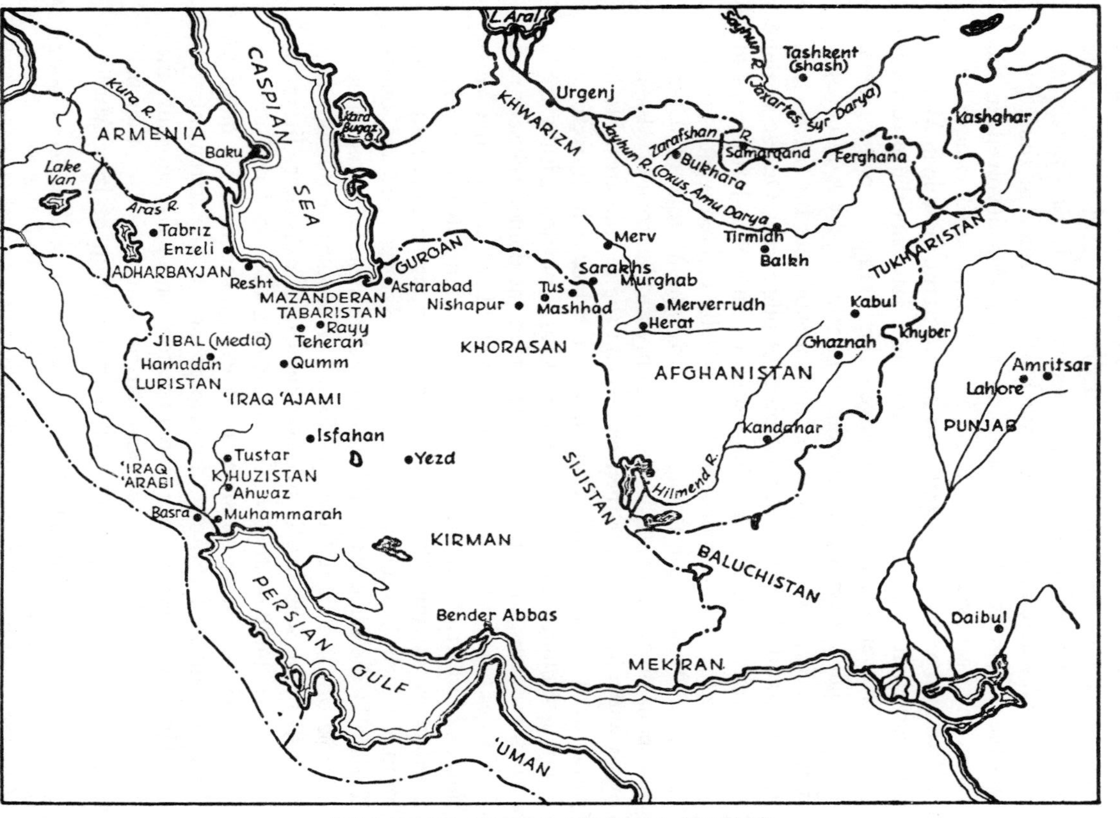

THE EAST OF THE ISLAMIC EMPIRE

the mosque in Kufah with columns appropriated from the buildings of the Sassanids and the churches of Hirah. Under Mu'awiyah the mosques in Kufah and Basra were further elaborated.* Next to the mihrab, or prayer niche, in the direction of Mecca (*qiblah*) the mosque was adjoined by the state buildings, since in the capital and the provinces the conduct of divine worship devolved on the caliph and his governors. 'Uthman himself is supposed to have built in a wooden screen (*maqsurah*) for himself in the mosque in Medina, for protection against attack. Under the Umayyads the provincial governors everywhere also followed this example. In Jerusalem, 'Abd-al-Malik, when the rival caliph ibn-az-Zubayr was in occupation of Mecca, had attempted to create a substitute for the Ka'bah, inaccessible to his subjects, as an object of pilgrimage. On the sacred rock plateau to which 'Umar himself at his entry into Jerusalem had laid claim for Muslim worship, Abd-al-Malik erected what is today called the Dome of the Rock (incorrectly, the Mosque of 'Umar). The Jami' al-Aqsa, named in connection with the story of Muhammad's night journey, was then erected on the temple area. He had those parts of Justinian's Church of St. Mary which were still standing included in the building, making a portico with a triple row of columns, to which were later added the domed transept and four aisles.† In Damascus itself, the capital of the empire, the Muslims had hitherto been satisfied with an unpretentious small mosque. Even in pagan times the central part of the city contained a large temple which had been rebuilt by the Romans, perhaps under Trajan, in the same style, though on a larger scale, as the famous Temple of the Sun at Palmyra. Columnar remains of this building are still to be seen in the neighborhood of the mosque. In 379 a church was built on this pagan temple site, dedicated to John the Baptist, which was restored under Arcadius, the son of Honorius. This had remained entirely Christian property. The statement that the Muslims directly after the conquest occupied one-half the church for their own worship and left the Christians the other half in gratitude for this capitulation is an invention of later Muslim

* At that time the floor consisted simply of sand, which the believers shook from their hands on arising from prayer. Ziyad was afraid that this shaking of the hands might in time be taken for a part of the ritual of prayer, and hence had the sand replaced with gravel; al-Baladhuri, *Kitab al-Futuh*, 277; M. J. Goeje, review of Wellhausen, *Arab. Reich* in *Museum*, 1902.

† Architectural history and designs in E. Diez, *Die Kunst der islamischen Völker*, Berlin, 1915, p. 12 ff.

tradition, which could no longer understand such favoring of the Christians. Whereas the earlier caliphs had heeded the rights of the Christians, in 705 Walid simply took the church away from them,* and reconstructed it, by including the south wall together with the adjoining portico of the former temple, into a triple-aisled colonnade with the arcades resting on piers, a transept modeled on the *chalke* in Byzantium, and a timber roof. The lofty stone cupola erected over the transept no doubt first arose at the instigation of the Byzantine mosaicists charged with the decoration of the interior. On the example of Syrian churches the corners of the central aisle of the transept were connected with the rotunda of the dome by semicircular niches. The capitals of the columns were gilded and the walls ornamented with marble intarsia and overlaid with mosaics depicting cities and trees of all kinds. A new minaret was built on the foundation of an old tower in the southwest corner of the old portico; on the north side of the vestibule of the mosque stood "the Minaret of the Betrothed." Around the court toward the north a lofty arcade was erected. Once again the model for this combination of colonnaded portico and vestibule, imitated by numerous mosques in its turn, is found by H. Thiersch in the Chalke of the Aitherios in Byzantium, and the Augusteion, in which the vestibule of the imperial palace was laid out as the principal court, with a ceremonial chamber for audiences and receptions, which again was based on classical models. These structures were erected in the provinces through the use of *corvée*. An Egyptian papyrus from Aphrodite tells of the efforts devoted to this building. The laborers were foreigners without exception; literary tradition reports the enrollment of twelve hundred workers from Byzantium; we learn from papyri that a Persian was also engaged there. In view of all this, it goes without saying that the style of construction could not be uniform. Foreign technical skill still had to be turned to later also; in the twelfth century the great clock of the mosque was installed by a Persian. Unfortunately, this oldest monument of Muslim architecture in Syria has suffered a good deal from the malice of fortune. Three times, in 1069, 1400, and 1893, the building was consumed by fire almost to the foundation walls.

'Iraq, the most important province in the empire after the nuclear territory of Syria, was governed under 'Abd-al-Malik and Walid

* See H. Lammens, *Le Calife Walid et le partage de la Mosquée des Omayyades de Damas, Etudes sur le siècle des Omayyades*, Beyrouth, 1930, pp. 269-302.

by Hajjaj ibn-Yusuf, who took over this office in 693, as mentioned above. His position there was very difficult; the inhabitants were completely barbarized by the long-drawn-out wars for the caliphate. In Kufah the excitement over the disturbances under the false prophet Mukhtar was still causing trepidation. The Kharijites were still ranging about outside the gates of Basra. A new sect had turned up among them, the Azraqites, who regarded anyone who differed with them and refused conversion as an infidel, subject to death, together with his wife and children. Al-Muhallab ibn-abi-Sufrah had already fought against them under Mus'ab. After his master's fall he had submitted to 'Abd-al-Malik and been left in his command. In 688 the Azraqites had elected a new caliph, Qatari ibn-Fuja'ah of the Tamim tribe, also famous as a poet, who constituted a persistent threat to 'Iraq from Khuzistan and gave Muhallab a great deal of trouble, especially since 'Abd-al-Malik's first two governors, out of jealousy, failed to give him adequate support. It was Hajjaj who first placed new troops at his disposition, with which he was able to pursue the rebels as far as the interior of the Persian province of Kirman. Then dissension broke out among the rebels. Qatari moved with the Arabs farther toward Tabaristan, while the clients stayed behind in the city of Jiruft and elected a new leader. Here Muhallab was able to overpower them easily. In Tabaristan, Qatari's Arabs had sorely oppressed the natives; the leader of the natives consequently summoned the governor of Rayy to his aid, who inflicted a crushing defeat on the Arabs. Qatari himself perished in the battle (697 or 698). Another Kharijite leader, Shabib, of the Shayban tribe, made 'Iraq insecure for two years out of Mosul. He was a genuine brigand leader, who was favored by the Christians in the country and thus was able to defy Hajjaj's troops from constantly shifting hide-outs; it was only in 697 after the Caliph sent reinforcements from Syria that he was defeated along the Dujayl River and drowned in its waters. Hajjaj's gratitude to the Syrian troops for this assistance aroused the discontent of the local aristocracy. After the province of Kirman, governed from 'Iraq, was swept clean of the insurrectionaries, Hajjaj sent out a particularly well-equipped army (the "Peacock Army") under the command of 'Abd-ar-Rahman ibn-al-Ash'ath, a descendant of the old royal house of Kindah, to subjugate the bordering country of Sijistan, ruled at that time by a prince of Turkish origin. When this expedition failed to achieve its object rapidly enough for the tempestuous governor, and he pressed for speed, ibn-al-Ash'ath left the decision to his captains, knowing that to them both Hajjaj and this war in the barbarians' country were equally detestable. For that matter, they were also ready to swear allegiance to him at once if he would lead them back home in a war against Hajjaj. So he concluded peace with the Turks and slowly moved westward, being joined by the garrisons in Persia. When Hajjaj advanced against the rebels they defeated him and seized Basra, while Hajjaj was still in control of the suburbs. From there the governor succeeded in pushing back the rebels, who now turned toward Kufah. Once again the Caliph sent out a Syrian army under the command of his son 'Abdallah and his brother Muhammad. These had been given the task of negotiating with ibn-al-Ash'ath first, being authorized even to hold out the prospect of recalling the hated governor. But since even after this he persisted in refusing his obedience, the government troops passed over to the attack and defeated him first at Dayr al-Jamajim and then at Maskin, where some of his supporters deserted him. 'Abd-ar-Rahman fled to the Turkish prince of Sijistan, who actually freed him from an Arab commander, but then handed him over after all to Hajjaj's emissaries. He killed himself on the way, in 704, by jumping off the battlements of a castle.

It was not until after Hajjaj had put down this final uprising of the 'Iraqi Arabs that he could concern himself properly with the consolidation of his regime, which was based on the military power of Syria. In 702 he constructed midway between the two ceaselessly turbulent cities of Kufah and Basra a new city called Wasit ("Mid-City") as the seat and stronghold of the regime. During his lifetime he tolerated in Wasit, besides the Arab military from Syria, only Transoxanian Turks, who had come to Basra for the most part as prisoners of war and deportees, though voluntarily also, and were now settling in the new city. It was not until after his death that Arameans and Persians were permitted to settle there. Together with its sister city Kaskar on the other bank of the Tigris, this creation of Hajjaj's, thanks to its strategic location, maintained its position among the cities of 'Iraq even under the 'Abbasids, when it had to relinquish its role as seat of the government to Baghdad.

Hajjaj then harvested, under Walid, the fruits of the hard work he had performed under the latter's predecessor. The new ruler preserved complete confidence in him, especially since he felt obligated to him for having supported his succession to the throne against the claims of 'Abd-al-'Aziz. He was now energetically concerned with restoring the prosperity of the country, devastated by twenty years of war. This was primarily a question of resuming the operation and the continual supervision of the canals which carried the water of the two rivers throughout the country, and the dams which protected its fertility against the desert, which would burst at the slightest deterioration. He took energetic steps against the exodus from the countryside engendered by the big cities. He provided for security and confidence in business affairs by revising the system of currency and measures, and is even supposed to have taken an interest in the exact transmission of the text of the Qur'an, perhaps not without political grounds, since the Qur'an reciters ever since the days of 'Uthman were always ready to stir up feeling against the government. They repaid him for this attention by spreading the anecdote of his having been a schoolmaster as a youth in his native Taif. The only contemporary poet who was in his favor for a time was Jarir, who had already been prominent in 'Iraq, under Mus'ab, and had fought out his duels with his poetic adversary Farazdaq; just as 'Abd-al-Malik had used the Christian al-Akhtal in his struggle against Medinese opposition, so his governor utilized Jarir to proclaim his glory and unmask the secret opponents of Syrian rule in the country. In June of 714, after twenty years of beneficent rule, Hajjaj died, only just past his fifty-second year.

Walid was succeeded by his brother Sulayman, in the order their father had established in advance. During the last years of his life Hajjaj had vigorously opposed this and advised the Caliph to elevate his son to the succession. The hatred he had aroused in Sulayman by this could now be vented by the latter only on his captains. Directly after his ascension to the throne he deposed the governor of Medina, 'Uthman al-Murri. The governor of Khorasan, Qutaybah ibn-Muslim, whose conquests in the east had given him great prestige, wished to forestall this fate and summoned his troops to an uprising against the Caliph. But the banu Tamim, with whom he had fallen out, announced their opposition and killed him. The governorship of 'Iraq was given by the new caliph to Hajjaj's worst enemy, Yazid, the son of the distinguished general al-Muhallab ibn-abi-Sufrah. After his father's death he had succeeded him as governor of Khorasan, but soon fell out with his superior in 'Iraq. Hajjaj had married his sister, but brusquely rejected her mediation;

he managed to have the Caliph depose Yazid and even kept him imprisoned for a year. Then Yazid succeeded in escaping to Ramlah and joined the successor to the caliphate, who then sent him to 'Iraq, where he could assuage his revenge on his predecessor's followers. The finances alone were put in charge of a technical official by the Caliph, reputedly on the request of Yazid, who wished to evade the hatred of the population groaning beneath the pressure of taxation; but the Caliph may only have been carrying on the old and tested practice. Yazid soon came into conflict with this director of finances, since the latter refused to comply with his demands on the state treasury. Accordingly he began seeking a more profitable post and had himself transferred by the Caliph to Khorasan, retaining, however, supreme authority in 'Iraq. His military successes in the east were unimportant, and in addition he made himself so hated through his extortions that before his death the Caliph was even thinking of calling him to account. His fate was consummated under the Caliph's two successors.

Sulayman held court at Ramlah in Palestine, where he had already lived as a prince and won the devotion of the inhabitants. In Dabiq in North Syria he maintained a great assembly camp for the war against the Byzantines, which he often inspected himself. But he was unable to achieve any decisive successes. It is true that after vainly besieging Amorium in the autumn and winter of 715 his troops penetrated westward as far as Pergamos and Sardis and surrounded Constantinople for a year; but he had to retire again without success.* Sulayman died at Dabiq only a year later, in September 717.

In accordance with the testamentary instructions of 'Abd-al-Malik, his brother was to have ascended the throne after him; but Sulayman had had allegiance sworn to his son Ayyub instead. Since Ayyub died before him, however, Sulayman let himself be persuaded by the theologian Raja' ibn-Haywa to transfer the caliphate to his pious cousin 'Umar ibn-'Abd-al-'Aziz, who in fact was able to assume it unhindered.

'Umar II, a son of the long-lived governor of Egypt, 'Abd-al-

* The only result of these *razzias* (raids) was to flood the slave market with Greek prisoners of war. Once, when Sulayman was in Medina on his way back from the pilgrimage, he placed four hundred Greeks at the disposal of his local favorites, who could think of nothing better to do with them than slaughter them, as we learn from a boastful song of Jarir, a poet who took part in this.

'Aziz ibn-Marwan, and on his mother's side a descendant of the first 'Umar, of which he was very proud, was born in Medina and had passed his youth there in the midst of the pious successors of the companions of the Prophet. He was still intimately connected with them in 706 when Walid appointed him governor of the Hijaz; a permanent council of ten pious connoisseurs of the tradition made sure his conduct of the office was in accord with the Sunnah of the Prophet. But since he granted asylum in Medina to refugees from 'Iraq, Hajjaj managed to have the Caliph recall him, though Walid did not withdraw his favor from him.

As soon as he became caliph, 'Umar II ordered a halt to the advance of Muslim arms in Asia Minor, in order to have a free hand in the interior, where he intended to realize the ideals of political life he had cherished since early youth in Medina. It was only in the far west that his love of peace proved incapable of restraining his governors, who crossed the Pyrenees and fell on southern France, where they set up a fixed headquarters in Narbonne, perhaps even during his reign. He sought to win over the old adversaries of his house, the 'Alids, by placing at their disposal the oasis of Fadak, which the Prophet had reserved for himself after the conquest and which had then become state domain, and abolishing the execration of 'Ali from the pulpit which had become customary under his predecessors. He also conciliated the Christians wherever possible; in compensation for the Church of St. John in Damascus which had been absorbed by Walid, he ceded them the Church of St. Thomas in the Ghutah, although ever since the conquest it had served as a mosque, in violation of the terms of capitulation. He also lessened the burden of tribute of the Christians in Cyprus, in Aylah (on the Gulf of 'Aqabah), and in the South Arabian Najran. He made the inferior legal position of the newly converted clients (*mawali*), which had led to so many uprisings in 'Iraq, equal to that of the Arabs, and by approving exemption from taxation for mawali fighters in Khorasan, in addition to their pay, he consolidated the empire for his successors.

But his most important concern was financial reform. The tax policy introduced by 'Umar I had failed of its effect, since many Muslims in the conquered provinces had acquired property in land and claimed tax exemption for it; and since, on the other hand, many tax-bound country dwellers went over to Islam and were able to escape the tax by settling in the metropolises, Hajjaj had simply prohibited this migration and imposed the land tax on Muslim property also. In contrast, 'Umar II held fast to the principle of tax freedom for all Muslims. But he reintroduced the practice established by 'Umar I, that the totality of the conquered country belonged to the Muslim community, and hence he forbade the individual Muslim in future from acquiring anything from it. If a tax-bound peasant went over to Islam, his land reverted to the village community; if he wished to continue cultivation he had to rent it, and this rental served to pay the taxes the community had to collect. 'Umar's intentions at any rate were good, and they did not, as has been thought, arise in an unworldly theological mind; but during his brief reign—he died on February 9, 720—it was not granted him to execute them with energy, and his successors clung to the more comfortable practice of Hajjaj.

'Umar's successor, Yazid II, the third son of 'Abd-al-Malik, had to put down another uprising of the 'Iraqis directly after he became caliph. Yazid ibn-Muhallab, the governor of Khorasan, had been imprisoned for debt by 'Umar II because he was unable to pay off the statutory fifth part of the booty of his last campaign, which he had exaggerated out of braggadocio. Nor could he expect any mercy from Yazid, who was married to a niece of his old enemy Hajjaj. Accordingly he fled to Basra from his imprisonment in Aleppo, and there summoned his tribe, the Azd, and their South Arabian kinsmen to a holy war against the Umayyads as the enemies of religion. Persis and Kirman also joined him. At first Yazid attempted to negotiate with him, then sent out against the rebels his predecessors' best general, Maslamah ibn-'Abd-al-Malik, who had proved his mettle in the battles of Asia Minor. A battle took place on August 25, 720, near the village of al-'Aqr, between Wasit and Kufah. The rebels were routed, Yazid ibn-Muhallab himself was killed, his family outlawed, the men killed, and the women and children, contrary to all custom, sold into slavery.

Yazid II, like his cousinly namesake, is regarded by the anti-Umayyad tradition as an impassioned amateur of sport and music, as well as singing girls, who left the concern of his provinces to his governors. In reality his brief reign remained filled with trouble even after the pacification of 'Iraq. He unified the administration of Mecca and Medina, and in Egypt instituted a revision of the register of the tribes, which was the basis of their pensions. He even attempted to remedy the abuses following in the wake of 'Umar II's financial reforms by such unpopular measures as the reintroduction of the land tax abolished in various provinces by his predecessors. He was also opposed to the latter's friendliness to Christians; he not only took away a few of their churches but also ordered the destruction of religious images.* It is difficult to credit such a man with taking the death of a favorite singing girl so to heart, as later tradition tries to make credible, that he died as a result in January 724 in the castle of Arbad (Izbid, according to others) in Transjordan.

A number of these desert castles in Moab, in which Umayyad rulers occasionally sought to forget the cares of state, have been so well preserved to this day that they allow us a glimpse into their construction. The most famous among them, Mshatta, the "Winter Camp" (of which considerable portions of the façade frieze were presented by Sultan 'Abd-al-Hamid to Kaiser Wilhelm II as a gift and are now displayed in the Kaiser Friedrich Museum in Berlin), is an example of the first of the two types represented in the desert, that of the Bedouin encampment cast in stone.† A square space with sides 157 yards long each is enclosed by a wall flanked with towers. The southern side reveals a magnificent façade with the gate, again framed by two towers, in the center. The interior is divided into three aisles. In the center the gateway and gateway area lead through an open court with a cistern in the center, into the prince's gallery, terminated by a triapsidial domed chamber. This was adjoined on the right and left by two barrel vaults with the depressed pointed arches characteristic of Persian art and later of Islamic art. As shown by the indentations, it was originally planned to build a number of rooms in both, but this was never done. The gate façade is ornamented by friezes, which alternate from horizontal to vertical lines and are crowned by a flat coussinet profile. The columns of the portico bear capitals of imported marble painted over in blue-gray, the favorite colors of Mesopotamia. The capital of the triumphal arch and the display ground of the exterior façade are wrought on the flat surfaces like lace or tapestry. The portico façade displays the same acanthus motif as the columns, but

* The authenticity of the edict relating to this is attested to, contrary to Wellhausen's doubts, by Christian and Muslim witnesses; see Caetani, *Chronographia Islamica*, II, p. 1284, 19.

† See E. Diez, *Die Kunst der islamischen Völker*, p. 23 ff.; the same author in the *Encyclopaedia of Islam*, III, 612-14; H. Lammens, *La Badia et la Hira sous les Omaiyades*, in *Mélanges de la Faculté Orientale de Beyrouth*, IV.

wrought in dark black. The throne room is characterized by niches flanked with columns, which later recur in the prayer niches of mosques.

If Mshatta's Umayyad origin, while remaining extremely probable,* cannot be demonstrated with certainty, inscriptions preserved in another castle east of the northern end of the Dead Sea, the Qusayr 'Amrah discovered by Musil, constitute direct evidence of its construction in the first half of the eighth century; unfortunately the name of the builder cannot be definitely determined here either. On one wall of this castle four princes are depicted, supposed to represent the empires conquered by Islam. These are designated in the Arabic and Greek superscriptions as Caesar, Chosroes (of Persia), Nagashi (negus of Abyssinia), and Rodoriq (Roderick, the last Spanish Gothic king). Next to these four rulers of world empires stand two other figures without superscriptions. Since these are designated in sequence according to the geographical position of their domains, M. van Berchen has determined the third figure next to the Persian to be the ruler of an empire lying further to the east, accordingly either Metchuo (Kapghan, the *khagan* of East Turkestan who was murdered in 716) or even the emperor of China himself. In the background two more heads are visible, which must be referred to smaller princes conquered by Islam. The third among them must belong to a prince of a country east of Abyssinia; this may be one of the Turkish or Indian princes, possibly Daher of Sind (conquered in 712). On the basis of this, Walid I might be regarded as the builder. The building, of reddish limestone, contains a principal chamber roofed by three barrel vaults; opposite the entrance it is terminated by a low barrel-vaulted niche with two chambers on both sides, likewise barrel-vaulted and in the shape of an apse. The space is illuminated by six small window openings on the front walls of the barrel vaults. On the east three small chambers adjoin the main one, which are roofed by a barrel vault, a cruciform vault, and a pendentive cupola in order. They constitute a bathing establishment, with benches along the walls and a system of drainage pipes. All four chambers are adorned with wonderfully preserved paintings, the last creations of Hellenistic art on Asiatic soil. The front wall

* H. Lammens (*Encyclopaedia of Islam*, IV, 1112) suggested it was erected for Walid II, but the passage adduced by him from Severus ibn-al-Muqaffa's history of the patriarchs of Alexandria (163/4) does not definitely refer to Mshatta.

of the niche in the main chamber depicts a bearded man in state robes with a halo, on a throne under a canopy borne on columns, obviously the Caliph; at the right stands a woman with right arm uplifted, at the left a man with a staff, both pointing to the occupant of the throne. The semicircle is surrounded by a chain of desert flying birds (Pterocles, in Arabic *qata*) as so often described by the poets; the sea surges around the foot of the throne, with fish and a fishing boat. In the center of the west wall stands a nude woman at the edge of a cistern; at the right can be seen nude athletes in various postures. At the left stand the above-mentioned figures of potentates. The remaining wall surfaces show horse racing, battue hunts for wild asses and antelope, genre scenes, and symbolic female figures. In the domed chamber the zodiac and the northern skies are portrayed. The central bathing room contains bathing scenes with nude women. Two crescent-shaped spaces (lunettes) in the third chamber depict the creation and fall of man; on the east front wall there sits a woman in an advanced stage of pregnancy at the left, and at the right, with his back toward the spectator, a man; below, between the two of them, lies a kicking infant. On the west front wall a woman is standing near the dead body of a man, and the angel of death, Azrael, is warding her off. The barrel vault depicts the ages of man in half-length portraits. The squares surrounding them, like the walls in general, reproduce the most variegated likenesses of animals and birds. Besides these two desert castles (*badiyah*), the ones best preserved, we are also acquainted with the Muwaqqar, built by Yazid II, which on the Sassanid model reposed on vaulted terraces, but of which only the foundations are still standing. The Roman fortifications on the border of Provincia Arabia were also partially reconstructed into castles for the Umayyads.

Yazid II was followed by his brother Hisham,* who generally maintained his residence in Rusafah on the Euphrates. He had the good fortune of finding in Khalid ibn-'Abdallah al-Qasri another governor for 'Iraq worthy of his great predecessors Ziyad and Hajjaj. Since Khalid, having sprung from an insignificant tribe, stood above party, he succeeded in curbing the mischief-makers among the Qays. But he performed his greatest services for the land by continuing, in the grand style, the amelioration works already begun by Hajjaj. By drying out the swamps on the lower Tigris,

* G. Gabriel, *Il califato di Hisham, studi di storia omayyade, Mém. Soc. Arch.* Alexandrie, VII, 2, 1935.

around Wasit, he reclaimed extensive areas for cultivation, which yielded him great revenues.

The fact that in this he did yeoman work for his own pocket did him no harm in the Caliph's eyes, since he never failed to meet his tax obligations to the court in Damascus. When he allowed himself to be seduced into grain speculation, however, his opponents succeeded in having him dismissed after fifteen years in office. But as soon as his strong arm ceased ruling in 'Iraq, tranquillity also went by the board. A great grandson of 'Ali, by the name of Zayd ibn-'Ali, asserted his family's claim to the caliphate, in Kufah. He took the oath of allegiance with a promise to take the Book of God and the Sunnah of the Prophet as his guide, to fight against unrighteous rulers, to defend the weak, to secure justice for those despoiled of their pensions, to distribute government revenues equally, and to recall the soldiers fighting in distant countries. Although the governor Yusuf ibn-'Umar ath-Thaqafi put down this revolt without any difficulty, after the 'Alid had been killed in street fighting, this was only the first of a long series of successive Shi'ite movements which led to the fall of the Umayyad power. In the ninth century, descendants of this same Zayd founded a state in Yemen which has outlasted the tempests of centuries as the sole surviving 'Alid state.*

Hisham also resumed the war against the Byzantines, which had been conducted very sluggishly since the last futile attack on their capital in 716/17. But these battles led to no lasting success under his regime either, since in winter his troops generally had to abandon again the positions gained during the summer. Once, in 714, the Caliph had to take a hand himself when the Byzantines, after having inflicted a serious defeat on the Arabs at Akroinos in Phrygia the preceding year, attacked the city of Melytene; but he succeeded in repulsing them once again.

Under Hisham the Arabs exerted greater pressure in their advance westward. In the war against the Christians in Spain the Muslims had hitherto often been hindered by disunity between the Arabs and the Berbers, who felt themselves discriminated against. The Berber Munazah had even seceded, established his independence along the northern border, and made an alliance with Eudo, duke of Aquitaine. Hisham now installed a new governor in Spain, 'Abd-ar-Rah-

* As the Zaydites claim for an 'Alid only spiritual leadership (imamate), repudiating extreme Shi'ah tenets, the antagonism between them and the Sunni majority is not so sharp.

man ibn-'Abdallah, who overcame Munazah and then turned on Eudo, whom he defeated between the Garonne and the Dordogne and pursued in the direction of the Loire. But here, between Tours and Poitiers, he was confronted in October 732 by Charles Martel. The Austrasian Franks stood firm against the onslaught of the Arabs, and during the night the latter withdrew, their leader killed. Although his successors resumed their forays into Gaul, they were frequently hampered by internal disturbances.

The Berbers in Africa were discontent, since, although good Muslims and zealous fighters in the Holy War, they were always treated nevertheless like subjects bound by tribute. In consequence Kharijite emissaries from 'Iraq found a favorable ground among them for their preachings, agitating and inciting against the Umayyad caliph. When the Berbers came to court with one more of their complaints and were simply refused admittance, a tremendous rebellion broke out which set Africa in flames from Morocco to Qayrawan. The African emirs were not equal to dealing with them even with the help of the governor 'Uqbah, who came over from Spain. In 741 Hisham had to send out a Syrian army under Kulthum ibn-'Iyad against the Berbers, but this army also succumbed to their savage courage. In a great battle on the river Nawam in 741 Kulthum himself was killed, and it was only with great difficulty that his nephew, Balj ibn-Bishr, was able to fight his way through to Spain with the remaining third of his army. It was not until a year later that a victory assured the Arabs at least of the possession of Qayrawan.

Hisham's greatest fault was his avarice. The state was regarded by him only as a domain to be exploited; in consequence he kept driving his governors into further extortions from his subjects. He had the tribute of Cyprus increased and that of Alexandria doubled. Like the Berbers in Africa, the Persians and the Turks in Transoxania were driven to despair by his policies, which in the east prepared the ground for the emissaries of the 'Abbasids. His death on February 6, 743, left the empire in the most wretched of conditions.

Hisham's successor was his nephew Walid II, the son of Yazid,* who had inherited an artistic talent and a merrymaking disposition from his father. Since his uncle did not favor him for the throne, he had had to spend his youth far from court in a desert castle in

* See F. Gabriele, *Al-Walid ibn Jezid il califfo e il poeta, Rivista di studi orientali,* XV, 1934, 1-64.

Palestine. When he made his entry into Damascus after Hisham's death, he was greeted by jubilation on the part of the populace in general as their emancipator from his predecessor's extortionist economy. But he disappointed their hopes: he soon withdrew again to this desert castle as caliph also and there devoted himself to sport, wine, and poetry.

Just as Islam had hitherto exerted only a meager influence on the living habits of its Arab adherents, so in substance their poetry also remained true to their ancient traditions. In the new countries, Syria and 'Iraq, life had risen to a higher standard than in the old homeland. Intertribal animosities had taken on far more passionate forms, and the struggle between the Qays and the Kalb had been raging for decades. These tribal feuds, as we have seen, constituted the substance of poetry during the Umayyad efflorescence under 'Abd-al-Malik and Hajjaj; the court poet, al-Akhtal, and his adversaries Jarir and Farazdaq, fought against each other with a hitherto unheard-of ruthlessness, and a whole host of minor poets attempted to meddle in their strife and share their fame. The political poem set the tone here later also. During Hisham's reign al-Kumayt's poetry defended the claims of the Prophet's family to the caliphate, and especially of the Fatimids. Only in Arabia proper, poets had struck a tenderer note. For Mecca and Medina, after playing out their political role, had become the homes of a carefree *joie de vivre*. Love of women, mentioned in old poetry and its continuators in Syria and in 'Iraq almost exclusively in the inevitable introduction of the qasidah, now brought to life the independent genre of the love poem. In Mecca, under 'Abd-al-Malik, 'Umar ibn-abi-Rabi'ah, a member of the old aristocratic Makhzum clan, composed his tender, extremely individual personal songs, all dedicated to flirtation, generally with elegant women who joined in the pilgrimage to Mecca; they altogether ignore the agony of love and the pain of separation, the only things touched on in the old poetry. This art, a novelty for Arabia, was enthusiastically welcomed throughout the land. Walid II now laid open a new field for poetic hedonism: the drinking song. Although wine had also played a part in the poetry of the pagan Arabs, it had primarily served as a subject for the poet's boasting. The Prophet's interdiction had neither eliminated the enjoyment of wine from the world nor been entirely able to suppress its being extolled in poetry. But Walid II may nevertheless be considered the real creator of the Islamic drinking song, which later on was zealously cultivated under the 'Abbasids. In this he followed the tradition of 'Adi ibn-Zayd, a

Christian poet who had flourished under the last of the Lakhmids in Hirah. He had been made acquainted with him by his drinking companion, al-Qasim ibn-Tufayl, himself a Christian from Hirah.

In the gay life the Caliph led among women, singers, and poets he soon ran through the money hoarded by Hisham, so that he had to squeeze the governors just as much as his predecessor. He alienated his kinsmen by designating his two sons as his successors, although they were minors and born of slave mothers to boot. They set up on the throne against him Yazid ibn-al-Walid ibn-'Abd-al-Malik, who accepted the oath of allegiance in Damascus without opposition, although Walid resisted the troops sent against him and fought more bravely than had been expected. He then withdrew to his castle at Bakhra', south of Palmyra, and while reading the Qur'an, like 'Uthman before him, received his death stroke on April 17, 744.

Walid's assassination began the end of the dynasty. Since the Umayyads themselves had undermined the prestige of the caliphate in Syria, hitherto invariably loyal, the revolutionary propaganda of the Kharijites, which had already made great progress in the provinces, now gained ground there also. Political disintegration set in. Walid's successor, Yazid III, died the same year (September 25). 'Abd-al-Malik's clan encountered an opponent in a grandson of the caliph Marwan ibn-al-Hakam and son of a Kurdish slave woman, Marwan ibn-Muhammad,* whose father, as governor of Mesopotamia and Armenia, had directed the campaigns against the Byzantines for a period of many years. Marwan II himself had fought in the Caucasus for twelve years, and on the basis of this experience reorganized the Islamic military. The old system of paying the soldiers out of the revenues secured from tribute could no longer stand the test of these campaigns, which demanded a more rigid discipline. In consequence Marwan replaced the old tribal organization of the army by newly formed regiments led by professional soldiers. The old armies had fought in extended lines, in front of which the individual duels, which generally decided the outcome of the battle, were fought out. Instead of these Marwan now instituted small, very mobile tactical units.

Marwan had refused to recognize Yazid III and also declared him-

* His nickname of "the Wild Ass of Mesopotamia," which sounds so strange to us, is not meant in mockery, but in praise; the wild ass is regarded as the noblest of the animals of the hunt.

self against the latter's successor, Ibrahim ibn-al-Walid. He advanced into Syria, ostensibly representing the claims of Walid's heirs, and defeated the government troops moving against him before the Anti-Lebanon. Their leader Sulayman, a son of the caliph Hisham, had both of Walid's sons put to death on the retreat to Damascus and then fled the country with all the money accessible. On December 7, 744, Marwan himself accepted the oath of allegiance in Damascus, but then removed his residence to Harran, where he could prop himself up on the Qays, who were devoted to him. This irritated the Kalb in Syria into an uprising, which, however, he suppressed the same year. Then he raised up an army among them which was supposed to be united with his own troops in a campaign against 'Iraq, which had not yet submitted to him. On the march there, however, the Syrians in Rusafah, where Sulayman lived, persuaded him to lead them as caliph. He seized Qinnasrin, and in consequence Marwan had to interrupt his march into 'Iraq; he defeated Sulayman ibn-Hisham, who fled first to Hims and then to Kufah. Since Hims had surrendered only after a siege of many months, Marwan had its walls leveled and then removed the fortifications of Baalbek, Damascus, Jerusalem, and other Syrian cities as well. It was not until the summer of 746 that he was really master of the whole country.

Meanwhile, in the east of the empire the authority of the Umayyads had entirely vanished. In Kufah the 'Alids had now proclaimed 'Abdallah ibn-Mu'awiyah, a great-grandson of 'Ali's brother Ja'far, as imam. The latter asserted that the spirit of God had descended on him through his forefathers from the Prophet, and so laid the groundwork for the extreme Shi'ite doctrines of posterity. Although the Zaydites joined him, and he was occasionally able to overpower the Kufah fortress, Walid II's governor in 'Iraq, 'Abdallah, a son of 'Umar II, succeeded nevertheless in defeating him eventually. But since freedom of withdrawal was granted him, he went to Media, where numerous followers soon flocked to him. The Iranians had long been well acquainted with the notion of legitimacy fostered by the 'Alids. He maintained his residence first in Isfahan, then in Istakhr (the old Persepolis), and extended his rule to the neighboring provinces of Khuzistan, Fars, and Kirman. Since he offered asylum in his territory to the Kharijites defeated on the Tigris by 'Amir ibn-Dubarah, one of Marwan's generals, the latter attacked and defeated him at Merv ash-Shadhan in 747. He fled to Khorasan, but as a troublesome competitor was put to death there by Abu Muslim, the ‘Abbasid champion now to be discussed.

Since ‘Umar II's son ‘Abdallah refused to recognize Marwan, the latter dispatched Nadr ibn-Sa‘id al-Harashi to ‘Iraq as his governor. After fighting for four months, they were compelled to unite against a common enemy. Although the Kharijite movement had been repressed by Hajjaj and his successors, it had not been smothered. Now it broke out again in northern Mesopotamia among the Rabi‘ah tribe, which begrudged the Qurayshites the caliphate. They elected Dahhak ibn-Qays ash-Shaybani as caliph and advanced against both the Umayyad governors battling before Kufah. Although the latter now turned in unison against the Kharijites, they were no match for them; they were defeated and had to evacuate Kufah. ‘Umar's son made peace with the Kharijites and had himself confirmed as governor in Maysan and Fars by their caliph; after his master's fall he died of the plague in a Harran prison in 750.

The Kharijites after about twenty months in Kufah returned to Mesopotamia and seized Mosul. Marwan, still occupied in Syria, now ran the risk of losing the chief support of his regime, Mesopotamia. After an unfortunate battle, his son, whom he had sent out against the rebels, had to withdraw behind the walls of Nasibin. Meanwhile Marwan's hands were freed and he turned against the Kharijites himself. In September 746 he inflicted a decisive defeat on them: their caliph fell and his successor also perished. But it was not until the following year that their power was definitely broken, when Yazid ibn-Hubayrah, Marwan's general, succeeded in wresting ‘Iraq away from them again. Marwan could then leave the further pacification of the east in charge of his general, while withdrawing himself to his residence in Harran.

But now, when Marwan seemed to have attained his goal, his life work was again imperiled from the east. For some time the governor of Khorasan, Nasr ibn-Sayyar, had been warning of the machinations of the ‘Abbasids, who were assembling their followers there under black banners, but Marwan had felt himself incapable of heeding his urgent requests for help.

In Khorasan * the national-Iranian opponents of Arab rule united with those pious Muslims who upheld the principle of legitimacy and maintained that the government of the Umayyads from the very beginning had been no caliphate but a secular kingdom hostile to

* See G. van Vloten, *De Opkomst der Abbasiden in Chorasan*, Leiden, 1896.

God. Dominion in the theocracy, according to their view, was due the family of the Prophet, that is, the descendants of 'Ali. But the 'Abbasids were able to turn the anti-Umayyad mood of the east to their own advantage. Their ancestor, the cousin of the Prophet and of 'Ali, was 'Abdallah ibn-'Abbas, who had made his peace with Mu'awiyah after 'Ali's death and been appanaged with the state treasury of Basra. Seeing no possibility of playing a political role, he transferred his attention to the study of tradition, which he enriched by rash fantasies and borrowings from the Jewish Haggadah, made accessible to him by converted Jews. Under 'Abd-al-Malik his son 'Ali had come to Damascus, but after Walid's death settled in Humaymah on the Syrian pilgrims' highway, and died there at a ripe old age in 736. During his own lifetime his son Muhammad had raised his claims to the Shi'ite imamate and transferred them to his son Ibrahim. Their emissaries had already been at work in the east of the empire for a long time, and in 746 Ibrahim sent to Khorasan, where the ground had been best prepared, Abu Muslim 'Abd-ar-Rahman ibn-Muslim, a Persian by birth. The latter began his activity in the territory of the Khuza'ah tribe and there, for the first time, held Friday services in the name of the 'Abbasids. But since there was still an older party leader in his way here, he left for Makhwan, where he now gave himself sovereign airs and so aroused the suspicion of the Arabs, but the same tribal animosity as prevailed in the center of the empire prevented them from turning against him in unison; some of the South Arabs even joined him. His supporters, who consisted mostly of Iranian peasants, were bound, on the Book of God and on the Sunnah of the Prophet, to obey whichever member of the Prophet's family would be agreed on. In particular he obligated the troops to unconditional obedience to the officers. It is said he was the first to win over to Islam the Persian landed nobility (the dihqans) in Khorasan, but his propaganda was based also on Iranian beliefs; he is said to have taught the transmigration of souls and given himself out as an incarnation of the Deity.*

Arab disunity enabled Abu Muslim to seize Merv, center of the fertile oasis of the Murghab valley. From there he took up the struggle against the governor of Nishapur, Nasr ibn-Sayyar, and so the war developed which finally led to the collapse of the Umayyad

* His disciple Hashim al-Muqanna' called him the last incarnation of divinity before Muqanna' himself (an-Narshakhi, *Tarikh Bukhara*, ed. Schefer, 64 f., quoted by W. Barthold, *Encyclopaedia of Islam*, I, 101).

empire. The first attack was not made by Abu Muslim himself but by Qahtabah ibn-Salih, of the Tayyi' tribe, who was one of the twelve heads of the 'Abbasid party in Khorasan as early as 718 and in Mecca in 747 was presented by Ibrahim with a black banner designating him his lieutenant. Upon returning to Khorasan he defeated Nasr's son at Tus; Nasr himself fled to Jurjan, and in June 748 Abu Muslim made his entry into Nishapur. On Nasr's call for help the governor of 'Iraq, Yazid ibn-Hubayrah, sent an army to Jurjan; Qahtabah met and defeated it on August 1, 748. Nasr died while in flight. The ruins of his army joined the remainder of the Syrian troops at Nihawend in Persia and were surrounded there by Qahtabah's son Hasan. A large Syrian army of relief under 'Amir al-Murri, the governor of Kirman, was beaten by Qahtabah near Isfahan on March 18, 749. After a number of months the Syrians besieged in Nihawend agreed to capitulate without bothering themselves about the Khorasanians, who were then massacred without mercy.

Qahtabah immediately moved to 'Iraq from Nihawend. At first he avoided the governor of this province, who came across the Tigris to meet him, and turned at once toward Kufah. When Yazid ibn-Hubayrah followed him, Qahtabah attacked his camp on August 27, 749, near Anbar and forced him to retreat to Wasit. During this nocturnal skirmish Qahtabah either drowned or was killed; but his son Hasan, who even before this had played a very independent leader's role, took up his command without incident and occupied Kufah.

This city had long been the center of 'Abbasid agitation. Abu Salamah, the "Wazir of the Family of the Prophet," who hitherto had been conducting it clandestinely and who through emissaries was in constant connection with Abu Muslim, now came into the open and took charge of affairs. The head of the house of Hashim had been arrested in Humaymah shortly before this, on the orders of the caliph Marwan, and taken to Harran. He had advised his people beforehand to take refuge in Kufah, designating his brother Abu-l-'Abbas as his successor. In October 749 fourteen 'Abbasids arrived in Kufah.

The *wazir* (vizier) Abu Salamah, who had only bound himself to Ibrahim on a personal level, was disinclined to subordinate himself to them without more ado, and attempted to keep them separated from the Khorasanians. He is even said to have begun negotiations with the 'Alids; but once again the latter had no man to put forward who could undertake to lead them. A representative of Abu Muslim led twelve Khorasanian chieftains to Abu-l-'Abbas, and they took an oath of allegiance to him. Now Abu Salamah was compelled to waive his objections, and on November 28, 749, Abu-l-'Abbas accepted a public oath of allegiance for the new dynasty in the mosque at Kufah. His first speech from the pulpit was interrupted by an attack of fever, but his uncle Da'ud took his place. He attempted to prove by God's Word that his house had a better claim to the caliphate than the 'Alids, and laid special emphasis on the emancipation of 'Iraq by the Khorasanians from the yoke of the hated Syrians. In any event the Caliph still felt somewhat insecure in Kufah and went over to the Khorasanian encampment with Abu Salamah, but then left him and went to Hirah. Soon afterward he was relieved of Abu Salamah, who was assassinated by one of Abu Muslim's intimates.

The troops operating on the upper Tigris were commanded by 'Awn al-Azdi, appointed by Qahtabah. He had to relinquish command to the 'Abbasid 'Abdallah ibn-'Abbas after the fall of Kufah. Marwan advanced against the Khorasanians, and a battle took place on the left bank of the Great Zab River, which after a struggle of nine days ended with a defeat for Marwan. Pursued by the Khorasanians, he fled by way of Harran and Damascus to the Egyptian coastal city of Farma. The Syrian cities as a whole surrendered to the new rulers without opposition; Damascus alone resisted for a time. Marwan was killed during a final battle at Busir in lower Egypt, in the first part of August 750.

The last refuge of the Umayyad power, the camp-city of Wasit that Hajjaj had founded in the swamps of the Tigris, held out for another eleven months in spite of the disunity prevailing there between the encircled North and South Arabs. It was not until the governor Yazid ibn-Hubayrah learned of Marwan's death that he entered into negotiations. The terms agreed to after forty days of negotiations and approved by Abu-l-'Abbas himself, were nevertheless violated: the captured officers, among them the governor himself, were executed.

The 'Abbasids proceeded against the fallen dynasty with unheard-of savagery. Throughout Syria the Umayyads were hunted down and extirpated like wild beasts. Even the tombs of the caliphs, with the exception of those of Mu'awiyah and 'Umar II, were desecrated.

Only one of the caliph Hisham's grandsons succeeded in escaping to Spain, and there founded a new empire.

Out of hatred for Marwan the Syrians had previously looked almost indifferently on the fall of the dynasty to which they owed so much. But this cruel war of extermination finally called forth a repercussion. In Qinnasrin the Qays raised the banner of Abu Muhammad, a Sufyanid. But they were routed in July 752, and while in flight Abu Muhammad fell at the hands of the 'Abbasid executioners in the Hijaz. To be sure, his followers refused to believe in his death; they continued hoping for his return as for that of the Messiah, who would restore to Syria the vanished days of empire. Since this hope failed them after all, he was absorbed into the Islamic eschatological system as the forerunner of Anti-Christ. The last remnant of the pro-Umayyad sects which, like the Shi'ites, combined political aspirations with gnostic piety, lives on today in the Kurdish Yazidis around Mosul, on Mt. Sinjar, and scattered northward as far as the interior of the Caucasus.*

With the decline of the Umayyads not only the Syrians but the Arabs in general lost their absolute sovereignty in Islam. Their homeland very soon relapsed into total barbarism. The newly converted non-Arabs, whom they had hitherto treated as second-class Muslims, now became their equals. Since the 'Abbasids owed their victory to the Iranian East, and since the military organization of the Khorasanians assured them of their own share in the victory, the Iranians soon gained a preponderance in Islam. They were, however, unable to repress the Arabs entirely, who were still to be found in controlling positions among the officers and functionaries, and who possessed a powerful backing in the dynasty of the Prophet's clan. In the new empire, consequently, Arabic retained its position of uncontested authority in official intercourse, in the ensemble of intellectual life, and above all in religion.

* M. Guidi has demonstrated the Yazidi connections, formerly generally overlooked, with the extremist supporters of the Umayyads, after M. Taymur; see *Rivista di studi orientali*, XIII, 1932, 266-300.

2. The Islamic Empire and Its Dissolution

1. *The First 'Abbasids*

THE first 'Abbasid caliph, Abu-l-'Abbas 'Abdallah, was destined to rule only a short time; consequently he lives on in history primarily as the annihilator of the Umayyads—called as-Saffah, "the Blood Pourer," the name he gave himself in his speech of acceptance in the mosque at Kufah. The real founder of the rule of his house became his brother Abu Ja'far 'Abdallah al-Mansur,* who succeeded him on the throne in June 754. He still had to secure his authority against the claims raised by his uncle 'Abdallah ibn-'Ali. The latter was stationed in northern Syria with the army set up against the Byzantines, but was very soon defeated by Abu Muslim.

But this faithful servitor, to whom the 'Abbasids primarily owed their rise, also had to experience the ingratitude of the new caliph very soon thereafter. He was, to be sure, rather too conscious of his own services. Even in 754 he had demanded as-Saffah's permission to escort the pilgrims' caravan to Mecca and appear there as his deputy. But as-Saffah had subordinated him to his brother (al-Mansur), and Abu Muslim had shown the latter far too great an excess of initiative. Mansur's first concern was to remove Abu Muslim from Khorasan, the firm foundation of his power. Although Abu Muslim rejected the offer to assume the governorship of Egypt, he did allow himself afterward to be lured to Babylonia, and there, near the old capital of Mada'in, he was killed before the eyes of the Caliph. He found an avenger in the person of a Persian, Sundbadh, who raised

* Actually al-Mansur-billah, "whom God has made victorious"; these royal names of pious complexion were borne afterward by all the 'Abbasids; for his reign see Nöldeke in *Orientalische Skizzen*, Berlin, 1892, pp. 112-162 (*Sketches from Eastern History*, tr. by J. S. Black, London and Edinburgh, 1892, 107-145).

the banner of revolt in Khorasan and penetrated as far as Media; but there, between Hamadan and Rayy, he was defeated by the Caliph's troops and killed.

The 'Alids, who up to the very last may have been living in the hope that the Khorasanians were working on their behalf, did not reconcile themselves at once to the rise of their cousins. But like their ancestor, they lacked energy and political acumen. It was in Medina in particular, the chief seat of the clan, by this time widely scattered, that they conducted their agitation against the new dynasty. The governor installed by Mansur had many of them imprisoned and also initiated a zealous search for their ringleader, Muhammad, a great-grandson of Hasan and, through his grandmother, of Husayn also. But this was just what precipitated the outbreak of the rebellion.

At the end of 762 the 'Alids revolted, set free their captive kinsmen, and had the famous theologian Malik ibn-Anas (founder of the Malikite school dominant throughout North Africa today) absolve them of the oath of loyalty taken to the 'Abbasids, as having been extorted by force. It was of course easy for the Khorasanian army sent out immediately to Medina by Mansur to overcome the unsophisticated insurrectionaries, who thought they could protect themselves adequately by a moat on the model of the Prophet's. After courageous resistance Muhammad was killed and his family's estates were confiscated; otherwise the city, which could no longer constitute a threat to the Caliph, was treated gently.

Far more substantial concern was aroused by the uprising of the 'Alids in Basra, under Muhammad's brother Ibrahim. But the latter also lacked political ability. Although he succeeded in seizing Basra and with the money extracted there also won over Persia and Susiana, he could not be persuaded to turn against Kufah, where Mansur was stationed with only a few troops. Mansur's general, 'Isa ibn-Musa, who had put down the uprising in Medina, advanced on Susiana at once and achieved control of the country, though only after some violent fighting. Ibrahim himself, who had finally decided to advance on Kufah, was killed in a battle with 'Isa's troops at Bahamra, south of Kufah, on February 14, 763.

After his decisive victory over the 'Alids, Mansur energetically promoted the construction of a new imperial capital, which he had embarked on soon after becoming caliph. His brother had established a residence in Hashimiyah, on the left bank of the Euphrates near

Anbar. But the proximity of Kufah, whose unruly inhabitants had caused the Umayyads a great deal of trouble, could easily become dangerous for the new dynasty in the future. After careful consideration Mansur decided on a small Christian village on the west bank of the Tigris, called Baghdad, for reconstruction as the capital of his empire. The choice was excellent: the region owed its rapid efflorescence not only to the ruler's whim but to its favorable position, which assured it of substantial importance even after the total dissolution of civilization in Babylonia. On the west bank of the Tigris the Caliph, by a mass levy of forced labor, erected palaces for his court, mosques, and government buildings, attracting tradesmen by favorable terms of construction. Building materials were taken principally from the old Sassanid residence at al-Mada'in. The system of canals was elaborated and bridged over, and waterworks and fortifications made it possible and secure to live there. A series of surrounding localities were comprised in the precincts of the city, of which Karkh (Aramaic *karkha*, "city") was the most important. On the east bank, on which the chief part of present-day Baghdad lies, Mansur erected at first only a camp for his son Mahdi. He gave the sites around the city to his kinsmen, clients, and officers as fiefs. He named his work Dar as-Salam or Madinat as-Salam, "House (or City) of Peace," but its ancient name really remained in popular use.

From the very beginning the tone of the new capital was quite different from that of Damascus. Although Arabs continued to keep going in and out of Mansur's court too, they no longer approached the Caliph, as in the time of 'Abd-al-Malik, as though he were *primus inter pares*. No tribal *shaykh* resided in Baghdad, but a successor of the Persian great kings. Later an interest also arose in the Persian books about ceremonial procedure at the court of the Sassanids, and an attempt was made to imitate it. Rank and dignity at the court and in the state were now no longer hereditary privileges of the nobility, but were distributed according to the favor and caprice of the caliph. The honorary garment *khil'ah, khal'ah* (whence our gala), unknown under the Umayyads, became the outward sign of such favor. While the Umayyads in the main had been content with a hajib who was supposed to regulate audiences with the caliph, a continually growing swarm of court functionaries and court flunkeys now screened the caliph more and more from the public. The caliphs withdrew from the conduct of affairs almost entirely, leaving them to their wazirs. But they exercised power over life and death directly: the executioner, a phenomenon hitherto unknown to Arab civilization, always accompanied the caliph; the leather bag for his victims' heads always lay near the throne in readiness.

The 'Abbasid empire also owed Mansur the principles of its government. For the most part he retained the procedure, already tested under the Umayyads, of the Byzantine and Sassanid chanceries. He always tried to place able governors at the head of the individual provinces. Although in this he was unable to disregard his clan, still he was never hesitant about appointing even clients and freedmen to the highest offices. He had an excellent check of provincial administration in the institution of the postal directors, already present under the Umayyads but not really elaborated until his reign. These postal directors were in charge of the entire news service of the government, but their principal duty was to keep the Caliph abreast of his governors' conduct in office. Their regular and careful reports were also of benefit to the general welfare; their information on sowing conditions, for instance, made it possible to take proper precautions against any crop failure. The registers of the postal stations set up by them constitute one of the sources out of which in the next generation the science of geography arose among the Arabs.

The experts in the holy tradition and the law, who in Medina had hitherto constituted an anti-Umayyad cabal, were attracted by Mansur to his court; now, after all, the theocratic ideal they had dreamed of was fulfilled, since power was once again in the hands of the Prophet's family. To be sure, the founders of two schools of law, among the oldest surviving today, had themselves been sympathetic to the 'Alids. Abu Hanifah, the founder of the school of Hanafites, was the grandson of a slave captured during the conquest of Kabul, whom his master, of the Taymallah tribe, had set free; his followers composed a genealogical tree for him which traced him back to one of the ancient Iranian kings of legend. As client of the Taymallah, he lived in personal independence by trading in silk in Kufah. He had been a supporter of Zayd ibn-Ibrahim's uprising in Basra, and in 767 died in a Baghdad prison. In Kufah he had held public lectures and handed down legal opinions. In these he adhered strictly to tradition and allowed no more space to deductive speculation than any other teacher of law. It was the competitive envy of the later leaders of schools which first raised such reproaches against him. His contemporary in Medina, Malik ibn-Anas, the founder of the Malikite school, has already been met with as a follower of the 'Alids; he was punished for this by flogging after the collapse of their revolt. The later caliphs, however, held him in great esteem, and Harun ar-Rashid visited him shortly before his death while on pilgrimage. While Malik's disciples spread his doctrine primarily in Spain and North Africa, the Hanafites soon entered the service of the central government. As the first *qadi-l-qudat* (supreme judge) of Islam, Abu Yusuf obtained official authorization for Abu Hanifah's doctrine and wrote a basic work for Harun ar-Rashid on the land tax, after one of al-Mahdi's secretaries who had emerged out of the Umayyad administration had already given an account before him of actual conditions in a book on land taxation.

Mansur was constantly preoccupied with securing the frontiers of his mighty empire and expanding them wherever possible. Although the almost incessant wars against the Byzantines had no more success under his reign than under the Umayyads, and the campaigns against the Turkish Khazars in the Caucasus, against the Daylamites on the south bank of the Caspian Sea, against the Turks on the other side of the Oxus, and against the Indians also failed to bring about any substantial expansion of power, nevertheless they demonstrated that an energetic central government was very well able to brave storms similar to those which decadent generations to come could no longer control. The dynasty was frequently imperiled by the rise of sectarian movements in Khorasan, the borderland of Islam where it came into contact with Buddhist and shamanistic ideas, and where the Iranian national religion in particular was still having a powerful aftereffect on people's minds. It is true that Mansur himself had shaken off Abu Muslim, and in 758 when fanatics from Khorasan appeared before his residence in Hashimiyah to revere him as the incarnation of divine majesty, he simply had them hewn down, since they refused to be pacified by soft words. But in 778 Hashim, a Persian from Merv and former secretary of Abu Muslim's, turned up among his followers, claiming to be the new incarnation of the Deity after the Master's death; since he always appeared before the multitude in a gold-embroidered veil which, like that of Moses, was supposed to obscure the refulgence of the divine majesty from profane eyes unequal to it, he survives in history under his by-name of al-Muqanna', "the veiled."

From his Sanam fortress near Kesh in Transoxania, he subjugated the entire province while another Kharijite uprising broke out in Khorasan. It was only after defeating various armies that he was shut up in his fortress, which he set fire to and died in together with his wives and followers (780). The communistic doctrines of Mazdak, of the Sassanid epoch, had already been resurrected the preceding year in the province of Jurjan, and under Harun flared up once again in a dangerous rebellion.

In North Africa also, where Mansur's rule, in any case, probably did not extend very far beyond Qayrawan, he had another Berber uprising to suppress. The Berbers, though yielding to Islam, held firm against all attempts to win them over for Arabism, and have preserved a lively sense of nationality down to the present day; in consequence the Kharijites, almost eradicated in the center of the empire, again and again found among them a favorable terrain for their propaganda.

In the beginning Mansur had intended his cousin 'Isa ibn-Musa, who had performed great services for the dynasty in putting down the 'Alid uprisings, to be his successor to the throne. But as his son Mahdi grew up, he conceived the desire to transfer the succession to him. Accordingly he compelled 'Isa, who only relinquished his claim after great pressure, to release the people from the oath of allegiance they had already sworn to him in 767. On Mansur's death on October 7, 775, on the way back from the pilgrimage, which he was fond of leading himself, Mahdi ascended the throne unhindered.

Despite all the pomp of an Oriental grand monarch observed under Mansur, because of his personal frugality he was able to accumulate a substantial treasury. Consequently Mahdi found it possible at his court to satisfy the claims of an already very refined way of living. To poets and singers he was an openhanded Maecenas. But in addition he did a great deal for the welfare of the empire by constructing a network of highways and improving the postal system. Thanks to its favorable position, Baghdad under his reign developed more and more into a principal entrepôt center for trade with India, but he also showed insight in his patronizing of indigenous industry. The above-mentioned sectarian movements in the Persian provinces imposed on the Caliph the necessity of supervising more sharply the intellectual life of his subjects in the center of the empire as well. Not pure Zoroastrianism but rather Manicheanism, particularly in 'Iraq, still exercised a great influence on those among the new converts not entirely satisfied by the rigid formalism of Islam, and very nearly became the religion of the educated classes. Mansur himself had already had the writer 'Abdallah ibn-al-Muqaffa' put to death. Ibn-al-Muqaffa' (his Persian name was Roz-bih) was the son of a tax collector in the service of Hajjaj ibn-Yusuf and as a supporter of 'Ali ibn-'Isa, the uncle of the first two 'Abbasid caliphs, went over to Islam. He translated the Middle Persian account of Persian history, the *Khudhayname*, as well as the Persian translation of the Indian book of fables *Kalilah and Dimnah* into Arabic, and composed a few discourses on political wisdom in the Iranian genre. He is said to have aroused Mansur's displeasure when as secretary he prepared an ambiguous draft of the amnesty decree for the Caliph's uncle Abu-l-'Abbas 'Abdallah. Whether this alleged treachery was the sole cause of the cruel punishment meted out to him by the governor of Basra may be doubted; he may have made himself suspect of participation in the politico-religious activities of the Iranians which, as we have seen, became a burden to the Caliph. Under Mahdi the same fate met the poet Salih ibn-'Abd al-Quddus, who in his religious discourses in Basra had openly preached the dualism of the Persians. He attempted to escape the animosity this aroused in theological circles by fleeing to Damascus, but Mahdi had him brought back and crucified in 783 as a *zindiq*. At that time this was what heretics were generally called; it was a name which, under the Sassanids, originally branded anyone who dared put out a new and nonorthodox explanation (*zand*) of the Avesta, and which was then applied to Manicheans and Mazdakites in particular. In the same year the blind poet Bashshar ibn-Burd, whose poetry had openly professed the fire worship of his ancestors, was put to death; since he was simultaneously a notoriously slanderous poet whose satire did not spare the Caliph himself, tradition, as in the case of ibn-al-Muqaffa', has sought the cause of his tragic end in this political aberration. But around the same time Mahdi entrusted the inquisition against the heretics to a special official (*'arif*), who is said to have been active at first for three years. Under his successors this inquisition was then also directed against doctrinal opinions within the intellectual framework of Islam proper, which though otherwise innocuous, for one reason or another were disagreeable to the government.

After a reign of ten years Mahdi left the throne to his son Musa in 785, with the royal name al-Hadi. Musa resisted the influence of his mother, Khayzuran, a Berber slave, who had already taken a lively interest in affairs during her husband's reign and had almost dominated him. Musa vainly tried to force his brother Harun, favored by his mother, to waive his rights to the succession, and on September 15, 786, no doubt at the latter's instigation, was murdered near Mosul in his harem. It was as early as this that the defects came to light by which the 'Abbasid dynasty finally perished.

Under Harun's twenty-three-year rule the 'Abbasid dynasty was at the summit of its power.* Since in this period material well-being simultaneously achieved a hitherto unknown efflorescence, later generations were all the more inclined to visualize the caliph Harun, with the royal name of ar-Rashid, as an ideal ruler, and ascribe to his personal merits what he merely owed to the favorable conditions of his time.

During the first years of his reign Harun left concern with affairs almost entirely to his wazirs. This office had long been hereditary in the family of the Barmakids,† the descendants of the high priestly family of the Buddhist monastery Naubahar in Balkh, which a later Persian tradition, for the sake of national pride, laid claim to as fire priests. After the assassination of Abu Salamah, Saffah himself had designated Khalid ibn-Barmak as his wazir, or rather his first secretary (*katib*). Under Mansur also the latter retained control of finances and particularly distinguished himself in the construction of Baghdad. But at the same time he was an able soldier, and not only had fought in his youth under Abu Muslim and Qahtabah but as the governor of Tabaristan from 765-69 had put an end to the last native principality, on Mt. Demawend, and at an advanced age even participated in the wars against the Byzantines. That he found an opportunity during all this to enrich himself, like all functionaries, was merely a matter of course. Consequently Mansur, shortly before his death, exacted from him nearly three million dirhams ‡ and then gave him the governorship of Mosul, which because of the proximity of the turbulent Kurds was a particularly important post. His

* G. Audisio, *Harun ar Rashid, Caliph of Bagdad*, New York, 1931. [N. Abbott, *Two Queens of Baghdad*, Chicago, 1946.]

† L. Bouvat, *Les Barmécides d'après les historiens arabes et persans*, Paris, 1912.

‡ Since state loans were still unknown at that time, such fleecing of officials who had sucked their fill in service constituted a regular means of refilling the empty state treasuries; there was a special technical term for this—*musadarah*.

son Yahya simultaneously assumed the governorship of Adharbayjan. Under al-Mahdi he was recalled to Baghdad. In 777, when Harun was appointed governor of the western provinces together with Armenia and Adharbayjan, he stepped in as head of his chancery. During Hadi's attempt to force Harun into renouncing his rights to the succession, Yahya remained faithful to Harun; he is even supposed to have lost his freedom for a while as a result. In gratitude for this, Harun elevated him to be his wazir directly after he became caliph; together with his sons Fadl and Ja'far he governed from 786 to 803 with unlimited powers, though during the first years of his office he was strictly supervised by the Caliph's mother. Whereas Fadl, as governor of the eastern provinces, achieved great merit through his military exploits and works of peace, Ja'far remained in the capital as the Caliph's favorite and had the provinces entrusted to him for administration, i.e. in this case for exploitation, administered by deputies. But his friendship must eventually have become tiresome to the Caliph. A harem episode is traditionally given as the cause of final displeasure: the Caliph had him contract a marriage of appearance with his sister 'Abbasah, so as to be able to enjoy the society of both at the same time, and Ja'far took undue advantage of this connection. But directly after his mother's death in 790 the Caliph is supposed to have taken away from Ja'far the state seal hitherto in his charge and transferred a portion of his affairs to his opponent and successor Fadl ibn-Rabi'. In the beginning of 803, when Harun had returned from the pilgrimage to Mecca, which he generally used to conduct in his own person, he had Ja'far executed during the night of January 29 and his head placed in display on the central bridge of Baghdad and the two halves of his body on the other two bridges. His father and brothers were arrested and their property confiscated. After the fall of the Barmakids, Harun transferred his residence to Raqqah on the Euphrates.

Harun's reign saw no lack of repeated uprisings in the interior of the empire. In Syria, in 796, the old hostilities between North and South Arabs had flared up again in bitter struggles; in Damascus the attendant disorder was taken advantage of by a pillaging mob. It was not until Ja'far made an exceptional appearance there in person and instituted a general disarming that order was restored.

In Africa uprisings against the Caliph's governors broke out continually. Here order was first restored by Ibrahim ibn-Aghlab, whose own father, a native of Merverrudh, had lost his life while governor of Ifriqiyah during an uprising in 767. In 795 the son had been entrusted with the governorship of the Zab region in southern Algeria on both sides of Biskra. When his father's successor, ibn-Muqatil, was expelled again by rebels, ibn-Aghlab came to his assistance in 799 and with great skill restored order. For a reward, Harun bestowed the country on him as a hereditary fief, in return for an annual tribute of forty thousand dinars. Ibn-Aghlab immediately set about the construction of a new capital city, 'Abbasiyah, about three miles south of Qayrawan. By the following year he was already able to receive here ambassadors sent by Charlemagne, who came ostensibly to ask for relics of St. Cyprian, but who in reality not doubt wished to initiate diplomatic relations and sound him out with respect to concerted action against Spain.*

Harun himself also owed his fame in the Occident to his reputed relations with the great king of the Franks, which he himself is supposed to have initiated by an embassy to Aix-la-Chapelle; Arabic sources, however, have nothing to say about this, and presumably it was only a case of Oriental merchants' passing themselves off without authorization as ambassadors of the Caliph.†

The struggle against Byzantium dragged on throughout Harun's reign and led to no greater success than compelling Emperor Nicephorus in 806, after the conquest of Heraclea, to bind himself to the payment of a tribute. In Iran also there was a continuous fermentation. When Rafi' ibn-Layth revolted in Samarqand in 805 and subdued all of Transoxania, the Caliph himself took the field against him. But he only got as far as Tus in Khorasan; there he sickened and died on March 24, 809.

Harun's reign was made particularly lustrous by the blossoms borne at that time by Arabic literature on the fertile soil of the ancient civilizations of Babylonia. The desert poets, who even under the Umayyads had exhausted themselves entirely in tribal feuds and petty jealousies, were succeeded by a new generation of urban poets. People had no time for the long-drawn-out qasidahs of the old poets, nor any understanding; these were broken up by the new art and an attempt was made to foster each element individually. The intellectual horizon, to be sure, was scarcely broadened. Love,

* Eginhardi Annales Francorum, year 801.

† See F. F. Schmidt in *Der Islam*, III, 409-11; W. Barthold, *ibid.* IV, 333 ff. Professional diplomats were as little known in the Orient then as in Europe; as a general rule theologians learned in law (*fuqaha*) were made use of.

hunting, and wine had been praised by the ancients, too; they, too, had mocked their adversaries in biting words, and on occasion sounded a more earnest note in laments over the transitoriness of earthly things. The love poem had already achieved its independence under 'Abd-al-Malik in the songs of 'Umar ibn-abi-Rabi'ah, and the caliph Walid II revivified the genre of the drinking song. All these themes were now cultivated further by the younger poets; they also borrowed their rhetorical flourishes not only from the colloquial language of their time, but generally from the vocabulary of the Bedouins, whose speech was still considered the ideal. In the eulogies of the caliphs and the Barmakids the old style is most often preserved and handled with skill by poets of non-Arab origin, too. The most famous panegyricist of the 'Abbasids, Marwan ibn-abi-Hafsah, was the great-grandson of a Khorasanian Jew, but usually lived in Yamamah and always returned there after his visits to the court of the Caliph where he delivered his eulogies. Khalaf al-Ahmar, the son of a freedman from Ferghana, had so integrated himself with the ancient poetry that he was able to imitate it deceptively.* But the most famous poet of the time, Abu Nuwas, the son of a Persian washerwoman, who had spent his youth in Basra and Kufah, also had such an extraordinary mastery of Arabic in all its forms that it was assumed that he had been able to achieve this virtuosity only through a protracted sojourn among the desert Arabs. But in his casual poems he makes room for the locutions of everyday speech. This poet had unmistakably genuine lyric talent, though he often also succumbed to an insipid straining after effect. In this frivolity of his not even religion was sacred to him, and the many open and covert salacious allusions in his diwan throw a characteristic light on the low level of his audience's taste. He himself also seems to have quite often played the role of a jester at court and in Baghdad society, which was the sole delight of his contemporary, Abu Dulamah.† But there was also no lack of more earnest singers who attempted to influence the demoralized society of the metropolis. Christian influences are unmistakable in the poetry of Abu-l-'Atahiyah, who in his youth had been well received at

* One of the most famous poems, still the most attractive to European taste also, the *Lamiyat al-'Arab* (translated by J. W. Redhouse, 1881, G. Hughes, 1896; cf. R. A. Nicholson, *A Literary History of the Arabs*, p. 80), which tradition ascribes to Shanfara, a pre-Islamic South Arab hero, is regarded by many Arab philologists as his work.

† The source of the motif of C. M. von Weber's comic opera *Abu Hasan*.

Harun's court because of his agreeable love songs, but then preached the renunciation of the world so single-mindedly that he attracted the suspicions of the smellers-out of heresy.

As under the Umayyads in Mecca and Medina before, the new love poety was principally spread by women singers, who also played a pre-eminent role in the social life of Baghdad. For a time a son of the caliph al-Mahdi by a Daylamite slave woman set the tone in Baghdad and Samarra as an amateur of music, which he himself is supposed to have enriched by a number of innovations. Under Harun and his successors the musical life of the capital was dominated by Ibrahim ibn-Mahan al-Mawsili, the son of a Persian tax farmer, and his son Ishaq. Both trained slave girls in singing and then resold them for high prices. Arabic literature is full of elegant love stories concerning these girls and their lovers, who are not always equal to the financial demands of the girls' owners.

If the rule of Arabic was still unquestioned in belles-lettres, nevertheless there was no lack of poets of Iranian origin, whose poetry often made a public display of their pride in their heritage and glorified the Persians at the expense of the Arabs. This tendency came to light even more strongly in the prose writing which was burgeoning at the same time. A Persian named ʻAllan, who was employed as a copyist in the court library under Harun and Ma'mun, composed a special work which put together the mutual insults of the Arab tribes in the old poetry. In consequence he was given the by-name of the "Shuʻubi," that is, the defender of equality of rights among the nations. The same tendency was represented in numerous writings of the period.*

The extent to which the intellectual life of the epoch was still dominated by Arabic and by the great past of the Arabs is also attested to by the two branches of science which at that time were the focus of interest of the educated world: philology and history. The former had arisen in connection with the Qur'an. It was necessary that the numerous new converts, born in communities of different speech, develop and perfect an understanding of the divine word and its proper application in effective prayer. It was just as urgent a need to enable them to achieve a complete mastery of the nuances of Arabic and its excessively rich vocabulary; whoever wished to survive in Baghdad society had to have not only a thor-

* See I. Goldziher, *Die Shuʻubijja und ihre Bekundung in der Wissenschaft*, in *Muhammedanische Studien* I, Halle, 1889, p. 147-208.

ough knowledge of the old poets, whose verses still set the standard in social intercourse, but also be in a position to produce independent work on the same pattern. That is why the great dictionary of Khalil of Basra stands at the cradle of the history of Arabic philology; its arrangement according to the origin of the sounds in the organs of speech, beginning with the deepest guttural *ayn* (so that it was simply called *Kitab al-'Ayn*), proved inconvenient, and the book was soon discarded in literary circles. But the method—elucidation of the vocabulary on the basis of poetical passages—established a pattern for all future study. Work on the poetic texts themselves also began very early, consisting of a discussion of the institutions of Bedouin life, which constituted the framework of the poems and to which city dwellers were generally alien, and the gathering of information concerning the poets themselves, leading up to attempts at literary evaluation. Khalil is also supposed to have created the basic concepts of meter and of a grammar, which, though going back to Aristotelian logic, was otherwise a completely independent production of the new civilization. One of Khalil's pupils, the Persian Seboya (Sibawayhi) performed the service of establishing this system in a canonical form for posterity, though in a very awkward style. His competitor was a teacher of Qur'anic recitation, al-Kisa'i, a native of Kufah, who had taught Harun himself and was entrusted by him with the education of his son al-Mahdi. Al-Kisa'i's disciple al-Farra' is said to have lectured on Qur'anic exegesis in a mosque at Kufah; however, he, too, usually lived in Baghdad and is said to have composed his book on grammatical definitions, lost to us, in the palace of Ma'mun. The literary-historical tradition of the Arabs retroactively constructed a contradiction between the two schools of Basra and Kufah, which was only dissolved in a later generation in the higher unity of the Baghdad school; but it seems that rivalries of individual scholars from both cities were unduly inflated.

Interest in historical tradition had been very lively even in ancient Arabia. Tales of the battle days of the Arabs, of the tribal feuds which generally arose out of quite petty motivations, took the place of the epic in verse which Arabia lacked, and had been enlivened by verses placed in the mouths of the heroes. The conquests now gave this art an unforeseen impetus. Individual tribes already had entire garlands of epic accounts of their participation in the grandiose contest of nations. Even under the Umayyads these had been collected in book form. A member of the Azd tribe in Kufah, Abu Mikhnaf Lut ibn-

Yahya, composed these accounts into a brilliant prose work of more than thirty individual essays, which are generally broken up into single scenes and dialogues. We owe the preservation of his writings to two scholars from Kufah, Muhammad ibn-as-Sa'ib al-Kalbi, and more particularly his son Hisham, from whom Tabari took it over for his great *Annals*. The father had taken a special interest in the genealogy of the Arab tribes, and attempted to fix the chronology of the Lakhmids in Hirah from the tomb inscriptions then still preserved in their churches. His son, who compiled his father's labors in a great work on genealogy still extant, is supposed to have won Mahdi's favor by reports on the weaknesses of the Umayyads, on the basis of which the Caliph's secretaries were able to answer an insulting epistle of the Umayyad ruler of Spain. We also owe him valuable information concerning the religion of the pagan Arabs in another work still extant, which, to be sure, as a good Muslim he entitled *The Book of the Overthrowing of the Idols*. Although, as a Kufan, Abu Mikhnaf's heart was with 'Ali, his account did not make this so blatant as the works foisted on him much later concerning the martyrdom of Kerbela and the false prophet Mukhtar. The Shi'ite tendency is much less veiled in the history of the Battle of Siffin, written by Nasr ibn-Muzahim, who died in Kufah in 827, which has come down to us in the original version and is still read today in Shi'ite circles as a national prose romance. Under Harun there also flourished Sayf ibn-'Umar al-Asadi, a Tamimite, who in his history of the conquests and of the apostasy of the Arabs (following the Prophet's death), as well as of the Battle of the Camel, was preoccupied with the glorification of his tribe and was fond of indulging in imaginative embellishments; his colorful account—entirely unreliable in detail, however—pleased the chronicler Tabari to such a degree that he conformed to it almost exclusively and so misled all the later historians who depended on him.

Medina, in contrast, was characterized by erudite historical research. Abu Ma'shar, who had come there as a slave from India and later settled in Baghdad, was the first to write a book on the campaigns of the Prophet; his principal interest was in a more exact chronology. In this he was followed by Muhammad ibn-Ishaq, who also went to Baghdad, presumably in order to escape the animosities of scholars interested exclusively in legalistic tradition. There he wrote for Mansur the first complete life of the Prophet, which has come down to us only in a later adaptation. His work was continued under Harun by the protégé of the Barmakid Yahya, Waqidi, whose works on the campaigns of the Prophet and the wars of conquest did not permit his secret sympathy for 'Ali and his house to emerge. His pupil and assistant ibn-Sa'd then collected in his *Book of Classes* (classified notes) all the information about the Prophet, his associates and their direct successors; this gave an impetus to the biographical literature which later generations cultivated with almost exaggerated meticulousness, to which we owe, in addition to a great deal of indifferent rubbish, the preservation of some information of great value for cultural history. Even in Abu Ma'shar and Waqidi the dates on the reign of the caliphs, the administrations of their governors, the leaders of the pilgrimage, and the summer campaigns against the Byzantines constituted the invariable framework of the annals, which were only seldom enlivened by a detailed account of important events. Continuing their work, and possibly impelled also by Persian official annals, Tabari, born at Amul in Tabaristan, became the great chronist of the empire. He began with biblical prehistory according to the late Jewish traditions gathered by the exegetes of the Qur'an and added a selection from the Arabic translation by al-Muqaffa' of the Middle Persian *Khudhayname*. For the history of Islam he used the previously mentioned sources, reproducing them with their authorities carefully aligned. In addition he compiled a vast commentary on the Qur'an equally based on all accessible sources. But the goal of his ambition was the founding of an independent school of law, which did not, however, survive for very long.

Directly after Harun's death the empire threatened to split up into two halves.* He himself had designated his first-born son Muhammad al-Amin, the son of Zubaydah, a granddaughter of Mansur, as heir to the throne, and at the same time entrusted him with the governorship of Syria, But he transferred the eastern provinces to his younger son 'Abdallah al-Ma'mun, born to him by a Persian slave, and at the same time decreed that any encroachment by the elder son on his brother's rights would entail the loss of the throne. Ma'mun's power was limited still further by the governorship of a third brother, al-Qasim, in Mesopotamia. Although directly after his accession to the throne Amin restricted Qasim's governorship to Qinnasrin, he did not yet dare attack Ma'mun himself, despite the

* G. Gabrieli, *La successione di Harun ar-Rashid e la guerra fra al-Amin e al-Mamun*, *Rivista di studi orientali*, 1929.

urging of his father's wazir Fadl ibn-Rabi'. At first Ma'mun still had to heed his brother's rights, no matter how much his wazir Fadl ibn-Sahl pressed him to restore the unity of the empire. He was still tied down by the threat of danger from the east. At the time of the Arab conquests in central Asia the Tibetans had carried on a series of victorious battles against China with the support of the Arabs of Kashghar. But afterward they felt themselves threatened by the advance of Islamic power, and accordingly had helped Rafi' ibn-Layth during his rebellion in Samarqand and were now threatening to attack Transoxania. But in 810 Ma'mun was compelled to forego his restraint, when Amin had his own son Musa named in the Friday prayers in addition to Ma'mun and so brought into question the right to the succession due him. When Ma'mun went further and broke off all connections with Baghdad, Amin declared him deposed and charged the marshal 'Ali ibn-'Isa to take the necessary action against him. But the latter was defeated by Ma'mun's marshal Tahir ibn-al-Husayn at Rayy and was killed. After a second army of Amin's was also annihilated, the troops he had sent to the east for the third time refused to advance any farther, coming to a halt just at Khaniqin on the 'Iraqi frontier. Riots also broke out against him in Syria and for a short time he was held captive in the capital, together with his mother, by Husayn, the son of his general 'Ali who had fallen at Rayy, although later Amin was set free by those who had remained faithful to him. After Arabia had joined in the oath of allegiance to Ma'mun, his marshals Tahir and Harthamah appeared before Baghdad. One quarter of the city after another fell into their hands, and finally Amin had to surrender. Although Harthamah had assured him of his life, and toward the end of September 813 personally fetched him from his palace in a boat, Tahir's men attacked and killed the Caliph.

Although Ma'mun had become sole ruler after this victory over his brother, at first he stayed on in Merv. His absence was exploited by the 'Alids in 'Iraq to fish in the troubled waters. At the beginning of 815 Muhammad ibn-Ibrahim ibn-Tabataba emerged in Kufah as pretender but was easily overcome by Harthamah; however, since after this new success Harthamah himself appeared dangerous to the Caliph and his wazir, they had him arrested directly after his entry into Merv and shortly afterward removed. The equally deserving Tahir ibn-Husayn was allowed to go with inadequate troops to Raqqah on the Euphrates, where disturbances never ceased. In 817 the Baghdadis offered the sovereignty to Mansur, a son of the caliph Mahdi; but he was faithful to the Caliph and attempted to restore order in his name. Ma'mun no doubt thought he could win over the sympathies of the 'Iraqis by betrothing the 'Alid 'Ali ibn-Musa ar-Rida to his daughter, on the advice of his wazir Fadl ibn-Sahl, in March 817, and designating him as heir to the throne; at the same time he replaced the black banners of the 'Abbasids with the green ones of the 'Alids. But the 'Iraqis refused allegiance to 'Ali and on June 24 raised up as caliph another son of Mahdi, the musical dilettante Ibrahim. At this point Ma'mun at last decided to take energetic measures in the center of the empire. The wazir Fadl ibn-Sahl is supposed to have been deceiving him previously with false reports on conditions in 'Iraq, his 'Alid son-in-law being the first to clarify them for him. In the east also a new danger was threatening. The doctrines preached by Abu Muslim and his pupil al-Muqanna', of the transmigration of souls and the incarnation of the Deity, had been resuscitated in Adharbayjan by a man called Babak, who gained a great many followers, and whose power, if it spread any further, would cut off the Iranian provinces from the west. Ma'mun, however, set out directly for Tus, to fortify himself through prayer at the grave of his father Harun. On the way there his wazir was murdered in his bath at Sarakhs. In Tus, too, his son-in-law was taken ill, ostensibly of some digestive disorder but probably of poison. He was interred near Harun's tomb, and since he was soon revered by the Shi'ites as a martyr, a new city arose around his mausoleum, called al-Mashhad ar-Ridawi, or simply Mashhad, which supplanted the ancient Tus entirely and today is the greatest Shi'ite sanctuary next to Kerbela.* Since soon afterward the wazir Fadl's brother Hasan, who was in command in Wasit, and particularly detested by the 'Iraqis, succumbed to insanity, or at any rate was held captive on this pretext, the Baghdadis gave up their rival caliph, and in August 819 Ma'mun made his entry into the capital. After his withdrawal from Khorasan a Kharijite rebellion broke out there. Ma'mun delegated its suppression to Tahir, who in a short time had control of the whole province. But he soon felt so secure here that in 822 he dared omit mention of the Caliph in the Friday services. Although this was equivalent to open insurrection, the Caliph never-

* See P. M. Sykes, *The Glory of the Shia World, the Tale of a Pilgrimage Translated*, London, 1910, 234-57; Diez, *Chorassanische Baudenkmäler*, Berlin, 1918, p. 89 ff.; R. Strothmann, *Die Zwölferschi'a*, Leipzig, 1926, p. 171.

theless dared not refuse the bestowal of Khorasan on Talhah, the son of Tahir, when the old war lord died. His descendants, who will be met with again, maintained their power for almost a century. These events really deprived the Islamic empire of its easternmost as well as its westernmost province.*

Another son of Tahir's, 'Abdallah, was of great service to the empire in the western provinces. Nasr ibn-Shabath, a supporter of Amin, had maintained himself even after the latter's death in the region of Aleppo, and it was not until 825 that 'Abdallah was able to overthrow him decisively. Now he still had to restore order and peace in Egypt. Here the old struggle between North and South Arabs had flared up once again during the war between the brothers: the Qaysites sided with Amin, the Kalbites with Ma'mun. The unity of the empire had scarcely been restored when an incursion of Spaniards, who had seized Alexandria after being exiled by the Umayyad ruler in Spain, conjured up new disturbances. But 'Abdallah very soon succeeded in forcing them to withdraw to Crete, and restored the machinery of government. After the death of his brother Talhah he then assumed the latter's inheritance in Khorasan. Egypt was taken over by the successor to the throne, al-Mu'tasim, and when the latter proved unable to cope with a Copt rebellion alone, the caliph Ma'mun had to intervene personally and suppress the uprising.

Although Ma'mun had not generally conducted his campaigns himself toward the end of his reign, he nevertheless found himself compelled to resume the struggle against the Byzantines in person. The help the Byzantines had continued to afford the still-unvanquished rebel Babak in Adharbayjan may have impelled him to an attack on Asia Minor in March 830. For three years in succession the Caliph took part in the summer campaigns, and also continued the battle after the emperor Theophilus sued for peace in 832 upon the fall of his strongest border fortress, Lu'lu'a, at Tarsus. The Caliph died on the third campaign at Budendun near Tarsus in August 833.

Ma'mun had done a great deal for Islamic culture during the twenty years of his residence in Baghdad by his personal interest in Greek science. The study of this in the Syrian monasteries had never entirely died down. In order to understand the theology of the

* See W. Rothstein, *Zu asch-Schabustis Bericht über die Tahiriden (Orientalische Studien, Th. Nöldeke gewidmet)*, Giessen, 1906, I, 155-170; W. Barthold, *Turkestan Down to the Mongol Invasion*, London, 1928, 207-22.

Greek church fathers, among whom Theodor of Mopsuestia in particular had dominated the Nestorian exegesis of the Bible, it had been necessary to go back again and again to the formal apparatus it had drawn from Aristotelian philosophy. But mathematics and natural sciences had always attracted a certain interest also, although among the Syrians the cultivation of intellectual matters lay exclusively in the hands of the clergy. Although the Alexandrian school of medicine, with its philosophic spirit, had died out after the Arab conquest, which cut it off from Byzantium, Syrians in Antioch and Harran continued to foster its tradition, and transplanted it to Baghdad. Still more important in this connection was the influence of the medical college founded earlier by the Sassanids at Gundeshapur in Susiana; thence hailed the famous family of physicians the Bokhtisho', of whom one Jirjis ibn-Jibril had treated the caliph Mansur in Baghdad, and whose members still practiced there even later. In Baghdad, Greek medicine encountered Indian. Harun ar-Rashid himself had once summoned Mankah, an Indian physician, to Baghdad, and the Barmakids had had Indian medical works translated into Arabic.* All these interests now received sympathetic patronage from Ma'mun. In his court library, the House of Wisdom (Bayt al-Hikmah), he attempted to unite the literary treasures of the Islamic as well as of foreign literatures; he had Greek works purchased in Asia Minor. Under his reign Abu Yusuf Ya'qub al-Kindi, "the Philosopher of the Arabs," one of the greatest minds in world history as he was called in 1552 by Cardano, began his literary activity, which was not only to transmit to his countrymen a knowledge of Aristotelian and neo-Platonic philosophy in translations and adaptations, but also to extend their intellectual horizon by studies in natural history and meteorology made in the spirit of that philosophy. Al-Kindi showed himself a child of his time in his cultivation of astrology, and even the study of the future from shoulder bones, as entirely serious sciences. Though he maintained a negative attitude with respect to the fraudulent claims of alchemy, he did not consider it beneath his dignity to take an interest in the distillation of perfumes. He even cultivated military science; his essay on swords enumerates more than twenty-five

* See E. G. Browne, *Arabian Medicine*, Cambridge, 1921; M. Meyerhof, *Von Alexandrien nach Bagdad, ein Beitrag zur Geschichte des philosophischen und medizinischen Unterrichts bei den Arabern Sitzungsberichte der Preussischen Akademie der Wissenschaften*, 1930.

varieties according to the country of origin, from Yemen to Ceylon and as far as France and Russia, describes the qualities of individual blades, and gives instructions as to the reforging of damaged swords by gradual cooling.*

Particular interest, in Baghdad, was taken in mathematics and astronomy. The works of Euclid and Ptolemy's *Megale Syntaxis*, the Almagest of the Arabs, were translated for Ma'mun by al-Hajjaj ibn-Yusuf ibn-Matar, after he had already dedicated a translation of Euclid's *Elements* to Harun. But Indian science was drawn on for supplementary material in this too. Ibrahim al-Fazari had already translated the Indian book of astronomy, *Sindhind*, into Arabic for Mansur; a résumé of it was prepared for Ma'mun by Muhammad al-Khwarizmi, who also adapted Ptolemy's *Geographike Hyphegesis* and composed the first independent textbook for algebra; as a result his name survives even today in the term algorithm for the formulation of a calculating method. Ma'mun also had an understanding for the practical problems of astronomy; he had Ptolemy's astronomical tables revised on the basis of simultaneous observations in Baghdad and Damascus, and a meridian degree calculated.

Ma'mun's attitude toward the theological problems of his time was of a piece with this patronage of Greek science. The spiritual labors of the first two centuries of Islam had been devoted primarily to the question of how the theocratic ideals based on the Qur'an and the tradition could be reconciled with reality. While 'Uthman's recension had brought work on the Qur'an text to an end quite early, questions concerning its correct reading occupied generation after generation of scholars. We have already met with Qur'an reciters, as religious-political fanatics, more than once; and in subsequent periods also they continued to play an influential role in public life. The interpretation of the Qur'an was generally still dominated by storytellers, who had appeared earlier under the Umayyads and in wartime not infrequently functioned as field preachers, spurring on the warriors of the faith by examples from sacred history. In times of peace the pious assembled around them in the mosques, just as swarms of idlers surrounded their profane colleagues on the street corners. There is a record, from the second century of the Hijrah, of an 'Iraqi who interpreted the Qur'an to

* See A. Zeki Validi, *Die Schwerter der Germanen nach arabischen Berichten des 9. bis 11. Jahrhunderts*, Zeitschrift der Deutsch. Morg. Ges. 90, 1937, 20.

Arabs and Persians, sitting at his left and right, in both languages. For the most part they borrowed from Christian legends and the Jewish Haggadah, which came to their knowledge distorted by many intermediaries. Such materials also constituted the Qur'anic commentary of Muhammad al-Kalbi, whom we have already met with as one of the fathers of Arabic historiography. A somewhat younger contemporary of his, Muqatil al-Balkhi, had already endeavored to formulate the legal material of the Qur'an and establish its religious terminology by precise definitions. This was then combined with the purely philological interpretation represented by al-Farra', the pupil of the Kufah grammarian al-Kisa'i. The ensemble of the material elaborated by this generation was then compiled by Tabari in his comprehensive Qur'anic commentary. The traditions concerning the life and teachings of the Prophet were also current at this time in an almost entirely oral tradition and were only occasionally put together in writings concerning individual questions or the material handed down by a particular student of tradition; it was not until the following generation that there arose the great canonical collections of tradition of Bukhari, Muslim, and others which later came to be revered by the community almost as much as the Qur'an. The application of the Sunnah of the Prophet, i.e. the model found in his life as reported in the tradition, then became the source of the science of *fiqh*, in which, as on most inferior levels of culture, jurisprudence and practical theology are still merged. In addition to the older schools of Abu Hanifah in 'Iraq and Malik in Medina, that of Awza'i emerged in Syria; for a time this was dominant in North Africa, until it was expelled by Malikite doctrines. In its country of origin it was soon outstripped by the school of Shafi'i, who could not prevail in Hijaz, the home of his family, against the pupils of Malik, nor in 'Iraq against those of Abu Hanifah, and consequently attempted to secure a new sphere of influence in Egypt; he died in Fustat on January 20, 820. He made a more thorough investigation into the principles of jurisprudence, though like his predecessors he did not question the primacy of tradition. Nevertheless Ahmad ibn-Hanbal in Baghdad felt himself forced to emphasize this even more sharply than Malik and Shafi'i. His brusque rejection of any middle path soon brought him into conflict with the government, and in Baghdad for a number of centuries later the fanaticism of his followers constituted a grave danger to law and order. In modern times his doctrine was revived by the Arabian

Wahhabi movement and gave petrified Islam a powerful impetus toward further development.

Islamic dogmatics had also evolved in the struggle around political questions which 'Ali's caliphate had engendered in the community. The Kharijites, who rejected 'Ali, went so far in their fanaticism as to declare every Muslim an infidel who committed a mortal sin. They were opposed by the Murji'ah, who held the profession of Islam, once made, to be inexpugnable, and left the decision as to the sinner's fate in the hereafter exclusively to God. This mild judgment concerning moral character enabled the supporters of the Umayyad regime among theologians to counter the bitterness of the opposition; but even the pro-'Alids could comfort themselves by it, as Abu Hanifah is said to have done. Then, under the caliph Hisham, when the agitation on behalf of the 'Abbasids dared come out into the open, though at first remaining dependent on 'Alid support, particularly of the moderate Zaydite faction, their followers sought a middle road between both doctrines, which made it possible to assume a distinct and neutral position in the struggle between the 'Alids and their adversaries. These representatives of the schism (*i'tizal*) bore the name of Mu'tazilites, which name was later also applied to the secession of two founders of schools from their teacher, the pious traditionist Hasan al-Basri (*d.* 728). They postulated for the sinning Muslim an intermediate position between faith and disbelief. Hasan's pupil, Wasil ibn-'Ata, is regarded as the first Mu'tazilite. His doctrine won over 'Amr ibn-'Ubayd, who was even more anti-'Alid than Wasil and consequently recognized not only Abu Bakr and 'Umar but also 'Uthman as rightful successors of the Prophet. He later became the religious counselor of the caliph Mansur. Both Wasil and 'Amr turned against their contemporary Jahm ibn-Safwan, who taught strict predestination, while the Mu'tazilites did not contest human free will; they nevertheless appear to have taken over from this opponent of theirs the doctrine of the creation of the Qur'an in time and of the attributes of God. In the beginning Wasil and 'Amr had entertained a rather intimate connection with the poet Salih ibn-'Abd al-Quddus and his circle, but a conflict between them soon arose, after which one of the most important concerns of the Mu'tazilites was the struggle against the strong Manichean influence on the religion of the educated classes. But in order to elaborate the doctrine of God's attributes, speculation by means of the formal apparatus of Greek philosophy was indispensable, even though its tendency, as is natural, was decisively rejected. Whereas the representatives of pure tradition considered God's Word, the Qur'an, as eternal as God himself, Mu'tazilite speculation concerning God's attributes resulted in the idea, already held by Jahm, that the Qur'an was not eternal but created. The Mu'tazilites succeeded in interesting the caliph Ma'mun himself in this theory, so that in 827 he declared it to be state dogma, and those who rejected it were delivered over to the inquisition, as the followers of Manicheism had been before. Their first victim was the fanatical traditionary, Ahmad ibn-Hanbal. While Ma'mun was encamped in Tarsus in a campaign against the Byzantines, Ahmad was arrested in Baghdad and taken to his headquarters in chains. Before he arrived, the Caliph had died. The prisoner was transported back to Baghdad, but his persecution did not cease under Ma'mun's successor either, and it was only the reaction which set in under al-Mutawakkil that brought him into favor once again. There used to be an inclination to consider the Mu'tazilites representatives of a liberal theology as against the orthodoxy; on the basis of what has just been set forth there can be no further question of this: they were just as fanatical as the orthodox theologians, from whom they differ not in methods but only in their particular dogmas.

After Ma'mun's death his brother Muhammad, who had been governor of Egypt, ascended the throne uncontested, with the royal name of al-Mu'tasim-billah, since the army, which at first had sworn allegiance to Ma'mun's son, 'Abbas, abandoned this claimant upon Mu'tasim's emergence. But the lack of security in 'Iraq was in itself a demonstration of how the prestige of the dynasty had suffered. In southern 'Iraq, in the swamps between Basra and Wasit, the Sassanids had settled an Indian people, the Jat (in Arabic, Zott), who, like their relatives the gypsies, had left their country for reasons unknown to us. While the Muslims had previously used them in the army without discrimination, they had turned refractory even under Ma'mun, and for years disrupted all traffic between Basra and Baghdad. Mu'tasim found himself compelled to take thoroughgoing measures, but it was not until 825 that he was able to conquer them decisively and deport them to the border fortress of 'Ayn Zarba in Cilicia. The rivalry between the Arabs and the Persians, to whom Ma'mun in the first years of his reign had shown special favor, had already impelled him to entrust his personal security to a corps of slaves, some of them Berbers, but principally Turks. The latter came from the lands beyond the Oxus, partially as tribute from indigenous princes and partially through the slave trade. Hitherto the control of this corps had always been in the hands of freemen; but Mu'tasim, no doubt to assure himself of still greater fidelity, also filled the officers' positions with his personal slaves. During his reign these pretorian leaders had already gained an influence on the government, and in a short time they became the real masters of the state. The threat they constituted to the Arabs must long since have become clear to intelligent men; thus ibn-Sa'd, who wrote under Mu'tasim, puts a prophecy in the mouth of one of the Prophet's associates, to the effect that one day the Turks would drive the Arabs back to their deserts.

Mu'tasim's most famous general was still, to be sure, a Persian, Haydar ibn-Ka'us, usually called Afshin after his forefathers, the former princes of Usrushana in central Asia. He succeeded in breaking the rule of the sectarian Babak in Adharbayjan after taking his fortress by storm in the autumn of 837. Afshin then turned on the Byzantines, who under Emperor Theophilus had attacked northern Syria and Mesopotamia. Afshin defeated the Emperor and after a lengthy siege took Amorium in Galatia by the use of treachery. But it may have been precisely these successes which aroused the Caliph's jealousy. Although after returning home he had put down another conspiracy intended to elevate 'Abbas, the son of Ma'mun, to the throne, he was accused of apostasy from Islam in 840 and left to die of hunger in a dungeon, since no one dared apply the otherwise customary punishment of crucifixion.

While during the last years of his life Harun had preferred the small country hamlet of Raqqah on the Euphrates to the agitation of Baghdad, in 836 Mu'tasim decided to found a new residence for himself a hundred kilometers above Baghdad, on the east bank of the Tigris at Samarra, whose probably Persian name was taken by the Arab ear to conceal an evil omen and was consequently altered in official usage to "Surra man ra'a" (i.e. "Its beholder rejoices"). He delegated its construction to one of his Turkish generals, Ashnas. Two canals branching off toward the east from the Tigris, together with the mainstream, gave the new installation the security of an insular position. Eight Christian monasteries had already been established there. The castle of Jawsaq was built for al-Mu'tasim first; his successors, of whom seven held court here for all of a half century, adorned the region with still more palaces and mosques.

Though of the magnificent structures erected during this brief period of efflorescence only ruins have come down to us, they give us a livelier view of the architecture of the 'Abbasid age than the capital Baghdad, whose monuments, in so far as they withstood the Mongol tempest, were abused by later generations. In the east, no less than in the west, Muslim architects went back to the traditions of the past. The most important building in Samarra whose foundations are still preserved, the castle of Balkuwara erected by the caliph al-Mutawakkil, is, in design, in the arrangement of areas, and in the conformation of the façades, modeled on the Middle Persian palaces of Ctesiphon. It is a rectangle with sides almost two-thirds of a mile long. On the western front, sloping away to the river in front of the terraces, there rose three brickwork arches which led to the living quarters and the public reception chambers. These were grouped in the form of a cross around three inner courts, surrounded by numerous chambers of state with baths and service rooms. To the east a garden with waterfalls adjoined the palace. In the north lay a great pond between grottoes and cisterns. Around the palace there stood buildings for the court attendants and barracks for the guards. The architects of the great mosque went back to an example even far more venerable. For their manarah (the tower for summoning to prayers), on a base three hundred and twenty-eight yards long, they manifestly took as their model the Babylonian towers with stairways, the *zikkurat*. The prodigious resources still available to these architects, although at that time the empire had already passed its zenith, are shown by the really gigantic dimensions of this mosque. It constitutes a rectangle very nearly two hundred and sixty meters long and a hundred and eighty meters wide, and the inner area, divided into twenty-five aisles, encompasses more than 44,000 square meters. This may be compared with the floor space of St. Peter's Church at Rome, with 15,160 square meters, that of the Aya Sophia at Istanbul with 6,890, and that of the Cologne Cathedral with 6,126 square meters.

2. *The Decay of the Caliphate and the Rise of Minor Dynasties*

Under Mu'tasim's son and successor al-Wathiq-billah (842-847) the Turkish generals had already so consolidated their power in Baghdad that the Caliph had to bestow on Ashnas the dignity of sultan and so acknowledge his rights as extending far beyond merely military functions. By the time Wathiq died, at an early age, Wasif, Ashnas's successor, was already able to put anyone on the throne who suited him. At first he put Wathiq's minor son Muhammad on the throne, still in accord, to be sure, with the highest civil authorities; however, soon afterward he replaced Muhammad with his uncle Ja'far al-Mutawakkil-billah. But the new caliph soon attempted to escape from the influence of the king-makers. The wazir ibn-az-Zayyat, who had been working against him, had to atone for this soon after Mutawakkil's accession to the throne three years later; the Caliph also removed the Turkish general Itakh, who had worked on his behalf together with Wasif. He hoped to find a prop among the orthodox Shafi'ites against the aspirations of the 'Alids, which kept continually reappearing. Ma'mun's counselor, the supreme qadi Ahmad ibn-abi-Du'ad, who had had a stroke directly after Mutawakkil's accession to the throne, had passed on his office to his son Muhammad. But no later than the second year of his reign the Caliph had him and his brothers arrested and their property confiscated. He transferred the office of supreme qadi to the Shafi'ite Yahya ibn-Aktam, who had already enjoyed great prestige under Ma'mun but because of his dislike of the Mu'tazilites had been forced to be content with various posts in the provinces. During his three years of office, which were all Mutawakkil's mistrustfulness and cupidity allowed him, he initiated a complete upheaval. The tomb of Husayn in Kerbela was destroyed and the pilgrimage there prohibited. All the theologians who had been held in custody for their opposition to the dogma of the created Qur'an, among them Ahmad ibn-Hanbal, were set free, and any further dispute concerning it was forbidden. But Christians and Jews, who as savants, and particularly as physicians, had played a great role at the court of his predecessors, and whom even Mutawakkil could not entirely dispense with, also had to suffer under the intolerance of the new regime; all newly erected churches and synagogues in Baghdad were torn down, humiliating insignia fixed on the costumes of the adherents of both religions, and the use of any riding animals but donkeys and mules forbidden to the infidels. At the very beginning of his reign the Caliph had designated his oldest son as his successor and held out the prospect of the throne's reversion to both his younger sons after him. But under the influence of his favorite, Fath ibn-Khaqan, he later shifted his preference to his younger son al-Mu'tazz. The power of the Turkish pretorians could not be broken even by the Tahirid Muhammad, appointed military governor in Baghdad in 851. Since the spendthrift Caliph was not always able to satisfy the demands of his guards, in 858 he attempted to escape their influence by settling in Damascus, but soon returned to Babylonia. Later on, when he was imprudent enough to make an attempt to confiscate the property of General Wasif in Media, the latter entered into a conspiracy with the heir to the throne, al-Muntasir; during the night of December 9-10, 861, the Caliph was assassinated in his palace, al-Ja'fari, newly erected before the gates of Samarra.

The patricide was able to hold the throne only six months; he made a vain effort to secure it for himself, by forcing his brothers to waive their claims and by patronizing the 'Alids. After he had been eliminated by poisoning, the Turks put a nephew of Mutawakkil's on the throne, Ahmad al-Musta'in-billah. But after a reign of only four years he lost his power, which long since, to be sure, had faded to a phantom, in a factional struggle among the Turkish generals. Bugha, to whom he owed his elevation, was forced to flee to Baghdad with him from his opponents, and in Samarra Mu'tazz was raised to the caliphate. The Tahirid Muhammad, whom he had appointed governor of 'Iraq and of both holy cities, attempted to help Musta'in while he was besieged in Baghdad, but after a quarrel with Bugha went over to his opponents, and so Musta'in, who could no longer hold out in Baghdad, was forced to abdicate in January 866, and in October of the same year was assassinated in Wasit.

Mu'tazz attempted to create a counterweight to the Turks, to whom he did after all owe his elevation, in his African bodyguard; but after four and a half years he also was dethroned and killed in July 869 by the Turks, whose demands for money he was unable to satisfy. His successor, Muhammad al-Muhtadi-billah, a son of Wathiq, vainly attempted to evade his predecessors' fate by cutting down on the expenses of the court in order to restore some order in the thoroughly chaotic financial system. However, even before he had completed the first year of his reign he was killed in a battle against Musa, the son of Bugha.

How weak the central government at that time had become through the pretorian economy and the incessant alternations of rulers is shown most clearly by a robber state of escaped slaves which sprang up under its eyes and almost before the gates of the capital, and for years continued to terrorize all of Babylonia. Near Basra there were great salt deposits, worked by squads of East African Negro slaves for the benefit of Basra entrepreneurs. Among these there arose a Persian, 'Ali ibn-Muhammad, who advertised himself as a descendant of 'Ali and of Fatimah through Zayd ibn-'Ali's clan (and for that matter may actually have been a member of this tribe, by this time enormously spread out) and summoned the Negroes to battle against their exploiters. He did not, to be sure, preach anything like a reform of social conditions, but only promised precisely these oppressed people, including slaves, an amelioration of their lot, freedom and riches. He did not base himself on the claims of his family, but rather professed the doctrine of the Kharijites, whose rejection of all national prerogatives must have seemed especially agreeable to his followers. He had made his first appearance on September 10, 869, and after only a short time controlled the surroundings of Basra. The armies sent out against him from Baghdad were regularly defeated, particularly since the colored mercenaries generally went over to his side. Nor were the inhabitants of Basra, who took the field against him themselves on October 23, 869, equal any longer to the savage courage of his men. On the site of his new base of operations, easily defensible because of its innumerable small canals and swamps, there soon arose a new city, Mukhtarah, "the Chosen," rapidly erected out of bricks, of course, but soon fitted out with the opulent booty. So he ruled the Tigris down to its mouth and then struck out at Khuzistan.*

But meanwhile a change for the better had taken place in the capital. Although the new caliph, al-Mu'tamid, a son of Mutawakkil, was absolutely incompetent himself, in 870—very soon after his accession to the throne—he made his energetic brother al-Muwaffaq-billah the imperial vice-regent. As soon as the latter had consolidated his position in Samarra in the summer of 871, he sent out an army against the Negroes, which in spite of initial successes was unable to come to grips with them to any extent. Even the Bedouin tribes of the surrounding region had already begun joining the rebels. On September 7, 871, they succeeded in surprising Basra during the Friday services. The rich city was despoiled, put to the slaughter—according to the lowest estimate 300,000 people lost their lives—and

* See Th. Nöldeke, "A Servile War in the East" in *Sketches from Eastern History*, tr. by J. S. Black, 1892, pp. 146-175.

set on fire. Muwaffaq himself, who had taken the field against the insurrectionaries in April 872, was defeated. Meanwhile a new danger arose from the east, which forced Muwaffaq to leave the Negroes to their own devices for a while.

In the province of Sistan in southeastern Iran, the border area between present-day Iran and Afghanistan, the Kharijites, who had been pushed back almost everywhere else, had held out for a long time; but in this remote region, which even in Harun ar-Rashid's time was under native princes and had been integrated only loosely into the provincial administration, the Kharijites had sunk to the level of mere brigands. In self-defense the populace finally took action against them. The leader of a band of volunteers fighting against them had seized the capital and driven out the subprefect installed there by the Tahirid governor of Khorasan. This leader of the volunteers had Ya'qub, a former coppersmith (*saffar*, hence his descendants' name of Saffarids), in his service. His bravery made Ya'qub so redoubtable that his former master soon assigned the supreme command to him entirely and settled down in Baghdad after a pilgrimage to Mecca. His brother's attempt to bring Ya'qub back under authority failed, and gradually the coppersmith, as emir, conquered the entire province, which he rendered a great service by rooting out brigandage. Only about seven years later, in 867, he was attacking the southern possession of the Tahirids in Herat. He tried to win the Caliph's favor by opulent gifts out of his booty. The slight importance still retained by the central government in these countries was shown when it willingly enfeoffed him with the neighboring province of Kirman at his own request, but simultaneously did the same for the governor of Pars, 'Ali ibn-Husayn. The latter attempted to forestall Ya'qub by occupying the country, but his general was conquered by Ya'qub and taken captive. Then Ya'qub advanced on 'Ali, defeated him on April 26, 869, and took possession of his capital, Shiraz. Since he was unable to hold Pars itself, he turned again toward the east and acquired the glory of a warrior of the faith by spreading Islam to Afghanistan. When he attacked Pars again in 871, the Caliph enfeoffed him with Balkh, Tukharistan, and Sind, to divert him from the west.

Meanwhile the power of the Tahirids in their native land of Khorasan had already become so debilitated that Ya'qub, favored by the treachery of some Khorasanian grandees, took possession of their capital, Nishapur, in August 873 almost without a struggle.

Upon the Caliph's order to evacuate the province again at once, he did not turn back but instead moved on Tabaristan also, on the southern bank of the Caspian Sea, whose ruler, a descendant of Zayd ibn-'Ali, had given asylum to the refugee Tahirid. Although he won an initial victory here also, he nevertheless soon saw himself forced to retreat because of the peculiar difficulties of the terrain. In the summer of 875 he turned on Pars again, without difficulty mastered the country for a second time, and then proceeded westward through Khuzistan. Since the Baghdad government was still occupied with the Negroes, it attempted to induce him to turn back by conferring on him the fiefs hitherto denied, of Khorasan and the neighboring territories, as well as Pars. But there was no stopping him and he continued advancing on Baghdad. About twelve miles below the city, at Dayr al-'Aqul, the vice-regent Muwaffaq went out against him with a great army. Here Ya'qub suffered the first serious defeat of his life, on April 8, 876. Muwaffaq did not, however, dare pursue him when he withdrew to the border of Babylonia. A treaty of alliance offered Ya'qub by the Negro prince was brusquely rejected. Muwaffaq once again entered into negotiations with him, but before these came to any conclusion Ya'qub died in Gundeshapur on June 5, 879.*

He was succeeded by his brother 'Amr, a former donkey driver and mason, who had long since proved his mettle as a military leader. Muwaffaq immediately concluded a treaty with him which confirmed his brother's conquests; in addition he conferred on him the rank, merely nominal, to be sure, of a military governor of Baghdad, which had previously adorned the Tahirids. But Khujastani, a former intimate of Ya'qub's, rebelled against 'Amr in Khorasan, defeated him on July 7, 880, and seized the capital, Nishapur. 'Amr was compelled to relinquish the country to him for a time and withdraw to his native country of Sistan. Two years later Khujastani was assassinated, and now 'Amr succeeded in winning Khorasan back again.

The menacing attitude Ya'qub had taken against Baghdad had been of benefit to the Negroes, who had not only conquered the important city of Wasit in Babylonia but also seized a particularly firm foothold in Khuzistan. Since Muwaffaq now had a free hand in the east, he cautiously but energetically resumed the struggle

* Th. Nöldeke, "Yakub the Coppersmith" in *Sketches*, pp. 176-206; W. Barthold, *Zur Geschichte der Saffariden, Orientalische Studien*, I, 171-196.

against these rebels. Ships had to be built for an attack on their city, enclosed on all sides by canals. The battle was joined by Muwaffaq's son, Ahmad Abu-l-'Abbas, later the caliph al-Mu'tadid. At first he contented himself with minor successes and attempted to induce the officers and especially the rank and file of the enemy army to desert. It was not until a year later, in the autumn, that Muwaffaq himself appeared in the theater of war; but after taking the second city erected by the Negroes, Mani'ah, "the Impregnable," he turned back to Khuzistan in order to purge it of their gangs. In the spring of 881 their capital city, Mukhtarah itself, was besieged, and for this purpose another city was erected opposite it on the other bank of the Tigris, a special camp-city called Muwaffaqiyah. The government troops succeeded a number of times in actually pressing into the enemy city itself, but it was not until July 883 that Muwaffaq ventured on a decisive attack, after his army had been reinforced by that of Lu'lu', a prefect of the governor of Egypt in command in Syria who had betrayed his master. The city finally fell victim to the latter's energy in August 883. This finally smashed the uprising which had so long devastated the richest province of the caliphate.

At this time the west of the empire, like the east, had also entirely withdrawn from the influence of the central government. During the preceding decades Egypt had generally been ruled by deputies of the 'Abbasid princes or of the Turkish grandees, who preferred living on their revenues in the capital in order to be able to pay personal attention to their interests in the ceaseless flux of the political situation. In 868 this sinecure had fallen to the Turk Bayakbek. He sent out Ahmad, the son of a Turkish slave Tulun from Bukhara, to Egypt as his deputy. Tulun had already been commandant of the Caliph's bodyguard under Mu'tasim; his son Ahmad had enjoyed a painstaking training and after a number of years in service on the Byzantine frontier at Tarsus had become so intimate with the caliph Musta'in in Samarra that the latter, after his abdication in 866, requested him as guard during his journey into exile at Wasit. But the Turk left the Caliph to his executioner and returned to the capital, where the new ruler was in the midst of distributing rewards to those who helped him during the upheaval. Ahmad's stepfather Bayakbek was one of them. In Egypt, Ahmad got so firm a foothold that Bayakbek's successor in possession of the province, the Turk Yarjukh, also left him in his post and attempted to bind him to his own interests by giving him one of his daughters in marriage. In 873 when Ja'far, the son of the caliph Mu'tamid, received Egypt as part of the western half of the empire, he reconciled himself to a fixed payment in money. For the first few years Ahmad retained at his side an independent director of finances, Ahmad ibn-al-Mudabbir, who had controlled this office in the country ever since 856. Since ibn-al-Mudabbir had made himself detested by excessively oppressive taxes and monopolies which encumbered many branches of the economy, and may also have appeared dangerous to the central government because of his wealth and influence, in 872 Ahmad succeeded in effecting his recall; although the office of an 'amil appointed by Baghdad survived for a long time. Ahmad gradually withdrew from his control by a fixed payment of tribute. When the caliph al-Muhtadi delegated the subjugation of the refractory governor of Palestine to him and gave to him the power to organize a slave army, he took advantage of the opportunity to create a continually expanding army of his own. He applied the most rigid discipline in an attempt to hold together the motley hordes, in which Greeks were later to predominate; but they turned dangerous even in his own time and under his successors really became formidable. He now retained the wealth of the country, based on its agriculture and a flourishing textile industry, within its own confines and increased it continually without disrupting economic life. The administration of justice, in accordance with Turkish custom, was in the hands of judges appointed by him, so that it was possible for the office of qadi to remain unoccupied for eight years at a time. The prosperity of the country enabled him to compete with the Caliph in the magnificence of his court. On the example of the new residence created in Samarra, Ahmad founded a new city quarter northeast of the old national capital of Fustat (Old Cairo) in an area given in fief to his officers and functionaries and therefore called al-Qata'i' (the Fiefs). It was dominated by his fortress on the cliff crowned today by the Citadel of Saladin. Here he transplanted the culture and the arts of 'Iraq, in which, as we have seen, Persian and Hellenistic elements were mingled.

When Muwaffaq usurped the guardianship of his brother as vicegerent, he attempted to raise the authority of the central government again in Egypt also; but although Ahmad agreed to some augmentation of his tribute, he simply ignored the command to leave his post and relinquish it to the governor of Syria, Amajur.

Instead, he himself advanced into Amajur's province on Amajur's death in 877 and had allegiance sworn to him there. Since Muwaffaq was still tied down by the Negroes in Babylonia, he was compelled to let Ahmad have his way in tranquillity. Ahmad's freedman Lu'lu', whom he left behind in Syria as governor, and who had a few of his own coins struck there, ceased his obedience in 881, perhaps through fear of losing a part of his territory to his rival, and joined Muwaffaq. Ahmad responded to this by challenging the Caliph to free himself from his brother's guardianship and place himself under his protection. He then left for Syria, where a rebellion had broken out on the Byzantine frontier. The caliph Mu'tamid attempted to escape from Raqqah to join him, but was stopped at the last moment. Ahmad was far from considering an open attack on Muwaffaq for his sake; nevertheless, he broke with the latter by no longer having him designated throughout his domains as the successor to the throne in the Friday services. His opponent's riposte was to have him cursed in the mosques. But Muwaffaq was also inclined to a peaceful compromise and refused to give troops for an attack on Egypt to Ahmad's freedman Lu'lu', to whom he was, after all, indebted for the subjugation of the Negroes. He even entered into negotiations with Ahmad; but before these came to any conclusion, Ahmad died in northern Syria in March 883.

His eldest son, 'Abbas, who had revolted against him once and was just as unpopular with the army as among his father's officials, was forced to swear allegiance to his younger brother Khumarawayh and soon afterward was removed. Muwaffaq thought this untried successor would prove easy game and consequently broke off the peace negotiations. Ahmad's governor in northern Mesopotamia joined forces with the governor of Damascus and refused allegiance to Khumarawayh. Although at first the insurgents were defeated while they were camped on the Orontes for the winter, Muwaffaq sent his son Ahmad, subsequently the caliph Mu'tadid, with an army to the help of the rebels, and the Egyptians suffered a serious defeat. Since no agreement could be reached with respect to the booty, Ahmad was abandoned by his ally and seems to have had only four thousand men still at his disposal in the spring of 885 when Khumarawayh advanced into Palestine with seventy thousand fresh troops. On April 6 a battle took place at at-Tawahin ("the Mills") near Ramlah. In spite of his superiority Khumarawayh soon conceded this battle as lost and set out on the road back to Egypt. But his opponent failed to exploit his victory and on encountering further resistance returned to Damascus, and when he found no reception there, moved on farther to Tarsus. Since he met with resistance here also, he left the field to Khumarawayh entirely. Consequently the latter could deal with his remaining adversaries with ease. In 886 a peace treaty was concluded which assured the Tulunids the governorship of Egypt and Syria together with the marches for thirty years, in return for a meager tribute. During the next four years dissension among his former opponents gave Khumarawayh an opportunity to extend his power into northern Mesopotamia as well. Muwaffaq and the caliph Mu'tamid died in 891 and 892, and the former's son Ahmad ascended the throne as al-Mu'tadid-billah. Khumarawayh concluded a new treaty with him and sealed it by his daughter's marriage with the Caliph, though this did not take place until two years later, in 896, when the princess had passed her twelfth year. The magnificence the Egyptian governor displayed in preparing her wedding trousseau embarrassed the Baghdad court, long since grown accustomed to far more impoverished circumstances, and gave rise to the rumor that the Caliph had only solicited the connection with him as a means of ruining his finances. Indeed, his prodigality had so exhausted his dominions that the power of his house soon disintegrated after he was murdered in Damascus in the beginning of 896, apparently in connection with some harem scandal. His first successor, Abu-l-Jaysh, was dethroned by his brother Harun only nine months later. The latter was unable to afford adequate resistance to the Qarmatians, who were ravaging Syria. The Damascenes themselves petitioned the caliph al-Muktafi (successor of Mu'tadid) to send his troops. After the latter had restored order there, it seemed time to remove the incompetent last of the Tulunids. While a fleet sailed out to the delta from Cilicia the 'Iraqi troops advanced through Palestine. After Damietta had fallen, Harun was assassinated by his kinsmen in his residence at 'Abbasah on December 30, 904. Fustat fell on January 12, 905; Ahmad's creation, al-Qata'i', was razed, and the last scions of his house were deported to Baghdad.

The rule of the Tulunids, measured by the achievements of their successors, seemed a golden age to later generations. Materially the populace had flourished extraordinarily under Ahmad's astute fiscal policy, which did away with many abuses and above all put a stop to the sucking dry of the country for the benefit of alien exploiters. Although as a result of the destruction of al-Qata'i' nothing has come down to us of Khumarawayh's magnificent constructions, the Mosque of Ibn-Tulun, erected by Ahmad in 876-879, has been preserved, at any rate as a ruin, and still conveys a lively sense of the artistic endeavors of the period. It was modeled on the great mosque at Samarra, but is only half the size. The principal nave was divided by five rows of piers, one of which is now in ruins, the adjoining naves by two window openings with pointed arches and small corner columns wedged in the wallwork between the piers and the outer walls. These consist of tile and are overlaid with stucco, the white surfaces of which are framed by graven ornamental borders. In addition to the window openings they display small circular niches and are crowned by a wealth of small crenellated wreaths. From the wall there emerges the mihrab, whose semicircle is set off from the wall only by two steps. On three sides outer courts adjoin the enclosing walls, and square the total circumference by closing it off against the profane world. The minaret, unique in Islamic architecture, and following a Samarra pattern, rises outside the mosque at its northern end. Its limestone structure does not show the spiral form native to Babylonia but is constructed in the shape of a square like the old Persian fire towers.*

While Egypt could be reconquered by the Baghdad government after almost forty years of independence, South Arabia was definitely lost to it around the same time. In this remotest province of the empire, Islam had been unable to transform social and political conditions in a thoroughgoing way. As in the time of the Sabaeans and the Himyarites, the aristocratic rulers remained in their fortresses and ruled uncontested in their sphere by the caliph's governors in San'a, if only they delivered their tribute with a fair degree of regularity. One of them, al-Hasan al-Hamdani, who died in a San'a prison in 945, after repeated conflicts with the political powers dominating his class, has given us, in his two books, *The Crown* and the *Island of the Arabs*, a portrait of his homeland swelled up with pride in its ancestral culture, the like of which cannot be displayed by any other province of Islam. For a time it appeared advisable to the 'Abbasid government to favor the rise of local centers of

* See E. Diez, *Die Kunst der islamischen Völker*, 44 ff.; Zaky Mohamed Hassan, *Les Tulunides, Etude de l'Egypte Musulmane à la fin du IX siècle, 868-905*, Paris, 1933.

power in addition to their own governors. Even Ma'mun, after the collapse of his 'Alid policy, sent out Khorasanian troops to South Arabia under the command of Muhammad, a proven soldier claiming descent from Mu'awiyah's putative half brother and governor in 'Iraq, Ziyad ibn-Abihi, who was able to bring the coastal strips as far as Shihr in Hadramaut and the beginning of the hill country under his power, while the real mountain country still remained subject to the governors in San'a. From his residence in Zabid he and his descendants were able to maintain their power in the country for a hundred and fifty years, though with numerous setbacks. The power of his second successor, however, was considerably curbed by Ya'fur ibn-'Abd-ar-Rahman, a native nobleman who revolted against Mu'tasim's governor. Ya'fur from his ancestral seat at Shibam extended his power southward, and his son secured recognition as governor of San'a. The 'Alids now took a hand in these involved circumstances. Ambassadors of the Qarmatians, of whom more presently, appeared in the outlying mountain country but were unable to maintain their position for any length of time, even though they continued their religious-political propaganda. A descendant of Zayd ibn-'Ali, on the other hand, succeeded in creating a position for his house here which survived the buffetings of many centuries and even at present still constitutes a potent element in Arabian history. After Zayd's adventurous attempt in 'Iraq to break the rule of the Umayyad caliph Hisham had miscarried, his descendants withdrew to the peripheral provinces. One of his great-grandsons, Hasan ibn-Zayd, who possessed the political acumen and energy generally denied his forefathers, had placed himself, in his residence at Rayy, at the disposition of the Tabaristan and Mazanderan notables on the southern bank of the Caspian Sea when they were seeking a leader against the oppression of the Tahirid governors. In protracted warfare he and his descendants survived here for more than half a century (864-928). Another of Zayd's descendants, Yahya ibn-al-Husayn, a grandson of al-Qasim ibn-Ibrahim, called Rassi after his family estates on Jabal ar-Rass, had given rise to the hope that because of his erudition and piety he might, as imam, restore the luster of their house. After a visit to his cousins in Tabaristan had convinced him of the impossibility of gaining a foothold there, he directed his gaze toward South Arabia, whose chaotic conditions were familiar enough in Medina. On March 16, 897, he appeared with only fifty men before the gates of Sa'dah, the principal resort on the pilgrims' highway between Mecca and San'a and only five days' journey from the latter. From here he sent out, as the imam al-Hadi ("the Righteous Guide"), a summons to obedience to the house of the Prophet. Just as the Prophet had been enabled by the tribal feuds he had been called upon to smooth over to assert himself as lord of Medina, so al-Hadi won a steadily growing following as arbiter between Muslims and Christians in the old bishopric of Najran, and later among the Bedouins of the region. But his power remained limited to Sa'dah and the neighborhood, since the Qarmatians and Ya'furites in the south of the country contested his rule there. When he died on August 18, 911, he nevertheless bequeathed his sons a secure foundation from which for a time his descendants could extend their power over the whole country.*

Under the caliph Mu'tadid, who succeeded his father Muwaffaq as vice-regent in 891 and his uncle on the throne in the following year, the lands around the core of the empire were shaken once again by a religious-political movement. In Shi'ite circles the doctrine was widespread that all injustice in the world would come to an end when the last imam, still living in concealment, appeared on earth as the Mahdi, "the Righteously Guided." After the collapse of so many attempts on the part of the 'Alids, their followers' hopes fell back on an expectation of the end of the world. While one group, who did not acquire political power till later, was awaiting a twelfth descendant of 'Ali as this Mahdi, the hopes of the others were bound up with the seventh, Isma'il, who had died in 762 even before his father, Ja'far as-Sadiq. Not only this accident, but no doubt still more the sanctity of the number seven, acknowledged in the Orient from of old, gave these "Seveners" the basis of their doctrine. This was combined with the Iranian ideology of divine grace, gnostic speculations of hermetic origin, as well as elements of Greek philosophy and the Manichean religion of the elite, into an esoteric doctrine which fitted in with the inclination to the formation of secret societies extant in the Orient as a heritage of the Near Eastern race, and at various periods was exploited by ambitious agitators for political purposes. It found literary expression a century later in the writings of the True Friends (called "the Brethren of Purity" by earlier translators), a kind of philosophical encyclopedia.

* C. van Arendonk, *De opkomst van het zaidietische imamaat in Yemen*, Leiden, 1919.

It first emerged as a sect in 'Iraq in 890 in the region around Wasit, where the slaves' rebellion had been suppressed only a short while before. There a man by the name of Hamdan Qarmat (probably an Aramaic word meaning "the Secret Teacher") established a meeting place for his followers which, on the example of the Prophet, he called Dar al-Hijrah. The whole sect were called Qarmatians after his surname, Qarmat. Complete community of property prevailed in this first cell of the new movement; the initiates held love feasts with paradisiacal bread, probably on the example of the Mandean gnostic sect indigenous in these regions from of old. 'Abdan, Hamdan's brother-in-law, is even said to have written a book concerning the initiation into the seven degrees of the sect. These degrees, the number of which was later raised to nine, led the man to be won, by way of a precise study of his religious faith, first to the conviction that the entire beauty of the faith had not yet become clear to him, and then to doubt as to its foundations; he became bound to the authority of the hidden imam and his representatives, whose persons were never revealed to him, and was shown that all previous revelations and religious laws merely represented a veil for an inner meaning which was not to be attained except by an allegorical explanation; the novice thus prepared was finally bound over to unconditional obedience to the society and its superiors, and freed from all dogmatic constraint and simultaneously from all fetters of law. One of the two superiors, who were supposed to have resided outside of 'Iraq, acting as "Lords of Purity," replaced 'Abdan with the more active Dhikrawayh ad-Dindani and sent him to Syria. Here he succeeded in 900 in inciting the Bedouins of the banu Ulays to rebellion against the already very considerably enfeebled Tulunid regime. The Lord of Purity was proclaimed caliph as Abu 'Abdallah Muhammad and ostensibly a descendent of 'Ali. The Qarmatians raged through all the cities of Syria with the utmost savagery; only Damascus was able to withstand their siege. Their caliph died in 901; his place was taken by his brother Abu 'Abdallah Ahmad, who, however, was captured two years later and executed in Baghdad. After Dhikrawayh was killed also in 906, the Baghdad government, which after the fall of the last Tulunids had resumed a firm hold on Syria, succeeded in suppressing the movement there and in 'Iraq.

But the Qarmatians had an enduring success in Arabia. By 894 the Lord of Purity had sent out Abu Sa'id Hasan ibn-Bahram al-

Jannabi to al-Ahsa, in the Bahrayn region of the Persian Gulf. With the help of the Bedouin tribe 'Abd-al-Qays, Abu Sa'id succeeded in founding an independent state here with a capital at al-Mu'miniyah, instead of the old capital of Hajar, the present-day Hufuf. He and his successors governed there as delegates of the hidden imam and with astute regard for ancient Bedouin tradition permitted the tribal elders to participate in decisions of policy. The son and successor of Abu Sa'id made repeated depredations in 'Iraq and crippled the pilgrim traffic (914-943); on January 12, 930, he even seized Mecca itself and carried off the Black Stone from the Ka'bah to his capital in al-Ahsa, where it remained for thirty years. The less successful attempts of the Qarmatians to get a foothold in South Arabia also have already been discussed.*

These struggles against the Qarmatians had entirely filled the reign of Caliph Muktafi (902-908), the son of Mu'tadid. His wazir, 'Abbas ibn-al-Hasan al-Jarjara'i, who during his reign had already concentrated in his hands all the power in the interior, without ever being able to make skillful use of it, attempted to perpetuate his position by raising Ja'far, the Caliph's brother, only just thirteen years old, to the throne as al-Muqtadir-billah. But his opponents assassinated him and proclaimed as caliph 'Abdallah, the son of the caliph Mu'tazz. The latter, however, was soon overtaken by the fate that had smitten the brother of one of his forebears, Ibrahim, ninety years before. Like the latter he had devoted his life, from youth on, to learning and poetry. His poetry had an aristocratic elegance in the style of the moderns, particularly of Abu Nuwas, without, however, remaining entirely free of imitations of the classical Bedouin poets either. The luxury still prevalent at the time in the court circles of Baghdad, despite the decay of power, not infrequently emerged in his poems as preciosity. But he was also the first to attempt to sing the deeds of his cousin the caliph al-Mu'tadid, in a heroic poem which, to be sure, frequently lapses into the arid accents of a rhymed chronicle. He was also the first to attempt comprising in a system the observations on poetic technique made by philologists influenced by Greek philosophy in innumerable poetic commentaries. Besides this he was a zealous student of literary history, and wrote the first history of modern poetry. The extent to which he was devoted to the joys of life is indicated by his work

* M. J. de Goeje, *Mémoire sur les Carmathes de Bahrain*, 2nd edition, Leiden, 1880. [B. Lewis, *The Origins of Isma'ilism*, Cambridge, 1940.]

on carousing and customs of tippling. This unfortunate prince was overthrown by Muqtadir's following on the same day he was to ascend the throne. Under the leadership of the eunuch Mu'nis, who had previously been police chief under Mu'tadid but then had been banished to Mecca and had only just returned to Baghdad, they had held the Hasan palace against attacks by the supporters of the rival caliph and then after a sortie had emerged victorious in the street fighting. Ibn-al-Mu'tazz had to seek refuge in the house of a friendly jeweler, and there was assassinated on December 29, 908, twelve days after he became caliph. Mu'nis attempted to exploit his influence over the youthful ruler to assure himself of his reward for the services he had performed for him, but the wazir ibn-al-Furat often proved an obstacle. The Caliph made two attempts to rid himself of this man, whose avarice and incompetence made his regime extremely vulnerable, but kept falling under his influence again and again until, after his third period in office, he had him executed together with his son al-Muhassin on July 18, 924.

Our information concerning the state finances under Muqtadir is based on a budget from 918/19 which has come down to us. Although most of the provinces were almost entirely independent of Baghdad, nevertheless they continued sending in huge sums as tribute. During the first few years of 'Abbasid rule the eastern provinces made payments in silver, whereas a gold currency prevailed in the countries taken from the Roman Empire, where gold mines had been worked since ancient times. The gold flowing into Baghdad then found its way to the east as well, and throughout the empire silver lost more than half its original current value. But the humbler silver currency won more and more ground as the power of the central government dwindled away. Under Muqtadir's reign the caliph was still acknowledged as actually sovereign only in 'Iraq, Khuzistan, Persia, Mesopotamia, Syria and Egypt, and as direct overlord in 'Uman, Adharbayjan, and Armenia. While in land taxes, shipping imposts, water excises, tolls, and market duties 'Iraq contributed 1,547,734 dinars (the dinar at that time contained over sixteen silver dirhams), the eastern provinces 6,213,283 dinars, and Egypt and Syria 4,746,492 dinars, the Caliph had to be satisfied with the payment of a lump sum of 226,370 dinars from Adharbayjan and Armenia. This was augmented by another 1,768,015 dinars from the revenues of the landholdings and pious foundations. The expenditures which had to be covered by these revenues served to maintain the two holy cities of Mecca and Medina, the pilgrim highway, the fortifications of the border areas, the salaries of the judges, the chiefs of the market police, and the courts of appeal as well as of the postmasters in all the provinces. But the largest sums were consumed by the Caliph's court expenses and the payment of his troops; yet the caliphs and their kinfolk were also often able to accumulate quite enormous sums. When Muqtadir started his reign, fifteen million dinars were found in the estate of his predecessor, to which Mu'tadid had contributed nine million. Nevertheless the budget quite often closed with a deficit, and since it was impossible at this time to cover it through loans, as in a modern state, the requisite sums were levied again in the form of monetary fines on wealthy private individuals, most usually officials who had been sucking their fill in well-lined sinecures. This procedure was so frequent that there was a special constitutional expression for it. In 914 Muqtadir confiscated the fortune of a jeweler, valued at four million dinars; monetary fines of fifty thousand to a hundred thousand dinars were not at all rare. Because of this insecurity of fortunes in cash, landholdings were naturally a form of capital investment very much sought after, especially since the burden on property in land was comparatively light. The land areas in the possession of local rulers were generally either altogether tax free or at most paid only a certain lump sum. A very popular method of withdrawing possessions from taxation and simultaneously protecting them against confiscation consisted in declaring them a foundation for pious purposes, e.g. for the poor, for the defense of the frontiers, for the two holy cities, etc.; the administration of these foundations was reserved to one's self and each oldest son in turn. In Egypt genuine family trusts developed out of these foundations. In this way Muqtadir's mother herself had attempted to secure her landholdings; without, however, any lasting success, since after the death of her son, when his half brother Qahir began his reign and she stubbornly refused to allow the reversion of her colossal foundations, he simply had them declared void by a judicial dispensation. But the state treasury suffered the greatest injury when the caliphs, for lack of cash, began to pay off their troops with property deeds in land, as first began to occur at the beginning of Qahir's reign. In the provinces, as we have seen, the military power and the finances were strictly separated. The 'amil associated with the emir guaranteed the central government a specific sum as the tax contribution of a province, and naturally successfully endeavored to arrange for not only this sum but also for a substantial personal profit, and his subordinates followed his example. If the emir succeeded, like Ahmad ibn-Tulun in Egypt, in seizing control of the financial administration as well, then his power was complete. Lack of money gradually forced the caliphs to install the Turkish generals as tax lessees in broad territories throughout 'Iraq also, in order to collect the pay for their troops; in this way their revenue was lost to the state treasury. When things went as far as providing for subcommanders and rank-and-filers in the same way, the damage grew beyond bounds. In their own interest the great lords at any rate maintained the irrigation establishments indispensable for the fertility of the soils, which required a continual expenditure of money; but the lower officers, as soon as they had bled their peasants sufficiently dry, would return the land to the government and demand richer allotments.* Life was very insecure, however, not only in the countryside, but in the cities of 'Iraq as well. For years the slave war and the incursions of the Qarmatians had crippled commerce and trade and traffic. The luxury of the upper classes was counterbalanced by the equally great impoverishment of the lower strata, in spite of the frugality of the Oriental and the still rather high purchasing power of the currency.

The factional strife among the rulers was added to by the tensions among the religious sects, which were continually inflamed anew by the preachers. This was not merely a question of the opposition between Shi'ites and Sunnites. Among the latter the fanatical Hanbalites in particular were continually stirring up dissension. Profounder spirits sought to escape from the cantankerous bickerings about religious-political and dogmatic questions into the tranquillity of contemplation. This tendency, however, had already emerged under the Umayyads in 'Iraq; Hasan al-Basri (*d.* 728) in Basra, the Shi'ite alchemist Jabir ibn-Hayyan, and the poet Abu-l-'Atahiyah in Kufah had worked along these lines. After Baghdad became the capital of the empire, the devotees of the contemplative life formed into groups there which instituted public lectures in the mosques and in their own quarters attempted to arouse and heighten the mystic mood by music. They had borrowed from the Christian monks the white

* A. von Kremer, *Uber das Einnahmebudget des Abbasiden-Reiches vom Jahre 306 H* (918-919), *Abhandlungen der Wiener Akademie*, 1887; C. H. Becker, *Steuerpacht und Lehnswesen, Islam* V, 81-92.

woolen garment (*suf*) on the basis of which they soon became generally known as Sufis. Christian influence was also unmistakable in the form of the contemplative exercises, but the origins of the movement were purely Arab and Islamic. Their basic motivations appear to us with the most clarity, next to the sermons of Hasan of Basra, in the confessions of al-Muhasibi, who was born in Basra in 781, settled in Baghdad at an early age, and died there in 837. Finding contemporary Islam split up into numerous sects and parties, he at first sought in vain for a religious leader. Like the solitary founder of Islam, he, too, recognized that the individual could find his soul's salvation only outside the community—only a profound study of the Qur'an would show him the right path, which by the most conscientious observance of its precepts and a rigid imitation of the Prophet would lead to God. The consciousness of having achieved divine grace by the strict observance of his commands fills the soul with thankfulness to God and an inner love for him. The mystic finds this path to God in a series of levels which lead him by way of remorse and patience to intimacy with God and finally to the contemplation of the pure truth (*haqq*). These attempts at attaining access to God for the soul in a way not prescribed by the orthodoxy could not escape its disapproval. Although al-Muhasibi's doctrine was not yet condemned in public, Ahmad ibn-Hanbal nevertheless declared that its connection with the intellectual methods of Mu'tazilite dogmatism was excessively intimate. The doctrines were further developed by Junayd, who had first been inducted by his uncle Sari as-Saqati into the teachings of the ascetic Ma'ruf al-Karkhi, in whose simplicity, however, he found no lasting satisfaction. He also rejected, to be sure, his new master's inclination to clothe his teachings in the language of the dogmatists. The focal point of his intellectual universe was the love of God; this was supposed to contain the human being so completely that in it he surrendered his entire ego to be dissolved in God. This kernel of all later mysticism was subsequently developed by Junayd's pupil al-Husayn ibn-Mansur al-Hallaj ("the Wool Carder") through rigid application. He was born in Persia in 858, the son of a Zoroastrian. At Tustar (Shustar) in Khuzistan he entered into the milieu of Sahl at-Tustari, an independent thinker who gave al-Muhasibi's doctrine of the necessary return to God the form of unflagging mortification since become classical, and borrowing from gnostic Shi'ite doctrines, spoke of the tower of light which encompasses in a mystical pre-existence the souls of all the believers and gives them the right to feel at one with God. Also enthralled by the luster of the capital, al-Hallaj joined Junayd in Baghdad. After spending about six years in his society he was induced to break with him by the consciousness Sahl aroused within him of having already ascended to the level of a union with God, which had remained an unattainable ideal for his master Junayd. He became a wandering preacher and set out on travels which led him as far as India, and on which he came into contact with the most famous physician of his time, ar-Razi (Rhases), to be initiated by him in Greek philosophy; he is also supposed to have encountered the leaders of the Qarmatians. After making the pilgrimage to Mecca once again, he returned to the capital in 908. His ecstatic doctrines, which culminated in a union with the divine will by yielding to suffering and the divine afflatus in the ascetic, so that the latter as divine witness has the right to equate himself with the divine truth, and in consequence dissolved the inviolability of the precepts of religious law, soon attracted a wide circle of pupils. His activities seemed to imperil the social order, tottering in any case, still further, so that the theologians found it easy to make his doctrine suspect to the rulers. For eight years he languished in prison. The caliph Muqtadir's mother and his chamberlain Nasr attempted to save him, but it was precisely their favor that drew on him the hostility of the wazir Hamid. After a trial lasting seven months he was sentenced to death by unanimous verdict of the supreme qadis of all schools and hanged on March 26, 922, on the square before the new Baghdad jail on the right bank of the Tigris, and his corpse decapitated and burned. It was his martyrdom that first made his doctrine really effective in the future; his pupils, who fled to Khorasan, there prepared the ground for one of the loveliest flowers of Islamic culture, the mystical poetry of the Persians and Turks.

The caliph Muqtadir had been unable to consolidate his power, persistently menaced by the Qarmatians, even after ridding himself of his wazir al-Furat. In vain he appealed to a provincial governor, Yusuf ibn-abi-s-Saj of Adharbayjan, for aid. In February 929 the unrestraint of his own troops forced the Caliph to abdicate in favor of his brother Muhammad al-Qahir. When the latter, or rather the police prefect who had elevated him to the throne, found himself unable to satisfy the army's demands for pay, Muqtadir, who had taken refuge with his old patron Mu'nis, was called back. But he believed himself unable to depend on the latter unreservedly and looked to the new police prefect, Muhammad ibn-Yaqut, for support against him. Although the latter had been able to subdue the disorderly Baghdad garrison, in July 931 on Mu'nis's insistence the Caliph had to banish him to Sijistan, but by February 932 had already recalled him and sent him out with an army against Mu'nis, who was advancing from Mosul. But when Muhammad, without daring to do battle, withdrew to the capital again, the Caliph himself at the head of his troops advanced against his rebellious generalissimo. He knew very well he was going to his death; consequently he had donned, over the silver kaftan, the black band of the 'Abbasids, and over that the mantle of the Prophet, and girded around himself the latter's sword with the red sword belt. In this way, after a short struggle, he fell on October 31, 932. Although Mu'nis wished to raise the Caliph's son Ahmad, who had taken the field at his father's side, to the throne, the latter's uncle Muhammad al-Qahir succeeded in again taking over the rulership he had already exercised once before for a short time. Cruelty and avarice were his most conspicuous traits of character. The wazir ibn-Muqlah, the police prefect Muhammad ibn-Yaqut, and the emir Mu'nis contended for influence over the Caliph. When he attempted to get rid of his wazir, the latter conceived a plan to overthrow him and replace him by Muktafi's son. When the conspiracy came to light prematurely, Mu'nis was deposed and executed, although ibn-Muqlah was able to save himself. Dressed as a beggar, the Wazir traveled around the country stirring up hatred against the Caliph. In April 934 the latter was attacked in his palace, blinded, and imprisoned, since he refused to abdicate. The throne was taken by Muqtadir's son Ahmad ar-Radi; but he had to relinquish the power to Muhammad ibn-Yaqut, and then, after the latter's fall in April 935, to ibn-Muqlah. But in April 936, when the Wazir was taken captive by Muhammad's brother Muzaffar, the Caliph sought a new prop. He appointed the governor of Wasit and Basra, Muhammad ibn-Ra'iq, to be *amir al-umara* (emir-in-chief) and not only gave him supreme command of the armies but also made him head of the entire government, even granting him the princely honor of having his name designated in the Friday services. By this he limited himself at first to the dignity of a religious supreme leader of the believers, which was all that remained to all his successors. But ibn-Ra'iq's government was also unable to restore any authority to the central government in the east of the empire, and he was able to keep the Qarmatians at a distance from Baghdad only by the payment of a tribute. Only two years later he was forced out of his office by the Turk Bajkam, who for a time curbed the Hamdanids and Buyids.

In the tenth century the war against the Byzantines was left to a genuine Arab dynasty. In 890 its founder, Hamdan, the emir of the Taghlib tribe, had seized the fortress of Mardin in upper Mesopotamia in alliance with the Kharijites. Although he was then taken captive by the Caliph, he was pardoned after his son Husayn defeated the Kharijites. In 905 Husayn's brother Abu-l-Hayja was appointed governor of Mosul under Muqtadir, and ruled there until his death in 929, supported from 920 on by his son Hasan. The latter extended his power over the whole of Mesopotamia and northern Syria. In 941, when the caliph Muttaqi had to flee to Mosul with his amir al-umara ibn-Ra'iq, who had meanwhile come to power again, from the al-Baridi brothers who were making repeated attacks on 'Iraq from their province Khuzistan, Hasan had ibn-Ra'iq murdered and forced the Caliph to transfer ibn-Ra'iq's office to him together with the honorary title of Nasir-ad-Dawlah. Together with his brother 'Alim, who received the title Sayf-ad-Dawlah at the same time, he was able to conduct the Caliph back to his capital. In 945, however, when the Buyid Mu'izz ad-Dawlah occupied Baghdad, he at once started a war against the Hamdanids which ended with their overthrow. As a Buyid vassal subject to tribute, Nasir survived in spite of various attempts to evade his obligations, until he was declared incompetent and imprisoned by his own family a year before his death in 968. His reign was the worst example of Oriental despotism; not content with the monstrous taxes which ground down his subjects, he was also preoccupied with bringing the bulk of the landed property in the country into his own possession. His son was still able to survive for a short time in Mosul, but after his death in 979 his brothers and their descendants lost their independence as vassals of the Buyids and the Fatimids.

Greater fame was won by Nasir's brother Sayf-ad-Dawlah. After perceiving the impossibility of maintaining his position in 'Iraq as the Caliph's major-domo against the Turks and the Buyids, he turned toward Syria and in 945 wrested Aleppo from the *ikhshid* of Egypt. After a futile attempt to extend his power to Damascus as well, he found his life's work in the struggle against Byzantium. Although he professed himself a vassal of the Fatimids when they came to power in Egypt, and consequently a Shi'ite, in his own territory he was sovereign. As in earlier centuries, the wars against Byzantium consisted of summertime raids and skirmishes around fortresses, in which the advantage swung back and forth between the Arabs and the Byzantines. Sayf-ad-Dawlah's very first campaign in 949 ended with a setback; the following year he won great booty, but on the retreat lost it again by falling into an ambush in a narrow pass of the Taurus, and with difficulty escaped to safety with a small band only. On both sides of the frontier there grew up a class of professional soldiers, who were enfeoffed by their chiefs with land booty, and who, during longer interludes of quiet, also exchanged cultural values. In 953 the Byzantine major-domo Barzos seems to have feared greater dangers for the empire; he threw a great army, in which Russians, Bulgars, and Khazars also served, against the border, but suffered a severe defeat at the hands of Sayf-ad-Dawlah near Mar'ash. Five years later John Tzimisces avenged this by defeating the Arabs in their own land, not far from Aleppo. Another severe defeat was inflicted on Sayf-ad-Dawlah in 962 by the major-domo Nicephorus. Aleppo itself, including the citadel, fell into the hands of the Greeks, who were devastating and pillaging the land round about. Two years later Sayf-ad-Dawlah could still successfully fend off an attack by the Greeks, although already crippled on one side by a stroke; he died in Aleppo in 967. His son Sa'd-ad-Dawlah and his grandson Sa'id-ad-Dawlah held Aleppo until 1002, by winning over their former Byzantine enemies in an alliance against the common menace of the Fatimid power in Egypt.

Sayf-ad-Dawlah owes his fame, next to his success in war, primarily to his sympathy for the arts and sciences. His cousin Abu Firas, who fought bravely against the Byzantines as his governor in Manbij and once spent two years in Constantinople as a prisoner of war, was a skillful poet who could also strike a more profound note, particularly in his elegies of captivity; one of his poems, in praise of the 'Alids, achieved great prestige among the Shi'ites and is still studied and expounded among them down to the present day. In 948 there came to Sayf-ad-Dawlah's court the poet al-Mutanabbi, the bearer of one of the last great names Arabic literature has to display; he owed his surname, under which he has become famous—al-Mutanabbi, "the Would-Be Prophet"—to a youthful escapade when as a Qarmatian agitator he attempted to effect a Bedouin uprising in the Syrian desert between Kufah and Palmyra. Even later his speech was still impregnated with Qarmatian images, preoccupied as he was with cultivating the Bedouin vocabulary he had acquired in the wilderness. For nine years he glorified the deeds of the Hamdanid prince in Aleppo, then left him as the result of a falling out, first seeking his fortune at the court of the Turkish ruler of Egypt, the ikhshid Kafur, later in Baghdad, and finally with the Buyid 'Adud-ad-Dawlah in Persia; on his way back from there in 965 he met his end in a robbers' attack near Baghdad. Mutanabbi still treated the ancient qasidah form very skillfully; while clinging to the classic models with excessive rigidity, he nevertheless vied with them in the wealth of his vocabulary and not infrequently surpassed them in the boldness of his figurative speech. Although his poetry was often sharply attacked by his contemporaries—to be sure, principally by the zealots of the purity of the ancient tongue—nevertheless his poems, begotten by an authentic Arab spirit, enjoyed the undivided approval of posterity, and even today they are, second only to the *Maqamat* of Hariri, still in the hands of all the educated, even in 'Uman, the remotest province of Arabia. In Damascus in 1936 the entire Arab world participated in a celebration of his millennial anniversary. But science was also cultivated with understanding at Sayf-ad-Dawlah's court. A place for contemplative endeavors was found there by the great Aristotelian al-Farabi, a Turk by birth, who had completed his studies in Baghdad. Although his writings were later shouldered out of literary circulation by those of Ibn Sina (Avicenna), and his intellectualist system was incapable of winning lasting influence in the Muslim world, nevertheless, as one of the most independent disciples of the Greek thinkers, he represents a very remarkable phenomenon in the history of Islamic civilization.

In the east of the empire around this time a new dynasty, destined for major political influence, had arisen among the numerous rulers usually limited to petty districts. In Tabaristan, on the southern bank of the Caspian Sea, a Daylamite by the name of Mardawij had overthrown the 'Alid Zaydites ruling there and made himself independent. His countryman Buyah (Buwayh) was in his service. Buyah's son 'Ali was governor of Karaj, southeast of Hamadan. There he revolted in 932 against his suzerain and occupied Isfahan after driving out Caliph Qahir's garrison. Although Mardawij was still able to punish this encroachment by driving the rebel out and returning the city to the Caliph, 'Ali, in alliance with his brothers, succeeded in extending his power in Iran still further and in 934 conquered Shiraz. Here he set up residence. In 933, when Mardawij was assassinated by his Turkish troops, 'Ali's brother ruled in Media, while the third brother, Ahmad, had conquered Kirman.

Meanwhile conditions in Baghdad had become ripe for his intervention. Ar-Radi's successor as caliph, Muttaqi (940-944), had been merely a plaything in the hands of the generals contending for power and of the governors, al-Baridi of Khuzistan, ibn-Ra'iq, and the Hamdanids, until the Turk Tusun seized him and had him blinded while he entered into negotiations with the ikhshid of Egypt. His son Mustakfi was equally powerless, and when the emirs controlling him could neither satisfy the troops' demands for pay nor ward off the famine threatening Baghdad, he welcomed as a savior the Buyid Ahmad who was advancing westward from Kirman. After a battle with al-Baridi and the emir Tusun, Ahmad seized Wasit and in December 945 made his entry into Baghdad. The Caliph designated him as amir al-umara with the honorary title of Mu'izz-ad-Dawlah; soon afterward, however, Mustakfi succumbed to the fate of his ancestors: he is said to have entered into dealings with the enemies of the Buyid. His successors al-Muti' (946-974), at-Ta'i' (974-991), and al-Qadir (991-1003) were still merely pensioners of the Buyids; they had to be content with the honorary rights of the coinage, still minted in their name, and the Friday sermon, which made mention of them as rulers. Their major-domos themselves, who resided partly in Baghdad and partly in Shiraz, could only maintain their power in interminable skirmishings with the mountain peoples of Iran who were showing increasing inclination to revolt, such as the Daylamites, and with the Arab tribes of Mesopotamia, among whom a few ephemeral dynasties after the Hamdanids continued to come to the surface. The descendants of the three brothers who had founded the dynasty's power fell out on numerous occasions over the inheritance. Beginning in 976, Hasan's son 'Adud-ad-Dawlah wrested the territories of all his cousins and brothers away from them and united Iran and 'Iraq under his rule once again. But by 983 this power had already dissolved again as the result of the contentions of his sons. In 1029 the ruler of the eastern provinces was removed by the Turk Mahmud ibn-Subuktigin; in 1055 the ruler of 'Iraq by the Seljuq Tughril Beg; both ended their lives in the dungeon.

The west had long since slipped out of the caliph's control. From 800 on, Africa, under the rule of the Aghlabids, was absolutely independent, even though the latter did not fail to send their sovereigns a respectful reminder of the expansion of their power by gifts from out of the booty. In the west their power extended as far as Bona, in the southwest as far as Zab, which was bounded by the domains of the Rustamids of Tahert, founded by the Kharijite subsect of Abadites; in the east they ruled Tripoli, which, however, was continually threatened by the Berbers of Jabal Nafusah, Kharijites also. Qayrawan, the center of their power, was entirely populated by the immigrant Arabs against whose pretensions the Berbers sought a prop in the doctrines of the Kharijites.

The wealth and power accorded the Aghlabids * by the favorable location of their territory, with its rich hinterland and harbors controlling Mediterranean commerce, is still testified to today by the mosque in their capital, Qayrawan, which, though it may fall short of the gigantic structures of Samarra and Cairo, nevertheless is one of the most magnificent of the religious edifices of Islam. Although named Sidi 'Uqbah after the earliest conqueror, the sole remainder of what he built is the mihrab built in behind the present-day prayer niche, which, like the entire building, stems from the time of Ziyadatallah I. The main portico is divided into seventeen aisles, the broader central one opening into a nave enclosed by double columns near the qiblah wall, together with which it constitutes a T-shaped transept. The Aghlabid Ahmad (956-963) had this wall adorned with fayence tiles, and crowned the mihrab with a dome; under him the famous pulpit of Baghdad plane-tree wood was also erected. Magnificent wooden doors close off the main portico from the court, which with its porticoes supported by piers all of which rest on double columns is particularly lovely. In 876, when the influence of the Malikite legists, distinguished for their fanaticism, became too great in Qayrawan, the seventh ruler of the house, Ibrahim II, founded a new residence for himself after the example of the 'Abbasids, nine kilometers inland in ar-Raqqadah.

The third Aghlabid, Ziyadatallah (817-838), began the conquest of Sicily. After alternating fortunes the Arabs succeeded in getting a firm foothold on the island by taking Palermo in September 831, and by 840 they had conquered about a third of Sicily. Not only

* M. Vonderheyden, *La Bérbérie orientale sous la dynastie des Benou Arlab*, Paris, 1927.

Aghlabid troops, however, participated in these successes, but also adventurers from Spain, who landed on the island in 830 and afterward were strengthened by reinforcements from their homeland. In 875 Syracuse also fell to the Aghlabids. But the disunity among the various branches of the Arabs was just as great here as in Spain, so that Ibrahim II had to come to Sicily in person to restore the prestige of his regime. His death immediately imperiled this brief success, and in 956 the disunity of the Arabs even forced them into a treaty with the Byzantine emperor Constantine VII (Porphyrogenitus). However, Tauromenium, which they had given up in this treaty, fell into their hands again in 965. The seventy-three years of peace the Arabs were destined to have in Sicily from then on were enough to spread their civilization over the island to such an extent that the Normans, who under Count Roger de Hauteville put an end to their rule in 1060, took over not merely the Arab system of administration, but also the basic elements of Islamic culture in intellectual life and in art. In 1154 the Arab Idrisi wrote his famous description of the earth at the court of Roger II. Their successor in control of Sicily, Frederick II of Hohenstaufen (1197-1250), cultivated this heritage in admiration of the science of the Arabs and their Greek teachers.

This rich colony, as a consequence of its shifting fortunes, had scarcely been able to consolidate the rule of the Aghlabids in Africa when they were threatened by religious-political disorders in the interior. In addition to the Kharijites who kept rekindling Berber opposition to the Arabs, from 780 on the Shi'ah itself entered the competition for the power. Idris ibn-'Abdallah, a grandson of Hasan, had escaped to northern Morocco by way of Egypt after an unsuccessful uprising in Medina, and among the Berber tribes living there had obtained recognition as imam, in the struggle against the Aghlabids extending his rule as far as Tlemsen; in 808 his son Idris II, who while still in his mother's womb had had to assume the inheritance of his father, done away with by poison, founded a new capital for the dynasty at Fas (Fez). Under his own sons the power of his house disintegrated through division of the inheritance, and from 930 onward his descendants lost their territories, partly to the Spanish Umayyads, partly to the Fatimids.

Though the Idrisids had made themselves a reigning dynasty only by force of arms, without gaining any influence for the special doctrines of the adherents of their family, nevertheless in the legitimate principle represented by them they prepared the ground for more fortunate successors in Africa. Around 890 an alleged descendant of 'Ali and Fatimah living in Salamiyah near Aleppo, Muhammad al-Habib, whose genealogical tree, however, was strongly contested, had emissaries recruiting for the Mahdi being awaited from his house. He professed adherence to the Shi'ite sect of the Isma'iliyah, who, like the Qarmatians related to them, were able to make Muslim dogma serve their political ends by allegorically interpreting the words of the Qur'an and recognizing only its inner meaning (*al-batin;* they were also called Batiniyah). A man named Abu 'Abdallah, who had been won over to this cause in South Arabia, gained the allegiance of some Kutamah Berbers present in Mecca on the pilgrimage, and they placed themselves under his command when he visited them in their own country. He gathered an army around him and in 909 defeated the last of the Aghlabids, Ziyadat-allah II, so decisively that he had to flee to Mesopotamia. The governor of Egypt refused to accede to Muqtadir's command to help the Aghlabid regain his empire. Abu 'Abdallah established himself in the Aghlabid residence at ar-Raqqadah and took the reins of government for a time into his own hand. Soon afterward the Fatimid Muhammad died, and his son 'Ubaydallah escaped the Caliph's machinations by fleeing to Africa. Here he emerged as the Mahdi. Although the governor of Sijilmasah held him captive for a time, his father's emissary, Abu 'Abdallah, freed him in 910 and raised him to the throne in ar-Raqqadah. He then erected a new residence in al-Mahdiyah along the near-by coastland. While all former princes of Islam, including the Spanish Umayyads themselves, held their land in fief at least nominally from the caliph in Baghdad, the Fatimids raised the claim of being the sole rightful heirs of the caliphate. Although 'Ubaydallah had to repress another uprising by Abu 'Abdallah, who saw his hopes disappointed, in a few years he had so consolidated his power that he could embark on conquests. His armies subjugated the west as far as Morocco, which after his death in 924 also fell to his successor as far as Ceuta, though here the Spanish caliph 'Abd-ar-Rahman III forced a retreat. But once again the rule of the Fatimids was seriously imperiled by an uprising of the Kharijite Berbers of the Zenata tribe in the Aures. Under the leadership of a fanatic named Abu Yazid, who had made his appearance riding an ass in the ancient prophetic manner, the courageous Berbers struggled with desperate savagery to regain their freedom. After Abu Yazid had subjugated the entire country, he confined the Fatimid caliph al-Qa'im to his residence in al-Mahdiyah for a whole year. But here his energies were exhausted. After he had given up the siege his troops were defeated; the leader fell into the hands of the new caliph, Isma'il, on August 19, 947, after his last fortress was taken by storm.

'Ubaydallah himself had also envisaged the conquest of Egypt; but an initial attack misfired. In 914 his army took Alexandria and the Fayyum region but was soon driven out again. Things fared no better for his son Abu-l-Qasim, who in 921 pressed as far as upper Egypt but was then decisively defeated by Muqtadir's general, Mu'nis. After 935 there arose once again in Egypt a power which kept the Fatimids from its borders for a generation. A Turk, Muhammad ibn-Tughj, whose grandfather and father had already served the caliph in Baghdad, came to Egypt as governor at this time and in two years was able to establish his power to such an extent that in 937 he could petition the caliph ar-Radi to elevate him above the rank of an ordinary governor by bestowing on him the title of ikhshid, which the rulers of his family in his native Ferghana had borne before their subjugation by Islam (just as in 1867 the Ottoman sultan 'Abd-al-'Aziz, by the title of khedive, elevated his Egyptian vassal Isma'il Pasha over his peers). At first he still had to defend this position in Egypt against the amir al-umara, ibn-Ra'iq, who was, however, finally compelled to concede to him the Sinai peninsula, indispensable for the defense of the country, as well as southern Palestine as far as Ramlah, in return for a payment of tribute. After ibn-Ra'iq's death he himself considered assuming the latter's position and was already negotiating with the caliph Muttaqi at Raqqah on the Euphrates. But the secure possession of a rich province attracted him more than the contending of the Turkish generals for the power in the down-at-heels center of the empire. In contrast he attempted to secure his position in Egypt through the building up of his Syrian outpost. Here he came up against the Hamdanid Sayf-ad-Dawlah, who was finally, however, compelled to leave him Damascus, which they had both been struggling for. In 946, when he died, the regime was taken over on behalf of his sons by an Abyssinian eunuch called Kafur; after the second one's death Kafur was also personally enfeoffed by the Caliph with Egypt in 966. He was still able to defend Egypt and Syria against Fatimids and Hamdanids, but after his death in 968, when a grandson of the first ikhshid, Abu-l-Fawaris Ahmad, barely out of his boyhood, began his reign, the fourth Fatimid caliph, al-Mu'izz, resumed his dynasty's plans of conquest. He had available to him in the person of Jawhar, a former Greek slave, an army leader who in 958 had already been able to secure the Fatimid domination of the west as far as Ceuta and Tangier. On February 5, 969, Jawhar set out with his army from Raqqadah and before the gates of Alexandria was already able to receive an Egyptian embassy announcing the submission of the country. Although in June the Egyptian army rallied its forces once again for resistance, Jawhar beat it back without any difficulty in a battle near the pyramids of Gizeh. At the beginning of July he moved into the national capital. As the Tulunids before him had created a new seat of government before the capital gates in al-Qata'i', so on July 9 he began staking off the future Fatimid residence between the old canal, at present filled in, which had once connected the Nile with the Suez, and the high ridge Muqattam. Just as the old Islamic cities had separate quarters for the Arab tribes, so the new city was divided up into blocks for the various categories of mercenaries: the Greeks, Armenians, Berbers, Kurds, Turks, and Negroes. The name of the new establishment, al-Mansuriyah, was changed into al-Qahirah al-Mu'izziyah ("the Conquering City of Mu'izz," whence Cairo) by the caliph Mu'izz, when he entered the country four years later.

Under the rule of the Fatimids, which lasted nearly two hundred and five years, Egypt enjoyed a fair degree of tranquillity, though enormous demands continued to be made on the country in the way of taxation. Mu'izz and his successor 'Aziz, with the help of Jewish and Christian officials, gave the country foundations of a sound administration, headed here also by the wazir. The third Fatimid to rule Egypt, al-Hakim Abu 'Ali al-Mansur (996-1020) made a special name for himself, though less by services to the country than through a variety of character traits probably based on psychic abnormality. In the first years of his reign he was meticulous about his duties as ruler and preoccupied with increasing the country's prosperity. Accordingly he summoned from Basra to Egypt the famous mathematician and physicist al-Hasan ibn-al-Haytham (Alhazen of the West), whose chief work, the *Optics*, eliminated the old Euclidian explanation of vision as an emanation of rays from the eyes and dominated this science in Europe also, until Kepler; al-Hasan had pledged himself to regulate the Nile floods which were the basis of the country's fertility. But since he was unable to translate his theoretical calculations into practice, he was forced to hide from Hakim's wrath until the end of the latter's life. The unlimited power at the Caliph's disposal, which was still sublimated by the nimbus of religion, finally must have deranged his mind. Hakim was bent on restoring the validity of the laws of Islam which civilization had rendered ineffective, such as the interdiction on wine, for instance, which had long since become a dead letter; he now had all vineyards, which in Egypt itself, to be sure, could not have been numerous, uprooted, and forbade the importation of all intoxicating beverages. Daily life was cut into still more deeply by the laws with which he attempted to restrict his subjects' search for pleasure; he prohibited not only banquets and music, but also chess, and finally even promenading along the Nile. He fought against the immorality of women, who in the big cities still found repeated opportunity for love affairs in spite of the harem life, by means of a system of moral checks exercised by old women; as this still appeared inadequate to him, he forbade all women in general to leave the house, and in order to effect this prohibition more thoroughly, laid penalties on the finishing of women's shoes. He restored the old fanatical clothing regulations for Jews and Christians, which were to distinguish them externally from Muslims, and made them still more stringent by making the Jews wear a bell and the Christians a five-pound cross around their necks. At his court he naturally favored the most extreme tendencies of the Shi'ah, which after the ancient Iranian example regarded the ruler of legitimate descent as an incarnation of divinity. It is probable that he himself was already laying claim to divine veneration. After his death Muhammad ibn-Isma'il ad-Darazi, and his successor Hamzah ibn-Ahmad al-Hadi in Syria, agitated on behalf of a new sect called Druzes after their founder, in which mystical-pantheistic and ancient pagan conceptions, in addition to the veneration of the divine Hakim, completely submerged Islam. In the Lebanon this sect found, among the courageous, freedom-loving mountain dwellers, enthusiastic supporters who have survived to this day and on many occasions influenced the course of Syria's history. Hakim's end has no doubt remained enigmatic not only for religious but also for political reasons. He is supposed to have fallen victim to a conspiracy his capricious regime engendered among the notables of his court; he is said to have been assassinated at their instigation in the early part of 1021 while riding before the gates of Cairo.

His successors as a rule submerged themselves in the luxuries of court life and proved incapable of curbing the unrestraint of the mercenaries or of redressing the economic ills of the country, afflicted just at this time by an excessive depression of the level of the Nile. It was not until the second half of the long reign of Hakim's grandson al-Mustansir (1036-1094) that an Armenian, Badr al-Jamali, who had begun his career as a general in Syria and in 1073 was provided with comprehensive powers, succeeded in breaking the tyranny of the Turkish generals and emirs and restoring order in the country. But he was unable to maintain the rule of the Fatimids in Syria, which had always been menaced by minor rulers, against the power of the Seljuqs, who in the meanwhile had risen in the East. By 1060 Aleppo was lost to the Mirdasids, a dynasty which had emerged among the Syrian Bedouins; Jerusalem fell into the hands of the Seljuqs in 1071, Damascus in 1076. Al-Jamali's son and successor, al-Malik al-Afdal, who after the death of both his father and the Caliph in 1094 had raised the latter's youngest son al-Musta'li to the throne and dominated him completely, was at first able to restore the Fatimid rule in Syria by taking away the Holy City from the Ortoqids, Seljuq vassals who had their seat in Jerusalem. But now Islam was to find a new and dangerous adversary here in the Crusaders, whose importance at first was manifestly underestimated in the general confusion resulting from the contention of petty Syrian dynasts for primacy. In 1099 Jerusalem fell into the hands of the Crusaders, who in the next two decades succeeded in restricting Fatimid rule to the coastal areas of Tyre and Ascalon in a series of battles of alternating fortunes. In 1121 al-Malik al-Afdal was killed by an assassin: the incompetent caliph al-Amir was resentful of his guardianship. Now the end came on the dynasty inexorably. Between Crusaders and Turkish rulers in Syria and unruly pretorians in the capital, peace could only be secured for the country for a brief space of time by an able general like Tala'i' ibn-Ruzziq, who was summoned to power by the wives of the assassinated caliph Zafir in 1154; but six years later he succumbed to an assassin's dagger himself. The last of the Fatimids, 'Adid, could no longer ward off the superior power of the Seljuq generals ruling Damascus; he had to appoint one of them, the Kurd Shirkuh, as wazir, and the latter's successor, Saladin, as we shall see, eliminated the final remnant of the mock power of the Fatimids formally as well.

In spite of their weakness, which made its appearance rapidly, the Fatimids, thanks to the administrative foundations laid by the first two caliphs, secured for Egypt extended periods of great prosperity. The magnificence of their court, regulated by an elaborate ceremonial performed down to the last detail, was unequaled by any of their rivals, and splendid structures like the mosques of al-Hakim and al-Azhar, the latter still flourishing today as the most celebrated institution of learning in Islam, bear witness to the lofty aspirations which inspired them.

The province of Africa from which the Fatimids had started slipped out of their grasp directly after their settlement in Egypt. Their first governor, Yusuf Bulukkin ibn-Ziri, made himself independent in 972. Under his grandson Badis the latter's uncle Hammad founded a new dynasty in Algeria; while wearing themselves out in this internecine strife the Muslims lost Sicily to the Normans under Roger, and their possessions in Corsica and Sardinia to the Genoese and Pisans.

3. *Persians and Turks*

Between the inhabitants of Tibet and China in the east, the Paleo-Asiatic (Sibirid) race in the north, and the Finno-Ugrian peoples in the west, the Turkish people on the broad plains of southern Sibiria and the steppes between the Caspian Sea and the Altai Mountains had emerged out of a racial and linguistic community which in primeval times may also have comprised the Mongols and Tungus. They were often led by great ruling figures such as have arisen among the leaders of minor patriarchally organized nomadic groups and are encountered again and again in the later history of these regions. At their entry into history, as they pressed forward from the slopes of Tien Shan out into the central Asiatic steppes, they already bore well-marked ethnic traits designated by anthropologists as Turanian. While Mongolian features appeared among the northerly groups, the southern branches preserved the moderately large graceful bodily form with the medium long face, powerful straight nose, high and steep forehead, and abundant hair.

In the sixth century A.D. we find them in possession of two powerful states, founded by two brothers, which stretched from Mongolia and the northern frontier of China as far as the Black Sea. The founder of the eastern state, Bumin, died in 552; his brother Istemi, who had subjugated the west, survived him by almost a quarter of a century. The Tang dynasty of China overthrew the northern state around 630, the western around 659. But in 682 the northern Turks freed themselves from alien rule and maintained their independence until 745. On the Orkhon in Mongolia, from the common tomb of two princes of this kingdom, Bilga Kaghan and his younger brother Kultegin, the oldest monuments of Turkish speech have come down to us: long inscriptions from the years 731 and 734, written in a runelike script for use on stone which was borrowed from the Iranians and was derived from the Aramaic script. These nomad states consisted of loosely organized tribal confederations, led by individual khans bound together under a supreme military war lord, the kaghan; the khan sprang from the nobility of the *begs*, to which the masses of the people still willingly subordinated themselves. The organization of functions, characterized by a fixed nomenclature, part of which survived in the Islamic Turkish states, already showed definite beginnings in the formulation of a public code of law, which was also borrowed by their successors; the Slavs, too, took over this old Turkish law from the Avars. National life culminated in the holidays which were associated with hunts and pillaging expeditions, and it was one of the main duties of the prince to provide munificently for them.

The realm of belief was dominated by the shaman, who by means of a trance, often artificially induced, could exorcise the power of the evil spirits dwelling below the earth and win the blessing of the friendly earth and water spirits and the tribal forebears in Paradise; it was only through the shaman that one might venture to come into contact with the Highest Being, the heaven as God (*Tengri*) who created the world and ruled over its seventeen upper strata that were inhabited by benevolent beings. Before the incursion of Islam a belief was widespread in the power of the destiny embodied in world and time, which was conceived of in a quite personal way as being filled with envy and a desire for vengeance against human grandeur.

A state formation of this kind could only survive while held together by an energetic leader who could exploit his neighbors by raids and impositions of tribute. The farthest western outposts of this state had already been subjugated by the Arabs around 700, under the Umayyads. Around 745 the northern kingdom also fell into the power of another Turkish tribe, the Uigurs, who had originally dwelt further north along the Selenga River. The latter permitted the Syrian Christians of the Nestorian sect, as well as the emissaries of Manicheans sent out by the Soghdians, freedom of preaching in their domains; in place of the older runes they introduced a later form of the Aramaic alphabet, which subsequently prevailed in the Mongol state also. In 840, when the Kirghiz overthrew the empire of the Uigurs in the north, the latter emigrated into the territory of present-day Chinese Turkestan, which had already been settled by Turks before them. Here Buddhist missionaries also appeared, and vied with Christians and Manicheans in creating for these Turks a flexible and powerful language, though at first it was used only in translated works. Of the two Uigur principalities, the one in Kanchu was annihilated in 1028 by the Tanguts, while the second survived down to the time of the Mongols. The Kirghiz, who had earlier driven them out of their ancestral domain, had already been subjugated by the Mongol tribe of the Kitai (still the Russian name for China). Its ruler is supposed to have requested the Uigurs, esteemed for their more advanced civilization, to return to their old habitations, which, however, they were no longer prepared to do. While at the beginning of the eighth century vassals of the West Turkish kingdom still controlled the borders of Iran, the latter were already subjugated under the Umayyads and delivered inexhaustible quantities of human beings to the slave market; it has already been related how these slaves appropriated the power in Baghdad under the ʿAbbasids, and how, for a time, individuals of this clan seized control of other provinces also.

Their former headquarters, Transoxania, Bukhara, and Samarqand, enjoyed relative tranquillity under the enlightened regime of the Samanids in the ninth century. The founder of this dynasty, Saman-khudat (i.e. Lord of the village of Saman in the region of Balkh), was an Iranian who had accepted Islam during the reign of the Umayyad caliph Hisham (724-743). Around 819 his four grandsons were installed by Ma'mun in the governorships of Samarqand, Ferghana, Shash, and Herat, and at first they were still subordinate to the Tahirids. The governor of Ferghana, Ahmad, managed to gain control of Samarqand as well. In 875 his son Nasr was enfeoffed by the Caliph himself with Transoxania; he installed his brother Ismaʿil as ruler in Bukhara, where he put an end to the disorder prevalent there since the wars with the Saffarids, and also forced the native aristocracy into submission. In 903, after a struggle with his brother Nasr, whom he relegated to the position of a nominal overlord, he also won Khorasan from the Saffarid 'Amr, as well as Tabaristan by a victory over Muhammad ibn-Zayd of the 'Alids. His successors also conquered Sistan and Jurjan, but they lost Tabaristan again to the Buyids, and in their ancestral land as well were limited more and more by the slowly expanding power of the national Turkish dynasty of the Ilek khans in Turkestan, who had originally stemmed from the areas north and south of Tien Shan and from there pushed westward.

In the first half of the tenth century, however, under the rulers Nasr II (913-942) and Nuh I (942-954) the Samanid territories were nevertheless the site of a flourishing culture. Transoxania's abundantly watered lowlands had long been cultivated and had produced great harvests under skillful regulation. The national consciousness of the Persians, enslaved so long by the political and religious hegemony of the Arabs, here reawakened. Although the Persians, from the beginning of 'Abbasid rule on, had largely outstripped the Arabs in the administration of the state as well as culturally, their achievements had nevertheless been of benefit to the latter, since the language of the Qur'an could no longer be expelled from public affairs any more than it could from literature. But here in the east the Persians for the first time bethought themselves again of the dignity of their mother tongue. Although the Persian landed aristocracy had never ceased the painstaking cultivation of the proud national memories in the sagas of kings and heroes, and no doubt the people also did not forget the art of poetry singing, the renewed fructification of this spiritual heritage was reserved for the Samanid court. Under Nasr II there flourished Rudaki, the first Persian lyric poet of whom we have any detailed knowledge. Although his speech was not free from Arabic words and his metrical system, like that of all his successors, was modeled on the Arabic, he preached a carefree, merry wisdom of life, inspired, despite the commandments of Islam, by love not only of women and of song but also of wine. Rudaki was also the founder of the most fertile branch of Persian literature, the epic-didactic. He cast into Persian verse the ancient and famous Indian book of fables, *Kalilah and Dimnah*, which the Sassanid emperor Chosroes Nushirwan (531-579) had already had his personal physician Burzoe translate into Middle Persian, and which under the first 'Abbasids the Persian ibn-al-Muqaffa' had translated into Arabic, as well as the story of Sindbad and the seven wazirs. Under Mansur ibn-Nuh (961-976) the wazir Bal'ami translated Tabari's great Arabic world history into Persian and so became the founder of Persian historiography, which was later to attain great heights. In strictly scientific fields, to be sure, Arabic retained its primacy here in the east also. Thus the famous philosopher and physician Ibn Sina (Avicenna), who began his career under the eighth Samanid, Nuh ibn-Mansur (976-997), used Arabic for his philosophic writings and his medical canon, which in the Middle Ages was also the basic book of medical science in Europe, and which dominated in Persia, until recently, the entire art of healing.

At the Samanid court Arabic geography also attained its scientific zenith, although it is true the Arabs had long shown an interest in the description of countries, which had been encouraged in South Arabia particularly by pride in the advanced civilization of the country before Islam, as is shown in the description of Arabia written by al-Hamdani, who died in a San'a prison in 945. By the ninth century the postal and information system which the Umayyads had borrowed from the Persian great kings and which was first properly elaborated by the 'Abbasids, had already established a network of communications for the use of imperial functionaries. Books on the land tax were also concerned with imperial organization. In Baghdad, the center of contemporary world commerce, an interest developed in foreign countries, empires, and peoples, which was emphasized in the lost geography of the journalist al-Jahiz. At the court of the Samanid Isma'il (892-907) the wazir al-Jayhani wrote a book, also lost to us, which in connection with an account of taxation gave a description of neighboring countries. Then, as a sequel to an older Islamic atlas (based on an adaptation of Ptolemy's geography prepared by al-Khwarizmi before 846), Abu Zayd al-Balkhi, in Isma'il's service in Balkh, wrote a cartographical work which was later adapted to conditions in the Fatimid empire, and was added to by a Spaniard to suit his own country. This was also the basis of the classic work of the Palestinian al-Muqaddasi, who in 978 enlivened the cartography by an elegant literary text and by material gathered from his own travels, about both the Samanid and the Fatimid domains. He was surpassed in breadth of vision by al-Mas'udi, who died in Egypt in 946, and whose wanderlust had led him by way of India as far as Ceylon and into the Chinese Sea; yet he regarded geography only as a groundwork for his broadly conceived works on history, unfortunately preserved only in excerpts.

The Samanids finally met their end as the result of the same evil as the 'Abbasids. Like them they were reduced to dependency on the Turks as a still-unexhausted reservoir of recruits for their armies, all the more so since they had broad areas populated by Turks under their rule. As in Baghdad, so in the Samanid army also, the Turks gradually penetrated into the officers' positions and from there passed over into the civil administration, where they soon became dangerous because of their highhandedness. The Samanid 'Abd-al-Malik I (954-961) had appointed the former Turkish slave Alptigin as supreme commander in Khorasan, primarily with the intention of removing him from the capital, where he had become too powerful. After his master's death Alptigin withdrew to Ghaznah in the Sulayman Mountains in Afghanistan, where his father had previously been governor. He himself died too early to become dangerous to the Samanids from there. But his former slave, later his son-in-law, Subuktigin, soon drove out his other heirs and began extending his power by conquests in India. He first appropriated Bost in Sijistan. Its ruler had called on him for help against a usurper; when he failed to pay the tribute promised in reward for the services rendered him, he lost his throne entirely. Subuktigin's campaigns were much more successful in India, where the disunity of the Rajputs cleared the way for him, and from where he brought back the richest spoils. In two victorious campaigns he compelled King Jaypal of the Punjab to turn over to him the important border area of Kabul, which controlled the passes into the rich Indian plain. Simultaneously he won the fame of a champion of Islam against the infidels.

Even at that time his right hand was his son Mahmud, to whom the Samanid transferred the governorship of Khorasan in 994. In 997, when Subuktigin died, he was first succeeded on the throne by his oldest son, Isma'il, who, however, proved an incompetent spendthrift. Isma'il's brother Mahmud then demanded that he abdicate, and the following year compelled him to do so by force of arms. Seven months after his father's death Mahmud ascended the throne as sultan. In the same year the Samanid Nuh also died; his successor, Mansur, was simply ordered by Mahmud to relinquish the latter's old province of Khorasan. But before it came to this, Mansur was blinded by a Turkish officer, and his brother 'Abd-al-Malik was raised to the throne in his place. Now Mahmud could pose as the defender of the legitimacy principle; he drove the rebel, together with his own new master, out of Balkh and there set up his own residence. 'Abd-al-Malik fled to Bukhara, where he fell into the hands of the Ilek khan of Turkestan and was taken away to Urgenj. The last of the Samanids, Muntasir, was killed around 1004 after a number of unfortunate adventures. Mahmud, however, received from the Caliph the official sanction his regime still lacked and the honorific name of Yamin-ad-Dawlah.

Mahmud's life was filled with incessant campaigning. He advanced into India repeatedly; in 1001 he conquered Kabulistan, then Multan and Kashmir soon afterwards, and tried to supplant Brahmanism by Islam everywhere. In 1006 he had to defend his possessions in the north against the Ilek khan, on whom he inflicted a bloody defeat on the plain of Balkh. Directly afterward he went to India again; he subjugated the Punjab, and here his descendants maintained themselves in their capital at Lahore another hundred and fifty years. On his pillaging expeditions, however, he pressed far beyond the Ganges; in 1025 he concluded his conquests in India by the occupation of Gujerat. Meanwhile he had also extended his power in the north, and conquered Khwarizm in the east and Georgia in the west. In 1026 he had wrested Rayy from the Buyid Majd-ad-Dawlah and removed the latter himself to his capital at Ghaznah.

But this crude soldier Mahmud was far from hostile to the arts of peace. He adorned Ghaznah with magnificent buildings, having the steps to his mosque and to his palace hewn out of the idol's image from the Hindu Temple of Somnath in Gujerat, which he despoiled in 1026. Since the city became desolate after the fall of his dynasty, today there survive of his monuments only the minaret of his mosque and his mausoleum, whose outer gates were removed to India in 1842 by the British on the mistaken assumption that they were also once part of the Temple of Somnath. But Mahmud could also bind scholars and poets to his court. During the last years of his life he had in his service the great scholar of the age and one of the greatest in the entire Islamic world, Abu-r-Rayhan Muhammad al-Biruni, who had followed him to Ghaznah in 1017 when Mahmud had absorbed the country of his former patron the Khwarizm shah Ma'mun. From Ghaznah, Biruni made a number of voyages of study through conquered India. He learned Sanskrit from native scholars, which enabled him to study the rich scientific and religious literature of the Indians. After his youthful work on the chronology of all peoples, which he composed in Jurjan in 1000, in 1017 he began his famous book on India, which as a complete portrayal of an alien cultural world is quite unique in Arabic literature, and was also of great service to European scholarship.* A Turk, Mahmud was devoted to the Sunnah and so preferred Arabic literature to Persian, whose representatives were generally Shi'ites. He also persecuted other heretics, not only their most radical fringe, the Isma'ilis, but also the scholastic theologians of Mu'tazilite tendency. It is, to be sure, very questionable whether he understood much of the book *Al-Yamini,* in which 'Utbi, postmaster in Ganj-Rustak, glorified his deeds, for this work is one of the first examples of that revoltingly tasteless rhetorical style overburdened with flowery images which during this age of decline penetrated from the writings of the Persian chanceries into Arabic historiography, and which has made the bombast of the Orient so notorious.

Mahmud had no understanding at all of the greatest Persian poet, the epicist Firdawsi, who was his subject and vainly strove for his favor. The Iranian saga of kings and heroes had hitherto been handed down primarily by word of mouth. But its foundations had already been laid in the Middle Persian prose works which ibn-al-Muqaffa' had translated into Arabic and so made accessible to Arab historians, in particular Tabari. In 957 a high official, Abu Mansur al-Ma'mari, had four men rework this entire tradition into a neo-Persian prose book for Abu Mansur, the son of 'Abd-ar-Razzaq, then ruler of Tus in Khorasan. The first attempt to give this material a form worthy of it was made by the poet Daqiqi, who lived at the court of the Samanid Nuh ibn-Mansur (976-997) but was killed by a kept boy when he had just completed about a thousand verses. Firdawsi of Tus took up his work around 990, when he was already sixty years old, and completed it eleven years later. *Shahname* (*The Book of Kings*) in which we encounter the essence of the Persian epic style at the summit of its perfection, and which with all its routine displays the master hand of a poetic genius, was dedicated by him to the ruler of his country, the sultan Mahmud; in many places he praised him as the mightiest and most kindly of rulers. But the hoped-for reward failed to appear; only later did the Sultan give him a gift—a paltry one. Firdawsi's receipt for this con-

* [E. Sachan translated the chronology, London, 1879, and the work on India, 2 vols., London, 1888, 1910.]

sisted of the mordant satire with which he prefaced his immortal work as a way of counteracting its eulogy of the Sultan. Then, in order to escape his sovereign's wrath, he removed to the west, to the court of the Buyid Baha-ad-Dawlah in Baghdad, where he wrote the epic *Yusuf and Zulaykha*, which in scope approximates the *Iliad;* it still testifies to the rare freshness of spirit of this man in his advanced seventies, though with his long practice the verses flow easily from his pen and the work in the judgment of the Persians, also, falls short of the *Shahname*. But the aging poet could no longer really acclimate himself to the quite different living conditions in 'Iraq, and consequently returned to his native city after making certain of Mahmud's forgiveness; he died there shortly after 1020. Firdawsi's work, which, in perfect poetic form, encompasses the ensemble of the mythical and historical memory of his people, and which, despite its range—about eight times greater than that of the Iliad—never falls into a stereotyped technique, has rightly been celebrated by the Persians as the greatest masterpiece of their literature; his style remained a model for the whole of the epic poetry of the Persians and later of the Turks. Because of this it was entirely appropriate that the people of Iran, awakened to a lively national consciousness under Shah Riza Pehlevi, celebrated as a national holiday the millennial jubilee of their greatest poet in 1934, though for lack of an established chronological tradition, the date, in fact, was somewhat arbitrarily chosen.

Since the Buyids had proved incapable of curbing the anarchy which had erupted in the center of the empire, the Persians here also were soon entirely expelled by the Turks. Among the Ilek khans in Turkestan and the sultans of Ghaznah a new clan sprang up which was destined to rule the entire Near East. Around 970 the Ghuzz chieftain Seljuq had advanced, together with his tribe, from the Kirghiz steppe to Jand, where the Sayhun–Syr Darya discharges into the Aral lake, and later from there to Bukhara. The Ghuzz or Oghuzz, who were also called Turkomans after their conversion to Islam, constituted that great Turkish tribal group which had founded the northern kingdom in the sixth century and since then had been wandering westward. After their entry into the Islamic sphere these Turks adhered to the Sunnah, whose clear and sober content of belief was suited to their simple minds and was embraced with all the energy of their souls, still unspoiled and capable of enthusiasm. Seljuq's tribe then participated in the wars between the

Samanids and the Karakhanids, as they did later on in those between the Ilek khans and the sultans of Ghaznah. But on their own account they also undertook raids which brought them as far west as Adharbayjan and 'Iraq. In 1040 Seljuq's grandsons Tughril Beg Muhammad and Chaghri Beg Da'ud also wrested Khorasan away from Mas'ud, the son and successor of Mahmud of Ghaznah, after their attempt to seize Samarqand and Bukhara had misfired. In Merv, Da'ud had his name recited in the Friday prayers; in Nishapur, Tughril Beg his own. Since dynastic quarrels soon broke out among the Ghaznawids, the Seljuqs were able to expand their power at the expense of Ghaznah. They won over Khwarizm as well as Tabaristan, and in 1043 even "Persian 'Iraq" (Media). It cost them only a slight effort to put an end to the Buyid dynasty in Persia. They continued moving their residence more and more to the west, first to Rayy and then to Isfahan.

It is no wonder that the 'Abbasid caliph al-Qa'im (1031-1075) desired this new ruler of the east as his protector instead of his Buyid guardian, who, moreover, had already been stripped of all his power by a Turkish officer called al-Basasiri. In 1055, while Tughril Beg was waiting in Hulwan, the Caliph offered him the khutbah, the designation by name in the Friday services, for Babylonia. The last Buyid, al-Malik ar-Rahim, died in a Rayy dungeon in 1058. But the Seljuqs were unable to deal with al-Basasiri so easily. He had fled to the north; and when Tughril Beg followed as far as Mosul, his stepbrother * Ibrahim ibn-Inal left him and returned to 'Iraq. It was only with the help of his nephew Alp Arslan, son of Da'ud, the ruler of Sijistan, that Tughril Beg succeeded in subduing Ibrahim, who on August 3, 1059, paid for his treachery with death. Al-Basasiri took advantage of this embarrassment by allying himself with the 'Uqaylid Quraysh ibn-Badran, an Arab prince, and occupying undefended Baghdad. While the latter removed the Caliph to Ana in Mesopotamia, al-Basasiri had the Fatimid Mustansir designated in the Friday services. As soon as Tughril Beg's hands were freed, he brought the caliph al-Qa'im back to Baghdad and received from him in return the honorary title King of the East and the West. Al-Basasiri fled to Wasit and was killed there at the beginning of 1060 in a battle with the Seljuq troops.

* In contrast to other information, in the Seljuq history of Sadr-ad-Din al-Husayni edited by M. Iqbal (Lahore, 1933, p. 19) he is expressly designated as the son of Tughril's mother.

When Tughril Beg died in 1063, he was succeeded by his nephew, Da'ud's son Alp Arslan, who during the last years of his father's life had already headed the regime in the latter's territory. At first he had to break the resistance of some kinsmen who refused to recognize him. But he was soon able to extend the boundaries of his domain in all directions. In the east he subjugated the principality of Subran between Bost and Kabul; in the west he personally conducted the war against the Byzantines on a number of occasions, though without achieving any lasting success. On August 26, 1071, he defeated the Byzantine emperor Romanus Diogenes at Malaskerd and took him captive; when freed, the latter was unable to put into effect the peace terms he had agreed to, since in the meanwhile Michael VII had ascended the throne. But Alp Arslan was able to wrest from the Fatimids their possessions as far as Damascus. In December 1072, while in the midst of a campaign beyond the Oxus to win back the ancestral homeland of his house, he was assassinated by a rebel whom he wanted to put to death.

He transferred the guardianship of his still-minor son Malikshah to the wazir Nizam-al-Mulk, who had already served his father as governor of Khorasan. This vice-regent—whose influence Malikshah tried repeatedly, and unsuccessfully, to escape, although his own throne had previously been assured only through the defeat of rebellious kinsmen by the Wazir—had almost unlimited power. Nizam also determined policy vis-à-vis the Caliph, whose court he kept under supervision by officials friendly to him. In 1083, when he encountered resistance in this, he avenged himself by opposing the Caliph's last direct vassal, the Marwanid ruler of Diyarbekr, and so reinforced his influence. Under Nizam-al-Mulk's rule Persia and Babylonia enjoyed once again a period of a certain prosperity, though the Wazir, or *Atabeg*, as he was called as guardian of the Sultan, owed his fame primarily to his patronage of theologians and scholars, for whom he made excellent provision by the founding of institutes of learning, *madrasah*s, in all the important cities of the empire. There is evidence of such institutes in Persia from the end of the tenth century on, but they were specially encouraged by the Seljuq wazir, who erected the Nizamiyah named after him first in Nishapur and then in Baghdad between 1065-67. While Tughril Beg's wazir had still ardently persecuted the Ash'arite theologians, whose deceased leader, 'Ali al-Ash'ari (*d.* 935), had been concerned with reconciling the dialectical method of the Mu'tazilites with orthodox thought, it was precisely this modern tendency that was favored by Nizam-al-Mulk.

Under his protection the last great theological thinker of Islam, Ghazzali, accomplished his work, first at Nishapur, then at the Baghdad nizamiyah. In his youth he had made a deep study of the juridical-theological systems of the scholastics and given a account of them in a series of brilliant textbooks. After his patron Nizam-al-Mulk was killed in 1092 by the dagger of a fanatical Isma'ilite, he studied the Isma'ili doctrines and wrote a number of polemics refuting them. His work on this also led him to a deeper study of philosophy. But in none of the doctrinal systems he studied with passionate zeal did he find any satisfaction in his quest for truth, and in consequence he lapsed for a time into an acute skepticism, for which he had shown an inclination ever since youth. In this spiritual crisis he underwent a decisive religious experience; as the Prophet himself had once been aroused to his office by fear of an accounting on the Day of Judgment, so Ghazzali also was seized by questions concerning the salvation of his soul. In 1095 he consequently gave up his magnificent position in Baghdad for the free life of a wanderer, in order to re-examine his beliefs altogether, torn between faith and reason. He became more and more attracted toward mysticism, which communicated to him the personal experience of religious certitude. He spent eleven years in tranquil seclusion, mostly in Syria, and wrote his work on the *Revivification of the Sciences of Religion*, which he published around the turn of the fifth century after the Hijrah (about 1106). According to one tradition the Prophet is supposed to have promised his community a man at the beginning of every century who would revive their faith, and Ghazzali manifestly felt this to be his mission. He performed the service of consistently applying the reconciliation of dialectics with theology begun by al-Ash'ari, and of providing the doctrinal edifice of Islam with a new structure based on the method of dialectics. At the insistence of the Seljuq sultan Muhammad, the brother of Barkiyaruq, who had come to the throne in 1104, and his wazir Fakhr-al-Mulk, son of Nizam-al-Mulk, he let himself be persuaded to resume his public teaching activities in Nishapur, but soon withdrew again to solitude in his native city of Tus and there died, at the age of only fifty-four, on December 19, 1112. Although his work was not always completely understood by his contemporaries–indeed, the orthodox fanatics in Spain are even supposed to have had his writings burned–nevertheless it was not lost to the future, and constituted a fertile element in the further evolution of Islam.

Next to theology the exact sciences also aroused a lively interest in the Seljuq era. One of Ghazzali's later compatriots was the famous mathematician 'Umar ibn-al-Khayyam, whose death probably took place in 1132. His algebra was the first to crown with success the attempt to solve cubic equations (of which he distinguished thirteen kinds) not only algebraically but geometrically. His reputation as mathematician caused the sultan Malikshah Jalal-ad-Din to charge him with a reform of the calendar; the Jalalian era suggested by him could not be put into practice, to be sure, although in precision it was superior to the Gregorian calendar. His fame in Europe rests primarily on the witty Persian quatrains under his name, which, sometimes frivolously, sometimes profoundly, preached a carefree enjoyment of life and dissolved the foundations of Islam in a mystic pantheism; for years they have enjoyed great popularity in the Anglo-Saxon world through the poetic paraphrases by Fitzgerald, and they were also made known in Germany by the diplomat Fr. Rosen. Since many of these quatrains recur in the collections of other poets, for a long time there was doubt as to 'Umar's authorship; now that his authentic theological and metaphysical writings have become known to us, the outlook represented in the quatrains can no longer be ascribed to him.

While the Persians of this epoch wrestled with the most advanced problems of religion and science, an Arab created a work which once again encompassed all the nuances of Arabic speech. The narrative prose of the Arabs, which in pre-Islamic antiquity had depicted the petty struggles of Bedouin tribes in images rich in episodes but lacking coherence, demonstrated its skill also in picturing the great events of the times of Islam's conquests and the struggles for power within Islam. We have already seen that stimuli from the Iranian cultural milieu were indispensable, initially, for shaping these ephemeral images into a continuous narrative for the imperial annals. Under the Umayyads there had already developed, in addition to the accounts of raids and battles, a constellation of narratives of famous lovers, the foundation of a body of short tales which was later brilliantly elaborated. But their cultivation generally was left to storytellers from among the people, since they appeared unworthy of the labors of serious-minded men. Examples of this art have been transmitted only by philologists, who found them useful in explaining the poems they were handing down. Materials from the rich narrative literature of the Indians were also introduced into Islamic culture by Persians at an early period. But today all we know of innumerable works of this kind is their titles, preserved in a bibliophile's lists dating from the end of the tenth century; only a portion of this material has come down to us in the compilation of the Arabian Nights, which did not arise until the thirteenth and fourteenth centuries. In the ninth century the pleasure in the word itself still overshadowed any interest in the actual construction of a literary work of art; this is shown particularly by the writings of a journalist who died in Baghdad in 869, al-Jahiz, who even in a work of his old age, the *Zoology*, in spite of an unmistakable endeavor to interest his readers in scientific questions, was incapable of elevating himself beyond a disorderly piling up of details, and consequently in innumerable essays and books showed a special preference for pointed anecdotes to depict classes and types of character in human society. Just as the individual verse was much more important to the ancient poet than its consistency with the qasidah, he and his audience also thought one single point more valuable than a well-constructed narrative. Pleasure in an aptly coined word had already developed the art of persuasive speech to great perfection even among the Bedouins. This rhetoric had also burgeoned in Middle Persian historical literature, which ibn-al-Muqaffa' made known to the Arabs. In religious discourse as well as in political writings of the chanceries under the 'Abbasids, and under the small dynasts par excellence, this art was lovingly cultivated. In the hands of the literary proletariat which grew up in the metropolises and in the milieux of the not always successful office-seekers it descended from this official sphere into a rhymed rhetoric which served the disciples of the philologists in their peregrinations from place to place as a means of finding favor or at any rate a brief respite in the support of some wealthy patron. These mendicants' addresses were called *maqamah*s, a term used earlier for religious sermons. As early as the second half of the tenth century Badi'-az-Zaman al-Hamadhani, a sponger on petty Persian princes, had elevated this genre to literary dignity; his "hero" gives eyewitness accounts, short and dramatically flowing in a skillful rhymed prose, of the experiences of a wandering *littérateur*. But while al-Hamadhani had retained the same form for an entirely different content, al-Hariri, who followed in his footsteps some hundred years later, restricted himself to such genre scenes exclusively. In contrast to his predecessor, who had been able to depend on his own experiences as a wanderer, al-Hariri was a well-to-do bourgeois who directed the court information bureau in his native city of Mashan, near Basra; he died there in 1122. His maqamahs, which relate the adventures of Abu Zayd of Saruj, had a great success. Though he fell short of his predecessor in imaginative power, he excelled him in the use of the hyper-artificial form which has remained characteristic of this genre ever since. His work found imitators in other literatures, such as the Spanish Jew Harizi in Hebrew, and the metropolitan of Nisibis 'Ebedyeshu' (*d.* 1318) in Syriac, and was given a most felicitous German paraphrase by Rückert in his *Verwandlungen des Abu Said von Serug*. Down to the threshold of modern times Hariri's maqamahs, together with the poems of Mutanabbi, have been regarded by the Arabs as the most perfect expression of their spirit.

The shortcomings of the state administration of the Seljuq empire even under Nizam-al-Mulk's regime were admitted by the latter himself in a remarkable treatise in Persian which he wrote, at the Sultan's desire, not long before his death in 1092, but which was not published until twenty-two years later. Since the writer took entirely for granted a knowledge of prevailing conditions, we are not given a great deal of insight into the internal organization of the empire. He warned the Sultan against the irresponsible influence of his personal friends on affairs of state, at the same time recommending the restoration of the old institution obligating the postmasters to provide information (which, however, the Sultan's father Alp Arslan had already rejected) and further control by secret agents. The law must have been in a parlous state: he warned against delegating trial decisions to a *mamluk* (slave) sent out by the court, who naturally was always inclined to exploit such a commission by the extortion of disproportionately high fees; in this we catch another glimpse of the degeneration of the old Turkish custom of having the administration of law exercised by officials appointed by the prince—though Nizam could not exonerate even the juridically trained judges of an inclination to abuse their office. He warned, rightly, against the accumulation of offices present even under the 'Abbasids. In military affairs we are acquainted with the important fact that there were feudal troops in addition to the mercenaries.

Nizam, who in general failed to take pains with respect to historical information or understanding, was mistaken in regarding this tendency as something entirely novel. It had already been in existence, after all, under the 'Abbasids, even though only as an abuse and an emergency measure. In the Ghaznawid state it is supposed to have been unknown, but for the Turks in the west, particularly the Osmanlis, it later constituted the foundation of the state structure. Further, he recommended that enfeoffed property be delimited with precision and that it be held in fief for specified periods of time. Shortly before his assassination Nizam al-Mulk added one more chapter to this memoir, warning the Sultan of the dangers threatening his empire from the Isma'ilis.

Malikshah also extended the boundaries of his empire. In 1089-90 he subjugated Samarqand and Kashghar. Syria was taken away from the Fatimids entirely, and minor vassal principalities arose in Damascus and Jerusalem. His cousin Suleyman, the son of Kutlumish, went on to Asia Minor for conquest; later we shall deal with what happened to him.

Under Malikshah's reign an internal enemy of the empire arose which for a long time was the terror of the whole Near East. It was not without reason that Nizam-al-Mulk warned the Sultan of the machinations of the Shi'ite sects. The Shi'ah, in the beginning a purely dynastic party under whose banners the newly converted Muslims struggled against the primacy of the Arabs, had not infrequently also served unscrupulous careerists as a mask for purely egotistic aims hostile to the government. Among the Shi'ite preachers wandering about the country seeking to win over the mob by promising them a mahdi to punish the injustice of the rulers, there emerged under Malikshah one Hasan Sabbah. Legend tells of his youthful friendship with Nizam al-Mulk and the great mathematician 'Umar al-Khayyam. In Egypt he was won over to the doctrine of the Fatimids, and decided in favor of Nizar, the son of the Fatimid caliph Mustansir. But Nizar failed to ascend the throne. Sabbah's supporters were therefore also called Nizaris. In 1090 he turned up in Persia as their emissary. With a small band of followers he encamped in front of the mountain fortress of Alamut, "the Eagle's Nest," in the Rudhabar district, sixty parasangs north of Qazwin,* and called upon the officer of Malikshah in command there to take

* See W. Ivanow in *Geographical Journal*, 1931, LXXXVI, 38-45, and *Islamic Culture* XII, 1938, 383-392.

the oath of allegiance to Mustansir. When the officer refused, he seized the fortress, which then became the seat of his power. In accordance with Fatimid propaganda he built up his order in various degrees. While the narrowest circle of initiates professed a libertinism which negated any limitations by morality or religion, their agents were trained in the severest fanaticism. The murder of an enemy of the true faith designated by their master was presented to them as a work well pleasing to God, the execution of which would assure them of the joys of Paradise. Such murderers were called *Fida'is*, "the Self-Sacrificers," or *Hashishis* (whence Assassins), those intoxicated by hashish, the narcotic element in hemp. The use of stimulants was widespread in mystic circles elsewhere as well; in the sixteenth century coffee was used for such purposes in South Arabia. Accordingly, what the Venetian world traveler Marco Polo reported who some two hundred years later (1271 or 1272) passed through the territory of Alamut, may be mere legend: namely, that the fida'is, while intoxicated by hashish, were placed in a section of the Alamut gardens fitted out as Paradise, with young women as huris, in order to make the assassins amenable to the orders of the leader by giving them a foretaste of the pleasures awaiting them in the hereafter. From Alamut the order succeeded in a short time in seizing other castles in Persia and Syria as well. The attempts of the Seljuq regime to suppress them collapsed, and were answered in 1092 by the assassination of Nizam-al-Mulk, although it is not entirely out of the question that the Sultan himself, who after coming of age grew weary of this minister's omnipotence, knew about this plot. Less than two months later, however, he followed him to death himself.

Barkiyaruq, whom Malikshah himself designated as his successor on the throne, at first had to struggle for his rights against the mother of his four-year-old stepbrother Mahmud and against his uncle Tutush, who was governor in Damascus. The caliph Muqtadi, who had been prepared to recognize Mahmud, paid for this with his death after Barkiyaruq's final victory in 1092. The struggle with Tutush lasted another year and did not come to an end until the latter was killed in a battle near Rayy in Persia, after he had already conquered Mesopotamia and compelled the caliph Mustazhir in Baghdad to nominate him in the Friday prayers. But still other kinsmen of Barkiyaruq's came out against him. In Khorasan his uncle Arslan Arghun made himself independent but was murdered by one of his slaves in 1096, and the country reverted to the empire. In 1099, however, Barkiyaruq's brother Muhammad, who ruled over Adharbayjan, rose against him and together with the third brother Sanjar, not yet twenty years old, whom Barkiyaruq had appointed governor in Khorasan, drove him to flight into the mountains of Damaghan after two unfortunate engagements. After numerous battles of alternating fortunes, a peace was concluded in 1103 in which Barkiyaruq recognized Muhammad as independent and placed his brother Sanjar under him as governor of Khorasan. When Barkiyaruq died, only one year later, leaving behind a minor son, Muhammad made himself sole ruler.

Under Muhammad's reign (1105-1118) the East enjoyed relative tranquillity once again. He took pains to eliminate the small parasite states which kept springing up in distant regions. In 1108 he defeated the Arab chieftain Abu Sadaqah, of the banu Mazyad, who from Hillah near ancient Babylon had usurped authority over the Bedouin tribes of Mesopotamia. He could not, however, destroy the gravest cancer of his empire, the Assassins, although he had their fortresses razed in various places and in 1118 his troops even surrounded Alamut itself. But before this fortress surrendered Muhammad himself died on April 18, at the age of thirty-seven, perhaps poisoned by some supporter of the Assassins. On hearing of this his troops lifted the siege at once, since they no longer knew to whom they owed allegiance.

After Hasan Sabbah's death (1124) his followers gained a foothold in Syria also, and on many occasions took a hand in the struggles with the Crusaders. In 1140 they seized the fortress of Masyad on the eastern slope of Jabal an-Nusayriyah; this was the residence of the Syrian subordinate of the Grand Master in Alamut, whom we shall encounter again as the Shaykh al-Jabal, "the Old Man of the Mountain," an important factor in the Syrian contest for power.

The Seljuq empire disintegrated very quickly into its component elements. The princes of this house lost their power entirely to their guardians, the atabegs, some of whom created, by efficient administration, conditions which were tolerable in smaller areas for a certain time.

4. *Islam in Spain and in North Africa*

In Spain also Islam had long since passed the zenith of its power. Under the last Umayyads the victorious wars against the Christians had been brought to a halt by the dissension between the Berbers and the Arabs, who here also were still split into Qays and Kalb. As their rule in Syria began to decline, about five hundred Arabs under the leadership of Balj ibn-Bishr had crossed from Africa into Spain and settled down in the military districts of Elvira and Jaen. 'Abd-ar-Rahman, "the Falcon of the Quraysh," grandson of the tenth Umayyad caliph, Hisham, had fled to North Africa from the 'Abbasids and found refuge at the court of the Rustamids at Tahert. Since no opportunity was offered there for winning a position worthy of his origin, he directed his gaze toward Spain, where the only support of the governor Yusuf ibn-'Abd-ar-Rahman al-Fihri, who was out of touch with the center of the empire, was the leader of the Qays, as-Sumayl al-Kilabi. In concert with the clients of his house, the Umayyad prince landed on Spanish soil at Almunecar in September 755 and turned at once on the Governor. On May 15, 756, he established his residence at Cordova and was recognized as emir. He succeeded in binding together the splintered forces of Islam and expanded his sphere of power in the struggle against the Christians, although his thirty-two-year reign (756-788) was filled with incessant warfare against insurrectionaries. Yusuf al-Fihri, the governor expelled by him, attempted to regain Cordova and fell in battle in 759, near Toledo. South Arabs and Berbers kept coming up against the Umayyad. Charlemagne, the founder of the powerful Frankish empire, once took a hand in these wars: In Paderborn, where he held a May festival in 777 after his victory over the Saxons, the Yemenite shaykh Sulayman al-'Arabi came to see him with some kinsmen of the emir Yusuf to ask for his help against the Umayyads. Since Charlemagne thought it advisable to be on good terms with the rising power of Islam, and since 'Abd-ar-Rahman was apparently represented to him as a usurper of legitimate rule, he promised the Spanish emissaries his support. The army he was to send out through the Pyrenees was to be joined at once by Yusuf, the governor of Barcelona, while Yusuf's kinsmen, together with their tribe, the Fihr, were to revolt against the Umayyads in the southeast. But this uprising broke out prematurely and was beaten down by the Yemenites. When the Franks appeared before Saragossa in 778, the inhabitants refused allegiance to 'Arabi, who was there, and shut the gates against the Christians. During the siege Charlemagne heard of a new Saxon revolt which had broken out behind his back, and as a result had to break off his Spanish enterprise at once. On the way back through the Pyrenees the Basques inflicted the legendary defeat of the Roncevaux valley on his rear guard under Ruotland, margrave of the Breton coast. Directly after the Franks withdrew, 'Abd-ar-Rahman pressed north. In 780 he added Saragossa to the Cordova realm, though for only a short time, and subjugated the Basques. When 'Abd-ar-Rahman died in 788, he left his son Hisham a well-organized state based on a strong army; to be maintained for any length of time it required rulers who were as ready as he was to risk everything for the maintenance of their power and shrink at nothing. Although his reckless energy had held down the germs of dissension rampant throughout the country, it had been unable to eradicate them. The Arab nobility accepted his hard hand only with reluctance, and the resistance of the new converts against the claims of the Muslim lords was already making itself felt here in the west also.

Nor could his successors deal with the still-unconquered Christian states of the peninsula so easily as had the founder of the dynasty. In Asturias a new spirit had appeared with Alfonso II's accession to the throne. In alliance with the Basques and the Franks of Aquitaine he succeeded in wresting Barcelona again from the third Umayyad, Hakam I, in 801 and even occupied Lisbon for a short time during a raid southward. In the interior of the country, Hakam, who succeeded to the throne when his father Hisham died in 798 after a reign of only seven years, was engaged in an incessant struggle for his kingdom, but showed the same energy as his grandfather in maintaining it. While the Awza'i school of jurisprudence had hitherto prevailed in Spain as in Syria, its place may have been taken even under his father by the doctrine of Malik, which already dominated all of North Africa. Its representatives, the fuqaha (singular, *faqih*) had been distinguished from the first by a particular fidelity to the law and a fanatical ambition. Consequently they took serious offense at Hakam's manner of life—devoid, in the style of his Syrian forebears, of any legal scruples—and together with the discontented nobility they carried on an incitement against him among the new converts. Twice, in 805 and 806, he had to suppress insurrections in his capital, Cordova. In Toledo the newly converted Muslims had united with their still-Christian countrymen into an independent city government and defied the Emir. It was not until he sent out as governor 'Amrus ibn-Yusuf, a convert blindly devoted to him, that he succeeded in subduing the city after luring its rulers into an ambush and butchering them one and all on the edge of a grave in the court of his newly erected castle. Like the 'Abbasids, 'Abd-ar-Rahman also had had to depend on a bodyguard of foreign mercenaries for protection against the hatred of his subjects. These foreigners were called "the Mutes." Toward the end of Hakam's reign there was another flare-up. In 817, incited by fanatical fuqaha, the inhabitants of the southern suburb of Cordova on the left bank of the Guadalquivir attempted to storm the palace of the Emir. After his guard had massacred the rebels, he had the suburb razed to its foundations and exiled its inhabitants, about sixty thousand in number, from the land and scattered them. While a third of them settled down in Fez, where their quarter was still called "the Bank of the Spaniards" later on, the others went on to Egypt and first got a foothold in Alexandria; in alliance with other adventurers they held the city for ten years against the 'Abbasid governors; after their subjugation they were removed to Crete.

Under Hakam's weak successor, 'Abd-ar-Rahman II (822-852), Toledo again made itself practically independent. In Cordova also new difficulties were arising for the regime because of the Christians, who hitherto had willingly submitted to the tolerant rule of the Muslims and had even been strongly influenced by the superior culture of Islam. Now, however, fanatical zealots like the priest Eulogius were stirring up their courage in the faith, so that many Christians sought to attain a martyr's laurels by malediction of the Prophet. In vain did a council called by the archbishop Reccafred at the instigation of the Emir condemn this wanton disdain for death; the influence of the lower clergy embarrassed the government again and again. The Emir was incapable of opposing this with the same severity as his father. It is true that a certain faqih Yahya ibn-Yahya, a disciple of Malik ibn-Anas himself, played a great role at his court, but the legist was principally concerned with securing supremacy in Spain for the master's doctrines. The Emir was influenced more by his favorite wife Tarub and her protégé, the Spanish eunuch Nasr, than by Yahya. These two shared their influence with the musician Ziryab, a pupil of Ishaq al-Mawsili, who was seeking to escape his master's jealousy; by the time he reached Spain he was so famous that the Emir personally went to meet him in Cordova in 822. In a short time he not only set the tone at court in music, but also pricked the Emir's ambition to vie with his Baghdad rival in opulent pleasure-seeking. Difficulties in the interior, which compelled the Emir to subjugate Merida and Toledo by force of arms, were still increasing when the Normans fell on Spain in 844 and occupied Seville. The Emir sent his court poet Yahya ibn-al-Hakam al-Ghazal to negotiate a truce with the Norman leader, who had his residence on one of the Danish islands; he brought back to Spain the first knowledge of the northern peoples.

During a long reign 'Abd-ar-Rahman's successor, Muhammad I (852-886), who had been thoroughly trained in the fanatical spirit of the fuqaha, added fuel to the conflict between the two elements of the population by making even conciliatory minded Christians atone for the guilt of their fanatical fellow believers. In their need the especially harassed Christians of Toledo turned to the king of Leon, Ordoño I, whose general, the count of Bierza, made a foray into Muslim territory in 854 and defeated the Emir's troops at Wadi Salit (Guadacelete); although the damage was compensated by three serious defeats of the Toledans, Muhammad could not make up his mind to a lasting and effective siege of the city, and so it maintained its independence for another eighty years. Its example had an inspiring effect on the Christians in Cordova also. Although the wave of martyrdom came to a halt here with the death of Eulogius and Leocritia (859), the example of these witnesses of the faith continued to have an effect throughout the country. Twenty-four years later when Muhammad sued for a truce with Alfonso the Great, he had to deliver to him the remains of Eulogius, who meanwhile had been canonized. Since Muhammad was concerned with improving the state finances, enfeebled by the prodigality of his father, he went so far in his parsimony that he neglected to care for the military defense of his realm. In the struggle with Asturias and Navarre he therefore often found himself in straits. In Aragon the convert Musa and his sons asserted their independence, and in Badajoz another convert, ibn-Marwan, rose against the Emir in 875 in alliance with Alfonso III of Asturias. In the north the contradiction between the Spanish national consciousness and the alien Arab rule overshadowed the religious strife between Christianity and Islam to such an extent that ibn-Marwan could conceive of instituting a new mixture of both religions for his people. The Spanish successes in the north also had a provocative effect on the hitherto placid population of the south. In 884 in the Serrania Mountains between Ronda and Malaga the renegade 'Umar ibn-Hafsun revolted against Umayyad rule and for years continued to hold out in his fortress of Bobastro even against Muhammad's successor Mundhir, who had already combated him while crown prince. After a reign of only two years the latter was poisoned by his brother 'Abdallah (888-912), who concluded an immediate peace with the rebels.

He was constrained to this not by any lack of energy but by the insecurity prevailing throughout the realm. For a long time the great Arab landholders, like the Emir himself, had maintained huge corps of slaves whom they occasionally armed in order to fight out their feuds. One of the landholders, Qurayb ibn-Khaldun, had seized the entire region of Aljarafe with such troops shortly after 'Abdallah's accession to the throne; but after the converts in Seville, in alliance with the Berbers settled in the surrounding mountains, renounced their allegiance to the Emir, Qurayb joined the Emir in defense of Arab supremacy and together they suppressed the Sevillians. But eight years later the Emir fell out with another Arab chieftain, Ibrahim ibn-Hajjaj; the latter eliminated Qurayb and allied himself with ibn-Hafsun. Since the feudal lords elsewhere were also showing themselves defiant of the Emir, he was compelled to cede Ibrahim the mastery of Seville even though Ibrahim was finally overpowered. Finally even the Christians in Cordova, under the leadership of Count Servando, entered into an alliance with ibn-Hafsun, whereupon 'Abdallah gathered his forces for a decisive blow. In 891 he attacked the rebel in his fortress Polei, south of Cordova, and forced him to fall back on Bobastro. Here ibn-Hafsun injured his position still further by apostacizing to Christianity and thus alienating himself from his subjects, most of whom professed Islam entirely out of conviction, without his new fellow believers' being able to lend him any assistance. In incessant battles 'Abdallah attempted to foil his numerous opponents, and in spite of some failures he eventually succeeded in fortifying the prestige of the regime.

In October 912 when 'Abdallah died, he was succeeded by his grandson 'Abd-ar-Rahman III, the son of Muhammad, whom 'Abdallah had had removed. The new emir became the most important Spanish ruler of the Umayyad house; during his reign, which lasted almost fifty years (912-961), he first managed to bring to a conclusion the pacification of the country begun by his grandfather under such enormous difficulties, and then re-established his prestige and influence abroad. In a short time his energy and gentleness succeeded in restoring the allegiance of the heads of the Arab nobility in the provinces of Jaen and Elvira, although ibn-Hafsun maintained his independence in mountainous Serrania retreats until his death in 917. By the following year one of ibn-Hafsun's sons, Sulayman, had to give up the struggle; another, Ja'far, attempted to save himself by embracing Islam again and was killed by his Christian followers as a result. The youngest son, Hafs, held out as long as 928 in Bobastro, the chief fortress, but then he also had to capitulate. Most of the other fortresses had surrendered before; they were razed and the notables of the country transplanted to Cordova. In 930 Toledo alone was still independent, and even this city-republic, which had now enjoyed its freedom for eighty years, was compelled to submit to the Emir after a siege of two years. In 920-924 'Abd-ar-Rahman also repulsed King Ordoño II of Leon, who in alliance with Sancho of Navarre had pushed back the Muslims beyond Merida in the south and as far as Tudela and Valtierra in the north, and pursued them beyond the frontiers.

While restoring the empire of his fathers in the interior, 'Abd-ar-Rahman had been attentive to the policy of the Fatimids, who at that time were attempting to expand their power in western North Africa as well as elsewhere. In 929, to oppose their claims, he assumed, like them, the title of Caliph and Commander of the Believers, to replace the designation Emir borne by his forefathers, and in accordance with the habitual ceremonial of the Orient bestowed on himself the honorific name of an-Nasir li-Din Allah ("Helper toward the Victory of God's Religion"). At the same time he created a fleet to ward off any Fatimid attacks. In 931 he forestalled them by occupying Ceuta in Morocco at the eastern exit of the Straits of Gibraltar. The petty rulers in the hinterland, who saw themselves threatened by the Fatimids, sought his protection at once, and so he was able to extend his power throughout North Africa as far as Tahert, which was conquered by the Fatimids in 908.

Like the 'Abbasids, 'Abd-ar-Rahman also sought to protect his power by a troop of foreign mercenaries made up of purchased slaves. The Turks of the east had their counterpart in Spain in the

Saqalibah, the Slavs, which was the name used for all the prisoners of war from all European countries. At this time a very lively slave trade, predominantly in Jewish hands, was flourishing in western Europe. Its victims were principally captives from the wars along the Slavic eastern marches of Germany who were sold into Spain by way of France; Verdun was a principal center for the preparation of eunuchs, who at that time were sought after in Spain also as harem servants, on the model of Baghdad. Other slaves were delivered by Byzantium from the raids along the coasts of the Black Sea; but the Spanish pirates themselves also provided the market with slaves by forays on the French and Italian coasts. Like the Turks in Baghdad, the Saqalibah in Spain very often achieved wealth and prestige through the favor of their masters. 'Abd-ar-Rahman considered them more reliable than the Arab noblemen who had often been such a danger to his ancestors. Accordingly he occasionally even placed Saqalibah officers at the head of an entire army. Thus in 939 the Slav Najdah led the army the Caliph sent into the field against Ramiro II of Leon and his Navarrese allies. But this made the Arabs so indignant that their passive conduct in the Battle of Simanca resulted in the worst defeat of 'Abd-ar-Rahman's life. Toward the end of his reign he also subdued his Christian opponents. Ramiro II had got into a feud with the count of Castile, and after his death his sons Ordoño III and Sancho contended for the throne. Since Sancho was supported by the Castilians, Ordoño concluded a peace with 'Abd-ar-Rahman and obligated himself to pay tribute. Sancho succeeded him in 955 and broke this treaty, but was driven out of his domain by his nephew and had to flee to the aging Queen Tota of Navarre. Together with her he appeared in Cordova personally to ask 'Abd-ar-Rahman for help. This was given him in exchange for a series of border fortresses, and Muslim troops re-established him in his dominions.

Under 'Abd-ar-Rahman's long reign, not marked by any further disturbances in the interior, Andalusia saw the burgeoning of the civilization which aroused the admiration of medieval Europe. Agriculture and horticulture, trade and industry, all reached a flourishing stage. The Arabs cultivated grains and introduced in Spain the growing of date palms; the remains of their orchards are still found today in the palm grove of Elche in the south of Valencia province. Artisanship excelled particularly in metal and leather goods; down to the present day Cordovan leather has kept alive the name of the

Andalusian capital in the world market. The annual revenues from taxes and tolls during 'Abd-ar-Rahman's reign were calculated at 6,245,000 dinars. A third of this is said to have covered current state expenditures; a third was deposited by the Caliph in his treasury, and the rest devoted to the buildings which give him a place worthy of the most famous builders of Islam.

The ruler's chief concern here, as in the Orient, embraced the worthy construction of the mosque. In Cordova the first conquerors had been content with confiscating half the Christian cathedral of San Vincenzo for their worship. The first mosque was erected by the founder of the Umayyad dynasty in 785-786. In twelve months the foundation of the building was completed; this haste led to the appropriation of columns from other churches, which were probably in ruins, and there was no particular concern about whether the capitals were suitable for the shafts or not. The Muslims also borrowed from the Visigothic architects the horseshoe arches which in alternating white and colored wedge-shaped stones and bricks connected the columns with each other and led up through a second nave floor to the originally richly carved and painted wooden ceiling. All his successors then set to work on the elaboration of the mosque. Hisham I erected the minaret; 'Abd-ar-Rahman II lengthened the eleven aisles by seven arches each and added a second mihrab. Muhammad I set off the maqsurah as court loge through the use of a balustrade; 'Abdallah, who must have been particularly concerned about his safety, connected this loge by a covered walk with his palace, bordering the mosque on the west, so that, just as under the Umayyads in 'Iraq, the castle (*qasr*) of the emir and the mosque constituted a unit. 'Abd-ar-Rahman III, the first to call himself caliph in Spain, in 951 replaced the minaret destroyed by an earthquake with a magnificent new structure which was the model for the famous Giralda of Seville as well as for many other minarets in the west. His successor, Hakam II, extended the eleven long aisles by fourteen arches each, about a hundred meters southward, and instituted (according to an inscription in 965) a new mihrab, the still-existing eight-cornered chapel of Zancarron with a cupola of a mussel-shaped fluted block of marble, as well as a new maqsurah of three rooms "which constitute the architectonic culmination of the mosque, with their crisscrossing arches, lobed arches, and the peculiar ribbed domes." * The vice-

* E. Diez, *Die Kunst der islamischen Völker*, p. 50.

regent al-Mansur finally added to the eleven long aisles still another eight with seven rows of columns. So the mosque numbered nineteen aisles with thirty-five columns each; the central nave leading up to the mihrab was in this way excluded from the principal axis.

A high wall, between two and three meters high, crowned by battlements, surrounded the whole building, stretching in a rectangle from north to south. Mighty substructures were necessary, since the foundation ground sloped toward the river. Twenty-one doors, ornamented with wrought copper and today mostly filled in, led into the interior; the windows and blind vaulted niches at their sides with tower-shaped buttresses articulate the façade of the mosque. A few of these doors were reserved for women and led to the galleries built in for them between the roofs; the women's loges otherwise characteristic of the Byzantine churches were not taken over by Islam. The courtyard, surrounded by galleries no longer in existence, which officials of 'Abd-ar-Rahman III saw completed in 957, surrounded a cistern with pillars and vaults of hewn stone. This provided the faithful with water for the ritual ablutions before prayer.

Under 'Abd-ar-Rahman the capital was further ornamented by the architecture of magnificent secular structures known to us only from the description of historians. His principal work was the suburb az-Zahra, which he named in honor of a favorite slave. At the foot of the 'Arus Mountain, about three Arabian miles north of Cordova, its construction was begun in 936. For twenty-five years ten thousand workers were occupied there. The city was built in three terraces on the slope of the mountain. The gardens lay below; in the center, the houses of the court functionaries; above them, the Caliph's palace. The main hall consisted entirely of multicolored marble and of gold. In the center there shone a pearl, a gift of the Byzantine emperor Leo. The eight doors rested on pillars of multicolored marble and crystal, under gilded arches of ebony and ivory set with jewels. In the sleeping chamber of the Caliph there was a well-basin adorned with twelve animal images of red gold. The castle extended 2,700 cords from east to west and 1,500 cords from north to south. The fifteen hundred doors were adorned with gilded iron and copper metalwork; the forty-three hundred columns had been imported partly from Africa and partly from Frankish territories. 'Abd-ar-Rahman's successors were incapable of maintaining this prodigious structure. In the second half of the eleventh century only a few portions of it were still standing, and today only a few heaps of refuse in so-called Old Cordova, a mile away from Cordova on the slopes of the Sierra, designate its former site.

This efflorescence of material culture was paralleled by that of the spirit. As for poetry, unfortunately we are better acquainted with its development in the later era of political decline of Moslem Spain. We may presume that originally it supplied here, as in Syria, the traditional accompaniment of intertribal feuds: eulogies and satires. At the court of the Umayyads, under the influence of the contemporary art of Baghdad, there was a burgeoning of panegyrics wallowing in grotesque flatteries. But as the Persians in the east invested the old forms of Bedouin poetry with new life, here the Spanish temperament affected them; the peculiar tenderness and profundity of emotion, that almost modern receptivity to the charms of nature and art and their portrayal with grace and insight, is manifestly, as already recognized by Count A. von Schack, a heritage of the Iberian-Roman stock merely clothed in the language of the Arab conquerors. Of the sciences theology and philology were also soon zealously cultivated in Spain. The enslavement to tradition of the dominant Malikite school saved Spain from the struggles concerning the form and the methods of study of the dogma which shook the spiritual world of Baghdad and the East. In contrast the interest for the past soon outstripped purely theological speculation here. We shall see that mysticism was given its definitive expression, which eventually prevailed in the east also.

The merit of having aroused an interest in the problems of philosophy belongs to a Cordovan, ibn-Masarrah, who around 900 * gathered around himself a group of disciples in a hermitage on the slopes of the Sierra de Cordoba; since he became suspect of heresy, he set out on a pilgrimage and did not return home until after the accession of 'Abd-ar-Rahman III. He resumed his teaching activities and died in 931. It is still impossible to determine how the pseudo-Empedoclean metaphysics grafted on to neo-Platonism came to his knowledge. The doctrine of emanation which derived the world from the primordially one God through intellect, the world soul and nature, led him to the conviction that the human soul must retrace this path and that its fate thus is not sealed in death. This path to perfection could best be trodden in a community, and in

* The date 912 given by Asin Palacios in the *Encyclopedia of Islam, Supplement*, is really that of 'Abd-ar-Rahman's accession to the throne.

many Spanish cities such groups arose on the model of Cordova, and held out in spite of orthodox persecution down to the thirteenth century.

Like the Persians in the east, natives of Spain were ready to emphasize the virtues of their forebears as against the Arabs. Under 'Abd-ar-Rahman III this was dared even by a qadi, Abu Muhammad 'Abdallah ibn-Hasan, who was held in such esteem that the Caliph himself attended his lectures.* In 942 the study of philology was introduced in Cordova by al-Qali, who had been born in Armenia and educated in Baghdad. Historiography, cultivated with great zeal in the Islamic east and in Spain as well, was almost exclusively an appendage of the court and consequently incapable of ever achieving impartiality in narration. Particular diligence was devoted to the history of the Muslim conquest, given its classic expression by Muhammad ibn-al-Qutiyah ("the son of the Gothic woman"), a contemporary of al-Qali, and, as throughout the east, to the history of scholars and outstanding individuals. In medicine and the natural sciences an attempt was made to emancipate Spain from the tradition of the Orient. 'Abd-ar-Rahman III had a new translation of the therapeutic doctrines of Dioscorides made from a copy in Greek sent to him from Constantinople. His son Hakam II, an enthusiastic admirer of scholarship, collected a library of (reputedly) four hundred thousand volumes, for the perfection of which he maintained agents everywhere in the east. He also promoted the spread of knowledge by founding twenty-seven schools in Cordova, with free instruction for the children of the destitute.

Hakam II al-Mustansir-billah, during his reign which lasted only fifteen years (961-976), was able to enrich the heritage of his father in the interior and to make the realm secure against attempts of his Christian neighbors, who gradually all had to submit to him. Crippled by a stroke during the last years of his life, he had to leave the administration of government affairs mostly to his not particularly capable first wazir, Ja'far al-Mushafi. The chief minister in Spain was known as the hajib; at the Umayyad court in Damascus this was the title of the chamberlain who regulated the prince's intercourse with his subjects and was thus enabled to acquire an influence on the conduct of affairs. In Africa the pressure exerted on the Spanish domain by the Fatimids had become much feebler

* Goldziher, in *Zeitschrift der Deutschen Morgenländischen Gesellschaft*, 53, 605.

after their removal to Egypt. But new difficulties arose out of the clash between two great Berber groups of the Zenata, who were subdued by the Umayyads, and the Sanhaja, whose name still survives in Senegal, the river which bounded their territory. By 940 one of their leaders, Ziri ibn-Manad, had established a firm center in Ashir south of Algiers; in 971, however, he lost his life in a battle with al-Hakam's vassals. His son Bulukkin was entrusted by the Fatimid

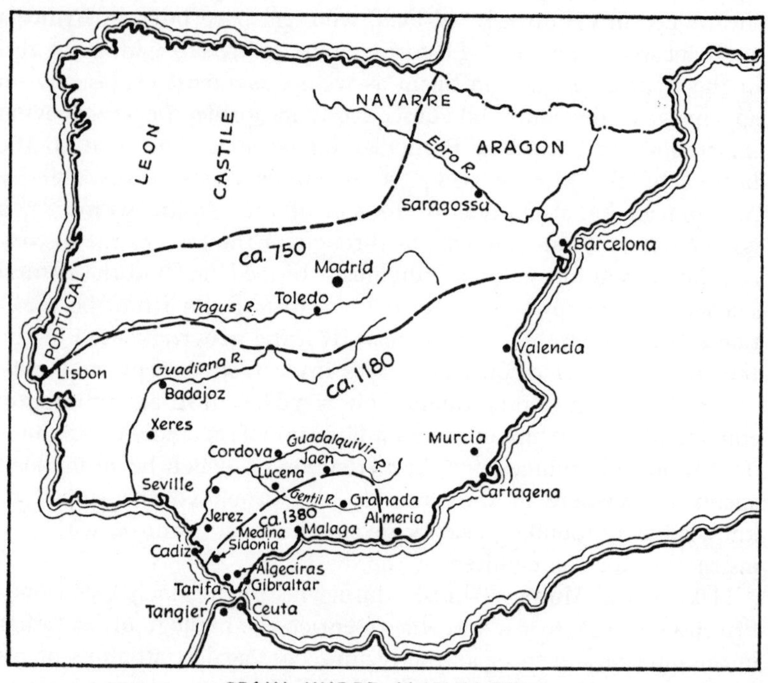

SPAIN UNDER MUSLIM RULE

Mu'izz, after his transfer to Cairo, with the administration of the African provinces and their capital, Qayrawan. He avenged his father's death by an attack on Umayyad territory which took him as far as Sijilmasah. In 973 he conquered Tlemsen and in 979 occupied Fez and Sijilmasah.

He had been emboldened to this by the continuing confusion of conditions in Spain. In 976 Hakam II had been succeeded by his sole surviving son Hisham, who was only ten years old. His Basque mother, Aurora-Subh, was his guardian, together with an Arab nobleman, Muhammad ibn-abi-'Amir al-Mansur. The latter had begun his career as steward of her estates and through her favor had risen to the position of finance minister; as such he had been able to moderate the heavy expenses of the troops fighting in Africa on special missions by skillful negotiations with the general Ghalib, who later became his father-in-law. Soon after Hisham's ascension to the throne, al-Mansur succeeded with the help of Ghalib, who was governor of Medinaceli, in depriving the hajib Ja'far al-Mushafi of his position and in restricting the influence of the Saqalibah pretorians, who were already playing a role in Cordova similar to that of the Turks in Baghdad. In alliance with the Caliph's mother, whose lover he soon became, he was able to keep the young prince at a distance from affairs by means of an exaltedly pious upbringing. In 978 he started the construction of a new government city before the gates of Cordova, al-Madinah az-Zahirah, which rapidly burgeoned into the seat of actual government. He did not shrink from buying the support of the still-influential fuqaha by destroying all the secular books in Hakam II's library when they accused him of philosophical interests. He liquidated the former African policy, which merely incurred heavy expenses while bringing very little into the country and imperiling its position, by retaining a firm hold only on Ceuta and allowing indigenous princes to rule in the hinterland as vassals of Cordova. It was only when the Idrisid ibn-Jannun attempted to renounce his fief obligations in 985 and restore his ancestral dominions that Mansur had him overthrown by his cousin and decapitated. In contrast he resumed a strong policy against the Christian states in the north. Breaking the opposition of his father-in-law Ghalib, he reorganized the army, replacing the unreliable Slavs by Berber and Christian mercenaries from Africa and northern Spain. So firm was his hold on the Christian mercenaries that he dared lead them against fellow believers. A victorious campaign against Leon won him the honorific title of al-Mansur-billah, but it was not until 987 that he decisively subjugated the country. In 985, on his twenty-third campaign, he took Barcelona by storm; in 997 he destroyed the famous Christian holy place of the peninsula, Santiago de Compostella, down to the very tomb of the apostle. He transferred his office as hajib to his son 'Abd-al-Malik in 991, and in 997 he assumed the princely titles of Sayyid and al-Malik al-Karim ("the Noble King"), so that the caliph, as in Baghdad, was restricted to his palace. On the way back from his fifty-second campaign, in which he had conquered Canales, al-Mansur died, on August 10, 1002.

His son 'Abd-al-Malik at first was able to take his position uncontested and continued his campaigns in northern Spain. But six years later he was poisoned at the instigation of his brother 'Abd-ar-Rahman. The latter, the son of a daughter of Sancho of Navarre and therefore called Sanchuelo, was unwise enough to attempt to secure, through a decree of Hisham, the succession to the throne in case of the Caliph's death. After he had left the capital for a campaign against the Christians in Galicia, an insurrection broke out against the usurper behind his back. The Umayyads who were excluded from the succession forced the caliph Hisham to relinquish the throne in favor of his cousin Muhammad II, who assumed the name of al-Mahdi. When 'Abd-al-Malik turned against him, the hajib was abandoned by his mercenaries and put to death before the gates of the city.

The new caliph had the vice-regent's city al-Madinah az-Zahirah destroyed; and attempting to break the influence of the Berber mercenaries, who had been reinforced by many Sanhaja, one of the African groups previously hostile to the Spaniards, he struck them off the pay lists. But since he was unable to set any new troops against them, he was overthrown in the same year and replaced by a grandson of 'Abd-ar-Rahman III, Sulayman. The latter had led the Berbers in the battle against the Christians in Calatrava and Guadalajara and then occupied Cordova. But al-Mahdi won the assistance of the general Wadih, in command in Medinaceli, and the counts Raïmund of Barcelona and Ermengol of Urgel. They defeated the Berbers before the gates of Cordova, and the unhappy capital atoned for the dissension of the pretenders in being sacked by the victors. The Berbers, however, still controlled the surrounding country, cutting Cordova off from the outside world. Accordingly there was a conspiracy in the city against al-Mahdi, who was unequal to a situation of this kind. He was killed in 1010 and Hisham II was raised to the throne again. But Wadih was unable to make peace with the Berbers on his behalf either; they finally forced the Cordovans to renew their allegiance to Sulayman. Since he had to leave all power to the Berbers, the Cordovans finally turned for help to a former governor of Ceuta, 'Ali ibn-Hammud, a kinsman of the former Idrisid dynasty of Morocco; but he had hardly removed Sulayman when he himself was overtaken by the same fate. Then two more of his kinsmen entered on a contest for the power with no less than seven Umayyad pretenders. Since none of them was able to assert himself the head of the city, after the fall of the last Umayyad, Hisham III took over the government of Cordova, forming an aristocratic republic like the one formerly in Toledo.

Muslim Spain was now turned into a patchwork of petty states. In the south it was principally the Berbers, in the east the "Slavs" who snatched the power in individual cities. These petty principalities had only the disunity of the Christians to thank for Islam's ability to continue its hold on the peninsula. Of these small dynasties only the 'Abbadids of Seville deserve brief consideration. In this city, as in Cordova after the disintegration of the Umayyad caliphate, the patricians had taken power. A brother of the 'Alid pretender of Cordova, Qasim ibn-Hammud, had consolidated his position in Malaga and attempted to extend his rule over Seville as well. But here the qadi Muhammad, of the South Arab family of 'Abbad, led the struggle for the freedom of his native city, and although he bore only the title of qadi, he succeeded in handing down his power to his progeny. He himself had already overthrown a series of the neighboring petty princes. His son 'Abbad, who succeeded him in 1042, continued this policy with success. While his father had still thought it necessary to authenticate his rule through recognition by an ostensible Umayyad, Hisham, after Muhammad's death 'Abbad felt himself sufficiently powerful to accept the oath of allegiance under the reigning name of Mu'tadid. He rid himself of all his opponents with needless cruelty. By skillful negotiations he warded off the blows of King Ferdinand I of Castile and Leon, who had energetically resumed the struggle against the Muslims. By the time he died in 1069 he was already able to leave his son Muhammad al-Mu'tamid in control of almost the entire southwest of the peninsula. In 1071 Mu'tamid succeeded in conquering Cordova as well, but lost it three years later to a pretender supported by the prince of Toledo. Just as al-Mu'tamid himself, when a thirteen-year-old, had led an army in the service of his father, so his own son 'Abbad was installed as governor in Cordova, where he lost his life. Mu'tamid was unable to avenge his death until 1078, when he regained Cordova and seized from the prince of Toledo the southern portion of his territory. While 'Abbad had still been able to purchase peace for himself from the ruler of Castile by payment of a tribute, Mu'tamid soon saw his domains imperiled by the latter's ambitious successor, Alfonso VI. In 1080 the Castilian moved on Toledo, which he was able to conquer, however, only after a five-year siege. But in 1082 he raided al-Mu'tamid's territory in order to avenge an insult to his Jewish tribute collector, and pressed as far as Tarifa. After the fall of Toledo, Alfonso demanded the return of the territories Mu'tamid had wrested from the princes of the city. To escape the Christian peril, Mu'tamid, together with other Muslim princes of Spain, turned for aid to the Almoravids in North Africa, of whose rise we shall soon give an account. He and his comrades had to pay dearly for this help. After the victory over the Christians they were all dethroned, one after another. Mu'tamid was taken to Africa and died a prisoner at Aghmat in Morocco in 1095.

This time of deepest political degradation for the Spanish Muslims still bore a rich cultural harvest. The more restricted the power of the city princes, the readier they were to increase the luster of their courts by generosity to the poets who glorified their deeds on the model of the eulogy long since rigid in form. Under al-Mansur the greatest master of this profession flourished in Cordova, Ahmad ibn-Darraj al-Qastali, whose skillful pen also played a political role. Spain had long since followed the Oriental custom of casting the state documents exchanged among the princes in as artistic a form as possible. His somewhat younger contemporary, ibn-Shahid, whose deafness excluded him from attendance at court, nevertheless won great prestige through his gay and witty verses; he composed a remarkable epistle in criticism of the art of his contemporaries and their predecessors in the form of an account of a journey through a valley of spirits. This form, a journey into the beyond, was borrowed some twenty years later by a poet in Syria, Abu-l-'Ala al-Ma'arri, as a means of passing in review all the most distinguished poets in Islam. For a time after the fall of the Umayyads the poet ibn-Zaydun gained a certain influence in the aristocratic republic of Cordova. A love affair with the poetess al-Walladah, of Umayyad blood, involved him in a literary feud with a rival, ibn-'Abdus, the chief minister of the city governor ibn-Jahwar. Although a letter replete with historical allusions, addressed to his rival whom he laid open to public laughter, did indeed bring him great fame, it also cost him the loss of his freedom, since his adversary put him under suspicion of being an Umayyad partisan. After managing to escape from the prison he had to avoid his native city for a long time and could only return after the death of ibn-Jahwar. The latter's son took him into his service, and as his ambassador ibn-Zaydun acquired an intimate knowledge of all the minor courts. As a result, falling into disfavor again in Cordova, he was given a hospitable reception in Seville by the 'Abbadid ruler Mu'tadid; he also maintained his position with the latter's son Mu'tamid, to whom he was of great service during the conquest of Cordova. Like Hariri's maqamahs in the east a half century later, his witty but basically trivial epistles represent a final endeavor of the Arab spirit to find an appropriate form of expression outside conventional poetry. In adroitness of form he was excelled by his rival at Mu'tamid's court, ibn-'Ammar, who had installed himself in the prince's favor when as his father's governor he held court in Silves. When ibn-Zaydun threatened to overshadow him by his services in the conquest of Cordova, he utilized the pretext of a Jewish revolt to have him sent back to Seville to quell it, and there ibn-Zaydun died shortly afterward. Ibn-'Ammar eventually allowed himself to be carried away by his ambition. In Murcia, which he had subjugated, he declared himself independent, which cost him his head in 1086. How great was the attraction exercised by Arabic literature on the Berbers, in spite of their tendency to assert their national character, is shown by the story of the rulers of Badajoz, the Aftasids. Their ancestor was one of the Berber mercenaries Mansur had brought into Spain. In 1022 one of his descendants succeeded the prince he had served as wazir, and then, according to the custom of the age, claimed an Arab genealogy for himself; his son al-Muzaffar, who succeeded him in 1045, turned aside from politics, after yielding to Ferdinand I without opposition, to seek literary fame as the writer of an entertaining book. The poet ibn-'Abdun was court secretary to his son 'Umar al-Mutawakkil, who after his brother Yahya's death in 1081 re-established his control of the ancestral domain until he lost it to the Almoravids in 1094. Ibn-'Abdun's elegy on the fall of this house, rich in historical allusions to the similar fate of other dynasties since Darius, has given the Aftasids in Arabic literature a fame entirely undeserved.

All these poets, and the endless multitude of their colleagues who generally had to be satisfied with much more meager rewards, clung tenaciously to the classic forms of poetry and its language, which had long since lost any trace of life. But the influence of the new converts of Spanish descent was nevertheless so great as to have an effect on literature also. At the court of the Umayyad 'Abdallah

(888-912) the blind poet al-Muqaddam al-Qabri had dared break through the monotonous qasidah form by dividing it up into stanzas; since in this he used the colloquial language, permeated by Spanish elements, it may be assumed he also imitated indigenous models in the stanza form. The success of this innovation was so great that even a *littérateur* like ibn-'Abd-Rabbihi, who was hailed as the first great poet of the west and who in his *Necklace* composed a work of entertainment entirely tied to the severest canons of the eastern tradition, and the first great poet of Spain, ar-Ramadi, who lived through the fall of the Umayyads and as a pupil of the great philologist al-Qali had a mastery of all the niceties of the Arabic classics, both devoted themselves eagerly to this popular artistic exercise. A second poetic form, originally native to Spain, the genre of the *zajal*, which was no longer controlled by quantity but by accent, was then introduced into literature by ibn-Quzman, who is said to have served in his youth the last Aftasid of Badajoz. His country's unhappy state, soon to be discussed, denied him external successes such as those previously offered by the small princely courts. A minstrel who had to make his art more attractive through that of a monkey, he wandered around the country as a mendicant poet until in his old age he landed in the service of a mosque in Cordova. He had to adapt himself to the baser instincts of his audience by a homosexual eroticism. So ended an art which had once come to great blossoming in Spain. Even under the 'Abbasids love poetry, which in early Arab times had been bound down to conventional forms, had blossomed forth. While the harem hampered association with free women, life with its slave girls, singing girls, and courtesans offered an opportunity all the greater for the cultivation of sentiment. Even pious theologians were not ashamed of such emotions, going so far as to work them into a kind of system. In Baghdad, Da'ud ibn-'Ali (*d.* 884) had founded a new doctrinal scheme, which rejected all speculation even more rigorously than the Hanbalites and recognized the validity only of the pure literal sense of the Qur'anic text and of tradition, in consequence of which his pupils were called Zahirites (literalists) in contrast to the Batinites. His son Muhammad, who succeeded his father as head of the school when barely sixteen years old, in his youth composed a poetic anthology whose first part, the only one now extant, is dedicated to love, with an analysis of its expression in poetry. A Spaniard ibn-Hazm, of the same school, in his youth also wrote a work which offers a detailed investigation of all amorous desires and their concomitant phenomena, illustrated by poetical passages, for the most part from his own pen.* Here we find fully developed all those themes which later became current in the Occident in the poetry of the Provençal troubadours and the German Minnesingers; a Spanish influence on their art remains very probable, even though it will no doubt never be possible to trace the channels through which it was transmitted, via the north of the Iberian peninsula, since our knowledge of the civilization of the north in those days is too restricted.

Scientific research developed even more freely in Spain than poetry; unlike the latter, it did not depend so greatly on princely favor and was scarcely hampered by the constantly weakening authorities. One of its most brilliant representatives is ibn-Hazm, just mentioned. Born in Cordova in 994, the great-grandson of a Spanish convert to Islam of Gothic or Celto-Iberian descent and the son of a wazir of the hajib al-Mansur, he passed his youth on the estate of his family at Manta Lisham in the Niebla district, devoted, besides his scientific training, to the pursuit of love and of love poetry. The fall of the Amirids (Mansur's house) put an abrupt end to the splendor of his family. At first the civil war, which ruined its fortunes, drove him to Almeria, but after Sulayman's fall he became suspect of Umayyad machinations and was exiled after several months under arrest. In Valencia he served the Umayyad ʻAbd-ar-Rahman IV, who for a short time maintained his caliphate there. In 1018 he was able to return to his native city, and there, around the turn of the years 1023-24, for seven happy weeks he once again served an Umayyad, ʻAbd-ar-Rahman V, as wazir. In 1027 we find him in Jativa, where he ended his youth with the composition of his above-mentioned treatise on love. Soon afterward he began his great religious-historical work, the first of its kind in world literature: *The Decision on the Religions, Heterodoxies, and Sects,* in which he subjected not only the various tendencies of Islam but also Judaism and Christianity to acute analysis. Though in the beginning he had joined the Shafiʻites, who in Cordova were patronized by ʻAbd-ar-Rahman III as a bulwark against the ambition of the Malikite fuqaha, he now turned to the Zahirites, the implacable champions of the foundations of primitive Islam; in concert with them he took the field against all Ashʻarite dogmatism as well as against mysticism, saint cults, and superstition. We have no precise

*[*The Ring of the Dove,* tr. A. R. Nykl, Paris, 1931.]

information about what he did during the second half of his life, in which he wrote a great number of other historical and theological works. In the chaos of the epoch he was unable to gather a school around himself. In the decade 1038-1048 he found refuge with the governor of the island of Majorca, from which a fanatical Malikite drove him out as the result of a dispute. He was able to live out the evening of his life, at any rate, on his ancestral estate, where he died in 1064. While he had been unable to win any support for his doctrine, nevertheless it had provocative and stimulating effects as against the petrifaction of religious life in Spain.

Among the Greek sciences medicine was regarded most highly at the princely courts of Spain, as in the east. Abu-l-Qasim az-Zahrawi (Abulcasis of the Latins)—from az-Zahra, the caliph's suburb of Cordova—who died around 1023, wrote an account of the whole range of medicine; posterity regarded with particular esteem the section on surgery, with its detailed description of instruments, which was translated into Latin in the fifteenth century and spread in numerous printings.

In this cultural life the Jews also took a lively part. They had been widely scattered among the Visigoths throughout the peninsula and had served the Christian princes as financial officials. In the same way 'Abd-ar-Rahman III made his Jewish physician, Hasdai ibn-Shaprut, his financial minister. Under the Berber prince Habbus who around 1024 assumed the rule of Granada given up by his uncle Zawi ibn-Ziri, and ruled until 1038, a Jew, Samuel Naghdalah, even filled the office of wazir. Accordingly, the Jewish community, very numerous here since ancient times, bestowed on him for their part the Jewish princely title of Nagid. It is true that the work by which he sought literary fame was concerned exclusively with the field of Jewish lore, which in Spain at that time devoted particular attention to language study after the example of the Arabs. Solomon ibn-Gabirol, for a time patronized by Samuel, owes his fame among Jews to his Hebrew poems, which show clearly the influence of Arabic poetry. But he also made a deep study of the philosophy of ibn-Masarrah, giving an account of it in his book *The Source of Life*, which in the Latin translation by the baptized Jew, John Hispalensis of Toledo, also made his name, generally distorted into Avicebrol or Avicebron, famous among Occidental scholastics. To be sure, there was no lack of setbacks for the Jews in Spain. The revolt which broke out against them in Seville, and which the poet

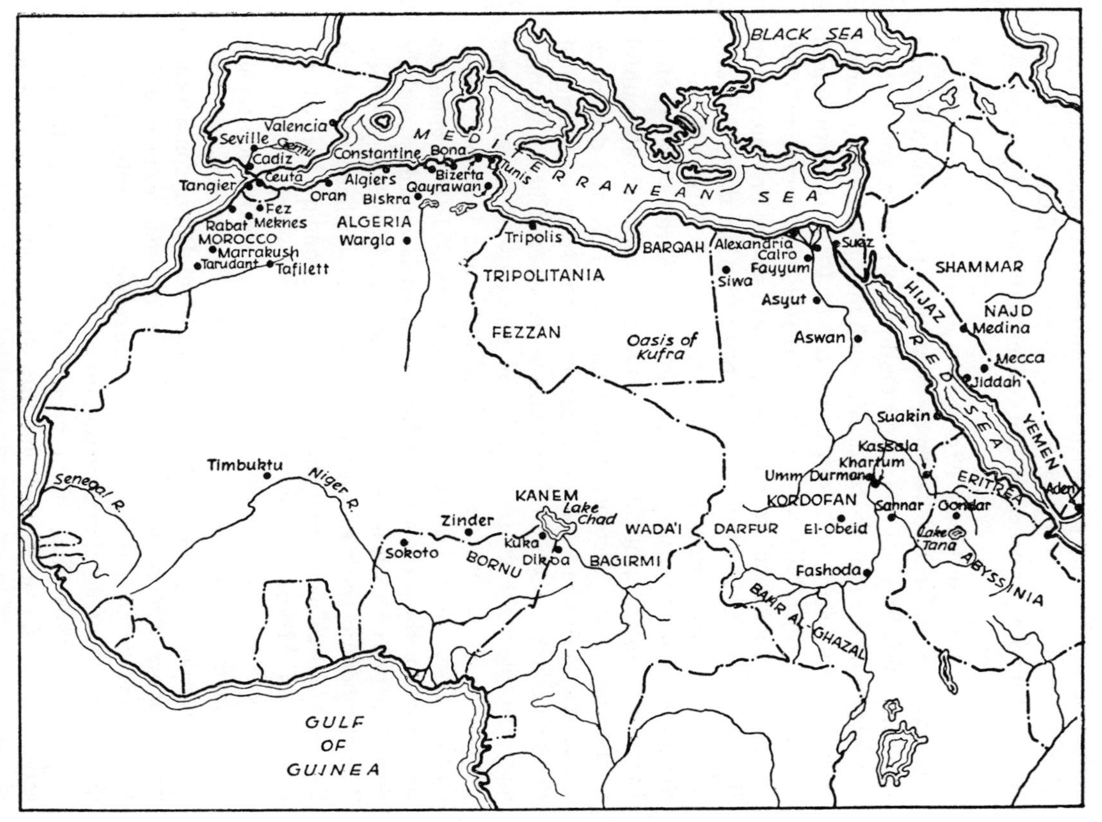
BLACK SEA
MEDITERRANEAN SEA
Valencia
Seville
Cadiz
Ceuta
Tangier
Constantine
Bona
Bizerta
Tunis
Algiers
Oran
Biskra
Qayrawan
Fez
Meknes
Rabat
MOROCCO
Marrakush
Tarudant
Tafilett
ALGERIA
Wargla
Tripolis
TRIPOLITANIA
FEZZAN
Oasis of Kufra
BARQAH
Alexandria
Cairo
Fayyum
Siwa
Asyut
Aswan
Suez
SHAMMAR
HIJAZ
NAJD
Medina
Mecca
Jiddah
RED SEA
YEMEN
Aden
Suakin
Kassala
Khartum
Umm Durman
ERITREA
KORDOFAN
Sannar
Gondar
El-Obeid
DARFUR
Lake Tana
ABYSSINIA
Fashoda
BAHR AL GHAZAL
Timbuktu
Niger R.
Senegal R.
KANEM
Lake Chad
WADA'I
Zinder
Kuka
Sokoto
BORNU
Dikoa
BAGIRMI
GULF OF GUINEA

ibn-Zaydun was supposed to quell, has already been mentioned. Under the Almoravids their position became so difficult that the father of the famous physician and philosopher Maimonides left Cordova around 1150, going first to Africa and then to Palestine; the son found a permanent abode for his activities in Egypt.

Meanwhile in northwest Africa, whose various petty states had hitherto been influenced partly by Spain and partly by Algeria, a movement was brewing which was destined to rule the entire western section of the Islamic world. Although in appearance the Berber tribes of the Sahara had been converted to Islam from the ninth century on, their religious training was still on a very low level. In the Bargwata tribe we even meet, as late as the first quarter of the second century of the Hijrah, in place of Allah the god Bakah, known to us from Roman inscriptions in North Africa. Down to the present day tribes may be found in North Africa which profess Islam only in name, but in reality have remained entirely faithful to the religion and customs of their forebears. It is true that every world religion had to make concessions to the religious feelings of the new converts; even in Egypt and Syria, where Christianity had already broken the ground for Islam, remnants of ancient pagan popular belief survived in the cult of saints and in some holiday customs. The efforts made by new converts in all Islamic countries to wrest for themselves the political and social equality initially denied them by the Arabs were particularly lively in North Africa. The democratic spirit of the Berbers was least inclined to submit to the Arabs. Almost from the beginning, in consequence, we encounter on African soil movements of revolt, which Islamic historians ascribe to the Kharijites; that the latter found such willing ears is an indication of the reaction of the Berber national spirit against the domination of the first-born of Islam. But in consequence any preacher who made an appeal to the national feelings of the Berbers and summoned them to resistance against the ruling powers could also count on abundant support.

In the Lamtuna tribe, of the great Sanhaja group which tented southward as far as Senegal and had subjugated the surrounding Negro peoples, Yahya ibn-Ibrahim al-Jaddali succeeded in elevating himself to the leadership after the old tribal kingdom had collapsed in anarchy. In 1048-49 the chieftain had made the pilgrimage and become convinced of the need for reforming the faith of his people.

On the journey back, at Naffis, in the region later known as Marrakush, he won over the learned theologian 'Abdallah ibn-Yasin al-Juzuli, so that the latter moved on with him to work among his people as a teacher of the pure faith. Since in the beginning at any rate his preaching aroused little response, the master withdrew with a few devoted followers to an island in the Senegal and founded a *ribat*, that is, an outpost for the struggle against the infidels and simultaneously a settlement for exercises in meditation. His attempts at reform were directed not only against abuses in private life but primarily against those in the state, such as, for instance, excessively high taxation. In ten years the number of his followers had already grown to such an extent that he could summon them against the princes on the northern edge of the desert. The military command of his Murabitun, the Almoravides, as the Spaniards called them, was left by ibn-Yasin to the chieftain Yahya, and after the latter's death in 1056 to his brother Abu Bakr and his nephew Yusuf ibn-Tashfin; Zaynab, the widow of the prince of Aghmat after the conquest of his city, became the wife of Abu Bakr and played a decisive role in the reigns of Abu Bakr and Yusuf. In 1059, after ibn-Yasin had died in a battle against the Berber tribe of the Bargwata on the Atlantic coast, who followed a prophet of their own and were considered infidels, the two army heads also took over the government. Since dissension had arisen among the tribal kinsfolk who had remained behind in the south, they fell apart. Abu Bakr returned to the Sahara to restore peace; his nephew, to whom he relinquished his wife, continued the conquests in the north. In 1062 he founded a new residence in Marrakush (Morocco), and in 1070 he took Fez, in 1078 Tangier, and in 1080-82 extended his authority as far as the region of Algiers. When Abu Bakr made another attempt to enforce his power in the north also, ibn-Tashfin resolutely set him on the road back into the Sahara; Abu Bakr died there in 1087, and his nephew was now supreme ruler of the Almoravids from the northern coast of Africa down to Senegal.

The Fatimid vassal state in North Africa, already enfeebled by its partition between the Zirids in Tunis and the Hammadids in Algeria, had lost its valuable dominions on the islands of the Mediterranean to the Christians. The unscrupulousness of the Fatimid Mustansir had then further hastened the collapse of these regions. For more than a century there had been settled in Egypt, together with other Arab tribes, the Bedouin groups of the Hilal and Sulaym, especially notorious for their savagery. The caliph al-'Aziz, after heavy fighting, had forced them back from the delta into upper Egypt. Here they got in touch with the Qarmatians and became a menace to the Fatimid caliphate. In order to be rid of them Mustansir sent them to Qayrawan in 1052, to have them seek new headquarters for themselves in North Africa. By this he intended at the same time to punish the Zirid al-Mu'izz ibn-Badis, who had seceded from his authority and even renounced the Shi'ite profession in his territories. The Bedouins devastated the flatlands, so that the Zirid was restricted to his residence at al-Mahdiyah while in the other cities aristocratic republics developed. The formerly flourishing culture of the land was thoroughly destroyed by the intruders, and so they paved the way for the success of the Almoravids.

In Spain meanwhile King Alfonso VI of Castile-Leon had energetically exploited the weaknesses of the petty Islamic states. After the fall of Toledo the 'Abbasid Mu'tamid of Seville saw himself threatened directly; accordingly, in concert with his nearest neighbors, the princes of Badajoz and Granada, he sent an embassy consisting of the qadis of their principal cities to Yusuf ibn-Tashfin with the plea that he send them an army for aid against the Christians. Since Yusuf had just settled accounts with the Hammadids by taking Ceuta, he was prepared for this, merely requesting that he be left Algeciras as a point of support, while otherwise promising to respect the possessions of his allies. Since the emissaries lacked authority for such a concession, he dismissed them without a conclusive answer. Supported by a *fatwa* (opinion) of his fuqaha which declared that the occupation of Algeciras for the struggle against the Christians was admissible even against the wishes of its lawful rulers, he sent a fleet there in 1086, which ar-Radi, the son and governor of Mu'tamid, did not dare resist. Soon afterward Yusuf himself embarked for there and after appropriately developing his point of support advanced against Seville, where Mu'tamid, together with neighboring princes, humbly received him. On the news of his appearance Alfonso had given up the siege of Saragossa and advanced toward him as far as the region around Badajoz. At Zallaqah (Sacralias) on October 23, after Alfonso had rejected the proposal that he submit, a battle took place which ended with a devastating defeat for the Christians. In consequence Alfonso felt constrained to evacuate the region of Valencia and raise the siege of Saragossa. But the fortress of Aledo, between Murcia and Lorca, still served him as a base against Mu'tamid's territories. The Almoravid Yusuf returned to Africa, since his son, whom he had left behind in Ceuta as his deputy, had died. The three thousand Berbers who remained in Spain were unable to keep the Castilians in check. In Valencia the Cid, Rodrigo el Campeador, had established himself as the guardian of King al-Qadir, whom Alfonso had compensated with this city for the loss of his rule in Toledo. The Almoravid accordingly was soon sought out by suitors for his assistance from every part of Spain, but it was not until Mu'tamid decided to appear at his court in person as a suppliant that he determined to embark on a second military expedition to Spain. In the spring of 1090 he landed in Algeciras again and with his army, which was joined by the princes of Malaga, Granada, and Almeria besides Mu'tamid, advanced before the fortress of Aledo, which, however, withstood the first onslaught. It was necessary to make arrangements for a siege, which dragged on into the winter. In the camp outside Aledo, however, the dissensions and petty envies of the Spanish princes, particularly between Mu'tasim of Almeria and Mu'tamid, soon broke out again, and they were unwise enough to summon the Almoravid as arbiter. At the beginning of the winter Alfonso advanced with a strong army to the relief of Aledo. Yusuf abandoned the field to him, since in view of the unreliability of the Spaniards he was afraid of an open battle, and withdrew to Lorca. But Alfonso for his part was also not satisfied with removing his garrison from Aledo back to Castile after letting the fortress, well-nigh destroyed by the constant bombardments, go up in flames. Even during the siege Yusuf had lent a willing ear to the complaints of the qadis against the incompetence and lack of dignity of the petty Spanish princes. The help of legists now enabled him to realize a plan, undoubtedly already fostered for a long time, to seize the entire country. First of all he had the qadis of Granada and Malaga pronounce fatwas in which the princes, because of constant offenses against the commandments of the Qur'an, were declared unworthy of rule; to proceed with thorough certainty, he had this opinion confirmed by the most famous juridical savants of the east, among whom the great theologian Ghazzali did not fail to figure. The odious task of consummating this judgment Yusuf left to his kinsman, Zir ibn-abi-Bakr, while he preferred to return to Africa. The Spaniards were unable to offer any resistance to his Berber troops; the prince of Saragossa alone was able to purchase grace by costly gifts; but after his death in 1110 his son lost the throne at once.

When Yusuf died in 1106 he left his son the mightiest empire hitherto seen in the Islamic west. But the internal organization of his vast domains was worse than loose. His son 'Ali devoted himself entirely to his religious interests. The religious counselors who had contributed so decisively to the very foundation of the empire now gained the upper hand completely. But their religious life was absorbed in the most rigid legalism and would not tolerate even the slightest tendency toward individual piety. When Ghazzali's book *The Revivification of the Sciences of Religion* became known in Spain, it aroused a storm of indignation instead of self-analysis. The qadi of Cordova had 'Ali presented with a fatwa countersigned by his colleagues which condemned the restorer of Islamic orthodoxy as a heretic. The book was publicly burned in Cordova, and its readers were subject to the death penalty throughout the kingdom. It was no wonder that the hand of the clergy descended on the non-Muslims with still greater rigor. The Jews of Lucena, accounted the wealthiest in Spain, were only able to purchase freedom of worship by a heavy ransom. Others, like Maimonides's father, preferred to leave the country. The Christian *Musta'ribah* (Mozarabs), who had adopted Arabic everywhere, suffered no less from the fanaticism of the fuqaha. Consequently they may have given a sympathetic reception to the renewed attacks of the Christian princes, to which the Berbers, soon relaxed in the amenities of Spanish civilization, no longer set up any forceful opposition. On December 19, 1118, Alfonso I of Aragon succeeded in conquering Saragossa, the northern outpost of Islam which had so long been contended for. In 1125 he pushed on farther southward, and though he failed to attain Granada, his goal, he inflicted a bloody defeat on the Muslims at Arnisol near the Jewish city of Lucena. The most famous qadi of his time, ibn-Rushd, the grandfather of the famous philosopher, now ordered in a fatwa the deportation of the Christians, allegedly responsible for this defeat, to Morocco, where they were settled in Sale and Meknes. But in the Muslim cities, too, the dissatisfaction with the Almoravid regime soon became very great, since the Berber troops raged with no less savagery than the mercenaries of the petty princes before them and crippled commerce and trade.

However, a new ferment soon arose among the Berber tribes of

North Africa.* Theological dissension allowed a very dangerous adversary to emerge in opposition to the rule of the Almoravids. Throughout the Maghrib, in addition to the legal system of Malik, which since the emancipation from the yoke of the Fatimids in 1049 had regained its authority in Ifriqiyah also, there had prevailed with respect to dogmatic questions that rigid orthodoxy which ordained the interpretation of all anthropomorphisms in the Qur'an in a strictly literal sense and condemned any discussion thereof as heresy. Its representatives regarded as science only the hairsplitting casuistry based on the recognized textbooks. The rationalist doctrine of the Mu'tazilites had succumbed to this orthodoxy, as we have seen, even in the center of the Islamic world where for a time it had even enjoyed the protection of the government. In Baghdad, however, at the beginning of the tenth century, Abu-l-Hasan 'Ali al-Ash'ari (*d.* 935), having professed the Mu'tazilite doctrines up to the age of forty, then turned to orthodoxy and undertook to transform the latter dialectically and provide it with a scientific foundation. For a long time his pupils had to struggle for recognition of his method. Even in the first years of Alp Arslan's regime this method had been execrated from the pulpits as heretical. But the great Seljuq wazir Nizam-al-Mulk lent it his support, summoning the Ash'arites al-Juwayni ("Imam al-Haramayn") and al-Qushayri to the college founded by him in Baghdad; and in spite of the opposition of the reactionary Hanbalites, which still broke out on occasion in street rioting, al-Ash'ari's doctrine then finally prevailed in the east. His work was perfected by Ghazzali, who made the return to the Qur'an and the Sunnah the guiding line of his theology, but also acknowledged, in addition to the dogma, the rights of a moderate mysticism.

Around 1107 the Berber Muhammad ibn-Tumart of the tribe of the Masmuda, a native of Sus in the southwest of present-day Morocco, after a short stay in Cordova—where he had lived through the burning of Ghazzali's writings but had been aroused to further reflection by the works of ibn-Hazm—went to Baghdad to complete his theological studies at the source. There he had become acquainted with al-Ash'ari's teachings, which he espoused at once with the tenacity characteristic of his people. Upon returning home, he opened the battle against the anthropomorphic conceptions of

* R. Millet, *Les Almohades, Histoire d'une dynastie berbère*, Paris, 1923.

the theology dominant there; in contrast he laid major emphasis on the profession of unity, the *tawhid*, which gained his followers the name of Muwahhidun, whence the Spanish Almohades. In the sphere of practical theology he emphasized the unique value of the tradition as the norm of life, whereas among the Almoravids the juridical deductions of the fuqaha had been most highly esteemed. To give greater authority to his struggle against the abuses prevalent, he gave himself out as the Mahdi who was expected to fill the world with righteousness. Like the Almoravids before him, he militated against exactions not founded on the tradition of early Islam, which shows that the Almoravids had not lived up to their sermons in this respect.

After preaching to deaf ears in various large cities, including Marrakush, and being rejected everywhere because of his violent manner, he went to his tribe in the Atlas and successfully preached his doctrines to it. In Tin Malal, near the source of the Nafis River, he built a mosque and so laid the foundation for the first capital of the Almohads. As mahdi and imam he summoned to his side a council of his ten oldest disciples, to which was later added another council of fifty representatives of the various Berber tribes. He flattered the national consciousness of the Berbers by introducing the call to prayers in the Berber tongue. Since in the eyes of his community all other human beings were regarded as infidels, he was soon able to launch an attack against the regime of the Almoravids. The governor of Sus was the first to fall; in 1130 Marrakush was still holding out. Four months later ibn-Tumart died. His most faithful follower, 'Abd-al-Mu'min ibn-'Ali, who even during the Mahdi's lifetime had been his military deputy, carried on his work as his khalifah. Since he was an alien, the Council of Ten apparently concealed the Mahdi's death for another two years before proclaiming 'Abd-al-Mu'min as his successor. In the next ten years he defeated one Almoravid army after the other. Their power was declining steadily. In 1122, in alliance with the Zirid Hasan, they had attacked the Normans on Sicily; the latter revenged themselves by expelling the Zirid from his capital at al-Mahdiyah in 1148-49 and occupying the entire coast from Sus to Tripoli for a time. In Spain, too, the Christians were making more and more menacing advances.

The feeble Almoravid prince 'Ali died in 1143. His son Tashfin consumed himself in vain attempts to repel the forward movement of the Almohads. After being besieged in Tlemsen for a year, he fled along the coast to Oran in the hope of being able to escape from there to Spain with the fleet he had ordered up from Almeria. But before he reached his ships he fell off a cliff along the beach with his horse and was killed (1145 or 1146) while fleeing from the Almohad troops which had already occupied the city.

In Spain, after the collapse of the Almoravid power, a series of petty rulers had arisen once again, who were naturally unable to offer any further resistance to the Christians. In 1147 Alfonso I of Portugal was able to wrest decisively from the Muslims the capital of his domains, Lisbon, which had already been occupied once by the Christians at the beginning of the Almoravid regime but was later reconquered by Zir ibn-abi-Bakr in 1110. Alfonso VII of Castile pressed forward as far as Cordova the following year; but here the Almohads came up against him so that he had to leave the matter unfinished and withdraw. In 1149 the Caliph had smothered the last opposition to his rule in North Africa in a monstrous blood bath among the Berbers, and he could now proceed against foreign foes with greater energy. First he sent to Spain his general Barras, who in a bitter contest forced back the followers of the Almoravids as far as the Balearics. The Caliph himself freed the North African coast from the rule of the Sicilian Normans; he was already preparing after the conclusion of this campaign for a voyage to Spain when he was overtaken by death in 1163.

Under his son Abu Ya'qub Yusuf (1163-1184) and his grandson Ya'qub al-Mansur (1184-1199) the Almohads stood at the zenith of their power. Yusuf completed the pacification of Muslim Spain but was then killed during the siege of Santarem in a battle against Prince Sancho of Portugal. After his father had broken the moral control of the fanatical Malikites, he himself ventured to turn his favor to the representatives of hitherto proscribed philosophy. The two most important philosophers of western Islam, ibn-Tufayl and ibn-Rushd (Averroes), came to his court from Spain. Ibn-Tufayl of Guadix near Granada had at first settled down in Granada as a physician and then served the deputy of the Almohad regime as secretary; in 1154, on the recommendation of his chief, he went in the same capacity to a son of 'Abd-al-Mu'min who had his residence in Ceuta and Tangier as governor. Yusuf then summoned him to his court as his court physician. He owes his fame to the first philosophical romance which Arabic literature can show. Ibn-Sina

(Avicenna) had already produced a mystical allegory under the title *Hayy ibn-Yaqzan* ("Alive, Son of Awake"). Its hero was borrowed by ibn-Tufayl for his epistemological fantasy. The author has Hayy grow up on an uninhabited island as an orphan and in intercourse with nature arrive at the axiomatic foundations of civilization and the knowledge of the world and of God. Only in old age, when already in possession of his perfected *Weltanschauung*, does he become acquainted, through Absal, the wazir of King Salaman, the ruler of a neighboring island, with revealed religion, and both recognize the identity of their basic principles. But the king, to whom Hayy is presented by his friend, is incapable of elevating himself to the level of their beliefs; consequently they return to the lonely island to devote the rest of their lives to pious meditation, leaving the king and his people to the worship of symbols. That is too primitive a stage for the heroes of the story. The work, which two hundred years later was translated into Hebrew and then passed into almost all civilized languages through the medium of Latin,* is eloquent testimony to the freedom with which the reconciliation of mysticism and philosophy could be striven for under the Almohads. Ibn-Tufayl might have expected a continuation of his work by young ibn-Rushd, the grandson of a famous qadi of Cordova; ibn-Tufayl introduced ibn-Rushd himself at the court in Marrakush and in 1182 recommended him to be his successor for the office of court physician. But since ibn-Rushd had been for twelve years in the office of his grandfather and his father as the judge of Cordova, the Caliph released him. His principal accomplishments were his commentaries on the works of Aristotle, for which the Caliph himself had given the impetus. It was through them that Hellenistic philosophy was really opened up to the Occident in the Latin adaptation begun by Michael Scotus as early as 1230. In his own writings he sought to reconcile Muslim dogma with the results of philosophy. His position on the questions of the eternity of the world (which he defended as against a creation *ex nihilo*) and of knowledge of God called forth the opposition of the Spanish fuqaha, just as in the thirteenth century it compelled the Christian church to proscribe his doctrine. In the beginning Yusuf's successor Ya'qub, like his father, had held a protecting hand over him; but since the Caliph could not dispense with the support of

* *The History of Hayy ibn Yaqzan*, tr. by Simon Ockley (1708), revised ed. by A. S. Fulton, London, 1929.

the Spanish fuqaha for the struggle against the Christians, on whom he had to avenge the death of his father, he finally gave in to their insistence, banished the philosopher—who had to submit to a painful hearing—to Lucena, near Cordova, and had his books burned, with the exception of the medical, mathematical, and astronomical works. Soon afterward, on July 19, 1195, the Caliph won at Alarcos a brilliant victory over Alfonso VIII of Castile, though he was unable to exploit it since a revolt soon called him back to Africa. After restoring order there he lifted the judgment against the philosopher and summoned him to his court in Marrakush; but ibn-Rushd soon died, on December 10, 1198, and the next year the Caliph followed him.

The vast empire of the Almohads, which, like no other Muslim state before, included all of North Africa to the borders of Egypt, as well as Spain, very soon fell into decline under the feeble successors of its founders. At the very inception of his reign Ya'qub's son Muhammad an-Nasir had to suppress insurrections against it. Just after finishing off the revolt of the Ghumarah Berber tribe in the Atlas, he had to move off to the east of his domain to repress the rebellion of Yahya ibn-Ghaniyah in Ifriqiyah. After reconquering al-Mahdiyah, the residence of the Aghlabids, in January 1206, he left behind as his governor in the east 'Abd-al-Wahid ibn-abi-Hafs al-Hintati, the son of the Abu Hafs who had already been of such value to the founder of the empire, and whose descendants, the Hafsids, had made themselves independent later on in Tunis. An-Nasir also terminated the last remnant of Almoravid rule. On the Balearics the banu Ghaniyah dynasty had made itself independent after losing Spain. In 1207 an-Nasir dispatched against them a fleet from Algiers which succeeded in conquering Majorca for him. But he was unable to oppose any permanent resistance to the advances of the Christians. On July 16, 1212, Alfonso VIII of Castile had launched an attack on Muslim territory and inflicted at Hisn al-'Uqab, or Navas de Tolosa, an annihilating defeat on the Almohad ruler, in spite of the great superiority of the Muslim army. An-Nasir hurried back to Fez and soon afterward delegated the regime, hitherto controlled principally by his incompetent wazir ibn-Jami', entirely to his son Yusuf; he died at Rabat on December 25, 1213.

During his ten-year reign Yusuf al-Mustansir was completely under the thumb of his wazir, whose power was limited only by the Almohad aristocracy. Muhammad, the Hafsid governor in

Tunis, had sworn allegiance to Yusuf only with reluctance, and a general uprising broke out when the wazir ibn-Jami', after the Caliph's death, set 'Abd-al-Wahid, a brother of Ya'qub al-Mansur, on the throne. At Murcia in Spain a nephew of 'Abd-al-Wahid, 'Abdallah, took the oath of allegiance as caliph with the throne name of al-'Adil. At this the Moroccan shaykhs deposed 'Abd-al-Wahid and banished the wazir. But in Spain al-'Adil was confronted by a rival caliph, the governor of Bayyasah (Baeza), Abu Muhammad, claiming to be a descendant first of 'Abd-al-Mu'min, then of Hafs. King Ferdinand III heeded his call for help with joy, since Baeza itself was ceded to him. In 1225 al-'Adil was defeated and went to Africa, leaving the struggle against the rebels and the Christians to his brother Abu-l-'Ula. But in Morocco the shaykhs refused to pledge allegiance to him and elevated his nephew Yahya al-Mu'tasim to the throne. In the battle against the latter's followers al-'Adil was killed, and his brother al-Ma'mun emerged in Spain as the pretender to the throne. By further territorial concessions he purchased the assistance of Ferdinand in setting up his rule in Morocco. Having expelled Yahya, and considering all resistance broken after a blood bath among the shaykhs, he sought to secure his power by the extirpation of the Almohad doctrines professed by the nobility, and by a return to the Malikite system. This gave the Hafsid in Tunis, Abu Zakariya, the desired pretext for refusing him allegiance. Nor did his son 'Abd-al-Wahid II ar-Rashid gain anything when in 1232 at his accession to the throne he reverted to the Almohad creed. Abu Zakariya had no intention of relinquishing his independence, and his example was followed generally. Although in Tlemsen the Berber Yaghmurasan ibn-'Abd-al-Wad of the Zayan tribe acted in 1236 as ar-Rashid's governor, in reality he ruled absolutely independently, as did his descendants until 1393. But the final collapse of the Almohads was brought about by Berbers of the banu Marin of the Zenata group, who after the general defeat of their compatriots in 1145 had escaped subjugation by fleeing into the Sahara. By 1216 they had conducted a devastating raid through central Morocco out of the Muluyah valley. They first gained a permanent foothold in the territory of an Arab tribe, the banu Riyah. Although the troops of ar-Rashid's successor as-Sa'id succeeded in beating them back in 1244, under as-Sa'id's successors they resumed their advance. Their emir Abu Yahya ibn-'Abd-al-Haqq ostensibly opposed the Almohads in the service of the Hafsid. The prestige of the local Moroccan saints, always deeply venerated by the people, was spared by him, and he turned their influence to his own use. He provided for his kinfolk by rich appanages. He multiplied his combat forces by recruiting foreign mercenaries, and was able to wrest the important cities of Fez and Meknes, as well as Sale and Rabat on the coast, from the Almohads. In 1269, when a contest for the throne arose again in Marrakush, Abu Yahya's successor Abu Yusuf seized the capital; the last descendants of the Almohad dynasty were destroyed in the Atlas in 1275 by one of his governors.

In Spain, after the withdrawal of the Almohads, Muhammad ibn-Yusuf ibn-Hud, whose forebears had reigned in Saragossa, emerged in Murcia as champion against the Christians, and gradually united the most important cities of the country under his rule by exploiting the weakness of his Christian neighbors. In 1230, however, Leon was reunited with Castile after the death of King Alfonso, whereupon the Christians resumed the attack, defeating ibn-Hud at Xeres in 1231. An Arab pretender exploited his defeat at once in an attempt to gain power at his expense. Arjona, north of Jaen, was the headquarters of a descendant of the Khazraji chieftain at the time of the prophet Muhammad, ibn-Yusuf ibn-Ahmad ibn-Nasr, whose clan was called Banu-l-Ahmar. Directly in 1231 he declared himself ruler of Andalusia, and was able to establish himself in Jaen, Guadix, and Baza. In 1235 he seized Granada, which from then on remained the capital of his dynasty, the Nasrids. As a result of the strife among the Muslims, Cordova, the old capital of Muslim Spain, fell into the hands of the Christians on June 29, 1236. Two years later ibn-Hud, after losing another battle to the Christians, met his end at the hand of an assassin. To secure himself against his rivals for power, the Nasrid placed himself under the protection of Ferdinand I of Castile (1217-1252) as his vassal, in return for a heavy tribute, and in 1248 had to give him military aid against Seville. His successor Muhammad II (1273-1302) attempted to escape his feudal obligations by joining the Marinids in Morocco. In return for the cession of Algeciras and Tarifa, Abu Yusuf, like the Almohads and Almoravids before him, was prepared to intervene in Spain. The Marinid undertook the journey across the sea on four occasions. Though his troops injured the Christians in recurrent raids, they were unable to bring about any permanent shift in power. Since the Berber soldiers, a division of whom the Nasrids placed on their pay lists, soon became just as much of a burden to the country as before, Muhammad sought protection against his Marinid associate with Alfonso X of Castile, and even Yaghmurasan of Tlemsen offered to disrupt his neighbor's expeditions to Spain. Abu Ya'qub's second successor, Abu-l-Hasan, therefore definitely abandoned the Spanish policy of his predecessors, and so the Nasrids were able, by means of an adroit policy of constant shifting, to survive another two hundred and fifty years as the last Muslim dynasty of Spain in the narrow region along the Gibraltar coast as far as Almeria and in the interior as far as the mountain chains of the Serrania de Ronda and the Sierra de Elvira.

Even in this last of its refuges the civilization of Muslim Spain was granted a period of great brilliance. Two great thinkers whom Spanish Islam then produced ended their lives in the east. The mystic ibn-'Arabi,* born in Murcia on July 28, 1165, pursued theological and juridical studies in Seville from 1173-1202, then went on the pilgrimage to Mecca, from which he was not to return home. After far-flung travels, which led him as far as Asia Minor, he settled in Damascus, where he died in October 1240. In his homeland he had moved in the intellectual orbit of ibn-Masarrah's school. In Mecca he came under the influence of the pantheistic doctrines of the Qarmatians. In his enormously prolific writings, which culminated in the seventeen books of his *Meccan Revelations*, written between 1201 and 1231, and the quintessence of which he expressed in the *Seal of Wisdom*, he helped secure a decisive victory for this type of mystical doctrine over the older Sufi strivings for asceticism and purification. The thought of his countryman ibn-Sab'in, to whom a very shallow compilation of answers to philosophical questions reputedly asked by Frederick II of Sicily is ascribed, ran a similar course; on the pilgrimage to Mecca in 1270 he drew the logical conclusion of these pantheistic doctrines with a consistency unique in Islam and sought to unite his soul with God through suicide.

This small principality of the Nasrids can also boast of a great historian, whose life of ups and downs gives a characteristic illustration of the political life of this dwarf state in the fourteenth century. Muhammad ibn-al-Khatib as-Salmani Lisan-ad-Din, born in 1313, was the son of a court functionary under the Nasrid Yusuf (1333-1354), and after his father's death in the battle of Tarifa in

* [A. E. Affifi, *The Mystical Philosophy of . . . Arabi*, London, 1939.]

1341 entered the service of the wazir ibn-al-Jayyab as his secretary. In 1349, when the Black Death afflicted southern Europe and the Mediterranean countries, his superior also succumbed to it, whereupon ibn-al-Khatib was appointed wazir. He also retained the favor of the Sultan's son and heir during his first short reign (1354-1359). Since the new sultan was still a minor, General Ridwan acted as his guardian. This aroused the jealousy of Abu Sa'id, another general, who while the young prince was in the country seized the Granada fortress, the Alhambra, and proclaimed Isma'il, a brother of the prince, sultan, having put the wazir ibn-al-Khatib in jail. These disturbances gave the Marinid Abu Salim, who had only just ascended the Moroccan throne himself, the desired opportunity for interference. He secured free passage for the dethroned Muhammad V out of Guadix, where he had been holding out, and set free his wazir, who followed his master into exile in Morocco. While the Wazir devoted himself to scholarly labors in the coastal city of Sale, the Sultan worked toward restoration. In this, ibn-Khaldun, the supreme qadi of Morocco, who later also achieved great fame as a historian, was extremely valuable to him. Ibn-Khaldun had been born in Tunis in 1332, and had followed the Marinid Abu-l-Hasan, who conquered Tunis in 1347, to Morocco. He persuaded his master to confer the fortress of Ronda in Spain, still held by the Moroccans, upon the Nasrid, and from there Muhammad V succeeded in reconquering his capital of Granada. He was followed there at once by ibn-al-Khatib, who as wazir very soon gained unlimited influence in the government. In 1361 ibn-Khaldun also settled down there when he had to leave Morocco after the assassination of his patron, Abu Salim. For two years the two great scholars lived in Granada in intimate friendship, which did not, however, permanently withstand the inevitable rivalry between them. As ambassador of the Nasrids to Pedro the Cruel of Castile, ibn-Khaldun gained such confidence that Pedro even offered him the restitution of all the former estates of his family in Seville if he would enter his service. But he was wise enough to remain true to his own society, and when ibn-al-Khatib's envy became too obvious, preferred withdrawing to Africa to enter the service of the Hafsid reigning in Bijaya (Bougie). But ibn-al-Khatib's power was also on the decline. Since he made use of it for unscrupulous personal aggrandizement, as was the general custom of the time, his prince's suspicion was soon thrown on him by his detractors. He tried to escape his downfall by fleeing to Ceuta in 1371, making an inspection tour of the fortifications of Gibraltar a pretext. In Morocco he was received by the Marinid 'Abd-al-'Aziz (1366-1372) with open arms, having already assured himself of his favor at the time of his accession to the throne by neutralizing his uncle and rivals for the throne who were in Granada. The qadi raised an accusation of heresy against him on the basis of his writings, and secured a death sentence against him; but the Marinid refused to deliver him to his foes. However, he lost this patron of his through death only a year later, and in the inevitable struggle for the throne the pretender Abu-l-'Abbas al-Mustansir purchased the support of the Nasrid by promising to extradite the former wazir. Ibn-al-Khatib's successor as wazir, his disciple Muhammad ibn-Zumruk, well known as a poet, appeared in Fez to conduct the trial against him, but before the hearings began ibn-al-Khatib was murdered in prison in an act of private vengeance. His old rival ibn-Khaldun met a happier fate. In the ups and downs of politics among the rulers of North Africa he always succeeded, by leaving a sinking ship at the appropriate moment, in retaining an influential position. In 1378, while at peace in the fortress of the Arab princeling ibn-Salamah at Taughzut, he began his world history, and four years later in Tunis, whose libraries attracted him, his history of the Berbers. From there, when his position grew too precarious, he started out on a pilgrimage to Mecca, but stayed over in Cairo, where the Mamluk sultan Barquq gave him first a professorship, then the office of Malikite supreme qadi. In this capacity he was able to maintain himself against all intrigues. In 1401 he went along on the Mamluk campaign against the Mongols under Timur, who were threatening the Mamluk empire, and negotiated with the great khan the conditions for the surrender of Damascus. On March 17, 1406, death brought to an end a life which, though full of abrupt reversals, was buoyed up again and again by the benevolence of fortune.

The rivals also present acute contradictions in their literary activity. Ibn-al-Khatib is the type of the educated *littérateur* of those days, with all his weaknesses. One might almost think style meant everything to him; he demonstrated this not only in a collection of model letters but in his great historical works also, where he would sacrifice the authenticity of account to rhetorics. Historical context hardly meant anything to him; in his great history of Granada, and in his city chronicles of the east, his interest lay in the personal, where the fortunes of the colleagues of his own class, the literary people, were generally more important than their environment. In contrast, ibn-Khaldun never found leisure in his wildly agitated life to devote any particular attention to his style. He was fascinated by the fate of nations. His history of the Berbers is unique in Arabic literature as an attempt to portray the life of an entire people in all of its manifestations, on the basis of personal observation and a painstaking study of sources. But in particular he owes his fame to his *Prolegomena* with which he opens his world history. Whereas the latter never rises above the level of a chronicle on Tabari's model for Arabic literature, in his prologue—which grew into an independent work—ibn-Khaldun attempted to outline the first philosophy of history. His doctrine of state and society is, to be sure, entirely dominated by the Islamic legal system of the Shari'ah; but nevertheless he incorporated in it many of his own penetrating observations and conclusions, drawn from a turbulent historical epoch which he lived through partially in a position of leadership and always in the midst of the current stream of events. His sound, coolly reflecting judgment on all phases of Islamic science and civilization in his carefully construed and clear account has never been surpassed by any Muslim author.*

Two Maghribis have also left us the most richly colored portraits of the eastern culture of their time, such as no earlier period can display. The Spaniard ibn-Jubayr, born at Valencia in 1145, embarked on a pilgrimage to Mecca in 1183, ostensibly in order to purify himself from the sin of drinking wine, which, as secretary of the governor of Granada, he had been unable to avoid in the latter's company. He traveled by sea from Tarifa to Alexandria, and from there by way of Cairo and the Red Sea to Mecca. After visiting the holy places he turned back by way of 'Iraq, Mosul, Aleppo, and Damascus to Acre, where he took ship for Sicily. He had the good fortune to become acquainted with the Orient under the secure regime of Saladin, while it was still in an era of efflorescence, and related what he saw of it in a skillful style which was, nevertheless, free from the vagaries of the professional without belying at any point his education as a faqih. With the same love he portrayed the flourishing civilization he found in Sicily under the rule of William the Good, of the Normans, taking delight in stressing again and again that it was still predominantly Islamic. He ar-

* [N. Schmidt, *Ibn Khaldun*, New York, 1930; H. A. R. Gibb in *Bulletin of the School of Oriental Studies*, vol. 7, London, 1933, pp. 23-31. There are French translations by de Slane of the *Prolegomena* (1863-68) and of the history of the Berbers (1852-56).]

rived in Granada by way of Cartagena in 1185, and only four years later nostalgia drew him once again to the Orient, where he spent another two years. When he was seventy-three years old, he ventured on another trip to the east, but death overtook him before he could leave Alexandria. A century later ibn-Battutah, a native of Tangier, embarked on a pilgrimage to Mecca in 1325. The Orient exercised on this traveler, barely twenty-one years old, a still stronger attraction than on his predecessor, of whose work he, or possibly his adapter, made reckless use for the areas covered by both, according to contemporary literary custom. He stayed away not less than twenty-five years, and journeyed through all of Persia, Asia Minor, and Crimea. From there he accompanied a Greek princess, the wife of the sultan Uzbek, on a visit to her parents in Constantinople. From the Volga he set out through central Asia for India, and for two years filled the office of a qadi in Delhi. His attempt to accompany an embassy setting out for China brought him only as far as the Maldives, where he lingered for another year and a half as a judge. After finally succeeding in visiting the Chinese harbor cities of Zaytun (Tseu-Thung) and Canton, he came back to Arabia by way of Sumatra and finally arrived in Fez again in the late autumn of 1349. Three years later he took another trip throughout the Negro countries. Then he settled down in Morocco, where he dictated the accounts of his travels to a writer, leaving to him all stylistic concerns. In cosmopolitan breadth of outlook he can be compared only with his somewhat older contemporary, the Venetian Marco Polo, who also left to a secretary the literary shaping up of his reports. Both works constitute a most fortunate complement to each other for our knowledge of Asia, since the Venetian acquired a much more exact knowledge of the Far East than the Moroccan. The latter, in compensation, had a much more intimate acquaintanceship with the cultural conditions of the world he described. Neither was a learned geographer, but the Muslim's topographical data are more reliable than those of the Christian; only in the description of the "Land of Darkness" did he let himself be misled into copying from a literary source, since in southern Russia he evidently gave up the idea of the long, difficult trip into the land of the Bulgars, who then were still settled on the upper Volga.*

Arts and crafts in the Nasrid kingdom retained high standards

* [Ibn-Battuta, *Travels in Asia and Africa* . . ., tr. and selected by H. A. R. Gibb, 1929, 1939.]

down to the very last, and in particular founded the country's prosperity by the working of metals, which achieved a masterful perfection. The last and most magnificent monument of Muslim architecture in Spain, the Alhambra ("Red Castle"), was a work of the Nasrids. The mountain dominating the city had borne a citadel under the Umayyads, but the construction of this famous palace was first begun by Muhammad, and his descendants in the first half of the fourteenth century vied with each other in the construction of the seat of their realm. The Alhambra is only to a small extent built of stone and tiles; for the most part it is made out of so-called tapia, an artificial stone of earth, lime chalk, and gravel. Its arches, cupolas and ceilings are lightly joined together with boards and billets. Because of the ephemeral quality of the materials, the models of this technique, no doubt originally from Mesopotamia, have not come down to us anywhere. The hill of the fortress is enclosed by a circular outer wall crowned with battlements and dominated by numerous towers. Within the wall the palace lies imbedded in extensive parks. From the latter, two courtyards lead to the inner building. In the south, one comes to the so-called Court of the Myrtles which leads to the mighty Comares tower with the Hall of the Ambassadors in the north. The southeast of the Court of the Myrtles abuts perpendicularly on the Court of the Lions, which leads directly into the rooms of the tribunal; on the right into the Hall of the Abencerages, on the left to the Hall of the Two Sisters. The Court of the Myrtles takes its name from the myrtle goblets which enclose a section for its entire length; the Court of the Lions is named after the lions that bear the spring-well in their midst, in which the narrow watercourses meet on both sides. The panels of the court hall are adorned by paintings representing knightly and hunting scenes as well as ten princes sitting side by side along a long bench. "The floor was covered with squares of white marble; along the lower section of the walls there ran to a height of about four feet a covering of little plates of colored faience (*azulejos*); farther up, the walls were covered with stucco followed by a frieze close to the ceiling and above that, sometimes carried by small half columns, there was the roof which hung down, put together partly with pieces of wood, partly with small tiers and cells worked in stucco. Marble columns of the most elegant shape, and with capitals of an endless variety of form, were carried by consoles or wall strips, on which the roofing rested, and between which the arcade vaults of woodwork covered over by plaster were set. The predominant form of these arches was that of the elevated half circle with only a slight indication of the horseshoe form; but they very often acquired a pointed arch appearance through the stucco spread out over them. Niches of various kinds were set deeply into the walls; larger ones covered with pillows served as rest places; in smaller ones stood water jugs. And over all sections of the palace, over the walls, ceilings, columns, arcades, or niches, there were ornaments strewn about in luxurious variety; the azulejos were formed in the most variegated contortions into arabesques, the marble was chiseled into the most variegated shapes, the stucco was worked in relief in thousands and thousands of winding lines representing kaleidoscopic figures of all kinds—stars and octagons, plants and stone shapes. This was accompanied, moreover, by an astonishing number of inscriptions stretched out along the frieze, which wound around the arches, windows, and niches or were brought together into individual symmetrically placed medallions and treated in the same manner as the other embellishments and often represented mere arabesques to the untrained eye. These inscriptions, unlike other building inscriptions, do not give sober facts but speak to the observer in verses in a panegyric style, or in the languid description characteristic of Spanish poetry. Finally, the impression was heightened to the point of dazzlement through the copious and tasteful painting. The greatest splendors of color were poured out extravagantly over all the rooms of the palace. At the top, because of the stronger effect, there was a predominance of carmine reds, golds, and blues; farther below there were violet, purple, and orange. Even the white marble squares of the floor, according to all appearance, were painted." (Von Schack.)

The endless dissensions in the house of the Nasrids made it easy for Isabella the Catholic to finish them off when she decided in 1479, after the union of the two kingdoms of Castile and Aragon through her marriage with Ferdinand II, to expel the infidels from Spain entirely. Both sons of Abu-l-Hasan, the last emir of Granada—Abu 'Abdallah Muhammad (Boabdil of the Spaniards) and Yusuf—revolted against him. In this struggle, in which at last Boabdil was able to seize Granada, Isabella's spouse Ferdinand took a hand with subtle diplomacy. After he had taken away from the Arabs the smaller cities, sometimes defended with extreme bravery, Granada surrendered to him, following a protracted siege, on January 2, 1492. At first Boabdil was appanaged with a small fief, but later he withdrew to Fez, where he died. The last Muslims in Spain, in so far as they failed to emigrate, were conducted by the Inquisition into the bosom of the one and only saving church without heed to the terms of surrender; but great numbers poured back across the Straits of Gibraltar, fructified the civilization of Morocco, and bore it farther south.

5. *The Near East in the Age of the Crusades and the Rise of the Mamluks in Egypt*

We turned away from the history of the east after the death of the sultan Muhammad, when the empire of the Seljuqs fell into dissolution. Even before this a new power had appeared in Syria which vied with the Turkish emirs and atabegs in the atomization of the former caliphate: the Crusaders. This is not the place to give an account of the significance of the Crusades for Europe. For the Islamic world the Christian knights were merely troublesome competitors of the Turks for power in Syria, and their particularly stubborn concentration on Jerusalem, which Muslims also regarded as holy soil, gave the struggle against them, at least under Saladin, another undertone of religious fanaticism. This is shown principally in the popular writings arising at the time, in which the campaigns of conquest of the Prophet and of his companions are displayed as sublime examples for inspiring the warriors of the faith.

When the first Crusaders, under Godfrey of Bouillon and a number of French and Norman leaders, appeared in Syria, the country was divided among various Seljuq emirs who were at sword's points with each other themselves and had no interest in helping the emir who was to be attacked first, Yaghi Siyan of Antioch. On June 3, 1098, after a lengthy siege, this city, though excellently protected by a mighty girdle of walls stretching out over the surrounding hills, fell through treachery into the hands of storming knights. Meanwhile Jerusalem was occupied by the Egyptians, who, however, relinquished the city to the Franks on July 15, 1099, without serious opposition. From Antioch the Crusaders extended their power into northern Syria; in 1098 Baldwin I had already founded a principality in Edessa. In 1100, when Godfrey of Bouillon, who had been elected king of Jerusalem, died, Baldwin took his place. In 1101 he charged Count Raymond of Toulouse with the conquest of Syrian Tripoli as the seat of a county. But it was not till after a siege of eight years, during which Raymond died in 1105 in the fortress constructed for the encirclement of the city on the mountain opposite Mount

St. Giles, that that city, dominating a fertile countryside, fell into the hands of the Christians, who subsequently held it for a hundred years.

Not until the second quarter of the twelfth century did the position of Islam, now entirely undermined by the contest of the Seljuq princes for hegemony in Syria, find a new support in a dynasty which fought its way to the top, and which for at least some time was able to rally the forces of the Muslims for an energetic fight against the Christians. Mosul had been ruled since 1127 by the Turk 'Imad-ad-Din Zengi, initially as atabeg, i.e. guardian, of the Seljuq princes Alp Arslan and Farrukh Shah. Since he was not only a skillful strategist and diplomat but also an excellent administrator, he was able to extend his sphere of influence more and more; at his death in 1146 it comprised nearly all of Mesopotamia as far as the north, where the Ortoqids still held Mardin, and a large portion of Syria. Zengi was so attentive to his subjects that the population sometimes called on him for help against their own former bloodsuckers. Justice and personal security, which in these areas had long been unknown concepts, were brought into repute by him once again. At his accession to power the main mosque of Mosul had lain in a broad field of ruins; at his death the square surrounding it was densely built up. His great and final work was the reconquest of Edessa (1144), which had been in the hands of the Franks for nearly half a century. It is true that even at the height of his success the insecurity of the foundations of his power was brought home to him by a plot which his ward, the Seljuq prince Alp Arslan, was brewing behind his back. After suppressing this without much difficulty Zengi was murdered by his own slave on September 15, 1146, in the midst of the siege of a castle of the 'Uqaylids (Qal'at Ja'bar) on the left bank of the middle Euphrates.

Zengi's two eldest sons divided his realm beween them; it was in fact difficult to maintain as a unit against its many enemies. The older son, Sayf-ad-Din al-Ghazi, took over Mosul, together with the title of atabeg, and Mesopotamia as far as the Khabur; the younger, Nur-ad-Din Mahmud, took Syria, with Aleppo as residence. The latter inherited his father's virtues of ruler to a heightened degree. While for centuries Muslim rulers almost without exception had looked on their possessions only as vast domains for exploitation, he was the first to feel any responsibility to God for the well-being of his subjects. Almost without any personal needs, he applied the wealthy revenues of the state which he acquired by able administration, and which, however, did not prove an excessive burden on his subjects, not only to the consolidation of his position in a world of enemies—and this, to be sure, demanded great expenditures for fortifications—but primarily to cultural objects, mosques, and retreats for dervishes, lodging houses for travelers, hospitals, and institutions of learning. In Damascus he founded the oldest school for the science of tradition (Dar al-Hadith) and the hospital named after him (Muristan) which soon burgeoned into an advanced school of medicine. He was buried in the madrasah named after him.

His foreign policy was directed primarily to the expulsion of the Franks. Immediately after Zengi's death Count Joscelin II had occupied Edessa again with the help of the Christian population, which consisted mostly of Armenians; this treachery was soon avenged by Nur-ad-Din in a frightful punitive expedition to which nearly all Christians fell victim. The fall of Edessa, however, revived the idea of the Crusades in Europe once again. In St. Bernard of Clairvaux, Pope Eugene III found an inspired preacher for the struggle against the infidels, and in 1146 King Louis VII of France and the Hohenstaufen Conrad III willingly complied with his flaming summons; but even on the march into Hungary their armies suffered such heavy losses through hunger and disease that only a few enfeebled remnants reached the Holy Land. Nevertheless it was decided there to undertake a new attack against the Muslims. The first attractive goal was Damascus, which at that time was ruled by the Mamluk Mu'in-ad-Din Anar for the Burid Mujir-ad-Din Abaq, the descendant of a Seljuq atabeg. When the Christians appeared before the city, the Mamluk turned for help to Nur-ad-Din; but before he could draw near, the Franks raised the siege. Their disunity soon gave Nur-ad-Din an occasion for attack. Count Raymond of Tripoli felt himself threatened by the young Count Bertrand of Toulouse from the latter's fortress at 'Arimah, and sought protection against him from Nur-ad-Din and Mu'in-ad-Din, whose troops indeed leveled 'Arimah to the ground and carried Raymond captive to Aleppo. For a number of years there were minor skirmishes and forays between the Muslims and Franks. In these Mujir-ad-Din, who was more afraid of the preponderance of Nur-ad-Din than of the Franks, since they were split up into petty principalities, proved more and more unreliable. In April 1154 Nur-ad-Din put an end to his rule and appanaged him first with Hims, then with the smaller town of Balis. This constant petty warfare with the Franks, which revolved principally around the possession of the fortress of Harim between Antioch and Aleppo, appeared to take a dangerous turn only once, when in 1158 the emperor of Byzantium, Manuel I (Comnenus), appeared in Syria to chastise Prince Raynald of Antioch for a raid against Cyprus. Baldwin III might almost have succeeded in gaining an alliance with him against Nur-ad-Din, but Nur-ad-Din through compliance with the Byzantines, who were concerned primarily with the security of the borders and scarcely inclined to further adventures, succeeded in eliminating the peril.

In Zengi's and Nur-ad-Din's service a Kurdish clan had meanwhile risen to the top, which was destined to obliterate Turkish hegemony in the Near East for some time to come. Two brothers, Ayyub and Shirkuh, sons of the Kurd Shadhi, had begun their career in 'Iraq, where the elder Ayyub governed the city of Takrit for the 'Abbasid caliph. An assassination in which the younger Shirkuh became involved forced the family to emigrate. Shirkuh entered the service of Zengi, Ayyub that of the Burid of Damascus. When Nur-ad-Din attacked Damascus, Ayyub was in command of the city while Shirkuh led the besiegers. There was, however, a peaceful reunion between the two brothers. From then on Ayyub governed Damascus for Nur-ad-Din, and Shirkuh was enfeoffed with Hims, where his descendants ruled for another century. A broader field was destined for Shirkuh himself.

In Egypt the wazir Tala'i' ibn-Ruzziq, who had restored at least a brief term of peace to the country torn by military insurrections, had been assassinated shortly after the accession to the throne of the last Fatimid, al-'Adid (1160). While the Caliph himself was deprived of nearly all means of power, a struggle took place between the son and successor of the murdered wazir Ruzziq and one of the latter's functionaries, Shawar, to whom he had delegated the important governorship of upper Egypt with the official seat in Qus, when the Wazir attempted to recall the ambitious governor. Shawar was victorious (January 1163); but since his sons shamefully abused their father's power, one of his officials, Dirgham, in concert with the Caliph, revolted against him in August of the same year. Shawar abandoned the field to him without opposition and sought help from Nur-ad-Din in Damascus. The task of reinstating him was delegated to Shirkuh, the governor of Hims. The battle-tried

Syrian troops defeated the Fatimid mercenaries and in May 1164 reinstated Shawar in Cairo in his office. But a conflict broke out at once between him and Shirkuh, and to get rid of his inconvenient helper, Shawar did not balk at summoning King Amalric of Jerusalem. The Franks shut up Shirkuh in Bilbays, but granted him freedom of withdrawal into Syria when they saw themselves threatened in the north by the fall of the Harim fortress besieged by Nur-ad-Din. Three years later Shirkuh appeared in Egypt again, but was once more compelled to withdraw after his initial brilliant victory, since his nephew Saladin, Ayyub's son, was shut up by Shawar and his Frankish allies in Alexandria and the city could not be held. As a result Egypt had to pay an excessive price for the help of the Franks. In addition to a high tribute, they demanded that their garrison be stationed in Egypt and a high commissioner be stationed in Cairo. A quarrel broke out over this very soon, and Shawar was besieged by the Franks in the old city of Cairo, Fustat. In this emergency the caliph 'Adid himself turned for help to Nur-ad-Din, who sent Shirkuh to Egypt for the third time, although meanwhile Shawar had succeeded in purchasing the withdrawal of the Franks, after letting Fustat, which he could not hold, go up in flames. When he tried to evade his obligations to the Syrians again, he was invited by Shirkuh's nephew Saladin and a number of other officers to negotiations at the burial place of the imam ash-Shafi'i, and was attacked and killed on January 18, 1169. 'Adid designated Shirkuh as wazir in his place, and when Shirkuh died only two months later, the office was passed on to his nephew Saladin with the honorific title of al-Malik an-Nasir, while Nur-ad-Din confirmed him as commander of the Syrian troops.

With unshakable energy and unusual diplomatic talent Saladin (Salah-ad-Din) succeeded in clambering out of this still rather critical situation into such a powerful position as had not for a long time been granted any prince of Islam. In Cairo first of all he had to eliminate the unreliable Negro corps of the Fatimids. The Franks at once recognized the danger to them of a powerful ruler in Egypt and again asked for help from Europe. And indeed a Byzantine fleet and an army from southern Italy appeared before Damietta. On Saladin's request Nur-ad-Din dispatched Saladin's father with auxiliary troops. As the siege of Damietta began to draw itself out and the Byzantines could provide for their needs only with difficulty, Amalric let himself be induced to withdraw by a payment of money.

Whether Saladin really needed Nur-ad-Din's advice in order to get rid of the last Fatimid is open to doubt. Anyhow, he had the 'Abbasid caliph named in the Friday prayers instead of the Fatimid in 1172. Soon afterward 'Adid died. Although Saladin did not suppress the Shi'ite sect by force, it lost its natural support with the decline of the Fatimid dynasty, and the Sunnites very soon regained Egypt.

Saladin's growing power necessarily aroused Nur-ad-Din's mistrust of his loyalty as vassal. As soon as the Franks withdrew, Saladin envisaged the conquest of Palestine as his next political goal, since no power had ever before been able to maintain a permanent hold in the country of the Nile without this glacis in the east. In 1172 he seized the harbor of Aylah on the Red Sea as a basis of operations for this. But when Nur-ad-Din wanted to gain a foothold in southern Palestine and requested him to lend him military aid for the conquest of the Crusaders' fortresses Kerak and Shawbak east of the Jordan, he evaded this obligation by pointing to the still-unsettled conditions in Egypt. Nur-ad-Din had already begun gathering troops to punish him for this, but he let himself be placated once again by a servile letter. When Saladin had another rebellion to suppress in Egypt in 1172, Nur-ad-Din decided to attack him, but he died in Damascus on May 15.

His son Isma'il al-Malik as-Salih, just eleven years old, was at first recognized without opposition not only by his own emirs but by Saladin as well. But his cousin Sayf-ad-Din al-Ghazi of Mosul, who had come into Nur-ad-Din's territory together with troops to lend him aid on his march to Egypt, continued in occupation of the Mesopotamian cities in which he had set up his quarters. Isma'il's guardians, who saw themselves simultaneously threatened by the Franks, acquiesced in the surrender of the areas taken by Sayf-ad-Din, considering they would have better assurance of his protection by withdrawing to Aleppo with the youthful prince.

Saladin's possession of Egypt, however, was not secure as long as it was not united with Syria, particularly in view of the menacing proximity of the Crusader states. He had just beaten back an attack of the Sicilian Normans, whose fleet had appeared before Alexandria, when the death of Amalric of Jerusalem relieved him of a dangerous foe. Playing the role of a faithful vassal of Isma'il, he reproached the latter's guardians for compliance toward the ruler of Mosul. Saladin advanced before Damascus under the pretext of reinstating Isma'il in his rights there. After occupying the city—the citadel was not surrendered by its commandant until a few months later—he entered into negotiations with Isma'il's guardians. Since the latter rightly mistrusted his intentions, they preferred appealing to the Franks for help. Then Saladin passed over to the attack, occupied Hama and Hims, and at the end of 1172 surrounded Aleppo. Since he encountered courageous resistance here, he offered to relinquish Hama and Hims again in exchange for recognition as Isma'il's governor in Damascus. When this offer was rejected he advanced against the united troops of Isma'il and Sayf-ad-Din in Hama in open battle, in which he won a brilliant victory. Now he besieged Isma'il in Aleppo for the second time and forced him to conclude a peace which limited him to that city alone. At the same time Saladin assumed the title of an independent sultan, which the 'Abbasid caliph confirmed through an embassy.

During the first siege of Aleppo the commandant had dispatched a hired hashishi against Saladin, who escaped his murderous steel only through a lucky accident. In Syria after 1169 a new Old Man of the Mountain, Rashid-ad-Din Sinan, had reorganized the frightful order and created an impregnable base in the fortress of Masyad (Masyaf) on the eastern slopes of the Nusayri Mountains. After the peace treaty of Aleppo, Saladin thought of getting rid of him, but very soon had to give up the siege of his fortress and concluded a peace with the master which was then honorably observed until his death.

Even before Saladin had secured his power in Syria, he attempted, in a policy of long-range vision, to consolidate his rule in Egypt at the southern gate of the Red Sea as well. In 1173 he sent his brother Turanshah there, when the small dynasties in control, the Hamdanids in San'a and the Najjahids in Zabid, were threatened by a fanatic and overrun. Around 1159 a mahdi had emerged in the Tihamah, as so often in Islamic history, and, supported by the Bedouins who were devoted to him, had conquered Zabid. His grandson 'Abd-an-Nabi, who had followed him in 1162, maintained his position for eleven years. Saladin's overlords must also have considered the removal of this heretical usurper a work pleasing to God. After the Egyptian expeditionary army had dealt with him without any difficulty, Turanshah dethroned the other rulers in San'a and Aden, and until 1228 he and his descendants ruled the land as vassals of their Egyptian kinsmen.

The borders of Saladin's sphere of power in Syria were continually being disturbed by the Crusaders. In 1177 in an attempt to ward off their advances in southern Palestine, he suffered a perceptible setback at Ramlah; he was only able to make up for this two years later by a victory at Marj 'Ayun. The peace when concluded was exploited by Saladin to expand and consolidate his power in northern Syria. In 1181 Isma'il, the prince of Aleppo, died and bequeathed his domain to his cousin 'Izz-ad-Din Mas'ud of Mosul; but the latter preferred to leave Aleppo to his brother Zengi II in exchange for the Sinjar Mountains bordering his ancestral lands. Before the new ruler could establish himself in Aleppo, Saladin occupied his territory; in the following years he also attacked Mesopotamia and forced 'Izz-ad-Din under his suzerainty.

The peace with the Crusaders, which Guy of Lusignan, who succeeded Baldwin V as king of Jerusalem, was also anxious to preserve, was frequently broken as a result of the unruliness of his vassals. Raynald of Chatillon, the lord of the Kerak fortress in ancient Moab east of the Dead Sea on a precipitous spur of the mountains which dominated the caravan highway from Damascus to the Hijaz as well as to Egypt, kept disturbing the traffic of the pilgrims as well as of commerce through repeated raiding forays. Saladin would no longer close his eyes to this, and in the beginning of 1187 he decided on a great stroke. While he himself advanced into the Kerak region, he had his Syrian troops assembled in Harim, and he united with them at the Lake of Gennesareth (Galilee). Thereupon the King of Jerusalem also gathered a great army of knights in Saffuriyah. But instead of awaiting Saladin's attack in this strategically favorable position, he let himself be induced to march against him toward Tiberias, which Saladin had occupied. To the west lies the chalk plateau of Hattin (Hittin), uneven, waterless, with a steep northerly drop. There Saladin inflicted an annihilating defeat on him; the King himself fell into his hands. The fortresses all over the country, divested of their garrisons, fell one after another within a short space of time, and in September 1187 Saladin appeared before Jerusalem, which was forced to surrender in the same month.* In the presence of nearly his entire house Saladin once again took possession of the Holy City on behalf of Islam and destroyed all Christian places of worship on the consecrated soil. Without delay he also attempted to eliminate the last remnants of Frankish rule

* M. W. Baldwin, *Raymond III of Tripolis and the Fall of Jerusalem, 1140-1187*, London, 1938.

in the Orient; but Tyre, defended by Conrad of Montferrat, withstood his attack. Tripoli was relieved by a Christian fleet under the command of William of Sicily, a Norman. In Europe the fall of Jerusalem had resuscitated the idea of the Crusades. The Hohenstaufen Frederick I, Philip of France, and Richard the Lion-hearted of England, whom the Pope was first compelled to reconcile to each other, took up the cross. Acre, which Saladin had had fortified as strongly as possible after taking it, was surrounded by the Crusaders as early as August 1189. Saladin hurried to its relief, but in 1191 Philip and Richard the Lion-hearted appeared with fresh troops for the besiegers, who held the harbor and so had a great advantage over the Muslims. On July 12, 1192, the garrison surrounded in Acre surrendered. When Saladin refused to pay the high ransom demanded for it, a savage massacre of prisoners on both sides ensued. Since there was no question of any military decision, Saladin's brother al-Malik al-'Adil began peace negotiations with Richard the Lion-hearted. The latter, weary of the war, was anxious to return to England in order not to lose his realm at home, and so peace was concluded on November 2, 1192. Saladin retained his conquests as far as Lydda, Ramlah, and Ascalon, and allowed Christians to visit Jerusalem as unarmed pilgrims.

Saladin was granted only a few months' enjoyment of the peace finally attained. At the end of November he moved from Jerusalem to Damascus, where in February 1193 he fell ill and died, only fifty-five years old. In Europe, as a result of his wars with the Crusaders, Saladin has become one of the most famous reigning figures of the east, but in Oriental memory also he lives on, along with Harun ar-Rashid and the Mamluk Baybars, as the symbol of one of the happiest periods of history. And indeed few Islamic princes can be named who, like him, free of any self-seeking, were concerned only with the well-being of their dynasties and their subjects. His nobility toward his conquered enemies had to be acknowledged even by them. As a zealous patron of science he found grateful biographers among scholars. His secretary Muhammad al-Katib al-Isfahani, who had previously been in the service of Nur-ad-Din in Damascus, and who accompanied him on all his campaigns, gave an account of the conquest of Jerusalem, unfortunately in an overloaded ornamental style which gives the impression that mastery of language was of greater importance to him than his subject. Smoother is the account of his life from the pen of his army judge and qadi in Jerusalem, Baha-ad-Din ibn-Shaddad. The most important of Saladin's functionaries, al-Qadi al-Fadil of Ascalon, who had begun his career under the last Fatimids, and under Saladin controlled the entire administration from the beginning, kept an official diary during his stay in office, of which, unfortunately, only some excerpts have been preserved; of his state papers also only drafts have come down to us, which unfortunately were chosen not for their historical importance but for their stylistic beauty. A living portrait of the culture of his time was handed down in the memoirs of the knight Usamah of the princely family of banu Munqidh, settled in Shayzar north of Hama. Under the Burids in Damascus, Usamah had contracted friendly relations with the Frankish knights; he then participated in Nur-ad-Din's campaigns against them and, already advanced in years, joined Saladin in Damascus. Although well versed in all the stylistic arts of his time, as his other works show, he disdained them in his memoirs entirely. In an amiable, gossiping tone he relates his numerous adventures in war, in peace, and especially on the hunt, and is remarkably dispassionate in his judgments of both Muslims and Christians.*

But Saladin was also a patron of Sunni theologians, with whose aid he encompassed the decisive extinction of the Shi'ite tendencies of the Fatimids in Egypt. Only once did he find himself compelled to establish a court for heresy. In Aleppo, where his son al-Malik az-Zahir represented him as viceroy, a Persian immigrant from Asia Minor, as-Suhrawardi, applied himself to gnosticism based on neo-Platonism and neo-Pythagoreanism, after study of Aristotelian and Platonic philosophy. Such was the basis for the doctrine, already hinted at early by Christian and Islamic mystics and philosophers, that a spiritual light permeated the world as an irradiation of divinity and as the real essence of all things. He developed his philosophy of illumination, which survived in the dervish order he had founded in Asia Minor. These lines of thought at once aroused orthodox suspicion and the allegation that he represented the doctrine of the Qarmatians hostile to the state. So in spite of Saladin's mildness, nothing was left for him to do but confirm the death sentence handed down by the judges against the heretic (1191).

Saladin was an active builder in Jerusalem and Cairo. In Jerusalem he was responsible for the restoration of the Jami' al-Aqsa (used

* Translated by Philip K. Hitti, New York, 1929.

as a palace by the Crusaders) as a mosque, with new ornamentation in mosaic and marble and a costly pulpit brought from Aleppo and still extant. In Cairo he erected the first four-aisled madrasah at the grave of the imam ash-Shafi'i. His military aims were served by the construction of the citadel of Cairo, whose completion he did not live to see. As early as 1179 he had formed the plan of combining Cairo and Fustat into a single fortified unit. In the east, between the two quarters, he began with the citadel, erected on the model of the Crusaders' fortresses. It was going to be his residence at the same time. Cairo was to be shielded against attacks from Syria by a wall pushed forward as far as the Muqattam hill in the east; but only the northern wall was built, while the remaining fortifications were never really embarked on in earnest.

Before his death Saladin himself divided up his empire among his survivors. His eldest son al-Malik al-Afdal, as head of the house, inherited the sultanate together with Damascus and southern Syria; of his brothers, al-Malik al-'Aziz got Egypt, and al-Malik az-Zahir, Aleppo with northern Syria; their uncle, al-Malik al-'Adil, Saladin's brother, was given the possessions in Mesopotamia. Only a year after Saladin's death dissension broke out among his sons. By playing them off against each other, their uncle was able to eliminate them all one after the other; it was only in Aleppo that Saladin's descendants survived until the incursion of the Mongols (1260). By 1200 al-'Adil had united almost the entire empire in his hands, and the collateral lines in Aleppo and Yemen acknowledged him as sovereign. Yet even during his lifetime he divided his domains among his sons. In Egypt he installed Kamil; in Damascus, Mu'azzam; in Mesopotamia, Awhad, Fa'iz, and Ashraf successively as his deputies.

In spite of these disturbances the Ayyubids held their territories against the Crusaders as well as against their neighbors in Asia Minor. Around this time the idea of the War for the Holy Land had practically sunk into oblivion. Not until 1217 did King Andrew of Hungary revive it and arm an expedition against Egypt. Al-'Adil had just died (1218) when the Crusaders appeared before Damietta. Since Kamil first had to establish authority in his own country, he was unable to prevent the seizure of the fortress dominating the eastern arm of the Nile delta. But the Crusaders could not withstand the co-ordinated attack of the Ayyubids; the next year Damietta was free again. Soon afterward the complex machinations of European politics led to a renewed flare-up of the struggle for the possession of Jerusalem. The Hohenstaufen Frederick II, who had come to the throne as the ward of Pope Innocent III, had not only had to approve, out of gratitude for the support accorded him, the expansion of the ecclesiastical state consummated at the expense of the empire, and to waive the exercise of any influence on the episcopal elections in Germany, but had also to vow a crusade (1215). The fulfillment of this vow, however, was very far from his intentions, since as heir of the Normans in Sicily he was thoroughly preoccupied with constructing a modern regime there which would enable him to win back Italy. Like the Normans, he also favored Arabic culture and maintained Arab mercenaries. As he kept postponing the date for the beginning of the crusade, Gregory IX excommunicated him in 1227. To absolve himself he had to set out for the Holy Land from Brindisi in 1228. The sultan Kamil had started negotiations with him even before this to secure his aid against Mu'azzam, the Sultan's brother, in Damascus. When Frederick II landed in Palestine, Mu'azzam had already died and Kamil had handed over Damascus to his brother in addition to his Mesopotamian holdings. Nevertheless, negotiating continued, and in exchange for a promised guarantee of his Syrian possessions, Kamil surrendered Jerusalem together with Bethlehem and Nazareth and corridors to both Jaffa and Saida (Sidon) before any blows were exchanged. On March 18, 1229, Frederick was crowned as spouse of the ruler of the Holy Land, Isabelle of Brienne, in the Church of the Holy Sepulcher in Jerusalem. But this apparent diplomatic coup was approved by neither the Christians nor the Muslims. Indeed, the Pope had an interdiction laid on the city by the patriarch of Jerusalem as long as Frederick remained there.

But Kamil used the peace purchased in Palestine to expand his power in the north at the expense of the Seljuqs of Iconium. This aroused the jealousy of his brother Ashraf in Damascus. Kamil was relieved of this adversary by death, when he appeared before Damascus, but he himself died directly thereafter (1238). Only two years later his son 'Adil in Egypt was pushed out by his brother as-Salih, who in 1244 was able, with a force of Khwarizmi Turks who had fled before Chingiz Khan, to reconquer Jerusalem, which had already been temporarily occupied in 1239 by Da'ud, prince of Kerak, after the expiration of the treaty concluded with Frederick II. In contrast, Salih lost Damascus to his uncle as-Salih Isma'il, who after the death of his brother Ashraf had been forced to leave the city to Kamil. But after the conquest of Jerusalem, Damascus also fell into Salih's hands in 1245, and thus almost the entire empire of Saladin as far as Aleppo and northern Mesopotamia was reunited. Yet his reign was a series of struggles with his rivals from his own house, with the Franks and with the Khwarizmi Turks, who were ready to place themselves at the command of the most lucrative offer. In 1248, while lingering in Damascus to arm for a campaign against Yusuf II of Aleppo, he was overtaken by the news of another incursion of the Franks in Egypt. Louis IX, the Saint of France, had landed in Damietta and secured possession of the city, since at the news of Salih's illness the discipline of his army had collapsed. When Salih died on November 23, 1249, his death was concealed by his wife, the former slave girl Shajar-ad-Durr, until his son al-Malik al-Mu'azzam Turanshah arrived from Mesopotamia. When the latter, who had grown up entirely removed from conditions in Egypt, favored the Mamluks he had brought with him from Mesopotamia at the expense of the Egyptians, a conspiracy against him took place and he was assassinated at the beginning of 1250. But meanwhile he had succeeded in reconquering Damietta, where Louis IX fell captive. To shut this port of entry, so often menaced from the sea, the city was razed and its inhabitants resettled. After Turanshah's assassination the Mamluks elevated Salih's widow as queen; her general Aybeg stood at her side as atabeg and soon became her husband. While she had well-nigh absolute authority in Egypt, Aybeg had to defend her power in Syria, where she was not acknowledged. When he attempted to rid himself of her in 1257, she anticipated him and had him murdered in his bath. However, she found no support among the Mamluks and directly afterward was murdered herself, whereupon the Mamluk al-Mansur Nur-ad-Din 'Ali came to power.

In spite of all this tumult the Ayyubid regime meant a period of prosperity for Egypt and Syria even after Saladin's death. Its attention was devoted to agriculture, which could be maintained at its peak only through persistent tending of the irrigation system, no less than to commerce, continually imperiled by the insecurity of the trade routes. The enmity with the Christians did not prevent it from concluding a series of trade agreements with European states. The relationship to the crusading knights, in constant alternation between animosity and peaceful intercourse, also led to a many-sided cultural exchange; together with other chivalric usages the heraldic system of the Ayyubids also seems to have been transplanted to the Occident.* Like the 'Abbasids before them, the Ayyubids had been compelled to prop themselves up on purchased slaves (mamluks), since the inhabitants of their dominions had long since grown unaccustomed to military service; but in addition they had often taken into their service entire Turkish hordes which, driven by the Mongols, had appeared in the Near East. Then, as so frequently, a new race of rulers arose from among their leaders, which survived in Egypt and Syria until the Ottoman conquest. Aybeg, the first in the series, belonged to Salih's guard stationed on the Nile island of ar-Rawdah; consequently he and his successors were called the *Bahri* (River) Mamluks. Aybeg's son 'Ali and his guardian Qutuz were followed in swift succession by Baybars az-Zahir Rukn-ad-Din. The latter had participated in Turanshah's assassination and evaded punishment by fleeing to Syria, but returned to Egypt after Qutuz assumed power. At this time the Mongol tempest was overwhelming all of the Near East and threatening Egypt with annihilation. So Qutuz put him in command of the vanguard of the troops drawn up in Palestine against the Mongols. In the Battle of 'Ayn Jalut in 1259, in which the Mongol tide came to a standstill for the first time, to recede slowly thereafter, Baybars distinguished himself by personal valor. He was hoping to be enfeoffed with Aleppo as reward, and when he had to withdraw in disappointment he murdered Qutuz and was proclaimed sultan by the emirs. Accordingly he must be accredited with the fact that in Egypt alone, among all the countries of Islam, the even course of cultural development was not interrupted by the Mongol invasion, of whose devastating effects an account will shortly be given. But as it turned out, Baybars was an extremely able ruler. In order to consolidate his throne against any possible Ayyubid pretenders, he gave refuge in Cairo to a scion of the clan of the 'Abbasid caliphs just overthrown by the Mongols in Baghdad and well-nigh exterminated, and was confirmed by him as co-regent after taking an oath of allegiance to the caliph. This first 'Abbasid appears to have had somewhat more energy than Baybars found agreeable. He set out at the head of Baybars's troops to recapture Baghdad; however, the Mamluk allocated troops in such feeble numbers that the Mongols soon

* See Yacoub Artin Pasha, *Contribution à l'étude du blason en Orient*, London, 1902. [L. A. Mayer, *Saracenic Heraldry*, Oxford, 1933.]

finished him off with ease. From then on all his successors in the caliphate were merely puppets in the hands of the Mamluks.

Baybars defended himself against his enemies with extraordinary valor, but frequently by astute and guileful diplomacy as well. In Palestine he still had to deal with the Franks, but he managed to wrest one of the most powerful fortresses, Hisn al-Akrad, from the grasp of St. John's Knights, and the city of Safed from the Templars. The Assassins had to cede Masyaf and a series of smaller castles, but he did not entirely dissolve the order, since he wished to make further use of its murderers for his own purposes. He lured the last still-independent Ayyubid, the prince of Kerak, to Cairo, and breaking his promises, had him and his son eliminated. In the north he held the Armenian kings of Asia Minor in check by continually repeated incursions into their territory; in the south he attached Nubia to Egypt as a vassal state. Again and again the Mongols in 'Iraq were prevented by circumstances in the interior of their Asiatic empire from avenging their first defeat, even though Baybars frequently still had to ward off minor raids into his domain. He was protected against a repetition of the European crusades by a treaty with the Byzantine emperor Michael Paleologus, who had freed his empire from the rule of the Frankish knights. In the interior, Baybars consolidated his empire by an information service modeled on the Iranian-'Abbasid postal system. In Cairo he erected for himself a magnificent monument in the mosque, nowadays in ruins, for which he procured the materials in 1267/68 from conquered Jaffa. The surrounding wall, still standing, is set up out of quarry stone with masonry; the main structure, of brick. Six rows of columns connected by pointed arches lead into the interior and bear a transept, which is covered in front of the mihrab by a cupola overspanning three aisles. The other sides of the court comprise two-aisled halls of columns. The outer wall is divided by three jutting portals, and at the corners by rectangularly salient towers, and is decorated at the gates with niches, medallions, and rhomboids.*

Baybars's regime was considered by posterity, like those of Harun ar-Rashid and Saladin, an age of splendor for Islam. At a very early time a wreath of romantic tales became twined around him, in which his exploits were merged in a fantastic historical image with fixed motifs drawn from the rogues' romances native to Egypt from

* See E. Diez, *Die Kunst der islamischen Völker*, p. 58.

of old; even down to the threshold of the present, the Baybars romance, added to by generations of storytellers, has formed, in addition to the chivalrous romances of 'Antar, the Bedouin stories of the banu Hilal, and the fairy tales of the Arabian Nights, a very popular source of entertainment for the Egyptians.

Eight years before his death Baybars had already had allegiance sworn to his oldest son, Barakah Khan, as his successor on the throne; accordingly, after his death in 1277, the latter could ascend the throne unhindered; but he was deposed two years later. An army chief named Qala'un, who had already proved his mettle under Baybars, assumed the guardianship of Baybars's son Salamish, only seven years old, but soon afterward preferred taking his place as an independent ruler. Qala'un was just as successful as Baybars in defending his power in Syria against the Mongols; he expanded it at the expense of the Franks and freed it of the emirs, whom he had had to endure at first as associates. At his death in 1290 it was also granted him to pass his empire on to his son, whose descendants maintained it for four generations, down to 1382, though they always had to be confirmed in office by an election. Subsequently, however, in Barquq there came to the throne a member of the corps of troops Qala'un had formed out of Mongols and Circassians and quartered in the towers of the Cairo citadel. These were called *burjis* ("of the citadel"). These latter put a stop to any further hereditary succession, electing anyone they found most convenient, sometimes simply the oldest one in their midst. After this the power of the sultan, theoretically unlimited, fell into steady decay. His decisions were dependent on a state council composed of the principal Mamluk chieftains. These jealously stood guard over the maintenance of the purity of their estate. Special functionaries kept supplementing it through purchases on the principal slave markets, which were supplied particularly from southern Russia and the Caucasus; the young slaves were trained in the citadel of Cairo and then distributed among the emirs, in whose service they could expect promotion. In addition, however, the Mamluks maintained a recruited body of troops paid by fiefs, which in part again turned into a hereditary estate; to this, for instance, belonged Khalil, the famous author of a manual of Malikite law still authoritative for his school, who died in 1365 and that same year, together with the garrison of Cairo, participated in the defense of Alexandria against an attack by the king of Cyprus. Only the positions of magistrates and the professorships in the madrasahs were reserved for native scholars, but in the civil service, where notaries and chancery executives had the topmost positions, Jews and Christians were shown preference.

This persistent insecurity in the political situation, which granted none of the rulers a long reign and scarcely allowed one of them to die a natural death, entailed a corresponding insecurity of life and property for the entire court and government milieu such as can only have hovered over the heads of the old nobility during the worst days of the Roman Empire. Even the ablest officials seldom survived an effective period of more than three years, and many a qadi was appointed and removed again more than ten times during a lifetime. In addition there was the moral constraint of the orthodox fuqaha, who for years even persecuted such a pious and rigidly believing man as the Hanbalite ibn-Taymiyah * because he failed to conform to the opinion of their school in all points and militated against many aspects of the popular religion such as veneration of prophets and saints. Baybars himself had recognized the Hanbalite doctrine as orthodox by conceding a supreme qadi in Cairo to it as well as to the other three schools of law. But the Hanbalites, like their founder in Baghdad before, aroused the feelings of the other schools again and again by claiming to be the sole representatives of the unfalsified doctrine of Muhammad. So ibn-Taymiyah, who had succeeded his father as teacher in Damascus in 1282, also became suspect of heresy as the result of an answer to a question put to him from Hama: he contradicted the Shafi'ite doctrine and was removed from office. The Shafi'ites summoned him in 1305 before their tribunal in Cairo and sentenced him to prison. When his former patron, the sultan al-Malik an-Nasir, came to the throne for the third time, he gave him the office of Hanbali teacher in the madrasah founded by him and took him along with him to Damascus in 1313. But in 1318 ibn-Taymiyah aroused new irritation by a fatwa concerning divorce, and now even his patron could no longer protect him, although after five months he was released from the imprisonment he had been sentenced to and could resume his teaching. In July of 1326, however, his enemies secured his arrest once again on the basis of an opinion he had handed down as early as 1310 concerning visits to prophets' and saints' burial places. In the citadel of Damascus he was able to keep up his literary activity, at least in the beginning, but when paper and pen were

* [H. Laoust, *Essai sur . . . Ibn Taymiya*, Cairo, 1939.]

denied him he died of grief at the insult, on September 29, 1329. While his contemporaries had attempted to use force in suppressing his doctrine, it lived on nevertheless in the restricted milieu of his school, and four hundred years later gave an impetus to the Wahhabi movement and so to the Islamic modernism of the present day. In other fields besides theology Syrians and Egyptians developed under the Mamluks a very prolific production, which created for us also some very valuable work, particularly in the historical field, but was almost entirely devoid of any originality.

The economic foundation of this excessively prolific writing during the Mamluk period was the system of pious foundations (*waqf*) created under the 'Abbasids, which in Egypt and Syria had assumed fantastic proportions.* As in 'Iraq earlier, the form of the foundation served to preserve great properties against the intervention of the state by yielding at least a certain income to the founder and to his descendants. But since these foundations continually alienated broad strata from earning a living and led to a life of contemplation in honor of God as religious leaders or dervishes and at the same time withdrew large areas from intensive cultivation by private enterprise, they bear a good portion of the blame for the economic decline of the East. Most of the foundations, though, were erected in the towns, and the waqfs yielded income from rent for small shops and industrial establishments.

The ruling class, the Mamluks, lived on the usually generous grant of fiefs which could not develop into family properties since transmission of estates was unlawful. Indeed, at the death of the holder the survivors had to pay back to the treasury, which maintained a special bureau for this, the pay received in advance for a period of service prematurely broken off by death, and it took a special decree to soften the rigors arising out of this procedure. It goes without saying that the peasants on these enfeoffed lands, who were forbidden to leave them, were delivered over mercilessly to the caprice of the holder.†

Moreover, the economic regime was marked by numerous oppressive exactions which, although branded again and again by the religious legal code as an abuse, nevertheless formed the backbone of the state finances. Great was the role of compulsory transactions

* See C. H. Becker, *Islam*, I, 93 ff.

† [A. N. Poliak, *Feudalism in Egypt, Syria, Palestine and the Lebanon*, London, 1939.]

in which the government bought up the most important provisions and resold them to retail traders at fixed prices; in times of need, to be sure, this was also a means of preventing speculation. In spite of these limitations commerce flourished extraordinarily during the Mamluk period, since at that time Egypt and Syria were still the transit country for the rich Indian trade of the Italian merchant republics, who were frequently able to insure their privileges through treaties with the Mamluks; subsequently these formed the basis of the capitulations which influenced Egypt's history down to the modern era.

In this way great revenues flowed in to the Mamluk sultans, which enabled them to build on a scale rivaling that of the most lustrous periods of Islam. Since, from the time of Qala'un on, their architectural monuments were generally built in quarry stone, such as offered by the chalk of the Muqattam and the porphyry and granite of upper Egypt, their work has withstood decay better than that of their predecessors and today still determines the urban lay-out of Cairo. The first place is taken among them by the burial sites. The form of their mausoleums, with the beautiful towering domes, was carried over from Turkestan into Egypt. Thus the Mamluks, although they had been torn away from their homes in early youth and generally sprang from the lower classes, nevertheless regarded the art of their homeland, whose representatives sought refuge among them, as their real ideal. From the Persian style, as it prevailed among the Fatimids and the Ayyubids, the Turkish cupola was distinguished by the elevation of its polygon or circle from the rectangle or square of the supporting structure by means of wall consoles at the corners or by rows of mutually supporting triangles; in this the Indian wood style survived, out of which the stone cupola developed. Under Sultan Hasan (1347-1351) a new style appeared in Cairo, which developed in the façades of the mosques. Their lofty, smooth stone walls were segmented in level niches reaching as far as the roof sill and closed off with the horizontal stalactite rim. In the niches windows were installed; the wall generally was crowned by a wreath of battlements. The gate usually lay in the corner in a deep niche, led up to by a free stairway. This style, in which the Babylonian-Assyrian art survives, must have been transplanted from northern Mesopotamia and the Kurdish mountain lands, where it had been preserved as though in an area of relics, to Adharbayjan and Asia Minor in the north and to Egypt in the south. Brilliant examples of this style are the burial mosque of Sultan Hasan and the madrasah he erected with special separate halls of teaching for all four rites.*

6. *Turks and Mongols: the End of the Caliphate*

While it was the Turks who by centuries of persistent maladministration inflicted the worst damage on the once so flourishing civilization of Iran and Mesopotamia, it was reserved to the related tribe of the Tatars or Mongols, at the beginning of the thirteenth century, to bring that work of destruction to completion. In his chronicle for the year 617 H (1220 A.D.) the Arab historian ibn-al-Athir, in a moving lamentation, rightly calls their breaking into the Near East the greatest misfortune to come upon the humanity he knew. Maybe economic factors played a great role in this case, as previously in the emergence of the Arabs from Arabia for world conquest; e.g., possibly the struggle for grazing land between sheep herders and raisers of horses may have played a role; but as usual in history it was a powerful personality, in this case Chingiz Khan, that gave the impetus which welded together Mongols previously accustomed to roam along the borders of the empire of China, and their tribal kinfolk in the north who lived by hunting and fishing. It was this new force and leadership that now swept over the countries of ancient civilization with the bloodthirstiness and destructive fury characteristic of their race.

The east of the former empire of the caliphs, after the collapse of Seljuq rule, had become a plaything of Turkish rulers whose endless warfare devastated the once thriving civilized countries. It is impossible to give a detailed account here of the unspeakably sad spectacle; only the most important facts can be touched on briefly. From 1097 on Sanjar, one of the heirs of the Seljuq sultan, in a peaceful reign had for a short time reunited Persia and the Oxus countries. In Khwarizm he had had to recognize as vassals Muhammad, the son of Anushtegin, whom Barkiyaruq had installed previously, and who had established his independence as Khwarizm shah; and in Sijistan an ostensible descendant of the Saffarids, Taj-ad-Din Abu-l-Fath ibn-Tahir. The independent rulers of Transoxania, the Ghaznawids, who, true to the ancient tradition of their house, regarded the pillaging of India as their life's work, were also more or less

* See E. Diez, *Die Kunst der islamischen Völker*, 142 ff.

subject to Sanjar. But Atsiz himself (1128-1156), the successor of the first Khwarizm shah, had made an attempt to extricate himself from the influence of the Seljuq sultan. In punishment for his rebelliousness he was deposed but as soon as Sanjar had left his country he revolted again, and in order to divert Sanjar toward the east, incited the still pagan Mongol tribe Karakhitai against Samarqand. Since 916 these kinsmen of the Turks, about whose prehistory something has already been said, had ruled as the Liao dynasty in China, which as a result is still called Kitai by the Russians. From there the Jurjenes, a Tungus people, had expelled them around 1125, forcing them westward. At first the Mongols attacked the Kirghiz country along the Yenisei, then Kashghar and Khotan in the south. Now Sanjar suffered a serious defeat on September 9, 1141, on the other side of the Oxus. From then on their prince ruled an enormous area stretching from the Yenisei in the north to Balkh in the south, and from Khwarizm, whose shah became his vassal, in the west as far as the Uigur empire in the east, and had his residence near Balasaghun along the Chui, the principal river of present-day Russian Turkestan. In their lands the Christianity introduced by Nestorian missionaries was still contending with Islam, which finally remained at an advantage because of its widely ramified connections.*

Atsiz took advantage of his suzerain's misfortune. Although it is true he was incapable of retaining a permanent hold on those portions of his territory he had gained, and was finally compelled to renew his allegiance, his son Il Arslan, who followed him on the throne in 1156, established the sovereignty of the dynasty of the Khwarizm shahs, who acquired a decisive influence over the history of central Asia, though only for a short time.

Soon afterward the creation of Mahmud of Ghaznah also fell victim to the new Turkish bands. In the mountainous country of Ghor, between the valley of the Hilmend and Herat in Afghanistan, princes of the indigenous house of Suri were settled as vassals of the Ghaznawids. A prince of this house was executed by the Ghaznawid Bahram Shah at whose court he lived. To avenge him

* Out of a dim awareness of these conditions, and by deforming the title Gurkhan, there arose in Europe the widely spread saga of the empire of Prester John in the Far East; see G. Oppert, *Der Presbyter Johannes in Sage und Geschichte*, 2nd edition, Berlin, 1870; F. Zarncke, *Der Priester Johannes*, Leipzig, 1879 (Königliche Sächsische Gesellschaft für Wissenschaft, VII, XIX).

his brother attacked Ghaznah in 1148 and forced the Sultan to flee to India. But from there he returned with fresh troops and defeated the Suri, who fell into his hands himself and was executed. In revenge for this the latter's brothers gathered together the savage hordes of their people and in 1150 conquered Ghaznah and razed the city to the ground; only two minarets still indicate its site today. From then on Bahram Shah lived in India, with his residence at Lahore.

When the Ghorids then turned toward Herat, against Sanjar's domains, the Seljuq sultan came out to meet them. They were defeated, and their chief was allowed to return to his land only after two years in captivity. Less fortunate was the outcome of Sanjar's campaign against the Turkoman clan Ghuzz, whom the Karakhitai had expelled from their grazing lands, and who in consequence, driven by necessity, had fallen on his land. They had wished at first to submit peaceably, but had been driven to revolt by the highhandedness of the tax officials. In 1153 they inflicted a severe defeat on him and kept the Sultan himself captive for three years. Soon after succeeding in escaping from their custody he died, in 1157.

After their victory over Sanjar the Ghuzz clan fell on his dominions, plundering and slaughtering. His heir was his nephew Mahmud, who was soon dethroned, however, by his guardian Mu'ayyad. The latter, after Il Arslan's death, took a hand in the struggle between his two sons for the throne of the Khwarizm shah, was defeated in 1174 by the elder, Takash, and killed. After protracted warfare between the brothers, in which the Ghuzz ranging throughout the country also took part, Takash was able to seize control of the whole kingdom after the death of his brother in 1193. Under his reign, until 1200, Khwarizm was left in peace at any rate by the Ghuzz, who were in the midst of an onslaught on the remainder of the Ghaznawid dominions in India. But after his death his successor, 'Ala-ad-Din Muhammad II, was attacked in 1204 by the Ghorid Mu'izz-ad-Din. The latter's army was defeated and in its retreat well-nigh pulverized by the Karakhitai; this defeat also had repercussions on Ghorid * rule in India. Soon afterward a struggle for power among the emirs broke out there, but the former Turkish slave Iltutmish succeeded once again in uniting the entire realm under his control.

* [A dynasty in Afghanistan.]

In Persia the Khwarizm Shah came into contact with the sphere of influence of the 'Abbasid caliph an-Nasir (1180-1225), who had first liberated Baghdad from the rule of the mayors of the palace and then proceeded to extend his sway eastward out of his base in Babylonia. This last politically talented descendant of the house of 'Abbas attempted to eliminate the weaknesses of his still very much encumbered power by an astute patronage of the Shi'ites. For centuries now there had been veterans' associations (*futuwa*) in 'Iraq * which had no doubt first arisen along the borders among the warriors of the faith, but then became active in the interior of the empire and during times of political turmoil not infrequently terrorized the populace, occasionally degenerating into criminal gangs; in peacetime, however, they entered into relations with the Sufi orders. An-Nasir attempted to turn these associations to his own advantage by reorganizing them and placing himself at their head. Since 'Ali, the son-in-law of the Prophet, as a hero's ideal, to a certain extent was their guardian patron, he gave the latter's descendants a sphere of activity, innocuous for his own power, in this new futuwa association and took advantage of their prestige. Since this knightly order zealously cultivated sport, other princes also considered membership in it to be an honorable distinction, although the association did not accord the Caliph any more extensive political influence he might have been hoping to achieve through it. That the grand master of the no longer very dangerous order of Assassins, despite his Shi'ite tenets, swore allegiance to the Caliph was not of great consequence. But no sooner was Takash tied down in the east than the Caliph's wazir conquered Khuzistan and the bordering Persian provinces; in 1196, when Takash had a free hand again, he reconquered these acquisitions as far as Khuzistan. In 1214 the Caliph advanced northward, where in Media a Mamluk named Mengli had seized power. Against him the Caliph supported a kinsman of the overthrown prince, the Pahlawanid Uzbeg of Adharbayjan, and after his victory the latter installed his mamluk Oglumish as governor. When he sought an alliance with the Khwarizm shah 'Ala-ad-Din Muhammad II, an-Nasir had him murdered by an Assassin. The Khwarizm Shah now decided to cut away the foundations of his troublesome adversary's power by summoning an ecclesiastical council in 1217 for considering the question whether the dignity of the caliphate was not rather suited to the descendants of 'Ali, whose

* See F. Taeschner, *Islamisches Ordensrittertum zur Zeit der Kreuzzüge*, *Die Welt als Geschichte*, 1938, 387-402.

partisans, the Shi'ites, were still very widely spread throughout Persia. An 'Alid from Tirmidh, 'Ala-al-Mulk, was set up as rival caliph, and the Khwarizm Shah already began equipping an army to set him on the throne in Baghdad when he had to turn back because of the unusually early onset of winter.* Before he could resume his plan the following year a frightful calamity irrupted over the countries of Islam which radically transformed the political situation.

Among the peoples of the Asiatic interior another great migratory movement had broken out. The easterly neighbors of the Turks were tribes who, originally related to them, had preserved a Mongolian racial type. One of these tribes, the Karakhitai, who were first after the Huns to embark on the migration westward, has already been met with. At that time their kinsmen were still settled in present-day Mongolia and southern Siberia. The Chinese refer to them by a name appearing as early as the Orkhon inscription—Tatars—and divide them into three groups according to their stage of development. They called White Tatars their immediate neighbors behind the Chinese wall, who manifestly had already been strongly influenced by Chinese culture. North of the Gobi desert there dwelt the Black Tatars, who were nomads; Nestorian missionaries had already gained ground among them: the Kerayits who lived along the upper reaches of the Onon and Kerulen rivers, as well as along the Tola, professed Christianity. North of them were settled the forest peoples, who still led a purely hunter life and looked on their just-mentioned tribal kinfolk as degenerate weaklings. Shamanism was still in full bloom among them, and the belief in a supernatural world of spirits assured the conjurers-up, i.e. the shamans, great influence on the life of the people. In one of these tribes, the Taijiut, who were settled near the borders of the Black Tatars, the chieftain Yisukai of the Burchig clan had a first son, Temuchin, born to him in 1155; at his father's death in 1167 Temuchin could have been left no sort of established formal position of authority; indeed, it is doubtful if his father ever had possessed one himself. His personal courage soon secured Temuchin a

* In memory of his rescue from this danger the Caliph had the Talisman gate erected in Baghdad which was later to serve as a powder tower and was blown up by the Turks in the First World War during their withdrawal before the British; on it the Caliph had himself portrayed between two dragons, grasping both by the jaws; according to M. van Berchem's interpretation these embody his two rivals, the Assassin and the 'Alid.

following of adventurers with whom he undertook raiding expeditions against his more civilized tribal kinfolk. The Chinese government was always ready to play these troublesome and disorderly neighbors against each other and so hold them in check. In 1161 the Chinese dynasty of the Kin had annihilated a Tatar tribe called Mongol (Moghul) with the help of their neighbors settled along Lake Buyir-Nor. But when these latter themselves then became too powerful for the Chinese, they assembled the Christian Kerayit against them, and the adventurer Temuchin also participated in the strife. He began his political career as avenger of the Mongols, and took the same name for his followers and later on for his entire people. Around 1202 dissension among the former allies placed Temuchin in dire straits so that he had to withdraw to Lake Baljiyuna with a small band of followers. There were three Muslims among them already, probably Iranian merchants, who at that time often used to come to the Far East on their trading journeys. Two of them accompanied him for a long time on his military expeditions and may have given him advice on the organization of his empire. By 1203 Temuchin had already attacked and exiled from the country his former allies and brothers-in-arms, now turned opponents, so that all the tribes of eastern Mongolia acknowledged him as ruler. In 1206 he was also able to subjugate the powerful Christian tribe of Naiman in western Mongolia. At that time (though according to some accounts even a few years earlier) he had the reigning name of Chinghiz Khan bestowed on him by a shaman, under which he has survived in the memory of posterity. He also summoned then the first parliament (*kurultai*) at which a banner with nine white horse's tails indicated his dignity as ruler and at which he laid down the primary foundations of his empire. The core of his power was formed by his guard, ten thousand strong, of which one thousand served as his bodyguard. They were subject to a rigorous but just training always supervised by the Khan in person, and every private was considered equal in rank to the higher officers of the line. Chinghiz Khan borrowed from the Naiman the use of the Uigur script for state affairs. At first the Khan certainly never planned a systematic expansion of his empire. His expeditions during the next few years were simply forays on a grand scale with the object of riding the steeds of his conquered enemies and embracing their women.*

* Cf. Rashid-ad-Din, ap. W. Barthold, *Enc. of Islam* I, 857.

After ravaging the Tangut country he attacked the empire of the Kin in northern China the following year. In 1214 a peace was concluded which was sealed by the Khan's marriage to a Chinese princess. But no later than 1215 the war broke out again, leading to the conquest of Peking. The Khan, however, had scarcely left the country when the Kin won their freedom again. The princes driven out by the Mongols turned westward and fell on the Karakhitai empire, already enfeebled by the defection of the Khwarizm shah Muhammad, who afterward defeated the Karakhitai at Talas in 1210 and also conquered Transoxania (Ma wara an-nahr). The rest of the country fell into the hands of the Naiman prince Kuchluk, whose neighbors, the prince of the Uigurs in the south and the khan of the Karluk in the north, as well as the prince of Almalik in the Ili valley, placed themselves under Chinghiz Khan's protection.

After the conquest of Peking, Chinghiz Khan in 1215 sent his son Juchi toward the west against the people of the Merkit, who had been allied with the Naiman and expelled from their seats along Lake Baikal into the Kirghiz steppes. While on this campaign, Juchi encountered an army of the Khwarizm Shah sent to subjugate the Kipchak tribe, neighbors of the Merkit. Since the battle remained undecided, Juchi apparently preferred to ignore it as based on a misunderstanding. The Khwarizm Shah, however, thought it advisable to learn through an embassy to Chinghiz Khan concerning the latter's resources.* Trade relations between the two empires had no doubt existed previously.

All the more incomprehensible is the behavior of the Khwarizm Shah in the conflict which broke out in 1218. At that time three Muslim merchants with opulent gifts appeared before him in Transoxania as emissaries of the Mongol khan to greet him as "his most beloved son," i.e. in the diplomatic language of the period as his vassal. However, though our sources state that the Shah expressed his irritation at this to the ambassadors only after the audience, nevertheless it is scarcely to be assumed that the assassination of the ambassadors which took place at the frontier station soon afterward and the pillaging of their caravans could have been accomplished

* Later narrators hostile to the 'Abbasids have interpreted this initial Muslim embassy to the Mongols as one of the caliph an-Nasir, who used it to seek Mongol aid against the Khwarizm Shah.

without his knowledge, especially since he had a second embassy massacred instead of according them the desired satisfaction.

Chinghiz Khan could not allow this grave insult to go unpunished. Although a portion of his army was still tied down by the war against the Kin in China, he assembled the pick of his troops under his own command and that of his sons in a battle against Khwarizm, for which the Muslim princes of the Karluk and of Almalik were also compelled to provide military aid. With incomprehensible blindness the Khwarizm shah Muhammad failed to concentrate all the forces of his empire, although he would then have been numerically superior to the Mongols. Since he had reason to mistrust the troops from the territories only just subjugated, he contented himself with strengthening the border fortifications and in Samarqand he himself awaited the attack of the main Mongol force, which was advancing in four columns and driving the inhabitants of the surrounding villages as the shock troops and as sappers for the siege of the cities ahead of them. While Chinghiz Khan's sons were besieging the border fortifications, the Grand Khan himself pressed through at once to Bukhara, which after a brief siege was taken and practically reduced to ashes, amid horrible atrocities. At the news of this misfortune the Khwarizm Shah, discouraged, retreated to Balkh, then to Nishapur. While occupying Samarqand and the other larger cities himself, Chinghiz Khan sent a few detachments in pursuit of the Shah. With a certain amount of energy and with the troops still at his disposal the Shah could easily have marched against the Mongols, for his Turkish soldiery knew that under no circumstances would they be spared by the Mongols, and in the individual garrisons they defended themselves with the utmost valor. Muhammad finally found his last refuge on a small island in the Caspian Sea, where his pursuers had lost trace of him; he died there on January 11, 1221. He was succeeded by his eldest son, Jalal-ad-Din Mangubirti.

While the Mongols continued their work of destruction along the southern shore of the Caspian Sea and then broke out over the Caucasus into southern Russia, to return to their homeland across the Volga, Jalal-ad-Din had first of all gone back to Khwarizm, which was still spared by them. But the Turks there were devoted to his younger brother Oslag, for whom the throne had previously been intended, and refused allegiance to him. In consequence he went to Ghaznah, and there succeeded in assembling an army for battle against Chinghiz Khan, who meanwhile had conquered Khwarizm and Khorasan. Jalal-ad-Din was able to defeat an advanced detachment of the Mongols near Perwan, in the mountains between Bamiyan and the valleys of Kabul and Ghaznah, but dissension broke out among his emirs, and in consequence the Khalj tribe and the Turkomans abandoned him; he was in no position to risk another advance against the Mongols with the remnant of his army which was still true to him. As a result he fled to India; but his Mongol pursuers set a trap for him along the steep banks of the Indus, which he did not dare cross, and pulverized almost his entire army, while he himself saved his life only by a desperate plunge through the tearing river (November 1221). In India afterward he was able to group another petty combat force around himself of scattered Turkish adventurers. For a time Chinghiz Khan ceased his pursuit, and while continuing the massacres in the former lands of Khwarizm slowly withdrew to Mongolia.

For three years the Khwarizm Shah held out in India, then he betook himself to the Persian province of Kirman, which had been conquered by Buraq Hajib, the guardian of his brother Ghiyath-ad-Din Pirshah. Here and in the mountains of the Median-Persian border he had roved about for another few years with Turks and Mongols, until in August 16, 1231, he fell victim to a Kurd's thirst for vengeance. However planless the manner in which his battles had all been fought, nevertheless he had been the last defender of Islam against the pagans and as such deserves the admiration with which his secretary an-Nasawi described his life. The other Muslim princes, the Ayyubids in Syria as well as the Seljuqs in Asia Minor, vied with each other in fawning on the Mongols in order to be at least tolerated in their own states as Mongol vassals.

After his triumph over Iran, Chinghiz Khan recuperated for a few years in the newly subjugated steppes and then in his home country, and in 1225 set out on another campaign against the Tangut kingdom in Hsia, the present-day province of Kansu, which comes like a wedge between north and south China. During the siege of their capital he died, a few days before its surrender, in August 1227. During his lifetime he had already divided up his empire among his sons, according to Mongol custom. The eldest son, Juchi, remained in the western countries he had conquered; there he soon felt himself so independent that his father had already considered leading him back to obedience by force, but he died six months before his father. His second son, Chaghatai, was regarded as the best connoisseur of the legal code established by his father; as such he exercised the greatest influence from his residences in the Ili valley, without laying claim to any particular sphere of authority, but after Juchi's death became his heir. While the youngest son, Tului, according to Mongol custom, inherited his father's "house" (that is, the tribal seat in eastern Mongolia), the third, Ogotay, was proclaimed great khan (*ka'an*) by Chinghiz Khan's orders and set up his residence along the Orkhon.

Ogotay and Chaghatai died close together in time, at the turn of the year 1241/42. Feuds now broke out among their heirs which granted the countries of Islam another period of grace. At the parliament of 1235 Juchi's second son, Batu, was charged with bringing eastern Europe under Mongol rule. In 1236 he set out in the company of sons of Chaghatai, Ogotay, and Tului, and in 1237 conquered the capital of the Volga Bulgars. In 1237-1240 Russia was conquered, Poland in 1241/42, Hungary and Dalmatia in 1241/42. On Christmas day of 1241 Batu crossed the frozen Danube and conquered Gran; in the spring of 1242 he went on to Bulgaria, and in the winter of 1242/43 returned to the Volga region by way of Wallachia and Moldavia. Even on this expedition conflict had broken out between himself and his cousins. In December 1241 Ogotay had died, and it was not until 1246 that his eldest son Geyük, who had rebelled against Batu during the Balkan campaign, was proclaimed great khan. But only two years later on the expedition westward which Batu was preparing to fend off as an attack on his territory, Geyük was surprised by death. As senior of his house Batu sought to nominate his successor. At a parliament convoked by him, his brother Berke succeeded in securing the proclamation of Tului's oldest son, Mangu, as great khan. Since the sons of Chaghatai and Ogotay had not participated in this, they were all assassinated together with their kinsmen when they turned up later anyhow for the oath of allegiance, because they were reproached with having treacherous plans. So the Mongol Empire was divided between two spheres of authority whose marches were formed by the steppe between the rivers Talas and Chui. While Batu's descendants, as rulers of the "Golden Horde," decided the fortunes of eastern Europe, Mangu's brother Hulagu carried his rule on into the Near East.

On his westward course Hulagu crossed the Amu-Darya on

January 1, 1256, and received the immediate oath of allegiance of the petty princes of Persia and the Caucasus. Among them there appeared also the prince of the Assassins, whose name had long since lost its magic; but in the possession of a series of very strong fortresses the Assassins still represented a force to be reckoned with. The last Assassin prince, Rukn-ad-Din, who had just succeeded his father (who had been murdered, doubtless not without the son's knowledge), was not, however, accepted among Hulagu's vassals, and fled upon this rejection to the fortress of Maymun-Diz in the Alamut district. The famous mathematician and astronomer Nasir-ad-Din at-Tusi lived with him. The latter advised him, no doubt in the hope of saving his own life in this way, to surrender himself without any resistance. But even while being transported to the Khan's encampment Rukn-ad-Din was assassinated. His followers were ferreted out and slain throughout Persia. But at-Tusi was received graciously and accompanied his new master as his court astrologer on his further expeditions, and was then charged with the foundation of the famous astronomical observatory at Maragha in Adharbayjan.

It was Hulagu's object from the very beginning to create as the vassal of his brother a new empire for himself in the west. Since Persia lay at his feet, the 'Abbasid realm in Babylonia was his closest neighbor. Here again, since 1225, the energetic an-Nasir had been succeeded by weaklings. The Mongol hardly needed any urging by Shi'ite Persians like at-Tusi to direct his attention to this easy plunder. After some negotiations, in which the last of the 'Abbasids missed the right moment for surrender at a point when he was surely incapable of gathering his forces for serious resistance, Baghdad fell into the hands of the Mongols on January 17, 1258. The city itself was mainly spared, but the Caliph, after his palace had been sacked, was executed together with many of his kinsmen, though a few escaped to Egypt, where, as already related, the Mamluk Baybars, in order to legitimize his rule, raised one of them to the throne as mock caliph under the name of al-Mustansir-billah. This shadowy existence continued to be led by his descendants down to the Ottoman conquest (1516/17).

Directly after the fall of Baghdad the petty Syrian princes also announced their submission. But in the Turkish Mamluks of Egypt the Mongols encountered their first successful opposition. The

Mongol demand to surrender was answered by an attack in Palestine; on September 3, 1260, the Mamluks inflicted a decisive defeat on Hulagu's army at 'Ayn Jalut near Nablus, while he himself was entangled in a war with the Golden Horde, whose khan Berke felt himself menaced by Hulagu's newly aspiring power. The Mamluks, particularly the sultan Baybars, then gradually wrested all of Syria from Hulagu and his successors the ilkhans, and the central Mongol power, meanwhile fallen into dissolution through splintering, could provide its western branch with no assistance.

Among these ilkhans only one more, Hulagu's great-grandson and Arghun's son, Ghazan, deserves mention (1295-1304). It is true he shortened his life, like most of his people, through the Mongol hereditary vice of drunkenness; nevertheless, in the short reign granted him he attempted to make up to a certain extent for his ancestor's crimes against Persia. Like his forefathers, who as pure-bred warriors had never sought any kind of spiritual community with their subjects, Hulagu himself had remained a pagan, even though he showed favor to the Buddhists and, to please his Christian wife Dokuz Khatun, to her own coreligionists. Ghazan, on the other hand, had been brought up in Buddhism, but shortly before his accession to the throne, when he took the field against one of his cousins, went over to Islam together with his entire army, and to the Sunnite denomination at that, which, however, his brother and successor Uljaitu Khodabanda (1309) exchanged for the Shi'ite. As indicated by the coins minted during his reign, Ghazan no longer wished to act as deputy of the Great Khan resident in Peking, but had himself designated as ruler "by the power of heaven." With respect to his kinsmen and the Mongol emirs he imposed his authority with ruthless severity; even the emir Nauruz, to whom he owed his throne, very soon fell victim to it. He encouraged the economic development of his empire. While land taxes hitherto had been imposed according to the whim of the Mongol governors and their Persian officials, he ordered first of all a new general survey to serve as the basis of taxation. In a tax decree of 1304 he ordered that the subjects were to be notified on taxation data at the entrances to the villages or at the mosques, churches, and synagogues, and even among the nomads at their grazing grounds by means of inscriptions on wood, stone, or metal, or on chalked boards. This account by his historian Rashid-ad-Din has been expressly confirmed by two inscriptions in Ani and in Angora from the time of his successors.* He encouraged new settlement in the innumerable areas bereft of their inhabitants as a result of the Mongol whirlwind and since then lying fallow. The new settlers were exempt from taxes. He gave renewed confidence to commerce and affairs by substituting a full-weight metal currency for the arbitrarily valued paper money introduced by his predecessors on the Chinese model. Thanks to these measures the state revenues during his reign went up from 1,700 to 2,100 tomans, or around twelve million dollars. He regulated anew the juridical situation in Persia, thrown into a muddle by the extremely simple and indefinite Mongol common law, and restored the validity of Islamic law. He established a common supreme court for the two realms of law. He adorned his capital of Tabriz with magnificent buildings, providing the local mosques and institutes of learning with opulent foundations. He also had an observatory and in connection with this founded a school for secular sciences, which he, like other Mongol princes, esteemed particularly because of their practical application. At his command, and, according to the record, with his personal collaboration, his court physician and all-powerful minister Rashid-ad-Din wrote a detailed history of the Mongols in Persian, which was named the *Ghazan Chronicle* (*Ta'rikhi Ghazani*).

Under Ghazan's brother and successor, Uljaitu Khodabanda, the power of the ilkhans was maintained at its peak. The city of Sultaniyah in northern 'Iraq, on the watershed between the rivers Zanjan and Abhar, which because of its wholesome mountain climate amid pastures and hunting grounds had always attracted the Mongols, and which had already been fortified by Arghun, was raised by him at the birth of his son Abu Sa'id to the status of capital. It could not, however, maintain its position after the fall of the dynasty as against the more favorably located Tabriz. Uljaitu strengthened his power in the interior by eliminating the princes of Jilan and Herat; his attempts to secure a foothold in Asia Minor and dam up the Mamluk power remained unsuccessful, as did his endeavors to secure the help of the Christian powers of Europe for that purpose.

Under Ghazan and his successors—and soon under their kinsmen also as far away as China—Persian, along with Turkish, became a language of state affairs and international intercourse. Mongolian proved to be too clumsy, and in any case there could be no ques-

* See W. Barthold ap. P. Wittek, *Festschrift Jacob*, 348.

tion of an independent intellectual life among the Mongols. It is true that for his state chancery Chinghiz Khan, as mentioned above, had taken over from the Naiman the use of the Uigur script, a descendant of the Syriac form of the Semitic alphabet on which our own is also based, and which Nestorian missionaries had been spreading as far as the interior of Asia for centuries. It also served for writing East Turkish, and had supplanted the runelike script, also descended from a perversion of the Semitic alphabet, in which the oldest Turkish khans known to us had left us accounts of their exploits on the shores of the Orkhon in the eighth century. But the Turks also had not developed an independent literature of any consequence which could compete with Persian, though the Uigurs, at their headquarters in Turfan at the southern foot of the Tien Shan, had created an abundant literature of translations, under the influence of Buddhist and Manichean missionaries, in which the Uigur script was first put to use; remnants of it have been made accessible to us by the German Central Asiatic expedition in particular and first explained by the genius of the German scholar K. F. W. Müller. A lyric and epic national literature, once richly developed among the Central Asiatic Turks, is known to us only in fragments, through quotations in the oldest and most comprehensive textbook of Turkish for Arabs, by Mahmud of Kashghar (1073). The first independent Turkish literary monument, after the Orkhon inscriptions, first arose half a century after the decline of the Uigur kingdom in Kashghar, where in 1069-70 Yusuf Khass Hajib of Balasaghun drafted for the sultan Bughrakhan Hasan ibn-Sulayman Arslan a great didactic poem on the wisdom of life, for princes in particular, entitled *Kutadhghu Bilig* (*The Science of Being Happy*), based on the ideas of the philosopher Ibn Sina (Avicenna), in a meter taken from Persian literary models; he places his teachings in the mouths of allegorical figures of his own invention—a Prince Kun Toghdu as representative of justice, a Wazir Ai Toldu as representative of happiness, and the latter's son Oktulmish and his friends Alig and Ot Okturmish; in spite of their naïve pedantry they give us many valuable insights into the structure of society and state in the author's cultural milieu. The overwhelming influence of Islam is not yet to be detected in this work, though in the national literature which soon sprang up on this model, and in which the ascension of the Prophet and the lives of the saints provided the most important subjects, it became more and more evident. Only in individual cases was the Uigur script made use of; it was forced out steadily by the Arabic script, in which the original of the *Kutadhghu Bilig* may also have been written down. The further evolution of East Turkish literature, in which the Persian influence became more and more important, did not take place until the period of Timur and his successors, in the fifteenth and sixteenth centuries.

During the Mongol tempests Persian literature had found a refuge in the southwest of Iran, in the province of Fars. In 1148 one of the so-called Seljuq atabegs, of the house of Salghur, had made himself independent there, and his dynasty survived for 130 years as tributaries first of the 'Iraqi Seljuqs, then of the Khwarizm shah, and finally of the Mongols. From 1256 to 1291 under one of these rulers, Sa'd ibn-Zengi, the poet Sa'di—who took this name after his patron—in his native city of Shiraz, where he settled down after a turbulent, migratory life, wrote his two chief works, of a moralizing nature, the *Gulistan* or *Rose Garden*, of mingled verse and prose, and the *Bustan*, or *Pleasure Garden*, entirely in verse; the first of these works (which since 1654 has been naturalized in Europe by the German translation of the Silesian Olearius,* i.e. Ölschläger) is regarded by every Persian down to the present day as the classic expression of an aspect of the national character strongly predominant until the national revolution, the "inclination to bigotry and fiddle-faddle," and as such is closest to his heart. For a long time after the collapse of the ilkhans' rule the peace and quiet of the rose city, Shiraz, also belonged to the past. Around 1340 the emir Abu Ishaq ibn-Mahmud Shah Inju succeeded in seizing the city; but he lost it in 1353 to Muhammad, the Muzaffarid who boasted of authentic Arab origin as a descendant of one of the tribes settled in Khorasan during the conquest. He was followed in 1364 by his son Shah Shuja', who had destroyed his father's sight in 1358 and put him in prison. Under him there flourished the most famous of all Persian lyric poets, Shams-ad-Din Muhammad, known by the poetic name of Hafiz ("He who knows the Qur'an"), a Shi'ite (of the Twelvers) who could not draw a free breath until after the death of Muhammad, who was a fanatical Sunnite. The new sultan Shah Shuja' was sympathetic to him and upon the suggestion of one of the poet's friends, the minister Qiwam-ad-Din Hasan, gave him the professorship for Qur'anic exegesis at the madrasah in Shiraz, which he filled until he

* [Olearius, Adam, *The Voyages and Travells*, 2nd ed., London, 1669.]

died in 1389, after surviving the invasion of Timur. From the time when he published his diwan, in 1368-69, his name has been celebrated throughout the Persian-speaking world. His poems praise the beauty of nature, particularly when newly roused in spring, as he enjoyed it so often along the banks of the canal laid out by the Buyid Rukn-ad-Dawlah in 950 for the irrigation of the Shiraz plain, and of the promenade of Musalla, in which he also found his last resting place. They echo the yearning song of the nightingale, glorify the joys of youth, wine, and, with a tender reserve, the homosexual love widespread in the Orient for ages; they mock at all hypocrisy and cant as well as at every other kind of philistinism, and bear witness to a great and liberal spirit, which under the mournful conditions of his homeland learned to despise all other values of existence and sought a substitute for them in pleasure alone. By later investing these completely secular songs of his with an additional significance (reminiscent of the reinterpretation of the extremely sensuous Song of Songs by the Christian church) this refined mocker and aesthete found admirers in pious milieux as well. By virtue of their perfect form, as matchless examples of the *ghazel*, or love lyric, they have served as guide to all later Persian and Turkish poets.

But the greatest mystic poet of Islam, Jalal-ad-Din Rumi, born in Balkh in 1207, grew up abroad in a non-Persian land. His father, Baha-ad-Din Walad, had fallen into disfavor with the Khwarizm shah Muhammad and been compelled to leave the country. In 1226, after protracted wanderings, he found a patron in the Seljuq prince 'Ala-ad-Din Kaykobad at Konya in Asia Minor. He received a professorship there, in which he was succeeded after his death in 1230 by his son. Soon afterward, however, the latter encountered the mystic Shams-ad-Din Tabrizi, who won him over entirely to a life of contemplation, and in whose name he published his diwan. He founded the widespread and, until the national revolution in Turkey, very influential order of the Mawlawis, or Dancing Dervishes, who sought their way into mystic ecstasy to the music of the flute. His chief work, the *Mathnawi* (Mesnevi) gives an unsystematized six-volume exposition in fables, stories, and reflections cast in highly poetical language of the basic ideas of mysticism, yearning for a pantheistic dissolution of the ego; among his followers his work was valued almost as highly as the Qur'an, and for centuries it determined the intellectual outlook of the best elements in the Ottoman Empire.

3. The Ottoman Turks as the Leading Power in Islam

1. *The Origins of the Ottoman Empire and its Expansion down to the Time of Suleyman I*

WHILE around the middle of the thirteenth century numerous Turkish tribes were still contending for booty on the ruins of the caliphate—created by the Arabs, undermined by the Persians, and destroyed by the Mongols—there arose in its northwestern border area, in Asia Minor, the power which was destined not only to survive all other Turkish states, but to become the leader of all Islam for nearly half a millennium.*

For centuries there had been conflicts along the borders of Syria and Asia Minor, with alternating but never decisive success, between Muslim raiding parties and Byzantine mercenaries. On both sides there had developed a frontier society of Islamic *ghazis* and Greek *akritoi* who despite the antagonism of the religions, which were splintered on both sides into all sorts of sects, cultivated kindred ideas of chivalry and promoted a cultural exchange between Islam and Christianity. When the Seljuqs set up their empire, Alp Arslan attempted to secure its frontiers by an attack on Anatolia. On the Armenian highland he defeated the Byzantine emperor Romanus Diogenes near Manzikert in 1071 and took him prisoner. Although he himself had no thought of attaining any lasting acquisitions here, but freed his captive after the conclusion of an honorable peace treaty, nevertheless this victory in the long run did create entirely new conditions.

* See M. F. Köprülü, *Les Origines de l'Empire Ottoman*, Paris, 1935; P. Wittek, *The Rise of the Ottoman Empire*, London, 1938; H. A. Gibbons, *Foundation of the Ottoman Empire, History of the Osmanlis, 1300-1403*, Oxford, 1916.

In the border areas, on the Taurus and in Cilicia, there arose independent Armenian principalities, which later developed into the kingdom of Lesser Armenia. In Malatya (Melytene) the governors of Armenian descent who had split off from Byzantium were ousted by the Greek Gabriel, who had his possession of the country confirmed by the caliph in Baghdad himself. However, the weakness of the borderland, no longer defended by the capital, also lured the Turks into renewed forays. Alp Arslan's kinsman Kutlumish had revolted against him in 1063 and was killed in battle. Kutlumish's son Suleyman was sent to Asia Minor in 1072 by Alp Arslan's son and successor Malikshah in order to remove him from the center of the empire, together with the Turkish bands who were still ranging about throughout the empire, imperiling its tranquillity. In a bold advance Suleyman wrested the northwest of Anatolia from the Byzantines and set up his residence in Nicaea in 1081, in threatening proximity to Byzantium itself. But this most extended outpost of Islam was lost again during the First Crusade. Suleyman's real goal, however, remained a position of authority in the east. By 1084 he had seized Antioch, and he was killed in 1086 during an attack on Aleppo. His son Kilij Arslan attempted to create a new base for himself in southeastern Asia Minor for the execution of his father's plans. Here he met with a rival, the Turkish leader Danishmend, who may have been of Armenian origin. With the aid of bands of Turkish border fighters he established a domain in Sivas, abandoned by Byzantium, and extended it in the north as far as Ankara, Amasia, and Niksar (Neocaesarea) and in the south as far as Albistan. In 1101 he wrested Malatya from Gabriel, after Bohemund's attempt to relieve the Greek had failed. Since it did not occur to him to concentrate his power, based only on plunder, into a stable government, it dissolved again when the Byzantines, with the help of the Crusaders, reunited the west of Anatolia with their empire. But Kilij Arslan did not succeed until after Danishmend's death in 1106 in winning Malatya and establishing himself in Mayafariqin; from there he attempted, like his father, to establish a new sphere of authority in the east. He lost his life during an advance on Mosul in 1107, in a battle on the banks of the Khabur.

After that his successors limited themselves to Asia Minor. His son Mas'ud took Konya (Iconium), which the German emperor Barbarossa had occupied for fourteen days, May 18-26, 1190, before being killed in the flood tides of the Calycadnus in Cilicia while marching off to the Third Crusade. The plain between Konya and Kayseri, very fertile under irrigation, with a Greek population still uninfluenced by the frontier community, provided him and his successors with a base for the foundation of an Islamic state which, after the example of the caliphs, allowed its subjects a separate religion and cultural life in order to secure from the revenues of their toil a lordly existence for the conquerors. As ancient Byzantine soil their realm continued to be called Rum.* In a surprise attack in the pass of Chardak (Myriokephaloi) his son Kilij Arslan II finally succeeded in securing his frontiers against Byzantium by decisively defeating and imposing a peace on the emperor Manuel, who was also attempting to restore his rule in the east. After a number of battles with Danishmend's successors, in which the Byzantines and the kings of Lesser Armenia also took a hand, he was able to wrest Malatya from them in 1177 and put an end to their regime in 1180.

Under his sons, who held their dominions from him while he was still alive, the Seljuq power disintegrated. But after the foundation of the Latin empire by the Frankish knights in Byzantium, Kaykobad and his son Kayka'us exploited the latter's weakness to extend their power toward the south and north. They won the important harbor sites of Adalia (Antalya) on the Mediterranean and Sinope on the Black Sea. This opened their kingdom to world trade, and by favorable commercial treaties with the Italian city-republics it was able to exchange its abundant agricultural produce at an advantage. The resulting flow of capital into the country enabled the emirs to patronize a flourishing architecture and the artistic handicrafts.

Richly ornamented façades are particularly characteristic of Seljuq building. Their mosques and madrasahs are effective primarily by virtue of magnificent gate structures. Images of plants and animals are intermingled among the bands of script and the geometric border ornamentations. In these, Turkish popular art was freed from the hostility to images of the older Islamic art, born of Semitic abstraction; but in the Turkish cultural milieu animal ornamentation remained limited to profane constructions, such as, for instance, the city wall of Konya, while the same style, by way of Armenia and Russia, also engulfed the church façades of western Europe.†

But wealth, for the Seljuqs, had calamitous consequences also. Softened by luxury, they grew more and more unaccustomed to

* See P. Wittek, *Le Sultan de Rum*, in *Mélanges Boisacq*, Brussels, 1938.
† See E. Diez, *Die Kunst der islamischen Völker*, p. 125.

military service and left the profession of arms to Greek, Armenian, and Arab mercenaries. In 1239, under the reign of Kaykhosraw II, a popular reaction took place against the degeneracy of the emirs; the rebellion, however, led by the dervish Baba Ishaq, was drowned in blood. But the Mongols were already pressing against the borders of Asia Minor and inflicted a serious defeat on the troops of Kaykhosraw II at Közedagh in 1243. Kaykhosraw was still able to purchase his independence from the Mongols in return for the payment of a heavy tribute, but after his death in 1245, when bickerings over the throne broke out among his sons, Hulagu interceded and divided up the lands along the boundary of the Kizil Irmak (Halys) between his two sons 'Izz-ad-Din and Rukn-ad-Din. The former attempted to ally himself with the only successful opponents of the Mongols, the Egyptian Mamluks, and was punished for this by being deprived of his dominion, while his brother was subjected to the supervision of a Mongol functionary with the title of *perwana*. Soon afterward the latter deposed him, to rule alone as guardian of Rukn-ad-Din's son Ghiyath-ad-Din. The Turkish emirs now summoned Baybars into the country, who had defeated the Mongols at Albistan in 1277 and pressed forward as far as Kayseri. But since he found no support within the country, he soon had to withdraw again, and then Abaka inflicted severe punishment on the emirs as well as on the perwana, for not having gone out against Baybars. The independence of the kingdom was definitely over with.

But in the frontier lands the ancient ghazi ideals revived once again. In the wake of the Mongols numerous religious leaders and heads of orders had streamed into Anatolia from central Asia. They resuscitated the idea of the Holy War against the Byzantines, while the latter, occupied with the restoration of their power in the Balkans, allowed their resistance in Asia Minor to slacken. In this way western Asia Minor was overrun by the Turks once again, and the emirs of the ghazis set up independent domains in the different provinces. These principalities were not put an end to until the Osmanlis. In ancient Lycaonia and Isauria the Karamans were settled, in Kütahya (Cotyaeum) the Germians, in Mysia the Hamids, in Magnesia the Sarukhans. While the foregoing ghazis advanced by land, one of the oldest and most important of these emirates arose by way of the sea. From the coasts of Lycia and Pamphylia, Turks under the leadership of the Menteshe clan, in alliance with Byzantine seafarers who had lost their livelihood through the dissolution of the fleet in 1284, pressed into Caria and pushed up the Maeander. From these coasts, which even in antiquity had harbored a pirate state rising to menace the Roman Empire itself, they ravaged the shores of the Aegean Sea, and even conquered Rhodes, until the Knights of St. John drove them out in 1310.* Seeing themselves hemmed in, they allied themselves with their northern neighbor, the emirate of Aidin, which was further disturbing the Aegean Sea, until an alliance of the Venetians with Cyprus and the Knights of St. John broke their power by occupying Smyrna in 1344.

Among the Turks who took up the struggle against Byzantium with particular success were the Osmanlis. Legend has the following to relate of their origins: The Kayi clan, of the Turkish tribal federation of the Oghuzzes, is supposed to have had to retreat before the Mongols pressing forward in Khorasan, and to have accepted the protection of the Khwarizm shah Jalal-ad-Din Mangubirti, who showed them the way to grazing grounds in northwestern Armenia. After the assassination of their patron, their chieftain Suleyman is supposed to have decided to lead his people back to the steppes of inner Asia, away from the chaos of petty states contending for the ancient lands of civilization. But when he was killed while on his wanderings, at the ford over the Euphrates near the heights of Aleppo, his third son Ertoghrul led at least the smaller section of the tribe, about four hundred families, back to Asia Minor and with them entered the service of the Seljuq sultan of Iconium, 'Ala-ad-Din II. The latter enfeoffed him with the border marches against the Byzantines at Sogud in the Karasu valley and on the mountains of Domanich and Ermeni-Dagh, and left it to him to expand his holdings at the expense of his Christian neighbors. His son Osman, reputedly born in 1258, is supposed to have removed his residence as early as 1288 from Sogud farther southward to Melangenon, which he conquered and rebaptized Karajahisar.

But this saga cannot withstand historical criticism. Osman's son Orkhan, in the inscriptions on the mosque at Brusa which he had built in 1334, designated himself simply as "Sultan, son of the Sultan of the Ghazis, Ghazi son of the Ghazi, Marzuban of the Horizons,

* See P. Wittek, *Das Fürstentum Mentesche, Studie zur Geschichte Westkleinasiens im 13.-15. Jahrhundert* (*Istanbuler Mitteilungen*, published by the Istanbul Section of the Archaeological Institute of the German Reich II) Istanbul, 1934.

Hero of the World." * Sultan of the Ghazis is what one of his father's contemporaries called himself, the emir of Aidin on the Maeander, who accepted this title from a leader of the Mawlawi order in Konya. In the same way Orkhan's father Osman had already had his sword girded round him by his father-in-law, the dervish Shaykh Edebali, as Ghazi ("Warrior of the Faith"); and later also the Osmanli sultans in Stambul were likewise girded round with the sword of Osman by the imam of the Mosque of Ayyub on the Golden Horn, and so invested with their rank. After Osman resumed the war against Byzantium, ghazis poured in to him from all sections of Anatolia and from the most variegated Turkish tribes. The *akhis*—artisans' and merchants' associations organized on the pattern of the dervish orders and already spread over all of Asia Minor—followed the ghazis into the youthful state, where they served the warriors in the exploitation of their booty; but they could not have played a dominating role in the foundation of the state, as may have been thought. They were followed further by the 'ulama as representatives of Islamic civilization. In finances, Christians and Jews proved indispensable as in all the Islamic states.

From Karajahisar, Osman directed the striking power of his people, constantly being reinforced by immigration from every Turkish tribe, to the Propontis and the Black Sea, and in the west as far as Yenishehir, which controlled the ford over the Gokjesu. In 1300 he bequeathed Karajahisar to his son Orkhan once again as fief. The Mongols, who at that time were putting an end to the rule of the Seljuqs of Konya, left the Osmanlis unmolested in the extremest northwest of Asia Minor.

In 1326 Orkhan crowned the work of his father, while the latter lay on his deathbed at Sogud, with the conquest of Brusa, at the foot of the Olympus (Kashish-Dagh). He then had his father's corpse interred in the castle church, which was straightway turned into a mosque; Brusa thus became the holy city of the Osmanlis. Here, in the new capital of the realm, there soon arose magnificent buildings, of which the oldest mosque, the Ulu Jami, an unadorned hall of columns of rectangular form and with five naves, each of four cupolas in a row, was, to be sure, not built until Orkhan's successor Murad I. In 1327 Nicomedia (Izmid) also fell into Orkhan's hands, and now as a true believer of Islam he expressed his apprecia-

* See P. Wittek, *Deux chapitres de l'Histoire des Turcs de Roum*, *Byzantion* XI (1936) 285-318, p. 315.

tion of knowledge, whose cultivation always constituted one of the great titles of glory of Muslim rulers, by creating the first Ottoman institute of learning (madrasah), whose direction he delegated to the Egyptian-trained Da'ud al-Qaysari.

The Byzantines attempted to save Nicaea at least, but their army of relief was defeated at Philokrene in 1330. The city had to surrender to the Osmanlis, and under their rule soon revived again as the seat of the faience industry and of a number of institutes of learning. In 1335 the contention among Orkhan's dynasty for the throne of the neighboring ghazi state of Karasi in ancient Mysia, with the capital at Bergama (Pergamon), offered an occasion for interference in that country; but it does not seem to have been decisively subdued until 1345.

Soon a need for more rigid organization became evident. As the emirs themselves—the Ottoman rulers frequently still called themselves this until 1473—traced back their territorial rights to an enfeoffment by the sultan of Konya, so for their own part they enfeoffed again their fellow tribesmen and comrades-in-arms of proven courage with estates in the conquered territories, in return for the obligation to provide horsemen for the general draft. This military objective of the fief received its expression in their being grouped into *sanjaq*s, i.e. banners. After its conquest Brusa was turned into the capital of a new sanjaq, which was given to the crown prince Murad and named Khudawend (Ruler's Land). Later on there were two of these sanjaqs—Sultan-Onu, or In-Onu, comprising the tribal seats of the Osmanlis in the southeast, and Koja-Ili, the coastal regions in the northwest, named after their conqueror and first bey, Akche Koja.

In Osmanli religious life, as among the other Turkish tribes, Shi'ite tendencies, represented by the influential dervishes, were still entirely dominant. The legal code of the realm was theoretically supposed to repose only on the divine law laid down in the Qur'an and in the Sunnah as revealed in the oral statements of the Prophet. Although this Sunnah was in no way disavowed by the Shi'ites either, nevertheless in contrast to the Sunnites in the narrower sense they recognized only the imams as bearers of the tradition of the Prophet, rejecting all bearers of the tradition not belonging to the family of the Prophet, who were regarded by the Sunnites as having equal authority. However, since even these two sources of law were inadequate for settling every question of life, now much more complicated and resting on entirely different economic foundations, it was necessary to recognize new and purely temporal regulations in addition to divine law; for even at that time this was too rigid for anyone to have ventured adapting it to new conditions, as the jurists during the first few centuries of Islam had still been able to do. Thus there arose among the Osmanlis, in addition to the Shar'-i Sherif (Holy Law), the Qanun (Canon); its capacity for development was recognized from the outset and it was further added to by later sultans.

The first secular statutes are traced back to a brother of the sultan Orkhan by the name of Alaeddin, who, we are told, as a youth renounced the world, but then returned to the court to place his legal knowledge at the service of the state. In consequence he is traditionally regarded as the first wazir of the empire. His efforts are said to have been directed at first to three points: the coinage, the regulation of dress, and the organization of the army.

The right of placing his name on coins had long been regarded in Islam as a token of the prince's sovereignty, along with the mention of his name in the Friday prayers. As vassals of the sultans of Konya the Osmanli emirs in any case had had to allow the latter's coins free circulation in their territory for a long time, even though their historians are concerned with ascribing to them the exercise of minting rights as early as possible. But the report that Alaeddin did not have silver coins minted in Orkhan's name until 1328 is decidedly the only trustworthy one. This new coin was adapted to the coinage introduced by the Seljuqs on the Byzantine pattern. Its par weight is supposed to have amounted to six *qirat*, i.e. a quarter of the dirham current in other Muslim countries. The coin was named, as throughout Asia Minor, *akche* (white piece), in translation of the *aspron* (asper) in use throughout Byzantium since the tenth century. The oldest coins preserved show, on the averse, the profession of faith; on the reverse, the name of the prince in the colloquial form Okhan with the wish: "May God prolong his rule"; the name of the father as a title is absent, as well as indications of the year and the place of minting.

A modern Westerner may be surprised at the regulation of clothing which also was part of the first principles of the life of the Ottoman state. But on older levels of civilization clothing is an essential attribute of the personality, such as only the military uniform is today—not merely an external though necessary appendage

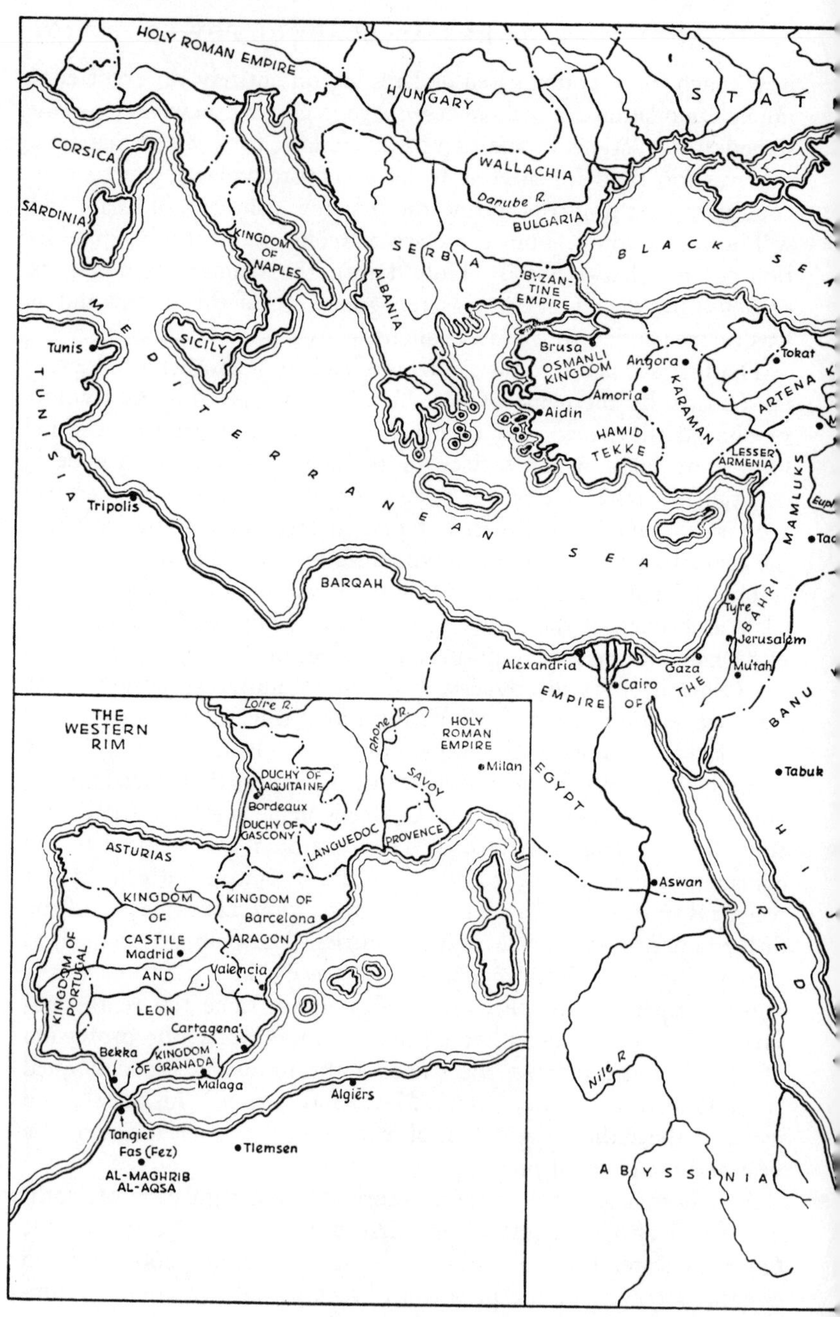

ISLAMIC DOMAINS

KIPCHAKS
Volga R.
Astrakhan
CASPIAN SEA
Lake Aral
Syr Darya (Jaxartes) R.
KHWARIZM
CHAGATAI
KINGDOM
FERGHANA
Urkend
Khiva
Samarqand
TRANSOXANIA
Amu Darya (Oxus) R.
Balkh
TUKHARISTAN
Merv
Kabul
KINGDOM OF THE SHOPANIDS OF ADHARBAYJAN
Tabriz
MAZANDERAN
KINGDOM OF THE SERBEDARS
Sebzevar
KINGDOM OF HERAT
Herat
GHOR
SUBRAN
DELHI EMPIRE
Hamadan
KINGDOM OF THE JALAIRIDS
LUR
KINGDOM KUHISTAN
Kandahar
KINGDOM OF SIJISTAN
Baghdad
Tigris R.
Yezd
Kelat
Indus R.
IRAQ
KHUZISTAN
KINGDOM OF FARS
KINGDOM OF THE MUZAFFARIDS
KINGDOM OF MEKRAN
Basra
Kuwayt
PERSIAN GULF
Hormuz
Kaj
Qatif
BAHRAYN
'UMAN
'Uyaynah
Dar'iyah
YAMAMAH
RUB' AL-KHALI
NAJRAN
YEMEN
San'a
Ma'rib
HADRAMAUT
Aden
Islamic Domains ca. 1350
Scale
0
500
1000 km.
0
500 mi.

CA. 1350

mostly dependent on the taste of the wearer. Clothing does not merely mark off the social classes, but peoples as well, and since the rights of the latter in the Islamic state were extremely varied, the legislator could not avoid being concerned with their marked differentiation as well. Just as the fez distinguished the Osmanli from the European, from the time of its introduction by Mahmud II down to its abolition by Mustafa Kemal in 1925, and as it still distinguishes the Egyptian down to the present day, so in the Orient for ages the headgear was considered really the characteristic article of clothing. As the token of adherence to the army and to the court, Alaeddin laid down white for the tall, cone-shaped felt cap worn at that time, as it still has been in various regions of Persia until recently. The Sultan himself, and the beys on ceremonial occasions, enwrapped the felt with the turban, the use of which did not become more general until later on.

In the organization of the army the Sultan and his brother are said to have had at their side as technical adviser the army magistrate of Bilejik, Kara Khalil Jandarli Khayr-ad-Din Pasha, although other sources do not indicate his appearance until the reign of Murad.* The Turks had distinguished themselves since their emergence from the steppes as skillful and recklessly bold horsemen; but they still lacked any sense of tactical organization. Though they were superior to the degenerate Byzantine mercenaries in the open field, still, fortified positions required other soldierly abilities. The creation of an infantry proved most essential. At first an attempt was made to form this from among the Turks themselves. For the duration of a campaign, a daily pay of one akche was granted possessors of military fiefs selected for infantry service, who were divided up into groups of ten, a hundred, and a thousand men. But this arrangement did not withstand a test. The unaccustomed service seduced the people into immoderate demands, so that after a short while Orkhan had to decide to dissolve this force.

Reputedly on Jandarli's advice, he reintroduced the old Islamic custom of taking a fifth of the booty for the state treasury, and so found the means of paying for a standing army. He attempted to find a substitute for the Turkish infantry among the Christians, who were accustomed to such service. But since according to one of the

* See Fr. Taeschner and P. Wittek, *Die Vezierfamilie der Gandarlyzade und ihre Denkmäler, Islam* 18, 60-115.

most important principles of Islamic constitutional law only Muslims could bear arms, the Christians selected for the new corps had to be converted to Islam by force. A beginning was made with a thousand Christian boys who were snatched from their families by force and compelled to deny their faith, but in return were bound to the person of the ruler by the prospect for a brilliant career. Like the Christian knightly orders created for the struggle against the infidels, this New Force (*Yeni Cheri*, whence Janizary) was also given a semireligious organization, supposedly as early as 1330. Asia Minor had always been a particularly fertile soil for all sorts of religious brotherhoods devoted to the cultivation of a mystic-ascetic life as well as to social welfare, particularly the care of foreign travelers; their membership proper was joined by numerous lay brethren such as the previously mentioned akhis. Thus the Janizaries joined the order of the Bektashis; its alleged founder, according to the legend, had given his blessing to the corps at its very inception. The cavalry was also given a firmer organization under Orkhan. As its basic stratum he created a paid elite troop, the four squadrons (Bolukiati Erbe'a)—in the beginning only 2,400 men strong; later as much as 16,000—to whose protection the great imperial standard, since Selim I the banner of the Prophet, was entrusted. But in addition there remained the feudal cavalry, the Musallamun ("the Tax-exempt"), who were under the command of the sanjaq beys.

With these newly organized troops Orkhan kept exerting more and more energetic pressure against the coasts, and soon the largest and most important harbors attempted to secure their commerce by formal submission to his rule. Although his first attack on Byzantium itself, which he undertook in 1337 in order to punish the emperor Cantacuzene for having agreed to a protective alliance with the Seljuqs against him, ended in a grave defeat, nevertheless the emperor had become so fearful of Orkhan's power, pressing in on him from his immediate vicinity, that for the time being he preferred an alliance with him; in 1345 he strengthened this by giving his daughter to him in marriage. It is true this did not prevent the Osmanlis from pressing forward: in 1357 under the command of the crown prince Suleyman they succeeded in establishing themselves in Kallipolis (Gallipoli) on the Thracian Chersonese; soon after this success, however, Suleyman died and was buried on Thracian soil.

Orkhan's second son Murad, who followed him on the throne in 1362, at once directed his gaze to the Balkan peninsula, where at that time innumerable petty rulers were rending each other in incessant warfare. But before he could set out for there, he still had a coalition of opponents in Asia Minor to overthrow. In Angora, which his brother Suleyman had incorporated into his father's realm in 1354, the administration, as was natural in a remote border city, had remained principally in the hands of wholesale merchants formed into an akhi association; the latter thought they could exploit the occasion of the change of ruler to rid themselves of the burdensome alien rule in alliance with the neighboring Karaman Seljuqs. But in a swift campaign which led him as far as Tokat, Murad overthrew his adversaries * and was able to turn his immediate attention to the Balkan war. He set up his headquarters in Demotika, and the Balkan princes fell victim one by one to the Osmanlis, who were firmly pursuing their far-reaching political aims. In 1362 the Byzantines lost Adrianople, which remained the capital of the Osmanli emirs from 1366 to the fall of Constantinople. In vain did Pope Urban V summon Christians to a crusade for the rescue of Constantinople. Although an army of knights under Amadios of Savoy secured a foothold in Gallipoli for a short time, it was unable to agree with the Byzantines on its further course and soon had to withdraw. The Palaeologi became more and more dependent on the Turks, for whom later they even had to provide military aid at the conquest of Philadelphia (Ala Shehir).

The disunity of the Balkan Slavs facilitated their subjugation by the Osmanlis. In 1371, while Murad was in Asia, the Serbs under the Mrnjavcevic Vukashin attempted, by an attack, to ward off the yoke threatening them but were bloodily defeated at Chirmen on Maritza by Hajji Ilbegi and lost their possessions in Macedonia. This was followed by the occupation of Sofia and Nish in 1385-86. The conquest of Macedonia was effected by Khayr-ad-Din Pasha Jandarli from Gallipoli (where in 1385 he had the great mosque, Eski Jami, erected) together with the army general Evrenos Beg, who after the overthrow of his Karasi house had been employed by Suleyman. From Gumuljina, which Evrenos had conquered, Zeres, contended for by Serbs and Byzantines, was taken, and from there Salonica conquered and northern Greece as far as Acarnania ravaged by forays. The Bulgarian czar Shishman III had had to divide the empire of his father Alexander with his brother Srasimir

* See P. Wittek, in *Festschrift Jacob*, 354.

residing in Vidin (1364) and had become Murad's brother-in-law; but when Murad's advance on the Balkans made him apprehensive, he nevertheless joined an alliance of the Serbs and Bosnians. Their united armies were confronted at Plochnik in 1387 by the Turkish marshal Lalashahin, who was defeated and whose army was almost totally annihilated. This victory was possible only because of Murad's renewed preoccupation with Asia. His oldest son and governor in Europe, Sawji, had revolted against him in alliance with a Byzantine prince and the Seljuq emir of Karaman; but these allies were defeated at Konya in 1386. In 1388 'Ali Pasha, the son of Kara Khalil Jandarli, was able to avenge the defeat of the Osmanlis in the Balkans. He crossed the Nadir pass with thirty thousand men and conquered the cities of Tirnovo and Shumla. The czar Shishman was hemmed in at Nicopolis on the Danube, but was granted a peace in return for the payment of tribute and the surrender of Silistria; when he broke the agreement, he was shut up again in Nicopolis, this time having to surrender unconditionally, but retained his throne and his life. The following year another great coalition was formed against the Osmanlis. On June 15, 1389, this time led by Murad himself after his sons Bayezid and Yaqub, as well as the vassals of Sarukhan, Menteshe, Aidin, and Hamid had rallied the Asiatic troops, the Osmanlis were confronted by the Serbs —with Bosnian, Magyar, Bulgar, and Albanian auxiliary troops—on the Field of Blackbirds (Kossovo Polye), the source of the three rivers Ibar, Vardar, and Drin. The decision wavered back and forth for a long time, and the resistance of the Christians inflicted many serious casualties on the Osmanlis. Murad himself was killed—according to Turkish versions treacherously murdered by a Serbian warrior, Milosh Kobilich, who lay wounded on the battlefield; according to the Serbian epics he fell in his tent beneath the dagger blows of twelve valiant warriors who had mutually bound themselves to this deed. But finally the Serb king Lazar, abandoned by his allies, was captured by the Osmanlis and decapitated on the spot together with his company, reputedly on the orders of the dying Sultan. The crown prince Bayezid, in command of the left flank, rallied the wavering ranks of his soldiers and led them to final victory over the Serbian forces enfeebled by the fall of their prince.*

* M. Braun, *Kosovo, Die Schlacht auf dem Amselfelde in geschichtlicher und epischer Uberlieferung* (*Slav. balt. Quellen und Forschungen*, published by R. Trautmann, VIII) Leipzig, 1937.

The new ruler, even more than his ancestors, devoted himself entirely to military matters, which he no longer conducted as the leader of ghazi bands but as the head of a great state, and his neighbors very soon came to feel the weight of his hand. In 1390 the Byzantines lost their last possession in Asia Minor, the city of Philadelphia, at the overthrow of which the young emperor Manuel himself had to provide the Sultan with military aid against his own loyal subjects. Three years later the Bulgars were definitely subjugated; after the fall of their prince Shishman, the patriarch Euthymius led their final resistance in the capital of Tirnovo.

By now, to be sure, these successes had aroused the concern of the west. Pope Boniface IX had the war against the infidels preached in France, in the Alpine countries, and in southern Germany, and in the spring of 1396 the idea of the crusade, seemingly long since forgotten, once again assembled a strong Western European army of knights around King Sigismund of Hungary in Buda. But the lack of discipline of these warriors of the faith altogether neutralized their enthusiasm. All of Sigismund's efforts for a tactical command remained unsuccessful, and thus on September 27 Bayezid was able to inflict a serious defeat on them in Nicopolis. The pursuing Osmanlis penetrated as far as Styria. The Crusaders' allies, the Latin rulers of the Peloponnesus, were punished by Bayezid with the devastation of their territories. In 1394, at the height of his success, Bayezid, by an embassy to the caliph Mutawakkil residing in Cairo, had applied for the bestowal on himself of the title Sultan of Rum, in order to give an official religious sanction in the eyes of the Islamic world to the power already exercised by his ancestors before him; the Mamluk sultan Barquq, the guardian of the Caliph, could not refuse his approval, since he necessarily perceived in the Osmanli his sole ally against the Mongol danger menacing both of them.

For the Ottoman kingdom was already being threatened from the east by a grave danger which procured another interlude of grace for the Greeks in Byzantium. Another great military hero had arisen among the Mongols, who once again visited all the horrors of barbarian devastation on the Islamic world. Around 1369 Timur, of Kesh in Transoxania, a descendant of Chinghiz Khan born in 1336, had dethroned the Chaghatai emir of Khorasan and Transoxania (a descendant of Chinghiz Khan's second son Chaghatai), who had merely served as the titular head of a regime in the hands of the

Turkish military nobility. Timur turned the latter's dominions into an empire of his own with the capital at Samarqand, which, in contrast to the nomadic traditions of his predecessors, was elevated to a fixed residence and embellished by Persian craftsmen with magnificent buildings. As a good Muslim he patronized the scholars and the clergy, particularly the dervish order of Naqshbandiyah. Not satisfied with this, however, he attempted to regain the entire inheritance of his ancestor Chinghiz Khan, and annually spread warfare throughout the lands from Moscow down to the Ganges and westward as far as Syria. Bayezid saw in advance that a struggle with this world conqueror would not be spared him, and consequently from the very first years of his reign strove to fortify his position in Asia against him. In 1391 he wrested Konya from the emir of Karaman, his brother-in-law, whom his father had still spared, and the following year, after the emir had lost a battle against his general Timurtash, he took away his remaining possessions. Then the Turkomans in Kayseri, Tokat, and Sivas also submitted to him, and in 1393 the emir of Kastamuni lost his dominions. The dethroned princes fled to Timur and carried on agitation against Bayezid. When Bayezid then also disturbed the Armenian lord of Erzinjan in his possessions, the Khan, who looked upon the latter as his vassal, appeared in Asia Minor in 1400, conquered Sivas, and had the garrison massacred, including Bayezid's oldest son Ertoghrul.

Timur had at first been content with this chastisement of Bayezid, and had marched on to inflict a victorious pillaging expedition on the Mamluk Faraj of Egypt. Perhaps, recalling the resistance once offered by the Egyptian Mamluks to Hulagu, he wanted to cover his flank. He spent the following winter of 1401-02 on the high plain of Karabagh in Transcaucasia, between the rivers Kura and Aras, and there armed for a decisive battle against the Osmanlis.

With the beginning of the spring of 1402 Timur began the attack and came to the plain of Angora by way of Erzinjan and Sivas. Here, at the end of July, Bayezid accepted battle at Chibukabad, although his counselors strongly advised him against it, in view of the scarcely reliable mood of the troops and the greatly superior numbers of the enemy. In this struggle against their fellow believers the Osmanlis lacked the fanatical enthusiasm which otherwise inspired them; in any case the Christian auxiliaries followed Bayezid's banners only with reluctance. In spite of this the battle, on the morning of July 20, 1402, began not unfavorably for the Turks. The armored Serbian cavalry attacked the lightly armed Mongols with great vigor, but Bayezid recalled them out of fear of encirclement. The Mongols pursued, and when they came into the Turkish lines the Seljuq troops, who caught sight of their former princes on the enemy's side, were induced to desert. The courageous resistance which Bayezid and his ten thousand Janizaries offered until evening could no longer hold off defeat. When the Sultan turned to flee, at the onset of dusk, he was taken captive together with his son Musa, while the latter's brothers Muhammad and 'Isa escaped to Karamania. In the beginning the victor treated the captured ruler with generosity; it was only after he had made an unsuccessful attempt at escape that he made his custody more severe by taking him along with him in an iron cage. Bayezid died on March 8, 1403, at Akshehir in Hamid, and the victor accorded him burial in the mosque at Brusa.

In Asia Minor, Timur reinstalled the dethroned Seljuq princes in their rights and conquered Smyrna, which Umur Beg of Aidin had lost to the Byzantines. But he left Rumelia to the Osmanlis under Bayezid's son Suleyman, who was compelled to take the country from him in fief. Then he moved eastward again to his residence in Samarqand. On January 19, 1405, when Timur died in Otrar on a campaign against China, Asia Minor was left to its own devices.

Timur's sons, Shah Rukh and Miran Shah, divided his empire into an eastern and a western half, whose boundary was formed by the rim of the Iranian plateau. Miran Shah, the ruler of 'Iraq, Adharbayjan, and parts of the Caucasus, was compelled to submit to his brother, and was killed in a battle against the chieftain of the Turkoman group calling itself the Black Sheep (1408). The latter and their rivals the White Sheep contested the possession of the northwest provinces of Shah Rukh, who after his brother's death united the whole empire under his rule. As patrons of poetry and the sciences he and his descendants, among whom may be mentioned Ulugh Beg, distinguished for his interest in astronomy (1447-52), performed great service to Persian and East Turkish literature. Abu Sa'id, Ulugh Beg's successor (1452-69) re-established a position of great authority from 'Iraq to the borders of India, but perished in a battle against Uzun Hasan, of whom there will be something to say in connection with the Osmanlis. After Samarqand, Herat, Husayn Baikara's residence from 1469 to 1506, became a flourishing center of Islamic learning and art. In the east, however, the Timurid empire was hard pressed by the Turkoman tribe of the Uzbegs under their leader Shaybani; in 1500 he removed Baber, a grandson of Abu Sa'id, from his throne in Samarqand and forced him to emigrate to India, where he founded the empire of the Great Moguls. In the west the position of the Timurids became untenable after Shah Isma'il reconstructed a unified Iran out of the Shi'ite monk-state of Ardabil, as will be related.

Struggle for the inheritance broke out among Bayezid's sons directly after his death. The most energetic among them, Muhammad, had fled from Angora eastward and established himself in the mountains around Amasia and Tokat. From there he attacked his older brother 'Isa, who had seized Brusa and rejected his suggestion to divide the Asiatic possessions with him (1403); defeated him at Ulubad, and then advanced into Brusa, while 'Isa fled to Byzantium. His brother Suleyman, who refused to be satisfied with Rumelia alone, sent him to Asia Minor again with fresh troops; but 'Isa was defeated again and met his death in Karamania. Toward the end of 1404 Suleyman himself crossed the Hellespont, drove Muhammad from Brusa, and the following year from Angora too. At this point, however, Rumelia was attacked, with the support of the Serbs under Muhammad's orders, by the fourth brother, Musa, who had been captured at Angora but had been set free by the Seljuq emir in Germian; however, he was defeated by Suleyman at the Golden Horn near Constantinople and driven back to the Dardanelles.

Suleyman's unrestrained behavior trifled away the sympathies of his entourage; consequently when Musa three years later attacked him once again, he was betrayed, even before the battle, and in July 1410 was killed by peasants while in flight.

But Musa refused to recognize Muhammad as sovereign; he began his regime with an expedition of revenge against the Serbs, on whose betrayal he blamed his defeat of three years earlier, and conquered Thessaly. When he then bore hard on the emperor Manuel, the latter concluded an alliance with Muhammad against him, by means of Musa's own ambassador, who was supposed to be collecting tribute in Byzantium but went over to Muhammad. Their first joint attack in 1410 ended with a defeat at Yajigiz. Muhammad was then tied down for two years by battles with the emirs of Smyrna and Angora in Asia Minor. It was not until 1412 that he could attack in Europe again. While Musa's troops were encamped before Constantinople, he pushed forward directly north as far as Nish, in order to unite with the Serbs who had taken the field against Musa. Together with them he advanced southward the following summer. On July 10, 1413, Musa advanced against them on the narrow plain of Chamurlu, in the river bed of the Asker, east of Sofia, but after valiant resistance was defeated, captured while in flight, and strangled to death in his brother's camp. The victor rewarded the Serbs and Greeks for their help with territorial concessions.

Most of the vassal states in Europe and Asia also recognized Muhammad after brief resistance. But at the attempt to force the Venetians on the islands of the Aegean Sea to swear allegiance to him, he came into conflict with the mother city and at first had to waive his claims, after his fleet suffered a serious defeat at Gallipoli on May 29, 1416.

But the extent to which the foundations of the state were shaken by the Mongol emergency and the subsequent fratricidal wars is shown in a remarkable sectarian movement which was directed against Islam itself. The former army magistrate and chief minister of Musa, Badr-ad-Din Mahmud of Simawna, a close relation of the Seljuq emir of Konya, had settled down in Nicaea after his master's defeat. Here the revered jurist, who had demonstrated his intimate knowledge of Islamic law in a textbook used for a long time, succumbed to a fanatical mysticism, which no doubt originally went back to the belief in the Mahdi so widespread among the Shi'ah, but which eventually alienated him from Islam entirely. His new doctrine, which prescribed ownership in common and the recognition of Christians as the equals of Muslims in their worship of God, was enthusiastically taken up by the peasants of Asia Minor, who were generally sorely oppressed by their feudal lords and among whom Christian ideas survived everywhere mingled with ideas from the paganism of ancient Asia Minor. His disciple and former house steward Burkluje Mustafa gathered his followers around him on Mt. Stylarios at the southern tip of the Gulf of Smyrna opposite the island of Chios. His bands, led by fanatical dervishes, were soon raiding back and forth as far as the region of Magnesia. The governor of Aidin, the Serbian convert Shishman, received the order to suppress the dangerous movement, but when he imprudently ventured into the gorges of the Stylarios was fallen on there and annihilated together with all his troops. Things went scarcely any better for his successor Ali Beg, who was, however, able to save his life. Now Muhammad's son Murad, barely twelve years old, who had his residence in Amasia as governor, had to combine his troops with those of the Rumelian *beylerbey* Bayezid Pasha and turn on the insurgents, whose power was finally broken at the Karaburun promontory. Mustafa ended on the cross as a martyr for his faith. His teacher, Badr-ad-Din, had fled to Wallachia beforehand, and there had gathered his remaining followers and occupied a Balkan mountain pass. When Muhammad himself advanced against him, Badr-ad-Din's troops went over to him on the news of Mustafa's downfall. The last of his followers, with whom he continued roving about for a time, finally surrendered him, and at Zeres in 1416 he was hanged for high treason.

In 1421, when Muhammad died at Adrianople, his successor Murad II had to defend his throne first against a pretender allied with Emperor Manuel of Byzantium and passing himself off as Bayezid's son Mustafa (who had been killed at Angora), and then in Asia against his own brother Mustafa, only thirteen years old. When he tried to punish Emperor Manuel, after subjugating the rebels, by the seizure of Salonica, the Venetians stood in his way and purchased the city from the Emperor. At first Murad recognized their possession of this city in return for a payment of tribute, but only in order to gain time for rearming. In 1430 he passed over to the attack, and on March 29 the Osmanlis took Salonica by storm. It was only gradually that the city, terribly devastated and then resettled by Muslims, with a harbor which assured her of an important trade at all times, gradually burgeoned again.

When Murad then attempted to carry his power northward over the Balkans, the Magyars opposed him. The victories won against his armies here by the Transylvanian Rumanian John Hunyadi even revived the idea of a common crusade of Christendom against the infidels. A proclamation of Pope Eugene IV met with an enthusiastic welcome in Hungary and Poland, closest to the peril, and also in Germany and France. In July 1443 a crusading army set out from Buda and on December 24 won a brilliant victory at Jalowaz between Sofia and Philippopolis, which the winter, however, made it impossible to exploit. Then, after George Kastriota (Skanderbeg), who had been brought up as a hostage at the Ottoman court, also successfully raised the banner of revolt against the Osmanlis in

Albania, Murad had to sue for peace, and this was granted him by a conclave in Szegedin in 1444 for a period of ten years.

But the Pope, who saw his plans being nullified by this, incited the Magyars to break the peace, oaths sworn to infidels not being binding. Under the pretext that the Turks had not evacuated a number of Serbian fortresses in accordance with the treaty, they invaded the Balkan countries in September of the same year to move along the coast of the Black Sea and join the Venetian fleet in Gallipoli. But Murad advanced against the Christians on November 9 beneath the walls of Varna and won a brilliant victory, thanks to the lightmindedness of King Vladislav, only twenty years old, who, jealous of Hunyadi's initial successes, abandoned the post assigned him and was killed in an attack on the Janizaries.

It was not for another four years that Hunyadi, who was governing Hungary on behalf of the minor son of the fallen king, attempted to wipe out the disgrace of Varna. At the end of September 1448 he advanced into Serbia, and on October 17 Murad confronted him on the field of Kossovo. Two days later the Wallachians, after heated battles, went over to the Osmanlis; in his attempt to beat his way through to the Danube, Hunyadi fell into the hands of the hostile Serbs and was compelled to conclude a very unfavorable peace.

In many respects Murad's reign meant the end of the ancient culture of the Osmanlis. Under him the old nobility of officials was still able to maintain its influence, which it later lost to the renegades (new converts). Religious life still moved in the orbit of mysticism, which also set the tone in literature. The poems of the East Turkish mystic Ahmed Yesevi were already known in Anatolia in the thirteenth century through the dervish orders which spread his doctrines; his art, expressed in popular language and genuine Turkish syllabic meter, was taken up in Anatolia by Yunus Emre, who lived past the beginning of the fourteenth century. In addition there flourished at the courts of the Seljuq emirs a secular poetry based on Persian models. After the disintegration of the Seljuq empire into the small principalities which divided up its heritage, when the general level of education declined, Turkish began to force out the standard literary languages, Arabic and Persian, more and more; an entire popular religious literature in prose elucidating the Qur'an and cultivating meditation was already arising. At Murad's court, which encouraged scholars, poets, and musicians, arose the first longer works in Turkish prose, the earliest ones, to be sure, based on translation.

On February 5, 1451, when Murad died, the first act of his son and successor Muhammad was to order the death of his brother Ahmed, and from then on, as a result of the melancholy experiences of earlier generations, fratricide at the new ruler's accession to the throne almost became the domestic law of his dynasty. Muhammad was unjustly accounted as ungifted because at the hour of peril at the Battle of Varna his father had resumed the command after having already delegated it to him.

As on almost every other occasion of an accession to the throne, the emir of Karaman immediately attempted to shake off the sovereignty of the Osmanlis; while Muhammad was occupied with the suppression of the rebels in Asia Minor, the emperor Constantine IX imprudently threatened to put up Prince Orkhan, a grandson of Suleyman, against him as a pretender if he did not double the annual sum allocated to him for the custody of the Prince. By this he sealed his own fate. Muhammad had scarcely returned to Europe at the end of 1451 from the campaign against Karaman when hardly seven kilometers from the gates of Constantinople, at the narrowest point along the Bosporus, which was dominated along the Asiatic side by an outer fort set up by Bayezid, he erected the mighty castle of Rumili Hisar. When the Emperor sent ambassadors to protest against this action, he had them decapitated. This was his declaration of war.

Imperiled Byzantium received aid only from the Genoese colony on Chios. The Pope made his support contingent on a union of the two churches, which the fanaticized rabble of the capital rendered hopeless, although the Emperor was prepared for even this sacrifice.

The Emperor's combat forces were scarcely sufficient to man the Byzantine line of walls, in length more than a five-hour walk, but for almost two months the city's fortifications offered resistance to the still unpracticed Ottoman artillery. It was only by a general frontal assault on May 29, 1453, that the enemy forced his way into the city; the Emperor was killed in the street fighting. Toward midday Muhammad himself appeared in the city, ordered his murderous troops to halt, and took ceremonial possession of St. Sophia Church for Islam. The Genoese in Galata, who had kept neutral during the siege, were granted favorable terms of capitulation, which assured them freedom of life and property in return for the delivery of all weapons, as well as freedom of trade in return for the payment of all legal taxes and duties.

The Christian powers of the Occident had decided too late to dispatch a fleet in aid; it arrived in the harbor of Negroponte in time to hear of the fall of Constantinople.

Before Muhammad set up his residence in Constantinople, the natural focal point of his empire, he returned to Adrianople in 1453 to wait for the restoration of Constantinople's destroyed fortifications. However, he regulated the conditions of the subjugated Greeks at once. As his ancestors had not disturbed the ecclesiastical constitution of the Bulgars, so he also recognized, for that matter in entire accord with old concepts of Islamic statesmanship sanctified by the religious tradition, the entire sphere of authority of the Greek hierarchy. Indeed he even increased its powers, by delegating to it civil jurisdiction over its communicants.

Muhammad's immediate concern was to increase the capital's shrunken population. After he installed a resolute representative of the national church hierarchy in the patriarchate, numerous Greeks who had left before the catastrophe began returning to their homeland at his summons. They settled around the patriarchate, on the western bank of the Golden Horn. Their wealth, which was based on trade, as well as their skill, which later made them indispensable to the Porte in its intercourse with the Occidental powers, always assured them of a favored position. In addition Muhammad also compulsorily settled representatives of the other nations of his empire in the capital, in particular great numbers of South Slavs.

But Muslims from Asia also poured into the new center—to which, to an ever increasing extent, most of the communicants of Islam gradually became subject—in order to exploit the commercial advantages of the city, uniquely favored by its position, and particularly in order to make use of the pious foundations created there through the generosity of Muhammad and his successors for the benefit of learning. Istanbul very soon became the intellectual focus of Islam.

St. Sophia Church was decided on as the chief mosque directly after the conquest, and it required but few alterations to be adapted to the needs of the Islamic ritual. Since orthodox Islam proscribes any image of a living creature, the magnificent gold mosaics on the vaults, so characteristic of Byzantine art, had to be covered by limestone chalk. The qiblah, the direction of prayer toward Mecca, was stamped into the Christian plan of the church by introducing the mihrab, the niche designating the qiblah, between the central and southern side window opening of the apse. To the right of this, on the great southeastern column of the church, the minbar, the pulpit for the Friday sermon, was erected, opposite the maqsurah, the sultan's loge with its gilded latticework. However, the gigantic inscriptions, some of them in letters nine meters high, executed in gold script on a green background on enormous round shields on the walls and columns of the mosque, containing the names of God, the Prophet, and the first caliphs, were first introduced under Murad IV (1623-1640). On the exterior its adoption for Islam was marked by the towers for the prayer callers, the minarets, the first of which Muhammad himself had already had built; under Selim II and his successors three more were added. The latter also had a bronze crescent moon of a diameter of thirty meters erected on the principal dome. As the original outline of many a German dome was thrown out of shape by the additional burial chapels of bishops, so in the course of time the Aya Sophia was submerged by all sorts of augmentations—*turbahs* (mausoleums) and madrasahs, but particularly by buttressing works.

But Muhammad also considered the construction of new buildings one of his most important duties as ruler. At the central point of the city, on the grounds of the Apostolic Church, formerly the burial site of the emperors, he had the Greek architect Christodulos erect the mosque bearing his name (Mehmediye or Sultan Mehmed Fatih Jami), the most perfect monument of Ottoman architecture, in the years 1463-1469 (1473). The original construction, however, was destroyed repeatedly by earthquakes, most recently in 1767, so that the present-day structure can only suggest the original design. In this, as demonstrated by Gurlitt, he had merged the outlines of the Apostolic and the Sophia churches. The cruciform interior is crowned by the vast central dome, which rests on four columns between four equally wide half-domes; four smaller dome cupolas cover the corners. The interior gleams in the bright light of the six rows of windows arranged one over the other. Two slender minarets loom over the mosque, which, together with its extended subordinate buildings for schools, baths, kitchens, a so-called *khan* (a living and sleeping room for foreign traders), a poorhouse and hospital, dominates the entire peak of the hill over the old bridge. Right of the main portal could be read on a marble tablet in golden letters the prophetic words, now come to pass: "They shall conquer Constantinople! Happy the prince, happy the army, who shall accomplish this!"

Besides ten other mosques Muhammad also constructed in 1459 the one near the grave of the martyr Abu Ayyub al-Ansari, who had perished in 678 during the first Arab attack on Constantinople; at the outset of the final siege Shaykh Ak Shams-ad-Din, in a vision, had "discovered" it near the Cosmidion suburb and so been able to whip up the religious enthusiasm of the troops. Near this mosque, entirely constructed of white marble, in the mausoleum of the martyr--a simple, square domed structure with no side aisles–the sultans, after the accession to the throne, were ceremonially girded round with the sword of Osman by the *buyuk chelebi*, the head of the Mevlevi dervish order, and near by a number of sultans, together with their relatives and high dignitaries, found their last resting place. To the individual mosques were soon added rich libraries into which the treasures of the three Islamic literatures poured in unparalleled abundance, institutes of learning with lodgings for professors and students, hospitals, kitchens for the poor, inns, baths, and wells, which the Sultans vied with their wazirs in founding.

The design of the most important secular buildings in the capital also goes back to the conqueror. He restored the city walls and at the southwest tip of the city along the Sea of Marmara built the Castle of the Seven Towers (Yedi Kulle) which later served as a state prison and on occasion even saw the ambassadors of the European great powers within its walls. Muhammad built dockyards and arsenals in the harbor, and even the core of the bazaar was his handiwork. In 1454 he began on the construction of his palace, the Serai, on a hill in the interior of the city, which later became the seat of the *serasker* (war minister). He began a new palace in 1464 at the eastern tip of the city, washed by the Sea of Marmara, where the Greek emperors had previously had their residence, until Manuel Comnenus removed his headquarters to the Blachernae on the Golden Horn, north of the Fanar. The only secular building remaining today from the period of the conqueror is the Chinili (Faience) Kiosk, begun in 1466, completed in 1472, and restored in 1599, in which a part of the national museum is housed today.

The first objective of Muhammad's policy was the consolidation of his rule in the north of the Balkan peninsula, where it was still threatened by the proximity of the warlike Magyars. To gain a firm base of operations against them he had to liquidate the independence of Serbia. The pretext for this was presented by his relationship through a forced marriage with a member of the former dynasty of Lazarevich. In 1454, when he thereupon requested Prince George Brankovich to surrender his country, the latter fled to Hunyadi in Hungary. Although the Magyars expelled the Osmanlis from the once-conquered fortress of Semendria and inflicted a serious defeat on Muhammad's general Firoz Beg at Krushevatz, they had to be content with holding the Danube line, since the reinforcements expected by them from Europe did not arrive. In 1456 Muhammad himself with a powerful army surrounded Belgrade from the landed side. But Hunyadi, with a motley army made up of Crusaders, principally of the lower classes inspired by the monk Capistrano, threw himself across the Danube into the beleaguered city and on June 22 beat off a major assault of the Osmanlis in a bloody battle. Muhammad himself was badly wounded in this and had to lead his army back to Sofia. But that same year both the valiant defenders of Belgrade died, Hunyadi on August 14, Capistrano on October 23. Then, two years later, when George Brankovich also died and dissension broke out among his heirs concerning the succession, Muhammad was able to subdue Serbia without much effort, and to shatter the strength of the people by massacres, enslavement, and transplantation to other sections of the empire.

Meanwhile, in the Peloponnesus he had attacked the Paleologi who had revolted against his rule in alliance with the Albanian George Kastriota. Order was restored here to the accompaniment of frightful atrocities, which gave Muhammad more and more pleasure with each passing year.

In the same year he also eliminated the last Greek dynasty in Asia Minor, that of the Comneni in Trebizond, who had up to then hoped for support by the khan of the Turkomans of the White Sheep (Ak Koyunlu), Uzun Hasan. From his tribal seat in Diyarbekr the latter, in warfare with his rivals the Turkomans of the Black Sheep (Kara Koyunlu) who were professing Shiʿites while he and his tribe were Sunnites, had founded a substantial domain in Armenia, to which he later added Persia and Mesopotamia after a victory over the Kara Koyunlu. In 1458 David, the last Comnenus of Trebizond, had given his niece Catherine, the daughter of his brother and predecessor Kalo-Joannes, to Uzun Hasan in marriage. While Muhammad was occupied by an uprising of Isfendiyar-Oghlu in Sinope, Uzun Hasan, who as early as 1457 and 1460 had made known his claims to hegemony in eastern Asia Minor by means of embassies in Constantinople, attacked Osmanli territory and plundered the country around Tokat and Amasia. In the spring of 1461, as soon as Muhammad had a free hand, he turned against the Turkomans. After their vanguard had been defeated by Ahmed Pasha, Uzun Hasan dared not put into play his undisciplined mounted hordes against victorious Janizaries. His mother Sara Khatun, who had proved a skillful diplomat in earlier clashes, appeared in Muhammad's camp in person and was able to dissuade him from any further attacks on her son. But she was unable to achieve any clemency for Trebizond. The city was occupied by the Osmanlis, the last emperor was deported to Istanbul together with his nobles, the civil population for the most part was sold into slavery. A portion of the imperial treasury, however, was placed by the victor at the disposal of Sara Khatun for her daughter-in-law.

Muhammad's activities in the Peloponnesus had already brought him on many occasions into conflict with Venice, the only power which could still offer him any resistance on Greek soil. The war, long since inevitable, broke out in the autumn of 1462 as the result of some triviality. The main burden of the war fell on George Kastriota, whom the Venetians had induced to break the truce. Muhammad himself took the field against him; he surrounded him in Kroia in 1466, and when George died two years later, the independence of Albanians was over with. He erected the stronghold of al-Basan in the heart of their territory. Then the Venetians themselves came to feel the Osmanli hand. In the summer of 1470, after a hard siege, they lost the city of Negroponte on Euboea, which they had had in their possession for 264 years.

But the *signoria* of Venice succeeded once again in finding an ally against the Osmanlis. Uzun Hasan had conquered Persia in 1467.* His rival, the khan of the Kara Koyunlu, Jahan Shah, who had held this country up to then, attacked his tribal seat at Diyarbekr, but was defeated by Uzun Hasan on November 11, 1467, and lost his life while in flight. While Uzun Hasan advanced southward to the siege of Baghdad, Jahan Shah's son Hasan 'Ali won the assistance of the Timurid Abu Sa'id. The latter set out from Khorasan in March 1468 and occupied all of northern (Persian) 'Iraq. But when, in an attempt to expel Uzun Hasan from Karabagh, he then

* See V. Minorsky, *La Perse au XVè siècle entre la Turquie et Vénise*, *Publications de la Société des Etudes Iraniennes*, No. 7, Paris, 1933.

encircled Mahmudabad, on the steppe south of the lower reaches of the Araxes, he was taken captive and delivered over to a dynastic rival, who had him killed. Hasan 'Ali was killed in Hamadan by Uzun Hasan's troops, and the latter could then seize all of Persia unhindered. The Venetians had already sent an ambassador to Uzun Hasan in 1463 to win him for an alliance against the Osmanlis. The ambassador returned to Venice in 1471 accompanied by a Turkoman ambassador. Then Caterino Zeno, whose mother was a sister of the Trebizond wife of Uzun Hasan, was dispatched to Tabriz. That same year the signoria sent out to Persia Giosafo Barbaro, accompanied by an ambassador of Uzun Hasan, with six large mortars, six hundred rifles, muskets, and ammunition, protected by two hundred fusiliers with their officers. But he only got as far as Cyprus, where a Venetian fleet under P. Mocenigo was operating along the southern coast of Asia Minor and had occupied a number of coastal areas. In 1472 Uzun Hasan sent out an army from Diyarbekr into Ottoman territory, where Tokat and Kayseri were plundered. After an exchange of notes with the Turkomans, the style of which continually grew sharper and sharper, Muhammad himself set out for Asia Minor in March 1473. Uzun Hasan had set up his headquarters in Erzinjan and inflicted an annihilating defeat on the Osmanli vanguard at Terjan on August 1, 1473. On August 12, while he was in pursuit of the Ottoman army, which was already on the way back to Trebizond, the main body of the army under Muhammad himself advanced against him north of Erzinjan, on the watershed between the upper reaches of the Euphrates and the Chorokh. For a long time the cavalry battle wavered back and forth, but the Janizaries and the Osmanli artillery finally determined the outcome. On the advice of his grand wazir, Muhammad dispensed with the pursuit of Uzun Hasan in view of the difficulties of the terrain. In vain did the Venetians attempt to induce Uzun Hasan into a new attack on the Osmanlis. Uprisings of his brother Uways and his son Oghurlu Muhammad, and, after he had suppressed these, his preoccupation with the reorganization of conditions in Persia and 'Iraq, prevented him from resuming his designs on Asia Minor. After his death on January 6, 1478, his empire, like all preceding state formations of this type, sank into nothingness.

In Europe, after the resistance of the Albanians was broken, Osmanli raiding parties poured out of Bosnia over the Venetian countryside. On January 26, 1479 the republic was finally ready for an honorable peace. It waived all its possessions in Albania, including Durazzo and Antivari, and gave up Euboea and Lemnos as well as the inhabitants of Taygetos in the Peloponnesus. In return for one payment of 100,000 ducats and an annual duty of 10,000 ducats it purchased freedom for its trade in the Levant and the right to install again in Galata near Istanbul a bailiff to represent its interests.

The Venetians could find a certain consolation in the fact that shortly before this the position of their most dangerous competitors in the Levant, the Genoese, had also become almost untenable. The latter's trade had hitherto derived its greatest advantages from their possessions along the northern shore of the Black Sea, particularly from Caffa in the Crimea. But here they fell out with the Tatar chieftains, and since their khan Mengli Ghiray took the side of the Genoese, the chieftains called on the Osmanlis for help. Muhammad sent out his fleet at once, and on June 6 Caffa was forced to surrender. The Genoese colony was annihilated for good, and those of its inhabitants who were not made slaves were transported to Istanbul. But the Tatars became feudatories of the Sultan.

Now the St. John's Knights on Rhodes were the only power in the archipelago which had not yet submitted to Ottoman rule. After an attack on their strongly fortified island had failed in 1480, Muhammad undertook a second campaign against them the following year. While on this he died in his camp at Tekfur Chairi, between Scutari and Gebse in Asia Minor, on May 3, 1481, at the age of fifty-two.

Muhammad had been the truest representative of the old Osmanli, with all his virtues and faults. His inflexible energy, inexhaustibly striving after new goals, was coupled with a cruelty which by far surpassed even the harshness of his times. It is necessary to go back to the Assyrian "great kings" to find parallels to his treatment of war prisoners, in which sawing in two was particularly popular. But the same man who perpetrated such atrocities in warfare that even his subordinates sometimes refused to execute them concentrated in his person the entire intellectual range of his cultural milieu. He proved his devotion to Islamic lore and to poetry not only by material support of their representatives; he was fond of trying his own skill as poet, and he succeeded in handing on for posterity many of the verses he considered worthy. His poetry, to be sure, like that of all his compatriots, moved in the fixed orbit of its Persian models, and its intellectual content never escaped the narrow confines of the amorous dalliance known from Hafiz, meant half mystically, half sensually. The extent of Muhammad's esteem for Persian is indicated by the commission he gave the Anatolian poet Shehdi to write in Persian a poem on Ottoman history in imitation of Firdawsi's *Shahname*, the diwan of one of his court poets, Hamidi, includes Persian as well as Turkish poems. The prose of his period also was dominated in consequence by the artificial style, overladen with foreign words, which had developed in the Persian chanceries. But Muhammad also showed an understanding for the artistic past of a despised raya people; in the summer of 1458, while pacifying Greece, he granted Athens its autonomy, enchanted as he was with the still-magnificent remains of classical antiquity. He also showed understanding for the renaissance burgeoning in Italy. He once had the Ragusan tribute paid in manuscripts from Italy. He passed beyond the Islamic interdiction on images to such an extent that the year before his death he commissioned a Venetian, Gentile Bellini, to paint his portrait, which is still preserved in the Layard collection in Venice.

After Muhammad's death his empire lapsed once again into fratricidal warfare. He himself seems to have destined the succession for his younger son Jem, who had his residence in Konya as the governor of Karaman; in any case the grand wazir attempted without delay to elevate the latter by keeping the Sultan's death a secret for a time. But his plans were seen through by the Janizaries; they stormed the castle in Scutari, murdered the grand wazir, and, once their fury was unleashed, plundered the houses of the Jews and the foreign merchants. Then, after the older prince Bayezid, till then governor of Amasia, entered Scutari on May 20, he had to grant them not only a pardon for their excesses but also an increase in pay, which from then on was demanded at every change of ruler as a fixed contribution.

Meanwhile Jem had been recognized in Brusa as sultan and had suggested to his brother a division of the empire into a European and an Asiatic half. Bayezid did not acquiesce in this, but attacked him in Asia and defeated him at Yenishehir on June 23. Jem fled to the Mamluk sultan Qaitbay in Egypt and then, after an unsuccessful incursion into Asia Minor, whither Karamanoghlu Qasimbeg had called him, to the St. John's Knights on Rhodes, in the hope of allying himself with them and with the western powers against his brother. But the knights afterward concluded a favorable peace with Bayezid, required a rental for Jem's custody, and interned him in southern France. In 1488 they delivered him to Pope Innocent VIII, who was planning a crusade against the Osmanlis, and whose successor Alexander VI * had to surrender him to King Charles VIII of France, who was besieging Rome around the turn of the year 1494/95. But even beforehand he is supposed to have given the pretender poison at Bayezid's instigation, as a result of which Jem died in Naples on February 25, 1495.†

This hostage whom the European powers had in their hands for so long may have acted as a codeterminant on Bayezid's pacific policy, but it also corresponded to his inclinations. Like his brother, he had inherited poetic talent from his father, and his brooding mind also took pleasure in the cultivation of the sciences. He sought to do justice to his duties as ruler principally through magnificent buildings for public use. He had the network of streets and bridges his ancestors had already begun throughout the empire elaborated by Greek and Bulgar master craftsmen; although primarily intended for military purposes, this was of invaluable service to general traffic too. But his chief work was the mosque in Istanbul named after him, which he had erected in the years 1497-1503 opposite the older Serai. It is distinguished from all the edifices in the city by the opulence of the material and the Persian style of the decoration. Pointed arches of alternating black and white marble on costly pillars of jasper and *verde antico*, with elegant stalactite capitals, surround on four sides the forecourt, shadowed over by lofty cypresses and plane trees, and bear richly jointed domed porticoes. In the center of the court there rises the octagonal well house, borne on columns. Four tall gates in the Persian style open outward. This mosque is also distinguished by the position of its minarets, which rise, not as elsewhere, on the corners, but freely on independent side wings. It gave its name to the entire surrounding city quarter, Bayezid (today Beyazid), which includes the former palace of the serasker, now the seat of the university.

This peace-loving prince was also incapable of preventing the conflicts along the northern marches of his empire, since they kept

* In the Appartemento Borgia, painted for the Pope by Pinturicchio, a portrait of Jem can be found in the third room (called "Of the Lives of the Saints") in the picture of the disputation of St. Catherine of Alexandria before Emperor Maximianus.

† See L. Thuasne, *Djem-Sultan*, Paris, 1892.

springing up automatically out of his people's expansionism and the insecure political conditions of their neighbors. Although the incursions of the Osmanlis into Transylvania were beaten back, they subdued Bosnia entirely and by devastating attacks obviated the attempts of the Poles to conquer Moldavia.

Bayezid had kept the peace with the Venetians at the beginning of his reign, and tranquilly looked on as they conquered Cyprus and Naxos. But their relations with France aroused his suspicion, and in 1499 another war took place. After three campaigns of alternating fortune, Bayezid concluded in 1503 a peace with Venice in which he contented himself with the acquisition of Durazzo, Lepanto, and Messenia. His readiness for peace was no doubt codetermined by the danger threatening his empire in the east; in Persia, as will be related in the chapter after the next, a native dynasty under Shah Isma'il supported by the Shi'ah (which was still widespread in the Ottoman Empire also), succeeded the Turkomans. There was reason for apprehension.

Bayezid's last days were filled with savage contention for the succession, since his sons had no desire to wait for his death. He had destined the throne to his favorite, Ahmed, and even wanted to abdicate in his favor. To prevent this the younger Selim, who had the by-name of Yavuz, "the Grim," after his martial tastes, which gave him greater popularity in the army, demanded a governorship in Europe instead of the one he had in Trebizond. When this was refused him, he appeared before Adrianople in 1511 with twenty-five thousand men and in defiance of his father seized the sanjaqs of Semendria and Vidin, since his ostensible plan to conquer a new empire for himself in the north met with enthusiastic approval among the Janizaries. It was not until he had seized Adrianople by force that the old Sultan gathered his strength for armed resistance and defeated him at Chorlu on August 3, 1511. Since Selim had had to flee to the khan in Crimea, Ahmed was already thinking of ascending the throne in Istanbul itself; but an uprising of the Janizaries compelled him to return to Asia. In April 1512 Selim appeared before Istanbul again and was enthusiastically welcomed by the garrison. He forced his father to renounce his throne. On the journey to his birthplace, Demotika, where he was thinking of ending his days, Bayezid died on May 26, poisoned, as has generally and no doubt rightly been thought, at the instigation of his son.

Ahmed established himself in Brusa but was by 1513 conquered and killed. His son Murad escaped to Persia. In Bayezid's very last reigning year the Shi'ites in Asia Minor under Shah Kuli, trusting to the help of their fellow believers who ruled in Persia, had revolted; after Selim had put down this uprising, he initiated a general religious persecution against the Shi'ites living in his domains. To avenge its victims Shah Isma'il attacked in Asia Minor immediately. Selim summoned the believers to a holy war against the heretics, and defeated the Shah in the valley of Chaldiran, between Lake Urmia and Tabriz, on August 23, 1514. He then advanced into his opponent's capital, Tabriz, and from there was already considering the further expansion of his power in Asia.

But here the second Islamic great power, that of the Egyptian Mamluks, barred his path. Like all powerful rulers of the Nile valley, Circassians had long since seized Syria and from there extended their power farther and farther northward. Even under Muhammad II there had been friction along the marches of Asia Minor and Syria. In addition the Mamluks suspected the Ottoman sultan of competing with them in the caring for the holy cities and the Meccan pilgrims, which had always been regarded as a privilege of the most powerful Muslim ruler. The unmilitary regime of Bayezid had been exploited by the Mamluks to extend their power not only in Lesser Armenia and Cilicia, but also toward the north.

There, where the Ottoman and the Egyptian spheres of authority came into contact with that of the Persians in the valleys of the Taurus, from Mar'ash over Albistan and Malatya as far as Kharput, the Turkoman dynasty of the Dhu-l-Qadr had been dominant since the middle of the fourteenth century. Selim was the son of a princess of this house. Although her father, 'Ala-ad-Dawlah, had been installed in his rule by Muhammad II, he had only been able to defend himself against a rival with Egyptian help. In 1507 he had fallen out with Shah Isma'il for having refused him the hand of a daughter of his, and lost Kharput and Diyarbekr to him. Nevertheless, his grandson Selim accused him of ambiguous behavior during his war with Shah Isma'il; in consequence, while on his way back from Persia he ordered Sinan Pasha to punish him for it. The graybeard 'Ala-ad-Dawlah was killed in the battle. His principality was given to his nephew 'Ali Beg, who had accompanied Selim on the Persian campaign; it was only under Suleyman that it was definitively incorporated into the Ottoman Empire. The aging Mamluk sultan, Qansuh al-Ghuri, attempted to protect himself against this incursion into their joint sphere of interest by an alliance with Shah Isma'il. When Selim set out on a new campaign against the Shah, Qansuh went to Aleppo, ostensibly as a mediator of peace. But Selim was already on Syrian soil and arrogantly turned back the Egyptian embassy. A battle took place near Dabiq, north of Aleppo, on August 24; since the Mamluks had entirely neglected the development of artillery, as a weapon unworthy of them, they suffered a crushing defeat, and their ruler fell while in flight. The whole of Syria now lay at the victor's feet, and he was able to draw into Damascus on September 26.

At first Selim was willing to leave the Mamluks in possession of Egypt if they would acknowledge him as sovereign in the pulpit prayers and in their coinage. Since the new sultan Tumanbay refused to do this, Selim attacked him on his own ground. By January 21, 1517, he was stationed before Cairo, and on the following day his superior artillery inflicted a decisive defeat on the Mamluks. The residence itself did not fall into the hands of the Osmanlis until after bloody street fighting. Tumanbay had escaped into the delta area but was soon betrayed into the hands of his enemies; he was hanged in Cairo on April 13, 1517.

Among the hostages captured in the battle and brought back to Cairo there was also the last scion of the 'Abbasid caliphs, whose descendants had been permitted a semblance of authority by the Mamluks after 1261 in order to legitimize their regime. According to legend, the 'Abbasid was taken to Istanbul and made to transfer to Selim the caliphate over all orthodox believers in Islam. In reality Selim had already designated himself caliph beforehand in the prayer from the pulpit; in this capacity he also took into his charge in August 1517 the keys of the Ka'bah. Egypt retained only a loose connection with the Ottoman Empire. The famous scholar Shams-ad-Din ibn-Kamal Pasha, who was first charged with the regulation of Egyptian finances, calculated in this office that the revenues the Sultan could expect from this new acquisition of his were scarcely worth mentioning. Yet even under Suleyman the tribute from Egypt, whose great economic potentialities swiftly revived, was set at a high figure. But the Mamluk begs, supported by their rich landholdings, soon acquired so much political power that the Sultan's governor had to content himself with the collection of the tribute.

Selim's conquests caused such a sensation in Europe that Pope

Leo X grew fearful for the safety of Christendom, and began planning a new crusade. Selim's name has lived on for the Turkish people as that of one of the greatest of military heroes; it was because of this that the Young Turks named the German cruiser *Göben*, which escaped the British Mediterranean fleet in August 1914 and passed into their possession, *Yavuz Sultan Selim*. But this same sultan, like Muhammad Fatih, the conqueror of Constantinople, also tried his hand at Persian verse; his diwan was published by Paul Horn in 1904 on the orders of Kaiser Wilhelm II and presented as a gift to Sultan 'Abd-al-Hamid in a de luxe edition of the Imperial Printing Office. Under Selim, as a consequence of the political opposition to Persia, the Sunnite form of Islam forced the Shi'ite tendencies surviving in Anatolia from the beginnings of the empire entirely into the background.

When Selim returned to Adrianople in 1518, he may have brought back plans of conquest against the west. In any case he was already arming against the St. John's Knights on Rhodes when he died of an illness on the way back from Istanbul to Adrianople on September 2, 1520.

His son Suleyman * ascended the throne without a struggle. As crown prince he had kept himself very much in the background, since his father, in recollection of his own rise, always regarded him with mistrust; but he was now able to develop his brilliant qualities to the full. He at once set about the solution of the most important task left him by his ancestors, the securing of the northern marches. Louis II, a minor, had been ruling in Hungary since 1516, and the magnates, preoccupied with internal feuds, defended the border so badly that under the command of the Sultan the Osmanlis were able to take Belgrade in 1521. After this success Suleyman cut short the campaign in the north in order to carry out his father's last plan and conquer Rhodes, whence the St. John's Knights, to the shame of the Ottoman name, were still lending support to the freebooting expeditions of the Christian pirates. At the end of July 1522 the siege of the fortress began, but it was not until December 21, after frightful losses on both sides, that the grand master of the order capitulated, in return for freedom of withdrawal for all knights, security of person and of property, and a tax exemption of five years for the native Christian population of the island.

* See Fr. Babinger, *Suleyman der Grosse*, Stuttgart, 1922, 2 vols.

Suleyman's designs on his neighbor in the north were furthered to a very substantial degree by French policy and its opposition to the house of Habsburg. It was then that friendly relations developed between the courts of Paris and Istanbul which for centuries thereafter assured the French of a leading position among the great powers in Oriental politics.

In 1526 Suleyman resumed the war against the Magyars. In the unfortunate Battle of Mohacs on August 28 their king, Louis, barely twenty years old, was killed, together with the cream of his men. On September 11 Buda was occupied by the Osmanlis for the first time, and went up in flames. A war for the Hungarian crown flared up between Ferdinand of Austria and Voivode John Zapolya of Transylvania. Suleyman took the latter's side and in September 1529 conquered Buda once again and had him crowned there. Then he moved up before Vienna, but on October 15 had to give up the siege of the city as a result of inadequate supplies. Equally unsuccessful was the campaign of 1532, in which Suleyman was held up for the whole of August by the small Hungarian fortress of Güns and had to content himself with devastating the open country until Güns fell on August 28. This modest success was again brought into question by the fleet of Emperor Charles, which, under the Genoese admiral Andrea Doria, was battling successfully along the coasts of Morea. The following year Suleyman announced his readiness for a peace treaty recognizing the *status quo* in the possessions of both parties, for conditions in Asia were claiming his attention.

Since 1524 Persia had been ruled by Isma'il's son Tahmasp, who accorded the Sultan's claims to the caliphate no more recognition than his father had done. After the Persian governor in Baghdad had deserted to the Sultan, but been subdued again by the Shah, Suleyman took this as a pretext for initiating a war against Persia. In the summer of 1534, since the Shah had had to retreat before a Turkish general, Suleyman was able to advance to the Persian capital at Tabriz and to take possession of Baghdad in November without a struggle. After establishing order in these border provinces, which he had no mind to relinquish again, he returned to Istanbul at the beginning of 1536.

Here his major concern now became his sea power, as a means of wiping out the disgraces of the last war. In this he was served by the corsair Khayr-ad-Din Barbarossa. The latter, a Greek from Mytilene in Lesbos, together with his brother 'Aruj, for years had been imperiling the coasts, particularly in the western Mediterranean, by their piracy. The entangled political conditions of North Africa had enabled them to establish themselves there. The Hafsid sultan of Tunis, Muhammad, had already delegated the governorship of the island of Jerba to 'Aruj. In order to bring this piratical pestilence under control, the Spaniards had attacked North Africa a number of times and had occupied the small mountainous islands lying opposite Algiers at cannon's range, from which they controlled the entry into the harbor. After the death of Ferdinand the Catholic, the Algerians, hampered in their most important vocation, summoned 'Aruj for help against the Spaniards. 'Aruj seized the city and its fertile countryside, and though unable to expel the Spaniards, warded off their encroachments on the mainland with much bloodshed. But in 1518, when he carried his power farther westward to Tlemsen, he was killed in a battle with the Spaniards, who had cut off his retreat. He had left behind as governor in Algiers his brother Khayr-ad-Din, who then assumed command of his troops. Seeing himself threatened by the Algerian rulers from all sides, he requested support from the sultan Selim, who had just conquered Egypt. The latter took him into his service as beylerbey and sent two thousand Turks with artillery to his aid, whom he was permitted to reinforce by mercenaries with the rights of Janizaries. In 1519, on an action undertaken against Tunis, he was cut off from his base of operations by treachery and had to resume his freebooting on the island of Jijelli. With the booty gained he succeeded in building up a new army and finally conquering Algiers, and also in rooting the Spaniards out of their mountain eyrie of Peñon. In 1534 he even occupied Tunis, but by June 1535 lost it again to the Spaniards under Charles V. In order to prosecute the sea war against the Spaniards with greater vigor, Barbarossa removed to Istanbul soon afterward, having been appointed *kapudanpasha* in 1533. In 1537, at his instigation, Suleyman declared war on the Venetians. Within three years the latter lost all their possessions in the Aegean Sea as far as Crete, Tinos, and Mykonos. But his interest was still directed primarily toward his political aspirations in North Africa, although he himself was never to stand on its soil again. For this reason he supported in Istanbul with the utmost zeal an alliance with Francis I of France against Emperor Charles V, whose attack on Algiers in 1541 had been successfully warded off by his troops. When the war between France and Spain broke out again, Barbarossa led a Turkish fleet against the Italian coasts and laid siege to Nice; but the Peace of Crespy in 1544 forced him to withdraw. Barbarossa died two years later, leaving the Sultan a well-equipped fleet with battle-hardened crew which was often to prove an effective instrument of the Sultan's policies.

Suleyman had won a great victory against the Habsburgs on land and added a valuable province to his empire. In 1543, when John Zapolya died, he advanced into Hungary, to prevent the recognition of Ferdinand as king. On September 2 he entered Buda, had the principal church of the city transformed into a mosque, and established an Ottoman provincial administration for Hungary. In 1547, after the Turks had gone on to conquer Gran and Stuhlweissenburg, Ferdinand was compelled to conclude a peace for seven years.

In 1550, at the summit of his power, Suleyman began the construction of a magnificent mosque in Istanbul, which was to overshadow even the Aya Sophia as one of the most beautiful monuments of Ottoman architecture. For this he set aside a spacious area north of the old Serai and placed a number of old churches as well as antique materials at the disposition of the architect, Sinan. The forecourt here also was built with great opulence, particularly by means of a Persian royal gate on the fourth of its wings on the main axis of the mosque; four minarets rise above the corners of the forecourt. The principal structure of three aisles is crowned by a majestic dome, borne by four powerful square columns, which exceeds that of the Aya Sophia by five meters. All the walls and columns in the interior of the mosque are inlaid with varicolored marble, and the rear wall together with the mihrab is ornamented with magnificent Persian tiles. The nine windows of this wall were painted by the most famous glass painter of the time, Serkhosh Ibrahim, in magnificent, deeply glowing colors. Sinan, the architect, as he himself relates in his autobiography which was printed in 1865 in Istanbul, had been inducted into the Janizary corps under Selim I (in the boy levy) and had taken part in the campaigns of Belgrade, Rhodes, and Mohacs as combatant and in the siege of Vienna as chief of the corps of engineers. After a protracted sojourn in Baghdad he entered directly into the service of the Serai and was soon appointed chief architectural director. In this capacity he displayed remarkable energy: seventy-five large and forty-nine small mosques, forty-nine madrasahs and seven institutes for the study of the Qur'an, seventeen public kitchens, three hospitals, seven viaducts, seven bridges, twenty-seven palaces, eighteen caravanserais, five treasure houses, thirty-one baths and eighteen burial chapels were erected by him on his imperial master's orders.

But the house of Suleyman was already being prepared for the fate which as a result of the harem system scarcely one of the Ottoman rulers was entirely spared, the falling-out between sons. His first-born, Mustafa, the favorite of the army, was made suspect to him by a favorite of Russian descent, Roxolana-Khurram, and her son-in-law, the grand wazir Rustam, so that he himself had him strangled in his tent at Eregli on a Persian campaign in 1553. But open warfare later broke out among Roxolana's sons also. Mustafa Riza, the *lala* (tutor) of the second son, Selim—at Rustam's instigation, we are told—had sown discord between him and his younger and more gifted brother Bayezid. In 1559 the brothers were to exchange the sanjaqs governed by them: Bayezid was supposed to exchange Konya for Amasia, and Selim, Magnesia for Kütahya. Bayezid defied this command and summoned his troops, was defeated at Konya on May 30, 1559, and fled to Persia. But the shah delivered him to Suleyman, and on September 25, 1561, his father handed him to the executioners. Thus the most incompetent of his sons, Selim, a libertine and drunkard, became the uncontested successor to the throne.

Toward the end of his life Suleyman's star paled in foreign affairs as well. By 1551 warfare had broken out again in Hungary. The Osmanlis were being fought at sea by the Spanish fleet in alliance with the Knights of St. John who were established on Malta from 1530 on. In spite of all his efforts Suleyman never succeeded in expelling them from there. To make up for this he attempted at least to put a stop to the dragging pace of the Hungarian campaign. Already ill, he set out with a powerful army from Istanbul on May 1, 1566; but he only got as far as Szigeth, which under Zriny's command resisted him for a month. He died there in the night of September 5-6; only two days later the ruins of the fortress fell into the hands of the Janizaries. Occidental historians have distinguished Suleyman by the honorific name of "the Magnificent," whereas the Osmanlis honor him as Kanuni, "the Legislator." He surpassed all his predecessors in the expansion of external power, which contrasted all the more strikingly with the decay which rapidly set in under his successors. Accordingly, his death provides us with an appropriate vantage point from which to review the course traversed by his people in its internal evolution.

2. *The Civilization of the Osmanlis at the Zenith of the Empire*

Suleyman was not only a great military leader but simultaneously an important organizer, who perfected the institutions founded by his ancestors and completed them. The foundation of the Ottoman state was still the feudal system, which had been taken over by the first rulers on the Byzantine model and which Suleyman had codified in detail. Meritorious soldiers were first appanaged with a small estate, which the former peasant proprietors had to continue cultivating as raya, or subjects, and which yielded an annual revenue for the incumbent of 3,000 to 20,000 aspers; for this he had to provide two to four horsemen for military service or sailors for the fleet. Such a fief was called a *timar*, in a Persian translation of the Greek word *pronoia*, similar to the Latin *cura*. Only personal service could assist the feudal vassal to a larger estate, a *ziamet;* but his son unqualifiedly had to begin with a timar. The possessor of a ziamet, the *za'im*, whose revenues went as high as 100,000 aspers and more, had to provide one man for each 5,000 aspers. A silver asper was normally supposed to have the weight of one-fourth of a drachma; under Muhammad II, 40 aspers were still worth one ducat, but under his successors the currency deteriorated to such an extent that 60 aspers equaled one ducat. Still larger fiefs, the *khass*, were bestowed on provincial governors and were not subject, like the timar and ziamet, to inspection by the *defterdar*s charged with the supervision of the fiefs. Under Suleyman I the enfeoffed land in Europe supplied about 80,000 horses, that in Asia about 50,000. But in the subjugated Persian provinces the formation of new enfeoffed estates was no longer possible, since no one desired to assume the obligations bound up with these areas devastated by incessant military campaigns.

The enfeoffed force of mounted vassals originally constituted the core of the Ottoman army. Their weapons were bow and arrows, the use of which was retained longest among the Asiatics; a light lance, and a short sword; occasionally an iron mace and a small round shield. Mail shirt and spiked helmet made entry only gradually; in former times the turban was the general headgear. Care of the horses was recorded as the principal duty of the feudal vassal; the neglect of this might even entail the loss of the fief.

The military fiefs were grouped together in banners, or sanjaqs; at first there were only two such sanjaqs, but they later grew to 290. They were governed by beys, as even among the Arabs the banner, or *liwa'*, had been the symbol of the delegation of supreme command over an army. Originally there stood above the sanjaq beys the two beylerbeys, one for Anadolu (Anatolia) and one for Rumeli (Europe); they also bore the title pasha. The former's headquarters were at first at Ankara and from 1451 on at Kütahya, and the latter's at Sophia. The beylerbey of Rumeli was of higher rank and in token of this had three horse's tails on his banner, whereas only two were due his Anatolian counterpart; he also represented the sultan as supreme commander, to whom even the princes had to yield.

It was only with the continued expansion of the empire in Asia that new beylerbeys were appointed, who, however, were inferior in rank to the Anatolian although their armies were larger. Still later a number of sanjaqs were combined to form *pashalik*s or vilayets, of which there were no fewer than seventy at the beginning of the nineteenth century. This in itself created a destructive element in the state administration, originally constructed along lines of rigid centralization.

The feudal system, which had stood the test excellently in the small ancestral Ottoman homeland, soon fell into decay in the continually expanding empire. The ruler was compelled to leave to the beylerbeys the appanagement of at least the smaller fiefs up to a yield of 6,000 aspers. But the latter did not refrain from handing over available timars, rather than to tested warriors, to their own protégés, often to slaves, of whom reciprocal military services could not be expected at all. They soon went even further and dismissed tried feudal vassals if there was even the slightest doubt of their Osmanli origins. Suleyman I attempted to curb these abuses by his *Kanunname*, handed down in 1530. He withdrew from the beylerbeys the right of arbitrary enfeoffment; henceforth they were to submit an application (*tezkere*) concerning the person entitled to investiture with a fief, on the basis of which the Sublime Porte itself (Babi Ali, as the official seat of the grand wazir) would issue a notice of investiture (*berat*) and have it entered into the feudal register. The hereditary rights of the sons of feudal lords were regulated with precision. A fief could never descend directly from father to son; the latter could claim only a smaller estate, until he himself rose through his own military accomplishments. The size of the initial fief was supposed to depend on whether the father had fallen in the field or died in bed. Minor sons could also be assigned a timar, which they lost, however, if by the end of their nineteenth year they had not presented themselves for military service.

But Suleyman's Kanunname did not eliminate all abuses either. Very many feudal fief holders omitted to have their tezkeres as submitted by their beylerbey confirmed by the Porte, in order to save themselves the tolls, often raised arbitrarily according to the whims of the Porte's officials. Not infrequently the estate of a deceased *sipahi* was parceled out in order to enfeoff a number of sons with smaller timars, whose holders then only had to present themselves alternately at military levies. Finally the hereditary succession even of women was permitted in such Asiatic fiefs. But the owners of major feudal estates also sought to withdraw more and more from their military obligations. The financial intendant of Sultan Ahmed I, Aini Ali, complains in his Kanunname that of ten *timarli*s who contended for the revenues at harvesttime not a man appeared in the field when it was a question of military service. But neither Aini nor the grand wazir Nasuh Pasha succeeded in their efforts to regulate anew at least the muster rolls, and Nasuh's violent end in 1614 was at any rate partially the result of these reforming efforts of his.

Thus it came about that, instead of the feudal troops, mercenaries more and more constituted the core of the army. Among them the mounted sipahis of the Porte were the oldest corps. The French diplomat Ghislain de Busbecq,* who represented the Habsburg emperor Ferdinand 1555-1562 as ambassador to the sultan Suleyman II and set down his excellent observations on the Ottoman Empire in a number of works, praises the beauty of their horses, whose harness gleamed with gold, silver, and jewels. They themselves wore clothing of brocade or silk in scarlet, hyacinth yellow, or dark blue colors. Their weapons were bow and arrow, a small shield, a light lance, a short sword often ornamented with jewels, and a mace at the pommel of the saddle. Manual firearms were not introduced until the Persian campaign of 1548, but this first attempt was a total failure, whereas artillery was already very well known. The European wars first imposed the introduction of the new weapon on the

* [*The Turkish Letters*, Oxford, 1927.]

Osmanlis with compelling necessity; nevertheless the sipahis, until the end of the sixteenth century, still relied principally on bows and arrows.

The four squadrons, which had been founded by Orkhan himself, were substantially increased, especially in the great campaigns of Selim and Suleyman; in 1534 their number had risen to 11,500. The three first divisions were recruited from the ichoghlan, the Christian boys captured in warfare and brought up in the Serai, whereas the fourth division, the less highly regarded foreign legion, was recruited from adult converts. During the Persian wars this corps notably decayed. The shah used to devastate his border provinces at the approach of the enemy and withdraw the inhabitants into the interior, so that the attacker had a great deal of difficulty in provisioning men and horses. Consequently a sipahi revolt took place as early as 1586 which could only be pacified by compliance with their demand that the Sultan himself lead them into Persia. Then, at the turn of the sixteenth and seventeenth centuries, when the financial plight of the Porte held up payment of the soldiers, the sipahis in repeated mutinies declared they were incapable of covering the costs of a campaign with their pay any longer. In the course of time the disproportion between the prescribed and the actual state of this corps grew greater and greater.

The spirit of ancient Asiatic nomadism, which had been considerably softened in the feudal troops and in the sipahis by civilization and discipline, still survived with unbroken force in the *akinjis*, the unpaid mounted vanguard of the army, which was compensated exclusively by tax exemption and resorted to plunder. It consisted primarily of the tenants of the feudal estates, seeking compensation as freebooters for the plight imposed on them by the oppression of their lords. In the years 1477-78 these bands bore all the terrors of devastation into the flourishing plains of the Venetian mainland and the high valleys of the Styrian Alps; for a century they ravaged Hungary and dragged hundreds of thousands off to slavery.

Similar was the role played by the auxiliary troops from tribute-paying Moldavia and Wallachia, the Crimean Tatars, the Georgians, and the Kurds. The khan of the Crimea also held fifty thousand men in readiness to fall on Poland's flank whenever the occasion presented itself. The same service was performed by the Georgians and Kurds with respect to the Persians.

The core of the army, however, was still formed by the Janizaries;

the Christian boys selected for their replacements were brought up in the four pageboy chambers in Adrianople, in the old and new Serai in Istanbul, and in Pera. Their inmates fell into five classes; their training, though rigorous, was thoroughly humane, since they were not to grow up to be cripples and cowards but men. In the highest class, that of the sultan's personal pages, there were never more than twenty-five to thirty young men; this was the preliminary school for the highest state and court offices, and most of the grand wazirs came up out of it. Although the selection of Christian boys for these pageboy chambers existed under Murad II (1421-1451), it was not firmly organized until the reign of Selim I. Every five years, later on more often as well, and finally every year, the levy of boys was assembled in Europe, in all the Balkan countries, and in Greece; later in Hungary also; only a few localities privileged by treaties, such as Istanbul, Galata, and Rhodes, were exempt from this tax. In the beginning only every fifth boy was selected; later all the able-bodied ones between the ages of ten and fifteen were taken. There was no lack of abuses in all this. The officials allowed wealthy parents to buy their sons' freedom; also they failed to deliver all the draftees to the pageboy chambers, but sold many of them to slave dealers on their own account. However, the brilliant future awaiting the Janizaries softened the rigors of the selection very considerably; indeed, it even aroused the envy of the Turks, who not infrequently strove to smuggle their own sons in among the Christian boys. It was not until the end of the seventeenth century that the levy of boys gradually went out of usage.

At first the age limit for entry into the Janizary corps was twenty-five; it was not until after the Persian wars had shattered the organization of the army that it was lowered. As an elite corps its number hardly ever exceeded fifteen thousand. Any further increase of the Janizaries was also gainsaid by the unruliness which early arose among them. They not only insisted on more and more expensive gifts at the accession of a new sultan to the throne, but on the Persian campaign, for instance, compelled Selim I to sacrifice to them the heads of the grand wazir, the army magistrate, and their own leader. An attempt was even made to make them innocuous by separation, quartering them temporarily in border garrisons. In 1581, for instance, only four thousand men among them were stationed in Istanbul itself. The permission to marry, accorded the Janizaries toward the end of the sixteenth century, meant one more step along

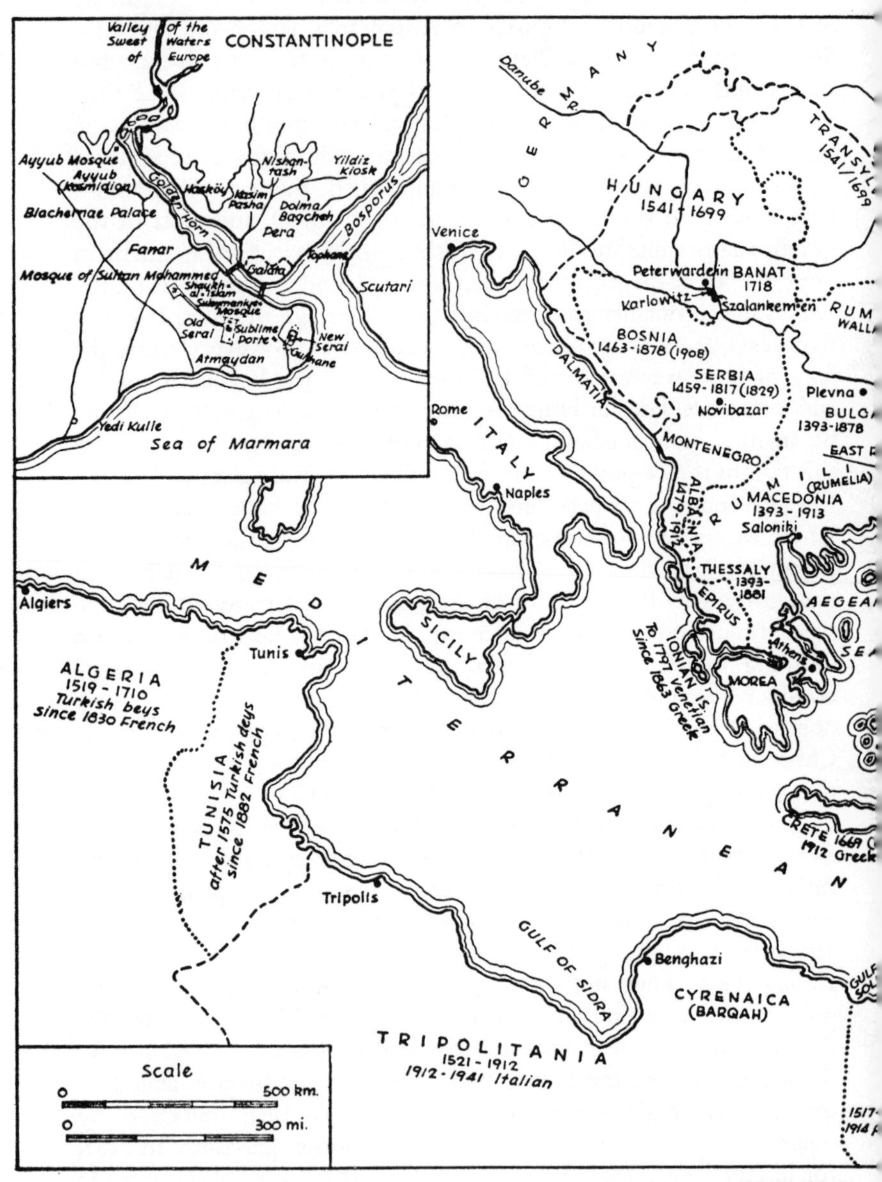

THE OTTOMAN EMPIRE

EXPANSION AND DECLINE

the path of decay. The consequence was that membership in the Janizary corps was soon simply made hereditary, regardless of military ability. The unfortunate Persian wars of Murad III then led to an undiscriminating reinforcement of the corps, which by 1660 had even grown to 54,222 men. In addition about the same number of men were carried on the muster rolls who made no claims for pay but were content with tax exemption; nor did they perform any military service in return, but were ready at all times to support the parent corps during mutinies. Since in the course of time the pay sank more and more, the Janizaries were increasingly compelled to earn a livelihood by some handicraft, while their officers tried to improve their position by service with the foreign ambassadors.

While firearms only gradually made their way into the infantry and the cavalry, the Osmanlis had paid great attention to artillery warfare from the very beginning; Muhammad II himself had had cannon casters and instructors brought in from Germany and Hungary for this branch of the army. Even under Bayezid II there existed corps of *topji*s, or artillerymen, whose number grew to a thousand under Selim I. Later Suleyman was principally concerned with the training of a light field artillery and the necessary supply train.

A great burden for the Osmanli armies from the very beginning had been the great train that had to accompany them, since their marches in Hungary and in Persia carried them through previously exhausted or intentionally and systematically devastated regions. The army which besieged Vienna in 1529, for instance, had no fewer than 22,000 camels for the transport of flour. In addition there were the same number of mules. The care of these fell on the corps of the *voinak*, mostly Bulgarian peasants, who as a rule served without pay merely in return for tax exemption and certain other privileges. On the march the light artillery together with the corps of the weaponsmiths, the *jebeji*s, formed the vanguard; they were joined by the Janizaries, followed by their *agha* with the two army judges and the accountants. Then came the sultan himself in the midst of his house troops and personal pageboys. Behind him was the place for the field insignia, the imperial banner, from the time of Selim I the banner of the Prophet, and the six standards of the various army divisions, as well as the six small banners of the sipahi mercenaries. The center was closed off by the grand wazir and the other wazirs with their numerous entourage. Then came the two beylerbeys of Rumelia and Anatolia with the mass of the feudal cavalry; on a campaign in Europe the former had precedence, in Asia the latter. The rear guard was brought up by the baggage and supply columns.

At the beginning of the battle the two beylerbeys advanced into the first line; in this the left wing was regarded as the place of honor. Both wings were reinforced by one division of artillery and akinjis each. Then followed the sipahis, while the Janizaries stood somewhat to the rear in the center. Behind them the sultan had his place with the field insignia and the dignitaries.

All European accounts are full of praise for the discipline of the Ottoman army. There was no place in it for either wine, gambling, or whores, of which there was never a lack in European armies of the time. The war against the unbelievers was actually still felt as a religious duty; during the efflorescence of the Ottoman army this contributed a great deal to insure victory over the Christians.

Their entire history impelled the Osmanlis to warfare on land; only the force of circumstances, not their own inclination, led them out to the sea. The victory of the Venetians at Gallipoli on May 29, 1416, fundamentally impressed on them the necessity of creating a navy. But Muhammad II was the first to invest the Ottoman name with the dignity worthy of it on the sea also. In the spring of 1456, 180 sailing vessels set out from Gallipoli to ravage the shores of the Aegean Sea. Selim I energetically continued the preparations, and Suleyman increased the number of the ships to 300. During his reign the pirate Khayr-ad-Din Barbarossa, as mentioned above, carried the terror of the Ottoman name as far as the Spanish coasts. But the Ottoman fleet really lacked the backbone which made their Latin adversaries so strong at sea, a powerful merchant marine. As against that, to be sure, they were quite superior in material wealth, since the forests along the shores of the Black Sea represented an inexhaustible store of timber, in spite of heedless exploitation. The requisite metals were provided by the mines of Moldavia and Wallachia, though sailcloth had to be procured from France.

The direction of shipbuilding lay mostly in the hands of Venetians; the workers were usually Greeks, who, however, very much to the disadvantage of the industry, were not permanently employed at the arsenals but brought together according to need. At the same time the swiftness with which the Ottoman dockyards worked not infrequently set Europe in astonishment; but the care in the selection of the materials and in the execution left a good deal to be desired. The real cancer of the Ottoman navy from the beginning was the dishonesty of the administration, which was to be handed down in an unbroken tradition to modern times. Even during the reign of Selim I the construction and arming of individual ships was left to the captains, of whom in 1592, for instance, 460 drew pay for themselves and their galleys while scarcely 150 performed any real service. The crews usually consisted of Christians, Italians and Greeks, generally runaways whom the substantial bounties to be gained from the fitting out of every Ottoman fleet attracted in droves to Pera. A still more unreliable element in the crews were the galley slaves shackled fast to the ship, with whom under Selim forty ships could still be manned, but whose number declined sharply after the beginning of the seventeenth century. An attempt was made to fill the gaps which arose by a regular conscription among the native subjects. The whole of the empire was divided into districts which had to provide a fixed quota for service in the fleet. The draftees could buy back their freedom and were then replaced by the captain with much cheaper slaves. Since Europe was already overburdened by the draft for the land army, the fleet got mostly Asiatics, usually debilitated and no longer equal to heavy duty. In consequence the proxy system was elaborated more and more, until it finally developed into a very lucrative fleet tax. Almost all sections of the land army were gradually drawn into armed service with the fleet; the Janizaries here also were the best, whose boldness, particularly in the boarding fights, was very much feared by their Christian adversaries.

The Ottoman fleet consisted of heavy battleships, *maons*, of which the largest, built in 1575, contained 576 slave oarsmen, and light cruisers, *chektiri* or *kadirgha*, with an average of 150 oarsmen. The fleet artillery was so weak at first that it made use of only twenty heavy guns on each galley. But after the unfortunate experiences in the Battle of Lepanto, the combat strength of the ships was so increased in this respect also that they were equal to those of the Venetians, at any rate in the number of guns.

From Barbarossa's time onward the pirate ships of the African Barbary Coast constituted a very substantial element of the Ottoman fleet. Whenever the sultan armed for a war at sea, these freebooters joined his fleet in droves, in order, under its protection, to damage the commerce of the Christians. Since their fast sailing vessels were excellently manned, their help was not unfavorably regarded in the beginning. But their unruliness soon brought them into disrepute with the Porte, especially since in peacetime they were almost continually responsible for diplomatic difficulties.

With the development of the fleet itself the functions of its chief had also increased. At first the sanjaq bey of Gallipoli directed the marine forces. But Barbarossa, as the beylerbey of the sea, was simultaneously charged with the governorship of the islands in the Aegean Sea, and eventually his domain encompassed fourteen sanjaqs. Since in outfitting the fleet it was possible for him, even with a certain degree of honesty, to secure substantial profits, this position was one of the most lucrative and most desired in the entire official hierarchy. Although after the Lepanto catastrophe the fleet was reconstructed with remarkable energy, it never managed to restore its prestige by a great victory. Its activities were more and more restricted to the patrolling of the coasts; in 1576 only forty of the three hundred galleys available were still completely armed; the rest were decayed and disarmed in the docks and wharves.

At the summit of the army and state which arose out of the feudal system stood the sultan. Originally the Osmanli emirs were still feudal vassals of the Seljuq sultans of Konya; but Orkhan laid claim to sovereign prerogatives by the right of coinage and the designation of his name in the khutbah, in the public Friday services. The title of sultan, which the Seljuqs, particularly since the Crusades, had borne with the approval of the caliph as champions of Islam, was secured by Bayezid I, as mentioned above, from the 'Abbasid caliph in Cairo, although his ancestors had borne it unofficially, so to speak, even before him. After the fall of Constantinople, Muhammad II assumed the title of Sultan al-Barrayn wal-Bahrayn, i.e. "Ruler over the Two Lands and the Two Seas." The titles of *khunkiar* and *padishah* were more colloquial. Murad I had already called himself the khalifah of God after the conquest of Adrianople; it was only according to a later legend that Selim I somehow made the 'Abbasid caliph in Cairo yield this title to him in 1517. It was not until the peace treaty of Kuchuk Kainarji in 1774, when believers of Islam came under Christian rule, that the Ottoman diplomats hoaxed the Europeans into believing that the caliph, like the pope, was regarded as the supreme spiritual leader of all Muslims and consequently had the right to claim nomination in the Friday services also in territories ruled by Christians as Austria still conceded to 'Abd-al-Hamid after the annexation of Bosnia. But, nevertheless, even in ancient times the loyalty toward the ruler rooted in the Turkish character itself was fortified still further by a certain religious sanction, so that his subjects were more unconditionally at his command than those of any contemporary Occidental ruler. He also had unlimited authority over all state resources, and only material powers, in particular the highhandedness of the Janizaries, were able to hamper it temporarily. Theoretically he even passed as the private owner of the state, and the net yield of taxation, after the covering of current expenses, flowed into his treasury, the Khaznah of the Seven Towers (Yedi Kulle). We have only inexact estimates of the size of the Ottoman state budget. During the last years of Muhammad II's reign the Byzantine Chalcondylas reckons the total revenues of the state at 4 million ducats. According to Venetian reports, however, by the middle of the sixteenth century this sum had already risen to 10 or 15 million, of which 2 million annually flowed into the sultan's treasury. Individual rulers, particularly Murad III, accumulated stupendous sums there and withdrew them from circulation. However, in public emergencies heavy claims were made on the treasury, and during a change of rulers it was often exhausted by the demands of the Janizaries. Public opinion took it for granted that the sultans would engage in extensive building, and in fact only a few failed to do so.

All political power theoretically, and for a long time in practice as well, remained in the hands of the sultan. But with the rapid growth of the empire the office of wazir, who at first had been only the sultan's first counselor, had steadily increased in importance. Muhammad II, in the first paragraph of his basic constitution for the state, the Kanunname, had already elevated the wazir to be the *de facto* regent of the empire.* As the padishah's plenipotentiary he was supposed to unite all the threads of administration in his own hands and decide on all affairs of state, including matters of life and death, with absolutely independent authority. As a symbol of his power the grand wazir bore the imperial seal with the *tughra*, the

* "Know first, that the Grand Wazir is the chief of the Wazirs and Emirs. He is the greatest of them all and the unlimited administrator of all affairs. The trustee of my estate is my *Defterdar* (Book-keeper), and the former is his overseer. Standing up and sitting down the Grand Wazir has precedence over all others in rank." *Kanunname'i Osman*, Istanbul, 1330, p. 10.

reigning sultan's monogram.* The ceremonial of the court also insured his position as deputy of the sultan. Like the latter, on fixed days of the week he accepted the homage of the functionaries of the court and the state; he appeared in public only in the midst of a brilliant entourage. His palace at the Sublime Porte (Babi Ali), in which he assembled the heads of the state for counsel, was thus made the real seat of the government. Suleyman I, in the diploma by which he elevated Ibrahim Pasha, the son of a Greek from Perga, to the grand wazirate in 1524, also transferred to him a substantial share of his own sovereign power. Ibrahim filled this office for many years, sustained by the full confidence of the Sultan, who was friendly toward him and even gave him his own sister in marriage. But the family strife which darkened the last years of the ruler shattered the Grand Wazir's position as well. He fell under the suspicion, hardly substantiated, of aspiring first to the Hungarian throne and finally to the throne of Osman itself. On March 15, 1536, he was found slain on his couch, which he had in the Serai in the immediate proximity of the Sultan. Only his second successor, Muhammad Sokolli, a Slav from the village of Sokol in Bosnia, again attained a position of similar authority; but he was astute enough to avoid the dangers the former had succumbed to. He aspired to increase not so much his power as his wealth. He was able to raise to fabulous heights the revenues of his position, substantial in themselves, by bribe-taking. The pashas in the provinces had to repurchase their posts annually with gifts; the pasha of Cairo is said to have paid more than 100,000 zechinos a year to Sokolli. Offices thrown open by death were awarded to the highest bidders. This was augmented by gifts from foreign powers. The German kaiser had to triple in secret the annual gift of 3,000 talers stipulated in the recent peace treaty. In 1573 Venice purchased an ignominious peace for 15,000 ducats. The example laid down by the highest imperial officials naturally had a corrupting effect on all branches of the administration. On October 11, 1579, Sokolli was killed by an assassin, perhaps only in an act of personal vengeance, and the importance of the office then also sank abruptly from its former heights. The destructive effects of the harem system, of which

* However, in decrees concerning finances and in decisions based on religious law (*shar'-i sherif*), the defterdars and the army judges also bore the tughra; *op. cit.* p. 16.

Muhammad Köprülü relieved the state only a century later, were to blame for this.

When Muhammad II transferred to the grand wazir his almost unlimited power, he at once placed the "wazirs of the dome" at his side, with the intention of restricting him appropriately. But the intention was never fulfilled. Although the external badge of their dignity, the three horse tails, made them equal to the grand wazir, their influence was never considerable. Their number, limited at first to four, later rose to six. What was denied these wazirs by their constitutional position they often attempted to achieve in other ways, and so as a rule they played an important role in the intrigues which continually imperiled and undermined the power of the grand wazir.

Just as the *kurultai* of the Mongols used to have assembled around the khan not only the princes of his house but also the ensemble of his army chiefs for deliberating on questions of vital importance to the state, so among the Osmanlis in the earlier period there was also the Diwan, a plenary assembly of all the office heads of the state which for important matters, especially when it was a question of deciding on peace or war, was convoked on horseback as in the nomad period. But the Diwan evolved more and more from this kind of assembly of leaders into a ministerial council, whose presidency Muhammad II, toward the end of his reign, generally left to the grand wazir. Only the so-called Pillars of the Realm (*Erkani Devlet*) still participated in it, i.e.: (1) the two army judges, one from Anadolu, and the other from Rumeli, who after Selim's great conquests were joined by a third for Africa; (2) the two beylerbeys for Asia and Europe; (3) the two defterdars for the financial administration of the two halves of the empire, likewise joined later on by a third for Africa; (4) the agha of the Janizaries as representatives of the army; (5) the kapudanpasha, or beylerbey of the sea, an office first created for Khayr-ad-Din Barbarossa, as representative of the fleet; (6) the *nishanji* for the monogram of the sultan. As in the earlier Islamic states on the Persian model, these highest of the imperial functionaries bore titles which were meticulously balanced off against each other in great detail, and which, indeed, were considered so important that Muhammad II at the end of his Kanunname had them formulated with precision for every single level of rank. The Diwan convened regularly on four days of the week from Saturday to Tuesday in a hall in the second courtyard of the Serai. The deliberations, interrupted twice by a communal meal, lasted from morning till late afternoon. Originally every subject had access to the sessions and could submit his requests and complaints, which were then generally referred to the individual offices to be dealt with. Since the sultan no longer conducted the chairmanship in person he received the Diwan at the end of its weekly councils in a ceremonial audience in order to receive a report on its decisions.

Since the two governors-general of Asia and Europe had a seat and a voice in the Diwan, it was, to be sure, still able to exert a certain influence on the administration of the provinces. But if the venality of the officials even in the central government was very great, in the provinces it often was boundless. Since the pasha had to buy his office from the grand wazir every year all over again, he naturally shifted the price off again onto his subordinates, who in their turn extorted it from the subjects. Every one of the twenty beylerbeys, indeed every one of the 290 sanjaq beys, sought to surround himself with a court, the expenses of which had to be covered by his administrative district. Their subordinates, the *subashi*s, always exploited the police power at their disposition for shameless extortions. Things were still worse for the regions of which the produce had been leased by the sanjaq beys to private individuals for a specified term. But it was only seldom that the oppressed populace rose to help itself, as for instance in Cyprus, where Greeks and Turks united practically tore to shreds the beylerbey, hated because of his avarice and cruelty.

Like the ensemble of the administration, originally the exercise of the law also had a military basis. At the summit of the judicial hierarchy, accordingly, even at a later period there still stood the army judge, whose office, no doubt on an Egyptian Mamluk pattern, had been created by Murad I. Muhammad II and Selim I then placed at his side one colleague each for Europe and Africa. The scope of authority of these army judges, however, was not limited to military affairs but extended to the total corpus of civil law. They appointed all judicial functionaries, the qadis and their deputies, the *naib*s; they also constituted the highest court of appeal, which was limited only by the judicial power of the grand wazir and the sultan. In hierarchical degree they were followed first of all by the senior mullas, the judges of the capital and of the provincial capitals, and the junior millas, who were the judges in ten provincial cities of the second class, such as Baghdad and Sofia. The lower stratum of the judges fell into three classes, the *mufettish*, or investigating officials, the qadis proper, and their deputies, the naibs.

The qadi possessed the highest judicial authority in his district. He alone, in the absence of any assessor, decided on civil and criminal cases according to the principles of the Shar'-i Sherif (the religious law based on the Qur'an and the Sunnah) and also had charge of all notarial matters and the preparation of testaments and other deeds. The advantages of the rapid procedure characteristic of Ottoman law were, again, counterbalanced by the venality of the judges; as early as 1394 Bayezid I vainly attempted to curb this ancient root-evil of Islamic jurisprudence by introducing fixed court fees.

After Selim I the entire judicial and theological hierarchy was subject in its turn to the mufti of Istanbul as Shaykh al-Islam, but his authority was exclusively theoretical. He had to hand down his opinion, or fatwa, on petitions concerning litigious questions, but lacked the power to see to it that his judgment was executed, though it is true that scarcely any judge would have dared to refuse compliance with the sentence passed by him. Muhammad II and Suleyman I expressly confirmed the mufti's exceptional position at the summit of the entire officialdom. And in fact the bearers of sovereign power had every interest in supporting his authority, since they themselves had to have recourse to it in difficult political situations. Thus Selim I had the mufti decree permission for war against the fellow believers in Egypt, and in 1570 Selim II secured from the famous mufti Abu Sa'ud approval of the totally unjustified breach of peace at the beginning of the Cypriote war against Venice. Later sultans, however, often disregarded this religious authority, which may have been a survival from the mystic Shi'ite period of the state, especially since its holders not infrequently became involved in political intrigues.

The confirmation of ecclesiastical officials in the capital was also incumbent on the mufti, whereas in the provinces this was a matter for the army judge. The actual nomination, on the other hand, was generally left to the founders of the individual mosques. In small communities, particularly in the countryside, an imam had sole supervision of all religious functions; in larger houses of worship, on the other hand, there was a division of labor. In such cases the imam was restricted to the conduct of the five daily prayers. Above him in rank there was the Friday preacher, the khatib, on whom it was also incumbent to strengthen the religious spirit of the community by exceptional meditative exercises. The menial functions, on the other hand, were taken care of by the sextons, the *qayyim*s, in addition to whom the *muwaqqit*s, determiners of the prayer periods according to the position of the sun, and the mu'adhdhins, the prayer callers, constituted special classes.

Training for religious office had been regulated by a venerable tradition and established by Muhammad II once again in a special decree. The aspirants were trained in the madrasahs, great numbers of which were established in noble competition by the sultans and their wazirs, in the capital and in the provinces, and generally adjoining the mosques. Their inmates fell into three classes. The actual students were called softas, from a combination, occurring not only in European writers, of the Arabic word *sufi*, a mystic, and the Persian *sukhta*, "inflamed" (i.e. by love of God and of knowledge). A census taken under Murad II indicated ninety thousand of them throughout the empire. As easily inflammable academic youth, they not infrequently, especially in later times, intervened in decisions concerning political questions. The *mu'id*s, or tutors, stood over them. After finishing his studies the young scholar bore the title of *danishmend*, or savant, and now had the choice of three careers, as teacher, cleric, or magistrate, open to him. However, anyone who wished to enter one of the higher classes, the junior or senior mullas, had to devote another seven years while still danishmend to studies at a madrasah. To this was added an examination before the mufti; whoever passed it was qualified for a position as *muderris*, a professor or teacher at a madrasah. These again fell into ten classes, graded according to the importance of the cities, out of the highest of which the junior mullas emerged. The holders of the higher offices in the hierarchy of the 'ulama frequently came into the Ottoman Empire from Egypt, more rarely from Persia, and after being in service there a while often returned to their native lands.

The religious life of the people was affected more by the dervish orders, very widespread in Asia Minor from of old and later in Rumelia also, such as the Naqshbandis, the Mevlevis, and the Bektashis, than by the official clergy. The system of ascending degrees in esoteric doctrines had always been cultivated with great success in the Islamic orders. While in the initiated circles no reluctance was shown in drawing the ultimate conclusions of a pantheistic mysticism, which not only dissolved the dogma of Islam but also unfettered its believers from its moral commandments, the religious sense was nourished in the people by exercises in ecstasy. Though speculation on the superstition may on occasion have played a not inconsequential role in this, and though the superstition itself may have been exploited for purely material purposes by unscrupulous superiors of an order, nevertheless it cannot be denied that to a great extent the orders exercised a civilizing effect under conditions of barbarism.

The scholastic life of the Osmanlis was almost entirely devoid of originality and moved in the fixed channels of tradition. Science for the Muslim did not mean the acquisition of new information but the most comprehensive mastery possible of the material elaborated by preceding generations. The highest esteem was bestowed on knowledge of religion and of the religious code, which was not to be separated from and which also dominated the civil law. Since canonical literature was written in Arabic, the theological writers among the Osmanli scholars also used Arabic as a general rule; only for the lay world were certain edifying books clothed in the national tongue. Not boldness or depth of thought but a retentive memory and patient industriousness are the virtues of the Osmanli scholars.

While the Osmanlis acknowledged the Arabs as their teachers in the strict sciences, they sought to imitate Persian models in their historical writing. The oldest historians actually wrote in Persian, and although the use of the mother tongue spread later on, its vocabulary in such works was entirely impregnated with Arabic and Persian borrowings; the style was an imitation of the high-flown bombast of Iranian rhetoric which for centuries had been seeping into Persian and, for a time, Arabic historiography from the court chanceries. But from the point of view of content the Osmanlis accomplished something outstanding and definitive for historical writing. It is true we have only very meager, largely confused and romantic information concerning the beginnings of the empire and its first few centuries, which we would be incapable of interpreting with any assurance without the Byzantine historians. But for nearly all the more important events of later history there are exhaustive and as a rule very valuable accounts by eyewitnesses, usually, indeed, by high officials who personally participated in the evolution of the events. But at an early time a beginning was made in the orderly recording of national history. The first work of this kind was written by the dervish Ahmed Ashikpashazade in Bayezid I's reign, still in a quite popular and largely legendary style. After the sixteenth century the Porte itself took a hand in the writing of history by appointing official historians; the first of them was Sa'd-ad-Din,* the prince-trainer, army judge, and mufti, who died in 1599.

It was only in the field of geography that Occidental learning made any headway among the Osmanlis. Even before the age of the great discoveries, Latin explorers had drawn up sailing manuals and atlases of their voyages. Their example was followed in the sixteenth century by the Turkish admiral Piri Re'is with a description of the coasts of the Mediterranean, with which he had become familiar on numerous voyages under his uncle Kemal Re'is and later under Barbarossa. In preparation for the war against Spain and Portugal, however, he had also collected information concerning their discoveries in America. Since the information concerning this was kept secret by these states, he must have learned of it through Italian agents. In Gallipoli, on the basis of it, he drew a map, based on that of Columbus, describing the Atlantic Ocean, with America and the western coasts of Europe and Africa, on which the names appear in the Italian form brought to him by his informants, and gave it to the sultan Selim in Cairo in 1517; since it was supposed to serve political ends, it was not published as was his sailing manual but stored away in the Sultan's palace and not found again till 1929, in the library of the Serai. Likewise a second map, of which a fragment has only recently turned up in the same place, was given by him to the sultan Suleyman I in 1529, three years after the completion of his sailing manual; it also contains the discoveries of the Portuguese in South and Central America as well as in Newfoundland, with which he had meanwhile become acquainted.† While kapudanpasha of Egypt, Piri Re'is conquered Aden in 1547 and Masqat in 1551; then, after besieging Hormuz on the Persian Gulf, he withdrew upon news of the advance of a hostile fleet but was shipwrecked on the Bahrayn Islands and was able to return to Suez with only two galleys; in Cairo he was sentenced to death because of his mishap. A century later one of the greatest of Osmanli scholars, Hajji Khalifah, who had taken part in the Asiatic campaigns as an administrative official of the army and so become acquainted with a large portion of the

* ['Abdi Pasha was first to hold the title of historian royal, in 1663.]

† See E. Bräunlich, *Zwei türkische Weltkarten aus dem Zeitalter der grossen Entdeckungen*, in *Berichte über die Verh. der Sächs. Akademie der Wiss. in Leipzig, Phil.-hist. Kl., Vol. 89, 1937.*

empire from his own observation, prepared a Turkish translation of the *Atlas Minor* of Mercator and Hondius (Arnheim, 1621) with the help of a convert in 1654-55; after dedicating a cosmography under the title of *World Survey* to the sultan Muhammad IV in 1648, he completely readapted this work on the basis of the atlas named above and other European sources, but in 1657 was surprised by death before its completion. The preceding year he had published a history of Ottoman sea power.

The originality of the Osmanlis in belles-lettres was even slighter than in their science. In earlier centuries, to be sure, as nowadays also, there must have been an abundant store of folk songs and tales in the areas of Turkish speech. The national song form was filled by the dervishes with a mystic religious spirit; particularly in the poems of Yunus Emre, which for a long time survived in the milieux of the dervishes and their followers and were widely imitated. This art flourished not only in the focal regions of the empire but also in the eastern border districts. The dialect of eastern Anatolia and of Adharbayjan was used in the fourteenth century by Nesimi, the poet of the Hurufiyah sect, who was executed in Aleppo in 1404/-05 as a heretic; and in the sixteenth century by Fuzuli, whose home was in Baghdad. Popular tales from the lives of the Prophet and the martyr Husayn, which were particularly popular in Shi'ite circles, and of the dervish saints, as well as of the prehistoric sultans and heroes, also spoke in simple prose to the hearts of the peasants and soldiers; but such works also were composed by preference in a metric form, like the famous *Muhammediye* of Yaziji-og̃hlu of Gallipoli, completed in 1449, which was also highly esteemed by the Turks on the other side of the Black Sea. But the "intellectuals" generally looked with disdain on such works. Just as the Arabs in science, so in poetry the Persians were regarded as models, whose imitation was considered the sole task worthy of a cultivated mind. With characteristic thoroughness the Osmanlis devoted themselves to the study of Persian poetry. In the philologic elucidation of the Persian classics their accomplishments were pre-eminent. Sururi, who flourished under Suleyman I and was tutor of Prince Mustafa, for whom he wrote his famous commentary to the works of Sa'di, and the Bosnian Sudi achieved particular distinction in this field. For a long time the Persian language was clung to, together with the Persian forms, and Selim I himself composed a great diwan in Persian. But in their own speech as well the Osmanlis made an effort to imitate all genres of Persian poetry. The crown of all poetic creation was considered to be the ghazel poetry, which, however, sought glory only in the continually renewed formulation of a narrowly restricted realm of sensations and ideas; a number of sultans also participated in this; down to the nineteenth century its most pre-eminent master was considered to be Baqi, who died in Istanbul in 1600, whose musical diction concealed the shallowness of his poetic sensitivity. The mystically and romantically inclined *mathnawis* of Jalal-ad-Din Rumi and of Jami, as well as of Nizami, were also widely copied. Even the satirical eulogizer of *gourmandise*, the Persian Abu Ishaq, found an Osmanli imitator.

Although the Osmanlis were never very strong numerically, they were able to control wide areas because of the system of military enfeoffment, which distributed them everywhere as prosperous gentry. And, to be sure, the ranks of the dominant race were never sealed fast. Even under the Seljuqs a mingling of the Turks with the native population of Asia Minor had taken place. When the Venetian explorer Marco Polo came through the country in 1272, he found the Turks still cattle-breeding nomads, while Greeks and Armenians were the sole masters of the cities. But the maladministration of the Byzantine proprietors of latifundia first drove the rural Greek population into the arms of the Turks, who penetrated into the cities also in the fourteenth century. The records of the Greek patriarchate during this time show us how the church of Asia Minor, formerly so prosperous, dwindled away before Islam and the Turks.* From the very beginning the Osmanlis also accepted every new convert who joined their court and their army as a full citizen. Even among the first four families of the Ottoman military aristocracy, one, that of Mikhaloghlu, was of Greek descent; it stemmed from Koze Michael, lord of Chirmenkia Castle at the foot of the Bithynian Olympus, who accepted Islam in 1308 and then became one of the most loyal paladins of Osman and his son Orkhan and was granted the rank of commander of the akinjis. For a long time the Osmanlis, by means of the levy of boys, were able to capture and absorb the flower of the male youth of the subject peoples. These *ajem-oghlan*, as we have seen, were also the source of the highest officials of the civil administration. According to a compu-

* See A. Wächter, *Der Verfall des Griechentums in Kleinasien im XIV. Jahrhundert*, Leipzig, 1903.

tation of H. Gelzer,* during the greatest efflorescence of the Ottoman Empire, between 1453-1623, only five out of forty-eight grand wazirs were of Turkish blood: one was a Circassian from the Caucasus, ten were of unknown origin, the remaining thirty-three converts, namely six Greeks, eleven Albanians and eleven Slavs, and one Italian, one Armenian, and one Georgian. In the Balkans the advantages of the Osmanli social position no doubt also lured many of their subjects into accepting Islam, such as the majority of the Albanians and the entire Bosnian nobility, which by virtue of this was able to preserve its old power over its domains. But these Muslims were no longer absorbed into Turkdom like the populace of Asia Minor. Albanians and Bosnians, as well as the Bulgar converts to Islam, the Pomaks, and the Cretans, retained their national languages. This is the explanation why the Balkan peninsula could not be held by the Osmanlis permanently. The Christian subjects, the raya, in the countryside, particularly in the remoter provinces, were, quite apart from political injustices, still further oppressed by heavy forced labor. They had to provide for the defense of the state by payment of the poll tax, which in 1590 amounted to a zechin with a value of about two dollars. In return for this they enjoyed the military protection of the Osmanlis. In the capital itself and in its surroundings, where the central power could easily be appealed to for help against the arbitrariness of the lower administration, the Christians, who were grouped according to nationality and denomination into millets, enjoyed complete civil and religious freedom, especially the Greeks (Rum Milleti). Their patriarch had even greater powers under the Ottoman rule than formerly in Byzantium. Baptisms, weddings, burials, and pilgrimages were held entirely in the open, and even as a rule with impressive magnificence. On the high holy days the Turkish authorities themselves even saw to it, by stationing a Janizary guard at the church gates, that divine worship could be held undisturbed.

Since in principle the Ottoman state did not concern itself with questions of religion, it actually became an asylum of religious liberty for the Jews driven out of Spain and Portugal at the beginning of the sixteenth century. Around 1590 the ghetto in Istanbul already contained about twenty thousand inhabitants. At first the Jews gained access to the sultan's palace as buffoons and jugglers,

* In *Geistliches und Weltliches aus dem griechisch-türkischen Orient*, p. 179.

particularly under Selim II, who was very fond of such enjoyments. But they also made themselves indispensable as physicians. The physician Nathan Salomon Ashkenazi, originally from Germany, even achieved great influence over Muhammad Sokolli. Under Selim II a Jew, Joseph Nasi, played a role similar to that of Michael Cantacuzene. His real name was Juan Miguez; he had immigrated from Portugal to Constantinople in 1550 with a very considerable fortune. Under Selim, whose lust for pleasure he had been able to exploit with great skill while the latter was still heir to the throne and governor in Kütahya, the lease on the wine tithe was bestowed on him in addition to the revenues from ten islands in the Aegean. He was allowed to designate himself in relations with Europeans as the duke of Naxos, and was represented in the Aegean by a Spaniard as governor. Even after Selim's death he retained the revenues, since in any case, at his death, because of his childlessness, his fortune would revert to the sultan's treasury. The Armenians, who in modern times were to become the most dangerous business competitors of the Greeks and the Jews, were still playing a very modest role in Istanbul around this time, though they had their own patriarch, who had to pay an annual tax of a thousand ducats; they gained their livelihood, as for that matter many of them still did in the nineteenth century, as house servants and petty tradesmen.

While the raya in the capital as a rule were all very good at accommodating themselves to the existing conditions, in the provinces the hope for emancipation from alien rule still survived. As often as the European powers won a victory in the struggle with the Porte, the Greeks in the Balkan peninsula were ready to join them. But, as we have seen, those who really bore aloft the idea of emancipation were the Albanians, among whom it did not die out even after their subjugation and under the heaviest of pressure. The Slavs, particularly the Serbs, kept the idea of emancipation alive through their national poetry, which in glowing colors glorified the wars against the Turks, and in particular the exploits of a hero, King Marko, son of Vukashin.

3. *The Rise of the New Persian Empire and the Turkish-Persian Conflict*

From the time of the Mongol tempest on, Iran had been the football of the feuds between tribal rulers of Mongol and of Turkish origin. We have seen how in 1469 the Turkoman Uzun Hasan, of the horde of the White Sheep, after defeating his rival Jahan Shah, the chief of the Black Sheep, had succeded in bringing the whole of Adharbayjan, Armenia, and Iran as far as Khorasan, still ruled by the Timurids, under his dominion, and how, after a conflict with the Osmanlis in which Venice supported him, he had afterward fallen back. His son Khalil, succeeding him in January 1478, was defeated by July of the same year by his brother Ya'qub, barely fifteen years old, and was killed in the battle, so that the latter could take possession of his father's dominions.

It was in his reign that the monk state of Ardabil, already mentioned, which was destined to become the starting point for the development of a homogeneous Iranian state, appeared on the scene. The combination of a contemplative life with warlike political aims, directed first against the infidels but later also against heretics within Islam itself, has been met with by us quite often before, as in the Almoravids in North Africa. Around 1334 the Sufi shaykh Ishaq Safi-ad-Din, who traced his descent to an 'Alid who ostensibly immigrated from South Arabia, died in Ardabil, in eastern Adharbayjan, a good day's journey from the southwestern shore of the Caspian Sea. He had married the daughter of his religious teacher Zahid, from Gilan on the southern shore of the Caspian Sea, and gained great prestige with Rashid-ad-Din, the wazir of the ilkhan of Persia. Like his descendants down to the third generation, he remained content with the repute of his saintly life, without seeking after temporal power. Safi's grandson, Khoja 'Ali, became so famous that Timur, after his victory over Bayezid, gave him and his descendants Ardabil and its district as pious endowment. This property, as well as the leadership of the order, was handed down within the founder's clan, not according to primogeniture, but according to the free choice made by the supreme head among his sons. Among his following outside of Ardabil, who were scattered as far as Anatolia, he was represented, as were the heads of other orders, by a khalifah.

The fanatical adherents of the Ardabil shaykhs, who professed the Shi'ite doctrine with increasing vigor, were soon bound to attract the attention of the neighboring secular rulers. Around 1350 the shaykh Sadr-ad-Din, Safi-ad-Din's son, had once been imprisoned by the contemporary Mongol ruler of Adharbayjan. In 1447, after the still-youthful Shaykh Junayd had fallen out with his uncle and guardian Ja'far, the latter urged his son's father-in-law, the khan of the Black Sheep Jahan Shah, to banish Junayd from the country. After adventurous wanderings through Asia Minor, Junayd found refuge on Jabal Arsus along the Gulf of Alexandretta in an old Crusaders' fortress, in which he assembled his followers. Since his Shi'ite machinations seemed suspicious to the Mamluk sultan Jaqmaq, the latter wanted to have him arrested; but he escaped to Janik on the Black Sea. Here again he succeeded in assembling numerous followers; with them he initiated a holy war against the kingdom of Trebizond, but the Ottoman sultan Muhammad II deprived him of his victory by making Trebizond tributary to his empire. However, he was given a hospitable reception in Diyarbekr by the latter's adversary Uzun Hasan, and in his territory was able to expand his order unhindered. In 1459 he returned to his homeland as the son-in-law of Uzun Hasan; to forestall another banishment by the khan of the Black Sheep he initiated a holy war against the Circassians; while advancing through the territory of the Shirwan shah he was attacked by the latter and on March 4, 1460, was killed in a battle in the Karasu valley.

At Amid, a month after Junayd's death, his wife bore his son Haydar, who grew up under the protection of Uzun Hasan and in 1470 was installed in Ardabil as his father's heir. After he had outgrown the guardianship of his uncle Ja'far, Uzun Hasan gave him in marriage his eldest daughter by his marriage with the Trebizond princess Despina Khatun. The second son of this marriage was Isma'il, born on July 17, 1487, the future founder of the Safavid dynasty. Haydar, who in the main had been left to his own resources after his grandfather's death, gave his order a new organization, which, as usual in the Orient, was expressed by the introduction of a new headgear; this was the red Haydar cap with twelve tassels in token of the twelve Shi'ite imams, which gave its wearers among the Osmanlis the designation of *Kizilbash*, "redheads." His supporters were descended from various Turkish tribes; among them the descendants of the Anatolian prisoners of war whom Timur had left behind for the shaykh Khoja 'Ali occupied a favored position. In 1483 Haydar began his military undertakings by a successful foray against the Circassians, for which transit was allowed him by the Shirwan shah. But he had to avenge his father's death on the latter; in 1488 he attacked him under the pretext of a renewed expedition against the Circassians, and shut him up in the fortress at Gulistan. The Shirwan shah escaped when a relief army of his emirs forced Haydar to withdraw; however, he had to flee at once to another fortress after Haydar had defeated his troops once again. But meanwhile Haydar's cousin, the Turkoman sultan Ya'qub, had sent out an army against him while he was laying siege to the fortress at Derbend. On July 9, 1488, battle took place at the foot of the Elburz Mountains between the Kizilbashes and the Turkomans, in which Haydar was killed. Ya'qub took his sons, together with their mother, from Ardabil to Istakhr in the province of Fars.

At the end of 1490 Ya'qub died, and in the warfare which broke out among his sons for the inheritance Haydar's sons were released from prison in order to summon their supporters to the aid of Rustam, Despina's grandson, against Ya'qub's son Baysonkur. Haydar's oldest son, Sultan 'Ali, and his Kizilbashes defeated the latter in 1493 and set out to assume the leadership of the monk state in Ardabil. But before Sultan 'Ali reached his homeland, Rustam had him attacked in a village near by and he was drowned during the engagement after being thrown into a rapids.

His two brothers Isma'il and Ibrahim were kept hidden from their pursuers by their followers in Ardabil, and Isma'il was then brought to safety to Gilan, whose ruler, although a vassal of the White Sheep, was on good terms with his family. There he lived in concealment until Rustam lost his throne and his life in 1497 through his cousin Gevdeh Ahmed.*

Just thirteen years old, Isma'il, reputedly with only seven followers, set out on the road to assume his father's inheritance. But from Ardabil he was at first turned back again by the Turkoman sultan 'Ali Beg Chakarlu, and withdrew again to Astara on the Caspian Sea. There, however, he again gradually assembled a great band of followers of Turkish blood, particularly from Anatolia and Syria, and in the spring of 1500 he was already able to set out on a holy war against the Christian Georgians. But this only served as a pretext for him to avenge his father's death on the Shirwan shah. Farrukh Shah was killed in battle at Gulistan, which was the end of his dynasty, who had regarded themselves as the descendants of the Sassanid Nushirwan. After seizing Baku, Isma'il turned against Alwand, the khan of the White Sheep in Adharbayjan. The victory over the latter opened the way to Tabriz, and there Isma'il was crowned shah of Persia. Although the Shi'ite clergy of the city

* See W. Hinz, *Irans Aufstieg zum Nationalstaat im 15. Jahrhundert*, Berlin and Leipzig, 1936.

indicated to him that of its 300,000 inhabitants at least two-thirds were Sunnites, he immediately elevated the Shi'ah to be the state religion, and in token of this forced all his subjects to execrate the first three caliphs.

After another victory over Alwand he turned against the latter's brother Murad, from whom he wrested the control of Shiraz in 1503, and extended his power as far as Astarabad and Yezd. He then conquered Mesopotamia and 'Iraq without much effort and so became master of the holy places of the Shi'ah, Najaf and Kerbela; at that time an extremist Shi'ite sect which regarded 'Ali as God and whose leaders claimed divine veneration for themselves was established in Huwayzah; he acted against these heretics with the same severity as against the Sunnites.

After Isma'il had subjugated all of Persia in this way, the only enemies opposing him were the Osmanlis in the west and the Uzbegs in the east. His conflict with Bayezid has already been related above. The Turkish tribe of Uzbegs under the khan Shaybani, who had developed his military abilities in the wars among the Mongol princes in Turkestan, had seized power there, and swept away the remaining Timurids in Khorasan and Herat in 1494, thus becoming a neighbor of the Persian state. It cannot be decided with certainty whether or not Shaybani, a resolute champion of the Sunnah, irritated Shah Isma'il into challenging him to return to the true faith, but it seems well attested that after the custom of the time they kept up a correspondence with each other of increasing acerbity. The direct occasion for their collision was provided by an incursion of the Uzbegs into the Persian province of Kirman. In revenge Isma'il undertook a campaign against the east in 1510, which simultaneously offered him an opportunity to visit the second great sanctuary of the Shi'ah, the burial place of the imam 'Ali Rida (Riza) at Mashhad. Near Merv in Tahirabad a battle took place on the first or second of December, in which Shaybani was defeated and killed. In token of this Isma'il sent his stuffed corpse to Sultan Bayezid, while he had his skull encased in gold to use as a drinking vessel. But the Uzbeg power was by no means broken by this and for a long time continued threatening the eastern frontier of Iran. After his defeat at Chaldiran, Isma'il also made peace with the Osmanlis, and it was not until after Selim's death that he ventured on a new enterprise in the west, a campaign against the Christian kingdom of Georgia. Shortly afterward, on May 23, 1524, Isma'il, only thirty-eight years old, died on a visit to Ardabil.

The foundation of the Safavid power has been referred to as constituting the rise of Iran to national statehood. But quite apart from the fact that the concept of nationality was entirely alien to its environment, a ruling dynasty of Iran in whose veins Turkish and Greek blood ran, in addition to Arab, and which was propped up in the capital on Turkish troops, can scarcely be called national. The scholars with whose help Isma'il brought the Shi'ah to power in Iran were largely of foreign descent, and since they wrote in Arabic, could not very well feel at ease as representatives of the Iranian people. Isma'il's reign, filled with strife, was not precisely favorable to literary accomplishment, and the few poets of his time met with greater patronage at the small courts of the Turkomans and the Timurids than at his own; one of the most famous among them, Hilali of Astarabad, was even of Turkish origin and owed his career to the patronage of the great eastern Turkish poet Neva'i. It may very well be doubted whether Isma'il's Persian subjects regarded his dominion as a prop of their national dignity, if during the religious disorders they even felt such a thing at all.

The reign of Isma'il's son Tahmasp, who assumed his inheritance at the age of ten and ruled for fifty-two and a half years, was filled with incessant warfare against his enemies, the Uzbegs in the east and the Osmanlis in the west. 'Ubayd Khan, the son of Shaybani Khan, conducted no fewer than seven campaigns against Persia from 1525 to his death in 1540. Next to holy Mashhad, Herat in particular had to suffer from the incursions of the fanatical Sunnites, who inflicted a regular and rigorous persecution on the Shi'ites. An account has already been given of the Osmanli campaigns against Persia. In the interludes between battles against his Sunnite enemies Tahmasp conducted seven campaigns against the Christian Georgians, which, however, brought him no lasting successes, even though numerous Georgians entered his service afterward. It goes without saying that the long reign of the Shah, who sought glory in the most painful compliance with every commandment of Shi'ite Islam, however petty, and during the last years of his rule secluded himself almost entirely in his palace, did not precisely redound to Iran's blessing, particularly since public security was continually being disturbed by robber bands as a result of the military upheavals. The Venetian ambassador to his court, Vincento d'Alessandri, has given an account of how the Shah once resolved to alleviate the oppressive burdens of his subjects' taxes because of an angel's having appeared to him in a dream and threatened him on account of it. From his autobiography we know that in general dreams played an important role in his life; on the basis of a dream in which the imam 'Ali Rida admonished him, he renounced the enjoyment of wine in his twentieth year and had all wine resorts in the country closed down.

When Tahmasp died on May 14, 1576, he had made no arrangements for the succession. His oldest son Muhammad Khudabanda, who resided in Herat from 1536 to 1556 as governor, and had exchanged this office for the governorship of Shiraz as the result of a dispute with a high officer, had been almost blind for a long time, and in consequence, according to the general attitude of the Orient, was excluded from the succession to the throne. His second son, Isma'il, who in contrast to his father and brother was filled with martial energy and in consequence was the favorite of the Kizilbashes, had already distinguished himself in the wars against the Osmanlis, especially in 1552 by a bold and successful enterprise against the governor of Erzerum, Iskender Pasha; but when he was governor of Khorasan, where he had succeeded his older brother in 1556, his independent war plans had aroused his father's suspicions, and from 1557 on he was kept in confinement at the Kahkahe fortress in the Sawalan Mountains between Ardabil and Tabriz. Among the Shah's other seven sons Haydar was his favorite; he had already ordered his ambassador to the Porte to see to it that the Porte should not exercise a disturbing influence on his succession to the throne. The Georgians at the court took his side, and the Ustajlu tribe of the Kizilbash; no doubt he also had the sympathies of his Persian subjects. But Isma'il's partisans, before he had yet escaped from his confinement, had seized possession of the palace in the capital of Qazwin under the command of his half sister Peri Khan Hanum and murdered Haydar.

On May 23 Isma'il, freed by his jailer on the news of Haydar's assassination, set out for the capital, which he entered on June 13, and finally, on August 22, he ascended the throne of his fathers. The new shah, whose mind had been deranged by his lengthy imprisonment, now concentrated all his energy exclusively on the consolidation of his power. In a short time he had all his brothers, except Muhammad Khudabanda and his sons, assassinated; though the latter's oldest son Husayn was also assassinated, and his brother 'Abbas, later the shah, only escaped the same fate by accident. The new shah alienated the pillar of his house, the Kizilbash, by his openly displayed dislike of the Shi'ite sect; he avoided having their formula stamped on his coins and forbade the public malediction of the first three caliphs; the confusion of his character, deranged by intoxicants, makes it impossible to decide what induced this attitude in him, whether it was the hope of so reconciling the hereditary enemies of his state, the Sunnites, or merely the desire for revenge on the memory of his father, who had cheated him of his life. A short time after an heir was born to him he died in the house of a boy lover, probably from poisoning, on November 24, 1577. His ambitious half sister was already considering the assumption of the imperial regency on behalf of his minor son, but the chiefs of the Kizilbash elevated the half-blind Muhammad Khudabanda to the throne.* It is indicative of the weakness of the state that soon afterward a Kalandar dervish could advertise himself as the murdered Shah in the Kurdish province of Luristan and maintain his rule there until 1582.

Directly after his accession to the throne Muhammad Khudabanda rid himself of his ambitious half sister Peri Khan Hanum and the minor son of Isma'il. In his place his wife, the daughter of a Mar'ashi sayyid from Mazanderan, conducted the affairs of state until she was assassinated by one of the Kizilbash chiefs. Since the weakness of the state was taken advantage of on all sides by its enemies, Shah 'Abbas's second son, who up to then had been filling the governorship of Khorasan, after the assassination of his older brother, intervened in the capital, forced his father to abdicate in October 1587, and had both his younger brothers blinded and imprisoned in Alamut.

The forty-three years of the reign of 'Abbas "the Great" (1588-1629) † led Iran to the zenith of its power. The Shah, barely seventeen years old at his accession to the throne, soon rid himself by murder of Murshid Kuli Khan, who had previously been in attendance on him during his governorship and had assisted him to the throne. With an astute perception of the dangerous position of his state he straightway concluded a humiliating peace with the Osmanlis, who since the death of Isma'il II had been attacking Persia

* See W. Hinz, *Schah Esmail II, Mitteilungen des Seminars für orient. Sprachen*, 1933, 2, 9-99.

† A. Bellan, *Chah Abbas, Les grandes figures de l'Orient*, III, Paris, 1933.

repeatedly. He ceded the provinces of Adharbayjan, Georgia, and a part of Luristan, which they had occupied, and bound himself to cease execration of the first three caliphs throughout his domain and to have his cousin Haydar Mirza sent as hostage to Istanbul. This gave him a free hand for the pacification of the country in the interior and for the repulsion of the Uzbegs, who had been making repeated depredations on Khorasan, until, after the death of the khan 'Abd-al-Mu'min in 1598, he succeeded in expelling them from the country. Soon afterward there appeared at his court two English knights of fortune, Sir Anthony and Sir Robert Sherley,* who finally enabled him, with the help of a cannon caster accompanying them, to provide the Persian army with artillery, the lack of which had continually insured its inferiority to the Turks. To make himself independent of the Kizilbash, from whom his ancestors had suffered so much, he founded on the model of the Janizaries a corps of troops of Georgian and Armenian converts to Islam, and a new Turkish bodyguard, the *Shahsevens*. Then, toward the end of the reign of Muhammad III, after the Ottoman Empire had become involved in a long-drawn-out war with Austria and was threatened in Asia Minor by the uprising of the Jelali sect, he initiated a war with his new army in 1602 and won back not only Tabriz but also Shirwan and Baghdad, which, to be sure, reverted to the Turks a number of times during his reign. In the Caucasus also he restored Persian rule, and secured the borders in the east as far as Merv and Balkh. In March 1622, with the support of some English ships, he wrested the island of Hormuz in the Persian Gulf from the Portuguese and founded a new base of trade in the harbor of Gumrun, which he built up as Bender 'Abbas.

From Qazwin, made somber by so many sad events, he removed his residence to Isfahan. There he transplanted the Armenians from Julfa on the Araxes, who transferred the name of their old homeland to the suburb set up by them. He adorned Isfahan itself with magnificent buildings, like the great mosque, the Palace of the Forty Columns (Chihil Sutun), and the great bridge over the Zende-Rud, and by the laying out of the Four Gardens. As earlier in the peace treaty with the Osmanlis he had softened the harshness of the Shi'ite belief, his tolerance now went so far as to permit the Carmelites a settlement in Isfahan. During his long reign the intellectual life of Persia burgeoned again. Among the scholars at his court,

* [D. E. Ross, *Sir Anthony Sherley and His Persian Adventure*. S. C. Chew, *The Crescent and the Rose*, Oxford, 1937.]

Muhammad Baqir ibn-Muhammad Damad was especially famous, inspiring the Shah himself with reverence; he carried on studies in philosophy and natural history in addition to theology, even making his own observations on bees. There was also the many-sided Baha'-ad-Din al-'Amili, who attempted to encompass the totality of contemporary knowledge. The great philosopher Sadr-ad-Din ash-Shirazi, on the other hand, whose metaphysics has exercised an influence down to our times as an element in the formation of the new religion of the Bab, preferred a life of contemplation in the holy city of Qumm. Poetry and music also revived under his reign.

But even this monarch, who otherwise towered so far above his ancestors, thought nothing of having his oldest son Safi Mirza assassinated when his popularity among the people seemed to make him dangerous. In the spring of 1629, when he died in his summer residence of Farakhabad in Mazanderan, he was succeeded by his grandson Sam Mirza, who assumed the name of his father, Safi, at his accession to the throne.

The reign of this grandson of his was one of the most unfortunate periods in the history of the long-suffering nation. An incompetent tyrant, he attempted to prop up his power at home by continually renewed acts of savagery. Although abroad he was able to repulse the incursions of the Turkomans in Khorasan, he lost Kandahar in present-day Afghanistan, which Tahmasp had conquered and 'Abbas had won back, to Shah Jahan of Delhi, and Baghdad to the Osmanlis.

But under 'Abbas II, who had followed his father on the throne in 1624 at the age of ten, Persia underwent another brief period of prosperity and good fortune. He regained Kandahar; otherwise he only had to repress an uprising of the Georgians under Tahmurath Khan in 1659. He treated all his subjects with equal justice and without regard to their beliefs, so that the Christians also enjoyed full religious freedom. Although at the insistence of the clergy he endeavored to restrict the enjoyment of wine, he himself later succumbed to dipsomania, which cut short his life.

Although his son Safi, who assumed the name of Suleyman at his accession to the throne in 1666, continued his father's xenophile policies, like the latter he was addicted to tippling and while in a fit of drunkenness not infrequently allowed himself to be swept away into acts of bestiality against those around him. His son, Sultan Husayn, who succeeded him in 1694, was a degenerate weakling; he left the state power entirely to the Shi'ite clergy, who abused it in a ruthless persecution of the indigenous Sunnites. Among the mullas Muhammad Baqir-i-Majlisi distinguished himself in particular by his blind raging against the Sufis. As will be related later on, this was the cause of the overthrow of the dynasty and the transfer of the power to the Afghans.

4. *The Decline of the Ottoman Power down to the End of the Eighteenth Century*

While governor of Magnesia, Selim II was surprised by the death of his father, during the Hungarian campaign of 1566 before Szigeth, and at once hurried to Belgrade, where he awaited the return of the grand wazir Muhammad Sokolli with his father's dead body. He first had to purchase his entry into Istanbul by extravagantly high payments to the Janizaries. He continued to leave affairs of state to the Grand Wazir, who in February 1568 concluded a peace treaty with Austria in return for a tribute of thirty thousand ducats and the reciprocal acknowledgment of the territorial *status quo*. In spite of his slight military bent he soon was persuaded into another war against Venice by his Jewish favorite, Joseph Nasi. The latter's covetousness had been aroused by the island of Cyprus, a valuable possession of the republic, and he induced the Sultan to declare war on the signoria when it refused to make the cession of it demanded by him in 1570. Without encountering any considerable opposition, the Osmanli troops were able to seize possession of the island. The Venetian fleet meanwhile was lying in wait at Crete, waiting for help from the west. It was not until May 1571 that the republic succeeded in persuading Philip II of Spain and the Pope Paul V to provide assistance, and in September the allied fleet assembled in the harbor of Messina. Under the command of Don John of Austria it was decided to seek out the Ottoman fleet, which was lying in the Bay of Lepanto, the old Naupaktos, at the exit of the Gulf of Corinth. It had just arrived from Cyprus after plaguing the coasts of Crete and the Ionian islands, and had been reinforced by forty ships under the beylerbey of Algiers. The kapudanpasha decided to abandon the secure anchorage of Lepanto, against the advice of his subordinates, who pointed to the weakened condition of the crews as the result of numerous desertions, and to advance against the Christian fleet, which had entered the gulf on October 7. The latter's superior combat strength inflicted an annihilating defeat on the Ottoman fleet; the beylerbey of Algiers alone succeeded in saving the left wing with forty ships. But Don John did not exploit his victory. He did not even attack Lepanto itself, although the Christian populace of the hinterland was simply waiting for this to rise against the Osmanlis. The allies quietly withdrew, and only the following year the Sultan was able to send into battle almost as strong a fleet. Thus the Venetians, who had also remained at a disadvantage in Dalmatia, lost the will to further resistance and in March 1573 concluded a peace treaty in which they ceded Cyprus. Only a year afterward, on December 12, the Sultan's vitality, weakened by excesses, gave way as the result of a stroke.

His oldest son, Murad III, ascended the throne unhindered. Since as crown prince he had passed as having a serious temperament, it was expected of him that he would follow in his grandfather's footsteps; but he became submerged even more deeply than his father in the pleasures of harem life and left to his mother, Nur Banu, and to his chief wife, Safiyah, of the Italian family Baffa, the decisive influence on the course of affairs.

After the Venetians were abandoned by the western powers, they endeavored to goad the elderly Shah Tahmasp of Persia into a war against the Sultan. But after his weakling son Muhammad Khudabanda came to the throne in his place, the Ottoman war party did not let the favorable opportunity of another encounter with their ancient enemy escape them. In 1577 the Osmanlis attacked the Caucasus and conquered Tiflis; in 1579 they erected the fortress of Kars, of great use for the consolidation of their power. But not until 1585 did they succeed in moving the theater of war to Persia itself and in taking the former capital of Tabriz. How 'Abbas the Great purchased peace from the Osmanlis after his accession to the throne has already been related.

During the Persian war the Osmanlis had also reinforced their influence in southern Russia, which in 1581 and 1583 served them as an area of deployment against Georgia. The disturbances among the Cossacks also offered them another opportunity to interfere in Poland. The Polish kings, Stephan Bathory and (after 1587) Sigismund, could actually be considered *de facto* vassals of the Sultan.

After the truce of 1583 the embers of war had been smoldering on in petty feuds along the Austrian border; ten years later they flared up in bright flames again. In June 1593 the governor of Bosnia had suffered a frightful defeat during a raid at Sissek in Hungary, and to avenge this the great war was to be resumed. But before this took place, Murad III died, on January 16, 1595.

He was succeeded by his son Muhammad III, the last Ottoman crown prince to whom a governorship in Magnesia was to be freely granted in preparation for his vocation of ruler. The next year he himself took the field and had the good fortune to participate in the first brilliant action at arms of his troops in this war, the victory over the Habsburg imperial forces at Keresztes. But after that the war continued only at a limping pace, which was not altered in any way by Muhammad's death in 1603 and the succession of his son Ahmed. Not until the Hungarian grandee Bocskai, elevated to be prince of Transylvania, took the side of the Osmanlis did fortune turn in their favor. This led to the peace treaty of Sitvatorok in 1606, in which, however, the Sultan dispensed with the tribute hitherto paid to him in the form of an honorary gift.

Even in the Battle of Keresztes, an Osmanli victory, an evil long crawling and seriously menacing the existence of the state had come to light. Not only had the Janizaries long since lost all respect for the Sultan's authority, but the timarli levy, particularly the Asiatic one, also proved unreliable. More than three thousand men of them, we are told, fled the severity of the grand wazir Chigala at that time and were hunted down by their own countrymen on his orders. In 1599, after their return to their homeland, the commander of the Janizary division of the Segbans, 'Abd-al-Halim Kara Yaziji, placed himself at the head of the malcontents among whom the tendencies of ancient Ottoman life may have been reviving, and seized Edessa. The Porte thought it could mollify him by appointing him governor of Amasia, but this merely gave him the power for further excesses. By April 1600 he was able to defeat the governors of Damascus and Baghdad in open battle near Kaysaniyah. He himself was killed in battle soon afterward, whereupon his brother took his place. The latter maintained himself for a time with success, but then was lured into Europe by a promise of the governorship of Bosnia and during the siege of Buda in 1603 was killed together with the greater portion of his troops.

That same year a mutiny in the Ottoman garrison of Tabriz broke out which offered Shah 'Abbas an occasion to seize possession of the city. Thus the Porte saw itself forced into a war on two fronts. The war against Persia was all the more burdensome since there was a series of continually renewed uprisings on the part of marauding chieftains in Asia Minor, of the Kurd Janbulad, the hereditary governor of Klis near Aleppo in Syria, and the Druze prince Fakhr-ad-Din in the Lebanon. After the peace treaty of Sitvatorok it was possible at any rate to defeat Janbulad, who now fled to Fakhr-ad-Din in the Lebanon, and to wipe out the most dangerous of the rebel leaders in Asia Minor. After the Osmanlis had retaken Tabriz also, 'Abbas acquiesced in a peace treaty which, although relieving him of the payment of the tribute, regulated questions of territory just as provisionally as the peace treaty of Sitvatorok for Hungary.

In 1617 Sultan Ahmed died, and his brother Mustafa, as the oldest prince of the house, succeeded him according to the ancient law of succession, but only three months later had to yield to his young nephew Osman II. In the border feuds with the Poles a great battle took place at Jassy on September 20, 1620, which made the Sultan take the field himself. But at the very walls of the Choczim fortress his ambitious plans collapsed; in 1621, having achieved nothing whatever, he had to acquiesce in a treaty of peace. Since, not without reason, he ascribed this failure to the Janizaries, his grand wazir was able to induce him to attempt to get rid of them and again prop himself up on the Asiatic provinces of the empire. A campaign against Fakhr-ad-Din in Syria and the pilgrimage to Mecca were to enable him to carry out this plan. But the Janizaries learned of his intention through treachery and forced him to give up the campaign. Upon his refusing to deliver to them the grand wazir, he was shut up in the Serai and the semi-feebleminded Mustafa set on the throne again. At the behest of the new grand wazir, Osman was assassinated in Yedi Kulle on May 30, 1622. Only two years later the more sober elements in Istanbul won the upper hand again. On September 11, 1623, Mustafa was forced to renounce the throne in favor of Murad IV, the fifth son of Ahmed, a boy eleven years old. It took him until 1632 to succeed in tearing loose from the fetters of Janizary rule and getting rid of their leaders, with the help of the elder statesmen. He restricted the number of Janizaries by suspending the draft of boys and organized for himself new and reliable troops.

During this tumult in the capital, Osmanli rule in Syria suffered a heavy blow. As early as 1603 the Druze prince Fakhr-ad-Din in the Lebanon, in alliance with the Kurd Janbulad, had revolted against the Porte, and even after the latter's defeat was left in possession of his territory in return for an annual tribute. The enterprising Duke Ferdinand I of Tuscany entered into relations with him in order to open up new channels for Florentine trade, while Fakhr-ad-Din, with his help as well as that of the Pope and of Spain, hoped to conquer Palestine. In 1610 he occupied Baalbek and even threatened to seize Damascus. When a Turkish fleet appeared along the coast in 1613, he fled to Leghorn. In Tuscany, Ferdinand's son Cosmas I had begun his reign; he was too cautious to consider a plan for a new crusade. During Fakhr-ad-Din's five-year sojourn in Florence, his astute mother held his domain on behalf of his grandson Ahmad 'Ali against the pasha of Damascus. After his return he had to continue recognition of his son as emir, but on his behalf conducted the war against the Osmanlis. During the Persian war he was then able to extend his rule along the Syrian coast as far as Antioch. In 1631 he came into open conflict with the Porte by refusing winter quarters in his territory to an army intended against Persia and expelling it by force of arms. Two years later another Ottoman fleet appeared along the Syrian coast in revenge for this breach of the peace and occupied all the harbors. Simultaneously the Ottoman governors attacked the Druzes by land. Fakhr-ad-Din's son 'Ali let himself be lured into a decisive battle on the plains on October 15, was miserably defeated, and both he and his uncle lost their lives. On November 12 Fakhr-ad-Din had to capitulate in his last refuge and was taken to Istanbul. There he was beheaded on April 13, 1635, after his nephew Melhem had made a vain attempt to restore the honor of his house by an armed uprising.

In 1623 the war with Persia had broken out again, since the Ottoman governor had surrendered Baghdad to the shah. For fifteen years guerrilla warfare for this city dragged on simultaneously in the Caucasus and Adharbayjan. In 1635 Murad IV took the field against Armenia with his newly formed army. In 1638 he succeeded in reconquering Baghdad, and the year after he concluded peace with Persia.

Murad IV did not long survive this happy ending of the Persian campaign. On February 19, 1640, he died of drink. After his brother Ibrahim came to the throne, the evils of indiscipline and women's rule, which Murad had held in check toward the end of his reign, made their entry again into Istanbul. During his first two years the grand wazir Kara Mustafa had been able to restrain these influences with some success, but in doing so had made numerous enemies by injuring many private interests through economies in the army and navy, a reform of the coinage, and a reorganization of the system of taxation. Consequently it was easy for the dowager sultaness and three favorites of Ibrahim's to stir up the Janizaries against him, and when the latter demanded his head on January 31, 1644, the Sultan dared not oppose them.

In spite of Ibrahim's insignificance the Osmanlis during his reign succeeded in gathering their forces for another great military undertaking in Europe. The Venetians were still in control of the entry to the Aegean Sea from Crete, but Istanbul had long since learned to despise them, since at every conflict on the Dalmatian frontier or with the Barbary states they retreated and tried to buy peace for money. A plan grew ripe to rob them of their last possession in the Levant, and by 1644 the arsenals were diligently rearming. On June 1 of the following year the Porte opened hostilities by the order to have all Venetians throughout the empire arrested and their property confiscated. The Ottoman fleet, without encountering any serious resistance, landed on Crete and conquered Canea by autumn, though afterward the Osmanlis advanced only slowly. A conspiracy was consequently formed in Istanbul to ascribe the blame for the sluggish conduct of the war to the Sultan, who was squandering the resources of the state in insane luxury. On August 9 he was deposed, and was strangled to death ten days later. The conspirators raised to the throne his minor son Muhammad IV.

Three years later the noxious influence of the grandmother on the young Sultan was also broken by a palace revolution, and the queen mother was already directing her gaze to the man who was destined to reorganize the state. This was Muhammad Köprülü, from Kopru on the Halys near Amasia, whither his grandfather had migrated from Albania. He appears to have come into the Serai as a levy-boy, but soon rose from subordinate court service to state service, was paymaster of the grand wazir, then became pasha in Damascus, Tripolis, and Jerusalem, and was back in the capital as an important minister, the wazir of the dome. At this point his enemies succeeded in an intrigue against him, and he withdrew to his native country. From there the grand wazir Mugri Boynu ("Crooked Neck") recalled him to the capital.

Meanwhile the Venetians in their war of desperation for their position in the Levant had been vainly endeavoring to gain the aid of the other powers. They were unable to relieve Candia but made some progress in Dalmatia, and in 1651 succeeded in defeating the Ottoman fleet at Paros.

Now that this defeat had heightened the misery of the Ottoman Empire to a maximum, Köprülü's hour had come. On September 22, 1656, he, by this time an octogenarian, took over the office of wazir only on condition that the Sultan allow him unrestricted power and free control of all offices. With ruthless severity he extirpated the spirit of rebellion by means of mass executions, without sparing even the favorites of the Serai. He restored financial order by openhanded borrowing from the Sultan's private exchequer as well as by secularization of the pious foundations and curtailment of the incomes of the clergy. Before his death in 1661 he secured his succession by his son Ahmed, who successfully elaborated his father's reforms without recourse to his savage means.

The internal renaissance of the Ottoman state was also soon given expression in energetic measures against its neighbors in the north. In Transylvania, Prince George Rakoczy, who had made an attempt to evade his feudal obligations toward the Sultan, was replaced by the compliant Apafy. When the emperor, pressed by the Magyars, refused to recognize Apafy, the Porte threatened war. In Europe there came to life the idea of the common obligations of Christendom in defense against the Turkish peril, for which the Venetians had so long been hoping in vain. Even Louis XIV of France answered the papal summons for aid against the Turks, despite his good relations with the Porte, by ordering the German princes associated with him in the Augsburg League to place twenty thousand men at the disposal of the German emperor. This offer embarrassed the Viennese court, which was still attempting to avoid war and negotiate. But in April 1663 the Sultan lost patience and his army launched an attack in Austrian Hungary. When the Osmanlis threatened Vienna itself, the emperor called for the help of the Augsburg League and even of Sweden. But even after two victorious battles, of which the one of St. Gotthard on the Raab, under the command of the count of Montecuculi, became especially famous, he concluded a peace treaty in 1665 in order to regain a free hand against the French policy.

Now the Osmanlis could devote their entire strength anew to the war on Crete, where the siege of Candia had not yet made any progress. The Venetians were still hoping for the help of at least

France, but Louis had no desire for an open break with the Porte. He had formally apologized in Istanbul for the help he had afforded the emperor. There was still greater irritation against him there for his compulsive measures against the Barbary states; on July 23, 1664, for defense against piracy at sea, he had taken Jijelli, which, however, the French could not hold after October 31, and bombarded Algiers and Tunis in 1665. Consequently after the peace treaty of Aix-la-Chapelle he only permitted individual officers to enter the service of Venice. It was not until the summer of 1669 that a French fleet with seven thousand men sailed for Crete. But neither this assistance nor that of the emperor and of the duke of Brunswick could save the hard-pressed fortress any longer. On September 6 it had to capitulate, and in the subsequent peace treaty the Venetians surrendered Crete.

After the Osmanlis had restored their dominion over the eastern Mediterranean, they sought an expansion of their power in the northeast as well. In 1668 the Cossack hetman Doroshenko, hitherto a subject of the Polish crown, passed over to the protection of the Porte. But not until 1672 did the Porte demand from Poland the cession of the Ukraine, after assuring itself that Louis XIV would not interfere. King Michael of Poland, after losing the border fortress of Kameniecz following a short siege, had already waived claim to Podolia and the Ukraine in a humiliating peace treaty. But only the following year this treaty was broken by Marshal Sobieski. On November 11 he was victorious at Choczim, and won the crown (as John III, 1674-96), since King Michael died soon after. But he also was unable to win any lasting success in the subsequent campaigns, and when, emboldened by a victory at Lwów, he ventured across the Dniester in 1676, he was encircled at Zuravna and in October had to accept a peace treaty in which he again ceded the greater part of Podolia and the Ukraine. The same year Ahmed Köprülü, just past his fortieth year, died on a voyage to the sultan's camp near Adrianople.

Poland owed these indulgent peace terms only to a conflict with Russia which was menacing the Porte. The Osmanlis had interfered in the Ukraine in the wars of the Cossacks against the Russians; after heavy losses on both sides a peace was concluded in 1681, in which Kiev and its surrounding territory fell to Russia.

As soon as the Osmanlis had a free hand in the east, they turned their entire strength against Hungary again. The Magyar grandees, led by Count Tokoly, had suggested to the Sultan the subjugation of the remaining Hungarian territory under Austrian rule in return for an annual tribute, and in May 1683 the Turkish army initiated a campaign against the emperor from Belgrade. In expectation of further help the latter's troops slowly withdrew to Vienna. On July 17 the capital was encircled by the Osmanlis under the grand wazir 'Umar Mustafa. But now, in spite of Louis's threatening attitude, a great army appeared from Germany and in concert with a Polish corps defeated the Osmanlis at Kahlenberg on September 12 and forced them to give up the siege. Although dissension broke out between the Germans and King Sobieski of Poland as a result of the latter's claims, the plan was now energetically conceived of rewinning the whole of Hungary, and through the mediation of the pope an alliance was formed on March 31, 1684, between the emperor and Sobieski, which Venice also joined, for a war against the Turks.

In Hungary the Osmanlis now suffered one defeat after another. In 1686 the German imperial forces appeared before Buda, and after a siege lasting two months this city, which for 145 years had been the bulwark of Osmanli rule in Hungary, fell into their hands.

Of the other members of the alliance only the Venetians did their duty; but their successes also came to an end with the occupation of Athens in 1687, which only the following year they had to evacuate again. From 1684 to 1687 the Poles endeavored in vain to reconquer Kameniecz. In 1687 Russia joined the alliance, but her attempt to seize the Crimea also ended in defeat.

But after the Ottoman army suffered another heavy defeat at Mohacs in Hungary in 1687, an insurrection broke out against the grand wazir Suleyman, which at once spread to Istanbul. Although the Sultan sacrificed the Grand Wazir, he was reproached for having neglected the welfare of the state in the pleasures of the hunt. A convocation of the 'ulama in the Aya Sophia on November 8 declared him deposed and on the advice of the Qa'immaqam, the deputy grand wazir Mustafa Köprülü, Ahmed's son, elevated to the throne Suleyman II, a brother of the deposed Muhammad IV.

The following summer the imperials advanced before Belgrade, which was taken by storm on September 6, 1688. The Viennese court was already considering the expulsion of the Osmanlis from Europe. But the latter gathered their forces once again when a new grand wazir, the above-mentioned Mustafa Köprülü, stepped to the head of the state after a severe defeat at Nish. He was an able statesman, and his efforts to restore financial order were successful; but he lacked any military experience, although he did reconquer Belgrade in September 1690. When he attacked Hungary in the following year, he was killed on August 19 in the unfortunate Battle of Szalankemen.

In 1695 an energetic sultan, Mustafa II, finally ascended the throne again as successor of his uncle Ahmed II. He personally assumed the supreme command in Hungary and was able to relieve Temesvar. But he found an opponent worthy of him in Prince Eugene of Savoy, who annihilated the Sultan's army at Zenta on the Theiss on September 11, 1697. Now another Köprülü, Amujazade Husayn, assumed control of the administration. Since in 1695 Tsar Peter had also resumed the war against the Osmanlis and in 1696 had conquered Azov, the Sultan accepted the mediation offered him by Britain and the Netherlands. At Karlowitz, on January 26, 1699, the peace treaty was signed in which the Porte was compelled to relinquish to the Habsburgs Transylvania as far as Temesvar, almost all of Hungary, and the greater portion of Slovenia and Croatia; to the Poles, Kameniecz, all their conquests in Podolia, and the Ukraine; and to the Venetians, Morea and a few places in Dalmatia.

After this inglorious peace treaty the Sultan withdrew to Adrianople and left the government almost entirely to the mufti Faizallah, who had ejected Köprülü and made himself profoundly detested through avarice and nepotism. Consequently an insurrection broke out in July 1703. The Sultan was invited to Istanbul, to answer before his Diwan; when he failed to appear, he was deposed and his brother Ahmed was elected padishah.

With the cession of Azov, which was effected soon after the Treaty of Karlowitz, the Black Sea, hitherto an Ottoman lake, became accessible to the Tsar. At this point, after he encountered a formidable adversary in the Swedish king Charles XII, the Porte willingly entered into relations with Charles and after his defeat at Poltava accorded him asylum in its fortress at Bender. But it was not until the end of 1710 that it began arming against the Tsar, since it could not come to any agreement with him concerning the extradition to his territories of its protégé. Consequently Peter was forced to abandon his operations in the Baltic province and turn southward. He was almost captured by the Osmanlis together with his entire army on the Pruth, and had only the venality of the grand wazir to thank for being able to withdraw again in July 1711 on indulgent terms; he had to evacuate Azov and level the fortifications of Taganrog.

If the Porte approved this apparently unfavorable treaty, it did so because it was more anxious to regain the territories lost by the Treaty of Karlowitz than to expand its power in the northeast. In 1714 a conflict in Montenegro provided pretext for war against Venice, and in a short time the republic lost its last possessions in Morea and in the archipelago. But now the Habsburg intervened in the war. On August 5, 1716, Prince Eugene won a victory at Peterwardein, in October conquered Temesvar, the last Ottoman fortress on Hungarian soil, and the following year Belgrade itself. But his victorious course was soon hindered by Spanish policy in Italy, which compelled the emperor to acquiesce in the peace proposals of the Osmanlis. In the treaty concluded at Passarowitz on July 21, 1718, the latter ceded to the emperor Belgrade and the entire area up to the point where the Aluta discharges into the Danube, while the Venetians had to give up Morea.

But the Porte saw itself compelled once again to turn its attention to conditions in Asia, since disturbances had broken out among its old opponents in Persia. The last descendant of Shah 'Abbas, Husayn, who had been ruling since 1694, had come into conflict with the Afghans, who had placed themselves under Persian protection in order to escape conquest by the Mongols of India, but had hitherto been able to preserve their independence. When the Shah attempted to pull the reins in tighter, their leader, Mir Ways, revolted and maintained his independence as prince until his death in 1715. His second successor, Mir Mahmud, then passed over to an attack on Persia and in October 1722 dethroned the last of the Safavids in Isfahan. These disturbances were exploited by Tsar Peter to secure possession of the Caucasian province of Daghestan. The chieftain of the Lezghians, who had established themselves in Shamakhi, the capital of Shirwan, sought the protection of the Porte against him, became a vassal of Turkey, and was enfeoffed with Derbend. But since Peter had already pressed forward as far as Baku, the Porte had to agree to his annexation of the country as far as the point where the Kura discharges into the Araxes.

The Persians were in no position to resist him. The Afghan Mahmud was successfully opposed by Husayn's son Tahmasp, but the latter was forced back to Mazanderan by Mahmud's successor

Ashraf. At this point, however, after Ashraf brought forward his claim for recognition as second imam, an equal of the sultan, a war broke out which in spite of a victory of the Afghans in 1726 ended with the surrender of their claims. But their rule in Persia did not endure. They were opposed in Khorasan by the leader of the Turkoman tribe of Afshar, Nadir Kuli, and together with Tahmasp were defeated by him at Dangun in October 1729 and at Shiraz in January 1730. Ashraf was slain in Baluchistan while in flight.

Tahmasp at once attacked the Ottoman possessions on Persian soil also, in order to regain the empire of his forebears in its former dimensions. When the Sultan appeared to hesitate in initiating a campaign against him, a Janizary uprising broke out in Istanbul, as a result of which Ahmed III was dethroned on October 1, 1730, and his nephew Mahmud I made sultan. But it was not until two years later that order was restored in the capital by a bloody hunting-down of the rebels, to which fifty thousand men fell victim.

The Shah's vassal Nadir, however, who in his honor had assumed the name of Nadir Tahmasp Kuli Khan, revolted against him and had the Shah's son 'Abbas, still in the cradle, crowned. Then he concluded a treaty with Russia and energetically opened hostilities against the Osmanlis. After three fortunate campaigns he himself took over the regime on March 10, 1736, since the infant 'Abbas had died, and concluded a peace treaty with the Porte in which the latter gave up all its previous acquisitions as far as Baghdad. Before his accession to the throne the Turkoman Nadir had forced the Persian grandees who hailed him as their savior to renounce the Shi'ite tenets introduced by Isma'il I, as contrary to the faith of his forebears. He did not, however, demand a reversion to the Sunnah, but granted them the status of a new (fifth) orthodox school named after the imam Ja'far Sadiq. Although, in the peace treaty with Turkey, Nadir wanted to secure a special prayer area in Mecca for the new school, nevertheless this remarkable reformation did not endure beyond his own reign.

During this war the Porte had already had numerous fallings-out with Russia because of the Crimean Tatars. But circumstances in Poland bound the hands of the empress Anna, although she had determined to continue the advance to the Black and the Caspian seas begun by Peter. An attack on the Porte was prevented by the maritime powers, which in the interest of their commerce endeavored to put a halt to further Russian expansion. After the termination of the Polish disturbances in the autumn of 1735 Russia attacked the Osmanlis, but at first got no farther than Azov. The Habsburg emperor, who was bound by treaty to the support of Russia, at first attempted mediation, and only intervened in the war in 1737. But his troops suffered one defeat after another, and in 1739 he ceded to the Osmanlis Belgrade, which had only just been encircled. In the treaty, which was signed at once, the emperor waived claim to all the acquisitions of Passarowitz, and now Russia also was forced to sign a peace treaty in which she gained merely Azov, in a completely leveled condition. The thanks due France for her diplomatic support during this war were accorded her by the Porte in 1740 in a renewed recognition of the French protectorate over the Christians in the Orient.

After Nadir Shah had restored the boundaries of the Safavid empire, he was lured into a campaign southward by the riches of the Mongol state in India, whose military weakness was quite evident. After overrunning Ghazni and Kabul without much difficulty in June 1738, he sent his son Riza Kuli to Persia as regent. He turned first on Lahore, which fell to him in February 1739. The Moghul Muhammad Shah advanced against him from Delhi and was captured after his army was crushingly defeated on February 24, 1739. Nadir marched into Delhi, but in May he reinstated the Moghul as ruler, after he had ceded all provinces north of the Indus. The incalculable tribute Nadir imposed on the Moghul, which also included the famous diamond Kohinoor and the Peacock Throne, enabled him to relieve all Persia for three years from any tax obligations. After the Indian campaign Nadir turned toward the eastern border of his empire to pacify the Uzbegs in Bukhara and Khiva, who kept attacking Khorasan repeatedly, and as a matter of fact he succeeded in doing so without shedding any blood; he installed their khan as feudal vassal and obligated him to recognize the Oxus as boundary. On a campaign against the Lezghians in the Caucasus an attempt was made on Nadir's life in Mazanderan on May 15, 1741, the instigator of which was declared to be the heir to the throne, Riza Kuli. In punishment the Shah had his son blinded, and from then on developed increasingly into a bloodthirsty tyrant. Since the Ottoman government refused to comply with the demand for recognition of the fifth orthodox school introduced by Nadir in Persia, he undertook a campaign against its Mesopotamian possessions; the pasha of Baghdad, however, was able to divert Nadir by adroit negotiations; the Shah was content with a pilgrimage to the holy cities of 'Iraq and had the legality of his religious reform authenticated once again by a conclave of the 'ulama in Najaf. Uprisings in the interior of his empire had prevented him from proceeding with greater energy against the Turks in Mesopotamia, and in 1746, when the Porte dispatched a new army against him, he contented himself, although he had won a brilliant victory at Erivan, with a restoration of the boundaries of the time of Murad I and waived recognition of his religious reform by acknowledging the sultan as caliph. The incessant uprisings in his empire were repressed by Nadir with continually increasing cruelty, attested to by the pyramids of skulls along his marching routes. In 1747, on one of these campaigns, Nadir was assassinated at Fathabad in the territory of the Kurds of Kuchan by the chiefs of his own tribe, the Afshars, in alliance with the Kajars.* His nephew 'Ali Kuli, who succeeded him as 'Adil Shah, lost his empire only one year later in wars with the ubiquitously arising pretenders. Among the latter a South Persian, Karim Khan of the Zend tribe, eventually emerged victorious. From 1750 to 1779 he ruled the entire empire from Shiraz but wished to be regarded only as the agent for the last scion of the Safavids, Isma'il III, whom he held in confinement at Abada. Under him the rose city once again experienced a period of prosperity still attested to today by a number of its most beautiful buildings. After his death, however, bloody feuds broke out in his tribe which cleared the way to the throne for the Kajars, as will yet be related.

As a result of the decline of its Persian adversary's power the Ottoman Empire was granted a protracted period of peace, which was not disturbed by its neighbors in Europe either. In 1757 an able sultan had come to the throne again in Mustafa III. During the first years of his reign he left the rule to his grand wazir, Raghib Pasha, who until his death in 1763 succeeded in maintaining order in the state finances and in preserving the organization of the army from decay. Frederick the Great hoped to use his help in inducing the Porte to launch an attack on Austria during the Seven Years' War, and in fact a treaty of friendship was concluded with Prussia on March 29, 1761; the Sultan, however, fortified in his love of peace by the 'ulama, could not be induced to intervene in the war.

* See L. Lockhart, *Nadir Shah, a critical study based mainly upon contemporary sources*, London, 1938.

It was the development of the Polish question which brought the Porte back into active participation in European politics. The enfeebling of Poland by Catherine had at first been tranquilly regarded in Istanbul, although Russia was also supporting the Georgians against the Osmanlis and creating embarrassments for the Crimean khan. But finally the Confederation party in Poland succeeded in inducing the Sultan into a defense of his influence in the northeast. The destruction of the city of Balta on the Bessarabian border gave the mufti, despite his colleagues' love of peace, the impetus to issue a fatwa approving the war against Russia.

Now the lengthy neglect of the Ottoman army was atoned for. The Russians defeated the Crimean Tatars, who had opened the campaign under Khan Kirim Ghiray, and took Choczim, while the Ottoman army was stationed in the Dobruja. In 1770 the Russians advanced through Moldavia and Wallachia as far as the Danube and took Kilia, Bender, and Braila, after making the Rumanian grandees swear allegiance to Catherine. At this time a Russian fleet first appeared in the Aegean Sea with the venturesome assignment of conjuring up and supporting a Greek uprising. A number of fortified places in the Morea were taken, but could not be held, by the Mainote pirates. In July 1770 the Russians managed to annihilate by fire the Ottoman fleet in the Bay of Cheshme along the coast of Asia Minor. Istanbul itself had already begun to fear an attack; but the Russians did not take advantage of their victory.

The next year brought the Russians another victory; they were able to subdue the Crimea after storming the isthmus of Perekop. The mediation of Prussia and Austria, in return for which the Porte waived all claim on Poland, brought about a truce in June 1772, but no agreement could be reached concerning the fortifications in the Black Sea, although the Porte was ready to surrender the Crimea itself. Meanwhile the Osmanlis had reorganized their army to such an extent that they were able to block the forward advance of the Russians in the Balkans; the latter had to give up the siege of Silistria and Varna and retreat across the Danube toward the end of 1773. By this time the Sultan himself had determined to assume the command of his army; but on December 24, 1773, he succumbed to an illness.

He was succeeded by his insignificant brother 'Abd-al-Hamid. In July 1774 the grand wazir Muhsinzade fell into a trap at Shumla and lost a large part of his troops through desertion. Accordingly he decided to sue the field marshal Romantsov for peace. In Kuchuk Kainarji, southward of Silistria, the treaty was signed on July 22, 1774. The Porte surrendered the most important fortresses on the Black Sea (Kerch, Yenikala, and Kinburn), ceded greater and lesser Kabarda in the Caucasus to Russia, and allowed her fleet passage through the Dardanelles; it had to recognize the independence of the Tatars in the Crimea and grant an amnesty and freedom of worship to the inhabitants of Moldavia and Wallachia. Its prestige in Europe had now sunk so low that an expulsion of the Osmanlis appeared to be only a question of time. Austria took advantage of this plight by annexing Bukovina on some flimsy pretext directly after the peace treaty, without the Porte's being able to prevent it. In 1783 Catherine put an end to the independence of the Crimea by subjugating the Tatars. This also had to be assented to by the Sultan in 1784 in the Convention of Ainali Kavak.

The prospect of compensating for its losses to Russia appeared to open up for the Porte once again in 1784 when the peoples of the Caucasus, Muslims as well as Christians, revolted against Catherine's protégé, Prince Heraclius of Georgia. But the Porte's attempt to reconquer the Crimea was shattered by the superior generalship of Suvorov, who successfully defended Kinburn and in December 1788 stormed Ochakov, after the Ottoman fleet had already been annihilated that summer along the coasts of the Crimea. In February of the same year Josef II of Austria also declared war on the Porte, but his armies made only slight advances in Serbia and Transylvania. In the middle of this war Selim III had to ascend the throne, on April 7, after the death of 'Abd-al-Hamid. He was also to carry on the war only with great losses, and it was not until the death of Josef II that the Austrian peril at any rate was first checked. With the mediation of Prussia and the sea powers the peace treaty of Zistova was concluded on August 4, 1791, in which the Porte retained the Danube principalities as far as Orsova. After violent warfare in Bessarabia and the Crimea as well as on the Danube, it was followed on January 9, 1792 by the peace treaty with Russia at Jassy, which established the Dniester as boundary and definitively granted the Crimea to Russia.

The end of the eighteenth century saw the Ottoman Empire driven entirely from its position of attack into one of defense, and only the rivalry of the European powers appeared to insure its continued existence in Europe. The decay of its power was paralleled by a decline in its intellectual life. None of the sultans and wazirs of the period had the slightest interest in literature. Poetry, despite the political antagonism to Persia, was still dominated by the Persian classics, though a few attempts were made to introduce popular styles into literature; but the misery of the times found some expression even among the poets in bitter lamentations and biting criticism of social abuses. In prose, artificiality of language increased more and more. A sole brilliant exception was the travel account of Evliya Chelebi,* who died shortly after 1679, and whose *Traveler's Chronicle*, for precisely this reason, was not fully appreciated by his contemporaries. Evliya was descended from an old family of soldiers and had personally participated in the campaigns in Russia, Transylvania, and Hungary. In times of peace he roved through the entire empire as far southward as Syria and Egypt. If one ignores his predilection for fables and miracles, a reflection of the age, his work must be considered unique in the fullness of its information concerning conditions in the Ottoman Empire, not only in all of Osmanli literature but also in the culture of Islam as a whole. Although in the eighteenth century a number of travel works also arose, such as Resmi's account of his embassy to the court of Frederick the Great, none of them could rival Evliya for vivacity of portrayal.

* [Partial translation by J. von Hammer-Purgstall, London, 1934, 1850.]

4. Islam in the Nineteenth Century

1. *The Ottoman Empire and Egypt*

AT THE turn of the eighteenth and nineteenth centuries the Ottoman Empire, which still laid claim to primacy in Islam, had sunk very low. Its northern neighbors, Austria and Russia, had already wrested away many of its valuable possessions; in Asia the Tsarist empire had pushed forward directly on to its borders after the abdication of King Heraclius of Georgia in 1784. Syria and Egypt had become well-nigh independent under Jazzar Pasha and the Mamluks. Among the raya peoples in Europe aspirations to independence were coming to life everywhere. The army had entirely decayed, for institutions once the basis of its grandeur had long since outlived themselves.

Internal politics in the empire, aside from a number of recoils, was consequently entirely dominated by the quest for reforms (*tanzimat*). There was a desire to turn to the advantage of the empire those institutions which were regarded as the foundations of the superiority of the European nations, without at the same time encroaching on its basic character. It was in the army, which after all constituted the foundation of the entire state, that the innovations were begun. In this way the predominance of the military, which was to prove fateful for all subsequent development, was carried into the adaptation to European civilization. It was primarily a question of creating a new and really efficient corps of troops in the place of the Janizaries, who had long since been transformed from the shield of the capital into its scourge. Sultan Selim III had already made one attempt to found a new militia. Since at that time French diplomats, even after the revolution, were still very influential at his court, he took French institutions as a model, being advised in this by Napoleon's ambassador, General Sebastiani. But even before the new corps was adequately drilled, and before it could be used for the repression of an uprising which had broken out in the Balkans, the Janizaries formed a conspiracy with the garrisons of the Bosporus fortresses and on May 29, 1807, forced the Sultan to abdicate, after driving all the advocates of reform together on the Atmeydan and slaughtering them.

His cousin Mustafa IV, who had naturally drawn his support from the reactionary elements in the army, could only hold the throne for a year and was then overthrown by the governor of Silistria, Mustafa Bayraktar. Since Selim had already been executed, Selim's brother, Mahmud II, succeeded to the throne. But the reaction was still so powerful that Bayraktar soon had to yield to it, and Mahmud was also compelled by his failures in foreign affairs to postpone the plans for reform which were to make him the founder of modern Turkey. In a war against Russia he lost Nicopolis, Silistria, and Ruschuk, and the tsar was induced only by the Napoleonic peril into signing the peace treaty of Bucharest on May 28, 1812, in which, renouncing any further conquests, he recognized the Pruth as boundary. Still more dangerous for the empire were the uprisings of the raya nations. As early as 1804 the Serbs had revolted under Karageorgios. In the final campaign they had lent the Russians energetic support; in thanks for this the Russians made semi-autonomy for them, with their own courts, a condition of the peace treaty. But since their principal grievance, the obligatory tribute, was not eliminated, they continued the struggle; after Karageorgios had fled to Austria, Milosh Obrenovich took his place. In 1820 the Greek revolt broke out, which, spurred on by the sentimental Hellenic enthusiasm in Europe, not only resulted in the loss for the Porte of a province which did not happen to be very valuable, but in particular also led to endless diplomatic complications. Nevertheless the Sultan succeeded in breaking the independence of the grandees–the *ayan* in Rumelia and the *derebeys* in Anatolia–and in restoring the prestige of the central authority in the provinces.

In all these battles the Janizaries again proved a complete failure. Mahmud, however, had turned to good advantage the waiting period imposed on him by the reaction, and gradually filled the most important offices with men devoted to him personally. In the spring of 1826 he was finally able to resume Selim's plans. Under the protection of Anatolian militiamen, whom the governor of Beikos had assembled on the eastern shore of the Bosporus, he issued the order for the foundation of a new regular corps, which received the name of *muallem eshkinji* (drilled guard). The instructors necessary for this were sent to him by the governor in Egypt, Muhammad 'Ali. The Janizary officers had been won over to his plans, but the subordinate officers agitated against the innovation all the more intensely. On June 18 a parade of the new corps was ordered in Sweet Water Valley near Istanbul. To prevent this the Janizaries revolted three days beforehand. They first demanded only the abolition of the drill regulations introduced for the new corps. But the Sultan, with the approval of the 'ulama, ordered the Prophet's banner unfurled as though for a war against infidels and had the Janizaries encircled on the square before their barracks, the Atmeydan, by the quickly mobilized troops. The mufti solemnly pronounced the malediction against them, and then began a general blood bath which none escaped. About a thousand Janizaries were killed in the other sections of the city. Their banner and their badge, the Janizary cap, were dragged through the mud, their mosques and habitually frequented cafés destroyed. The related dervish order of Bektashi and the closely associated corporations of firemen and porters were dissolved; indeed, even among the cannoneers and the Bosporus watchmen, who this time remained loyal though they otherwise used to make common cause with the Janizaries, all those suspected of reactionary inclinations were done away with.

But the western powers did not allow the Sultan the time to pluck the fruits of this bloody reform. On July 7, 1827, France, England, and Russia concluded the treaty of the Triple Alliance, which was then joined by Prussia, in order to force him to liberate the Greek people, since meanwhile Ibrahim, the son of Muhammad 'Ali, with his Egyptian auxiliaries, had borne hard on the rebels in Morea. Their last fortress, Missolunghi, had to capitulate on April 23, 1826, after a siege lasting six months. The imperial fleet appeared along the coast of Morea to debark four thousand infantrymen and five hundred cavalrymen in aid of Ibrahim. But before the harbor of Navarin, where the fleet lay at anchor, it was now confronted by the united Mediterranean squadrons of the allied powers, which denied Ibrahim, who had assumed its command, any further operation on the Greek coast. Since Ibrahim refused to comply in this interference with the supreme authority of his military overlord, on October 20 the disastrous sea battle took place in which the entire imperial fleet of over one hundred vessels was annihilated in a six-hour engagement.

The Porte responded to this monstrous onslaught, which took place in the midst of peace, by the seizure of all foreign vessels lying in the Golden Horn, and after futile negotiations the representatives of the Triple Alliance left Constantinople in mid-December. But it was not until May of the following year that Russia, after thoroughgoing preparations, opened the campaign. During the first year her armies failed to advance either on the Balkans or in the Caucasus. In the spring of 1829 Prince Diebitch assumed the command of the Russian armies in Europe. He had Shumla, which had previously held up their advance, encircled, and pressed forward as far as Adrianople. There he dictated a peace treaty to the Sultan on September 14. Russia was content with the cession of the Danube islands and the Turkish territory lying in the Caucasus between the provinces of Imeretia and Georgia. But the Sultan had to become a party to the London Treaty; that is, recognize the independence of Greece.

While Mahmud was still engaged in a vain endeavor to heighten the efficiency of the state by means of reforms, his Egyptian vassal, Muhammad 'Ali, had already far outdistanced him on this path. This most important man in the history of modern Islam was born in January 1769 at Kavala on the Macedonian coast, where his uncle occupied the office of a *mutasallim* (vice-governor). In the latter's Diwan he was given a practical introduction to affairs without having enjoyed any real schooling, and by the time he was twenty he was already successfully speculating in tobacco, the principal article of commerce of his homeland. This remote province, however, was too narrow for his ambition.

In Egypt the Mamluks had maintained their power even after their conquest by Selim in 1517. For the Ottoman Empire this country, apart from its contributions in the way of tribute, principally served as a base of operations for the maintenance of its power over Syria and Arabia. It was only after Egypt came into Napoleon's line of vision as a gateway of attack on British hegemony in India that it was drawn into world politics. In 1778 Britain concluded a commercial treaty with the Mamluk 'Ali Bey, who had maintained his independence of the Porte for a short time, in order to secure its shipping in the Red Sea. In July 1798 Napoleon undertook the expedition to Egypt on the pretext that the maladministration of the Mamluks was endangering the property of French citizens, and put a temporary end to their rule by the victory near the Pyramids, though Nelson's victory at Abuqir on August 1 was already making the French position in the country untenable. The sultan Selim III, however little he had concerned himself with the country beforehand, could not regard this encroachment on his sovereign rights with tranquillity. Consequently in the summer of 1799 he sent out a few ships with troops to Egypt. Muhammad 'Ali's uncle was also supposed to provide a contingent of three hundred men. He sent Muhammad 'Ali along with his young son who was to command it, as a mentor; and soon after the landing in Egypt, Muhammad 'Ali assumed the formal command as well. In the subsequent warfare, which forced the French to evacuate the country in 1801, he distinguished himself to such an extent that he leaped upward to a generalship. After the withdrawal of the French, Khosrev, a former Abkhazian slave, had been appointed pasha. Since he soon became entirely absorbed in the intrigues of the imperial palace, Egypt meant nothing more to him than a lower rung on the ladder of his ambition, and all his efforts were devoted to his being able to leave the country very soon again with a substantial fortune. Since Muhammad 'Ali maintained a more rigid discipline among his Albanian troops than the governor, he gradually succeeded in subjecting all of lower Egypt to his rule by skillfully playing off the Mamluks against Khosrev. In 1803 the latter was recalled from his no longer lucrative post; his first successor remained only a few months, then Muhammad 'Ali had himself expressly declared the bearer of authority, on the basis of the religious law, by the clergy of the al-Azhar Mosque in Cairo, for centuries highly esteemed throughout the Muslim world as an institute of religious learning. In November 1805 he was *de facto* master of the entire country, and in April 1806 the Porte had to acknowledge and confirm him as wali. He temporarily allowed the Mamluks to rule in Upper Egypt in return for a high tribute. But when they initiated negotiations with Britain, whose debarkation troops he had repulsed at Rosetta in April 1807, he invited their chiefs to Cairo in March 1811, ostensibly in order to take counsel concerning a campaign against the Wahhabis in Arabia, and there, on the eleventh of the same month, had them, three hundred in number, massacred.

Thus Muhammad 'Ali became absolute ruler of Egypt, as no

other pasha had ever been before him. His Albanian troops, however, still too deeply influenced by the Ottoman army, did not prove their mettle in the campaigns against the Wahhabis, which occupied him until 1815. Upon an attempt to accustom them to a severe discipline, a mutiny broke out in Cairo in 1816, which, however, he easily subdued. Then he dissolved the corps entirely, and to make up for it, drafted the fellahs (peasants) into military service. With this new corps, armed with European weapons and drilled on the French model by Captain Sève, later pasha, he subjugated Nubia, Sennar, Danqalah (Dongola), and Darfur in a series of campaigns which, to be sure, hardly consisted of anything more than great slave hunts.

But Muhammad 'Ali also paid heed to the economic development of the country. He not only embellished Cairo and Alexandria with numerous buildings in the Ottoman style but also had the harbor of the latter city built up and united by a canal with the western arm of the Nile. But he regarded the land exclusively as a domain from which it was his sole endeavor to extract a maximum yield. In 1815 he laid his hand on the total produce of cotton, hemp, and flax; two years later also on indigo, sesame, and other oil plants. But these revenues still failed to satisfy his avarice. By 1812 he had absorbed all the pious foundations and all the enfeoffed estates. At this point he set up a commission to test the title deeds of all real property. Anyone lacking one, and this of course constituted the majority of the hereditarily established peasants, from then on could cultivate his land as a tenant of the pasha. According to ancient Oriental usage, he conscripted all wood and construction workers in order to build a fleet, and bought up all imported timber at fixed prices. His reckless customs policy, which was felt to be all the more oppressive since it weighed more heavily on goods originating in other Muslim countries than on European goods, brought about an intolerable rise in the cost of living.

Muhammad 'Ali showed great admiration for the blessings of European civilization, in so far as it gave promise of increasing the productivity of the country. The first institute of learning founded on the European model was a mathematics school with English methods of instruction. Otherwise, however, the French had the preponderance at his court. In addition to a number of men honestly concerned with the improvement of the country, he had to pay off a horde of swindlers before finding a man competent enough to install his factories. In spite of all the blunders of his egotistic policies, to Muhammad 'Ali belongs the merit of having opened the country to the influences of European civilization.

Muhammad 'Ali's growing power aroused concern in Istanbul lest sooner or later he should outgrow his position as provincial governor in relations with foreign countries as well. At first, to be sure, he carefully avoided anything that might appear offensive to the reverence due the Sultan. Thus he had lent military aid without protest against the rebellious Greeks. His son Ibrahim conducted the ruins of the imperial fleet that had been annihilated at Navarin to Alexandria, together with the Egyptian ships, in order to have them reconditioned. When the Porte ordered him to send his own fleet to Istanbul at the same time as the Turkish, he placated it with a remittance, always welcome. In return for the assumption of a portion of the Russian war debt he was even appanaged with Crete.

But every great power which ever arose in Egypt before had had to stretch out its hand toward Syria. The Porte had promised to grant Muhammad 'Ali that country also for his help in the Greek war, but did not keep its promise. However, he was of no mind to relinquish it, and easily found a pretext to come to grips with the pasha of Acre. The fellahs who had been groaning under his agrarian policies had migrated into Syria in droves, and he could not, of course, admit that the Sultan's subjects had freedom of movement within the empire.

In the autumn of 1831 Muhammad 'Ali sent his son with an army into Syria, and the latter surrounded 'Abdallah Pasha in Acre. But although the fleet supported the army, the siege of the fortress dragged on until May of the following year. Muhammad 'Ali responded to the moderate order of the Porte to withdraw his troops with a request to be enfeoffed with the provinces of Acre and Damascus. Meanwhile, with the help of the prince of the Lebanon, Bashir Shihab, who had joined him after lengthy procrastination, Ibrahim subdued all of Palestine. Then, on May 26, 1832, after Acre had also fallen, he was able to advance as far as Adana, the capital of Cilicia, without encountering any opposition. Meanwhile the Sultan had been arming against his mutinous vassal, and an army fifty thousand strong under Husayn Pasha, a former Janizary, was now advancing southward. Husayn was at odds with the minister of war, Khosrev Pasha, and the latter was able to see to it that his adopted son Muhammad Pasha was made Husayn's chief of staff.

In order to forestall his superior officer in the victories to be expected, the subordinate commander advanced on Homs (Hims) by forced marches, and when the Egyptians came out against him, there joined battle at once, with his soldiers exhausted and hungry. In a few hours Ibrahim's victory was decided. After Muhammad had united with the main body of the army again, a second battle took place at Baylan, the pass over the Amanus, which, as a result of Ibrahim's superior tactics, again ended in a victory for the Egyptians. Husayn returned to Karaman and there had to relinquish his command to the Circassian Rashid Pasha. Ibrahim was not to be delayed in his pursuit by the severity of the winter, to which his troops were unaccustomed. On December 21 he defeated the Turks at Konya for the third time. The way to the Bosporus lay open to him. But the European powers could not allow that. Russia sent two divisions of the fleet to the aid of the Sultan, and with the mediation of Russian and French diplomats a peace treaty was concluded on April 8, 1833 at Kütahya, in Ibrahim's headquarters, which insured Muhammad 'Ali's enfeoffment with Syria. When he demanded Adana-Cilicia in addition, the cession of the latter was also granted him. But before the Russian fleet left the Bosporus the Tsarist diplomats succeeded in inducing the Porte to sign the Treaty of Hunkyar Iskelesi in July 1833. Both powers obligated themselves to reciprocal aid in case of attack; but since a secret addendum relieved the Porte of any further obligations, in return for a promise to bar the Dardanelles in case of need, in reality Turkey thus fell into a kind of dependent relationship to Russia.

In Syria, Ibrahim's troops were greeted almost as emancipators by the populace groaning under Turkish maladministration. But soon the Syrians were bitterly disappointed. It is true that under the orderly administration of the Egyptians the numerous subsidiary exactions with which the officials had been accustomed to filling their pockets went by the board; but in return the Syrians lost the last remnant of their personal liberty. The Egyptian regime began with a general disarmament, which was put into effect among the Druzes also as the result of the treachery of their own prince. With ruthless harshness general military service was introduced, and the exorbitant duties were felt to be all the more oppressive since they flowed into Egypt undiminished. In only a few months the mood of the country entirely reversed itself in favor of Ottoman rule, although almost another two years went by before the enserfed populace dared revolt against the closely knit military power of the new overlord. In May 1834 an uprising of the fellahs in the mountains of Nablus and Hebron broke out, which because of the rough terrain gave Ibrahim a great deal of trouble. It was only through treachery that he finally subdued the dangerous movement.

Muhammad 'Ali was not so fortunate in Arabia as in Egypt and Syria. There his power came up against the resistance of a great national revival. In Najd, the highland of the Arabian interior, Muhammad ibn-'Abd-al-Wahhab of the tribe of Tamim was born around the turn of the seventeenth and eighteenth centuries. He devoted himself to the study of theology and jurisprudence, and according to ancient custom attended the colleges in the capitals of the Islamic East. In Baghdad he became acquainted with the doctrine of Ahmad ibn-Hanbal, the founder of the last of the four orthodox schools, who with the most rigid consistency had advocated the principle of the exclusive validity of the tradition as against the inclination among the older legal authorities to make concessions to reason. He further studied the writings of Ahmad ibn-Taymiyah, who in the fourteenth century had revived the teachings of ibn-Hanbal. These studies aroused in him the conviction that the dominant form of contemporary Islam—that is, particularly among the Turks—was permeated with abuses. After his return to his homeland he first sought to restore the original purity of doctrine and of life in its restricted milieux. But when he stormed against the veneration accorded Sa'd, the local saint of his native town of 'Ayinah,* and enforced among his followers the due punishment of an adulteress—stoning—which, though canonical, had long since been outmoded, he was banished. In 1740 he turned to an opponent of the shaykh of 'Ayinah, Muhammad ibn-Sa'ud, who lived in the fortified settlement of Dar'iyah only six hours away, as chief of a clan of the 'Anayzah. Here he met with a friendly reception and, shortly afterward, sympathy for his doctrines. He rejected any veneration of the Prophet or of other saints, which in imitation of Christianity and more primitive religious usages had been present in Islam for centuries, and declared those Muslims guilty of it to be pagans, who according to the Qur'an were to be fought against until conversion or extirpation. With ruthless strictness he insisted on his followers' attendance at Friday services. Any ostentation of dress, particularly the use of silk, and also any adornment of the houses of worship and of tombs

* ['Uyaynah.]

were proscribed by him. By a consistent extension of the interdiction decreed by the Prophet on all means of intoxication he forbade the enjoyment of tobacco, against which, to be sure, at its initial introduction into the Orient, nearly all jurists, including the non-Hanbalites, had declared themselves. This reformer, accordingly, was no more distinguished by any abundance, or for that matter originality, of thought than the Prophet himself had been. But like the latter he was capable of inspiring his followers and making their sleepless passion for feud useful to his cause. In the course of ten years Muhammad ibn-Sa'ud subjected an area of about thirty square miles to the new doctrine and to his rule. It was not until 1757 that the successor of the prince of al-Hasa, who had once expelled the reformer from 'Ayinah, gathered his forces for a struggle against him; but he was defeated and lost his domains to the Wahhabis, who now spread out westward also. When Muhammad ibn-Sa'ud died in 1765, he was succeeded by his son 'Abd-al-'Aziz, who had already distinguished himself in warfare during the former's lifetime. He continued his father's policy of conquest and by 1788 had advanced as far as Kuwayt, the sole harbor on the northeast coast of Arabia. He had secured the hereditary succession for his house the preceding year by having his son Sa'ud confirmed as his successor by Muhammad ibn-'Abd-al-Wahhab at a great people's conclave. When the latter died in 1792, he was also followed in his religious office by his son as mufti.

The successes of the Wahhabis gradually became burdensome to their neighbors. The sharif Ghalib of Mecca, whose 'Alid forebears had ruled the Holy City since the tenth century, at first believed he could deal with them alone, but the army he sent to the Najd in 1790 was of no avail and on the retreat was even sorely defeated by Sa'ud. During the following years the Wahhabis continued their northward advance, so that finally the pasha of Baghdad found himself compelled to take defensive measures against them. In 1797, with about seven thousand Turks and double the number of Arabs, he attacked al-Hasa, the richest and most fertile province of the Wahhabis; but instead of moving on their capital, Dar'iyah, at once, he held off for a month while laying siege to the citadel of al-Hasa. Then, after Sa'ud himself advanced against him, he dared not attack him but concluded peace with him for six years. But the Wahhabis had learned disdain for his power and in 1801 attacked his territory. Their objective was Kerbela with the burial place of Husayn, the Prophet's grandson, deeply revered by all Shi'ites. On April 28, the day of the Bayram festival, the city fell into their hands. The magnificent domed building over the grave of Husayn was destroyed and enormous booty dragged off.

After nearly all the Bedouin tribes of the Najd had joined the Wahhabis in the course of the following years, they launched an attack on Mecca in 1803, at the time of the pilgrimage in April. Although the city was full of foreign pilgrims, it surrendered after brief resistance. The sharif Ghalib fled to the harbor city of Jiddah; the leader of the Syrian pilgrim caravan, 'Abdallah, the pasha of Damascus, had to leave the city three days later. The same year, however, Prince 'Abd-al-'Aziz was overtaken by vengeance for Kerbela; on November 4 he was murdered at the mosque of Dar'iyah by a Shi'ite zealot.

His son Sa'ud, a grandson of the reformer through his mother, raised the siege of Jiddah and had the Sharif return to Mecca as his vassal; as such the latter had to waive his most lucrative source of income, the customs revenue at Jiddah, since according to the strict theory of Islamic law this had always been regarded as an unlawful exaction. In the spring of 1804 Medina fell into the hands of the Wahhabis. The site of the idolatrous pilgrimages to the grave of the Prophet came to feel the martial wrath of the conquerors more harshly than Mecca. The Turks, settled there in great numbers, were expelled from the country. The magnificent domed structures over the holy burial place were destroyed and all precious objects removed from it. Thus the whole of the Hijaz was now in the hands of the Wahhabis.

In his capacity as caliph the Sultan was bound to free from domination by heretics the holy places subject to his protection, and he charged the governor of Egypt, Muhammad 'Ali, with this task. But it was not until 1811, after the elimination of the Mamluks, that the latter's hands were free. Meanwhile the Wahhabis had attacked Najaf and Damascus once again; although the latter city was successfully defended, they extended their sphere of authority in the north as far as Aleppo. After carefully arming, Muhammad 'Ali sent his son Tusun at the head of the cavalry into Arabia by land, while his fleet transported the infantry to the harbor of Yanbu'. In October the united Egyptian army moved on Medina but was attacked near the battlefield of Badr, famous from the history of the Prophet, and in spite of heroic resistance was almost completely shattered. Tusun owed his life only to the valor of a Scottish convert, Thomas Keith, whose Muslim name was Ibrahim Agha. But now, while Sa'ud and the main force of his army pushed on farther northward plundering, Tusun had time to strengthen his army in Yanbu' with reinforcements. In November 1812 he conquered Medina; the following January the sharif delivered Mecca into the hands of the Egyptians, and in the summer the latter were also able to occupy Taif.

But since the power of the Wahhabis in their homeland was still unbroken, Muhammad 'Ali decided to step to the head of the army himself. After arriving in Arabia he first seized the sharif Ghalib, who, now really discontent with the guardianship of the Egyptians, secretly favored the Wahhabis; he was taken away to Salonica and three years later died there in an epidemic. In November, Tusun suffered another severe defeat at Tarabah, which cost him his entire artillery. Since warfare with the Wahhabis only held out the prospect of further losses, Muhammad 'Ali turned his gaze from the Najd, which promised little benefit, to the riches of South Arabia instead.

Sa'ud died on April 27, 1814. He is described as the paragon of an Arab ruler. He associated with the Bedouin shaykhs on a footing of absolute equality, but could always impress them by his personal qualities, above all by eloquence, still very highly regarded in Arabia. He lived with his family in Dar'iyah in a house somewhat above the city. His sole luxury was his horses, of which he is supposed to have possessed about two thousand. His administration, though very simple, restored public security, unknown in Arabia for centuries. Juridical disputes were no longer settled by recourse to private means but were decided by magistrates who were paid by Dar'iyah and not allowed to collect any fees. Every violent theft was made the responsibility of the tribe in whose territory it had taken place. Instead of the blood vengeance the acceptance of the blood price, which hitherto had been accounted shameful, was recommended and often put into effect by force. The ancient tribal prerogative of withdrawing a criminal from punishment by placing him under tribal protection was now no longer recognized. The penal code was applied entirely according to the regulations of the Qur'an. The performance of religious obligations was enforced with relentless severity; a breach of the fast of Ramadan on occasion was punished with death. There were no arbitrary exactions; only the poor-tax was collected according to the principles established in the

Qur'an. An expensive burden for the believers, to be sure, was the military expeditions, since everyone had to arm himself and provide his own mount and food, with no other compensation than the prospect of a share in the plunder. The state revenues consisted of a fifth part of the booty; the poor-taxes; and the rents from the confiscated landholdings of the tribes and cities which had revolted again after their subjugation. The poor-tax, in so far as it was collected from city dwellers and peasants, flowed into the public treasury and served, aside from its specific purpose, to pay magistrates and teachers and for the construction and maintenance of mosques and public wells. The taxes of the Bedouins flowed into the private treasury of the Prince, out of which he covered not only his household expenses but also the expenditures for his bodyguard. The total revenues from both sources were estimated at one and a half million of Maria Theresa dollars.

Sa'ud was succeeded by his son 'Abdallah, who, though he had already proved a courageous warrior, nevertheless now appeared no match for the danger threatened by the Egyptians. Muhammad 'Ali avenged his son's latest defeat by a setback he inflicted on the Wahhabis at Basal. But then he left northern Arabia and attacked the 'Asir tribe in the wild mountainous territory in the south of the Tihamah. At the news of his victories a number of Bedouin chieftains from the northern Najd offered their help against the Wahhabis to his son Tusun, who was lingering in Medina. Thereupon Tusun broke into the province of Qasim; but here a peace was imposed on him by Prince 'Abdallah in which the latter, though surrendering the holy cities, secured the evacuation of the Najd and the extradition of the shaykhs who had abandoned him. Muhammad 'Ali refused to ratify his treaty; he himself had meanwhile departed from Arabia and left the continuation of the war to his adopted son Ibrahim.

In August 1816 Ibrahim set out from Cairo; upon arriving in Arabia he attacked Qasim again. The Wahhabi prince retired before his tenacious energy to his capital in Dar'iyah and was encircled there in April of 1818. In spite of the primitive fortifications the Egyptians had to lay siege to the city for the entire summer, since their great distance from their base of operations made the problem of supply very difficult. On September 9, 1818, 'Abdallah, who only had four hundred men of his colored bodyguard around him, surrendered. He died in Istanbul at the hands of the executioner. The city of Dar'iyah was leveled to the ground. Ibrahim installed a Turkish official as governor of Najd and withdrew to Medina.

Muhammad 'Ali was not so fortunate in his designs on South Arabia. All his efforts ran aground on the 'Asir region, whose inhabitants successfully warded off the Egyptian attacks for twelve years (1825-1837). His interest in these regions gradually declined, since he was largely preoccupied by his relations with the Porte. After the British occupied Aden in 1839, he definitely gave up his plans in Arabia, and also left the invariably expensive occupation of the holy cities to the Porte again.

Egyptian rule had not been of extended duration in Najd either. The Wahhabis again rallied round the representative of their dynasty who had escaped at Dar'iyah, Turki, a cousin of 'Abdallah. In Riyad, not far from Dar'iyah, the latter founded a new state, which soon gave the Egyptians a great deal of trouble. Although Turki was assassinated by a usurper in 1832, his brother Faysal, with the help of his officer 'Abdallah ibn-Rashid, succeeded in ensuring the succession for himself. As reward 'Abdallah received the hereditary governorship of the Shammar tribe. In 1838 Faysal fell into the hands of Muhammad 'Ali's troops and was taken to Egypt. His successor 'Abbas, however, helped him to escape; he returned to the command of the Wahhabis and in 1849 forced the last Egyptian governor to leave the country. After Faysal's death at the end of the sixties, dissension broke out among his sons over the succession. In this way their vassal, the prince of the Shammar, succeeded in overshadowing them. 'Abdallah ibn-Rashid first had to win for himself the authority granted him by Faysal. After doing away with the shaykh of the Shammar, he succeeded, by an astute mitigation of Wahhabi fanaticism and by his good relations with the Turkish governor in Medina, in consolidating his position. His residence at Hail soon surpassed Riyad, since he was able to attract trade there, and toward the end of the nineteenth century his was the sole important princedom in Arabia. He was succeeded in 1845 by Tallal and in 1876 by Muhammad ibn-Rashid. The religious doctrine of the Wahhabis led a quiet existence among them, but in India, where Sayyid Ahmad of Rai Barela transplanted it after his pilgrimage in 1822-23, it created disturbances emanating from Patna for decades to come, since its adherents kept proclaiming a holy war against the non-Muslims. The awakening of the Wahhabi movement to new life in Arabia during the First World War also will be recounted below.

After Ibrahim's victorious campaign in Syria, Sultan Mahmud's predominant concern was the regaining of this province. For this a more thoroughgoing reorganization of the army was needed than had taken place after the annihilation of the Janizaries. Hitherto he had been unable to win European instructors because of the jealousy of the great powers, but in the summer of 1836 two Prussian general staff officers, von Moltke and von Berg, passed through Istanbul on a trip and were presented to the Sultan. On the suggestion of the serasker, who had learned a great deal from them at their very first conference, the Sultan requested the king of Prussia to grant Moltke leave for a protracted sojourn in his empire, and had Moltke accompany him on a trip through Rumelia. The suggestions of Moltke, particularly for the system of fortifications, so impressed the Sultan that he asked Frederick William III to send him another four officers as instructors. The reorganization of the army, begun by Moltke and continued by numerous Prussian officers after him, substantially strengthened the Ottoman Empire's powers of resistance. The head of the guards and the chief of the artillery, who had hitherto held the same rank as the minister for war, were now subordinated to him. This transformation of the army was accompanied by similar changes in the highest state offices. Temporarily the title of grand wazir was abolished in 1837 and his functions were delegated to the *bash vekil*, the chief minister, who at the same time had the portfolio of the interior. In May 1838 there again followed a much more far-reaching measure. All state functionaries, who formerly were paid directly by the public, in the lower grade and through their subordinates in the higher, were granted fixed salaries.

In spite of all the warnings of the Russian diplomats and the Prussian instructors, Mahmud persistently sought a pretext for war against Muhammad 'Ali. In February 1837 the latter had again rejected the offer to enfeoff him for life with the hereditary possession of Egypt and the governorship of the Syrian coast in return for the cession of the Syrian interior. After that, in August 1838, the Turkish army under Hafiz Pasha had drawn up at Malatya, where fever and dysentery raged among the troops. The pretext for war was then provided by a district near Mar'ash, which was occupied by the Egyptians but claimed by the Porte as its absolute possession. In January 1839 the Sultan gave his troops their marching orders, but canceled them at once at the remonstrances of the European diplomats. Meanwhile he was merely waiting for a more favorable season to renew the orders for attack in April. Under enormous hardships the Turkish army crossed the Taurus and assembled at Birejik on the left bank of the upper Euphrates. As soon as the Turks had crossed the river, the populace, long since dissatisfied with Egyptian rule, revolted in favor of the Sultan. Up to then Ibrahim had been cautiously holding back, since his father wanted to avoid any appearance of aggression in the eyes of Europe. It was not until the middle of June that he received the order to advance, and on the twenty-fourth of that month he established contact with the enemy at Nasibin. The Turks unexpectedly withstood a bold frontal onslaught, but suddenly their cavalry guard rushed at the enemy without orders, were forced by the artillery to turn tail, and then overran their own infantry. At once all discipline in the Turkish army vanished, the Kurds shot at their own officers, and it was only with difficulty that the serasker could defend himself against the onslaught of mutineers. Here something unheard of in military history took place: entire battalions of the victorious army went over to the enemy, and the Egyptian cuirassiers joined the Turkish cavalry in a disorderly rout. Under these circumstances it was impossible for Ibrahim to contemplate a pursuit of the Turks retreating toward Mar'ash and Malatya.

The news of this catastrophe no longer reached the Sultan Mahmud. He died on June 30, 1839, after a reign lasting thirty-one years, only fifty-four years old, but long since enfeebled by an immoderate consumption of alcohol. In spite of his failures in foreign policy, which also prevented the maturing of his perhaps hasty plans of reform, Mahmud will always be considered one of the best rulers of the house of Osman. Like Peter the Great in Russia, with whom he was fond of comparing himself, he became for the Turks the founder of a new era, though this has been contested by Young Turk critics.

He was followed on the throne by his sixteen-year-old son 'Abd-al-Majid. At the news of the Nasibin defeat the grand admiral Fawzi Pasha, out of animosity to the grand wazir Khosrev—this office had been restored at the change of regime—conducted the fleet to Alexandria with the support of the French admiral Lalande. Muhammad 'Ali had long been entertaining the scheme of assuming the government of the entire empire as the sultan's major-domo, and the situation now appeared favorable to this plan. Consequently he instituted festivals of rejoicing throughout his provinces at the young Sultan's accession to the throne, and always referred to himself as the latter's most faithful servant. He summoned the Turkish generals to join him on behalf of the ruler against the Grand Wazir and the Russians. But his intrigues were unsuccessful, since the European powers, except France, opposed his policies, and internal difficulties tied his hands. After the ruthless levies of the preceding years Egypt lacked replacements for its army, and all of Syria was merely waiting for a defeat of his troops to revolt against him. There was a substantial ebb in his exchequer; a marauding excursion into the Sudan to replenish it ended in wretched failure.

Meanwhile the minister of foreign affairs, Rashid Pasha, had returned to Istanbul from his post as envoy extraordinary in London. There he had become an enthusiastic supporter of a constitutional and parliamentary form of government. He intended to introduce Turkey into the ranks of the liberal states by means of a constitution which would lay down in modern phraseology the basic rights of citizens and proclaim the abolition of the crying abuses in the state administration, and thus gain the sympathies of England and France, insure Turkey against violation by absolutist Russia, and in particular outshine Muhammad 'Ali in European public opinion. The young Sultan, who was flattered at being able to assume the luster of a national savior in the eyes of all Europe, easily allowed himself to be won for the plan, and in all secrecy a constitutional proclamation was elaborated. On November 3, 1839, all the dignitaries of the Porte, the delegates of the Osmanli populace of Istanbul and of the raya nations as well as the diplomatic corps, were invited to the kiosk of Gulhane on the southern side of the Serai (Seraglio) on the Sea of Marmara, in order to hear the imperial edict (*hatti-sherif*) of Gulhane.

This document contained no new ideas which Mahmud had not endeavored to translate into practice. The dual consideration of sparing the feelings of the Islamic population and winning the sympathy of the Christians seduced the author into the inconsistency of praising the ancient statutes of Islam as the true salvation of the state, and nevertheless simultaneously recommending new institutions to remedy the ills engendered by their infraction. The Sultan promised all his subjects, regardless of nationality and religion, security of life, honor, and property; a cheap and equitable apportionment of taxes; and to the Muslims in particular a regularized military service and a restriction of the period of service to four or five years. Three of the abuses of the former regime felt to be particularly oppressive, which, though long since declared void, had reappeared again and again—the monopolies, the leasing of provincial taxes to the highest bidders, and the confiscations—were definitely abolished, and the death penalty was made dependent on a judicial verdict handed down after a regular investigation.

The ambitious Rashid was not satisfied with the eulogies he had reaped in the European press for this theatrical coup, as the Russian ambassador called it. He felt he had to reinforce his liberal ideas in the eyes of the world by an example of popular representation. But of course the election of its representatives could not be left to the entirely unprepared populace; they were, rather, culled out by the government. These representatives responded to the Sultan's speech from the throne, introduced after the British example, by an address of thanks, and were then graciously dismissed.

The bitter scorn the Porte reaped for this vulgar speculation on the credulity of European public opinion frightened it away from any repetition of the farce.

Meanwhile the Sultan had been relieved of any concern over his obdurate Egyptian vassal by the European powers. While France, to consolidate its colony Algeria, was aiming at a protectorate over Egypt, Lord Palmerston considered the highway to India imperiled by any power which united Syria and Egypt, and induced the four great powers into a concerted *démarche* against Muhammad 'Ali. At Austria's suggestion a congress in London took counsel on the Egyptian question. The British motion to leave Muhammad 'Ali only Palestine in addition to the hereditary possession of Egypt was opposed by France. When the radical ministry of Thiers, which had assumed control of affairs in Paris on March 2, 1840, intervened on behalf of its protégé as though Turkey lived only by its grace, the Russian diplomats succeeded in shattering the harmony hitherto prevailing between France and Britain. On July 5, 1840, Britain concluded with Russia and the two German powers the so-called Quadruple Alliance, with the obligation to defend the integrity of Turkey and in case of need to constrain Muhammad 'Ali by force to relinquish Syria; Palestine alone, though, without Acre, was to be left to him.

After the negotiations attempted by the Porte once again in Alexandria proved futile, the Sultan declared Muhammad 'Ali, as an enemy of the state, to have forfeited his offices and dignities. The Mediterranean squadrons of the allies, twenty-two major war vessels, to which the Porte added two frigates and a number of transport ships with six thousand landing troops, assembled off the Syrian coast to attack Ibrahim. When the allied fleet appeared before Beirut, there flared up anew a rebellion of the Maronites of the Lebanon, which had already broken out before but been suppressed by Ibrahim. After the allies had landed in Juniyah, a few hours north of Beirut, the Maronites rushed to the coast in droves and took custody of the guns brought along for them. But the British general Smith contented himself with encircling Beirut, and the commandant of the city, Suleyman Pasha, succeeded in breaking out in October, after supplies had run out, and at Baalbek joined forces with Ibrahim, whose army, however, was already completely demoralized.

In November, Sir Charles Napier began the siege of Acre, the famous fortress which had heroically defended itself against Napoleon after his withdrawal from Egypt in 1799, against the Porte's punitive expedition in 1822, and against Ibrahim in 1832, and on whose completion Muhammad 'Ali had spent enormous sums. After four hours of murderous bombardment, in which the explosion of a powder magazine cost the lives of a quarter of the garrison, the survivors sought to escape, but were captured after a bloody battle and the fortress taken. At this news Ibrahim turned toward Damascus, there extorted another forty million piasters and then fled before the rebels to Egypt, leaving behind ammunition and weapons.

In the second half of November, Sir Charles Napier appeared with the fleet before Alexandria and forced Muhammad 'Ali to accept a convention in which he bound himself to return the Turkish imperial fleet and evacuate Syria. In return the Admiral promised him a guarantee for his hereditary rule in Egypt. After Muhammad 'Ali, in an epistle to the Grand Wazir, had consigned his fate to the grace of the Sultan and delivered the fleet, his constitutional position in Egypt was regulated anew, with the collaboration of the powers. He was to pay Turkey an annual tribute of thirty million piasters, limit his army to eighteen thousand men, leave the appointment of senior officers to the sultan, introduce the same laws and taxes as in the remainder of the empire, and acknowledge the validity for Egypt of treaties concluded by the Porte with foreign powers. The right of selecting 'Ali's successor among those of his sons surviving him, which at first had been granted the Sultan, was replaced at the London conference by the hereditary succession of the oldest son in the family.

To the Porte fell the difficult task of regulating conditions in Syria, which the war had upset still further. In the Lebanon for centuries there had been settled indigenous princes of the houses of the Tanukh, Ma'n, and Shihab. In the same way as Mahmud had previously broken the power of the derebeys (valley princes) in Asia Minor, the Porte now had to make an attempt to bring the Lebanon also under the direct authority of its provincial governor. Emir Bashir, who had once delivered the country to Ibrahim, had fled to Malta on a British warship in October 1840; his oldest son was feebleminded; and the youngest was also unfitted for the succession. But France, which, after all, laid claim to a protectorate over the Christians in the Orient and so also over the Maronites (Syrians united with the Roman church), was not disposed to allow a Christian principality to perish without more ado. Under pressure from the powers the Porte appointed one of the aging Bashir's nephews governor, but it simultaneously fomented a revolt of the Druzes, which made necessary the military garrisoning of the entire Lebanon. Upon the complaints of the Christians the Porte appointed a commission which forced the populace into petitioning the Sultan to introduce a Turkish administration. In August 1842 the powers effected the division of the Lebanon into two administrative districts, under one Druze and one Maronite notable, who bore the title of *qa'immaqam*. In the mingled districts, such as the important settlement of Matn on the highway to Damascus where a predominantly Maronite population lived under Druze shaykhs, each one of the two regents was to appoint a deputy. Since the powers still insisted on the Druzes' making amends for the damage inflicted during the 1842 revolt, civil war broke out anew in May 1845. At this point the Porte had both parties disarmed, and placed at the side of the two qa'immaqams a collegium with administrative and judicial powers, composed of representatives of the various classes of the population.

Muhammad 'Ali died in 1848; since Ibrahim's death had preceded his by eight months, he was succeeded by his son 'Abbas Pasha, a fanatical Muslim who had a profound contempt for European education. Directly after he began his reign the plan was put forth of connecting the Mediterranean with the Red Sea by a canal. Since French capitalists had an interest in this, Britain opposed it, and promoted the rival project of a railway across the Isthmus of Suez, construction of which was actually begun in 1851.

However, it was not this question of communications, of such consequence later on for the entire world, which determined the fate of the Orient during the following years, but another circumstance which, though always treated by the Porte as a bagatelle, now created a pretext for the European powers to decide the mastery of the Orient. This was the notorious question of the holy places. The areas in and around Jerusalem consecrated by memories of the life of Jesus and of the Apostles, from the time of the Crusades onward had been in the common possession of the six Christian denominations–the Roman Catholics (here called Latins), the Greeks, Armenians, Syrians, Copts, and Abyssinians. The three last-named churches, because of their weakness, had voluntarily submitted to the guardianship of the Armenians, who as the financial power of the Orient were indispensable to the Porte. The Greek church, however, as the representative of the ten million Orthodox subjects of the Sultan and by virtue of the protection of Russia, was superior to them. The Latin priesthood, mostly of Spanish and of Italian origin, enjoyed the foreign privilege of extraterritoriality and the protection of the French foreign office. The rights of these individual sects were handed down only by word of mouth and were by no means sharply delineated with respect to each other, and consequently often led to litigation before the local Muslim authorities. In the Church of the Holy Sepulcher, which was held in common by all sects, there were outbreaks of physical violence among the priests, whose numbers were as great as their functions were negligible, so that during the Easter holidays a Turkish guard had to maintain law and order at the Holy Sepulcher.

In the summer of 1847 a star with a silver inscription which had been suspended over the birthplace of the Saviour had vanished from the Church of the Nativity in Bethlehem. The Greeks were accused of having removed it; the authorities charged with the investigation, however, came to no conclusion. In 1849, when the French government again became accessible to clerical influence, it zealously seized on this occasion, which simultaneously gave it the desired opportunity of combating Russia's influence in the Orient. Accordingly, on the basis of a capitulation of 1740, its ambassador in Istanbul was ordered to demand for the Latins a considerable extension of their previous rights. But Russia threatened the Porte with breaking off diplomatic relations if it altered the proprietary status of the holy places. After negotiations and council meetings lasting nearly two years the Sultan decided that everything in Jerusalem was to remain as before, but that in Bethlehem the three keys to the principal gates of St. Mary's Church and the Crypts of the Nativity were to be handed over to the Latins. In this way, however, the Latins still lacked possession of the key to the principal entrance of the Basilica on the west, and the French ambassador, who shortly before had made a threatening reference to the honor of his emperor, had to declare his satisfaction with this absurd concession. But Russia intended to exploit this opportunity for the decisive expulsion from the arena of her political enemy in the east. She contrived to have the Porte transmit an order to the governor in Jerusalem that it was to be made clear to the Latins at the surrender of the keys that this did not also grant them the right to walk through the gates; further, to have all Greek rights to the holy places inscribed in the archives of the municipal courts and declare any further Latin claims null and void. When France also accepted this challenge with composure, the Russian general consul for Palestine demanded that the new firman of the Porte be publicly proclaimed in Jerusalem. The French ambassador protested against this and threatened the Porte, on the occasion of any further submissiveness to Russia, with a blockade of the Dardanelles. After the Porte nevertheless complied with Russia's demands, France once again dared not carry out her threat.

A new conflict was brought about by the Montenegrin question. The inhabitants of Montenegro were regarded by the Porte, although no effort had even been made to subdue them formally, as a part of the Rum Millet. Since the seventeenth century they had been ruled by priests, who bore the ecclesiastical title of metropolitan but among the people were simply called *vladika*, i.e. ruler. In October 1852, when the vladika Peter II died, his nephew and successor Danilo renounced the ecclesiastic primacy and began ruling as the founder of an independent and hereditary dynasty. This was rightly regarded by the Porte as insurrection, and it sent off its best general, 'Umar Pasha, to suppress it. The South Slav subjects of

Austria, to whom the Viennese cabinet was indebted for their behavior during the Hungarian uprising, took the side of their kinsmen, and at their request the emperor sent an envoy extraordinary to Istanbul to urge moderation upon the Porte. Russia felt itself bound to join in this and Menshikoff, her envoy extraordinary, by the time of whose arrival the Montenegrin incident was already over with, nevertheless behaved with such recklessness in Istanbul that Fu'ad Pasha resigned his office as foreign minister. Menshikoff now demanded that the Porte regulate the question of the holy places by a special treaty with Russia, and that it recognize the Greek patriarch as an independent church dignitary.

When the Porte rejected these impossible demands, the Ambassador took his leave, and on June 26 Tsar Nicholas issued to his people the famous manifesto in which he declared that the ancient Russian mission of defending the Orthodox faith compelled him, since the Porte had interfered with the rights of the Oriental churches, to have his troops advance into the Danube principalities, not to begin a war but in order to secure a guarantee for the restoration of these violated rights. A week later Russian troops crossed the Pruth. In Istanbul the old martial spirit came to life again at once. After an attempt at mediation on the part of the great powers had failed, a French and a British squadron steamed into the Sea of Marmara, to be enthusiastically greeted as allies by the Muslim populace. On October 4 the Porte declared war on Russia, and a fortnight later its troops under 'Umar Pasha crossed the Danube, though they were soon compelled to retire again. Although the Turks also took a Russian fort in Transcaucasia, they later had to withdraw to Kars, the principal fortress in Turkish Armenia. The western powers were still attempting to mediate, and did not send their fleets into the Black Sea until after the Russians had annihilated a Turkish squadron in the anchorage of Sinope. In the spring of 1854 the Russians made a new advance over the Danube but were held up by the fortress of Silistria. But now, after Prussia and Austria had demanded the evacuation of the Danube territories and the Germanic confederation was already gathering its troops along the Galician frontier, Russia gave in. Meanwhile the western powers had also assembled land forces in Istanbul, and with these attacked Russia in the Crimea in September. On the twentieth of the same month the Russians suffered a severe defeat along the Alma. Nevertheless the fortress of Sevastopol held out until September 8, 1855.

But in Caucasia the Russians had an advantage, although their Muslim subjects, the Lezghians, under the famous national hero Shamil, and the Abkhazians and Circassians revolted against them. After a lengthy siege Kars fell into their hands on November 28.

In order to secure the future of the peace treaty which was already under negotiation and to deprive Russia of any further pretext for intervention in the internal affairs of the Ottoman Empire, the western powers insisted on new reforms in Istanbul. Under their pressure a second edict of reform, the Hatti Humayun, was decreed on February 1. In this the Sultan first of all confirmed the rights granted his subjects in the Hatti-sherif of Gulhane. The secular affairs of the Christian nations were no longer to be conducted exclusively by priests, as before, but by an autonomously elected lay and clerical council. The contemptuous appellations of the Christian subjects, hitherto still in use in the pulpit address, were abolished. Muslim converts to Christianity could no longer, as before, be forcibly reconverted. Entry into the state institutes of learning and so into the civil service was opened to Christians. Christians were also to be drawn into military service, hitherto a Muslim prerogative, though they were to be free to hire a proxy. Christians in the provincial and communal councils were promised more effective representation than before. Under certain conditions foreign subjects were permitted to acquire land. Finally, a more just system of taxation, the adoption of an annual budget, and the elimination of all bribery were envisaged.

This new edict was not received by the subjects with the same enthusiasm as that of Gulhane previously. The Muslims grumbled at the loss of their ancient privileges; the Christians, made mistrustful by many melancholy experiences, expected no practical benefits from the new laws; in addition the contents of the edict were suspect to both parties because their origin in the European cabinets was unmistakable.

After the diplomats considered that they had done their duty in Istanbul, peace negotiations were entered on in earnest; they were concluded at the Paris congress in March 1856. All areas occupied by both sides during the Crimean War were returned. The powers guaranteed the independence of the Ottoman Empire and allowed it as a member of the "European Concert" to enjoy all the advantages of international law. The Dardanelles remained closed, as before, and the Black Sea was neutralized. Danube shipping was to be voluntarily regulated by a special commission. The Porte obligated itself to give Moldavia and Wallachia an independent national regime, and guaranteed them complete freedom of worship, legislation, trade, and shipping. The same liberties were conceded to Serbia, but it remained dependent on the Porte, which also retained its garrison rights.

Four years after the Treaty of Paris the European states were again provided with an occasion for intervention in the internal affairs of the Ottoman Empire. The dual regime of the Druzes and the Maronites in the Lebanon gave rise to continual conflict, particularly since the fanatical Old Turks there, feeling free from the persistent supervision of European diplomats, gave rein to their hatred of the Christians by an incitement of the Druzes. In May 1860 civil war broke out again and there was a reign of pillaging and murder until into the month of July, since the troops, unpaid for months, failed to intervene. More than thirty thousand Christians lost their lives in these atrocities, and the dangerous example in the mountains also had a provoking effect on the fanatics in the plains. In Damascus there began a persecution of the Christians, who would have been totally wiped out if the emir 'Abd-al-Qadir, famous from the wars of liberation of the Algerian Kabyles against the French, who was living there in exile, had not, together with his sons and a small force of men, saved many of them. This barbarism aroused such extreme indignation in Europe that the Porte found it advisable to dispatch Fu'ad Pasha with full powers to punish the culprits. France also sent six thousand men into Syria, while the other powers only made diplomatic representations. In the Lebanon and in Damascus savage sentences were handed down by the courts. Nevertheless the Druzes found a champion in Britain, which needed them as a counterweight to France's protectorate over the Christians. Its protestations held up the execution of the Druze leaders, which had already begun; 2,491 Druzes were deported to Tripolis, but only five years later were allowed to return home.

The sultan 'Abd-al-Majid had died on June 25, 1861. He was succeeded by his brother 'Abd-al-'Aziz, who had previously been held captive in his mother's house and had associated only with dervishes and exegetes of the Qur'an. The latter had stuffed his mind with fantastic daydreams of the caliph's religious dignity and international power. He began his reign with the best of intentions; he dissolved his predecessors' harem, announced his desire to be content with one wife, and restricted his entire court. But all Istanbul had an interest in the expenditures connected with the harem; consequently it was impossible for him to swim against the stream, and in a short time the new sultan developed into an arch-libertine. In addition he found himself in severe financial straits directly after his reign began. His predecessors had left behind a debt of 15 million pounds sterling, and by 1861 the deficit had run to 450 million piasters or 103 million francs. The following year the Porte succeeded in arranging for a British loan of 6 million pounds sterling, but in return had to put up with a British commissioner who supervised the expenditure of this capital. He was soon followed by financial representatives of the other great powers. At their suggestion a court of accounts and a state bank were founded, which did not, however, contribute a great deal to the regulation of finances because of the lack of competent officials.

Under 'Abd-al-'Aziz the Ottoman Empire definitely lost its most valuable provinces. In July 1856, in accordance with the Treaty of Paris, the Porte had appointed the boyars Balsh and Ghika qa'immaqams of Moldavia and Wallachia. The former died only eight months later and was replaced by his finance minister Vogorides, the son of the former prince of Samos. The definitive constitution of the principalities was to be deliberated on by an assembly to be called for the purpose. At the end of December 1858 it elected Colonel Cuza head of Moldavia, and soon afterward he was acknowledged in Wallachia as well. But Cuza squandered the country's resources in a regime of favorites and mistresses unheard of even for Oriental circumstances; his omnipotent counselor was a former Ostend waiter, Liebrecht, made director of the postal and telegraphic system. In February 1866 a conspiracy forced Cuza to abdicate. The provisional government succeeded in winning the young prince Carol von Hohenzollern for the vacant throne. On May 13 the chamber proclaimed the union of the two principalities under the hereditary sovereignty of the new ruler. Under his reign Rumania developed with great good fortune.

In July 1854 'Abbas Pasha, who had proven an incompetent despot, had died in Egypt, probably from poisoning; he was followed by Sa'id, the European-educated fourth son of Muhammad 'Ali. In December 1856 Sa'id made a decision heavy with consequences for the future evolution of Egypt: he granted Count Ferdinand de Lesseps, who as French consul had long been a friend of his, the right to build a canal through the isthmus of Suez. The Porte, to be sure, did not directly refuse to give the approval requested of it, however much the British foreign office worked against it, but in 1860 declared definitely that it would not oppose the opening of the canal. However, Lesseps had already begun construction beforehand. His patron Sa'id died on January 17, 1863. The successor, Isma'il, soon fell into financial straits because of his passion for squandering money. This was exploited by the British for a new attack on the project they opposed. Since cotton prices had gone up considerably as a result of the American Civil War, they suggested to Isma'il that he would be able to acquire great wealth by having the sixty thousand fellahs provided for forced labor on the canal plant cotton on the areas left by his predecessor to the canal construction company. When he now demanded land and laborers from Lesseps's board of directors, the latter at first declared that it would mean the ruin of the entire enterprise. Through Napoleon's mediation the matter was brought before a court of arbitration which granted the company, in return for a waiver on 60,000 hectares of land and four-fifths of the laborers, compensation of 30 and 38 million francs. Isma'il's decision to turn to cotton growing, in which he was soon joined by most of the great landholders, had almost more far-reaching consequences for the economic development of Egypt than even the building of the canal. While hitherto Egypt had not only been able to feed itself with its rich grain harvest but also supply its neighbors, cotton cultivation now involved it more and more in world economy and its crises, and it soon lost its independence. Lesseps substituted machines for the manpower he had been deprived of. In the autumn of 1869, after twelve years' labor, the canal, 93½ miles long, from 96 to 110 yards wide, and 35 feet deep, was completed. Beginning at Port Sa'id on the Mediterranean, it runs in a straight line through the Manzalah and Bellah Lake, then cuts across al-Jisr, an elevation of 16 meters, the Lake of Timsah, the Serapeum and the two Bitter Lakes, and discharges into the Red Sea at Suez and Port Ibrahim. On Nevember 17, 1869, the canal was dedicated in a brilliant celebration at which Isma'il cast aside all curbs on his spendthrift tastes and was able to bask among the representatives of the European princes–the Austrian emperor himself had come, Napoleon III had sent his queen Eugénie, King William I of Prussia had sent the crown prince–as their equal.

With a certain justice Isma'il could regard himself as the worthy executor of the political testament of his great ancestor. As early as 1866 he had succeeded in securing for his dynasty in Istanbul a direct succession on the European model, father to son (instead of the Turkish custom of succession by seniority), by offering the Porte, at this time hard pressed by a revolt of the Cretans, military aid and the raising of his tribute from 307,000 to 720,000 Turkish pounds. The following year he obtained the right of independent decree of all government measures with the exception of international treaties. Simultaneously the ancient Persian title of khedive, ("ruler") was bestowed on him, which elevated him far beyond the rank of a wali or governor-general and almost constituted acknowledgment of his sovereignty. Later, to be sure, the Sultan, incited by Britain and the older Egyptian princes, demanded that he give up his armored fleet, restrict his land army, submit an annual budget to the Porte, and without the Sultan's approval accept no loans and conclude no political accords. Since after the completion of the canal France no longer had such urgent need of his assistance as before, he no longer received any backing from Napoleon's diplomats against this humiliation. But in September 1871 his most violent antagonist at the Porte, the grand wazir 'Ali Pasha, died, and the latter's successor, Mahmud, showed himself much more accommodating to his ambitious designs. In June 1873 the Sultan issued a firman revising the constitutional position of the Khedive. His territorial power was extended by the grant of authority to him as qa'immaqam of Suakin and Massaua. The right of lineal succession was assured him. He was given complete independence in administration and legislation, after the Sultan, the year before, had already approved the new judicial constitution in accordance with the proposals of the international commission convoked in 1869. His powers of increasing the army as he saw fit, of concluding nonpolitical treaties with foreign powers, and of accepting loans were recognized. He also gained a freer position vis-à-vis foreign countries, when in 1875 consular jurisdiction in civil affairs was abolished and authority over them delegated to the mixed courts.

Isma'il's activities on behalf of the development of his country's civilization were also successful. He benefited agriculture by the establishment of new canals for irrigation from the Nile and by the introduction of the sugar industry. He built docks and harbors for commerce, new railways and telegraph lines, and improved the postal system. During his reign Cairo, Alexandria, and Suez were given gas- and waterworks. He raised the level of national education by increasing the state-supported schools, whose numbers rose under his reign from 185 to 4,817; Egypt owed him her first girls' school, a school of medicine, and a military academy.

Like the founder of his dynasty, Isma'il sought to extend his power in the south also. By annexing the sultanate of Darfur and the hinterland of Massaua he came into contact with the Christian empire of Abyssinia, which though still lying entirely under the spell of a medieval feudal form of government, nevertheless had at its disposal an army which was valiant though untrained. After the Egyptians had subdued Harar in 1875, they thought they would be able to penetrate into the interior mountain country of Abyssinia. But the first expedition which ventured into the interior was defeated at Gundet by Emperor John, and in 1876 a second army under the command of Hasan Pasha, one of the Khedive's sons, was even captured by the Abyssinians. In a third battle at Gura the Egyptians lost all their artillery. Fortunately for them a number of Emperor John's vassals revolted, so that in 1877 he was ready for a peace treaty leaving the Egyptians at least Massaua, which was already threatened by the enemy.

These unfortunate campaigns, combined with the Khedive's prodigality, bordering on mania, shattered the finances of the wealthy country, which Sa'id had already burdened by a loan of 3 million British pounds. In vain Isma'il endeavored to increase the yield of his enormous domains by the latest inventions of European technique. But the steam plows and other machines procured at great cost, in so far as they were put to use at all, never served for more than a short time. By November 1875 Isma'il, in momentary embarrassment, had had to sell his Suez canal shares to Great Britain for 4 million pounds sterling; by 1876 the foreign debt had already risen to almost 100 million pounds. The example of his suzerain, who had relieved himself by a state bankruptcy in 1875, tempted him to emulation. In April 1876 he ceased payment of interest for a quarter of a year on his state and private debts. He paid no salaries to his functionaries and doubled the annual tax on the fellahs. But the European court in Alexandria, which had taken the place of the consular courts on the basis of the new judicial organization confirmed by the Sultan, sentenced the Khedive to pay his debts and decreed that his palace at Ramlah be sequestered. Britain and France appointed a commission for the investigation of Egyptian finances, and in 1878 this compelled the Khedive and his relatives to cede the bulk of their estates to the state and to levy no further taxes without the approval of a parliament composed of natives and foreigners. In the newly formed cabinet, which the Armenian Nubar Pasha headed, the Englishman Wilson was called in for finances and the Frenchman de Blignières for public works. But the infuriated Khedive proved incapable of enduring such tutelage, particularly since a reduction of his army was also suggested. He succeeded in fomenting a military uprising against the Christians which was meant to force the foreigners into a retreat. But only Nubar Pasha resigned his office, while Wilson and de Blignières entered the new cabinet under the leadership of the crown prince Tawfiq. Now the Khedive, supposedly at the instigation of an assembly of native notables, declared that the foreigners were dismissed; he simultaneously attempted to reduce his obligations to his creditors by means of his own decree. In May 1880 this got him a note of protest from the imperial German government, in which the other powers concurred. On June 26, at their urging, the Sultan declared Isma'il deposed and appointed his oldest son, Tawfiq, khedive.

During the seventies the Ottoman Empire, also, was afflicted by continual financial difficulties. In 1875 these reached their peak. The Porte had been making a vain attempt in Paris to negotiate a new loan and to make the Ottoman bank the tax-collector-general and cashier for the whole of the empire. If the sultan 'Abd-al-'Aziz had at that time been able to make up his mind to sacrifice a portion of his enormous private fortune, or at any rate curtail his court expenses, then possibly the worst might still have been avoided. But such sacrifices were not to be expected of him, and so nothing remained for the Porte but to make a declaration of state bankruptcy, even if the Russian ambassador had not in addition expressly advised this. In October the grand wazir decreed that during the next five years the Porte would be compelled by the deficit to pay only half the interest in cash, the other half in 5 per cent bonds. The only exceptions made were the first two loans, which arose in the Crimean War and were guaranteed by Britain and France, and the state papers found in the possession of the Sultan, amounting to about 144 million francs. During the preceding twenty years the Porte had made ten loans, the last at the most unfavorable rates of issue, with an average interest of 9½ per cent. At the moment of bankruptcy the outstanding debt, together with the current debts for armored ships, Krupp cannons, and Martin guns, was estimated at more than 6,225,000,000 francs.

In the Slav provinces of Rumelia there was a ferment everywhere, and the Russian consulates were accused, doubtless not entirely without justice, of participating in the work of agitation against the Osmanlis. In Herzegovina, where the Christians were sucked dry to the very marrow by their own nobility, which had gone over to Islam after the conquest, disturbances broke out as early as July 1875. The Porte gathered an army, but first attempted some reforms and appointed an administrative council which included Christian officials. When this new authority tried to begin its activity in the rebel areas it was hindered by the Muslims. In January 1876 an uprising also broke out in Bulgaria, since in its financial straits the Porte had issued an order to collect all arrears of taxes within four weeks. On May 6 a dispute over a Bulgar girl took place in Salonica between Christians and Muslims, in which the German and the French consuls were murdered. When as a result of this a European squadron appeared before Salonica, in Istanbul an uprising of the softas (the students of theology and law) broke out which overthrew the grand wazir and the shaykh al-Islam. The three imperial powers proposed a two months' truce between the Christians and Muslims; if no peaceable accord could be achieved within this time, then more effective measures would have to be taken.

The mad extravagance of the Sultan and his total incompetence generated a conspiracy; its inspiration was Midhat Pasha, who had performed great services as governor in the Danube province of Bulgaria and after 1869 in Baghdad, and who for a short time had been a member of the cabinet of the grand wazir Muhammad Rushdi Pasha as minister without portfolio. Early in the year he had sent an anonymous memorandum to the great powers, with the exception of Russia, in which he declared that the deposition of the Sultan was demanded by Islamic law, which required the chief of state to be in full possession of all his mental faculties. On the evening of May 30 the conspirators, of whom the war minister, Husayn 'Awni Pasha, was one, surprised the Sultan in his Dolma Baghcheh Palace on the Bosporus and read out to him a fatwa of the shaykh al-Islam which proclaimed his deposition. That same night Murad V was elevated to the throne. On June 5 'Abd-al-'Aziz was found lifeless in his palace at Chiraghan; supposedly he had slashed the veins in his wrists with a scissors. The new sultan had had a European education and bore a reputation for enlightenment. But his health had long since been undermined by an immoderate consumption of alcohol, and the frightful scenes at his accession to the throne had completely clouded his mind to boot.

In Bulgaria the Porte had considered it necessary to repress the rebellion with all its power. After the Crimean War it had settled the Circassian emigrants from the Russian Caucasus in Bulgaria, and it now turned them loose on the Christians. Together with the half-savage irregular cavalry, the bashi-bozuks, they extirpated entire settlements. These Bulgarian atrocities aroused such a storm of indignation in Great Britain that Gladstone, the leader of the opposition, demanded the downright expulsion of the Osmanlis from Europe.

The war party now gained the upper hand in Serbia also. On June 27 the Belgrade government, in an ultimatum to the Porte, demanded the removal of the Turkish garrisons and of the irregular bands from the Serbian frontier, and the appointment of Prince Milan as viceroy of Bosnia. On July 2 Milan issued a declaration of war at his headquarters in Deligrad; Montenegro also openly entered the war. While the Serbs were still held in check by the Turks during the summer of 1876, the Montenegrins won a brilliant victory on July 28.

Meanwhile Murad's mental disorder had become so notorious that on August 31 the shaykh al-Islam declared him deposed. On September 1 his brother 'Abd-al-Hamid II ascended the throne. Soon afterward Midhat Pasha assumed the direction of affairs as grand wazir. With him the tsar Alexander II agreed on the conclusion of a two months' truce in the Balkans, which the Porte, however, used only as a period for rearming. At Britain's suggestion an ambassadorial conference convened in Istanbul to secure peace once again by means of new proposals for reform. The great powers demanded that for the first five years the confirmation of the governor of Bulgaria be reserved to them, and that an international commission of control be appointed. Midhat Pasha attempted to ward off this encroachment on the Sultan's sovereignty by internal reforms. A commission composed of sixteen civil officials, ten 'ulama, and two divisional generals was charged with the drafting of a new constitution, and after severe conflicts passed the following resolutions, based on the Belgian constitution, which were published as *Kanuni Esasi* on December 23: the privileges of Istanbul, which had hitherto had a special administration and whose inhabitants were exempt from military service and income tax, were to be abolished; all subjects of the empire were to be known as Ottomans and to be personally free; Islam was to be the religion of the state, which, however, also protected all other recognized cults; the press was to be free within the limits of the law; all Ottomans with a mastery of the Turkish language could occupy any office in the state service according to their abilities; popular representation was established by two chambers, that of the deputies and that of the senators, who were not to be persecuted because of their opinions or voting; the chambers were to convene on November 1 of each year and to be opened by a speech from the throne; the laws initiated by both chambers were to become effective after being passed by both and approved by the sultan; the president and the members of the senate were to be appointed by the sultan for life; for every fifty thousand citizens there was to be one deputy, who might not occupy any public office except that of minister; the deputies were to be elected for four years, though they could be re-elected, and each one was to represent all Ottomans as a whole, not any single community, and the voters had to elect their deputy from among the inhabitants of their province; the president and two vice-presidents were to be chosen by the sultan from a list proposed by the chamber of deputies; the drafting of the budget was to be the business of the chamber of deputies; its sessions were open to the public; there was to be a supreme court composed of ten senators, ten state councilors, and ten councilors of the appellate court for legal decisions concerning the ministers, the presidents, the members of the appellate court, and those accused of sedition and high treason; the administration of the provinces was to be decentralized; elementary education was to be compulsory for all Ottomans.

At first the Porte attempted to evade the demands of the great powers by declaring it was unable to make any further concessions without the approval of the parliament. Since this had not yet been elected, the Porte convoked, as in similar circumstances before, a great council of over two hundred members, in which present and former dignitaries as well as representatives of the Christian and Jewish communities participated. On January 18, 1877, this council unanimously rejected the demands of the powers, whereupon their representatives left Istanbul. But Midhat Pasha's diplomatic adroitness succeeded once again in dividing his opponents. On February 28 a peace treaty was concluded with Serbia which restored the *status quo ante*. Since Montenegro demanded a territorial expansion which was rejected by the Ottoman parliament, convened on March 19, the truce was not extended.

On April 24 Russia declared to the great powers that its peaceable evolution was hampered by the disturbances in the Orient, and that in consequence it was compelled to intervene actively. The powers, which in the Treaty of Paris had guaranteed the independence and territorial integrity of the Ottoman Empire, declared their neutrality. Rumania had been unable to prevent the passage of numerous Russian officers and volunteers through the country on the way to Serbia, and later had to permit the passage of Russian troops, which could come to grips with the enemy in no other way. Since after this the Turks also ceased respecting its boundaries, Rumania signed a military convention with Russia in which it placed all its resources and means of transport at the latter's disposition. On May 13 Rumania declared war on the Porte, and on May 21 the country's independence was proclaimed in both chambers.

At the end of June 1877 the Russian general Gurko crossed the Danube, advanced to the Balkans, though there were still Turkish troops stationed on both sides of his path, and occupied the Shipka pass, which dominated the highroad to Adrianople. In his rear Osman Pasha occupied the Plevna junction, which dominated all the highroads to northern Bulgaria; but Suleyman Pasha, in command south of the Balkans, did not think of joining him but instead made a vain attempt to storm the Shipka pass. Now Prince Carol of Rumania intervened in the war but was unable to force Osman Pasha to capitulate until December 10, after a protracted siege. In January 1878 the Russians passed over the Balkans and occupied Adrianople. Here, on January 31, they concluded a truce with the Turks. Russia was compelled to surrender the old objective of its Oriental policy, the march on Constantinople, since the British fleet sailed into Besika Bay, and the British parliament approved an increase in armaments. On March 3 a provisional peace treaty was signed at San Stefano. Turkey acquiesced in the cession of the Kars fortress in Armenia, conquered by the Russians, and of the important harbor of Batum, and agreed to the establishment of an independent principality of Bulgaria, subordinate only to the suzerainty of the sultan, which was to reach as far as the Aegean Sea. But these terms were not recognized by Great Britain, which had secured the cession of Cyprus by Turkey in payment for its help. Since Austria was also arming, Russia had to put up with a revision of the peace treaty at a congress to be convened in Berlin. On June 13, 1878, the Congress of Berlin met and was in session for four weeks. With Bismarck's help Turkey salvaged southern Bulgaria, at any rate, as an autonomous province of East Rumelia under a Christian governor, while northern Bulgaria was elevated into an independent principality. Rumania, Serbia, and Montenegro were given their absolute independence, and Greece was also satisfied by a territorial concession. Rumania had to cede Bessarabia to Russia and obtained an entirely inadequate compensation for this in the Dobruja. Most portentous for the future was the right accorded Austria to occupy Bosnia, Herzegovina, and the sanjaq of Novibazar.

On February 5, 1877, Sultan 'Abd-al-Hamid, disappointed in the support expected from Britain, had already had Midhat Pasha, who had recommended the policy of dependence on the western powers, removed from his office as grand wazir and exiled for high treason. The constitution created by him never became effective. 'Abd-al-Hamid was now solely concerned with improving the training of his army by German instructors, but rejected any other reform along European lines. He attempted to secure his power by a reversion to the worst methods of Oriental despotism. Every free intellectual impulse in his empire was nipped in the bud. The protagonists of the idea of reform, the so-called Young Turks, had to leave the country and in Paris and Geneva formed new centers of intellectual life. Under the influence of the court camarilla, which kept the Sultan in constant fear of conspiracies, and which in the person of the court theologian of Syrian origin, Abu-l-Huda as-Sayyadi, also dominated him intellectually, he wrapped himself more and more deeply in unreal daydreams, laying continually greater emphasis on his religious dignity as caliph, by means of which he hoped to achieve dominion over all Muslims. In this idea, to be sure, the Sultan was in accord with broad strata of the educated classes, particularly among the clergy, the 'ulama. Islam for them still took the place of a nonexistent national consciousness, and they were dreaming of a pan-Islamic reaction against European hegemony.

The weakness of the Ottoman Empire, however, was so blatant that its dismemberment proceeded at a continually increasing rate. In North Africa, which, indeed, had never been more than loosely dependent on the Porte, Tunisia was lost to France as early as 1881.

In Egypt the weak Khedive Tawfiq had had to look on at the increasing restrictions of his financial sovereignty by the European commission for the settlement of debts. When the latter then effected a reduction of his army, the opposition of the officers was aroused. But they were prevented from united action first of all by their division into a Turkish and an Egyptian party. From the time of Muhammad 'Ali on, numerous Turks still remained in dominant positions in the army, and they favored their kinsmen. A native Egyptian leader emerged in the person of Ahmad 'Arabi, the son of a fellah, who had worked his way up to become colonel and commander of the Fourth Regiment. In January 1881, together with 'Ali Fahmi, the commander of the First Regiment, he set up a protest against the measures of the government of 'Uthman Pasha Rifqi, and so became the head of the National party, which simultaneously represented the interests of the fellahs against the great landholders of Turkish origin. After a number of incidents he was appointed war minister in February 1882. A conspiracy of Turkish officers against him led to a conflict with the Khedive. Against the latter's wishes the ministerial council convoked an assembly of notables. Since Britain considered the security of the Europeans in the country endangered, it arranged for a demonstration of the fleet before Alexandria, in which France joined. This heightened the tension in Egypt, and on June 11 a savage outbreak of xenophobia took place in Alexandria. Since 'Arabi was afraid of intervention by the great powers, he set about fortifying Alexandria. The British government under Gladstone still had no idea of occupying Egypt. Since France was encumbered by difficulties in Tunis and in Indo-China simultaneously, but particularly by its relationship to the German Reich, it recalled its fleet from Alexandria. Thus Britain felt solely responsible for the safety of the Europeans, and on July 11, since 'Arabi failed to stop the work of fortification, the navy bombarded Alexandria. The Khedive had appealed for Britain's protection beforehand and joined forces with its landing troops. On August 2, consequently, 'Arabi had himself proclaimed the deputy of the Sultan, who, however, branded him as a rebel. He advanced against General Wolseley's landing troops at Tell al-Kabir on September 13 with his deficiently armed troops, was defeated, and two days later captured in Cairo. The death sentence passed against him was revoked, and he was exiled to Ceylon, whence in 1901 he was allowed to return to Cairo.

The defeat at Tell al-Kabir determined the history of Egypt for half a century. Britain assumed control of finances and the supreme command of the Egyptian army, in addition to which a permanent British garrison remained in the country. Like the resident at the side of native rulers in India, in Egypt the consul-general Lord Cromer stood beside the Khedive as the real ruler of the country. During this period, accordingly, Egypt's history is part of that of the British Empire, in which it served as a glacis for securing the control of India, and it was not until after the First World War that it was able to win back its independence in two decades of tenacious struggle.

While from his Yildiz Palace, in which he secluded himself from the public more and more, 'Abd-al-Hamid was preoccupied with suppressing by means of a widely ramified system of espionage every impulse to freedom in the Ottoman Empire, he attempted to consolidate his regime by the improvement of commerce. The Oriental railway begun by Baron Hirsch with the aid of enormous and dishonest profits had remained unfinished, and it was not until 1881, after the dissolution of the contract with him, that it could really be pushed ahead in earnest. At the end of 1888 the rails between Belgrade and Constantinople were connected, with a stretch on Asiatic soil from Haydar Pasha to Izmid. With a ninety-nine years' guarantee of a minimum revenue, the Deutsche Bank then obtained permission to extend the railway as far as Ankara, which was reached in 1892. At once the plan emerged to push the railway through Anatolia and 'Iraq as far as the Persian Gulf. In this way not only would the most important countries of the empire be connected with the capital but their abundant natural resources would be opened to world trade. But at the same time this plan imperiled Britain's position in the Orient and Russia's designs on Persia. Although farsighted German statesmen advised against the risks of such an enterprise, the dominant figures, concerned exclusively with the promotion of economic interests, nevertheless pushed this plan of the Baghdad railway, and succeeded in interesting Kaiser Wilhelm II in it. In 1898, when the Kaiser visited Constantinople while returning from his trip to Jerusalem, he requested that the Sultan, who regarded him as his friend and was indebted to him for the training of his army by German officers under Von der Goltz Pasha, give the authorization to construct the harbor of Haydar Pasha to the Deutsche Bank, against the efforts of Britain and Russia, which had hitherto thwarted the further extension of the railway. In 1902 the permission for the building of the Baghdad railway was then given. From Brusa, where the branch line to Ankara turned off, it was to pass through Afyon Karahisar, Konya, Eregli, Bulghurlu, and by way of Nasibin and Mosul to Baghdad; traffic over the stretch as far as Bulghurlu could begin on October 25, 1904. While the railway in Anatolia served economic and strategic objectives, the most distinctive work of the Sultan, the Hijaz railway, was intended to raise his prestige as caliph throughout the Islamic world. While the holy cities could hitherto be reached only over the laborious caravan trails from Damascus through the desert or by water through the Red Sea, now they were to be united with the center of the empire by rail. The construction, pushed ahead primarily by the Sultan's private secretary, 'Izzet Pasha, a Syrian Arab, was accomplished as far as Medina by German engineers between 1900 and 1908. A third of the cost of three million Turkish pounds was procured by voluntary contributions of Muslims throughout the world.*

Of all the subjects of the empire who profited by the Anatolian railway, 'Abd-al-Hamid thought he had to fear the Armenians alone, among whom ambitions for an independent national life had long since been evident. Their compatriots, scattered over the entire Mediterranean area as far as India, had very often acquired great wealth and supported and kept alive such hopes. This most unfortunate of Oriental peoples, on the topmost central ridge of the mountain range between Anatolia, Adharbayjan, and the Caspian Sea, had preserved the racial type of the Anatolian primordial population in its purest form, but had borrowed their language from a stratum of Indo-European immigrants and adapted it to that of their forebears. In their country, filled with broad plains between high mountains, a feudal system had developed at a very early period, which once in antiquity had produced a centralized power but ex-

* See Auler Pasha, *Die Hidschasbahn, Petermanns Mitteilungen, Ergänzungshefte* 154 (1906) and 161 (1908).

cept for this had at nearly all times fallen an easy prey to neighboring states. After their subjugation by the Osmanlis, their neighbors in the south, the Kurds, had continually increased their power in the country. 'Abd-al-Hamid, although himself the son of an Armenian mother, believed he could rely on the Kurds as the safest foundation of his power. His own personal bodyguard in Istanbul, the Hamidiye Regiment, consisted principally of Kurdish recruits. In the provinces he allowed them a free hand, although he was anxious to restrict the power of their beys and suppress all nationalist stirrings among them. As industrious artisans and energetic though unscrupulous businessmen, the Armenians were economically more advanced than their neighbors. Those resident for a long time outside the country had often accumulated great fortunes and were inclined to bring influence to bear on the European powers on behalf of their compatriots. The example of the Balkan nations also aroused the Armenians, despite their entirely different position, to a desire for a certain degree of independence, such as East Rumelia had obtained at the Congress of Berlin. Such desires, however, awakened the mistrust of the Sultan; it is certain that in 1905 he failed to oppose the inhuman butchery of the Armenians carried out by the Kurds, in alliance with the Turks, in nearly all the major cities of the country as well as Trebizond, Edessa, and even Istanbul. These atrocities, which were repeated the following year in the vilayets of Bitlis and Van, not only impaired the prestige of the Ottoman Empire throughout the civilized world but also shook the foundations of the regime.

The Greeks were dissatisfied with the rectifications of the frontiers granted them in the Treaty of Berlin. In particular the desire to incorporate into their kingdom the isle of Crete, inhabited predominantly by their kinfolk, repeatedly inflamed popular passion. In 1896 a rebellion broke out on the island, the leadership of which was assumed by Prince George of Greece. In connection with this, warfare broke out in Thessaly also in the spring of 1897. But the military weakness of the kingdom proved so calamitous that the great powers had to preserve it from a total collapse. The peace treaty dictated by them as a result merely brought the mainland Greeks an insignificant frontier rectification, though Crete was given the status of an autonomous province under a Christian governor.

Still more difficult for the Ottoman Empire did conditions prove in Macedonia, where Turks, Greeks, Albanians, and Wallachians, Bulgars, and Serbs dwelt higgledy-piggledy. Because of this, all three bordering Christian states contended for this fertile province, particularly valuable for its tobacco. In the autumn of 1902 Bulgar bands were formed there which roved about the countryside terrorizing the other Slavs, and which could not be subdued even by the Turkish military. In consequence Russia and Austria demanded that the Porte install a European inspector-general and a police corps under European officers. But an Italian general put in command of the *gendarmerie* was also incapable of restoring order; instead the other groups, after the example of the Bulgars, also took to guerrilla warfare. Even when the great powers compelled the Sultan to submit the state finances to their supervision, they could contribute nothing in the way of calming the inflamed passions. Austria attempted to take advantage of this situation to extend its influence as far as Salonica by a road from Sarajevo through the sanjaq of Novibazar, which was subject to its administration. This aroused the jealousy of Russia and of the other great powers, which now demanded the appointment of a governor-general under their own control.

This new humiliation conceived for their mother country aroused profound indignation among the officers of the Turkish troops stationed in Macedonia. In June 1908, after the meeting at Reval between King Edward VII and Tsar Nicholas II sealed the entente Britain and Russia had concluded by the treaty of August 18-31, 1907, new plans were expected in Turkey for the partition of the empire, and this threatening danger increased the excitement in the officers' circles to the boiling point. The liberal movement of Young Turks, suppressed for so long by the Sultan, had nevertheless, in spite of all the contrivances of espionage, established a foothold in the army. In Macedonia, Enver Bey, who as military attaché in Berlin had been well acquainted with German army methods, and Lieutenant Colonel Niyazi, who had acquired military experience in the warfare with the Macedonian bands, assumed the leadership of a conspiracy whose immediate goal was the restoration of the 1876 constitution of Midhat Pasha.* Among civil servants the tele-

* According to data given by Mustafa Kemal concerning his own life, which he dictated to the editor-in-chief of the Istanbul newspaper *Vakit* at the beginning of 1922, and which are followed by A. Fischer in the *Leipzig Illustrierte Zeitung* No. 4,084 of October 5, 1922, as well as in Kemal's auto-

graph operator Talat was active on behalf of their plans. The conspirators, who called themselves the Committee of Union and Progress (Ittihad ve Terakki), obtained financial assistance from the *dönme*, the Jewish converts to Islam in Salonica, who dominated the business life of the city.

Niyazi escaped with a number of comrades into the mountains of Resna and was secretly supported by the local qa'immaqam. After he joined Ayyub Effendi in Okhrida, they both sent a telegram to the Sultan demanding that he restore the constitution. Shemsi Pasha, sent out to arrest them, was shot. Then Enver also left Salonica and carried on agitation for the committee in Tikvish. By now the conspirators were already feeling so secure that they proclaimed the constitution in Monastir on July 21, 1908, and in Salonica on the twenty-second and twenty-third. That same month, in a surprise march on Istanbul, which was occupied almost without a struggle, they forced the Sultan to recognize the constitution and appoint ministers acceptable to them. On December 17 it was possible to open the Turkish parliament.

This surprising downfall of the autocratic regime was received

---

biography in *Turkun Altun Kitabi Ghazinin hayati* (Istanbul, 1928), p. 20, and the version translated by J. Deny in the *Revue du monde musulman* (vol. 63, 1920, p. 46 ff.) from the *Devletsalname*, which is also the basis of the account in the official Turkish history *Tarih*, IV, Istanbul 1931, p. 140 ff., the founder of the modern Turkish state is also to be taken as the inspiration of the Macedonian insurrection. According to this, while stationed in the garrison at Damascus in 1906, he had already founded an officers' society, Vatan ve Hurriyet Cemiyeti, which also gained members in Beirut, Jaffa, and Jerusalem. While on furlough he is supposed to have slipped away from Smyrna in secret to his native city of Salonica, and there founded a local branch of his society. When this violation of his furlough became known, he was transferred after his return to Syria to a border command for refractory soldiers at 'Aqabah and only three years later transferred to the staff of the high command for Rumelia in Salonica. Contemporary reports of one of the leaders of the Macedonian movement, Niyazi, in his memoirs (*Hatirat*, Istanbul, 1326), and Yunus Nadis, the editor-in-chief of the Istanbul newspaper *Tasviri Efkyar* (*Ihtilal ve Inkilabi Osmani*, Istanbul, 1325), remarkably enough say nothing of this activity of his; cf. also the discussion of the question in the Turkish historical journal *Belleten* (I, Ankara, 1937, 289-309, 619-625). According to Major-General Imhoff (*Die Welt des Islams*, I, Berlin, 1913, 174), the first military committee in Damascus was founded in 1905 by Dr. Haji Mustafa, while Mustafa Kemal formed a new committee in Salonica. From data given by Imhoff and collected by him in Turkey, where he worked as an army instructor, it may be seen that secret committees existed in various places in Turkey and without knowledge of each other; consequently it is not surprising that there is no uniform tradition concerning the beginning of the revolutionary movement.

with enthusiasm by the entire empire. The Young Turks also believed they could still win the confidence and support of all the Christian nations in the empire by proclaiming the new Turkish constitutional ideal, which was to abolish all differentiations of class, religion, and descent. But the peace concluded by 'Abd-al-Hamid with the Young Turks was not enduring. By April 13, 1909, a conspiracy had already broken out against the new rulers. On April 15 the Sultan appointed Tawfiq Pasha grand wazir with the task of again putting into effect the Shari'ah, the holy law. Once again the army corps of Salonica intervened. In April its leader, Husayn Husni Pasha, accompanied by Mustafa Kemal as chief of staff, advanced on the capital, which after a brief struggle was conquered by Mahmud Shevket Pasha. On April 26 a national assembly met in San Stefano and, supported by a fatwa of the shaykh al-Islam, resolved to depose the Sultan. In his place his brother Muhammad V was raised to the throne. In the newly formed parliament the bourgeois groups, who called themselves liberal and advertised their program as one of "Freedom and Unity" (*Hurriyet ve Itilaf*), formed a party which was anxious to counteract the dominant influence of the officers. But the situation abroad did not allow the Ottoman Empire to develop its constitutional life in tranquillity.

Italy, then searching for a colonial region in the Mediterranean area for its continually growing population in order to put a stop to the repeated loss of its natural increase to countries abroad, had lost Tunisia—which, being an immediate goal, had already absorbed numerous Italian emigrants—to France, and was now directing its gaze toward Tripolitania, already being treated by the Ottoman Empire as nothing more than a lost outpost. But when the Young Turks, for reasons of honor, could not approve its cession, the exaction of which took them by surprise, Italy declared war on September 29, 1911, and on October 5 landed troops in Africa. The defense was assumed by Enver Bey and by Mustafa Kemal, who won his first military laurels here; but although the native Arabs and Berbers energetically supported the Turks, eventually they were defeated. In the peace treaty of Ouchy, Tripolis and Benghazi had to be ceded to Italy in 1912; the sole right reserved to the caliph was the appointment of ecclesiastical officials.

Even before the peace treaty was concluded with Italy, the Balkan states declared war on the Ottoman Empire in October 1912; although they still had a number of points of difference to be settled among themselves, they felt their common interests imperiled through the plan of the Turkish government to bind Macedonia more tightly to the empire by a new settlement of Muslim colonists. The Turks were no match for their united strength: the Bulgars laid siege to Adrianople while the Greeks conquered Salonica. The liberal ministry concluded a truce and was prepared to surrender Adrianople. Under Enver's leadership the officers protested against this dishonor and on January 13, 1913, forced the ministry to retire, and Mahmud Shevket took over the government. Since meanwhile Adrianople had fallen, the defense was necessarily restricted to the Chatalja line. But in May at the peace conference in London the Turks finally had to acquiesce, nevertheless, in the cession of all areas west of the line of Enos on the Aegean Sea and Midia on the Black Sea. But since their opponents could not arrive at any agreement concerning the division of the spoils, and so lapsed into a state of war, Enver resorted to arms a second time and reconquered Adrianople, which the Bulgars, in the peace treaties of Istanbul (September 1913) and Athens (1914) were finally compelled to surrender.

During these disturbances it was impossible for any consistent line of internal policy to develop in the Ottoman Empire. The ideal of an Osmanli community encompassing all citizens had soon fallen to pieces; in its place there gradually emerged among the Turks the idea of nationalism. Borne by the ideas of the French Revolution and by German romanticism, nationalism had seized on the peoples of eastern Europe first and led them to their great political victories. It is no wonder that this idea now struck root among the Turks. Since language represented the real tie of nationhood, it was not hard for the Turks also to seek a community of ideals beyond the political frontiers with their linguistic kin living under alien rule. A number of gifted writers had migrated into Turkey from the regions of southern Russia inhabited by Tatars, away from Tsarist oppression, and exercised a decisive influence on the evolution of the new Turanian ideal which encompassed all Turks. The new ideal was given its finest literary expression in a novel by the brilliant poetess of modern Turkey, Halide Edib. But this ideal could only have a disintegrating effect in the midst of the fermentation preceding the submergence of the old empire; it misled the Young Turks into an alienation of the Arabs of the empire, whom Islam should have united with them against the Christians: the Young Turks expected them to surrender Arab culture in favor of a purely Turkish education. It was only in the new Turkey created by Mustafa Kemal as a self-contained national state that the national idea could unfold its sustaining power.

In the field of social relations the solution of the feminist question by the Young Turks proved particularly fruitful. While in the rural areas and smaller cities, even before this, women had possessed equal rights as working companions at the side of their men, nevertheless in the upper classes they remained restricted to the spheres of the home and the harem, in which Islamic society held them enthralled. It is true that a few Turkish women, such as the above-mentioned poetess Halide Edib, were able to extend their education along European lines at the American College in Istanbul, but under the old regime any public activity was closed to them. It was the World War which first freed them of these fetters, since their labor was necessary as a substitute for the men fighting at the front. From then on, Turkish women adapted themselves to the life of their European sisters with surprising swiftness, until the new national state granted them political rights as well as freedom of work in all fields.

Turkey entered World War I on the side of the Central powers, with whom she hoped to be able to break the hegemony of Britain and France in the Near East. The magnificent deeds at arms of the Turkish army and of the fleet, strengthened by the transfer of the German cruisers *Göben*, and *Breslau*, renamed *Selim Yavuz* and *Midilli*, frustrated the British attack on the Dardanelles; as defender of Anaforta, Mustafa Kemal gave another demonstration of his brilliant military gifts.

The Turkish army under Von der Goltz, who on April 19, 1916, succumbed to spotted typhus, brought the advance into 'Iraq of the Anglo-Indian expeditionary corps under General Townshend to a halt, repulsed a British army of relief, and forced Townshend's division, surrounded in Kut-al-'Amarah, to capitulate on April 29, 1916. But over a long period of time 'Iraq could not be maintained against the superiority of the British; by February 1917 they were already able to reoccupy Kut al-'Amarah, and in March, Baghdad also fell into their hands. This secured for Great Britain the control of the Persian and 'Iraqi oil fields, the exuberant flow of which, according to a statement by Lord Curzon, led the Allies to victory.* The attack on the Suez canal could not be successfully executed; nevertheless Turkish troops pinned down considerable British combat forces. In December 1917, however, the British were able to press into Palestine. In Arabia the British agent T. E. Lawrence, as will be related in the history of the evolution of the Arab lands, had induced the sharif of Mecca into defection from the Ottoman Empire by holding out the hope of political independence. He advanced as far as the Syrian capital of Damascus with Arab troops at the beginning of October 1918 and was able to occupy the city, abandoned by the Turks.

The Turks achieved their only lasting successes on the Caucasus front. Although they had had to yield before the Russians there in July 1916, after the collapse of the Tsarist regime they pressed forward through Erzerum in May 1918 as far as Batum and Baku, the center of the oil industry.

But the enormous losses inflicted on Turkey by four years of desperate defensive warfare against infinitely superior opponents necessarily crippled its will to battle after its allies were forced to relinquish any hope for a final victory. Yilderim, the army group newly formed in the Orient under von Falkenhayn, which was to wrest Baghdad again from the British, was unable to save the desperate situation any longer, particularly since differences of opinion between the German and the Turkish leaders concerning its strategic application did not fail to appear. The collapse was sealed by the truce of Mudros on October 30, 1918. The leaders of the Young Turks left the country. Enver went to Russia and on August 4, 1922 was killed in Turkestan in the struggle of the Basmachis against the Bolsheviks.† Talat found a refuge in Germany and was assassinated in Berlin by an Armenian. Jamal Pasha, the war minister, went to Afghanistan to become an army organizer there.

Such was the end of the Ottoman Empire. Being the bearer of an outmoded, outlived principle, it had perished. From its ruins there arose, as will be related in the next chapter, the modern Turkish national state.

* See W. Ireland, *Iraq*, p. 24.

† Cf. the reports of his death in J. Castagné, *Les Basmatchis*, Paris, 1925, p. 60, and in G. Krist, *Allein durchs verbotene Land*, Vienna, 1937.

2. *Intellectual Life in the Ottoman Empire and in Egypt in the Nineteenth Century*

During the nineteenth century the spirit of the Turkish people, clinging to traditional forms, proved again far more capable of resistance to the influences of western civilization in the intellectual sphere than in political and military affairs. The first concession to the new era was the founding in 1831 of a daily newspaper, the *Takvimi Veka'i*, which was soon followed by other journals with literary tendencies, such as the *Terjumani Ahval* in 1860 and *Tasviri Efkyar* in 1862. The reform period known as the tanzimat also led to a transformation of the educational system. While elementary schools, except for instruction in the Qur'an, had previously been totally nonexistent, and any higher education could only be acquired in the religious madrasahs, in 1853 a special bureau was charged with the drafting of textbooks for elementary schools; in 1861 the first advanced girls' school was opened. In 1869 a university was even founded, which, however, succumbed two years later to the storm of reaction. Only a medical institute and a school of law were able to survive.

Until around the middle of the nineteenth century the Osmanlis held fast in literature to Persian contents and Persian style. In the course of the reforms of the educational system, however, a number of gifted young men were sent to Paris to study. Among them was Ibrahim Shinasi, who there concentrated primarily on French literature. After living in Paris for five years, where he is said to have participated in the revolution of 1848, he was appointed to the department of education, but shortly afterward he left the civil service to work in the first nongovernmental newspaper, *Terjumani Ahval*, founded in 1860. In 1862 he founded his own organ, *Tasviri Efkyar*, which withstood all the political storms until it was suppressed by Mustafa Kemal in 1925. In his journalistic activity Shinasi rendered great services to the Turkish literary idiom, which he freed from pomposity and led back to the simple structure of the people's speech. In 1859 he published the first Turkish translations of selections from French prose and poetry with the original on parallel pages (eleven pages in each language). This pamphlet showed the educated Turks that ideas well known to them in the original could be expressed in their own mother tongue as well, and gave rise to a flourishing literature of translations. His own poetical talent was not great and was bound by the old style. Yet he was the first to give the Turks a little comedy, *The Poet's Wedding*, which dealt with the problem of woman's position, so much discussed in literature since.

Shinasi's attempts found a fertile ground: it was generally felt that the old literature had outlived itself. All the younger authors turned to the new movement. Ziya Pasha continued the purification of the language in his translations from Rousseau and Molière. But Shinasi's most important disciple was Namik Kemal, to whom he transferred the editorship of his publication in 1864 when he left for Paris. Namik Kemal understood that it was not enough to adopt French ideas, that literature must treat "native" subjects to influence the people. But political activity interfered with his literary work. Since he had joined the Young Turk committee founded by Ziya, he had to flee with him to London in 1866. Not until after the death of the grand wazir 'Ali Pasha could he return home, in 1871. During the final turbulent years of 'Abd-al-'Aziz's reign, when there was a ferment everywhere in the Balkans, he came out in 1872 with the drama *Fatherland or Silistria*, which glorified the defense of this fortress against the Russians in 1854 and for the first time made familiar to the Turks the concept of a fatherland independent of the person of the sultan. The play aroused such storms of patriotic enthusiasm that it appeared dangerous to the government; consequently it was prohibited after the second performance and the poet banished to Cyprus. 'Abd-al-Hamid was still less able to endure his criticisms and the patriotic character and popular tendency of his art, and kept him, as if in honorable banishment, continually remote from the capital, lastly as *mutasarrif* (governor) of Chios. But his works kept his ideas alive and contributed a great deal to bringing the Young Turk movement to its goal.

The artistic ideals which Namik Kemal often had to sacrifice to his political aims were realized by his disciple 'Abd-al-Haqq Hamid, to whom it was granted to serve his country as diplomat in Paris, London, and Brussels and after the decline of the old empire to rejoice in the rise of the national state until his death on April 12, 1937, at the age of eighty-six. His dramas, influenced largely by the French classics but also by Shakespeare, in addition to his lyric poetry, opened new paths for Turkish literature, though they drew their source from the emotional life of European culture rather than that of the Turks.

But there was also no lack of endeavors to direct literature into purely popular channels. The only authentic Turkish prose alive among the masses of the people, but hitherto haughtily disregarded by the educated classes, had been cultivated by the public story-tellers, the *meddahs*, in their tales from the everyday life of the people. This art of theirs was introduced into literature by Ahmad Midhat. In his *Entertaining Tales,* though he still relied greatly on French materials, he had a wealth of acutely observed details drawn from reality, which he knew how to cast in an absorbing form. An authentically national content was then introduced into literature by Mehmed Tawfiq in his work *A Year in Istanbul;* this described the still-unspoiled life of the people as once lived in the capital, the merry women's conversation on long winter's evenings, the gay hurly-burly of the cafés and the excursions to the Sweet Waters of Europe at the tip of the Golden Horn. Husayn Rahmi penetrated into the life of the people still more deeply. He owed his education, which in his official career carried him to the position of a director of the archives of indirect taxes, entirely to the modern schools of Istanbul and had never learned French. As a son of the people he was particularly fond of glorifying the sound Anatolian peasantry, the hope of the country. But he showed the people as they really were, not balking at learning to know them by intimate association. He shares with his predecessors the didacticism and basic pessimism of his works, which, however, was no longer an emotional aping of the west but rooted in the circumstances and completely authentic.

In the field of lyric poetry also the restraining fetters of classicism were shaken loose. Mahmud Ekrem introduced the native folk song into literature, ennobling it in the foreign forms of the ballad and the romance. Perfection in this popular lyric form was attained by the poems of the Istanbul fisherman's son Mehmed Emin, which served as accompaniment to the victory of the Young Turk movement.

These national aspirations were accompanied by the newly aroused zeal for the purity of the language, in which Sami Frasheri achieved particular distinction. After the artificial and overburdened style of the old classical writers had been discarded and supplanted by the simple idiom of the people, an attempt was also made to free the vocabulary more and more of the ballast of needless foreign words, Arabic and Persian, which in the old literature had stifled the disdained Turkish. Ahmed Jevdet (*d.* 1880), the publisher of the highly respected newspaper *Iqdam* (*Progress*), published the original text and an Osmanli translation of the work of Neva'i in which the latter had glorified Turkish at the expense of Arabic at the court of the Timurids in Herat. Indeed, sometimes things went as far as an attempt to replace the foreign words already completely naturalized by long-since-obsolete Turkish ones. Nevertheless, in spite of these exaggerations, the endeavors of the purists had a sound core and were not unsuccessful.

Toward the end of 'Abd-al-Hamid's reign literature had to struggle against the greatest difficulties. Since he feared the Young Turks as opponents of his autocratic rule, it became continually easier for his entourage, the more he secluded himself from the world in his Yildiz Palace, to cast suspicion on the healthy progressive movements among his people. To the extent that their representatives did not keep silent of their own accord, their activities were paralyzed by a censorship vexatious beyond all bounds, which suppressed a translation of *Wilhelm Tell*, for instance, and would not even tolerate the use of the word fatherland. Thus literature during these years, propped up on contemporary French poetry under the motto of "*L'art pour l'art*," produced only the fruits of a morbidly pessimistic sentimentality. Its representatives rallied round the newspaper *Serveti Funun;* this published Khalid Ziya's novels, *Blue and Black* and *Forbidden Love*, which in spite of their artificial style laid the first real foundations of this literary genre among the Turks. Next to him Ahmed Hikmet dominated the interest of the readers with his simply written imaginative short stories, generally about a fairy-tale world.

The Young Turk revolution freed literature at once of the oppressive shackles of the censorship. Only a few poets, such as the lyricist Ahmed Hashim, remained true to the purely aesthetic ideals of the preceding period. In addition a young national literature soon embarked on an energetic course of development. Soon after the revolution the Turkish society Turk Derneyi was founded, which was succeeded four years later, in 1912, by the more active group of the Turkish Hearth (Turk Ocagi). In its journal *The Turkish Homeland* (*Turk Yordu*) the new ideal of Turkish nationalism was not only championed in literature but also by a profound study of history; the Osmanlis were vied with, as already mentioned, by a number of Tatar writers escaped from Tsarist Russia, in the development of the new ideas. But the leadership of this movement fell to Ziya Gok Alp, whom the Entente considered so dangerous that it exiled him to Malta after the occupation of Istanbul. By his symbolic poems *Kizil Elma*, and perhaps even more by his courses at the university, newly founded during the World War, and by his lectures, he inflamed the youth with the national ideal, to which the poetess Halide Edib gave the finest literary expression in her novel *Turan*. The catastrophe of the end of the war did not destroy this movement; in the new national state, as will be related, it has undergone a vigorous renaissance.

While in Turkey itself contact with European civilization gradually brought about a total upheaval in literary life, in the Arab countries, although they were subjected much earlier and much more enduringly to European influence, the old ideals were effective for a much longer time, and it was only in the period after the First World War that their gradual decline began. The political separation of Egypt from the Ottoman Empire, to which the other Arab countries, except for North Africa, continued to remain subject, prevented a unified development of Arabic literature. This was strengthened by the absence of any national objectives that the Muslims had in common with the much more active Christians. In Egypt the ruling stratum of Muhammad 'Ali's family and their following had far more interest in Turkish than in Arabic literature. It is characteristic that in the presses founded before the First World War in Cairo, not only were military regulations printed in Turkish, but also a whole series of works of classical Turkish literature, before any approach was made to do the same honor to Arabic writings. In Syria, the Maronites, largely in the service of the Christian missionaries who founded the American College in Beirut, and of its rival, the Jesuit University of St. Joseph, vied with each other in reviving the old literature and in restoring the purity of classical Arabic. Such, in the main, was the work of Nasif al-Yaziji (*d.* 1879 in Beirut) who in his poems sought to imitate al-Mutanabbi and in his maqamahs al-Hariri. The attempt of one Marun an-Naqqash (*d.* 1871 in Beirut) to create for his people a drama on the French pattern, but with Oriental content, remained isolated and found no imitators. Turkish censorship hampered the development of the press in Syria with the same severity as in Istanbul. Consequently many gifted journalists preferred to settle in Egypt, particularly since the British authorities had granted the press there far greater freedom. The Arabic literature of Syria under 'Abd-al-Hamid is typified by the president of the religious court in Beirut, an-Nabhani, a friend of the Sultan's imam, Abu-l-Huda, who displayed an immensely prolific literary activity, in the spirit of old-fashioned Islam, in opposition to the influences of Christian Europe.

In Egypt, in the beginning, the Muslims stood quite alone as bearers of Arabic literature, while the Copts first entered the scene in the new political conditions after the First World War. Muhammad 'Ali's interest in European civilization engendered a very extensive literature of translations: in addition to technical and scientific works, which were desired initially, French novels as well soon appeared in great numbers, which, often translated indiscriminately, not infrequently dominated public taste and constituted an obstacle to the pursuit of the national arts. An isolated effort, which found no imitators, was the translation of the *Iliad* by the Syrian Sulayman al-Bustani in stanzas of alternating Arabic meters, which catches the epic atmosphere well but in spite of numerous scholarly observations could scarcely bring the alien content any closer to the Arab public. In poetry there prevailed an imitation of the classical masters of the 'Abbasid era in the work of the war minister, Sami Barudi, who after the 'Arabi revolt was exiled by the British to Ceylon and could only return home when an old man; in exile he gave to his affliction an original and touching expression. Sami was descended from a Turkish family; Arab blood was likewise mingled with foreign in the veins of the Khedive's court poet, Ahmad Shawqi, who atoned for a rash word to his master during World War I with a British sentence of exile to Spain. He was also entirely submerged in the classical tradition and only struck out along new artistic paths after the war. In narrative prose the Syrian Jurji Zaydan dominated the field with his numerous historical novels of the Islamic past, which, though never very profound, nevertheless gripped the readers with their imaginative accounts in a simple style and so broke the ground for the efflorescence of this genre in the postwar period. Zaydan further endeavored to make familiar to the Arabs the results of European research into history and sociology. In Egypt also the drama, because of the absence of any tradition, could evolve only slowly. Only pieces in the light French style had any real success, although there was no lack of efforts to naturalize classic French tragedy. 'Uthman Jalal (1829-1898) turned after such an attempt to the comedies of

Molière in the hope of making their contents palatable to his countrymen by a skillful adaptation to Egyptian circumstances. In this he made the bold innovation of using the popular dialect instead of the classical language which still dominated the stage exclusively, but had so little success in this that his plays were not produced until 1912, only to vanish again from the stage. In the richly developed press of Egypt a new prose style evolved, which served the politicians who emerged under British rule as a successful instrument for their propaganda. Among the latter mention must be made of Qasim Amin (*d.* 1908), whose books *The Emancipation of Women* (1899) and *The New Woman* (1901) made current a discussion of the feminist question throughout the Islamic world; later, after Turkey had gone on ahead with its practical solution, Egyptian society also followed, at first hesitantly, but soon with lasting success.

The religious life of Egypt, however, was and still is dominated by Islam. This is principally due to the influence of a Persian, Jamal-ad-Din, who for political reasons preferred calling himself an Afghan after the country where he spent his youth. In 1870, when he had to leave this adopted country of his after the death of his patron, the emir Dost Muhammad, he first went to Istanbul, and there, preceded by his reputation as an important scholar, although he had published nothing, he received a friendly reception by the government and by scholarly circles, on whom his courses at the newly founded university as well as his lectures made a deep impression. Nevertheless, the shaykh al-Islam succeeded in making him suspect as a freethinker and in effecting his expulsion. He then moved to Cairo, where he was welcomed with open arms. Here, without any official connections, he was able to work freely until the 'Arabi revolt and aroused in the Egyptian youth the hope of possible liberation from European hegemony if it could absorb the material culture and scientific methods of the West for the purpose of defending Islam as a more advanced religion. After the British occupation he was exiled to India, but in 1883 could go to Paris, where together with his disciple Muhammad 'Abduh he published a weekly newspaper, *al-'Urwa al-Wuthqa*, which, though short-lived, was all the more influential. His subsequent fortunes will be encountered later on in the history of Persia. In 1885 his disciple Muhammad 'Abduh returned first to Beirut and in 1888 to his native Egypt, where his countrymen greeted him as the apostle of their liberation. He began his official career as qadi in the people's courts, and in 1899 was promoted to become mufti of Egypt. Up to his death on July 11, 1905, he exerted a profound influence on the reform of law, as well as of instruction at the venerable University of al-Azhar. He founded the modernist movement in Islam with the purpose of going back to the ideas of its founder in an attempt to purify them of all later accretions and so demonstrate their vitality even in an Oriental world completely transformed by the civilization of the West. His ideas have continued to dominate Egyptian religious life down to the present day.*

3. *North Africa*

Tripolis, Tunisia, and Algeria, ever since the Osmanli conquest in the sixteenth century, had been the seats of provincial governors with the titles of pasha, dey, and bey, who were even more independent of the central government in Istanbul than the pashas in Egypt and Syria, since from the seventeenth century onward the sultan had never had at his disposal a fleet of any consequence. In the summer of 1835 Yusuf, the pasha of Tripolitania, died. He was of the Qaramanli clan in control of the country since 1711. Two kinsmen contended for the succession, one of whom was supported by French influence and the other by British, since France and Britain had both seized a foothold in the country after Bonaparte's Egyptian expedition. In this conflict both Qaramanlis appealed to the decision of the Porte, which gladly seized the opportunity of restoring its authority in this lost outpost. It sent a division of the fleet to Tripoli and appointed the French protégé governor. But when the latter went to Istanbul to be installed in his office in person, he was detained as a prisoner of the state, and in his place Muhammad Ra'uf Pasha came to Tripoli as governor. The other claimant of the throne revolted against him and confined the governor in the citadel of Tripoli, which could only be held with difficulty. It was not until the grand admiral came to their aid with a squadron in April 1836 that the Turks were again able to subdue the interior of the country. The astute Hasan Pasha, who assumed the governorship the following year, succeeded in inducing the Berbers settled in the inaccessible regions to recognize the sultan's

* Ch. C. Adams, *Islam and Modernism in Egypt*, London, 1933. [H. A. R. Gibb, *Modern Trends in Islam*, Chicago, 1947.]

power at least nominally. Under Turkish rule an Italian colony soon sprang up in the city; it has already been related how the country fell into Italian hands in 1911.

Down to the beginning of the nineteenth century the beys of Tunisia and the deys of Algeria, as well as the Qaramanlis in Tripolitania and the rulers of Morocco, had diligently pursued a career of piracy, which, being directed against the Christians, was regarded by the Muslims as a meritorious war of faith. The Christian states had never been able to unite in a common action against them but had preferred to purchase the freedom of their shipping individually by payments of tribute. Toward the end of the eighteenth century France had even entered into cordial relations with the dey of Algeria. When Bonaparte armed for his expedition to Egypt, he was aided by the dey through deliveries of grain. But no agreement could be reached concerning payment. Two Jewish firms, Bakri and Busnach (the head of which, Naftali, had controlled the country and sucked it dry since 1780, until in 1805 he was overthrown by a Janizary mutiny and murdered together with many of his fellow Jews) had negotiated the transaction, and it was not until October 28, 1819, after protracted litigation, that a sum of seven million francs was granted them. But their creditors attached this money in France, while the dey demanded direct payment for his protégés. Consequently he had French ships stopped at sea and created difficulties for French commercial houses in his domain. His wrath was directed particularly at the consul Deval, whom he considered the real author of the procrastinations. On the morning of the Bayram festival, April 30, 1820, at a reception of the diplomatic corps, he lost control of himself, struck him with a cane, and had him shown out. When he refused to give satisfaction for this, France had the coasts of Algeria blockaded for two years. Since the government was trying to avoid war, it showed a mildness in its negotiations with the dey which the latter interpreted as weakness. In July 1829 another incident took place. The commander of the ship *La Provence* had been vainly negotiating in Algeria, and while leaving the harbor was fired on by one of the forts. France could not allow this new insult to go unavenged. On May 25, 1830, the war minister himself, de Bourmont, set out from Marseilles with six hundred sailing vessels and seven small steamers to transport an army of thirty thousand men over to Africa. On June 14 the French landed off Algiers, and four weeks later the dey had to capitulate. Bourmont then had Oran and Bône occupied from the sea, and pressed forward on land as far as Blida at the foot of the Lesser Atlas. Meanwhile the July revolution had broken out in Paris, and he was replaced by General Clauzel. The latter landed in Algeria on September 2 and at once conceived the plan of colonizing the country. By October he had already established the first model farm. He offered the province of Constantine to the bey of Tunisia, laying claim on behalf of France only to the Matijah, the fertile plain of Algeria. But his arbitrary action created irritation in Paris, and by the beginning of the following year he was recalled. His successors in command mostly dissipated their energy in petty skirmishes with Arabs and Berbers. In small-spirited fear of Britain the government was already on the verge of relinquishing the colony.

Meanwhile complete anarchy prevailed in the province of Oran. A young adventurer took advantage of this. 'Abd-al-Qadir was the son of a *murabit* (marabout), a holy ascetic, and as a young man had made the pilgrimage to Mecca twice. But since he was clever and courageous as well as pious, the tribes Hashim and Amir, weary of the perpetual strife, placed themselves under his command in spite of his youth—he was only twenty-two years old. In a short time he succeeded in driving the other chieftains from the field; then he assumed the title of "Commander of the Believers" and preached a holy war against the French. General Desmichel, in command of Oran, entered into negotiations with him, but the General's successor, Trézel, underestimated his power and with inadequate combat forces undertook an expedition into the interior. On July 26, 1835, he suffered a bloody defeat along the Macta, and from then on 'Abd-al-Qadir was regarded throughout North Africa as the savior of Islam.

In this emergency the French government again appointed Clauzel governor-general, in August 1835. He succeeded in driving 'Abd-al-Qadir from his capital at Mascara and in relieving the Turks besieged by the latter's troops in Tlemsen. Since Paris balked at the expenses of a major expedition, he was supposed to content himself with the conquest of Constantine. A youthful pretender promised him support against its ruling bey, who had procured himself the title of pasha from the Porte but was detested by his subjects for his extortions. Clauzel thought he could seize the country with seven thousand men, but in November, after tenacious fighting, had to retire, his mission unaccomplished. Because of this failure he was replaced in February 1837 by General Damrémont.

Meanwhile General Bugeaud had carried on a successful campaign against 'Abd-al-Qadir, who repeatedly upset the French positions in the west. But since the government first wanted to wipe out the disgrace at Constantine, Bugeaud had to conclude a very unfavorable peace treaty with 'Abd-al-Qadir on May 31 at the Tafnah River, giving back not only Mascara but almost the entire province of Oran and a substantial portion of the province of Algeria. 'Abd-al-Qadir, however, extended his authority beyond this eastward as well, by installing governors in Majjanah, Ziban, and Laghwat. He also advanced in the Sahara, and in November 1838, after a siege lasting five months, broke into the fortress of a murabit, Muhammad Tijani, who, depending on his prestige among the Berbers, had opposed him. He attempted to secure his rule primarily by training his troops on the European pattern.

Toward the end of September 1837 Damrémont set out with twelve thousand men against Constantine. On October 6 the bombardment of the city began; Damrémont wanted to begin the frontal assault six days later. During the preparations he was killed, and Vallée assumed command. After bloody battles which continued into the streets of the city, the *qasbah*, the fortress dominating the city, surrendered on October 13. After this victory the occupation of the country made rapid advances. Philippeville was built as a harbor for the newly acquired province. Blida was conquered from the Algiers base, and in October 1839 the troops of Algiers and Constantine were able to join at Bouira by way of the Atlas.

'Abd-al-Qadir considered these French advances an infraction of the Treaty of Tafnah; he proclaimed the holy war in Médéa, and his governor ibn-Salim attacked Matijah. For a moment weakly garrisoned Algiers itself was in danger, but then Vallée defeated 'Abd-al-Qadir at Shiffa and on May 18, 1840 occupied Médéa.

Toward the end of the year Bugeaud, the best of the French military men, was appointed governor-general of Algeria. In the spring of 1841 he opened the campaign from Médéa and on May 4 won a brilliant victory against 'Abd-al-Qadir. Then he returned to the coast, pressed from Mustaghanim into the interior again, and on May 18 conquered Taghdemt, 'Abd-al-Qadir's new capital, and from his Mascara base destroyed the castle of 'Abd-al-Qadir's father, where the Emir himself had often sought rest, and which had once been a dangerous center of Muslim fanaticism.

In the spring of 1842 Bugeaud occupied Tlemsen, and on February 9 the Emir lost his last fortified city, Sebdu. After that he roved about the country with his camp, which was about fifty thousand strong, and was harried by the French. On May 16 the Duc d'Aumale succeeded in catching up with him after strenuous forced marches and in overpowering the completely surprised enemy. Four thousand men, the Emir's treasury, and the families of a number of his most aristocratic followers fell into the hands of the French. But 'Abd-al-Qadir, valiantly defended by his bodyguard, escaped from his pursuers this time also and stepped into Moroccan territory. After Bugeaud had negotiated in vain with the Moroccans for his extradition, he himself crossed the border. At the same time a French squadron appeared off the Moroccan coast, threatening Tangier and Mogador. On August 14 a battle took place along the Isly, a tributary of the Tafnah, with the Moroccan army, 65,000 strong, under the Sultan's son. Although Bugeaud only had 6,000 men available, he succeeded in defeating these troops, which were poorly armed and completely undisciplined. Now the Sultan was prepared for peace. But he did not hand over 'Abd-al-Qadir. Even with the best of intentions he would scarcely have been capable of doing so, since the Berber tribes along the border had hardly any respect for his authority. The religious brotherhoods, in particular the Derkawa, fanned the flame of their fanaticism, so that they continued the guerrilla warfare against the French. In the spring of 1845 a new religious champion appeared on the scene, the murabit Bu Ma'zah, "the Man with the Goat," and led the Berber tribe of the Dahrah against the French.

When 'Abd-al-Qadir attacked Algeria again, Bugeaud had him hunted by eighteen flying columns throughout the autumn and winter of 1845-46 without laying him by the heels. After he had been defeated a couple of times in the spring, he retired again to Moroccan soil. But the Sultan finally was induced by the persistent representations of the French government to send out an army against him and expel him. On December 21 Abd-al-Qadir crossed the border river of the Muluyah under Moroccan fire, was soon encircled by the French troops, and on the twenty-third of the same month surrendered, after being promised that he would be removed to Acre or Alexandria, since he wanted to make the pilgrimage once again. But instead he was taken to Toulon and held captive in Amboise. Napoleon III gave him his freedom on December 2, 1852. He first settled down in Brusa, and after the earthquake of 1855 in Istanbul, and then in Damascus. It has already been related how he, together with his countrymen who had accompanied him into exile, rescued numerous Christians there in 1860 from massacre by the Druzes. He died there in 1883.

In Algeria, the French still had to struggle for a long time against the turbulent Berbers in the east of the province. In 1857 a prophetess, Lallah Fatmah, emerged in the Yenni tribe, whom all the surrounding tribes joined. Governor-General Randon himself had to march against her with thirty thousand men, and only after a number of bloody battles took the prophetess captive and then definitely subdued the Kabyle country.

In the south of the province the French had installed a native clan, the Uled Sidi Shaykh, as governors with far-reaching powers. In February 1864 a representative of this dynasty, Si Sliman, took offense at the conduct of some French officers and was provoked by his uncle Si Lala into an uprising. The commander-in-chief, Beauprêtre, at once hurried up from Tiaret but was betrayed by his native cavalry and hewed down together with his infantry company, though while in his death throes he was still able at any rate to shoot down Si Sliman, who was standing before him. This, however, did not bring the revolt to an end; Si Sliman's brother Muhammad and the murabit Si Lazrag assumed command. Since Napoleon III, confident of the security of the country, had sent the veteran occupation troops to Mexico and Indo-China, warfare in the south still dragged on for a long time. Although by the winter of 1864-65 the two leaders had already been killed, their adherents in the inaccessible mountains did not lay down their arms, and whenever pursued, found refuge on Moroccan soil. Although General Wimpfen punished their allies, in 1870 the rebels kept retiring farther and farther into the Sahara; it was impossible to subdue them decisively until 1884.

France's defeats in the war against Germany and the transition to a republican form of government in 1871 aroused in Algeria new hopes of regaining freedom. In particular the Muslims regarded as a token of weakness the decree of October 24, 1871, that naturalized all the Jews. Even at the beginning of the year disturbances took place at the conscription of the Spahis, particularly along the Tunisian border. The movement found an energetic leader in the *bash agha* of the Majjanah, Muqrani, at whose side again there were two murabits. He belonged to one of the wealthiest and most aristocratic of the families in the province of Constantine and had been showered with honors by the government for the loyalty he had formerly shown it. But when the civil administration was established, he resigned, since, as he said, he would never obey a Jew. Political discontent was supplemented in his case by another and personal motive. During a famine in 1867 he had incurred great debts in order to support his countrymen, as demanded by his Arab sense of honor, and the government had not made good its promise to recompense him. In the middle of March he called together a great tribal council and then declared war on the commander of the nearest military station. On April 8 he was joined by the master of the Rahmaniyah order, the shaykh al-Haddad, who was urged on by his ambitious son al-'Aziz. In short time all Kabylia from the sea to the Sahara had taken the field, and the rebels were already ranging about in the neighborhood of Algiers. Muqrani was killed on May 6 in an engagement in the wadi Sufla near Aumale. His place was taken by his brother Bu Mazraq, who in numerous battles was pushed back farther and farther south and on January 20, 1872, taken captive near Rouissat. After the rebellion had finally been suppressed, the Kabyles had to pay for the heavy costs of the war; their autonomous communal administration was abolished, and they had to relinquish no less than 453,000 hectares of land for settlement by French colonists. This, apart from a few unimportant uprisings, marked the extinction of the last Algerian movement of emancipation. The country was increasingly overrun by European immigrants, and its subsequent history belongs to that of the French colonial empire.

In Tunisia the bey had still maintained his independence, but had so flagrantly neglected his administrative obligations that toward the end of the seventies a third of the fertile country lay completely fallow. In his capital there dwelt numerous Italians, and their mother country had long since entertained the hope of here being able to follow France's example. But while no decision could be reached in Rome for fear of international complications, France intervened at the first opportunity to secure for herself this country too. In 1881, after a dispute with a French trading company, the bey was disarmed in his capital by a body of troops which had attacked

Tunisia under the pretext of punishing a Bedouin tribe for an encroachment across the frontier. Although he was allowed to remain on the throne in name, he was divested of any real power.

From 1544 on, Morocco had been ruled by an 'Alid dynasty, the sharifs, initially by the Sa'did line, which was succeeded in 1664 by the house of the Hasani Filali, who still rule in name. The incumbent representative bears the title of khalifah and commander of the faithful. Inasmuch as they based their rule on the legitimate principle of their descent from the Prophet, it would actually be appropriate to call them Shi'ites, but the Moroccan 'Alids have never had anything to do with the course of religious evolution embarked on by the Shi'ah in the East, in South Arabia, and particularly in Persia. Like North Africa as a whole, Morocco is also dominated by the strictly orthodox Sunnite school of Malik.

The house of Sa'd had come to power when the Portuguese were endeavoring to establish themselves in southern Morocco and the last Marinids were incapable of warding off their attacks. In 1511 the sharif of Tagmadaret assumed command of the warriors of the faith, and his son Muhammad, after forcing back the foreigners in 1554, was able to defeat the Turks of Algeria, with whose help the Marinids were hoping to win back their kingdom, and to impose his rule on the entire country. His son and fifth successor, Ahmad I, al-Mansur (1578-1610), extended the power of his house deep into the Sahara, conquered Timbuktu, and destroyed the kingdom of the Askia of Gao. In the midst of these external successes, which enabled him to maintain a brilliant court at Marrakush, he neglected the internal development of his domains. He contented himself with using his troops, of the southern Berber tribes and the Arabs of Tlemsen and Ujdah, whom he settled in the country around Fez, for the collection of taxes for the *makhzin*, the exchequer, instead of making his authority effective in the interior; and under his weak successors Fez made itself independent. The Andalusians, the Moors who had been driven out of Spain and were settled in Rabat and Sale, and who had become wealthy through their piracy at sea, lived in aristocratic city republics like those in their former homeland. A number of murabits also exercised temporal power over their followers in their *zawiyah*s, or monastic colonies. After the last Sa'did was assassinated in 1660, the head of the al-Hasani sharifian clan in Tafilelt, ar-Rashid, emerged from among them and gradually eliminated the petty rulers. His brother and successor Isma'il (1672-1729) created a powerful corps of Negro slaves, who were bound by oath to the canonical traditionary work of Bukhari and consequently were known as ʿAbid al-Bukhari, or Buakher. With them he held the Berber tribes in check and attempted to clean out the country of the foreign intruders who had taken advantage of the weakness of the Saʿdids. For almost two centuries (1471-1661) the Portuguese had been in occupation of the most important Mediterranean harbor, at Tangier; in 1661 the infanta Catherine of Braganza brought the city as dowry to her husband, Charles II of England. In 1684, after a siege lasting six years, Ismaʿil was able to wrest the city from the English. He drove the Spaniards from their bases along the Atlantic Ocean; Ceuta alone, which in 1580 had been won by Philip II at the time of his annexation of Portugal and which had remained in the possession of Spain even after the restoration of the Portuguese kingdom, defended itself for twenty-seven years (1693-1720) against the besieging troops of Ismaʿil, although the mother country, tied down by the Spanish War of Succession, was scarcely concerned for the valiant garrison. After Ismaʿil's death Morocco again fell into anarchy, in which the Negro troops used their power to raise up rulers and overthrow them. It was Ismaʿil's grandson Muhammad I (1757-1792) who first restored order and also attempted to curb the sea piracy of his subjects by concluding commercial treaties with the European powers, which, however, failed to bring his country the benefits hoped for. Under his successors the defects of the government became more and more blatant; they sought to protect themselves by the most rigid sealing off of the country against the pressure of the Europeans, who were allowed only diplomatic representation in Tangier.

Moroccan constitutional law made an express distinction between Blad al-Makhzin, the subjugated territory which paid taxes and provided troops, and Blad as-Saiba, the independent territory, which was about four or five times as large. In the Atlas only a vanishingly small area was part of the Blad al-Makhzin. Only a few tribes in the west, in the seaboard regions, were really subjugated; the others, though still nominally acknowledging the Sultan's authority, paid no taxes, merely sending gifts from time to time to Marrakush. A number of tribes in the inaccessible portions of the Atlas may not even have known of the existence of a sultan. The great Berber chieftains regarded themselves as just as powerful as the sultan, in whom they merely saw the leader of a remote and hostile tribe. In

1889, for instance, the Lakhmas tribe even refused to provide straw for the ten-thousand-man army of the sultan in their district, and that same year the same tribe simply barred passage through their territory to the Italian ambassador who was supposed to be bringing the sultan his credentials. In such cases the sultan had recourse to ordering a neighboring tribe against the recalcitrant one by granting it permission to "eat" the tribe, as it was called by a technical expression in Moroccan affairs. But this means was also not always effective, and many small tribes, for instance the Mezgelda, had defied the sultan for years on end. As a rule he had to enter into negotiations with the tribe, and his sovereign rights seldom went further than the granting of a nominal confirmation for the chieftain the tribe elected. It was always his most important concern to be on good terms with the murabits, who had great influence on the Berbers, and during their visits he never dared omit presenting them with opulent gifts.

There was no question of organized government in the Blad al-Makhzin either. The sultan's civil power was exercised by *qa'id*s, who in the major cities of Morocco, Fez, Rabat, and Meknes bore the title of pasha. Their primary duty was the collection of the taxes, secondly the maintenance of public order and the execution of any judicial sentences. According to ancient Oriental custom they received no salary, but on the contrary had to purchase their office. Consequently they were compelled to extort, in addition to the legal taxes and their revenues, the by-no-means-slight purchase price. Sometimes the sultan was in the same situation as the caliphs of Baghdad so often before him: in a territory previously subjected to his rule he had to confirm as qa'id an upstart who might often have begun his career as a highwayman, in order to preserve at least the semblance of his prestige.

The qa'ids provided the sultan with the *mkhazniyah*, mostly mounted feudal levies, part of whom formed his bodyguard in the residence, and part of whom, scattered throughout the country in the qasbahs at the exits of the Atlas valleys, maintained public security. To supplement these troops the sultans recruited a foot-soldiery (*'askar*) in all the major cities, which also received a certain amount of European drilling. At the beginning of the twentieth century it was under the command of a Briton, the qa'id McLean. However, the weapons and training of the troops left a great deal to be desired.

The sultan Hasan, who had mounted the throne in 1873 filled with glittering dreams of power and riches, exhausted himself in a struggle against conditions in his domain, which the limited power at his disposal made it impossible to alter, although he was able to extend the Blad al-Makhzin further southward and even make another advance into the Sahara. In 1894, when he died on a military expedition against a mutinous Berber tribe, he left behind a minor son, 'Abd-al-'Aziz, born to him by a Circassian slave woman, and he had designated this son as successor to the throne by relegating an older brother to the background. His most influential counselor, Si Ahmad ibn-Muhammad, succeeded in concealing his master's death until he had taken the dead body to Rabat, the residence of the successor to the throne. There he had the latter proclaimed caliph, and usurped the guardianship himself. After the death of his wazir in 1900 the young Sultan trifled away the sympathy of his subjects by a preference for the accomplishments of European civilization and by increasing taxes. Rebels against him arose everywhere in the country; Ruqi 'Umar Zarhuni of Taza in particular, known as Bu Hamarah, "the Donkey Rider" (the ancient Oriental designation for the redeemer-ruler) for a long time gave his regime a great deal of trouble, until he was captured in 1909 and executed.

France attempted to exploit this weakness of Morocco in order to expand her colonial territories westward. In 1904, after recognizing Britain's position in Egypt and granting Spain a more extended zone of influence for her old possessions in the north, France gained their approval of her aims. The French had already laid before the Sultan a plan for administrative reform to be put into effect with their assistance, when on March 31, 1905, Kaiser Wilhelm II, urged by his counselors who had been won over to the support of the quite indefinite economic interests of the Mannesmann brothers in the Moroccan mines, landed in Tangier on a trip through the Mediterranean and in a speech interceded on behalf of the independence of the Sultan; whereupon 'Abd-al-'Aziz secured the convocation of an international conference for the study of the Moroccan question. At the conference in Algeciras (January 15 to April 7, 1906) the sovereignty of the Sultan was recognized and the founding of an international harbor police and a state bank with European capital decided on.

Since even with this help 'Abd-al-'Aziz was unable to restore order and had to look on at the French occupation of Ujdah and Casablanca in 1907, his brother 'Abd-al-Hafiz, sustained by the general disaffection in the country, revolted against him and had him deposed by the fuqaha. In a short time he subdued the entire country and was also recognized by Spain and France after he had concurred in the Algeciras conventions. But Hafiz was no more equal to the difficult situation than his brother, and in 1911, when he was encircled in Fez by rebels, he even had to appeal to France for aid. This sealed the fate of the country, although Germany still attempted to secure a number of its economic claims by the "panther leap" (sending the gunboat *Panther*) to Agadir, after Spain had also extended its territory by the occupation of Larache and al-Qasr. However, Germany also eventually recognized the French protectorate, which was definitively regulated by a treaty with the Sultan on November 4, 1912. Hafiz's place was taken by Yusuf, and after his death in 1927 by his son Muhammad III. Marshal Lyautey, by warfare against still-recalcitrant tribes, restored the prestige of the government, and the Sultan was only its titular head. During the First World War, France maintained the position she had won, and in 1921-1924 she extended her rule over the entire country in exhausting guerrilla warfare. Only one more champion of Moroccan freedom arose, in the person of Abd-el-Krim, whose family had long been resident in the Rif in Ajdir, on the bay of Alhucemas. To obtain freedom for those of his tribal kinsmen not yet subjugated by Spain, in 1921, with a small body of men, which, however, rapidly grew and which was eventually joined by nearly all the tribes of northern Morocco, he took the field against the Spaniards. After inflicting heavy losses on them he also attacked the French zone, and was already menacing Fez when Spain and France united for a common action, to which Abd-el-Krim succumbed in the spring of 1926; he was sent into exile, first to Marseille then to Mauritius.* After that, Spain also consolidated its power in Morocco, whose courageous fighters were of great value in helping Franco's army conquer the mother country.

Intellectual life in all of North Africa has remained down to the present day on a thoroughly medieval level. Moroccan scholars have

* Abd-el-Krim, *Memoiren, mein Krieg gegen Spanien und Frankreich*, (adapted by J. Roger-Mathieu, editor of *Le Matin*), Dresden, 1927. His exploits caused a sensation throughout the Islamic world; in Cairo in 1925 no fewer than four accounts by Arabic authors appeared; cf. also A. Sanchez Perez, *La acción decisiva contra Abdelkrim*, Madrid, 1931.

continued the tradition-bound scientific labors of their ancestors in the old style, writing commentaries for canonical textbooks and comprehensive biographies. The sultan Hafiz himself took a lively part in these studies; he even developed into an author and had classical works printed at his own expense. In Algeria and Tunisia the Arabs, in spite of the elementary education provided by the French, also failed to attain anything higher intellectually. Consequently the Muslims of North Africa were not able to take up the intellectual struggle against alien rule until much later, although a reform party and a constitution party were founded in Tunisia, whose demands occasionally proved an annoyance to the protectorate regime, and after the newly installed bey Muhammad al-Habib began his rule on July 10, 1922, a few inconsequential modifications were effected in the government. Equally hopeless seemed the prospects of the ambitions for reform of educated Algerians under their leader, the physician Dr. Ibn (Ben) Jallul, and of the Moroccans under 'Allal al-Fasi, whom the French deported to Gabun in French Senegal at the beginning of 1938.

4. *The Sudan*

South of the Sahara, from the Senegal to the upper Nile valley, in the regions inhabited by Negroes, so-called Hamites of Mediterranean race, Nilotes, and Nubians, Islam had already been spread in the west by the Almoravids. As early as the eleventh century the princes of Ghanah, and their vassals the rulers of the Takrur (present-day Tukulor), as well as the king of Malli on the upper Niger, had already been converted to the religion of their overlords. In the thirteenth century Timbuktu was the center of Islamic culture, which was not strengthened but rather shattered by a Moroccan onslaught in 1591. It was not until the eighteenth century that Muslim propaganda received a new impetus, after the Takrur established a new theocratic regime in Futa-Jallon in 1720. In 1776 they subjugated the pagan Ful and imposed Islam on them. The Takrur 'Uthman Danfojo converted the Hausa and in 1802 founded the Sokoto state. His tribal kinsman 'Umar, while on the Meccan pilgrimage, had joined the warriors' order Tijaniyah, which was very influential in Morocco, and had been appanaged by their grand master with the Sudan. From 1838 on he subdued the major portion of the Sudan, which at his death in 1864 recognized Islam as the state religion. After 1890 his successors succumbed to the French colonists.

In the central Sudan, along Lake Chad, Islam was introduced into Kanem as early as the eleventh century, but did not gain a firm foothold until the sixteenth century in Bornu and Bagirmi and the seventeenth century in Wada'i.*

In the eastern Sudan the Nubians, who had been Christians down to the seventh century, were converted to Islam quite early by way of Egypt. The founder of a new dynasty, Sulayman, introduced Islam into Darfur in the sixteenth century; one of his successors subdued Kordofan in the eighteenth century. Still, Islam did not make any major advances until the Egyptian conquest in the nineteenth century. But alien rule simultaneously inflamed religious fanaticism, which found a leader in the person of the famous Mahdi.

Muhammad ibn-'Abdallah was born around the middle of the last century in the province of Dongola as the son of a poor schoolmaster, whose family, however, laid claim to descent from the Prophet. After the completion of his theological studies he entered the dervish order Samaniyah and in 1870 settled on the Abba isle in the White Nile, to devote himself to religious exercises in a cave along the river. He fell out with his teacher after the latter had absolved his order from the interdiction of gambling and dancing at the festivals of his sons' circumcision, and because he found fault with the master on this account he was expelled from the society. He then rejected any reconciliation. His severity was generally approved throughout the country, and he himself was soon able to gather around him many disciples, to whom in a number of writings he appealed to counteract the religious decay breaking in, since no help was to be expected from the government. Thus the idea must gradually have ripened within him that he was called to higher things. Like many another reformer in the past history of Islam, he promised the believers by the Prophet, his ancestor, that as the Mahdi he was called to fill the world with righteousness.

* See D. Westermann, *Der Islam in West und Zentralsudan*, *Die Welt des Islams*, I, 1913, 85-108; P. C. Meyer, *Erforschungsgeschichte und Staatenbildung des Westsudan*, *Petermanns Mitteilungen*, *Ergänzungsband* XXVI, Gotha, 1898; A. Brass, *Eine neue Quelle zur Geschichte des Fullreiches Sokoto*, *Der Islam* X (1920), 1-73.

He was fortified in this belief by his friend 'Abdallah ibn-Muhammad al-Faqih, later khalifah, of the Arab tribe Ta'asha Baggara in the southwest of Darfur. 'Abdallah impelled him to make a journey to Kordofan, since the stronger and more courageous tribes in the west appeared to be more easily won over for an uprising. On this journey Muhammad came into contact with all the secular and religious leaders and could convince himself of the disaffection prevailing throughout the country. There was dissatisfaction with the venality of the Egyptian authorities, and with the unfair distribution and violent collection of the very high taxes. In addition the Egyptian government, under the pressure of its British guardian, had proclaimed the abolition of slavery and so disturbed the entire economic life.

The Egyptian government's attention was gradually attracted to him, particularly since his former teacher cast suspicion on him repeatedly. In July 1881 Re'uf Pasha, the governor-general of the Sudan, sent a summons to Muhammad in Abba to come to Khartum and vindicate himself. But the Mahdi cast aside this presumptuous proposal; he now openly gave himself out as master of the country and preached the Holy War against the infidels, among whom he naturally also included the Muslims who did not acknowledge his mission. Re'uf underestimated his power and thought he could finish him off with two hundred men with guns in their hands. On the evening of August 11 these troops arrived at Abba island in a steamer. The huts were encircled and fired on. But the Mahdi and his followers, who still had no firearms, were lying in an ambush and did not break out of the tall grass until darkness. The Egyptian troops were almost all wiped out; only a few reached the steamer by swimming. In spite of this victory the Mahdi made up his mind to migrate into Kordofan in order to escape the threatening proximity of Khartum. He advanced unopposed as far as Jabal Jadir, where he annihilated troops sent out against him by the *mudir* of Fashoda. In May 1882 the government sent out after him an army of six thousand men. These veteran troops, who had only just subdued Darfur, had so poor an opinion of the dervishes that they neglected the precautionary measure customary in the Sudan of protecting their night encampment by an entanglement of thorns. They were attacked at night and routed.

This victory brought the Mahdi innumerable new adherents,

whose hearts he won, quite in the manner of the Prophet, by means of the rich booty. In the beginning of September he appeared before 'Ubayd. The merchants of the city had already negotiated with him, but the Egyptian garrison prepared for battle. After a first assault had been beaten back, the Mahdi encircled the city, and on January 18, 1833, it had to capitulate. He now made 'Ubayd his residence. Believers from the Sudan streamed there to see the Saint of God. Clad only in a jubbah and linen trousers, with a cord or a cotton cloth around his hips, before his followers he was humble in appearance and bearing. But in the interior of his house he had long since begun yielding to good living. Like the Prophet, he was filled with a strong passion for women, and like him accustomed to selecting from the spoils the most beautiful girls for himself.

His rule was organized as simply as possible. The due tithes, a fifth of the booty, and the property of anyone guilty of high treason, theft, partaking of spirituous drinks, or of tobacco smoking, flowed into the state exchequer in accordance with Muhammad's law. The casting of any doubt on the Mahdi's mission was punished by confiscation of property or by death. The study of the theology and jurisprudence hitherto authoritative was prohibited and all relevant books burned. Instead he recommended a diligent reading of the Qur'an and a few dicta of the Prophet, but proscribed their public discussion.

Egypt had meanwhile been occupied by Britain, and now Hicks Pasha was sent to the Sudan with ten thousand Egyptian troops. The advance of the army with its six thousand camels slowed down because of dissatisfaction with British rule. The Mahdi could arm for its reception in tranquillity. On November 3, 1883, he advanced against the Egyptians at Birket, about thirty-seven miles southeast of 'Ubayd. His first assault on their encampment was repulsed, but the following morning he attacked the army on the march and completely destroyed it.

After this victory the whole of the Sudan lay at the Mahdi's feet, and the Europeans and Egyptians settled in the major cities saved themselves by precipitous flight. In December 1883 Slatin Pasha, a former Austrian officer, who was the commandant of Dara, the capital of Darfur, surrendered, after having fought in vain against the Mahdi's adherents for a year. The British government was already prepared to relinquish the Sudan entirely and sent out

General Gordon, who had subdued the Taiping rebellion in China, to Khartum in order to escort the Europeans still living there back to Egypt. Gordon had formerly been governor-general of the Sudan; he thought he enjoyed special popularity there and so could maintain British-Egyptian rule against his orders; but his prestige had suffered considerably because of his struggle against the slave trade. He arrived in Khartum on February 18 and immediately sent a communication to the Mahdi in which he offered to recognize him as ruler of Kordofan, allow the free resumption of the slave trade, and initiate commercial relations with him if he would release his captives. The Mahdi answered him with the demand that he surrender, and on August 22 set out against Khartum and attracted combat forces from all sides as he slowly advanced. In October he invested the city; at first, however, the siege made little progress, since the Mahdists were no match for artillery. Since Gordon had omitted to relieve the city of noncombatants, supplies soon became critical. Although toward the end of 1884 a British army advanced up the Nile and defeated the Mahdi's outposts at Matamah, Fort Umm Durman surrendered on January 15, 1885, and on the night of January 25-26 the Mahdi, at the head of his followers, stormed the city. Gordon was killed in his palace.

For the time being the British had to leave the Sudan to its own devices. The Mahdi transferred his residence to Khartum, and here he stood at the zenith of his power. To guard his followers, who like him all had to wear the dervish tunic, against any influence inimical to his prestige, he sealed off his entire domain round about and forbade the pilgrimage to Mecca. A happy fate preserved him from experiencing in person the decline of his power. In the middle of June 1885 he fell ill of typhus and a week later died.

While still on his deathbed the Mahdi had once more expressly confirmed as his successor under the by-name of Abu Bakr the caliph 'Abdallah, who had been his right hand even during his lifetime. To him the faithful then swore allegiance without protest. He consolidated his power by relieving of their offices the other two caliphs appointed by the Mahdi. The emir 'Abd-al-Karim, who was besieging the Egyptian garrison in Kassala, was recalled because of some incautious remarks concerning the Caliph's authority, and had to deliver over the Negro troops personally devoted to him. 'Abdallah transferred his residence to Umm Durman, the Khartum fort on the left bank of the Nile which had first fallen into the hands of the Mahdists.

Meanwhile Kassala had fallen, and now the Egyptian troops also evacuated the other fortified points along the Abyssinian border. The Caliph appointed an emir in Gallabat, who soon advanced for an attack on Abyssinia; but during an incursion into the province of Amhara he was badly beaten by the governor, Ras Adal. To avenge this setback the Caliph sent out a great army of about sixty thousand men to Abyssinia. Ras Adal first advanced against him in the plain Debra-Sin and was crushingly defeated, whereupon the Mahdists marched against the then capital of Abyssinia, Gondar, burned it, since it had been abandoned by its inhabitants, and returned to Gallabat.

In the beginning of 1889 Emperor John of Abyssinia decided to avenge this disgrace and assembled his entire army. With two army divisions, of men from Tigré, his own tribe, and those of Amhara, he marched on Gallabat. On the very first day of the siege the Amharas were able to penetrate into the weakly fortified settlement. Jealous of this success, the Emperor had himself borne among his own warriors on his throne in order to spur them on. He was wounded and died the same evening, March 9, 1889. Bereft of their leader, the Abyssinians withdrew the same night, since a change of regime seldom passed off among them without disturbances. The Mahdists set out in pursuit and forced them to abandon their camp while in flight.

The equatorial province, hitherto held for Egypt by Emin Pasha (Dr. Schnitzler) had been occupied by the Mahdists in the summer of 1888, after Emin Pasha had removed to the east coast together with Stanley.

After these victories the Caliph decided to embark on the conquest of Egypt, already planned by the Mahdi. In May 1889 he sent out an army under 'Abd-ar-Rahman an-Nujumi to the north with the order to circumvent Wadi Halfa, take Aswan, and there await further orders. But even the garrison of Wadi Halfa inflicted heavy losses on him while on the march. At Toski the commander-in-chief of the Egyptian army advanced against him and completely destroyed his army. This year, 1889, brought a further misfortune; a famine broke out in the Sudan against which the Caliph was powerless, since, being surrounded on all sides by enemies, he could procure no supplies.

A certain compensation was offered in 1890 by the subjugation of the Shilluk, one of the bravest Negro tribes in the Sudan; they were attacked by water in their capital at Fashoda and could not hold for long against the Mahdists armed with machine guns.

The arbitrary regime of the Caliph embittered the Mahdi's kinsmen in particular, whose share in the power he had curtailed. Among the Mahdi's widows his chief wife in particular, whom he had named 'Aishah, Mother of the Believers, after the precedent of the Prophet, agitated against the Caliph, as her namesake 'Aishah had once agitated against the caliph 'Ali. The Caliph received timely notice of a conspiracy of the sharifs, as the Mahdi's kinsmen were called after those of the Prophet, through his informants. When they had assembled and were on the point of attacking him, he succeeded in encircling them, but spared them out of consideration for the believers and made them a number of concessions. After they had laid down their arms, trusting to this, he instituted a judicial process against them and banished them to Fashoda.

On the Abyssinian border the Mahdi state was threatened by the Italians, who had occupied Massaua after the withdrawal of the Egyptians and from there pushed on into the hinterland. There, they came into contact, in November 1893, with an army of the Caliph about ten thousand men strong, which was in the midst of a marauding expedition against the Arabs of the eastern Sudan, and defeated it. In the spring of 1894 they attacked Kassala. The Mahdist garrison, which was discontented with its leader, refused to fight against them and retired to Goss-Rajab. But Emperor Menelik of Abyssinia prevented a further advance of the Italians. The bloody defeat he inflicted on them at Adowa on March 1, 1896, also eliminated any further danger from this quarter for the Mahdists.

Meanwhile, however, the storm which was to put an end to their state was already gathering in the north. In the autumn of 1896 the sirdar Kitchener, the commander-in-chief of the Egyptian army, was ordered to undertake a campaign into the Sudan; and in a bloody battle at Umm Durman, in which the Caliph himself was killed, he shattered the Mahdi's empire. But this failed to bring about the extinction of his ideas. As late as July 1928 the British governor-general of the Sudan had to justify the necessity of holding a strong air force there by a reference to the danger, still threatening, though latent, of a new outbreak of Mahdism.*

* Lord Lloyd, *Egypt since Cromer*, II, London, 1934, p. 346.

Toward the end of the nineties a related movement arose among the Somali of the eastern horn of Africa.* Muhammad ibn-'Abdallah Hasan of the Ogaden tribe had made the pilgrimage in 1895, at the age of about thirty-five, and in Mecca had been recruited by Muhammad ibn-Salih, a disciple of the Sudanese mystic Ibrahim ar-Rashidi, for the dervish order Salihiyah founded by him, which had branched off from the Ahmadiyah. After returning home he had settled among the Dulbahanta tribe and worked among the Muslims along his teacher's lines on behalf of a more profound piety. He soon acquired so much influence among this tribe, just as among his own kinsmen of the Ogaden, that even the British administration of Berbera made use of him in order to smooth over fallings-out among the nomads. But in 1899 he put forth the claim of being Mahdi, and thereafter "the Mad Mullah," as the British called him, for almost two decades gave them, as well as the Italians and Abyssinians, a great deal of trouble with his miltary expeditions. Although the British had defeated his bands more than once, in 1905 both colonial powers were ready to leave him the Italian section of the Nugal valley as an independent dominion. But by 1908 he had already resumed his marauding expeditions against the Italian and British colonies. During the First World War the Italians succeeded in damming up his power by treaties with the tribal chiefs in northern Somaliland who were hostile to him. But it was not until the beginning of 1920 that Great Britain decided to proceed energetically against him; it was an easy matter for her air force to destroy his positions; pursued by the British camel riders and their Somali allies, he fled to his tribe, the Ogaden, and on November 23, 1920, died there. His attempt to unite his people on a religious foundation beyond all tribal rivalries, by attempting to rule only through dervishes as the Mahdi had done in the Sudan, had already been shattered in 1905 after his teacher in Mecca, at the instigation of the British and Italians, had excommunicated him, enabling the Qadiriyah, the other order spread among the Somali, to combat him as a heretic. After that he was merely one tribal chieftain among others, who was followed by his adherents only in the hope of abundant booty.

While the Mahdi's dervishes dominated the east of the Sudan, a new power had arisen in the west on the ruins of the former Egyp-

* D. Jardina, *Il Mullah del paese dei Somali*, trad. da Mario Quercia, Rome, 1929.

tian possessions. Bahr al-Ghazal had been ruled by the Arab Zubayr Pasha as a relatively independent governor of the khedive.* Toward the end of 1874, when he was recalled to Cairo in order to answer his detractors in person, he appointed his son Sulayman as his deputy, and the latter retained the office after his father was detained. While Gordon was combating the slave trade in 1879 as governor-general of the Sudan, Sulayman joined forces against him with Harun, the deposed sultan of Darfur. The Italian Gessi Pasha succeeded in capturing him after a lengthy pursuit, and Sulayman was prepared to surrender to him, but his foster brother Rabih, an Arab from Sennar, who had formerly served his father faithfully and hitherto had shared all his trials, dissuaded him from this, and when Sulayman insisted on his decision, Rabih left the camp with a few thousand of Zubayr's best warriors. He established himself in the mountainous territory of Dar Manga and from there undertook slave hunts toward the south. After conquering the ruler of the Negro state of Kuti and repulsing an attack of the sultan of Wada'i, who was trying to hurry to the latter's aid, he received in 1884 a summons to submit to the Mahdi. He rejected this with a reference to the grand master of the Sanusi order, who had declared the Mahdi a heretic.

The Sanusiyah are a religious brotherhood whose founder, Muhammad ibn-'Ali (born at Torsh near Mustaghanim in Algeria in 1791), after a lengthy stay in Mecca, where he had already founded a highly regarded dervish monastery, settled on Jabal al-Akhdar in Tripolitania in 1834. Within only a few years he had extended his order from there throughout North Africa. In 1855 the animosity of the dominant orthodox party compelled him to transfer his headquarters to Jaghbub, two or three days' journey southeast of the Siwa oasis. He also achieved great influence on the Negro states through his missionaries. In 1859, when he died, he was succeeded in the leadership of the order by his still-youthful son, Muhammad al-Mahdi, who died in Guro in 1901. The latter removed the seat of the order to Kufra in 1895 and to Guro in 1899. His nephew and successor, Ahmad, returned to Kufra in 1902. In numerous places in the interior of Africa, along the caravan highway to Mecca among others, the Sanusiyah had monasteries where they lived as diligent agriculturists and propagated their purely theocratic ideals

* See M. Thilo, *Ez-Zber Rahmat Paschas Autobiographie, Ein Beitrag zur Geschichte des Sudans,* Bonn-Leipzig, 1921.

while rejecting the claims of the Turkish sultan to the caliphate. After the Italians occupied Tripolis, the order participated in the struggle against them; in the First World War it allied itself with Turkey and in the winter of 1915-16 attacked Egypt after conquering the important harbor of Sollum. Even after the British reoccupied the latter in February 1916, the Sanusis threatened Egypt a few more times during the summer of 1916. But then their martial energies dwindled away, although a younger brother of the shaykh Muhammad al-'Abid continued fighting against the French in the Sahara until 1918. When General Graziani decisively subdued Tripolitania after the end of the First World War, the Shaykh went to Ankara in 1921 in the hope of being able to continue working there on behalf of his ideas; but since the Turkish national state struck out along different paths, he was soon condemned to inactivity.

After an attack on the Wada'i sultanate in 1887 miscarried, Rabih turned west toward Lake Chad. In 1892 he attacked the sultan of Bagirmi and after a siege lasting seven months conquered his capital at Bugoman. Bornu, one of the oldest and largest states in the interior of Africa, whose inhabitants, however, had long since forgotten the use of arms, fell into his hands in 1893. He removed his residence to Dikoa on the southwest shore of Lake Chad, which at the beginning of the nineteenth century had been capital of Bornu for a short time.

Rabih had generally allowed the native princes in his empire, which lay between Wada'i in the north, Sokoto and the later German emirate of Adamawa in the south and southwest, and the Mahdist state in the east, to remain as his vassals, but appointed his intimates counselors and supervisors; only in a few places did he install new governors. In theory he endeavored to put into effect the Islamic constitutional law; his supreme qadi was the Sokoto prince Haiatu, who, excluded from the succession in his native country, devoted himself to study. Since the taxes of the provinces, half of which were supposed to accrue to Rabih, were inadequate for the maintenance of his army, he continued to carry on extended slave hunts, which at the same time served to keep his men in constant military practice. As a rule he disposed of his human booty in Tripolitania; but the trade routes through the Sahara, after the French conquest of Timbuktu on January 10, 1894, were rendered insecure by the Tuareg, who had retired eastward.

In consequence he sought new market outlets in the west, and in

1896 attacked the Fulbe state of Sokoto; although he won a few victories, he nevertheless relinquished the plan because of the necessity of saving his strength for a conflict with the French, who for a long time had been aiming with tenacious energy at Lake Chad for the unification of their colonies in North and West Africa.

In 1897 Gentil, a civil servant of the French Congo territory, appeared at Lake Chad and initiated negotiations with the prince of Bagirmi; as a punishment, Rabih fired his vassal's capital. In 1899 the French administrator Bretonnet advanced against him with forty-four Senegalese riflemen. With this corps of men and with the four hundred warriors of the prince of Bagirmi he thought himself able to advance against Rabih, but was defeated on July 18 and killed, together with all his men. Rabih retired to the Kuno fortress. Gentil attacked him, traveling downstream along the Shari. At the end of October a savage street battle took place in which half the French were put out of action, but Rabih himself was wounded; nevertheless the principal fort was still being held. From the north Major Lamy advanced through the Sahara to Lake Chad, installed a new sultan in Bornu, and joined forces with Gentil in the Shari delta. A decisive battle took place on April 22, which ended in a dearly won victory for the French. Rabih himself was killed, his capital at Dikoa being occupied on May 1. Although his son Fadlallah, who had at first fled to British territory along the Benueh, succeeded in retaking Dikoa, soon afterward he was defeated and killed. The treaties of November 15, 1893, and March 15, 1894, divided the regions around Lake Chad between France, Britain, and Germany. On July 10, 1898, when the Mahdi state succumbed in the struggle with Great Britain, the French major Marchand advanced into the Fashoda territory of the Shilluk subjugated by the Mahdi's caliph in 1890; but on September 19 he had to retreat before Kitchener, and after lengthy negotiations Fashoda was incorporated in the Anglo-Egyptian Sudan on December 11. In 1904, after the conclusion of the Entente, the ill-omened name of Fashoda was changed to Kodok in order to eradicate the memory of this conflict between the two western powers.*

* See von Oppenheim, *Rabih und das Tschadseegebiet*, Berlin, 1902.

5. *Persia and Afghanistan*

In Persia, after Nadir Shah's power had distintegrated, a number of dynasties from various parts of the country had contended for domination. One of the most successful of the rivals in this struggle was the Kajars, who had come to Persia as one of the seven Turkish tribes in the army of the Safavid Isma'il I, and whom the shah 'Abbas I, in order to limit their power, had settled in three groups near Merv, Erivan, and Ganja in Georgia, as well as in Astarabad on the southeast shore of the Caspian Sea. After Nadir's death the leader of the Astarabad branch, Muhammad Husayn, had made himself independent in the Caspian provinces and then conquered Adharbayjan. But when he then turned against Karim Khan of Shiraz he came into conflict with another Kajar leader and was assassinated by him. His son, Aqa Muhammad, who had been made a eunuch by 'Ali Shah at the age of five, lived at the court of Karim Khan as a hostage. At the latter's death in 1779 he fled to Mazanderan and from there extended his rule over all Persia, in warfare which lasted ten years. He removed his residence to Teheran. In 1795 he subjugated Georgia, whose king Heraclius had allied himself with Russia in 1783 but had been abandoned by his protectors. The following year he had himself crowned shah of Persia. The Russian empress Catherine wished to make good the abortive policy toward Georgia and in 1796 sent out an army, which was already in occupation of Derbend and Baku when she died. Her weak son, Peter, at once recalled the army. In 1797 the Shah moved against Georgia again but after occupying Shisha on the banks of the Araxes was assassinated by two servants whom he had condemned to death for some trivial reason.

He was succeeded by his nephew Fath 'Ali, who first had to wrest the throne from his uncle Sadiq Khan. His immediate concern was the restoration of Teheran, devastated by the Afghans. But he spent only the winter months there; in the summer he lived according to the custom of his nomadic forebears in a great tent encampment on the plain of Sultaniyah. He treated Persia like a conquered enemy country, which he was not to govern but to drain of its last resources. His numerous sons were settled in the provinces as governors and followed his example.

While Russia and the Ottoman Empire alone had hitherto lain within the horizon of the foreign policy of Persia, Napoleon involved it quite early in the net of his far-reaching schemes. Even after his withdrawal from Egypt and Syria he had envisaged it as an operational base for an attack on India. When he came into conflict with Russia, he sent out a special embassy under General Gardanne from Warsaw to Teheran in 1807, after concluding a treaty with the Shah against Russia on May 7. The Treaty of Tilsit, however, soon nullified the Shah's hopes for his aid. Consequently the Shah turned to Britain with the request to send him officers who could continue the work with the Persian army begun by the French military mission. These British instructors, however, were unable to accomplish a great deal, since wars in Persia had hitherto been waged solely by mounted nomad hordes and there was no foundation for the training of an infantry.

Although at first the Shah had declared his readiness to participate in a campaign of Napoleon's against India, nevertheless, his principal objective remained the reconquest of Georgia, which in 1800 had been formally annexed by Russia when the last king, George XII, while on his deathbed, offered his crown to the Tsar. The Shah had still been able to repulse an initial advance of the Russians on Erivan in 1804; the coasts of the Caspian Sea were also still being successfully defended. But in 1812 a Russian army advanced against the Persians along the Araxes and inflicted a severe defeat on them, in which the British infantry commander was also killed, and which forced Persia to accept a peace treaty. 'Abbas Mirza, the successor to the throne who had led the army, waived all claim to the Caucasian provinces of Georgia, Daghestan, Mingrelia, Imeretia, and Abkhazia; ceded to Russia Derbend, Baku, Shirwan, Sheki, Karabagh, and the major portion of Talish in the province of Gilan on the Caspian Sea; and also bound himself not to maintain any more warships on this sea in the future—all in return for the mere promise that he would be supported in his forthcoming accession to the throne.

But since the boundaries were still not established with adequate precision in this peace treaty, dissension concerning it was continually breaking out, which led to a new war in the summer of 1826. The successor to the Persian throne, 'Abbas Mirza, the governor of Adharbayjan, crossed the Araxes and occupied Talish; but in September he was defeated near Ganja (Elizavetpol) and forced back over the river.

In the spring of 1827 the Russians under General Paskievic

crossed the Persian frontier. The fortified town of Erivan offered them successful resistance, but they were able to conquer the neighboring Echmiadzin, the residence of the Armenian patriarch, as well as Nakhichevan and the important fortress of Abbasabad. On July 18 when 'Abbas Mirza moved up to relieve it, he suffered a severe defeat, for which, however, he was able to make amends on August 29 by a victory over the Russians at Echmiadzin. But the miserly Shah denied him the resources for the continuation of the campaign, and so he had to leave the field to the Russians, who took Erivan on October 13. Now all Adharbayjan lay at their feet; they occupied Tabriz and in November sacked Ardabil, the revered birthplace of the Safavids. On February 21, 1828, the Shah had to acquiesce in the peace treaty of Turkomanchai, in which he waived claim to the provinces of Erivan and Nakhichevan and in his domains—on the model of the capitulations in force in Turkey—conceded the Russians extraterritorial rights, which were then also claimed by other European nations. The financial plight the Shah fell into by paying the Russian war costs was taken advantage of by Britain to obtain from him a waiver of the aid promised him in a treaty concluded in Teheran in 1814.

The Shah sought a compensation for the lost western provinces in Khorasan, which, though long a nominal portion of his empire, he only now began to exploit in earnest. A rather powerful Persian nobility had survived there; the country was ravaged by almost incessant incursions of Turkoman nomads. In the autumn of 1831 'Abbas Mirza was sent there, and in two years he subdued the country after having been compelled to lay siege to the major cities, on occasion for quite lengthy periods of time; the fall of Sarakhs, which was ruled by a Turkoman khan, forced his neighbor the khan of Khiva, who made a vain attempt to bring him aid, to cut short his marauding expeditions.

After this victory 'Abbas Mirza also intended to subdue Afghanistan. In this country, which in the time of the Safavids was divided between them and the empire of the Indian Moghuls, the Afghan tribes domiciled in the mountains had kept themselves relatively independent, and their natural increase was beginning to overflow, partly eastward into the Indian plain and partly westward into the low country of the Hilmend River. After the disintegration of the Safavid power, Mahmud, the chieftain of the Ghalzai tribe, had become shah of Persia, but his cousin and successor Ashraf had been dethroned by the Turk Nadir. After the latter's death a chieftain of the Abdali tribe serving in Nadir's army had risen to power in Kandahar, as ostensible guardian of Nadir's grandson Shahrukh, and had also subdued Khorasan. As shah he assumed the name of Durri-Durran; his tribe were known as Durrani accordingly. His successor, Timur Shah (1773-1793), removed his residence to Kabul; Timur Shah's son, Zeman Shah, was dethroned in 1800 by his brother Mahmud Shah. During his reign, filled with disturbances and intrigues, he lost Kabul to Dost Muhammad (whose brother Fath Khan had once helped him become ruler, only to be done away with afterward), and lost the rest of the country including Herat to the chieftains of the Barakzai tribe. After Mahmud's death in 1829 his son Kamran ruled in Herat. 'Abbas Mirza now summoned the latter to submit to him, and after his refusal decided to attack him. In preparation for the campaign he set out on a trip to Teheran, but died midway at Mashhad in Khorasan on October 21, 1833. His son Muhammad Mirza, who had meanwhile encircled Herat, hurried to Teheran at the news of his death in order to secure the succession to the throne, since the aging Fath 'Ali was already nearing his end. Fath 'Ali died on October 23, 1834.

The life at Fath 'Ali's court has been very clearly described for us in the memoirs of one of his sons, 'Adud-ad-Dawlah. In his large harem, women of the Kajar tribe and the other aristocratic clans of the country, about forty in number, had first precedence. The most elegant among them was Asiyah Khanum, the mother of the successor to the throne. Besides her, only one other woman, the mother of Prince Qasim, had enjoyed the Shah's favor. The others had to be content with honorary precedence, while the favorites, generally of an inferior stratum of society, among them the Jewess Maryam Khanum, dominated the Shah's heart. Court finances were managed by a former slave woman. Along with her the servingwoman of the coffee table had a favored position. One of their privileges was to bring a flea caught in the royal blouse to one of the princes, who had to purchase the honor of killing an animal that had dared afflict the sanctified body of the ruler with a large sum of money predetermined by the Shah himself. The prodigality displayed at the court, in spite of the miserliness of Fath 'Ali, was limitless. The favorite Ta'us Khanum alone is supposed to have spent no less than 12,000 tumans ($23,000) annually for her kitchen spices. The Shah attempted to provide for his extremely numerous family by opulent dowries on the occasion of a marriage. His official income from the revenues of the rather moderate land rents amounted to only 989,000 tumans, and from gifts on Nauruz (New Year's day), monetary fines, and confiscations to about 1,500,000 tumans annually. To be sure, the entire administration and the army had to provide for their own support.

Muhammad Shah first had to wrest the throne from his two uncles, Ferman Ferma, the governor of Fars, and Zilli Sultan, who governed Teheran and was supported by Amir ad-Dawlah, the chief wazir of the deceased shah. In Tabriz, where Muhammad maintained his residence, the British ambassador Campbell granted him an advance for the payment of his troops, who were then led to Teheran by the Englishman Bethune. While the pretender there offered no serious resistance, Bethune had to advance on Isfahan against Ferman Ferma and defeated him at Kumishah; he was captured and died on the way to his exile in Ardabil.

Soon after his accession to the throne, Muhammad resumed the enterprise against the Afghans he had begun while prince, since Kamran still refused to pay tribute and moreover occupied the province of Sistan claimed by Persia. In November 1837 he invaded their territory. But Herat defended itself bravely; the inspiration of the defense was an English lieutenant from the Bombay Artillery Corps, Pottinger, the nephew of the resident of Sind, who had come to Herat in disguise. The British officers had had to leave the Shah's service before the beginning of the campaign. Muhammad fell more and more under the influence of the Russian ambassador, the Dalmatian count Simonich, who had placed some Russian officers at his disposal for the conduct of operations. In June 1838 the British sent 387 sipahis to the isle of Kharak in the Persian Gulf and threatened the Shah with an attack if he failed to raise the siege of Herat. Dost Muhammad, the ruler of Kabul, had hitherto refused to be induced by the arguments either of the British or of the Russian agents into taking sides either for or against Herat. After one more frontal assault on the fortress planned by the Russians had failed, Muhammad was persuaded by the British ambassador to raise the siege, and on September 9 set out on the way back.

In order to forestall a repetition of the threat to the Indian frontier by way of Persia and Russia, the British occupied Kabul and

Kandahar in 1839 and in Shah Shuja of the Sadokzai tribe as emir found a pliant instrument of their policy. But in 1842 Dost Muhammad inflicted a bloody defeat on the British; they had to evacuate the country and recognize him as emir.

In spite of the failure of his policy Muhammad Shah continued to grant the Russians the greatest influence and tolerated the further extension of their rule over the Caspian Sea by the occupation of the isle of Ashurada. Muhammad Shah also generally used to sell the governorship of a province to the highest bidder, who naturally then endeavored to extort the purchase price again as quickly as possible, since he could never know whether he himself might not soon be bought out in his turn. Thus in 1846 a newly appointed governor of Kirmanshah confiscated all flocks and had them sold outside the country, heedless of the famine which instantly broke out in his province.

When Muhammad Shah died on September 4, 1848, he was succeeded by his oldest son, Nasir-ad-Din, at the age of sixteen years. His regime appeared to begin under good auspices, even though the rebellion of a young Kajar khan of Adharbayjan, who had found allies in Khorasan and was also supported by the Afghans, first had to be suppressed. The youthful Shah appointed as chief minister his military attendant Taqi Khan, the son of a cook in the service of Muhammad's wazir; Taqi dispensed with the title of wazir and functioned only as the *amiri nizam*, the commander-in-chief of the army. In the beginning his endeavors to abolish the numerous administrative abuses were successful and made him powerful enemies, of whom the queen mother was one; in 1851 it was possible to render him suspect to the Shah because of his popularity in the army; he was banned from the court and soon afterward killed. Nasir-ad-Din reaped what the senseless tyranny of his father had sowed. The rebellions which broke out at various places among the maltreated populace, for instance at Isfahan in 1850, were added to by a dangerous religious movement.

Its founder, the sayyid 'Ali Muhammad, was born in Bushir on March 26, 1821, and there had been trained for commerce but at a quite early age had begun devoting himself to religious questions. On the pilgrimage to Kerbela he became acquainted with the mystic doctrine of the Shaykhi * and after his return home he preached

* [A dissenting Shi'ite school of theology.]

in the Mosque of the Blacksmiths in Shiraz against the dominant Shi'ite orthodoxy. After the death of the head of the Shaykhis, sayyid Qasim of Resht, the school elected him the latter's successor. On the pilgrimage to Mecca he wrote a series of treatises which his adherents regarded as divine revelations. After his return to Shiraz, on May 23, 1844, exactly one thousand years after the disappearance of the Twelfth Imam, whose reappearance was awaited by the sect of the Twelvers, he felt summoned, according to his own account, as the *Bab,* or "Gate," by which mankind could be united with the Imam, the executor of the divine will. To be sure, this doctrine of the gate, after which its adherents were called Babis, had always been advocated by the Shi'ah and in particular by the Shaykhis. But 'Ali Muhammad went beyond it and designated himself later as the *Nuqtah-i-A'la* (the Highest Point) or *Nuqtah-i-Bayan* (the Point of Revelation), then as *Qa'im* (He who is to arise from House of the Prophet at the end of time) and finally as the incarnation of the divine revelation itself, which had last appeared on earth in Muhammad 1,270 years before him. He grew further and further away from the basic doctrines of Islam, to which at first he had still clung, with the further elaboration of his mystic doctrine. While in the beginning he merely desired to be considered the Imam Mahdi–whose coming had been foretold by Muhammad, as the latter himself had been promised by Christ as the Paraclete–later he called himself the Mirror, in which the believers might behold God himself. As Muhammad was revealed by the Qur'an, so the Bab was made manifest to his followers by his own book of revelation, the *Bayan.* The manipulation of numbers, which had already occupied a very extensive place in older Islamic mysticism, served him also as a convenient means of making his interpreting and reinterpreting of the prevalent doctrine palatable. The number 19 was particularly sacred to him, the numerical value of the letters of the Arabic words *wahid* ("unique") and *wujud* ("existence"); in consequence he divided the year into 19 months and these into 19 days and appointed a board of 19 community leaders. He went back again to ancient national ideas of the Zoroastrian religion in requiring burial to take place in stone coffins to avoid defilement by the earth; in declaring the principal festival to be the Nauruz, the New Year's festival, which, to be sure, had always been celebrated with great pomp under Islam also; and in introducing the greeting to the sun on Friday morning. He exempted women from the commandment of the veil and permitted them entry into masculine society. He prohibited the study of the hitherto authoritative jurisprudence and philosophy. Like Islam his religion also demanded world dominion, which was to emerge from the five holy provinces of Persia and no longer tolerate any infidels as rulers.

In 1845 the Bab sent out his apostles from Bushir to Shiraz. But they very soon attracted the attention of the government. On August 6 the governor of the province of Fars forbade them to preach any further and on the twentieth sent out riders to Bushir to arrest the Bab himself. After his arrival in Shiraz he was given a hearing and thrown into jail; but six months later he succeeded in escaping, and in Isfahan the governor, Minuchihr Khan, received him hospitably. After his patron had died in February or March of 1847, he was taken to Maku in Adharbayjan, where he spent three years in jail. Meanwhile his disciples were making zealous endeavors, with great success, to spread his doctrine throughout Persia. A particular sensation was caused by the conversion of the beautiful and poetically gifted young Qurrat-al-'Ayn in Qazwin, who first put his doctrine on the feminist question into effect by removing her veil and beginning to preach in public. Because of this her uncle, an esteemed divine, laid a curse on the Bab and was soon afterward murdered by a Babi in a mosque. In the summer of 1848 the Babists were already causing disturbances in Mashhad. Driven out of Balfurush, they entrenched themselves near the grave of the shaykh Tabarsi about twelve to fifteen miles south of the city. The new shah Nasir-ad-Din sent out troops to combat them. The Babis repulsed the first assault with success; in July-August 1849 they were induced to surrender by the promise of an amnesty, but regardless of this were massacred. In Zanjan the Babis held out for almost the whole year 1850 against far superior government troops. On July 8 of the same year the Bab himself was shot with one of his disciples in Tabriz.

But it was this martyr's death of their leader that first really aroused the Babis to resistance. The rebellion submerged the entire country and hastened the fall of the former prime minister. On August 15 a number of Babis made an attempt to assassinate the Shah while he was on his way to the hunt from his summer palace at Niyaravan. This called forth a new and bloody persecution of the sect, in which at the end of August, Qurrat-al-'Ayn was also put to death among the many other martyrs.

In order to escape these persecutions the leaders of the sect withdrew to Baghdad. Their chief was Subhi-Ezel, whose younger brother Baha-allah, however, was more prominent even then. In 1861-62 he wrote the work *Iqan*, which spread among the sect even more than the writings of the founder himself. Since the stay of the Babis in Baghdad, so near its frontier, still seemed menacing to the Shah's government, it solicited the Porte to transplant them still farther into the interior of the empire. Accordingly in the summer of 1864 they were taken to Istanbul and in December to Adrianople. In 1866-67 Baha put forth the claim there that he was the next manifestation of the divine will foretold by the Bab. Thus a schism arose, since his brother's party refused to recognize his claim. When the quarrel led to outbreaks of violence, the Porte had to separate them. Baha and his followers were exiled to Acre, Subhi-Ezel and his to Cyprus, where the British government allotted him a pension. After the death of Baha on May 27, 1892, his son 'Abd-al-Baha became the uncontested leader of the sect. He let the Islamic and mystical elements of its doctrine subside more and more in favor of a general religion of humanitarianism. He succeeded in winning for his doctrine an Englishwoman, Laura Clifford Barnay, who disseminated his writings in English and French translations and recruited followers for his religion. By 1893 Bahaists had already appeared in America, and there were soon Bahaist communities in all the major cities, which in addition to converts from every other religion include large numbers of colored people.

In foreign affairs, too, the initial years of Shah Nasir-ad-Din's reign were most unfortunate. In 1851 an incompetent youth, Sa'id Muhammad, had become ruler in Herat, and sought to be united with Persia by an alliance. Although in 1853 the Shah had obligated himself to the British government to send no troops to Herat, in 1856 he had the city occupied. At first Britain attempted to send out Dost Muhammad against the Persians in advance, but since he refused, the British were forced to land troops in Persia itself. After a number of unimportant battles for Bushir and Khuzistan, the Shah, in the Treaty of Paris in 1857, had to acquiesce in the evacuation of Afghanistan and the recognition of its independence. Nevertheless, in 1856 the Persians succeeded in expelling the emir of Masqat's representative in 'Uman from the harbor of Bender 'Abbas lying opposite his country, which the emirs had leased since 1798, and in securing recognition for the Shah's authority in the provinces of Sistan and Baluchistan, which had remained relatively independent. But after Ahmad Shah's time Afghanistan also laid claim to Sistan; Sher 'Ali, Dost Muhammad's son, who had followed him on the throne in 1863, reasserted this claim, and in 1872 a British boundary commission determined on a partition of the country in which there fell to Afghanistan only the infertile strips along its frontier.

On his northern marches the Shah, through the governor of Khorasan, had been able to take Merv in 1857 from the Turkomans who had kept the countryside in a state of constant terror of their slave-hunt raids, but the next governor lost the city again after a shameful defeat three years later. To an increasing extent the Shah was relieved by the Russians of any concern for the security of this frontier. Since the subjugation of the Kirghiz in the eighteenth century and the annexation of the Lesser Horde in the province of Orenburg in 1822, Russia had more and more frequently come into hostile contact with the khanates of the Uzbegs in Khiva and Bukhara. From 1849 on the Russians had been advancing in the valley of the Syr Darya, and here came up against the khanate of Kokand. In 1868 the emir of Bukhara was defeated and had to cede Samarqand; in 1873 Khiva was incorporated into the Tsarist empire, and in 1876 Kokand. In 1877-1881 the Tekkeh-Turkomans of the Kara-Kum steppes were subjugated, and in 1884 Russia's position in central Asia was rounded off and secured by the voluntary cession of Merv.

In Great Britain this Russian advance was naturally construed as a threat to India. And in fact after Britain refused to recognize the preliminary peace treaty of San Stefano following the Russo-Turkish war and threatened the Tsarist empire with the loss of its conquests, the Russian general Skobelev had been charged with the task of diverting the British from the Ottoman Empire by means of a thrust into Afghanistan. But before he had made adequate preparations for the difficult undertaking, the Congress of Berlin came to an end. His attack on the Tekkeh-Turkomans, still independent at the time, failed. Nevertheless, General Stolietov succeeded in pressing forward into Kabul with a military mission and winning the emir Sher 'Ali for an alliance against the British, who, the Sher 'Ali felt, had done him an injury in the drawing of the Sistan boundary. Britain could not regard this with equanimity and demanded that he now accept a British embassy with military escort; and when he turned this away at the frontier, Lord Roberts advanced into Afghanistan in December 1878 and in a short time occupied Kabul and Kandahar. Sher 'Ali fled to Turkestan and died in Mazari-Sherif in 1879. His place was taken by his son Ya'qub, who had revolted against him once before with the support of the Indian government and had been imprisoned by his father. In the peace treaty of Gandamak of May 28, 1879, he not only accepted a British embassy in Kabul but also ceded the Bolan pass and the Kuram valley, which made it possible for the British to march into his territory at any time. In the summer of 1879, however, when the Russians, though still in vain, attacked the Turkomans, a mob in Kabul cut down the British ambassador Cavagnari with his escort. Although Ya'qub personally apologized for this in India, Roberts was sent to Afghanistan for the second time, and although he was able to occupy Kabul, he was afterward really hard put to it to free himself from a popular army besieging him. Then Ya'qub was deposed and exiled to India. His nephew 'Abd-ar-Rahman, who had fled to Turkestan before Sher 'Ali, made an attempt to win the throne with the help of Russia, but soon found it more prudent to reach an understanding with Britain. A son of Sher 'Ali, Ayyub Khan, rebelled against him from Herat, and was defeated by Roberts before reaching Kandahar. From then on, 'Abd-ar-Rahman was master of the entire country. In Britain meanwhile the helm had been taken by Gladstone, who as a Liberal abandoned Disraeli's former imperialist policies; he at once withdrew the British troops and even made the Emir the concession that the British ambassador at his court must always be a Muslim. In this way Afghanistan again achieved a relatively extensive freedom in foreign affairs.

After peace was thus secured for all its frontiers, Persia under Shah Nasir-ad-Din enjoyed almost two decades of tranquil development, which, however, at first bore but few fruits because of the general backwardness of the country. By 1864 the Shah, who was interested in the achievements of western civilization in so far as they were able to reinforce his power and increase his revenues, had approved a British project for a telegraph line from Baghdad to Bushir by way of Kirmanshah and Hamadan; in 1870 the Siemens brothers connected it with the line running from London over Alexandrovsk, Odessa, Tiflis, and Tabriz. British technicians then built branch lines into the remaining provinces, which made it possible for the central government to supervise them with greater efficiency. In 1872 the grand wazir granted a gigantic system of monopolies to a British subject, Baron Julius de Reuter, in return for a commitment to build railways, open mines, and found a national bank. But the following year when the Shah attempted to extend his horizon by a trip through Europe, in St. Petersburg he encountered a strong distaste and in London no enthusiasm for these plans. Accordingly he rightly decided after his return to cancel the concession.

The Shah undertook two further journeys to Europe in 1887 and in 1889 to the Paris international exposition; but their expenses were out of proportion to any practical results for his country. He himself communicated to his subjects what he saw and experienced on these trips and on his pilgrimage to Kerbela in 1873 in his travel accounts, in a light and graceful style which gratifyingly contrasts with the bombast of the older historiography and has had a favorable effect on the formation of modern Persian prose.

On his last journey the Shah met the pan-Islamic agitator Jamal-ad-Din Afghani in Munich in 1889 and took him along with him to Teheran. Afghani had stayed a short time upon invitation at the Shah's court in 1886 but had had to leave because his prestige among the Persians appeared dangerous to the ruler. This time, too, the Shah, who at first had shown great interest in his ideas of reform, soon turned against him under the influence of the grand wazir Atabegi A'zam 'Ali Asghar Khan. Afghani sought refuge in the sanctuary of Shah 'Abd-al-'Azim at Teheran, which was regarded as an inviolable asylum, but from there for another seven months was able to continue influencing his worshipers, who soon afterward founded a reform party. But at the beginning of 1891 the Shah had him plucked from there and expelled over the Turkish border into 'Iraq. From London, which was the first place he went to, he not only carried on an agitation in Europe against the wishes of the Persian government but continued to influence his adherents in the country by means of open letters. Soon afterward 'Abd-al-Hamid invited him to Istanbul, hoping to be able to use him as an instrument for his pan-Islamic designs. He lived there until his death on March 9, 1897, in Nishantash, but was mistrustfully watched over by the Sultan, particularly after the assassination of the Shah, even though Turkey refused his extradition to Persia.

The Shah attempted to alleviate the financial straits he had got into through his expensive European trips by means of a state tobacco monopoly; in return for an annual payment of 15,000 pounds sterling and a quarter of the profits he transferred the control of all tobacco cultivation and tobacco trade to a European group of capitalists. This monstrous exploitation of one of the most widespread of their pleasures aroused a storm of indignation among the people, as whose champion the clergy then stepped forward. The most revered mujtahid in the country demanded abstention from smoking and met with obedience everywhere. Finally the Shah, after disturbances had already broken out, had to buy back the concession for half a million pounds, and so laid the foundation of the Persian state debt to the royal bank, which the Shah had founded in 1889 in order to satisfy de Reuter. But the discontent of the people was not to be mollified by this. In 1896, when the Shah was making preparations for the fiftieth anniversary of his accession to the throne, he was shot by a disciple of Jamal-ad-Din's while accepting petitions from his subjects according to ancient custom.

His son Muzaffar-ad-Din was escorted to Teheran from Tabriz, his seat while crown prince, by the British and Russian ambassadors, and ascended the throne unhindered. After the fashion of his father he set out directly on a trip through Europe, on the pretext of a cure at a watering place. His need for money, which he vainly attempted to cover by a loan in Britain, was met by a loan of 42 million roubles, which were soon squandered, from the bank founded in Teheran in 1900 by the Russian ministry of finance in return for a concession for the construction of a highway from Julfa to Teheran and for prospecting rights for coal and petroleum. To secure payment, the administration of the customs, with special patronage for Russian trade, was transferred to a Belgian official. 'Ayn-ad-Dawlah, the Shah's son-in-law and chief minister, was blamed by the people for these financial operations so injurious to the country, or for not having opposed the sovereign's ceaseless demands for money. Thus there gradually arose in the educated classes the desire to gain some influence over the government.

To be sure, there was as yet no press in Persia which could have given expression to the popular mood. Although in 1851, the third year of his reign, Nasir-ad-Din had had his decrees published in a journal, which was later followed by similar enterprises, popular edification was served only by the weekly paper *Akhtar* (*The*

Star), appearing in Constantinople from 1875 on. It was suppressed by 'Abd-al-Hamid in 1896 after the assassination of Nasir-ad-Din. Sharper attacks on the government were first made by the journal *Qanun* (*The Law*) founded in London in 1890 by the prince Malkom Khan, the son of an Armenian, together with Jamal-ad-Din; in it he first demanded popular representation. During the sixties he had founded a club in Teheran which was soon dissolved by the government. He was banished from the country, but in 1872 appointed ambassador in London.

The initial impetus to an uprising was given, as so frequently, by an occasion unimportant in itself, a flogging to which the governor of Teheran sentenced a number of tradesmen in December 1905 for profiteering in sugar. In Persia it had been the custom from of old to seek protection (*best*) in a mosque against violence on the part of the sovereign, as Jamal-ad-Din had done. In the same Mosque of the Shah 'Abd-al-'Azim in which Afghani had defied Nasir-ad-Din, those discontented as a result of the flogging sentences gathered in daily increasing numbers, and met with such powerful support not only from the clergy but supposedly from the crown prince and the predecessor in office of the unpopular minister as well, that the Shah was forced to promise the latter's dismissal. But the Shah had no intention of fulfilling his word after the crowd had dispersed, and consequently another *best* took place in the spring of 1906 which ended in the migration of the principal religious leaders to the holy city of Qumm, where, among many others of the pious, Fatimah, the sister of the Seventh Imam, lay buried. This threatened to paralyze the judicial system they had controlled. When 'Ayn-ad-Dawlah thereupon tried to compel the tradesmen by violence to open the bazaars, they sought refuge in the summer residence of the British embassy at Gulahak, in whose gardens twelve thousand men were finally encamped. Now the Shah had to yield at last, dismiss 'Ayn-ad-Dawlah, and recall the clergy from Qumm. But the people were no longer satisfied with this. Through the mediation of the British embassy the Shah had to promise the convocation of a popular representative body to be elected from among the princes of the royal house, the clergy, the nobility, the landholders, merchants, and businessmen. In October, a few days after he opened the national assembly (the *Majlis*), the Shah died.

His successor Muhammad 'Ali had no more pressing desire than to fill his empty exchequer by a loan, after the fashion of his father;

but the Majlis refused its assent. Consequently he recalled Atabegi A'zam 'Ali Asghar Khan, who had spent the preceding three years abroad, to make his will prevail against the national assembly. After the minister negotiated in vain with the more moderate members, he was assassinated by a fanatic. His place was taken by Nasir-al-Mulk, an astute administrator, who succeeded for a short time in restoring order in the country's finances by energetic measures of economy. But he was also incapable of mastering the prodigious political difficulties. After the promulgation of the constitution an abundance of newspapers had arisen, of which only a few, such as the *Majlis* and the *Suri Asrafil*, were genuinely concerned with the enlightenment of the people, while the majority, very short-lived sheets, merely stirred up political passions.* In the national assembly, in addition to farsighted statesmen like Taqizade † of Tabriz and his countrymen, eloquent mujtahids from Teheran, and a numbers of grandees, there also sat deputies from the southern provinces, which were still very backward. The driving force of the revolution were the *enjumens*, partly local representative bodies, partly debating clubs in which anarchist ideas and terrorism were preached; their emissaries, such as the murderer of Atabegi A'zam, called themselves fida'is like the Assassins before them.

In defense against these rising powers the Shah had founded his own trained Cossack brigades on the Russian pattern. In December 1907 he made an attempt to smash the national assembly with their help, but abandoned this intention again because of the energetic resistance of the enjumens, who obtained reinforcement from Qazwin.

Meanwhile Russia, which after its defeat at the hands of Japan directed its expansionist endeavors more and more toward central Asia, and Britain, which wanted to tie Russia to the West in order to divert her from India, had reached an accord which partitioned Persia into two spheres of interest. Since Britain wanted nothing more than a glacis for the defense of India and in consequence merely laid claim to the less valuable portions of southern Persia from the Afghan border as far as Bender 'Abbas, it left to Russia the northern part from Qasr-Shirin as far as the Russian-Afghan border, with the inclusion of Isfahan, Yezd, and Kakh. Although

* See E. G. Browne, *The Press and Poetry of Modern Persia*, Oxford, 1914.

† His picture is reproduced in E. G. Browne's *Brief Narrative of Recent Events in Persia*, London, 1909.

both empires recognized Persia's independence in name, it was no wonder that the Persians felt themselves betrayed by Britain, whose protection had made possible their first impulses toward freedom.

The Shah, however, still found it impossible to become reconciled to the limitation of his power by the national assembly, and all attempts to find a compromise collapsed. In February 1908 a bomb was thrown against his automobile which killed one of his escorts. At the beginning of June the Shah left the capital and from his summer residence sent out his Cossack brigade under Colonel Lyakhov to Teheran, to bombard the parliamentary building and place the city under martial law.

The nationalists in Tabriz, emboldened by the revolution against 'Abd-al-Hamid which had just been successfully carried out in Turkey, revolted against this act of violence and expelled the adherents of the Shah from the city. In August the Shah ordered his troops against the city and laid siege to it, and in April 1909 Russian forces occupied Tabriz.

But the nationalist cause gained a new champion in the southern Persian nomad tribe the Bakhtiyari, whose chieftain Sirdari Asad had just returned from a trip to Europe when the revolution broke out. He succeeded in winning over his tribe for the cause of freedom, leading it first against Isfahan, whose inhabitants he freed from the arbitrary regime of their governor. When in Resht a combat force was then also formed—composed of Caucasians, Turks, and Armenians, under the leadership of a former general, Muhammad Wali Khan, and an Armenian artisan, Yeprem (Ephraim)—he decided to use it for a march on Teheran, although the Russians and the British ambassadors sent him warning. But before the Russians could send their troops, already landed in Enzeli, to the aid of the Shah, the nationalists succeeded in seizing the capital after street warfare lasting three days, and in deposing the Shah, who sought refuge in the Russian embassy on July 16.

Asad-al-Mulk, a respected Kajar leader, assumed the regency for the ex-Shah's twelve-year-old son, Ahmad Shah, while the ex-Shah himself, after a pension had been granted him, traveled to Odessa. Although as chief of police Yeprem was anxious to restore order in the city, there was some petty jealousy between the Bakhtiyari leader and General Wali Khan, who had taken over the ministry of internal affairs and the war ministry respectively; the former drew his support from the extremists in the national assembly, the Inqilabiyun (revolutionaries), who drove the cautious Taqizade from Teheran, and with their help he pushed out the War Minister. The ex-Shah wanted to exploit these disturbances to seize the throne again. He was already marching on Teheran from Astarabad with a body of recruits, while adherents of his advanced to join him from Kirmanshah in the south. He was favored by Russia, but Britain obdurately opposed his reinstatement, and so he had to retire again, his objective unattained.

The revolutionary party now in control was primarily concerned with the restoration of order in Persian finances, completely deranged by the maladministration of the preceding regimes. Since it could expect little from the European advisers, who, after all, would only labor on behalf of the country's creditors, it turned to the American embassy with a request for aid. At the suggestion of the American secretary of state the official of the Union Trust in Washington, W. Morgan Shuster, was called to Persia as treasurer-general with four countrymen as assistants. This American, who was very energetic but up to this point totally unacquainted with the country's circumstances, certainly had the best of intentions of serving the country that had summoned him, and of whose melancholy circumstances he gave an account in an unembellished indictment,* but he soon went astray in his choice of means. In order to put into effect a genuine control of taxation, parliament gave him his own *gendarmerie*. His desire to employ as its chief the military attaché of the British embassy, who was on the verge of leaving office, was frustrated by the Russians. But his very first attempt to intervene with the aid of his troops miscarried.

Parliament had decided to confiscate the fortune of a brother of the expelled shah, Shuja'-as-Saltanah, for having supported the former ruler in his attempt to regain power. When Shuster tried to have this decision executed by his gendarmes, the Russian consul-general sent out Cossacks against him to prevent it, since Shuja' was supposedly in debt to the Russian bank. Thereupon Shuster had the latter's protectors driven off by a stronger force, as a result of which it was claimed two Russian vice-consuls were threatened. On November 5, in requital for this, the Russians demanded Shuster's dismissal; when it was refused, Russian troops, who had fought against the nationalists in Tabriz, Resht, and Enzeli, advanced on Teheran.

* *The Strangling of Persia,* London, 1912.

Under their pressure parliament was compelled to approve Shuster's dismissal on December 25.

The unfortunate country soon came to feel the weight of Russia's hand. In August 1911 Shuja'-ad-Dawlah, one of the most zealous of the expelled shah's generals, laid siege to Tabriz, the stronghold of the nationalists, with a corps of *shahsevens*, partisans of the (former) shah. On January 2, 1912, he succeeded in pressing into the city, where he decreed a frightful punishment of the nationalist leaders.* On the trivial pretext that Russian subjects in Mashhad, the holy city of Khorasan, were imperiled by the disturbances created by one of their own agents, the Russians even bombarded that great Shi'ite sanctuary, the burial place of the imam Riza, on March 29. From then on, northern Persia was apparently delivered helpless into their hands, since Britain was content with the establishment of order in its own sphere of interests in the south with the help of gendarmes under the command of Swedish officers. The national assembly was first convoked again in July 1914, after the crowning of the Shah, who had attained his majority, in order to accept his speech from the throne, in which he proclaimed Persia's neutrality in the threatening world war.

In the First World War, Persia for a short time became a Russo-Turkish war theater along its western frontier. In January 1915 the Kurds attacked Tabriz, but by the thirtieth of the same month were driven off again by the Russians. At Lake Van and in Urmiạ in the autumn of 1917 bitter warfare took place between Kurds and their old enemies the Nestorian Christians, who were supported by the Russians, in which the Christians underwent endless sufferings. After the victory at Kut al-'Amarah, Turkish troops crossed the frontier and were threatening Teheran; however, since they were more urgently needed in other theaters of war, they soon had to be recalled. In southern Persia the former German consul at Bushir, Wassmuss, who enjoyed great regard among the tribes in the hinterland of Tangistan, gave the British considerable trouble, though he failed to attain the goal of Lawrence, his British antagonist in Arabia, that of leading his friends themselves into battle.† Despite

* *The Reign of Terror at Tabriz, England's Responsibility (with Photographs and a Brief Narrative of the Events of December 1911 and January 1912, compiled for the Use of the Persian Committee*, by E. G. Browne, London, October 1912.

† Christopher Sykes, *Wassmuss, the German Lawrence*, Leipzig, 1937.

heroic endeavors, success also remained denied to the German group under von Niedermeyer, which was supposed to summon Persia and Afghanistan to battle against their old oppressors, the Russians and British.* The collapse of the Russian front gave the Persians in the north their freedom again, since the Bolsheviks renounced all claims inherited from the Tsarist regime. The next section will give an account of how this sorely tried country under an energetic ruler was destined to achieve renewed prosperity after the war.

* Oskar von Niedermeyer, *Unter der Glutsonne Irans*, Dachau bei München, 1925.

5. The Islamic States After the World War

1. *Turkey*

THE truce of Mudros on October 4, 1918, put the Ottoman Empire out of the war. Talat and Enver, who had concluded the treaty, could not conduct the peace negotiations, for in the enemy's eyes they were primarily responsible for Turkey's entry into the war. But 'Izzet Pasha and Tawfiq Pasha, who assumed the government one after the other, were also suspect to the Allies, and only the opponent of the nationalists, Damad Ferid Pasha, who took over on March 4, was agreeable to the victors. His faith in Wilson's twelfth point, which promised the Turkish parts of the Ottoman Empire uncontested sovereignty, was ignominiously disappointed. On May 15, 1919, Smyrna was occupied by the Greeks in accord with the Allies and Ferid's protest against this did not receive a hearing at the Paris peace conference in June.

In vain had nationalist groups in Istanbul attempted to bring the fate of their country under control. On November 29, 1918, Dr. Esat, a very ambitious but politically incompetent eye doctor, had brought together there a national congress of eight parties and numerous splinter groups, which dissolved again after a number of futile sessions. No greater success was destined the thirty former ministers and other dignitaries who rallied round the former chamber and state president, Ahmed Riza, under the name "National Unity."

Salvation could only come from Anatolia, with its closely knit Turkish population, in which the peasantry, still full of vitality in spite of the lengthy and murderous war, predominated. The Greeks, who had been responsible for unheard-of atrocities in

Smyrna, were revolted against by Turkish bands of volunteers under the blacksmith Efe Mehmed and Yuruk 'Ali, soon joined by regular troops under staff officers, who kept their enemies preoccupied in implacable guerrilla warfare. General Qasim Karabekir went to eastern Anatolia on May 3 and succeeded in delaying the surrender of arms to the British supervisory commission. Led by the former deputy Re'uf, the nationalists of Erzerum decided on May 30 to convoke a congress for the defense of the country.

At this point the Entente powers themselves gave the impetus to the career of the man destined to build up the new Turkey. They demanded that the government restore order in Anatolia, if necessary by force. No one seemed more suitable to the government than the veteran defender of Anaforta, Mustafa Kemal, whose Yilderim army group had preserved Turkish military honor in the battles in Palestine and around Aleppo. On May 15 he entered Anatolia and at once assumed command of the national movement, whose adherents from Istanbul had joined him. On June 21, 1919, he sent out a summons from Amasia for an all-Turkish congress in Sivas. Before this could convene, he opened the quite poorly prepared congress in Erzerum on July 23, which since then has been regarded as the Turkish national holiday. By August 7 this first congress had drafted a proclamation demanding the inviolability of Turkish Anatolia and summoning up the national forces for its defense.

Under Mustafa Kemal's presidency the congress then met at Sivas on September 4, with representatives from Rumelia participating. This congress endorsed the resolutions passed at Erzerum with only slight modifications. Ferid Pasha, still in command in Istanbul, now recalled Mustafa Kemal and on the latter's failing to obey his order declared him a rebel and sought to make him suspect to the Entente powers. But Mustafa Kemal meanwhile extended his influence throughout Anatolia, and succeeded in severing all communications between the Istanbul government and Anatolia. On October 2, 1919, Ferid had to retire. His successor, the former war minister Ali Riza Pasha, yielded to Mustafa Kemal's insistence and had the Turkish parliament re-elected, but convoked it at Istanbul while Mustafa Kemal demanded its transfer to Anatolia, justifying this by a reference to the Weimar national assembly. Although on January 6 Ali Riza had submitted reform proposals to the Entente which granted far-reaching supervisory powers to its commissioners, and although the parliament was reluctant to declare itself openly for Mustafa Kemal, on January 28 it accepted the so-called National Pact, which reaffirmed the resolutions of Erzerum and Sivas by demanding complete independence and liberty for all regions inhabited by a Turkish majority, inclusive of Istanbul and its region on the Sea of Marmara, and entrusting the fate of the remaining portions of the empire to a vote.*

This unmistakable expression of the national will was answered by the Entente's forcing Ali Riza to retire on March 7, occupying Istanbul on March 16, and having the nationalist leaders, including Ziya Gok Alp, taken to Malta. Ferid Pasha, who had assumed the government again on April 5, had Mustafa Kemal and his best-known collaborators, among them the poetess Halide Edib Hanim, sentenced to death by court martial.

The founder of modern Turkey thus found untenable any consideration for the Istanbul government. He convoked the great national assembly at Ankara, which opened on April 23, 1920, with 350 members and simultaneously elected him president and head of its executive committee and ministerial council.

Ferid Pasha had to acquiesce in the signing of the Treaty of Sèvres on August 10, since otherwise the Entente threatened to drive the Turks out of Europe entirely. If the treaty had been fulfilled in all details it would certainly have also meant the end of their national existence. For not only were the Arab provinces withdrawn from their dominion, but Smyrna and its hinterland were also to become autonomous, Armenia to form an independent state, Thracia to fall to Greece except for a narrow strip, and the Bosporus and the Dardanelles to be controlled by an international commission. An accord of the Entente simultaneously delivered Cilicia and southern Kurdistan to France and southern Anatolia as far as the Smyrna region to Italy for exploitation.

Although this ignominious act of violence called forth indignant declarations from the entire Islamic world, in particular the Indian Muslims, whose feelings Britain had to spare, and brought the Turkish army numerous volunteers from other Islamic countries, the Ankara government was at first prepared to accept the occupation of Smyrna by the Greeks and also to waive claim to Adrianople. In February 1921, at a conference in London, its delegate Bekir

* See G. Jäschke, *Zur Geschichte des türkischen Nationalpaktes (Mitteilungen des Seminars für orientalische Sprachen*, 36, Berlin, 1933, II, 101-116).

Sami proposed the creation of an autonomous province of Smyrna under a Christian governor. But neither the Greeks nor the Allies were satisfied with this, although they soon relinquished the plan of subduing the Turkish nationalists by an expeditionary corps under General Foch, in view of the considerable difficulties and the general war fatigue. While France had no desire to see its Syrian mandate imperiled by an adventure in Asia Minor, nor Italy its new possession in the Dodecanese hemmed in by the proximity of a greater Greek state, Britain encouraged the Greeks to press forward from Smyrna. The previous guerrilla warfare against Turkish volunteer bands now became a full-scale battle for western Anatolia. On March 23 the Greeks advanced against the important railway junctions of Eskishehir and Afyon Karahisar. While in the south they were able to occupy Afyon Karahisar for a short time, they were decisively defeated in the north at In-Onu during the first days of April and forced to retire to Brusa. But by July 10 they had advanced again in the direction of Kütahya for a decisive battle; after Kütahya, Afyon Karahisar and Eskishehir also fell into their hands. Mustafa Kemal, however, was assembling Turkish combat forces in Sakarya. The Greeks attacked him there on August 24, but after bitter fighting had to retreat on September 16. This victory over the infidels, which definitely decided the fate of the new state, was celebrated by the national assembly by bestowing the honorary title of ghazi on Mustafa Kemal.

France was first to draw her conclusions from the new situation. At Ankara on October 20, through Franklin-Bouillon, she concluded a treaty with Turkey in which she waived claim to Cilicia in return for a concession for the exploitation of the iron, chromium, and silver mines in the valley of the Harshit, which flows into the Black Sea, and by this set free about eighty thousand men and abundant war material for the war against the Greeks. Italy evacuated Adalia in January 1921. Turkey concluded a treaty with Soviet Russia on March 16, succeeded by an agreement on October 13 with the Soviet Republics of Armenia, Georgia, and Adharbayjan. In return for the cession of Kars she assured them of her protection. These two powers, which had previously been divided by the Armenian Republic created by the Allies, and both of which felt menaced by Britain's control of the Black Sea, had at first got into a conflict; in September 1920 Qasim Karabekir Pasha had occupied Erivan and in October Kars. In December a peace treaty was signed in Erivan with the soviet in power there. But the important harbor of Batum, which the British had occupied after the truce of Mudros but meanwhile evacuated again, became the goal, in March, both of the Red Army and of the Turks; but before a war broke out, a treaty with Moscow was concluded which granted Batum to the Georgian Republic.

The summer of 1922 passed by in futile negotiations, although Mustafa Kemal was finally prepared for far-reaching concessions to the Greeks and their British protectors. On August 18 hostilities were resumed. On August 26 Afyon Karahisar, which the Greeks thought they had made impregnable, was taken. After a second defeat at Dumlu Pinar a wild exodus of the Greeks took place, in which they burned down all the settlements they passed through. On September 9 the Turks were able to occupy Smyrna almost without striking a blow. However, half the city went up in flames, so that any recollection of Greek rule there was destroyed.

Now Mustafa Kemal decided to win back Thracia also. A conflict might almost have taken place with the British garrison of Chanak Kala on the Dardanelles, where General Herrington barred the passage of the Turks, as in July he had also held back the Greeks from an attack on Istanbul; but on October 11 the truce of Mudania was concluded, in which the Greeks waived claim to Thracia as far as Maritza. Lloyd George, whose eastern policy foundered as a result of these events, stepped down on October 19. On November 20, 1922, the peace conference of Lausanne was opened, but it dissolved on February 4, 1923, without result. On April 23 the delegates convened again and on July 24 finally produced the peace treaty. The Turks again came into possession of all Asia Minor and Istanbul with eastern Thracia, and the Greek populace of Asia Minor had to migrate back to the mother country, while the Turks still in the Balkan states returned to Anatolia in droves. Only the question of the possession of Mosul remained unsettled. The region around Mosul, economically very valuable because of its oil fields, was principally inhabited by Kurds, the majority of whom in the north were already under Turkish rule; how Turkey came to grips with its neighbor in the south will be related in the history of 'Iraq. In Turkish internal affairs the Allies waived claim to the special rights of the Christian minorities rooted in the ancient millet system, which had to be surrendered together with the Capitulations for the foreigners.

After this brilliant victory which the nationalists had won with their own strength and without the collaboration of the sultan Muhammad VI, who remained in Istanbul under Allied occupation, the national assembly declared Turkey a republic (*jumhuriyet*) on October 29, 1923, and elected Mustafa Kemal its president. For the time being it was desired to retain the caliphate, which was transferred to the Sultan's son, 'Abd-al-Majid. Although the new caliph made no bid for power personally,* Mustafa Kemal very soon perceived that a supreme religious leader recognized as such by the entire Islamic world could, even against his will, become a focal point for reactionary ambitions.

Mustafa Kemal was resolved to conduct the state founded by him along the pathway of European civilization, in which any backward glance to the Islamic past could only be a hindrance. Consequently he preferred to forego the advantages that being a spiritual center of Islam might have offered. A resolution of the national assembly of March 3, 1924, dissolved the caliphate and banished its incumbent from the country. Thereupon a new version of the Turkish constitution was proclaimed on April 20.† Indignation over this step was very great, particularly among the Indian Muslims who had set their hopes for protection against British imperialism on the newly resurgent Turkey, and of whom a few had even removed to Ankara. All attempts at re-establishing the caliphate in other countries of Islam necessarily miscarried, since conditions for it were nowhere to be found; the Ghazi energetically rejected the demand that he himself assume the caliphate.

The rupture with the Islamic past of the country, however, was not consummated without severe upheavals. The Kurds, an Iranian people whose homeland was split up by lofty mountain ranges, and which had never in history attained a political life in a state of its own, had been subjected to Ottoman rule in 1515, but one of them, the historian Idris of Bitlis, had been able to save the power of the

* Even the official *Tarih* IV, 160 ff., reproaches him only for speaking too respectfully of his ancestors, for signing a telegram to the Muslims in Finland as "Caliph of the Apostle of the Lord of Worlds," for not rejecting a few declarations of reactionary circles, for entering into relations with foreign ambassadors, and for having instituted negotiations in Ankara concerning the caliphate's exchequer.

† Text and translation in *Mitteilungen des Seminars für orientalische Sprachen*, Berlin, 1924, II, 137-251. [D. E. Webster, *The Turkey of Atatürk*, Philadelphia, 1939, pp. 297-306.]

heads of their noble clans by skillful negotiations. Although 'Abd-al-Hamid had repressed any national movement among them and had even forbidden the printing of the first Kurdish grammar by Yusuf Khalidi, he had utilized them for the oppression of the Armenians and even formed his mounted bodyguard, the Hamidiye, mostly of Kurds. The Young Turks had continued this policy of his and made use of the Kurds during World War I for combating the Armenians. But now, after they were separated from their brethren in the Mosul region, for which Britain and Turkey had long been chaffering, the desire for national independence and the hope to escape Turkish rule awoke among them also. The pretext for this was offered by the violation of Islamic law in the dissolution of the caliphate. On February 13, 1925 the hereditary head of the dervish order Naqshbandiyah, which was very influential among Kurds, Shaykh Sa'id, raised the banner of revolt. His intimate connection with the Kurdish nobility rapidly secured him mass support. Within a short time the thirteen eastern vilayets, in which a Kurdish population predominated, were in a state of insurrection. The installation as caliph and sultan of Selim, a son of 'Abd-al-Hamid, was demanded. Since an insurrection on the part of reactionary elements was necessarily to be feared in Istanbul, martial law was proclaimed there also. The Kurds first attacked Diyarbekr (Amid); the city fell into their hands on March 7 but was soon liberated again. Since their principal leaders had fallen in these battles, the Kurds lost the will to further resistance. Shaykh Sa'id, however, was not captured until June, and was executed in Ankara. In 1929 another revolt flared up among the Kurds in the region of the Ararat and Lake Van, but was suppressed by the swift dispatch of a major body of troops. To prevent any further uprisings the government had recourse to the method of deportation, often tested in Oriental history, and settled some of the Kurds in eastern Thracia.

This revolt, individual nests of which still had to be rooted out by emergency courts, drove Mustafa Kemal's government to further steps in the secularization of the state. The ministry for pious endowments (Evkaf) had already been dissolved by March 2, 1924, and combined with the ministry of education. In June 1925 all the dervish orders were prohibited, and in September all monasteries dissolved. All religious criticism of measures taken by the government was ruthlessly suppressed. In the year 1931-32 it even went so far as to limit the number of mosques, of which only one was to be allowed within a circumference of every five hundred meters; the number of preachers paid by the government was to be reduced to three hundred, and the obligation was imposed on them of providing practical instruction concerning agricultural questions, etc., in the Friday sermons, in addition to religious edification. Two of the most famous mosques of Istanbul were withdrawn from use for divine worship: the Aya Sophia was transformed into a museum and the Fatih Mosque into a depot. The religious law, the Shari'ah, which hitherto had still been valid in the sphere of domestic relations, was replaced by a civil code worked out along Swiss lines. This resulted in the end of polygamy, which, to be sure, had been practically restricted to the well-to-do classes, if only for economic reasons. In connection with this, family names, hitherto unknown in Turkey, were introduced by a law of July 2, 1934.

Turkish women, who had already stepped in to replace the male combatants in many jobs during World War I, were now given equal legal rights, and finally obtained the active and passive right of election too; in the new elections of the spring of 1935 seventeen women entered the Great National Assembly.

The assimilation of European civilization striven for by Mustafa Kemal also received outward expression in the law of November 25, 1925, which introduced the hat in the place of the previous national headgear, the fez, as under Mahmud II * the fez had once supplanted the turban. Soon afterward European clothing was introduced for all circles of the populace.

But Mustafa Kemal was not content with external adaptation of his people to the mores of the West; he also wanted to impregnate them with the spirit of Europe. To achieve this goal the Arabic script first had to be done away with. By March 24, after the Arabic forms of the numerals were replaced by those in international use, he had also decided to give up the Arabic script, which in any event was only very poorly suited to the representation of Turkish. On June 26, 1928, a commission was charged

* How great is the significance of the fez as the outer sign of being a Turk, though that may seem incomprehensible for the European mind, is shown by one of Ya'qub Qadri's short stories, "The Hat"; this relates the unfortunate end of a young Osmanli who for the sake of his Christian fiancée shows himself on the street with a hat on and is killed by the fanatical mob. In order to combat the resistance of reactionary elements to this measure, the Ghazi was compelled to undertake a propaganda tour in person through the province of Kastamuni wearing a hat.

with the adaptation of the Latin script to Turkish. It performed its task with great skill by taking a middle path between an as-exact-as-possible reproduction of the sound and traditional orthography. By August 2 the new script had already been introduced in Ankara; the Ghazi himself insisted on appearing as a teacher for it. On August 9 he announced the introduction of the new script in a speech at Istanbul and on November 3 it was made into law. Schools were erected everywhere in the country for people of all ages to learn the new script, which was naturalized in a surprisingly short time. On September 1 the hitherto customary instruction in Arabic and Persian, which had been regarded as indispensable for the understanding of Turkish literature, was eliminated from the *lycées*. The use of Arabic type for printing Turkish works was prohibited; innumerable productions of Istanbul printing presses in earlier days were exported to Egypt, Persia, and India. This brought about another rupture of Turkey with its past and with its Islamic fellow believers; the consequences cannot as yet be predicted.

As a substitute for the spiritual values of which all this involved the surrender, the Ghazi or Ataturk *—this name had been bestowed on him on November 24, 1934, by the national assembly, after passage of the law concerning family surnames, as "the expression of the gratitude and veneration of the nation for her greatest son"—intended to inspire his people with a new pride in their nationality. After the Young Turks had to give up their hopes of winning over all the subjects of the empire to the support of their political principle (of Turkey's being a country of one people, the Ottomans, with equal rights), the attempt was made to bind together the Turks with all their linguistic kin in a new national consciousness by the ideal of Turanism. Mustafa Kemal cast aside this idea with genuine statesmanlike insight. Instead he wanted to insure his Anatolian Turks of the glory of an ancient and civilized people, just as the modern Egyptians sought to raise their national self-consciousness vis-à-vis their British oppressors by pride in the primordial culture of the Nile land. Because of this he adopted the uncritical speculation of a few European scholars to the effect that the speech of the Sumerians, the creators of the ancient Babylonian civilization, was related to Turkish. In Anatolia some monuments of Hittite civilization had been discovered (through the excavations

* ["Father of the Turks, Foremost Turk."]

of a German scholar, H. Winkler, at Boghazköy) which had been created by peoples of Asia Minor and taken over by an immigrant Indo-European ruling stratum. By means of a bold historical reconstruction these Hittites were also claimed as the ancestors of the Turks. In this way it was supposed to have been the Turks who created the oldest civilization of the world. The idea soon emerged also that the Indo-European and Semitic languages were originally related to Turkish and developed from it, the demonstration of which was undertaken by bold etymological artificialities immune to all criticism. In order to support these hypotheses a fantastic "solar theory of languages" was fabricated, apparently among the immediate entourage of the President of the republic. This made it possible to justify as authentic Turkish linguistic material all the foreign words in which Turkish is so rich, and which former speech purists had sought to eradicate as far as possible and replace by the resurrection of archaic Old Turkish words. The French word *école*, for instance, was incorporated into the vocabulary as *okul*, by referring it back to *okumak*, or "read"; indeed, there was no aversion to affixing foreign word endings like the convenient French *-al* in *social*, etc., to genuine Turkish or Arabic words. Through this there arose a new written language which was practically incomprehensible to the ordinary man. Thus, above the seat of the president of the national assembly at Ankara, which was now called Kamutai, there was proclaimed the basic principle of the Turkish constitution: "Sovereignty is derived from the People"–in an inscription with the words *Egemenlik Ulusundur*, which, except for the ending *-lik* of the first word and the copula *dur* ("is") at the end, no one would have understood only a few years before. To be sure, these manifestations of an exaggerated national self-consciousness soon yielded again to more sober considerations; the Turks, after all, even though they felt compelled to surrender the traditions of their Islamic past, are still so rich in their own national heritage that they have no need to prop up their self-consciousness on borrowed tinsel. And in fact Turkish scholarship has now long since been endeavoring, with a high degree of success, to reclaim the authentic treasures of their culture by methodical investigation.

With the emancipation from the intellectual domination of the

* In 1931 disdain for the past went so far that valuable old documents of the finance ministry were sold to Bulgaria as scrap paper; but after a debate in the Great National Assembly at least fifty-three bags of such valuable material could be saved for the archives by repurchase.

reactionary representatives of Islam, however, its genuine religious values were also made accessible to the people. The Qur'an, which formerly could only be read in Arabic, was translated into Turkish for the first time in April 1931 and published with a Turkish commentary. In January 1932 excerpts from this translation were publicly recited for the first time at a mosque in Istanbul, and since then the call to prayers also has been heard in Turkish. Religious freedom even made possible a number of conversions to Christianity in 1932, which according to old Islamic law would have been punished with death.

Thanks to the energetic patronage of the President of the republic, the arts, which except for architecture had never received cultivation of any kind in the old empire, burgeoned with surprising rapidity. In the new capital, Ankara, which in a few years was to develop from a forsaken provincial nest into a modern metropolis, from 1927 onward architects, principally German, were at work reconstructing the city in the most modern European style; but in addition to them many Turkish architects have also been active, successfully endeavoring to adapt the foreign architectural ideas to the character of the countryside and of the people. German sculptors also created the first statues of Ataturk—which testify to the new cultural tendency against the old Islamic hostility to images—on the squares of every metropolis; their school has also given rise to native sculptors of importance. Painting, which in Persia and India was cultivated only as an adornment for books and in Turkey was formerly entirely neglected, awakened, particularly under French influence, many talents, who by 1936 could display their art in an exposition in Athens. Music preserved its purely Oriental character down to 1928; string instruments and flutes accompanied the monotonous and often melancholy melodies of Turkish popular singers. For a long time it was known that the President of the republic was determined to lead his people along new paths in this field also. In 1928 he had an Austrian composer summoned to the Conservatory in Istanbul. In 1934 a modern school for music was created in Ankara and entrusted to the direction of P. Hindemith and E. Praetorius, with the purpose of acclimating European music, but concerned with the enrichment and deepening of Turkish music also.

As in the plastic and pictorial arts, the Turks have also struck out along new paths in literature, intended to lead to the goal of the adaptation of their culture to the west. The leader of the Turkish feminine world, Halide Edib Hanim, who followed Mustafa Kemal to Anatolia and personally participated in the battles of liberation, after giving a gripping account of them in her novel *Shirt of Flame* * had to leave her homeland because of differences of opinion; in England she wrote her informative memoirs in English, and for some time she lived in Paris. The great lyric poet 'Abd-al-Haqq Hamid, who died on April 12, 1937, at the age of eighty, and the sensitive Ahmed Hashim † kept alive the tradition of the Young Turk era. Ya'qub Qadri ‡ the founder of the new type of novel, placed it at the service of the new cultural movement, and in addition to him Reshat Nuri, Sadri Ertem, and Shevket Sureya were able to give artistic expression to the new life of the nation born on Anatolian soil.

Ataturk was able to maintain Turkish internal politics in fixed channels as the leader of the People's party (*Halk firkasi*) which he founded, although during the first years even in the circle of his collaborators there was no lack of friction, sometimes vented in violent debates in the national assembly. By 1921 a so-called Second party had already been formed which in 1924 named itself the Liberal, and later the Republican Progressive party. This included political and religious reactionaries together with the heads of the former Young Turks, but also some of the earlier collaborators of Mustafa Kemal; in contrast the People's party assumed the name of the Republican People's party. Then, when during the outbreak of the Kurdish revolt a rigid union of all national forces proved necessary, the opposition party was dissolved on the basis of a decision of the independence court at Ankara in June 1925. A year later, in June 1926, a conspiracy was discovered in Smyrna which planned to do away with the President during his entry into the city by hired assassins. Eighteen of the principal conspirators, among them five former Young Turk leaders, were sentenced to death. Re'uf Bey, the former president of the national assembly and of the cabinet, and Dr. Adnan Bey, who had represented the ministry of foreign affairs in Istanbul, with his wife Halide Edib, were exiled for ten years, while the generals Qasim Karabekir and 'Ali Fu'ad Pasha were acquitted. Four years later another uprising, fomented by the dervish order the Naqshbandiyah against the government,

* [Transl. New York, 1924. Memoirs, New York, 1926.]
† See H. Duda in *Die Welt des Islams*, XI, 1928, 200-244.
‡ See R. Hartmann, *ibid.*, 1918, 264-282.

flared up in Menemen north of Smyrna; a small body of troops under the command of the lieutenant of the reserve Kubilai fell victim to it, but it was repressed with ease. In 1930 the Ghazi, primarily in order to emasculate foreign criticisms of his system of government, attempted once more to allow a parliamentary opposition. The former premier and ambassador in London, M. Fethi, was allowed to enter the newly elected national assembly at the head of the Independent Republican party; soon afterward the party was dissolved again, after a number of collisions between its adherents and those of the people's party. It was not until 1936, at the new elections, that thirteen independent deputies, among them two representatives of the Greeks and one each for the Armenians and the Jews, were elected, of whom it was hoped that they would further the efforts of the government and of the party by means of unbiased criticism and supervision. Since friction had sometimes broken out between the representatives of the People's party and the civil servants in the country, the principles of the party were included in the constitution by a law of February 3, 1937; the minister of internal affairs was simultaneously made secretary-general of the party, and its emissaries in the province were recalled. Thus the struggle between the authorities was definitively settled in favor of the state without infringing on its democratic character, since, after all, authority is derived from the national assembly which is responsible to no one but its electors. The prodigious progress which the economic life of Turkey under the Ataturk regime has made has already been described too often for it to require treatment here. Accordingly, let it be recalled here that although agriculture, to be sure, still constitutes the backbone of national prosperity, industry, which formerly was almost nonexistent, if one disregards the traditional carpet weaving, mostly carried on at home, has burgeoned with surprising rapidity as a result of farsighted guidance. This industry at the same time constitutes a secure defense of the state, which is propped up on an army equipped and trained in an entirely modern manner and a navy suited to its defensive requirements.

The major element in the foreign policy of the first years of the youthful state was the struggle for the possession of the old vilayet of Mosul, valuable for its still-untapped oil fields and consequently claimed by Britain on behalf of 'Iraq, placed under her mandate. It was demanded by Turkey on the basis of the National Pact, since its population in the main consisted of Kurds, as in the bordering provinces. In the Treaty of Lausanne a definitive settlement was postponed, and in case of its being impossible to come to an agreement was reserved for the League of Nations. After lengthy negotiations and investigations carried on by a commission in charge of the Esthonian general Laidoner, this region, also of strategic importance for Turkey, was assigned to the mandated area of 'Iraq on December 15, 1925; in the Ankara accord of July 5, 1926, Turkey complied with this decision, after she was assured of ten per cent of the future oil profits. After that the tense relationship to Britain vanished, thanks to an economic rapprochement and mutually confident collaboration, and on July 18, 1932, Turkey entered the League of Nations.

The treaty relationship of the Turkish Republic with the Soviet Union, concluded directly after the inception of the new Turkey, has always been held fast in spite of the fundamentally different conception of national and economic life on both sides, and was strengthened by visits of a Turkish delegation under Premier Ismet Inonu to Moscow in 1932, and of a Soviet delegation to Ankara under War Commissar Voroshilov. Communist propaganda, which in view of the absence of a substantial industrial working class would be unable to strike roots in Anatolia anyhow, is not tolerated. Turkey has also derived a certain amount of economic advantage from Russia, apart from the security of its eastern frontier.*

Turkey still had to regulate with its southern neighbor, French-mandated Syria, the question of the former sanjaq of Iskenderun (Alexandretta), where Syrians live together with a strong Turkish minority. In the treaty with France of October 20, 1921, a separate administration, with Turkish as the official language and guarantees for an undisturbed cultural life for the Turks, was agreed on. But it was only after lengthy negotiations between both states that this question, which greatly agitated Turkish public opinion, could be regulated by a treaty confirmed by the Council of the League of Nations on January 27, 1937, which assured the sanjaq of the complete independence of the internal administration and bound it to Syria only in matters of foreign policy.

By means of adroit diplomacy Turkey was able to reconcile completely its ancient enemies in the Balkan peninsula with its new

* See G. Jäschke, *Der Weg zur russisch-türkischen Freundschaft* (*Welt des Islams*, XVI, 1936, 23-38).

and independent political existence. It was most difficult for Greece to relinquish its hopes, nourished by the Allies during the war, of winning back the ancient colonial territory of Ionia. By means of an extensive exchange of populations, which at first involved Greece in great economic difficulties, a dangerous source of friction was done away with. When it was finally carried out, in 1929, both states were able to conclude a neutrality treaty the very next year; in 1933 this was followed by a frontier guarantee for ten years. By 1925 Turkey was able to conclude a treaty of friendship with Bulgaria, which was strengthened and extended by a neutrality treaty in 1929, although Bulgaria still stayed out of the Balkan Pact signed in Athens on February 9, 1934, in which Turkey, Greece, Yugoslavia, and Rumania bound themselves not only to maintain peace between themselves, but also to aid each other militarily in case of attack. The economic interests of the four states were also considered in a common economic council which in Athens in March 1937 decided on the joint regulation of the export of certain agricultural products. The last military restrictions still incumbent on Turkey from the peace treaties became obsolete with the reoccupation of the Dardanelle forts and of Adrianople by Turkish garrisons.

Thus Ataturk, when he died, much too early for his people, in Istanbul on November 10, 1938, after a long illness, could bequeath the Turks a state secure abroad and prosperous at home, whose direction was assumed by his collaborator of many years' standing, Ismet Inonu, the second president of the republic.

2. *Egypt*

With its occupation by the British in 1882 Egypt departed from the common destiny of the Islamic states. At first, to be sure, Britain had only laid her hand on the Nile land to secure her sea lane to India through the Suez canal; but once she had undertaken the control of its fortunes, she was soon confronted by new tasks. The Anglo-Saxons, with the practical sense characteristic of them, were always inclined to deal with these tasks one after the other in the order of their appearance, and avoid any decision on the country's future.* It certainly must not be designated as political hypocrisy, as cant, when British statesmen gave repeated assurances that they

* Cf. Lord Cromer's admission in the epilogue of his *Egypt*.

only envisaged, in addition to the securing of the interests of the British Empire, primarily the material and intellectual elevation of Egypt's inhabitants. Egypt, as perceptive patriots have also admitted, actually owes an extraordinary amount to the British administration. It would be idle to attempt a discussion of whether without British intervention 'Arabi Pasha's movement could have found a compromise between the pretensions of Muhammad 'Ali's dynasty, with its military-bureaucratic Turkish aristocracy, and the requirements of the indigenous population. Since Britain took control, it must be acknowledged that though it may not have solved the problem, at any rate it laid a most fortunate groundwork for its solution. It is true that the classes formerly in sole control must often have resented bitterly the harsh tutelage of the consul-general Sir Evelyn Baring (later the Earl of Cromer) from September 11, 1883, to May 6, 1907; but it is very much to be doubted whether without it the prosperity of the country and so the intellectual and moral rise of its inhabitants could have been achieved so swiftly. The history of the British regime cannot be related here; it belongs to that of the British Empire. Nor does the history of the alternating ministries, which only reflects the effect of British influence on the ruling circles, need to be presented here. But an attempt must be made to give a brief account of the manner in which the Egyptian people evolved under this dominion.

Even the British ambassador in Istanbul, Lord Dufferin, the first representative of his country's government in Egypt after the occupation, was anxious to improve the distressing condition of the rural population, the fellahs. Hitherto it had been general usage among Egyptian civil servants to fulfill their principal duty, the collection of taxes, by a generous application of flogging and other tortures against those in arrears. Through a command put into effect by Lord Dufferin, this administrative practice was outlawed. There followed the abolition of the forced labor which was incumbent on the fellahs in cleaning out the canals for the overflow from the Nile, though not until after some difficult diplomatic struggles with the representatives of the international commission of finance control, whose acquiescence had to be secured for the procurement of the money to pay for the free labor; it was not until the death of Tawfiq Pasha in January 1892 that a definite liberation from forced labor could be presented to the Egyptian people as a gift at the new khedive's accession to the throne. But the tax burdens incumbent on the population were still prodigious, since in addition it had to pay the expenses of the British occupation and of the British counselors assigned to individual ministries, who had a mandatory influence on all decisions, as well as of a series of other administrative officials. Under Lord Cromer's control, to be sure, the advisers in the finance ministry—initially Sir E. Vincent, and from 1888 on Sir Elwin Palmer—restored thoroughgoing order in Egyptian finances, though they were incapable of substantially reducing the state debt. Regard for the international financial control also led on occasion to not unobjectionable measures. Nor was success achieved in lowering the burden of taxation. No source of revenue was left untapped; as before, those subject to military service could purchase exemption, of which right, to be sure, only the well-to-do classes could make any use. But it is not to be overlooked that cotton cultivation, already introduced by Muhammad 'Ali and further promoted by Isma'il, was brought to undreamed-of success by British hydraulic engineers, who were able to put into effect experience gained in India. For this, prodigious dam structures were required which made possible an irrigation system independent of the hazards of weather. The dam already laid out by a French engineer between 1842 and 1863 at the entry to the delta, which had proved inadequate, was renewed between 1885 and 1890 by Scott-Moncrieff, and the cotton crop of the delta doubled. This was followed in the years between 1898 and 1902 by the enormous dam at Aswan, the work of Sir William Willcocks. Certainly it must not be ignored that Egypt was thus drawn into the perils of world economics, the crises of which it came to feel on many occasions, and so lost the capacity to insure the feeding of its inhabitants from its own soil. The Egyptians perforce regarded as particularly oppressive the fact that it never even occurred to Britain to do away with the privileged position of foreigners, favored by the capitulations, and often controlling economic life. But of particular weight is the reproach which must be raised against Cromer's administration, that, compared to the extensive funds applied to installations which also benefited British interests, it made completely inadequate sums available for the education of the people; e.g., in the years 1882 to 1902 hardly half the costs of the Aswan dam. His successor, Lord Lloyd, attempted to excuse him by saying that, apart from lack of the requisite means, it had not been Britain's intent to impose the influence of British culture on the country.* This, to be sure, would scarcely have been of service to the Egyptians, but it would have lain in their interests to promote their own culture as against the French culture adopted by the upper strata. It must not, however, be passed over in silence that even in an Egypt liberated from British tutelage the ruling circles have far less interest in questions of education than in economics, of which the dean of the faculty of arts of the University of Cairo, Taha Husayn, bitterly complains in a book which appeared at the beginning of 1939.

Under these circumstances there could scarcely be any question of an independent political life of the Egyptian people before the First World War. It was not until 1892, when the still youthful 'Abbas II (Hilmi), brought up in Vienna, came to the throne after the death of his father Tawfiq, that the first feeble movement of resistance, against the alien rule came to life. During Tawfiq's last years the Armenian Nubar Pasha, and from 1888 on Riyad Pasha, stood at the head of the Egyptian government, and at the slightest attempt to bypass Cromer's measures both had to retreat. When 'Abbas took over the government, Mustafa Fahmi, blindly devoted to Britain, was in charge of affairs. When he fell severely ill at the end of 1892 'Abbas took advantage of the opportunity to get rid of him and appointed as his successor Fakhri Pasha, a supporter of Nubar's son-in-law Tigrane, who had had charge of the ministry for foreign affairs but now preferred remaining in the background. Lord Cromer was not consulted about it in advance. But even this step was calamitous for the Khedive; under British pressure he had to dismiss the minister of his choice, though, to be sure, he did not have to endure Fahmi again, since Riyad Pasha entered the government. The Khedive suffered a second humiliation when he dared criticize the bearing of the army, led by British officers, during an inspection tour in Wadi Halfa. Thereupon he not only had to dismiss the undersecretary for state in the war ministry, Mahir Pasha, to be replaced by a compliant instrument of Sirdar Kitchener, but also publicly retract his criticism. After this he abandoned any further interference in the government and confined himself to the administration of his estates. He received no support against Britain from his suzerain 'Abd-al-Hamid. France also waived her influence in Egypt after Britain granted her a free hand

* *Egypt since Cromer*, I, London, 1933, p. 159.

in Morocco in the accord of April 8, 1904. The extent to which Britain felt herself master of the country is shown by the dispute over the 'Aqabah harbor in the Sinai peninsula. The Sultan had had the Hijaz railway, with which he hoped to consolidate his position in Arabia as caliph, pushed forward as far as Ma'an in the autumn of 1904, and supposedly was planning a branch line to 'Aqabah, which would have been of benefit to the pilgrims from Egypt. While Britain hitherto had scarcely bothered herself about conditions on the Sinai peninsula, she now dispatched a commission to determine the still-confused frontier against the Ottoman Empire, and forced the Sultan to relinquish his plans by threatening a demonstration of the fleet.

In all his conflicts with British power the Khedive had found no backing of any kind in the Egyptian people. In vain had he set his hopes in 1893 on 'Ali Yusuf, the founder of the newspaper *al-Mu'ayyad;* the small reform party which gathered around its editor was incapable of acquiring any political influence. The first tendencies toward the formation of a national will did not arise from the Khedive but from a representative of the bourgeois stratum, first called into being by the British administration, whose sons had received their education in France. To this belonged Mustafa Kamil, the son of an Egyptian engineer, who had studied law in Toulouse and there become acquainted with the influential French journalist Juliette Adam. After his return home he founded the Fatherland party (*Hizb al-Watan*) in 1894. He hoped to be able to win the public opinion of Europe for the libreation of his people, and sought to spread knowledge in all the capitals of the west as well as in Egypt itself. His newspaper *al-Liwa,* (*The Banner*), founded in 1900, and which from 1907 on also appeared in English and in French, gained a wide circulation. In 1904 the Sultan, whose Hijaz railway he advocated with the utmost warmth, bestowed on him the title of pasha; but the Khedive, intimidated by Cromer, began to fear his influence, and that same year withdrew his support.

The hopes of all Orientals were brought to extreme tension by the victories of the Japanese over the Russians, which were celebrated in the Egyptian poetry of the period as the model for all Asia in the struggle against European ascendancy. But it was an incident of no consequence in itself that first made the entire populace conscious of its unworthy position. On June 13, 1906, British officers at a pigeon shoot in the village of Dinshaway * in the delta had shot a woman; the indignant fellahs set upon them with cudgels, and one of them while fleeing was killed. Cromer ordered a merciless condemnation of the culprits, of whom four were publicly hanged on June 28, and seventeen flogged and then sent to prison. Not only in Egypt, but in Europe and in the British parliament also, this barbarous punishment aroused a storm of indignation which for long echoed in the Egyptian press and in nationalist poetry, and rocked Britain's position in the country to its foundations. Mustafa Kamil made energetic representations in London to the Liberal prime minister, Sir Campbell-Bannerman, and demanded Cromer's retirement. And in fact the latter left Egypt in May 1907, having no mind to co-operate in the concession to the wishes of the Egyptians demanded by the Liberals. His place was taken by Sir Eldon Gorst, who was prepared to execute this Liberal policy and so hoped to salvage Britain's position on the Nile. It is true that he at once encountered great difficulties, since the country was oppressed by a severe financial crisis and at the same time imperiled by an unusually low level of the Nile waters. Since Gorst at first attempted to win over the Khedive, Mustafa Kamil turned against him too, and on December 7, 1907, convoked a national congress of 1,017 representatives of the entire country. They elected him lifelong chairman, and in a flaming discourse he was able to inspire them with enthusiasm for his goal, Egypt for the Egyptians via the political education of the entire people. But on February 10, 1908, a long-creeping ailment put an end to his life. His party declined with him; in 1938 it was represented in parliament by only eight members.

Gorst not only played the Khedive against the Fatherland party but also summoned the Copts against it, since its founder was in sympathy with the pan-Islamic aims of the Sultan of Turkey. When the premier Mustafa Fahmi retired in November 1908, Gorst induced the Khedive to appoint a Copt, the former finance minister Butrus Ghali Pasha, in his place. The wild agitation which the nationalists unleashed against him led to his assassination on February 20, 1910, and to a schism between the Muslims and the Christian minority which threatened to plunge the country into civil war. When Gorst fell seriously ill in 1911, the British government sent out in his place the former sirdar of the Egyptian army, Lord

* Corrupted in British reports, and consequently in most European accounts, into Denshawi.

Kitchener. His energy at first succeeded in restraining the nationalists from any support of the Turks when Italy began the campaign in Tripolitania. Whereas Gorst had at first used the Khedive as a prop, Kitchener at once made him feel his own superiority. In the summer of 1912, when students made an attempt on the lives of both rulers, the ruthless severity with which he acted against its backers shattered the party of the nationalists. Kitchener attempted to counterpose the peasantry to the party's supporters in the strata of the bourgeois intelligentsia by a law withdrawing all small landholdings up to five faddans from distraint. The ministry for agriculture, which he founded, provided for the British interest in Egyptian cotton cultivation while simultaneously working against the former preponderance of the Khedive's Agricultural Society.

Finally, the time also seemed to have come to yield to the desire of the Egyptian people for the blessings of European parliamentarianism. Up to then there had been in force the Organic Law introduced by Lord Dufferin on May 1, 1883, which, in addition to the provincial councils, provided for a legislative council of thirty members, of whom fourteen were appointed by the government and the others elected by the provincial councils and the major cities, and for a legislative assembly, which consisted of the six ministers, the members of the council, and forty-six elected deputies. As a result of the constitution which was proclaimed on July 24, 1913, its place was taken by a parliament of eighty-one members, of whom fifteen were appointed by the government and sixty-six called up by indirect elections. Although this parliament had the right to approve taxes, it could not reject legislative bills of the government concerning which there was no agreement. The evolution thus initiated was abruptly broken off by the First World War.

On August 4, 1914, martial law was proclaimed throughout the country, and on September 10 war was declared on Turkey; the British government decreed a protectorate over Egypt on December 18 and replaced the khedive 'Abbas by Husayn Kamil as sultan. The real government of the country was taken over soon afterward by Sir Henry McMahon, formerly political secretary of the government of Simla in India, as high commissioner. His principal task was to make all the auxiliary resources of the country available not only for its defense on the Sinai front but also for an aggressive war against Turkey. In August 1915 a corps of Egyptian laborers was sent to Mudros. But even good pay soon could no longer win the fellah voluntarily for this work in the army which removed him from his home, especially not after a labor corps came under fire, and the government was compelled to make forced drafts. The thankless task the high commissioner had to fulfill, between the constantly more urgent demands of the high command, the passive resistance of the Egyptians, and the inaccessibility of the London government, preoccupied by its other problems, was surrendered by McMahon to Sir Reginald Wingate, former governor of the Sudan.

The sufferings the country had to endure in a war carried on not in its own interest were only feebly recompensed by the foreign money abundantly flowing in with the army, which first of all benefited only the tradespeople and not the fellahs, torn from their homes and robbed of their work animals. The difficulties which the constantly extended cotton cultivation involved for the feeding of the country finally increased to such an extent that in September 1917 the government was forced to forbid entirely the planting of cotton in upper Egypt; but since the prices for this commodity with a world-wide market reached dizzy heights,* it still remained more advantageous for landholders to pay the slight fine for the planting than to dispense with it. Since all measures designed to curb the famine remained ineffective, the war oppressed the impoverished populace all the more, while the well-to-do profited by it and were able to evade giving any assistance.

On October 9, 1917, Sultan Husayn, whose health had long since been undermined, died. Since Britain with his death lost her mainstay in the country, she considered the annexation of Egypt and her incorporation into the empire, particularly since the Sultan's son had expressly waived his claim to the succession. Finally, however, it appeared wiser to spare the feelings of the Egyptians, and the government was transferred to the Sultan's brother, Ahmad Fu'ad, although he lived in Italy as a rule and had almost become alienated from the country.

When the war came to an end, Britain was faced by an entirely new situation in Egypt. Wilson's promise that the world was going to be reorganized on the basis of national self-determination had found an enthusiastic echo there, too. As a result a man emerged

* While during the winter of 1914-15 the price still amounted to $12 a qantar, in 1918 the British government bought up the entire crop at a price of $42 a qantar; and in 1919 the price even rose to $200; see Lord Lloyd, *Egypt since Cromer*, I, p. 244.

who was to determine the fate of the country for the following decade, Sa'd Zaghlul Pasha. As his title alone shows, he was no novice in politics. Born the son of a fellah, he had studied law and as a lawyer was entrusted by Princess Nazili, the daughter of Prince Mustafa Fadil, a friend of the Young Turks, with the administration of her estates. As the son-in-law of Cromer's favorite protégé, Mustafa Fahmi, he played his first political role in the founding in 1907 of the People's party, with which Cromer hoped to checkmate Mustafa Kamil's Fatherland party. But it could establish no contact with the people and had to cease its activities as early as the second year of the war. In gratitude for his services Cromer appointed Zaghlul to the newly created ministry of education. Under Gorst he took over the ministry of justice, but after a conflict with 'Abbas Hilmi he resigned his office in April 1912 and soon afterward was elected vice-president of the new parliament. His natural eloquence soon gained him a constantly growing following; with its backing he was on occasion even able to venture on making serious difficulties for Kitchener. Out of distaste for him the Consul-General missed the opportunity which at the beginning of 1914 presented itself to him, of getting rid of the troublesome agitator when the latter's father-in-law tried to have him freed of his monetary difficulties by having him promoted to the post of head of the Egyptian Student Mission in Paris. Fu'ad's desire to have Zaghlul as minister had also failed to win Sir Reginald Wingate's approval. But now this ambitious man saw his hour strike. On November 13, 1918, he appeared at Sir Reginald's with his friends as the head of a delegation (*wafd*) of the Egyptian people and requested his approval of their traveling to England in order to demand the complete independence of their country from his government; whereupon the High Commissioner declared himself in no position to comply with this request. This was the natal hour of the Wafd party, which for two decades could regard itself as the uniquely accredited representative of the people. Since the other Arab countries at that time were still deluding themselves with the hope of representing their own interests at the peace conference, the Egyptians, to whom this was denied, felt all the more repressed, since after all they had made such great sacrifices for the victory of Britain. Sir Reginald recognized at once that Zaghlul and his supporters would be less dangerous at the peace conference, where they would have to move about on a terrain with which they were unacquainted, than in the country itself, where they could lay down to Britain rules for her behavior; accordingly he recommended to the British foreign secretary, who had called him home for an accounting, that he yield to the demand of the Wafd, but found no hearing. During his absence the government in Egypt resigned from office, and on March 3 Zaghlul threatened the Sultan with violence if he made an attempt to form a new government. In this position Sir Milne Cheetham, Wingate's deputy, thought the only way he could help himself was by removing the leaders of the Wafd. The secretary for foreign affairs agreed to his suggestion that they be deported to Malta, and on March 8 Zaghlul and three of his closest collaborators embarked aboard a British destroyer at Alexandria. The news of their arrest called into the streets the student youth, who also constituted the vanguard of all subsequent revolutionary movements, and in a short time the entire country was in a state of insurrection; on March 17 all communications with Cairo were cut, and in upper Egypt the small garrisons were besieged by the rebels. It was not until April 10 that General Bulfin succeeded in restoring order throughout the country by means of flying columns. Lloyd George, however, had meanwhile made up his mind to send General Sir Edmund Allenby, known from the campaign in Palestine, to Egypt with orders to maintain the protectorate at all costs. Directly after his arrival in Cairo, on March 25, he attempted to quiet the populace by a proclamation, and on April 7 promised to release the leaders deported to Malta. On April 9 Rushdi Pasha resumed office, but the disorders and the officials' strikes did not cease until Allenby on the twenty-second threatened the most rigorous application of martial law. Out of fear the functionaries returned to their duties, and in May, Sa'id Pasha was able to form a new government; but the rebels had tested their power and were prepared to apply it again at the first opportunity. This was provided when the British government, at Allenby's suggestion, assigned Lord Milner the task of leading a commission to investigate the political state of the country and make suggestions for a new constitution. The Wafd, however, did not wish to receive this from outside, but intended to determine for itself the future of the country. Incomprehensibly enough the British government allowed it time, the whole summer and autumn, to agitate against Britain, and when Milner entered Cairo on December 7, Sa'id had retired again and the excitement of the populace had discharged itself in a series of attacks on British soldiers; on December 15 the new prime minister, Wahbah Pasha, just barely escaped a murderous attack.

Under the pressure of these political disorders, which at the beginning of the new year were reinforced by economic difficulties, Milner's commission came to the conclusion that the position of Egypt, hitherto never definitively and constitutionally laid down, could only be regulated by a treaty with Britain; a draft of this provided for Egypt's independence if it would approve the maintenance of a British army in the country and the admission of British counselors in the ministries of justice and finance, bind itself not to enter on any treaties unfavorable to Britain, and grant her the right of protecting foreigners against any unfair application of Egyptian laws. These concessions, which after all were very far-reaching in comparison with previous conditions, nevertheless aroused lively opposition in the country. The deputies of the Wafd, however, were still in session in Paris, where they had gone from Malta, and Milner was compelled to invite them to a conference in London, which began on July 7. Zaghlul declared himself satisfied with the proposal of a treaty, but could not be induced to take a definite position with respect to certain points.

Lloyd George's government for a long time was unable to make up its mind to resume negotiations with Egypt on the basis of the Milner mission's report. It was not until February 22, 1921, that it asked the Sultan to appoint a delegation for the negotiations. The deliberations concerning this led to a change of ministers which brought 'Adli Pasha Yegen into the government, and were seriously upset by a declaration of Zaghlul's in which he demanded that before beginning negotiations Britain surrender the protectorate, the censorship, and the state of siege. On April 5 he returned to Egypt to receive an enthusiastic welcome from his supporters. On May 10, after 'Adli, by circumventing the Wafd, had composed a delegation selected entirely from among his supporters in the Turkish aristocracy of functionaries, disorders broke out again in Cairo and in Alexandria, where they were directed against Greeks and Italians in particular. On July 1, 1921, 'Adli Pasha journeyed with his delegation to London and left the field to Zaghlul, to continue consolidating his position in the country.

After fruitless negotiations with the British government 'Adli Pasha returned to Cairo on December 5, and three days later resigned from office. It was not until the eleventh that Sarwat Pasha was ready to form a ministry, after Britain had declared her readiness to abolish the protectorate and allow the formation of a ministry for foreign affairs. To support him, the High Commissioner had Zaghlul arrested, and when disorders broke out again over this, had him deported to Ceylon on December 29 and from there to the Seychelles. But it was not until February 20, 1922, after Allenby himself had forcefully explained in London the dangerous position, that the British government decided to declare the protectorate extinct and hold out the imminent prospect of doing away with the state of siege. Sarwat could then form his ministry at last, and on March 15, 1922 Fu'ad assumed the title of king of Egypt.

This failed, however, to eliminate the difficulties. The year 1922 passed in fruitless negotiations concerning the new constitution, in which the question of the Sudan was the primary focus of dissension. Although a series of British officials were leaving the service, assassinations against the British were continually being attempted. It was only after Fu'ad had waived his claim to the title of king of the Sudan that Yahya Pasha, who after a twice-repeated reshuffle in the cabinet, was appointed premier on March 15, 1923, and who was bound to no party, could proclaim the new constitution.* Britain hoped to win over Egyptian public opinion by releasing Zaghlul (who meanwhile, on March 24, had been transferred from the Seychelles to Gibraltar), but without permitting him to return home. However, neither this concession nor the abolition of martial law had the expected success, and so Britain perforce decided to allow Zaghlul to go to Egypt on September 17. After behaving cautiously with respect to the King and the High Commissioner in the beginning, he soon unleashed a lively agitation against the new constitution, and the elections for the parliament in January 1924 brought him a majority of 190 out of 214 deputies, so that the King had to charge him with forming a government on January 27, 1924.

In Great Britain at almost the same time the Labor party had come into power, and its leader, Ramsay MacDonald, thought he could express his sympathy for Egyptian aspirations toward independence no better than by releasing about 150 political prisoners. Trusting this sympathy, Zaghlul initiated a lively agitation in the

* Text and translation in *Mitteilungen des Orientalischen Seminars zu Berlin*, 1924, II, 1-82. [Royal Institute of International Affairs, Information Dept. Paper No. 19, *Great Britain and Egypt*, London, 1936; *Current History*, New York, 1927, pp. 532-538.]

Sudan which resulted in rioting, and was very disappointed when the British cabinet declared in the House of Lords on June 25 its firm intention of never again giving up the Sudan. His domestic policies at first served no other purpose than to provide his adherents with offices, and led to an attempt at his assassination. On July 25 he accepted MacDonald's invitation to London to negotiate with him personally the treaty to be concluded with Great Britain, but these negotiations did not begin until September 25; they were broken off at the end of October, since Zaghlul insisted on his demand that Britain evacuate Egypt completely. Soon afterward the MacDonald government was succeeded by a Conservative cabinet.

The anti-foreign excitement kindled by the nationalists was vented soon after Zaghlul's return on November 19 in the assassination of the sirdar of the Egyptian army and governor-general of the Sudan, Sir Lee Stack. Zaghlul attempted to evade Britain's justifiable demands for the expiation of this crime, which, to be sure, also included favoring the promotion of Sudan irrigation at Egyptian expense, but was compelled to yield when the High Commissioner lent them emphasis by occupying the customhouses. His place as head of the government was taken by Ahmad Ziwar Pasha on November 24. British demands on the latter were moderated, but although the customhouses were set free again on December 2, the new government went about the expiation of the crime very sluggishly. Britain did not even insist that the post of sirdar be filled again with a Briton.

Ziwar Pasha thought he would be able to base his power on the Wafd's opponents. In 1922 ʻAdli Pasha had founded a Liberal-Constitutional party (*Hizb al-Ahrar ad-Dusturiyin*); Isma'il Sidqi Pasha, one of its members, took over the ministry of the interior and purged the administration of the protégés of the Wafd. The King sought to strengthen his own influence by a Union party (*Hizb al-Ittihad*). Neither party, however, was capable of draining away the strength of the widely ramified Wafd, and Zaghlul again entered parliament after the new elections with such a powerful following that he was elected president. But instead of charging him with the formation of the government, the King dissolved parliament on March 24, 1924, and soon afterward took advantage of an insignificant difference of opinion in the cabinet in order to expel the Liberal ministers and govern only with the men in his Union party, to an increasing extent leaving the exercise of his power to the head of his chancellery, Nash'at Pasha.

But Zaghlul was of no mind to renounce his influence, particularly since the disappointed Liberals were seeking a combination with him. Since the government failed to convoke parliament, he himself summoned its members to convene on November 21, and when he found the parliamentary building occupied, moved with them into the Hotel Continental, where he was again elected president. Britain, if she did not wish to risk her prestige in the country, could not look on idly. Lord Lloyd, the new high commissioner, who had taken office on October 21, 1925, persuaded the King to dismiss his chief of chancellery by making him ambassador to Madrid.

Finally, however, the King had to make up his mind whether to agree to new elections, after his government had made a vain attempt to alter the electoral law in its favor. On May 25, 1926, the new elections again brought Zaghlul a majority of 144 out of 201 seats. Although he declared that he felt too old to take office again and intended to resign himself to the role of a "Father of the Fatherland," yet on the twenty-seventh he tried to take over the government. Since Britain was perforce afraid of new disturbances, when Zaghlul refused to waive his claims after Lord Lloyd's representations to him, the latter demanded the dispatch of a warship to Alexandria. Zaghlul's adherents, anxious about the results of their political activity, forced him to acquiesce in resigning, and 'Adli Pasha was charged with forming a government. But the power exercised by Zaghlul throughout the country through his supporters was still very considerable, even though he had to restrain himself in its use out of consideration for Great Britain. The immediate objective of his party was the strengthening of its influence in the Egyptian army. 'Adli Pasha refused to assume the responsibility for this; accordingly he turned a parliamentary incident, unimportant in itself, into a pretext for resigning office on April 18. Once again, however, the Wafd considered it more astute not to put forth its own leader but to allow the government to go to Sarwat Pasha. However, the war minister in his cabinet, Khashabah Bey, yielded to the Wafd's pressure for a reinforcement of the army and sought to exclude the influence of the British inspector-general whenever possible. After lengthy negotiations with the British resident, Zaghlul complied with the British demands endorsed by the government, which insured the influence of the inspector-general.

In July 1927 Sarwat traveled to England in order to resume negotiations there concerning the treaty between the two countries; although he obtained no binding promises, he was able to set out on his voyage home in August in the hope of having straightened his country's path to the independence desired. However, the draft of the treaty, still heavily overburdened with provisos, could only have been put through the chamber by means of Zaghlul's influence. But the "Father of the Fatherland" died abruptly, after a short illness, on August 23, leaving behind a gap in political life which could not be filled immediately. It was he who was primarily responsible for the awakening of the Egyptians, after a bondage of a thousand years under native and foreign rulers, to a consciousness of their right to self-determination. Though his effectiveness may have been subject to the defects inevitable for his time and his environment, the Egyptian people nevertheless owes him the deepest gratitude for his life, certainly not poor in personal sacrifices, which he dedicated to its service.

Meanwhile Sarwat resumed his negotiations in London in October, and in November brought home a draft which the British government demanded an unmodified acceptance of. But before he could lay the draft of the treaty before the parliament, he was compelled to resign at the end of January 1928 because the parliament and senate had passed a law striking out of the government's hand any weapon with which it might hitherto have been able to restrict the right of free assembly. After Zaghlul's death his party had plunged into an increasingly radical channel. His successor in the leadership, his secretary of long standing, Mustafa Nahhas Pasha, although not outdone by him in ambition and tenacity, was far inferior to him in statesmanlike talents. Responsibility for the fate of Egypt now fell on him, since on March 15 the King charged him with forming a government. Although the British government indicated to him with the utmost sharpness that it could not approve the new law of assembly that threatened the peace of the country, at first he was still able to evade the consequences through a compliant answer, with which the British government declared itself satisfied. In June, however, a public scandal gave the King a pretext to dismiss the Prime Minister.* But the King soon went even fur-

* Nahhas Pasha had obligated himself to Prince Sayf-ad-Din's mother, in return for a fee of 130,000 Egyptian pounds, to contrive her acquisition of the Prince's estates, seized by the King.

ther; namely, the prime minister appointed by him, Muhammad Mahmud Pasha, one of the wealthiest landlords in Egypt, dissolved parliament and deferred the new elections for three years.

During the King's unchecked rule he succeeded in regulating advantageously the question, vital for Egypt, of the allocation of the Nile waters between his country and the Sudan; he was already considering limiting some of the particularly oppressive capitulations, and above all, extending the powers of the mixed courts at the expense of the consular jurisdiction.

But the hopes of the Wafd, which still possessed the unbounded confidence of the fellahs, for regaining power again rose when in May 1929 the Labor party in Britain once more came to the helm. Its first step was the recall of Lord Lloyd, who had been remiss in his regard for the necessary development of Egypt toward independence. In June, Mahmud Pasha began new negotiations in London for a treaty regulating the relations of the two countries; but it was borne in on him that such a treaty could only be ratified by the Egyptian parliament. The proposals published in a white paper of autumn 1929 for such a treaty went considerably beyond the concessions made to Sarwat Pasha, which nevertheless had been designated as an extreme limit in the way of compromise on the part of the British government. Naturally the Egyptians might expect to succeed in winning still further demands if they only insisted on their point of view. Britain was, after all, prepared to withdraw her troops from Cairo and Alexandria into the Canal Zone, recall all British officers in the Egyptian army, and waive all claim to the European department in the ministry of the interior.

Since the King desired the ratification of the treaty with Britain, he had to acquiesce in ordering new elections. As was to be expected, the Wafd's adherents again won an overwhelming victory and the King had to delegate the government once again to Nahhas Pasha, who then, on March 31, 1930, resumed negotiations for a treaty in London. As his predecessor had already achieved enough for Egypt, he turned all his energy to the question of the Sudan. Since he insisted that the immigration of Egyptians was not to be limited any further, and since at first he wanted to recognize a joint rule of Britain and Egypt for only one more year, he had to return home with his mission unaccomplished, and soon afterward was dismissed from office by the King. His place was taken by Isma'il Sidqi Pasha, the leader of the People's party; by a new electoral law he forced the Wafd out of parliament and ruled as the King's henchman, until he had to retire in 1933 for reasons of health. When the King also fell ill, his irresponsible counselor at the court acquired so much influence that the new prime minister Yahya Pasha thought it necessary to appeal for British aid against him. Thereupon a storm of popular indignation swept him out of office, and the King had to put up with allowing his successor, Nasim Pasha, to reintroduce the electoral law abolished by Sidqi Pasha. Thus the Wafd came into power again.

While internal politics were exhausted in factional strife, in which student riots not infrequently decided the outcome, Egypt and Britain saw their common interests in the Sudan threatened by the behavior of Italy in Abyssinia. A European power firmly established there might after all, with the resources of modern technique, have a decisive influence on one of the most important tributaries of the Nile, rising in Lake Tana. Seeing one of the most important sources of the country's prosperity threatened, the Egyptian parties combined in a united front in order to bring the negotiations with Britain, which had so often foundered before, to a final conclusion. On December 12, 1935, the united party leaders petitioned Sir Miles Lampson, the high commissioner, to invite the British government to resume negotiations for the treaty. The latter declared itself ready if the Egyptians were prepared to discuss first the most important questions—the organization of the army, and the Sudan. Meanwhile 'Ali Mahir Pasha, who left the Union party, succeeded in bringing together a neutral cabinet, which relieved the party leaders of the concern of being called to account by the voters for the outcome of the negotiations. On March 2, 1936, the British commission under Lampson met with the Egyptians under Nahhas Pasha in Cairo; his seven fellow members of the Wafd were accompanied by six men from other parties, among them three former prime ministers, Mahmud, Sidqi, and Yahya. On August 26 the treaty was signed in London and ratified by the Egyptian parliament on November 15 and 18 and by the British parliament on November 24 and 25. It definitely eliminated the military occupation of Egypt by British combat forces, except that in defense of the Suez canal ten thousand men were still to remain in the coastal zone. In recognition of the absolute sovereignty of Egypt, Britain was to be represented in Cairo by an ambassador, who was to be accorded precedence over the representatives of other powers.

Britain was to sponsor Egypt's entry into the League of Nations. Both countries concluded an alliance and bound themselves not to enter into any relations with other countries detrimental to this alliance. In case of war Egypt bound herself to place all the resources of the country at the disposal of Britain, and if necessary to introduce martial law and censorship. Egypt was to build up her railway network according to the strategic points of view regarded by Britain as requisite. Without prejudice to the question of sovereignty the administration of the Sudan remained further in the hands of the governor-general, to be appointed by Britain, and to him the Egyptian troops were also subject; the immigration of Egyptians was to be limited only for reasons of public security and of health conditions. Britain declared her readiness to support Egypt in the abolition of the capitulations, with the ultimate object of dissolving the mixed courts as well. The treaty was initially concluded for twenty years, after the expiration of which any differences were to be submitted to the decision of the Council of the League of Nations.

With this treaty, foreign rule in Egypt was terminated; though her international position remained most intimately bound up with that of Great Britain, the path to her internal development was opened up. This was still decided by the inter-party struggle. The Wafd, whose leader, Nahhas, had been able to present the Egyptian people with their long-desired independence, very soon lost sight of moderation in the proper use of his prestige; in the "Blue Shirts," an unskillful aping of a famous model, he created a bodyguard from among his youthful followers. His increasingly autocratic behavior and his intimate connection with Makram 'Ubayd Pasha, the Copt finance minister, finally brought it about that under the leadership of Dr. Ahmad Mahir, 'Ali Mahir Pasha's brother, and an-Nuqrashi Pasha, some of Zaghlul's older adherents separated from him as "Sa'dists" (after Sa'd Zaghlul Pasha).

On April 28, 1936, King Fu'ad died. His son Faruq, born on February 11, 1920, was at that time at the British military academy at Woolich. During the last year of his minority, affairs were conducted by a regency council. At the end of July 1937, after assuming the government himself, he at once recognized the weakness of the Wafd, which with the attainment of independence had fulfilled its historic task and was an obstacle to the further development of the country. On December 30, 1937, he dismissed the prime minister

Nahhas Pasha and called to his place the veteran statesman Muhammad Mahmud Pasha. On February 2, 1938, he also dissolved the parliament, in which 170 Wafd members still maintained a majority of four-fifths. In the elections of March and April 1938, only 13 were returned to the Chamber, but without their leader Nahhas and his most prominent supporters. The Young Egyptian party (*Hizb Misr al-Fatat*), under the lawyer Ahmad Husayn, attempted to rally the youth, particularly of the middle class, on the ruins of the Wafd and whip up their enthusiasm for an extreme nationalist xenophobe program; they counterposed to Nahhas's Blue Shirts their own Green Shirts, whose organization, however, was dissolved shortly before the outbreak of war in 1939.* It was the new government's intention to raise the standard of life of the nation as a whole, and above all to improve the position of the fellahs by the moderation of the land tax and the development of the irrigation installations, and to protect the national industry by a duty on cotton textile goods, which, in addition to British imports, Japan had dumped on the Egyptian market; however, it attempted to further withdraw from British tutelage, and in token of this had doubled the Egyptian army to forty thousand men. The primacy of Egypt in intellectual fields and in Muslim circles, long since undisputed, will grow with her political prestige and also achieve the long-desired emancipation from the intellectual guardianship of Europe.

3. *Arabia*

At the outbreak of the First World War the Arabian peninsula, nominally a portion of the Ottoman Empire, had disintegrated into numerous petty spheres of authority. The Hijaz, with the capital at Mecca, was ruled by the sharif Husayn ibn-'Ali ibn-'Awn, of the house of Hashim, who had lived in Istanbul since 1893 as the "guest" of the sultan 'Abd-al-Hamid but in 1908 had been reinstated in the heritage of his ancestors of the house of the Prophet by the Young Turks. Najd was divided between the principalities of the Shammar, under the house of Rashid with the capital at Hail, and the old dynasty of the Wahhabis with the capital at Riyad. Of the typically Arab history of the house of Rashid, again and again confused by

* Its program is reported by B. Spuler in the *Orientnachrichten*, IV, 18 (of Sept. 16, 1938, p. 281); see also A. Fischer, *Die politischen Parteien Ägyptens* in *Forschungen und Fortschritte*, 1938, pp. 279-281.

unflagging family strife, it can only be noted here that its most important representative, Muhammad ibn-'Abdallah ibn-Rashid (1872-1897), with the support of the Turks, had succeeded in dethroning the older dynasty of the Al-Sa'ud in Riyad. Under his nephew and successor, 'Abd-al-'Aziz ibn-Mit'ab, however, the Sa'udid 'Abd-al-'Aziz ibn-'Abd-ar-Rahman, who had fled to Shaykh Mubarak of Kuwayt, subject to Britain, was able with help to reconquer his tribal seat of Riyad in 1902. Upon the death of the Rashidid 'Abd-al-'Aziz in 1906, his son Sa'ud came to the throne after protracted disturbances. But while in the latter's state the old spirit of Wahhabism was well-nigh extinct, ibn-Sa'ud was able to revive it again by founding the brotherhood of the Ikhwan in 1910. He obligated these followers of his to strict compliance with Islamic law. Just as the Sanusi order trained its members not so much to a life of mystical contemplation as to practical labors, so ibn-Sa'ud settled his Ikhwan, who at the same time constituted his standing army, in agricultural colonies in relatively fertile parts of the Najd, and so created, in the inconstancy of nomadic life, the initial centers of state organization. In 1913 he took advantage of the weakness of the Ottoman Empire, involved in the Balkans, by conquering, in agreement with the Anglo-Indian government, the province of al-Hasa, bordering on his domains and hitherto ruled from Baghdad. This gave him access to the sea. Instead of punishing him, Turkey sought to tie him to herself by appointing him wali of the Najd, without imposing any obligations on him.

The mountain land of the 'Asir, lying in the south of the Hijaz, which Muhammad 'Ali had made a vain attempt to subdue, though still nominally belonging to the Ottoman Empire, was entirely independent. Toward the end of the eighteenth century a member of the Moroccan branch of the 'Alids, Ahmad al-Idrisi, after making the pilgrimage to Mecca, had settled there, and among the populace—still on a very inferior level of culture—had acquired the reputation of a saint, which insured his descendants something like political authority. One of them, the sayyid Muhammad, who had studied in Cairo at the al-Azhar university and then for a time lived among the Sanusis at Kufra in Cyrenaica, grouped his followers together in the mountain lands in a somewhat more rigid organization; and in 1909, at the age of thirty-five, he refused allegiance to the Turks, was defeated together with the Zaydi imam

Yahya, with whom he had allied himself, but—with the help of the Italians—was able, like his ally, to free himself again.

In neighboring Yemen the dynasty of the Zaydites had been able to survive, although since 1850 the Turks had been endeavoring to subdue their country. During the severe battles of 1904-05, after perceiving that this remote outpost could not be retained by force, the government of 'Abd-al-Hamid was already prepared to leave the mountainous interior to the imam Yahya as a free possession. But the Young Turks could not reconcile this with national honor, and resumed the struggle, only to acquiesce in a peace treaty under the same conditions in October 1911.

In the coastal territories along the Indian Ocean and the Persian Gulf, from Hadramaut through 'Uman to Kuwayt, there were settled a number of petty Arab rulers who called themselves sultans or shaykhs and had all fallen into more or less direct dependence on Great Britain, which since 1839 had been firmly established in Aden and was preoccupied with the security of the sea lanes to India in the Persian Gulf.

By the spring of 1914 the sharif Husayn, who had already become acquainted with the weakness of the Turkish empire during his exile in Istanbul, was already seeking to initiate relations with the British in Egypt through his son 'Abdallah, in the hope of finally being able to make himself independent with their aid. When Turkey entered the war, he gave immediate assurances that he would accord no obedience to the shaykh al-Islam's summons to the holy war. Britain, however, wanted to draw him into a more active participation in the war against the Turks, after the miscarriage of their attempt to involve 'Abd-al-'Aziz ibn-Sa'ud. Accordingly the British government had pamphlets disseminated to the populace by means of runners and gunboats, and gave effective emphasis to its recruiting by blocking the imports of grain from Egypt, on which the inhabitants of the Hijaz were dependent. In July 1915 Husayn was finally ready in person to enter into direct negotiations with the high commissioner, McMahon. In a note of July 15 he was already speaking in the name of the Arab people, and offered Britain their support if she would promise the Arabs independence in the entire area from Mersina-Adana in the northwest as far as the Persian frontier, and as far as the Indian Ocean, and would declare herself in agreement with the founding of an Arab caliphate. In his reply of August 30 McMahon, though giving assurance that Britain had no objection to the transfer of the caliphate to a scion of the house of the Prophet, stated that the time for the establishment of definite boundaries for an independent Arab state had not yet come, inasmuch as many Arabs were still fighting on the side of the Turks. Although the Husayn-McMahon correspondence * dragged on until the end of January 1916 without Husayn's having obtained any binding promises, these being deferred by reference to the interests of France, he nevertheless undertook the obligation to stir up the tribes subordinate to him and sympathetic to a war against the Turks, and to participate in this with his own troops. His son Faysal had even ventured into the lion's cave by lingering in Damascus from January 1915 on as a guest of the Turkish general Jamal-ad-Din, and there using his previously established connections with the Arab officers' society, al-'Ahd al-'Arabi, and its fellow conspirators in the civilian society al-Fatat (Youth), to agitate against Turkish rule. But even before the Sharif could embark on open action against his overlord, he was cheated of the fruits hoped for from the victory by the accord entered into at St. Petersburg between the Russian foreign minister Sazonov, the British Oriental expert Mark Sykes, and the former French consul-general in Beirut, F. G. Picot, which was to regulate the future partition of the Ottoman Empire. This Sykes-Picot agreement, which only became valid for the Arab provinces after the Russian exit from the Entente, laid down that in Palestine an international administration was to be set up, the coastal territory of Syria lying north of it as far as a line fixed between the cities of Damascus, Homs, and Aleppo was to fall to France as her sphere of interest, and 'Iraq was to fall to Britain; only the Syrian interior lying in between was to be erected,

* This correspondence, which Ireland (*Iraq*, pp. 68-69) quotes only from the British archives, was published completely for the first time by George Antonius, *The Arab Awakening* (London, 1938, pp. 413-427), and in the beginning of March 1939, while the Palestine Conference was in session in London, in a white paper by the British government. Even in the final note of January 30, 1916, McMahon merely declares his readiness to have the question of the vilayet of Baghdad studied after the final victory, and his satisfaction at Husayn's recognition of Britain's obligations vis-à-vis France. T. E. Lawrence, in his last work, *Seven Pillars of Wisdom* (London, 1935, p. 66 ff.), also speaks no further of any binding promises of McMahon's. It is not surprising that vis-à-vis France it later seemed opportune to speak of these. It may be doubted whether the text printed in the Arabic newspaper *al-Manar*, vol. 25 (Cairo, 1924) No. 1, and the German translation based on it in the *Mitteilungen* of the Oriental Seminar in Berlin, II, 130-131, may be regarded as a ratified treaty; see also W. Ireland, *Iraq*, p. 177, n. 4.

together with the vilayet of Mosul, as an independent Arab state or federation of states.

The severe warfare for the Dardanelles and the war in 'Iraq, where in the beginning Britain sustained heavy losses, at first did not allow the translation into action of the negotiations initiated with Husayn. It was not until after the evacuation of Gallipoli that it appeared advisable to call up the forces of the Hijaz, from which General Murray, commanding in Egypt, at first did not expect very much. Faysal meanwhile had returned home and was threatening Medina, still occupied by the Turks, with a Bedouin force from

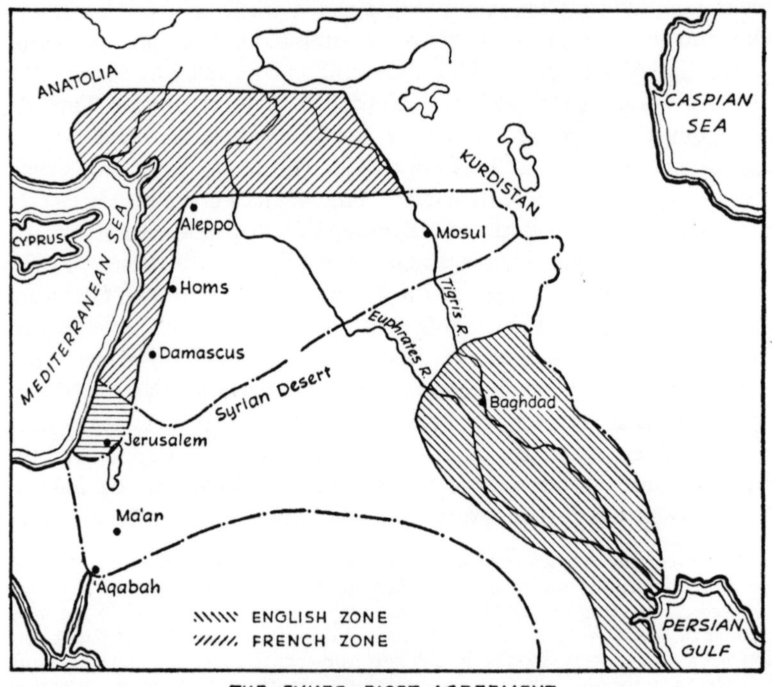

THE SYKES-PICOT AGREEMENT

Jabal Subh, while in the more southerly watering place of Rabigh, 'Aziz 'Ali al-Masri, a former colonel in the Turkish army, of Arab-Circassian origin, was endeavoring to train volunteers from Syria and 'Iraq. For the direction of the Arab enterprise the Arab Bureau in Cairo sent out to Hijaz T. E. Lawrence, famous afterward through his books recounting his experiences,* which were of great literary effect, and who almost became a national hero to British youth. He perceived at once that the most enterprising of Husayn's sons, Faysal, was already in possession of the most favorable position for the struggle against the Turks, and joined him; but no sooner had he got to him than he had to retreat before the Turks and retire to the harbor of Yanbu'. On Lawrence's advice Faysal decided to assemble his troops farther north near Wajh, whence the Hijaz railway could be threatened with the greatest ease. While Murray hoped to see the Turkish troops annihilated on their retreat from Wajh, Lawrence was anxious to secure a further point of support in the north. While Faysal remained in Wajh, Lawrence succeeded on July 5, 1917, in surprising the harbor of 'Aqabah with the help of a respected Bedouin shaykh. From there he hoped to be able to cover and facilitate Allenby's advance on the Sinai peninsula and in Palestine as though with a right flank. When Allenby had to transfer his troops to Flanders after the seizure of Jerusalem, thus postponing his advance, Lawrence returned to Faysal in order to prepare an attack on Medina and so divert Turkish troops from the Palestine front as far as possible. After the Hijaz railway was successfully broken at three points, Allenby attacked the Turks in Palestine by surprise and drove them over the Jordan. Thereupon Lawrence pushed on northward and was able to move into Damascus on November 30, 1918, with his troops reinforced by a division of Australians.

While Faysal and 'Abdallah were stationed in the field against the Turks, their father Husayn was preoccupied with the consolidation of his power in the Hijaz. With this object he had himself proclaimed by the grandees at Mecca "King of the Arabs" (October 29, 1916 †), and accepted their allegiance on November 2 according to ancient custom. By this he meant to insure at the outset the rights due him from the treaty he thought to have concluded with McMahon. But at once he experienced a grave disappointment, inasmuch as Britain, France, and Italy recognized him only as king of the Hijaz, informing him of this in a joint note of January 3. This

* *Revolt in the Desert*, London, 1927; *Seven Pillars of Wisdom*, London, 1935.

† Strothmann, *Islam* XVII, 38, states, after Toynbee, that Husayn was not proclaimed King of the Arabs until after the conquest of Damascus in October 1918; this contradicts data of other sources; see E. Topf, p. 23, Antonius, p. 213.

step was enough to show that he had overestimated his actual resources in romantic dreams of the greatness of his house and had falsely evaluated his position in Arabia. In Najd, meanwhile, as will be reported directly, 'Abd-al-'Aziz ibn-Sa'ud had come to power. He could not recognize Husayn's claim to suzerainty in Arabia, and no doubt it was not necessary for him to have been incited first by Khalid ibn-Lu'ayy, a hostile cousin of Husayn's, to induce him to attack Husayn's troops. On May 19, 1919, he won a decisive victory at Turabah, east of Taif, over their leader, the emir 'Abdallah. Instead of wiping out his disgrace, which had dealt a severe blow to his prestige in Arabia, Husayn concentrated his entire interest on the peace negotiations in Paris, which he still hoped would grant his presumptive claims. In deepest disappointment, accordingly, he rejected the treaties of Versailles and Sèvres, but by this merely secured his not even being invited at all to the Lausanne conference. After the British politicians and military men in March 1921 had laid down the basic lines for the treatment of the Arab question at a conference in Cairo, T. E. Lawrence was sent to the harbor city of Jiddah at the end of August to conclude a treaty with Husayn. In return for the continued payment of the previously received subsidies and the promise to protect him against attacks in the Hijaz, he was supposed to recognize the mandates over Syria and 'Iraq meanwhile established in San Remo. He was unable to acquiesce in this, although he could no longer expect any other proposals. The negotiations, which dragged on into the summer of 1924, finally ran aground, after Husayn had already reconciled himself to the conditions relating to Syria and 'Iraq, on his refusal to recognize the mandate over Palestine. The extent to which he still misjudged his position was shown on March 5, 1924, when he was induced, half reluctantly, by his son 'Abdallah, on whom Britain had meanwhile conferred the emirate of Transjordan, to accept, during a visit at the latter's residence in Shuna, the title of caliph, which had become free as a result of the deposition of Muhammad VI; but he failed to meet with recognition even in Syria, to say nothing of the Indian Muslims, who blamed him severely for this defection from Turkey. In any case his prestige in the Islamic world had suffered through his having done nothing to prevent the exploitation of the pilgrims in Mecca, long since traditional, to be sure, or to improve the administration of the country. His claim to the caliphate gave ibn-Sa'ud a pretext to combat him as a heretic, and when Husayn turned for aid against him to the British, they simply abandoned him in favor of the newly rising power. In the last week of August 1924 the Wahhabis advanced on Taif; they overran the town and slaughtered the inhabitants. The Meccans entreated Husayn to abdicate. He transferred the power to his oldest son 'Ali and fled to 'Aqabah. But ibn-Sa'ud was not now to be deterred in his advance; his subcommander, the sharif Khalid ibn-Lu'ayy, occupied Mecca on October 13. He himself first entered it on December 5, after calming the Sunnites, already apprehensive of a repetition of the atrocities perpetrated during the first seizure of the Holy City by the Wahhabis. 'Ali held out in Jiddah until December 1925 and then fled to his brother Faysal in 'Iraq. Accordingly, ibn-Sa'ud had himself proclaimed king of the Hijaz on January 8, 1926. Since ibn-Sa'ud also laid claim to 'Aqabah, the British expelled Husayn in June 1926 and granted him refuge on Cyprus. Toward the end of 1930 he was permitted to settle in 'Amman in Transjordan with his son; there he died in June 1931, finding his last resting place in Jerusalem. In him the fate of the house of Hashim had been consummated once again: like so many of his forebears of 'Ali's clan, in the conviction of his divine right he had finally lost any insight into the circumstances of this world and so fell victim to his conviction.

At the outbreak of the First World War the Wahhabi prince 'Abd-al-'Aziz was still too heavily preoccupied with the development of his domestic power to risk it by a strict fulfillment of his obligations as Turkish wali. Since he was advised by the British consul in Kuwayt, Shakespear, the Turks took the side of the Rashidid Sa'ud against him, particularly after the latter's guardian, Zamil, was assassinated by an ambitious cousin, Sa'ud as-Salih. Since the latter was supported by the Turks with gold and weapons, Shakespear finally succeeded in inciting the Wahhabis to attack. In January 1915 a battle took place at Jarrab. With his superior cavalry ibn-Sa'ud had already believed himself victorious when his infantry, advancing by another route, were attacked by surprise; thereupon the Bedouins of the 'Ajman tribe, whom he had once robbed of their pasturing grounds in al-Hasa, fell pillaging on his encampment, deciding the day against him. Shakespear, who could not be prevented from directing the fire of the single cannon possessed by ibn-Sa'ud at the time, fell in battle. From then on ibn-Sa'ud prudently held himself in reserve, particularly since the Anglo-Indian government also displayed no special interest in the Arabian theater of war after its initial failures in 'Iraq. The role assigned to it in the war against Turkey had been transferred meanwhile to Husayn by the British government. But the Anglo-Indian government believed it necessary to secure the war being conducted by it in 'Iraq through ibn-Sa'ud's aid, and dispatched St. John Philby to Riyad, who soon won the prince's complete confidence. Husayn's attempt to strike into Najd had been prevented by ibn-Sa'ud in the battle of Turabah. But before he armed for a final struggle against him, he still had to do away with the power of the house of Rashid, threatening him from the rear. In Hail the emir Sa'ud had been assassinated in the spring of 1920. This gave ibn-Sa'ud a pretext for turning against the latter's successor, 'Abdallah ibn-Mit'ab. After the latter had been defeated in April 1921 his place was taken by Muhammad ibn-Tallal, who defended the capital until November 1921. After its fall ibn-Sa'ud was able to restore the rule of his house throughout Najd. Its expansion northward was limited by the newly created mandatory states of Syria and 'Iraq. However, since the boundaries of the two were not yet determined, he succeeded in pressing forward in the west through the wadi as-Sirhan and in the east through the wadi ar-Rummah. But then Husayn's imprudent attempt to usurp the caliphate, as already told, gave ibn-Sa'ud a pretext—and in the eyes of believers the right—to drive him out and establish Sa'udi rule in the Hijaz. In order to allay the apprehensions raised in the Islamic world by the rule in its Holy Land of a prince it considered a heretic, he convoked an all-Muslim congress at Mecca in June 1926, after a congress in Cairo had discussed the caliphate question in May without arriving at any result. Since the delegates from Arabia were naturally especially numerous, and delegations from Russia, Afghanistan, Java, and the Sudan made up for the absence of the North Africans, the Meccan congress was twice as heavily attended (60:30) as the one in Cairo. The astute diplomacy of the Wahhabis enabled it to succeed in securing equal rights for the sects at the sanctuary, and so in securing freedom of the pilgrimage for the entire Islamic world, even though nothing has come of the intended periodic congresses and the levying of fixed contributions for them.* In 1930 ibn-Sa'ud had himself crowned in Mecca as king of Najd and the Hijaz.

* See Achille Sekaly, *Le Congrès du Khalifat et le Congrès du Monde Musulman*, Paris, 1926 (Collection de la *Revue du monde musulman*).

Ibn-Sa'ud's foreign policy was at first determined by his relations with his neighbor in the south. In 'Asir, after the death of the sayyid Muhammad in 1923, dissension had broken out among his heirs, which was utilized by the Zaydi imam Yahya to seize the coastal region with the important harbor of Hudaydah, which the British had evacuated on January 31, 1921. Against these encroachments the shaykhs of 'Asir sought help from ibn-Sa'ud and placed their country under his protection by a treaty concluded at Mecca on October 21, 1926.

The imam Yahya had meanwhile entered into relations with Italy, which hoped to make secure its colony Eritrea from the opposite coast and had long since seized an economic foothold in Yemen. On September 2, 1926, he concluded a treaty of friendship with Italy, in which the prospect of economic assistance and the provision of war material was held out in return for the promise to favor Italian enterprises and co-operate in the suppression of the slave trade. The crown prince Sayf-al-Islam Muhammad visited Rome on June 1, 1927, in order to negotiate with Italian industrialists. The help won in this way was overestimated by the Imam, who believed he could expand his territory at first in the hinterland of Aden at the expense of the British protectorate. Since Britain was actually interested only in Aden, in the beginning she was ready for concessions, although the Imam repeatedly attacked her wards, and did not make use of her air force until he demanded the return of all territory previously belonging to Yemen. Although the Imam yielded a portion of the territory occupied by him, he still held out for a long time against the conclusion of a treaty, and even was fortified in his resistance by a Soviet Russian trade delegation. It was only when he was threatened by ibn-Sa'ud that he acquiesced in a treaty. His boundaries with the Wahhabi-protected state of 'Asir continually gave rise to friction, which at the beginning of 1934 forced ibn-Sa'ud to take energetic action. In a swift advance his troops occupied the coastal regions of the Tihamah, together with Hudaydah. But ibn-Sa'ud contented himself, in the peace treaty concluded at Taif on May 20, 1934, with the recognition of his boundaries and waived any territorial demands.

The King of Najd and the Hijaz has been more concerned with the consolidation than with the expansion of his power. Although on occasion he has suppressed rebellions of individual Bedouin tribes, he has generally preferred, after the example of the Prophet, to secure his power by means of family alliances with the ruling shaykhs, in which the Islamic marriage laws and the ease of divorce have been of convenience to him. But he has also been successfully concerned with opening up his domains to civilization, in which St. John Philby has given him careful advice. The agricultural colonies of his Ikhwan have already been mentioned. He has addressed special attention to the question of transport, of particular importance because of the prodigious spaces to be traversed. Like the French and British in Syria and 'Iraq who substituted automobiles more and more for the camel caravans—the supply of camels during the First World War had brought the Arabs enormous profits—he introduced the automobile into Arabia, where the pilgrim traffic is now entirely motorized. He has long since used the telephone and radio in his administration, and has lately, particularly after becoming acquainted personally with the advantages of European medicine, been endeavoring to make the benefits of modern hygiene and medicine available to his subjects. Even education, which had hitherto, apart from Mecca and Medina, been entirely neglected in Arabia, has attracted his attention.

4. *Syria, Palestine, Transjordan, and 'Iraq*

Husayn's revolt against the Turks simultaneously raised the hopes of the Arabs throughout the Ottoman Empire. Of course differences in social structure and religion still made it impossible to speak of any community of national feeling in Syria. Apart from the national minorities of the Kurds, Armenians, and the scattered Circassians, the economic interests of the Bedouins, fellahs, and city dwellers were too variegated to make possible the unification of the population, split into Sunnites, Shi'ites, Druzes, and Nusayris on the one hand, and Catholics, Maronites, Melkites and Jacobites united with Rome, Greek Orthodox, and Nestorians on the other hand. Only the upper classes had the sense of belonging together against their Turkish masters, a feeling which had awakened under the influence of French culture, powerful in the coastal regions for more than a century, and the democratic ideas disseminated by the American University in Beirut. While the tyrannical regime of 'Abd-al-Hamid suppressed all freedom of thought, and in combination with the economic backwardness had driven many Syrians to emigrate to Egypt and to America, the rule of the Young Turks—who wanted to unify all citizens of the Ottoman Empire around a new constitutional ideal, by disregarding national differentiation, and accordingly suppressed the cultivation of Arabic by violence–strengthened the desires of the Arabs for liberation and self-determination. In the given political circumstances the adherents of this idea were forced into the formation of underground societies, following in this the example of the Young Turks themselves. In 1904 the Syrian Najib 'Azuri had founded an Arab patriotic society with the object of gaining France's assistance in the detaching of the Arab provinces from the Ottoman Empire; with the introduction of the constitution, however, he regarded his goal as attained and ceased publication of his newspaper *L'Indépendence Arabe*, founded by him together with the former French colonial official E. Jung. Directly after the proclamation of the Turkish constitution a number of Arabs living in Istanbul formed the Arab-Osmanli Brotherhood (al-Ikha al-'Arabi al-'Uthmani) in order to cultivate their national ideals in the framework of the new state; but after 'Abd-al-Hamid's *coup d'état* this society was suppressed. Warned by its fate, the Arab officials, deputies, and literati in Istanbul formed an ostensibly purely literary club (al-Muntada al-Adabi) in the summer of 1909, which was soon able to set up branches in Egypt and Syria and in particular endeavored to arouse Arab national feeling in the youth; the society dissolved in March 1915. Within the club a number of higher Arab functionaries, among them the former minister of Evkaf (endowments), Khalil Hamadah Pasha, and the general staff officer 'Aziz 'Ali al-Masri, whom we have already encountered in Husayn's service, formed a narrower association with political aims, the Qahtaniyah. From it there emerged the officers' club called al-'Ahd, later joined by a special 'Iraqi section which gave clear expression to its aims in a new name, ath-Thawrah al-'Arabiyah (The Arab Revolution). In the Lebanon, which had, after all, long since possessed an autonomous administration well-nigh free of Ottoman influence, an-Nahdah al-Lubnaniyah (Lebanese Progress) had been formed which advocated an occupation of the country by France, and accordingly was energetically supported by the French consul-general in Beirut. The Reform party (al-Jam'iyah al-Islahiyah), founded by Christians in Beirut, collaborated with it. Most of these societies soon dissolved in the La-Markaziyah (Decentralization League), founded in Egypt toward the end of 1912, which extended its net over the entire Arabic-speaking area. This was also joined by al-Fatat al-'Arabiyah (Arab Youth), founded by Arab students in Paris in 1911, which worked hand in hand with the 'Ahd, particularly among the civil servants in Syria.* At a congress held in Paris in June 1913 the representatives of these societies put together their demands, among which the restrictions of military service to the homeland and the introduction of Arabic as the official language were the most important, and the Young Turks, who had their own men at the congress, showed themselves disposed, under the pressure of the Balkan war, to make such concessions. But when the First World War broke out, Jamal Pasha, the commander-in-chief of the Fourth Army in Syria, refused to tolerate the activity of these societies behind his back, and after their correspondence with Picot, the French consul-general in Beirut, had fallen into his hands, he applied the full rigor of martial law to their members, of whom thirty-three were sentenced to death by court-martial at 'Aliyah in the Lebanon.

The hopes of the Arab nationalists were revivified and brought to extreme tension by the joint declaration of Britain and France of November 8, 1918, after the truce of Mudros, that their military objective, the liberation of the peoples oppressed by the Turks, had been attained, and that they were now prepared to set up independent governments in Syria and Mesopotamia which were to guarantee freedom of evolution for these countries.† Whether the sharif Husayn would have succeeded, if Britain had kept her half-promises, in bringing together under his rule these centrifugal groups of interests, may surely be doubted, despite the connections his son Faysal had made in Damascus. But the Sykes-Picot agreement and the Balfour Declaration of November 2, 1917, in favor of a national home to be set up in Palestine for the Jews, alone showed that the Entente had made quite different decisions concerning the fate of the Arab provinces of the Turkish empire. For France it was a question of prestige, and of finally deriving some political

* The best information on the organization of the Arab societies is in the Turkish green paper, *La Verité sur la question syrienne, publié par le Commandement de la IVème Armée*, Stamboul, 1916; cf. also G. Antonius, *The Arab Awakening*, p. 101 ff., Amin Sa'id (editor of the Cairo newspaper *al-Muqattam*), *Ath-Thawrah al-'Arabiyah al-Kubra* (a well-documented account forbidden by the French in Syria; see *Oriente Moderno* XV, 1935, p. 157) v. I, Cairo, n.d. p. 1-50; G. Kampffmeyer, *Dokumente zum Kampf der Araber um ihre Unabhängigkeit, Welt des Islams*, VIII (1926), p. 79-186.

† Ireland, *Iraq*, pp. 459 f.; Antonius, *Arab Awakening*, 435 f.

benefit from the right of protection claimed for centuries over Oriental Christianity and from her successful labors on behalf of the dissemination of French culture in Syria, even though her economic interests in Syria were not yet considerable. But Britain had to keep in mind the vital interests of her empire in 'Iraq, in order to secure the sea lanes to India against any attack from the Persian Gulf, round them off by the new airways, and finally to convert the rich oil fields of southern Persia and of 'Iraq to the use of her maritime dominion.

After Husayn had already buried his hopes, his sons still sought to save at least something. Faysal had reconciled himself to the French occupation of the Syrian coastal regions after the Sykes-Picot agreement, and hoped to be recognized as ruler at least in the interior, for which the prospect of an "independent" state was held out. Accordingly, in November 1918, he went himself to London, in order to negotiate with the foreign office and the Zionist leaders, and on February 6, 1919, together with Lawrence, laid the demand of the Arabs for complete independence before the peace conference at Paris, although the Syrian central committee in Paris had demanded a special position for Syria and the Lebanon under a French mandate. Since Faysal laid special emphasis on having the wishes of the populace itself heard, the Council of Four, on March 25, agreed to Wilson's proposal to dispatch two American experts to Syria, H. C. King and Charles R. Crane. This made Faysal believe he had attained his goal, and he returned to Syria during the first week in April. There he at once began working against France, and for this gained the support of the Turks and particularly of Britain, which provided him with money and his adherents with weapons. By the beginning of February the former secret society al-Fatat had already constituted itself openly as the Arab Independence party and convoked a congress which demanded an independent Syria with Palestine under Faysal as king, and while rejecting the mandate, solicited American or in any case British aid in the setting up of this state. The King-Crane commission * traveled through Palestine and Syria for six weeks, beginning June 10, and also declared itself for Faysal as king of Syria, recommending the mandate system, but rejecting the surrender of Palestine to the Zionists. Since Wilson had fallen ill soon after the return of the commission, its report had

[* H. N. Howard, *The King-Crane Commission*, in *The Moslem World*, April 1942.]

no influence on the fortunes of Syria. After France and Britain failed to come to any agreement, Lloyd George invited Faysal to London again in August 1919; and, provided with his instructions, the latter concluded an agreement with Clemenceau in Paris on November 27 in which France bound herself to recognize Faysal's state as an independent buffer state if he would accept France's help in its development. Soon afterward the British began to evacuate northern Syria, and as soon as the French moved in, they came up against Arab resistance at Tripoli, Baalbek, and other places. Upon Faysal's return to Syria his agreement with Clemenceau at first met with sharp criticism; nevertheless he succeeded in calming his followers by pointing to its provisional character, and a national congress at Damascus proclaimed him king on March 8, 1920.

But on April 25, 1920, the conference of San Remo transferred the mandate over the whole of Syria to France *; supported by this, General Gouraud, in command of Lebanon, handed Faysal an ultimatum on July 14, 1920, demanding recognition of the French mandate, supervision of the railways, the introduction of currency issued by him, and the punishment of the "revolutionaries." At first Faysal was disposed to compliance, but then, under the pressure of aroused public opinion, had to reject the ultimatum. His troops were defeated by General Goybet on July 22; Aleppo was occupied on July 23, Damascus on the 25th. In vain had Faysal waited for British help. In the Treaty of Sèvres of August 10, 1920, Syria as an independent state had been given over to France's mandate until it should be ripe for self-government; but this did not prevent France from breaking up Syria into four states: (1) greater Lebanon; (2) Damascus; (3) Aleppo, and (4) the 'Alawi state (the Nusayri territory north of the Lebanon between the Orontes and the Mediterranean). The cities of Beirut and Tripoli, as well as the Biqa' (valley; ancient Coele-Syria) were also incorporated into the Lebanon, so that Syria proper was entirely cut off from the sea; while the 200,000 Maronites, devoted to France, had previously formed a majority in the Lebanon, they were now joined by 135,000 Christians of various denominations, in addition to 30,000 Armenians, and 20,000 foreigners together with 250,000 Sunnites, 105,000 Shi'ites

* The world first learned what it might expect from these mandates on June 25, 1920, from the speech made by Lord Curzon, the British foreign secretary, in the House of Lords, in which he declared with gratifying frankness that the mandate of the League of Nations was a fiction, since it was only a question of the apportionment of the conquered provinces among the victors; see text in Ireland, *Iraq*, p. 263.

and 44,000 Druzes, and the traditional lack of unity made the internal development of the state very difficult. The formerly autonomous Druze territory in Hawran was joined on to Damascus. In all four states the power lay in the hands of the French officials, though Damascus obtained a Francophile Syrian as governor.

However, the Syrians were not to be calmed by this division, and they unleashed a lively agitation against it not only in the indigenous press but also through their compatriots in Europe. France attempted to meet it in 1922 by counterposing to Greater Lebanon the three remaining states as a Syrian Federation of States, but without making any essential alterations in their internal organization. The Constitution of May 22, 1926 transformed Greater Lebanon into a republic, whose costly administrative apparatus, however, had to be substantially simplified in the course of the following two years.

The Syrian federation received a federative council, which was to elect its president once a year; but since his decrees required the approval of the high commissioner, they meant very little in the otherwise independent administrations of the individual states. Consequently, only two years later, France abandoned this fictitious construction. General Weygand, Gouraud's successor, dissolved the federation on January 1, 1925, and combined Damascus and Aleppo into a Syrian state, while the independent 'Alawi state was left in existence.

The long-fermenting discontent of the Syrians, cheated of their hopes, broke out in July 1925 among the Druzes, for centuries proud of their independence, through the ruthless behavior of a French captain ruling them as commissioner. Although in September General Gamelin was able to relieve the punitive expedition encircled by the Druzes in Suwayda, the rebellion now flared up in Damascus as well as throughout the country. The French did not balk at arming Circassians and Armenians, and let them quarter themselves wherever they liked. Although General Sarrail was recalled after having Damascus bombed from the air and bombarded from the citadel, his successor, the civilian de Jouvenel, was driven to the same course of action in May 1926. Guerrilla warfare did not die out until the spring of 1927.

In August 1926 France was forced to replace the former military governors by sending to Syria M. Ponsot, an experienced administrative official, who in his seven years of service, though making amends for the worst blunders of his predecessors, was unable to satisfy the demands of the nationalists. In February 1928 he charged one of them, Taj-ad-Din al-Hasani, with the formation of a government and in April ordered elections to the national assembly, which were finally to give Syria a constitution. Although Ponsot omitted nothing in influencing the elections, they nevertheless ended in an overwhelming victory for the Radicals, who after parliament convened, elected Faysal's former premier, Hashim Bey al-Atasi, as president. On August 2 the constitutional committee installed by the parliament laid down a draft which entirely disregarded the mandate, demanding a republic with a president to be elected for three years and Islam as the religion of the state. Since the national assembly ignored the protest of Ponsot against its demands, which could not be reconciled with the mandate of the League of Nations, he had to prorogue it. It was only after lengthy negotiations with the party chiefs, who soon ceased presenting any solid front with respect to his objections, that Ponsot was able to introduce the republican constitution in 1930, and in June 1932 a parliament agreeable to him emerged from the elections, manipulated this time with greater success. It elected a president compliant to France. The following year Ponsot was also able to lay before the parliament the draft of a treaty with France which, like the treaty with Britain in 'Iraq, was to take the place of the mandate; however, since the draft failed to satisfy the expectations of the nationalists, it was rejected and Ponsot resigned. His successor, de Martel, dissolved parliament after it again refused to accept a draft of the treaty, and assumed solitary control of the government. In the first half of January 1936, when on the occasion of a memorial celebration for a leader of the nationalist party he had its offices searched by the police, indignation against his methods of government broke out in a strike of protest which paralyzed economic life for a number of weeks. At the end of February the High Commissioner found himself forced to yield. The French government declared itself ready to negotiate with a Syrian delegation in Paris concerning a treaty. The strike was ended on March 1. But only after Leon Blum had assumed the government in Daladier's place was a treaty satisfying to the Syrians concluded on September 9, on the model of which de Martel was able to conclude a corresponding treaty with the Lebanese Republic on November 13. The treaty, which was not to enter into effect for three years, limited France's military establishment in Syria to one garrison each in the Hawran and Lataqiyah, and two permanent air bases, while in the Lebanon her garrisoning rights remained restricted. France bound herself to secure entry into the League of Nations for both states. This would have fulfilled the most pressing wishes of the nationalists and cleared the way for a free evolution of both states, without France's giving up the possibility of further fulfilling her cultural mission in the east.

Still more bitterly than the Syrians were the Arabs in Palestine * disappointed in their hopes by the outcome of World War I, since at the side of the British they had made great sacrifices for the liberation of their country from Turkish rule. Husayn had always regarded Palestine, with the city of Jerusalem, holy to Muslims too, as an essential part of the Arab state he hoped for. The Turkish attacks against the Suez canal, however, convinced Britain again of the proposition so often demonstrated in history, that the control of Egypt could only really be secured by a glacis in Syria, and that the Sinai peninsula, which she had first taken with this perspective, was inadequate for this. In 1915 Lord Grey and Lloyd George seem to have approved a plan, emanating from the high command in Egypt, for incorporating Palestine into the empire. But in view of world opinion it appeared advisable to conceal this plan behind a humanitarian façade; a suitable pretext for this was offered by the demand raised at the first Zionist congress in Basel in August 1897, to create for the Jewish people a homeland in Palestine. Since France still raised claims to all Syria, the Sykes-Picot agreement spoke only of an international administration to be set up in Palestine, whose form was to be jointly determined by the Allies and the sharif of Mecca. It was Balfour who in November 1917 first declared himself openly in favor of the creation of a national home, in a letter to Lord Rothschild. Britain gained the support of the Jewish press for her plans in Palestine. But her plans aroused French opposition at the Paris peace conference, and only the threat of withdrawing her support in the plundering of Germany enabled Britain to have her way. At the San Remo conference she had the mandate over Palestine transferred to her on July 24, 1922, with no more talk of an international administration. On August 10 she then issued the constitution for Palestine, which in its ambiguous attitude, determined by the dual goal of British policy, contained within itself the germ of the country's hapless evolution. The high commissioner, to be

* [It is regrettable that on this controversial and tragic issue the author presents a partisan version in which a number of facts are inaccurately recorded. We did not deem it our task to change the text, but feel it our duty to forewarn the reader.—Tr.]

installed by the British government, received an almost absolute power, with the function of dividing the country into administrative districts, disposing freely of state lands, mineral deposits, treasures, etc., and appointing and dismissing officials. He was to have at his side a legislative council of ten officials and twelve elected members. In addition to the new secular courts to be set up, of which one was also provided for the district of Beersheba, in order to decide disputes among the Bedouins in accordance with their prescriptive law, the religious courts of the Muslims, Jews, and Christians held exclusive jurisdiction in all questions of personal status. English, Arabic, and Hebrew were to be recognized as official languages of equal right. Questions of immigration were to be decided by a committee consisting of at least eleven members of the legislative council; differences of opinion between this committee and the high commissioner were to be decided by the British foreign secretary. Foreign affairs for Palestine would be conducted by the imperial government, which would also defend the country with its troops. Although the British government at once explained that this constitution was not to serve as a means of erecting a Jewish state in Palestine, nevertheless there immediately arose among the Arabs of both religions the fear that their political and economic condition was threatened by Jewish immigration, particularly since Britain sent out as the first high commissioner a Jew, Sir Herbert Samuel. And in fact Jewish capitalists succeeded in procuring hitherto fallow lands from great Arab landholders, of whom many lived outside the country, and instituting Jewish agricultural colonies on them. In the cities, particularly in the new foundation of Tel Aviv, Jewish capital created flourishing industries and attracted more and more commerce. The unmistakable economic prosperity of the country could scarcely have been brought about by the indigenous population; moreover, the latter only benefited it to the smallest extent. Whereas Jewish immigration, constantly growing until 1925, from there on declined, and in 1927 was even exceeded by emigration, from 1933 on it swelled again considerably. In 1926 the number of Jews in the Palestinian civil service (678) had already exceeded that of the Muslims (632) but still remained far behind that of the Christians (1,244).* During the first few years contradic-

* It was precisely Christian Arabs who were primarily city dwellers; according to the census of 1931 only 21,318 lived on the land, as against 69,289 in the cities, while opposed to the 184,438 city-dwelling Muslims there were 491,196 fellahs and 60,000 Bedouins.

tions between Islam and Christianity, particularly profound in the Holy Land from of old, still hindered unity among the Arabs. It was only in 1928 that it was possible to convene an Arab congress in Jerusalem, which on July 23 demanded the creation of a popular representative body by the High Commissioner. The Jews, who would have been in a minority in it, combated the proposal with the utmost vigor; but the British government from its own standpoint also found it impossible to agree to it.

The high tide of Jewish immigrants from Germany, which began in 1933 and which swelled to 61,541 in 1935, at once called forth a violent reaction on the part of the Arabs. At this point Christians and Muslims came together in common defense; the rivalry of the leading Muslim families, which had hitherto still been extremely intense, now also receded into the background. As leader of the Muslims the mufti of Jerusalem, Amin al-Husayni, gained increasing influence. While previously collisions had taken place between Arabs and Jews, apart from the assaults on travelers, customary from of old, which even the police of the mandatory power had not been able to stop, these now grew more and more into a civil war. From 1935 on, Arab volunteers organized themselves to win for the Arabs the right of self-determination. The melancholy tale of these feuds need not and cannot be related here.

Britain's attempts to make amends for this greatest failure in her Oriental policy have up to now remained unsuccessful. In the summer of 1936 she dispatched a royal commission to Palestine to investigate the situation. Unfortunately the Arabs decided to boycott it, and only abandoned this imprudent behavior five days before its departure, so that it was referred principally to British and Jewish authorities. The commission, in its report of July 1937, arrived at the impossible proposal to split up the country, which by its structure can only constitute an economic unit, into three independent states, a Jewish one in the northwest (which, however, would still have included about 300,000 Arabs) and an Arab one for the remainder of the country, except for a new British mandate with the holy cities of Jerusalem, Bethlehem, and Nazareth. Although a storm of indignation against this plan arose among the Arabs, in the spring of 1938 Britain sent out another technical commission in order to investigate whether the plan might be executed if necessary by means of an extensive resettlement. Meanwhile the British government convinced itself that no solution of the difficult problem could be found on this path, and accordingly sought to convoke the leaders of the contending parties to a conference for an amicable settlement; but since it refused to admit to the conference the Mufti of Jerusalem, who had escaped to Beirut on October 19, 1937, before the threat of arrest, the conference could not be held until February 1939. Syria, 'Iraq, Egypt, and Sa'udi Arabia were also represented at it. But the Arabs refused to meet with the Jewish delegates, and so at the beginning of March 1939 the fate of the country still hung in the balance.

Transjordan—which on the basis of its entire history, belonged to Syria, and in the Sykes-Picot agreement was also included in the territory of the Arab state to be founded—was, under the mandate of San Remo in 1922, transferred to Great Britain as "lying between the Jordan and the eastern boundary of Palestine." It was tacitly claimed by Britain, for which it was indispensable as a buffer state against ibn-Sa'ud's kingdom and as a link with 'Iraq. This country, economically still quite undeveloped and inhabited mostly by Bedouins, moreover offered a good opportunity of making the Arab world forget Britain's breach of promise to the family of King Husayn. At the end of 1920 when 'Abdallah, Faysal's brother, who in the beginning had been envisaged as ruler of 'Iraq but had then had to yield to his brother, appeared with a small Bedouin force on the southern boundary of Palestine for the purpose of intervening in Syria, he was induced by the British officials to come to a halt, though not to retreat to the Hijaz. In December, Faysal had traveled to London and persuaded Churchill, then British colonial minister, that it was in Britain's interest to satisfy him and his brother. For this purpose Churchill himself traveled to Cairo in March 1921 and from there to Jerusalem. On his orders 'Abdallah was conducted by a British official on a special express of the Hijaz railway to Kerak and 'Amman, and there accepted the allegiance of the shaykhs whom the British high commissioner, Sir Herbert Samuel, himself had already prepared for the "independence" being granted them in a speech at as-Salt on July 12, 1920.* On March 28 he was received by Churchill in Jerusalem and confirmed by him as emir. Britain reserved for herself only the dispatching of a resident

* This account, which in some details diverges from Toynbee, is based on information given by Amin Sa'id, II, 11.

to the capital at 'Amman and the construction of two air bases in 'Amman and al-Jizah. But the British government considered it appropriate for the time being to leave matters in suspense.

In October 1922 'Abdallah himself went to London with his chief minister Rida ar-Rikabi, who had previously served his brother in Damascus, in order to bring about a definitive decision. But it was only on May 24, 1923, that Samuel was able to proclaim, during a visit to 'Amman on the occasion of the Muslim festival of the end of the fast, that Britain would recognize 'Abdallah's emirate if he would conclude a treaty concerning the rights of the mandate and give the country a constitution. This demand, which calculated on the further restriction of the Emir's power, in any case slight, created an uproar among the Bedouins, politically thoroughly immature, and revived ancient dissensions under the pretext of the formation of modern parties. Thus in August 1924, when the Emir was making the pilgrimage to Mecca, disturbances took place which overflowed as far as Syria. Accordingly, upon his return he was confronted by a British ultimatum which not only demanded the delivery of the culprits but which also entirely withdrew the financial administration from his influence. He had to acquiesce in a government whose three most important ministries were held by British officials. On February 20, 1928, a treaty was then concluded in London which divested him of all real power.* But Britain had underestimated the energies of the country. The indignation stirred up by the entire Arab press over the surrender of all rights exacted of the Arabs vented itself in disorders and strikes of protest, which Britain attempted to keep down by bombers. The constitution imposed on the Emir on April 16 also gave him and his people no rights as against Britain and accordingly encountered resistance on all sides. An assembly of the Bedouin shaykhs and the city grandees, convened in 'Amman in July 1928, rejected the British mandate in so far as it contravened its real purpose of preparing for autonomy, and demanded a freely elected parliament. Consequently in the autumn the populace offered the most violent resistance to the government's attempt to introduce elections along its own lines, and it was only in January 1929 that a "People's Representation" elected by only three per cent of those entitled to vote could be brought together.

* English text based on the white paper of March 26, 1938 in *The Near East and India,* vol. 33 (1928) pp. 427-429; Arabic text in Amin Sa'id, III, pp. 25-31.

There could be no question under these circumstances of the development of any political life in Transjordan. Parliamentary sessions often failed to take place because the deputies did not appear. The economic life of the country was particularly disturbed by the attempts of the Zionists to purchase or lease land for Jewish settlers. In 1933 the emir 'Abdallah himself leased to the Jews 65,000 dunams (one dunam equals 900 square meters) in the Ghor al-Kabid, for ninety-nine years, for 20,000 Palestinian pounds; when soon afterward he made a pilgrimage to the grave of the saint Abu 'Ubaydah 'Amir ibn-al-Jarrah, the people took this for an expiation of his treachery. But other great landholders as well, such as the shaykh of the banu Sakhr, Mithqal Pasha al-Faiz, favored Jewish colonization and founded a new party with the *Desert Echo* as organ. It also held a congress in 'Amman in order to discuss further plans for the economic development of the country. At a rival congress which Husayn Pasha at-Tarawnah convoked, Arab solidarity was emphasized. Under its influence a law was passed in April 1933 by the "People's Representation" which prohibited any sale or lease of land to the Zionists, or, as it was put, at the publication of the law in October, to any alien. Then the project for an agricultural bank, which Lord Melchett was thinking of founding together with two Egyptian Jews, also collapsed.

'Iraq, which was the first to rise to the dignity of an independent Arab state, had led a sort of separate existence within the Ottoman Empire for centuries. The Turkish administration here, as in Egypt, had never fully mastered the difficult conditions; at times the mamluks (slaves) had wrested the power for themselves, as in Egypt. The Bedouin tribes along the lower Euphrates had banded together around the middle of the eighteenth century, under the name of Muntafiq, into a confederation which gave the pasha of Baghdad a great deal of trouble. The Shi'ites settled around the holy cities of Najaf, Kerbela, and Kazimain were constantly in close touch with their fellow believers in Persia, and it was only with reluctance that they considered themselves subjects of the heretical sultan. Intellectual life was very backward among the Sunnites down to the beginning of the twentieth century. Thus the conditions for the development of Arab national feeling were far more unfavorable here than in Syria. Only the officers and functionaries who had received their training in Istanbul came into contact there with modern ideas; some officers had also been won over while in Syrian garrisons by representatives of the 'Ahd, and after returning to their homeland founded a few branches there.

During the war the conquest of 'Iraq was undertaken by an Anglo-Indian army corps, since the Indian government thought it had to protect its interests on the Persian Gulf itself. Soon after the taking of Basra the government officials assigned to the expeditionary corps began to introduce orderly administration according to methods tried out in India; they were planning to settle Indian colonists in 'Iraq and introduce cotton growing. But the military administration was a heavy burden on the country. As in Egypt the peasants were widely recruited for forced labor and often kept from their homes unwarrantably; indeed, even commerce in food was often not allowed until after the needs of the army were satisfied. It is true that the Muntafiq coalition was weakened by the settlement under favorable conditions of individaul groups as peasants, as had already been attempted by Midhat Pasha with great success; nevertheless the Bedouins were again very vexed when requested to pay taxes. By favoring some tribal shaykh an attempt was then made to enlist their support. The military authorities had at first coolly turned away the careerists who pressed in on them (such as Talib Pasha, who had volunteered to instigate a rebellion in southern 'Iraq against the Turks) and the deserters from the Turkish army, and had even deported them to Ceylon, India, and Egypt.

This policy, initiated by the Anglo-Indian military and officialdom, was intertwined after the taking of Baghdad with the general guiding principles of the British government, which were built up on the experiences of the administration in Egypt and on Lawrence's policy in the Hijaz. The task of keeping the initially conquered vilayet of Basra permanently under British administration, covering this up in Baghdad by an "Arab façade," in fact could be executed only with difficulty. The hope of successfully turning the Arabs into the war against the Turks proved delusive. But the truce of Mudros relieved the high command of this concern, and so it now was a question of reorganizing conditions in 'Iraq according to the Franco-British declaration of November 7, 1918. Unfortunately the civil administration was at the same time deprived of its ablest official, Sir Percy Cox, who went to Teheran in March 1918 as ambassador. While the foreign secretary, on the basis of Lawrence's suggestion, was considering setting up independent states in upper and lower Mesopotamia for both of Husayn's younger sons, 'Abdallah and Zayd, and thus, since Syria was intended for Faysal, rewarding the house of Hashim for its services and at the same time binding it to Britain, the civil commissioner, Sir A. T. Wilson, objected that such a partition was impossible, and that none of the Sharif's sons would be able to cope with the indigenous grandees. Consequently he proposed to institute a plebiscite on the questions of whether a unitary Arab state under British protection was desired, or whether what was wanted was an Arab ruler, and in this case, who was the favorite candidate. He obtained approval of this from the interdepartmental committee for the Near and Middle East.

In view of the backwardness of the great mass of the rural population the commissioner confined himself to consulting the shaykhs and great landholders in the tribal districts and the small cities; these, like some carefully selected grandees in Basra and Mosul, declared themselves in favor of a British regime, the Kurds asserting with particular emphasis that it was impossible for them to live under Arab dominion. The Shi'ites in the holy cities were divided: in Najaf, which, because of its strategic importance, was opportunely influenced by the British, a declaration in their favor was made; in Kerbela and in Kazimain the clergy branded anyone who came out for the rule of the infidels as an infidel himself. In Baghdad the Muslim deputies, although their selection was considered to have been manipulated with special caution, declared for summoning one of Husayn's sons.

In spite of this not very encouraging result of the "popular plebiscite," the British government believed it could propose a draft for a treaty which provided for a British high commissioner as supreme head of the state, with subordinated Arab provincial governors and a provincial council elected from the district councils. While he wanted to incorporate the vilayet of Mosul into 'Iraq as a province, he was directed by Curzon, who, before the conclusion of peace negotiations, was chary of introducing innovations, to set up Mosul as an Arab province separated from 'Iraq and surrounded by a series of autonomous Kurdish states.

Since in Syria meanwhile an independent state—destined, to be sure, for only brief existence—had been founded, from there a demand, supported in particular by officers of 'Iraqi descent, was raised, that 'Iraq, too, must finally be freed from alien rule. Nationalist agitation was vigorously promoted by a piece of careless meddling on the part of the Civil Commissioner. While the military authorities wanted to occupy the country only as far as al-Qa'im on the middle Euphrates, the Civil Commissioner considered it necessary to take possession of the more northerly Dayr az-Zor, which had already been absorbed into the province of Aleppo by the Syrian government, ostensibly to forestall any inroads by the Turks. The nationalists raised violent objection and induced the Bedouins into repeated attacks on caravans under British escort; when the British saw themselves forced to withdraw their excessively advanced outpost, it was celebrated as a victory of the Arabs and ascribed to fear of 'Abdallah's troops.

On March 8, 1920, the 'Iraqi section of the officers' society al-'Ahd proclaimed Husayn's son 'Abdallah king of 'Iraq. Accordingly it seemed damaging for Britain's prestige to delay any longer a declaration concerning the founding of a national regime. But the foreign secretary, Lord Curzon, persisted in an inability to overcome his doubts of the capacity of Oriental peoples for self-government, and above all believed he had to wait for the decision of the mandates commission convoked at San Remo.

The Civil Commissioner had meanwhile had an exhaustive investigation undertaken by a committee of his administrative officials under the legal expert Sir E. Bonham-Carter, of the question of how the former regime of martial law was to be converted into a peacetime form. The committee came to the conclusion that a self-government voluntarily assumed by the people under British mandate could best be brought about by a state council on the Egyptian model, concerning whose functions under the high commissioner opinions were still at variance. But at the end of April in Baghdad, when the mandate was transferred to Britain, waves of national excitement once again surged high. Fifteen delegates, who had received their instructions from a popular representative body in a mosque, demanded an audience with the Civil Commissioner, who received them on June 2 in the presence of forty grandees called in by himself and whom he regarded as Anglophile. But the latter also refused to hear of Bonham-Carter's proposals and demanded the convocation of a national assembly. He now had to perceive, himself, that his policy of governing the country according to principles tested in India, without regard for national desires, which he considered only artificially nourished, had run aground, and he recommended the recall of Sir Percy Cox, who was the only one who had sufficient prestige throughout the country to be able to introduce a mandatory government.

But so much tinder had already been accumulated in the country that an unimportant incident, the dispute over a lease, between a tribal shaykh and a British political official in Rumaythah on the lower Euphrates sufficed on June 30 to throw extensive areas of the country into insurrection. It was only after battles heavy in losses that the garrisoning army, which had to be strengthened by reserves from India, was able to dam up the insurrection, which by the end of September had leaped from the lower Euphrates, taking in the Shi'ite cities, to the Persian frontier—without, however, seizing Baghdad. But when Sir Percy Cox entered Basra on October 1 as high commissioner, half the country was still in disorder and could not be subdued before the spring of 1921.

Sir Percy Cox, assisted by Miss Gertrude L. Bell, intimately acquainted with the Orient for years through her archeological studies, and H. St. John Philby, the Arabian explorer well known through his skillful negotiations with ibn-Sa'ud, at first attempted to set up a provisional government under one of the Arab notables. After protracted opposition the aging *naqib* (marshal of the nobility) of Baghdad, the sayyid 'Abd-ar-Rahman al-Gilani, assumed leadership. Sayyid Talib Pasha, who had returned in February 1920 with Britain's permission, was to assume the ministry of the interior; a former high-ranking officer in the Turkish army, Ja'far al-'Askari, the ministry of defense, and a Jewish banker in Baghdad, Sassoon Effendi, the finances; an attempt was made to win over the Shi'ites by transferring the ministry of education to a scholar from Kerbela.

But the British government had meanwhile become convinced that it could only maintain its influence in 'Iraq if it were to put a monarch at the head of this government. Even though to raise one of the native notables to the throne might have been desirable in itself, nevertheless both candidates were handicapped, the Naqib by his age and Talib Pasha by his ambition, which had already made him many opponents. A Turkish prince, Burhan-ad-Din, whom many officers were considering, might have brought the state into conflict with Mustafa Kemal's Turkey. So the candidacy of the Sharif's sons had most to recommend it, and of these 'Abdallah was ready to retire in favor of his brother Faysal, whom the French had driven from Damascus. On the latter then fell the choice of the political and military representatives of Britain, whom Churchill had summoned to Cairo on March 12, 1921. His most dangerous antagonist, Talib Pasha, committed the imprudence of threatening an uprising of his partisans among the Bedouins if the government made any effort to influence the elections, and in consequence he was again removed to Ceylon. Miss Gertrude Bell put forth her entire influence on behalf of Faysal.

Faysal arrived in Basra on June 23 and was cordially received in Baghdad by the populace on the twenty-ninth, whereas while traveling through the minor settlements he was received with cool reserve. Accordingly it appeared necessary to secure his throne by a sort of people's assembly; since the outcome appeared uncertain in an elected national assembly, the authorities contented themselves with declarations from grandees and officials in the individual districts under the supervision of British counselors. On the basis of this "referendum" Faysal was proclaimed king on August 23 by Sir Percy Cox.

In his speech from the throne * Faysal envisaged a treaty which was to regulate the relationship of the country to Britain anew. Although the British government was prepared to circumvent the disagreeable word mandate as far as possible, it opposed with all the greater firmness the limitation of its influence. The first draft which the government recommended to the King came a long way to meet this demand, and accordingly was violently opposed by the nationalists. Faysal, supported by them, thought he was able to escape British tutelage and on August 14, 1922, accordingly accepted the resignation of his first cabinet under the Naqib.

When the two newly formed nationalist parties exploited the first anniversary of the day of Faysal's ascension to the throne by a demonstration against the mandate, a serious illness of the King offered the High Commissioner a convenient pretext for taking sole charge of the government. After the latter had banished some of the party leaders to the small, precipitous island of Hanjam in the Persian Gulf, and compelled some by means of threats to emigrate, the King, after his recovery, had to acquiesce in the Naqib's resumption of the premiership and his ratification of the treaty; directly after-

* Arabic text in Amin Sa'id, II, 105-107; English excerpt in Ireland, pp. 336-337.

ward, however, the Naqib resigned independently and 'Abd-al-Muhsin Beg as-Sa'dun took over the premiership.

The task of drafting a constitution which gave equal consideration to the wishes of the 'Iraqis and the demands of Britain proved just as difficult. To be sure, there were frequent complaints in Britain about the high cost of the Oriental policy, and after the fall of Lloyd George's cabinet on October 23, 1922, the demand that 'Iraq be evacuated was even used in the election campaign. 'Iraq for its part groaned under the burden of the British administration, whose representatives were paid much more than the native officials.* But the British government had no intention at all of giving up the country and was only concerned with the proper exercise of its influence, now on the King by means of the High Commissioner, now on the ministers and parliament by means of the advisers. Since Britain's hand in the constitution was flagrantly obvious, the Shi'ites offered the most violent opposition to the elections for the constituent assembly, which were set for October 1922, and it was only after their leaders were removed to their homes in Persia that the elections could be held and the constituent assembly opened on March 5, 1924.

The treaty with Britain was not ratified by the assembly until after lengthly discussions, whose excitement on occasion overflowed into the street, and after Britain threatened, if the treaty were not put into effect, to solicit the League of Nations for authorization to take new measures in 'Iraq. The pliancy of the assembly, however, was also affected by the quarrel with Turkey over the vilayet of Mosul, which 'Iraq was unable to win without British assistance. This fear could also be exploited by Britain in order to secure the concessions for the rich oil fields of Kirkuk; after a pipe line through the desert brought the oil to the Palestinian harbor of Haifa, one of the most important interests of the empire in 'Iraq was satisfied. Accordingly, the settling of the oil concession was followed on March 21, 1925, by the publication of the constitution of the state in its definitive form.

In the protocol of the treaty with Britain of April 30, 1923, it was agreed that the treaty was to expire after the entry of 'Iraq

* The fact that in any case foreigners were not entirely indispensable for the prosperity of the country is shown by the statistics, which from 1920 to 1931 indicate a decline in the number of British officials from 871 to 160 and of Indians from 2,035 to 36; Ireland, p. 367, note 2.

into the League of Nations. Up to that time Britain obligated herself to study every four years for twenty-five years the possibility of her recommending the admission of 'Iraq into the League of Nations, and whether the agreements concerning finances and the army might not be in need of improvement. When the first term expired in 1928, Faysal, together with Prime Minister Ja'far al-'Askari, personally endeavored in London to persuade the British government that 'Iraq was ripe for entry into the League of Nations; but he was put off until 1932. When the Labor party took power in Britain, there were hopes in 'Iraq as well as in Egypt of a liberal consideration for national desires. And in fact the new government held out the prospect of its sponsorship in the League of Nations for 1932 and declared itself prepared to conclude a new treaty with 'Iraq as well as with Egypt. Although the nationalists violently protested against the British reservations—of having free disposition of the resources of 'Iraq in case of war, and the permanent use of the air bases—a newly elected parliament was ready on November 16 to ratify the treaty, and from then on Britain really began dismantling its administrative apparatus. After 'Iraq had bound itself on May 30, 1932, to heed the rights of minorities and maintain a regular legal system, it was accepted into the League of Nations on October 3.

The final year of Faysal's regime was disturbed by a serious conflict. The Assyrians, Syriac-speaking Nestorians who had revolted in the First World War against the Turks—in so far as they had not been destroyed by their old enemies the Kurds—had settled in the vilayet of Mosul after the conclusion of peace and were treated particularly well by the British mandatory administration upon the recommendation of the Anglican clergy, especially since they also proved militarily serviceable. Trusting to this support, they had become the most bitter enemies of their Kurdish neighbors by fighting against them in British pay on the occasion of various uprisings. After British influence had declined and the government no longer made them any concessions, they were imprudently swept into an armed rebellion which Colonel Bakir Sidqi suppressed with inhuman cruelty.

When Faysal died on September 8, 1933, the general mourning in the country showed that his regime had been felt to be extremely beneficial. Though the counsel of the British high commissioners on occasion may have prevented him from taking any excessively bold steps, nevertheless he undoubtedly deserves credit for having firmly founded the power of the crown, which he had assumed, after all, as a foreigner and in the most difficult circumstances. His great tact enabled him in the midst of his socially and religiously divided people to find counselors always prepared to lend support to his political line, from its very inception correctly chosen and invariably adhered to, of guiding his country to independent political life and prosperity while carefully heeding parliamentary forms and recognizing the incontestable rights of Britain, with whose protection it could not dispense. Nearly all the cabinets formed during his reign took their orders from him and not from parliament, and whenever he intervened in government, it was for the well-being of the country. Under British mediation he placed himself on such good terms with the ancient enemy of his house, ibn-Sa'ud, the king of Najd and the Hijaz, who for a time had been inclined to extend his power northward at the expense of his neighbor, that on April 21, 1936, under his son, a treaty of friendship could even be signed with him.

Faysal's son Ghazi I came to the throne at the age of twenty-one, too young to continue his father's labors with the same success. His very first attempt after his accession to the throne to form a new ministry ran aground on the antagonism between his British and his 'Iraqi counselors, and so he had no decisive influence in the subsequent governmental shifts either. The insecurity of the political situation in the country was shown by the *coup d'état* of October 29, 1936. The oppressor of the Assyrians, Bakir Sidqi, whom the King had promoted to general out of a juvenile enthusiasm for his "heroic" deeds, while on maneuvers outside of Baghdad attacked the capital with his troops and airplanes in order to overthrow the cabinet of Yasin Pasha, who was accused of reactionary tendencies; during the negotiations the aging and valuable minister Ja'far Pasha was assassinated. After Yasin's withdrawal the government was taken over by Hikmat Sulayman, a brother of the Turkish grand wazir of 1913, Mahmud Shevket Pasha, together with Bakir's partisans. While Yasin Pasha had already acknowledged himself an admirer of Ataturk, it was only now that the new government really sought to imitate his methods. In comparison with Turkey, which is homogeneous and free of any foreign influences, 'Iraq under British supervision still had to contend with great difficulty for internal equilibrium in questions of minorities, colonization of the interior, and finances.

These stormy years were not particularly favorable to intellectual life in 'Iraq. Since the native forces, Shi'ite as well as Sunnite, which vied with each other in reviving the ancient literary tradition of the country, seemed all too encumbered for this, the government turned largely to Syria and Egypt to attract representatives of modern education into the country; nevertheless the latter were seldom able to maintain themselves for any length of time, since 'Iraqi regional patriotism took offense too easily. Thus, in 1927, a youthful Syrian was dismissed from his position as history teacher in the Baghdad teachers school for having written a book glorifying the Umayyads. Nevertheless, in 'Iraq also the spirit of modern education, particularly under the influence of the Egyptian press, is pressing gradually ahead and endeavoring to cut the ground away from the adherents of tradition, especially in poetry and historiography.

5. *Iran (Persia) and Afghanistan*

After the end of World War I, chaos well-nigh prevailed in Persia. True, the Bolsheviks had surrendered all their acquisitions and the claims of the Tsarist regime in the country directly after the Treaty of Brest-Litovsk; but the areas given up by the Russian troops were at once occupied by the British. Sir Percy Cox was able to conclude an accord with Persia on August 9, 1919, which, on the pattern of Egypt and 'Iraq, delivered over the army and the government to British "advisers." Simultaneously a Persian delegation in Paris endeavored in vain, without adequate instructions from their government, to arouse the interest of the Allies engaged in haggling over the fate of the world.

But the Bolsheviks also soon resumed an active policy in Persia. After the occupation of Baku in May 1920 they pursued the small flotilla of the White Russian general Denikin, which had fled to the Persian harbor of Enzeli on the Caspian Sea and there been disarmed by the Persians; bombarded the harbor, and followed the retreating British force inland as far as Resht, where they set up a provisional regime under Kuchuk Khan. They were already threatening Teheran, when the Persian brigade of Cossacks conquered Resht, only to retire again behind the British lines.

This failure was ascribed by the Persian officers of the Cossacks, perhaps not unjustly, to their Russian comrades. One of them, Riza Khan of Mazanderan, born in Sawadkuh on March 16, 1878, the son of a major, had fought out an engagement with the Russians when, under government orders, he removed a Russian commandant who had refused to surrender his position. With the same energy he now effected the dismissal of Russian officers, and created a truly devoted bodyguard for himself in the brigade whose fighting strength he restored.

While the British were still considering the final surrender of their lost outpost in Persia, the Persian ambassador Mushawir al-Mamalik was negotiating a treaty with Chicherin in Moscow in which Russia gave up the entirety of her possessions on Persian soil and waived all her rights in the capitulations.

The government in Teheran, headed by Shah Ahmad, was incapable of developing a clear political line, and so the Cossack officers in Qazwin decided, under the influence of Riza Khan, to intervene in the capital. For this they thought they needed a *littérateur*, skilled in speaking and writing, and found him in the person of the sayyid Ziya-ad-Din. With twenty-five hundred men Riza Khan drew up before the capital on February 2, in order to impose a new government on the Shah. After a brief battle with the *gendarmerie*, its Swedish commander joined the Cossacks. The Shah, who was already apprehensive for himself, acquiesced without opposition in the formation by Ziya-ad-Din of a new government, which called previous rulers, concerned solely with their advantage, to an accounting and lightened them of their dishonestly acquired fortunes in favor of the state exchequer. Riza Khan, who was appointed war minister and commander-in-chief (*sirdar i sepah*), with tireless labor transformed the few remains of the army scattered throughout the country, together with his Cossacks, into a new ready-to-fight corps. When Ziya-ad-Din, as premier, attempted to force on him British instructors, Riza Khan got rid of him and had one of the arrested provincial governors, Qawam as-Saltanah, appointed premier.

But the rulers in the provinces were still by no means disposed to yield to the new central power. In Gilan, besides Kuchuk Khan who had been installed by the Russians, a series of other gang leaders, likewise supported by the Russians, had to be overthrown; in Adharbayjan a Kurdish chieftain proclaimed a republic, and it was a question of finishing him off quickly before the Bolsheviks thought it worth their while to take his side. In the course of the years 1921 and 1922 the north of the country was subdued in destructive guerrilla warfare, and in 1923 Riza Khan also intervened in the south, where the British had completely undermined the prestige of the central government.

While Riza Khan was in the field, he had not bothered himself about the intrigues in the capital, which on three occasions led to changes of premiers. But in October, when a conspiracy of Qawam as-Saltanah against his life was discovered, he took over, in addition to the war ministry, the premiership. The Shah, who like his forefathers always had only his own advantage in mind, considered it advisable to escape his obligations by a European journey for an indefinite period.

There was enough in common between Riza Khan's position and that of Mustafa Kemal to expect of him the same conclusions as were drawn in Turkey with the abolition of the sultanate and the caliphate. But he was astute enough not to overestimate his position in the nationally far from unified and religiously—in spite of the Shi'ite primacy—disunited country. So he held himself cautiously in restraint when at the beginning of 1924 the demand for a republic was raised on two sides; while the party of renascence in the parliament thought it could later make use of the parliament to alter the constitution, Muhammad al-Khalisi, the Shi'ite mujtahid banned by Britain from Najaf, fought (perhaps under Bolshevik influence) for new elections to set up a "People's Republic." In March 1924 the question of the constitution led to violent debates in parliament, which were echoed in street riots and strikes. The republican movement was met by Riza Khan with a very adroit gesture. He traveled to the holy city of Qumm, and the clergy there, highly regarded throughout the country, charged him with defending the foundation of the state, and Islam, against any modern upheaval. When the proclamation he issued there still aroused no response, he resigned his offices and on April 8 retired to Rudhen. Thereupon his generals threatened to march on Teheran, and at once a delegation of parliament left to see Riza Khan and plead for his return. Parliament found itself forced to proclaim its confidence in him, and he resumed the direction of the government. After his troops subdued a rebellion which had meanwhile broken out among the Lurs, he devoted his entire concern to the building up of the army, which was equipped with modern weapons from French factories.

The last province of Iran which failed to yield to the central power was Khuzistan, for the most part inhabited by Arabs. Britain had secured its oil wells as early as 1905 by a treaty with the shaykh Khaz'al of Muhammarah. To protect the pipe line which ended in Abadan at the mouth of the Shatt al-'Arab, and which supplied British shipping in the Indian Ocean, Anglo-Indian army corps had occupied the south of 'Iraq at the outbreak of the First World War. Although the concession of the Anglo-Persian Oil Company at the time had been allocated by the government in Teheran, Britain had concluded a special treaty with Khaz'al, who ruled the entire left bank of the Shatt al-'Arab and the navigable lower reaches of the Karun from Ahwaz downstream, and granted him armed assistance against any attacks. Nevertheless it now allowed the treaty to lapse, when Riza Khan challenged him to meet the arrears in his tax obligations. In vain did the aging Khaz'al attempt to incite the Bakhtiyari tribe, which for a time during the Persian revolution had seized power, against Riza Khan. When the latter appeared in Khuzistan at the head of his troops, there was nothing left for the Shaykh to do but yield. In connection with this bloodless campaign, which restored the Iranian empire to its old boundaries, Riza Khan made the pilgrimage to the holy places of the Shi'ah in 'Iraq.

In spite of these great successes of the sirdar i sepah Pehlevi (as from then on Riza generally had himself called, assuming his old family name), Shah Ahmad, living in Paris succumbed to the foolish hope that his son Muhammad Hasan Mirza, left behind in Teheran, could still unite the partisans of the Kajars for a campaign in his favor. Although a motion in the parliament to solicit the Shah to return found no support, on October 1, 1925, he dared inform the Premier of his forthcoming departure for Iran. Riza Khan was astute enough to welcome this decision in his reply and to disseminate it throughout the country in circular letters. It was again the province of Adharbayjan which took command of the movement against the Kajars. As already so often in the revolution, it began with gatherings of seekers of asylum (best) in the mosques, etc. Their sympathizers in Teheran took their best in the military academy and deluged the Pehlevi premier with requests to prevent the return of the hated Kajar shah. On October 28 parliament finally convened and deliberated on the motion to depose the Kajar and transfer the executive power to the Premier until a national assembly gave the country a new constitution. Although the old champion of the constitution, the deputy Taqizade, courageously interceded for it once again, the motion was passed after a brief debate. On the same day Riza Khan had the successor to the throne taken from the palace of Gulistan and removed to Baghdad by way of Qazwin.

For the sake of form, a national assembly deliberated another six weeks on the new constitution, which summoned Riza Shah Pehlevi to be the hereditary ruler of Iran until he could take the oath on the new constitution in parliament on December 15, 1925. In April 1926 he ascended the Peacock Throne, glittering with jewels from Nadir Shah's Indian plunder.

This began an era of progress for Iran, which in a decade caught up with the omissions of centuries. The new shah was able to spare the feelings of the still-influential Shi'ite clergy with astuteness, and nevertheless to guide his Iranians successfully along the path of modern civilization. The veteran marshal proved to be a statesman in the grand style, who executed beneficial reforms in all spheres of political life. Majlis (parliament) was still in existence in name, but had nothing more to do but accept the Shah's laws. With sure insight he recognized that the opening up of the country by means of new channels of communications must form the foundation of all reforms; in 1925, accordingly, the revenues of the most important state taxes, on tea and sugar, the principal articles of consumption, were applied to railway construction. The north-south line from Benderi Shah, formerly Enzeli, on the Caspian Sea as far as Benderi Shahpur on the Persian Gulf was begun by the German firm of J. Berger in 1929 and continued from 1933 on by a Danish-Swedish consortium Kampsax. A miracle of modern technique, in three years the construction subdued the mountains of the north by means of seventy-five tunnels and numerous bridges; on June 5, 1937, the 461-kilometer stretch as far as Teheran, which was reached in fifteen hours, could be opened. The line goes on by way of Qumm and Sultanabad and passes through 150 tunnels in the Zagros Mountains. The branch begun simultaneously from the Persian Gulf was combined with the northern stretch on August 2, 1938.

In 1927 finances were reorganized; instead of the Imperial Bank founded in 1890, the Banki Milli assumed the issuance of notes; the basis of the currency is the riyal, worth four cents, of which 800 millions of notes were in circulation in 1937. An agreement with the Anglo-Persian Oil Company, which in Khuzistan employs twenty thousand Iranian laborers, was announced in November

1932 and in its new version assures the state of a due portion of its production and revenues.

In spite of Britain's violent resistance in 1928 the capitulations, unworthy of a modern state, were abolished. Instead of the religious law hitherto of sole validity, a new civil and penal code on the French model was put into effect.

Particular care was devoted to agriculture. The nomads whose backwardness had so often become a menace to the state were to be settled; for this purpose the crown lands near Bushihr were divided up in 1937. Agricultural schools and model farms spread modern methods. In 1934 two million tea-plants were distributed in the country. In order to tie the peasants to their work spiritually, a Tree Festival was introduced on March 15.

One of the worst obstacles to progress, the backwardness of women, conditioned by religious custom and ethics, was combated as early as 1926 with the abolition of the *chadur*, the most stringent form of veiling; since 1936 the veil has fallen entirely into disuse in Persia. In 1935 Princess Shemsi Pehlevi founded the first women's clubs and girl scout groups. In the same year a new marriage law was introduced which raised the minimum marriageable age for girls to fifteen years, introduced certificates of health for marriages, and granted women the right to divorce if their husbands wished to enter on a second marriage.

The school system kept growing steadily; in 1935 in addition to 6,621 boys 2,253 girls were graduated from school. On February 4, 1935, a university with a technical faculty and a conservatory was opened, in which Europeans also collaborated as instructors. It was followed that same year by the founding of the Iranian Academy, Ferhengistan, with thirty-seven members, which like its sisters in Damascus and Cairo was initially to serve for the purification of the language. The literature which under the Kajars, in spite of all the talent of the Iranians, was near decay, experienced a powerful renaissance, and particularly in the field of historiography has already had many gratifying accomplishments to its credit. Pride in the rich intellectual heritage of Iran's past has contributed not a little to the national pride of the Iranians; this was clearly demonstrated in the celebration of the millennial anniversary of its great poet Firdawsi in 1934. But the pre-Islamic past of the country has already been taken up, and in the reconstruction of the National Bank at Teheran the architect even dared go back to the bold architectural ideas of the Tag-i-Kisra, Ctesiphon of the Sassanians.

In foreign policy Riza Khan Pehlevi was able to promote, in addition to the interests of his own country, the cultural and religious community of the Near and Middle East. In 1925, directly after his assumption of the government, he provided for a definitive rectification of the boundaries in the south and the southeast by treaties with the British in Baluchistan and with Afghanistan. In June 1934 he initiated personal relations with Ataturk by a visit to Ankara. On July 8, 1937, a treaty was then concluded in Sa'dabad (the summer residence of the Shah, sixteen kilometers north of Teheran) with Turkey, 'Iraq, and Afghanistan, effective for five years, in which the three states guaranteed each other's borders and bound themselves to refrain from any interference in the internal affairs of another state, to settle any internal conflicts among themselves by means of peaceful negotiations, and not to conclude any offensive alliances of any kind with other powers. The marriage alliance Riza Khan envisaged between the Iranian crown prince and an Egyptian princess has closed the ring of Islamic states which have again achieved their freedom. A new epoch in human history will show what contribution the Orient, after having shaken off the shackles of the Occident, is capable of making on the path of progress.

Since the First World War, Iran's eastern neighbor Afghanistan also has energetically played its role in protecting the Islamic world from submergence by Russia and subjugation by Britain. The last attempt on the part of Britain to subdue the country ended in 1919, in spite of a military defeat, in the diplomatic victory of Afghanistan, since Britain ultimately gave up the attempt to bring the country under her control. Russia had to surrender the plan of incorporating Afghanistan in the ring of Turkish soviet republics founded by it, and no doubt permanently lost any prospect of drawing Afghanistan into its cultural orbit as a result of atheistic propaganda, which was also carried into the Islamic areas and forced many believers to emigrate into Afghanistan. The position of the dynasty was temporarily imperiled through its own fault. The emir Amanallah had succeeded his father, Shah Habiballah, assassinated on February 20, 1919, by rebels under the command of his brother Nasrallah. He had been able to suppress the rebellions of the Alizai in 1923, the Mangal in 1924, as well as of the Pathans, the majority of whom are domiciled in India under British rule; but his premature and overhasty zeal for reform proved his undoing. Following the example of Turkey and Iran, he attempted to place his country with one blow in the ranks of civilized states by introducing accomplishments of modern technique by reforms of legislation and administration, by improvement of the school system, and above all by founding a standing army. The discontent called forth among his subjects, still not ripe for his measures, vented itself in 1928 when he traveled through Europe to lay the groundwork for new reforms. It was in vain that after his precipitate return home he sought to subdue the insurrection, whose leader, Bacha-i-Saqqa, had himself sworn allegiance to as Habiballah II; in January 1929 he had to abdicate and leave the country. It was not until October that his cousin, Nadir Khan, could conquer the rebel leader, who had established himself in Kabul, and have him shot. Although he put an end to all of Amanallah's unpopular measures, he was assassinated in his palace on November 8, 1933, and his barely twenty-year-old son, Muhammad Zahir Khan, was raised to the throne. Up to 1939 the latter's regime had only once been disturbed: in January 1934 by the revolt of an adventurer, Muhammad Sa'di al-Kilani ad-Dimashqi, in Waziristan, which, however, was soon suppressed.

In 1923 a treaty with the neighboring state of Persia was concluded; in 1937 it was followed by the above-mentioned pact which made Afghanistan a part of the alliance of states under the leadership of Shah Riza Pehlevi. Even beforehand, on October 31, 1931, Nadir Shah had already given the country a constitution on the Persian model, which, however, reserved executive power to the shah and his ministers. Since then Afghanistan also has returned cautiously to the road of reform in the government's endeavors to bend European technique to its own uses. But the national idea has gained ground. In 1928 an academy was founded in Kabul to develop the native tongue, Pushtu, into a cultivated language. Up to then all written works, including the newspapers, were composed only in Persian; since then Pushtu has gradually been penetrating into the press also, and a knowledge of it is demanded of all officials. This youngest of the Islamic states, however, before it can occupy a position of equal rank at the side of its allies, will no doubt have a long way to go.

Review of Events, 1939-1947

by M. Perlmann

THE Second World War engulfed the Islamic countries: North Africa was the scene of grim battles; 'Iraq and Syria-Lebanon were occupied by Allied forces who were fighting pro-Axis nationalists in the former and Vichy French in the latter; Iran also was occupied by the Allies.

Economically the area was greatly affected by scarcities and privations resulting from wartime conditions. The usual channels of supplies, especially of industrial products, ran dry, and trade routes were disrupted. The lack of supplies from abroad caused rapid industrialization in an attempt to get a local supply of as many goods as possible both for the native population and the armed forces of the Allies in the area. Inflation in varying degrees resulted in the countries of the Middle East.

Military plans also caused a great expansion and improvement in transportation. The Trans-Iranian railway became of primary importance for lend-lease supplies to the U.S.S.R., and the British connected the Palestinian and Lebanese railways so that the lines ran through the whole of the Arab area. Air transport was developed tremendously.

Most of the Middle East has been tied to the sterling bloc, and considerable accounts are outstanding to the credit of its countries in London. On the other hand, from London came the initiative for the establishment of the Middle East Supply Center, first as a British, then as a British-American venture. This institution undertook the planning and regulation of the economic life of the Middle East to a great extent; and though its primary concern was how to save shipping space for purely military supplies, the result was that a great amount of knowledge and experience has been amassed about the economic structure and needs of the lands from the Sudan to Iran.

The battle of propaganda raged for years and could not fail to influence masses of people. Political consciousness and the feeling of self-importance were heightened during the war by the awareness of the crucial character of the battles fought on the fringes of the Middle East. This was enhanced, especially in Egypt; Cairo became a cosmopolitan center of Allied staffs, and there was a British cabinet minister for the Middle East. Masses of people came in contact with the great numbers of Allied soldiers and officials with their higher standard of living. The inflated prices of local products may have helped peasants in some countries to pay off debts and sometimes even accumulate cash.

Politically, prewar ideas and feelings mingled with wartime reflections on the great conflict and its interpretation by propaganda machinery and by local sources. The collapse of the French made an indelible impression. Great Britain retained a major role; but exposed to the rivalry of, and pressures from, the United States and the U.S.S.R., and hampered by home difficulties, the British are relaxing their grip.

The Turks succeeded in avoiding involvement in the war and planned on some form of a Balkan union linked with a strengthened Middle Eastern chain as provided under the Sa'dabad pact. If this had the blessing of the great Western powers, it encountered the definite hostility of the East.

The Arabs emerged shortly after the war with two new independent republics, Syria and Lebanon, and with Sa'udi Arabia having become unexpectedly a great and rich force due to her oil resources and American interest therein. Since the end of 1944 the Arab League has been functioning in an attempt to co-ordinate the policies of its seven member states.

None of the Middle Eastern states took part in military activities against the Axis.

In politics at home the old ruling cliques encountered more and more new forces, among them Leftists; social problems are forcefully coming to the fore.

Turkey

On May 12, 1939, an Anglo-Turkish mutual assistance pact was concluded. It was followed on June 23 by a similar pact with France.

Both Britain and France offered credits to Turkey, and France ceded to her the sanjaq of Alexandretta (Hatay), part of the mandated territory of Syria. On October 19 an alliance with Great Britain and France was concluded, and further substantial credits were opened to Turkey. Thus Turkey was drawn into the orbit of the Allies at the very beginning of the war.

Yet she maintained her nonbelligerence for years, claiming she was not sufficiently supplied with armaments. The Turks made efforts to erect a Balkan front against aggression, but the Soviets opposed that. The Turks were under constant pressure from the Germans and the U.S.S.R. in the days following the German-Soviet pact.

In 1940 the war closed in on Turkey: in the north and west Germany seized Rumania and Greece, and Italy attacked Albania and joined the war; in the south Axis missions sped to Vichy-controlled Syria. In February, German technicians in Istanbul shipyards and plants were dismissed, while the Soviet government recalled its technicians. On June 18, 1941, Turkey signed a ten-year nonaggression pact with Germany. Four days later Hitler attacked the U.S.S.R.

Now Germany pressed for a trade agreement; she needed, above all, Turkish chromite. The diplomatic wooing of Ankara continued. In December, President Roosevelt declared that the defense of Turkey was vital to the United States, and in March 1942 lend-lease supplies reached Turkish ports. After the American landings in North Africa the German pressure weakened, and chromite was not supplied to Germany. But all the attempts of Eden, Churchill, and Roosevelt to draw Turkey into the line of fire failed, although after the battle of Stalingrad (1943), Turkey, while still nonbelligerent, was more pronouncedly pro-Allied.

Relations with the Soviets continued to be strained. On August 2, 1944, relations with Germany were severed, and the suppression of Pan-Turanians was apt to be considered a friendly gesture toward the Soviets. Yet in March 1945 the U.S.S.R. denounced the 1925 treaty of friendship, neutrality, and nonaggression. Moscow was reported to demand a new regulation concerning the Straits, Balkan affairs, and territorial concessions in the Caucasus (Kars, Ardahan). On February 23, 1945, Turkey declared war on the Axis.

The end of the war devaluated Turkish exports, and this enhanced economic dislocation. Turkey still maintains a large armed force because of still-prevalent suspicions and the continuing "war of nerves"; one third of her budget is earmarked for defense.

During 1946 Russian demands were made clear as well as the stand of the other Allies: the main issue is whether only the Black Sea Powers—and the U.S.S.R. in particular as the decisive force among them—should decide the fate of the Straits, or whether the matter should be reviewed by a wider international forum.

On the eve of the war, attempts at democratization of the regime were under consideration. After the war they were resumed. In the 1946 elections to the new National Assembly 396 People's party deputies were returned, and 62 of the new Democratic party under Jelal Bayar also won seats.

The Arab League

It has been the aspiration of Arab nationalists to bring Arabic-speaking peoples together in some organization that would shape their unity in its various aspects, and more specifically their political unity. This ideal failed of realization after the First World War owing to the partitioning of the Arab countries and their lack of inner cohesion. Yet the ideal of unity was maintained by means of literary and personal contacts between the intellectuals and politicians of the Arab countries and through problems and trends which were common to the Arab countries to a considerable extent, such as the struggle against foreign domination.

On May 29, 1941, while the British were closing in on rebellious Baghdad and making the last preparations for the reconquest of Syria-Lebanon from Vichy forces, Mr. Anthony Eden stated in the House of Commons that Great Britain, in pursuit of her traditional friendship for the Arabs, would favor steps toward Arab unification. British officialdom in the East, anxious to wean the Arabs away from the Axis sympathies so widely held in the Middle East in those critical days, put this policy into practice. This favorable attitude of the British government spurred Arab statesmen to begin *pourparlers* on Arab unity. The negotiations were long and secretive. Egypt, till then aloof from the pan-Arab movement, became its spearhead.

The discord, suspicions, and jealousies among the Arab states and their leaders were strong, and though the countries were ready to pay lip service to unity, each had its own axe to grind. Half-Christian Lebanon was jealously guarding its independence; Syrian and 'Iraqian nationalists cherished a plan for Greater Syria, including

Lebanon, Palestine, and Transjordan, possibly federated with 'Iraq. Emir Abdallah of Transjordan thought of himself as the king of such a Greater Syria which would become the mainstay of the Hashimi house. But King Ibn-Sa'ud could not allow such a body to be formed. Indeed, he seems to have joined hands with King Faruq of Egypt to block this scheme. Popular pressure in the press, conferences of scouts, physicians, lawyers, women of different Arab countries gave further impetus to the negotiations. Throughout this time the Palestine issue was played up as the rallying point for all Arabs against Western imperialism and oppression.

On September 24, 1944, representatives of Egypt, 'Iraq, Syria, Lebanon, Transjordan—later joined by those of Sa'udi Arabia and Yemen—assembled in Alexandria, and after two weeks of deliberations "the Protocol of Alexandria" was published as a preliminary agreement to work toward "strengthening the intimate ties that bind the Arab states" in the "League of Arab States." Between February 14 and March 22, 1945, a conference of foreign ministers of the seven participants of the Alexandria conference met in Cairo to work out a pact or charter of the Arab League, the final and formal constitution of the new body.

The Pact of the Arab League establishes a league of the independent Arab states and provides for the possibility of future affiliation of independent Arab states (Par. 1). Its object is "to draw closer" the members, "co-ordinate their political action," "safeguard their independence and sovereignty, and consider generally matters concerning the Arab countries and their welfare." Co-operation is foreseen in matters of economics, communications, culture, nationality, health, and social affairs (Par. 2). A council heads the league, and one of its tasks is "to determine the means of co-operation with the international bodies that may be founded in the future to guarantee peace and security and to organize economic and social relations" (Par. 3). In the special committees "other Arab countries" may be represented (Par. 4). Force is eliminated in relations between members and arbitration made obligatory and binding where "independence, sovereignty or territorial integrity are not concerned" (Par. 5). Aggression against a member will be resisted if the council is unanimous on the subject (Par. 6). Unanimous decisions are binding; majority decisions are binding only upon those that accept them (Par. 7). Upon a year's notice a member may withdraw from the league (Par. 18), but if a member state objects to any future amendment of the pact, the withdrawal may be effected immediately (Par. 19).

A special annex contains a resolution on Palestine; "the Council of the League shall designate an Arab representative from that country to participate in the work of the Council."

At San Francisco the Arab delegations attempted to obtain recognition for the league as a "regional bloc," but failed.

The league exercised pressure for the demands of Syria and Lebanon and for the evacuation of foreign troops therefrom; opened propaganda offices abroad which are mostly devoted to anti-Zionist agitation, instituted a number of committees to elaborate plans for possible co-ordination, etc. While at the early stage of negotiations 'Iraq seemed to play an important role in the setting up of the league, at present the leadership seems to be in the hands of Egypt and Sa'udi Arabia.

On May 24, 1946, Foreign Secretary Ernest Bevin stated that he "would like to see the whole Middle East working together with Great Britain and the British dominions and eventually welded into a regional defense organization within the framework of the United Nations."

It is difficult to see what the league has achieved so far in anything that has to do with the internal life of its members, i.e., in economics, social work, legislation, education, etc. It is still in the stage of planning measures, and is absorbed in foreign politics.

Egypt

In August 1939 Muhammad Mahmud Pasha resigned and 'Ali Mahir Pasha formed a new cabinet. On September 3 a state of siege was proclaimed, and on that very day of the outbreak of the war Indian troops arrived in Egypt. Relations with Germany were severed, and nonbelligerence was maintained until the end of February 1945.

The situation became tense in June 1940 when Italy brought the war to the Mediterranean and to the Sudan, and invaded Egypt from Libya. Alexandria and Cairo were attacked from the air. But in December 1940 the Italians were defeated at Sidi Barrani. In 1941 the British conquered Italian East Africa and after suffering reverses opened an offensive in the desert front between Egypt and Libya, where Rommel headed strong mechanized forces of the Germans.

The latter advanced in the summer of 1942, when the famed battles of Tobruk and al-Alamein took place, but after reaching points only seventy miles from Alexandria the Germans were forced back in October-November 1943. Thus the country, defended by the British, escaped full-scale invasion.

In the meantime, following neutral cabinets of Sabri Pasha and Sirri Pasha, a government of the Wafd under Nahhas Pasha came into office on February 2, 1942, after forceful representations by the British, who wanted then to secure a friendly government with mass support to counter the widespread sulkiness of the populace toward the Allies and the war effort. But the imposition of the Wafd regime enhanced future friction with the court of King Faruq.

In March 1942 a new parliament assembled with a Wafdist majority. But a few weeks later one of the leading Wafdists, Makram ‘Ubayd, was expelled from the party. He had distributed a "Black Book" full of allegations of abuse of power and corruption among the Wafd leaders. Later he was expelled from the Chamber. He formed a small splinter group of his own and gave the court excellent ammunition against Nahhas and the Wafd, and for years violent discussions of the subject continued to exacerbate public relations.

In July the Middle East Supply Center was established, first as a British and then as an Anglo-American agency for regional economic planning, a venture crowned with considerable success. The British bought up Egyptian cotton so as to avoid an economic crisis and consequent resentment. Huge amounts of money flowed into the country through the armies stationed there and in payment for services and goods needed by them. In 1943 an American airfield opened near Cairo. A Soviet embassy opened in August.

Nahhas conducted conversations on Arab unity. Just after these were crowned with success in the announcement of the Protocol of Alexandria, he was dismissed by the King on October 8, 1944. Ahmad Mahir, leader of the Sa‘dists, became premier. He was assassinated on February 24, 1945, after reading the declaration of war to the Chamber, and was succeeded by Nuqrashi Pasha. The new Chamber on which they relied had 124 Sa‘dists, 74 Liberals, and 30 Makramites.

The end of the war brought almost immediately a rising tide of demands for evacuation of foreign troops, revision of the Treaty of Alliance, reforms, and the unity of the Nile valley (i.e., the incorporation of the Sudan under the Egyptian crown). Virulence in the press, demonstrations, riots, even terrorism, and xenophobia accompanied these demands.

Lord Killearn (Miles Lampson), the British ambassador, left Egypt after twelve years of service there. In February 1946 Sidqi Pasha formed a new cabinet. In April a British delegation arrived for discussions of the review of the 1936 Treaty of Alliance. The Premier even took a trip to London. Yet the negotiations broke down.

On December 9 Nuqrashi Pasha was charged with the formation of a new cabinet. On February 3, 1947, he stated that Egypt would ask the United Nations to annul the treaty of 1936.

Arabia

On February 4, 1940, diplomatic relations were established between the United States and Sa'udi Arabia. These were concerned with the extensive oil developments and large investments by American oil companies in Sa'udi Arabia, to which lend-lease was extended on April 19, 1943. In May the first United States minister was sent there; in October, Prince Faysal, son and foreign minister of King ibn-Sa'ud, visited Washington.

In January 1945 King Faruq visited Hijaz. In February, King ibn-Sa'ud met the late President Roosevelt. On March 1, Sa'udi Arabia declared war and joined the Allies, but made reservations about the Holy Places of Hijaz.

Behind these moves stands the basic fact that Arabia was forced out of her isolation by the development of her oil resources. Hundreds and thousands of foreigners were sent to Sa'udi Arabia's oil region on the Persian Gulf, and revolutionary changes in the destiny of the country and its people may be expected.

The Yemen is also being forced out of its traditional isolation. Thus it also established regular diplomatic relations with the United States in 1946.

'Iraq

King Ghazi was killed in an automobile accident on April 3, 1939. His son, the four-year old Faysal II, was proclaimed his successor, with Prince 'Abd-al-Ilah as regent.

When the war broke out in Europe, 'Iraq severed connections with Germany, but Italian agents continued the thorough propaganda work established by the Germans, especially in military circles, long in opposition to the groups conducting the affairs of state in Baghdad. On April 4, 1941, Rashid 'Ali al-Gailani effected a *coup d'état.* His government was intensely anti-British and in violation of the Treaty of Alliance opposed British landings in Basra. On May 5 he renewed diplomatic relations with Germany. This was at the height of the German pincers movement through the Balkans and North Africa. In a six-week campaign the British reoccupied Baghdad and re-established the Regent and his government on June 1.

The situation, however, was still unsettled for many months because the apparatus for propaganda left by Axis agents and the ex-Mufti of Jerusalem turned out to be deeply entrenched in the administration and to have aroused wide popular appeal. Only after Rommel's army was routed from al-Alamein and the Americans landed in North Africa–i.e., about a year and a half after the reoccupation of the country–did the government of 'Iraq venture to declare war on Germany (January 16, 1943), the first Arab and first Moslem state to do so.

In 1943, Nuri Sa'id Pasha, the country's leading statesman, became active on behalf of the projected unification of Arab politics. In 1945-46 he conducted negotiations with Turkey for a treaty "on economic and cultural matters."

The Kurd question continued to trouble the political life of the country; thus in 1945 another revolt of the Kurdish tribes was put down, and it was even suspected that it was not unconnected with events in Adharbayjan.

Syria and Lebanon

The French failed to ratify the proposed treaties with Syria and Lebanon, and on June 23, 1939, delivered Alexandretta (Hatay) to the Turks, evidently in order to draw them into the Anglo-French alliance in the approaching world conflict.

This undermined what remained of trust in French politics. When the war broke out, General Weygand had a considerable force stationed in Syria, and many of the nationalists, though not all, rallied to the French authorities. But the French debacle of 1940 and the Vichy regime contributed further to the anti-French orientation of Levant nationalists. After all, the first duty of a mandatary is the defense of the mandated territory against aggression, and the French seemed to have failed in that both before their defeat (by ceding Alexandretta) and after it (when German and Italian military missions arrived in the Levant).

In February and March 1941 there were clashes between the populace and the French. On June 8, immediately after the suppression of the 'Iraqi rebellion, British and Free French forces invaded Syria and the Lebanon, and after a month of hostilities an armistice was signed on July 14 granting free exit to Vichy French. Both the Free French and the British proclaimed their intention to establish self-government in Syria and the Lebanon. General Catroux, who headed the Free French, seemed to return to the ideas incorporated in the draft treaties of 1936; on September 16 he announced the independence of Syria and on October 23 the independence of Lebanon. Shaykh Taj ad Din al Hasani was proclaimed president and the Syrian nationalists entered the government.

On February 8, 1942, a British minister to Syria and the Lebanon was appointed, and in October the United States, too, appointed a diplomatic agent. The government had great difficulties on account of scarcity of supplies. What with accelerated development, and extensive military projects such as road construction, there was no unemployment. Political difficulties, however, continued. Axis agents were at work; some French elements displayed an opposition to Syrian freedom, while Britain and the United States urged the De Gaullists to implement it.

In 1943 the constitutions were restored and elections were held in July and September in Syria and the Lebanon respectively. Shukri Quwatli became president of Syria, Besharah al-Khouri president of the Lebanon. The new Lebanese chamber, led by the veteran Arab nationalist Riyad Sulh, clashed with the French when it decided to delete provisions incompatible with the sovereignty and independence of the country; i.e., to ignore the mandate and the mandatary altogether. J. Helleux, the chief French administrator, thought he could suppress the movement by arresting the President, the cabinet and as many deputies as possible, but the result was that resentment was aroused in the country, and Britain and the United States refused to back France. The French had to capitulate.

This success spurred the republics to demand control of the armed forces locally recruited and to refuse to grant any special status for the French. In February 1945 they strengthened their position by joining the Allies and thus securing representation at the San Francisco Conference.

Syria and Lebanon demanded evacuation of the French forces. Clashes occurred between the populace and the French, and the latter accused the British of having instigated the clashes in order to oust the French from the Middle East. Indeed, the Syrian-Lebanese affair contributed substantially to French resentment against the British. When the latter attempted to mollify the French, it was too late, for the unleashed forces of Syrian politics had deprived the French of the last vestiges of authority in the area.

In February 1946 both republics appealed to the Security Council of the United Nations, demanding the evacuation of British and French forces. The Security Council expressed its confidence in the great powers' intentions of early withdrawal. In April, Syria celebrated the evacuation of foreign troops. The last French units left Lebanon on December 31.

In Syria complications continued with the Druzes and Nusayris. Political organizations were dissolved in May 1946.

Palestine

On May 17, 1939, the British government issued a White Paper, and though it was disapproved by the Permanent Mandates Commission of the League of Nations in its June session, this document inaugurated Great Britain's new policy concerning Palestine. The White Paper lays down that free land purchases by Jews may take place only in a section later restricted to about 5 per cent of Palestine; that 75,000 new immigrants will be admitted within five years, after which further immigration will depend on Arab consent; that within ten years self-governing institutions will be set up. It was approved by the House of Commons by a small majority against the votes of Churchill, Leopold Amery, and the Labor party. While the Arabs were gradually moved to accept the White Paper as a basis, the Jews pointed out that it meant reducing the Jews in Palestine to the status of a permanent minority in an Arab state to come.

The outbreak of the war seemed to reduce local political tension and channelized energies into the war effort. On July 16 Italian raids began on the coastal cities. The Jews began volunteering for the British forces in 1940, and pressed for the organization of Jewish units. The government refused to approve of such separate units and wanted instead to recruit mixed companies. But the Arabs were still largely influenced by Axis propaganda; the ex-Mufti of Jerusalem escaped from his Syrian refuge to 'Iraq and Iran and via Turkey to Rome and Berlin (1941), whence he called upon the Arabs to assist the Axis against "the Anglo-Saxons and the Jewish menace." Therefore only a very small number of Arabs volunteered for the British forces. Ultimately, in September 1944, the Jewish Brigade was organized, and it fought on the Italian front. As early as 1940 Palestine became a British fortress, an important link between the North Africa front and the 'Iraqi pipeline, and in 1941 the basis for operations against the 'Iraqi rebellion and the Vichy forces in Syria-Lebanon. Industrialization, especially among the Jews, increased by leaps and bounds.

In 1940 the new laws on land sales were promulgated. Noncertified immigrants were turned away from the shores of Palestine. The ship *Patria* was not allowed to disembark its 1,771 passengers and suffered an explosion in the harbor of Haifa (55 killed, 190 missing). In February 1942 the vessel *Struma* was lost in the Black Sea with 758 refugees aboard. Then in 1943 came the reports of the systematic extermination of Jews in the furnaces of Hitler's Europe. All these events were bound to bring the resentment of Jewry, and especially in Palestine with its splendid record of co-operation in the Allied war effort, to a high pitch. Some even turned to the path of terrorism in the belief that if terrorism could have induced the British to pursue a pro-Arab policy, it could force them in turn to abandon such a policy. Abraham Stern, a young classical scholar, led a tiny group bent on terroristic acts against the British. He was killed by the police, but in Cairo members of his group shot Lord Moyne, Britain's minister in the Middle East. A broader military organization, the Irgun, numbering a few thousand, represented the extreme "revisionists" who had seceded from the Zionist Organization, which they found too committed to Britain. The Haganah, the central mass defense organization of the Jews of Palestine, carried out acts of sabotage in order to ease immigration. The British cracked down with searches, curfews, mass screenings and detentions, and accused leaders of the Jewish Agency for Palestine of abetting terrorism. Jewish authorities rejected these accusations, stating that they had always taken a stand against terrorism, but would not oppose uncertified entry into Palestine inasmuch as it is not this immigration which they consider "illegal" but the restrictions on the entry of Jews into Palestine.

In the meantime the political struggle of the Jews assumed new scope when a Zionist conference in New York on May 11, 1942, resolved (Biltmore Resolution) that the Jewish people should demand, not merely the abolition of the White Paper, but, in view of the necessity for drastic and broad measures to salvage the remnants of the Jewish people in Europe, the establishment of a Jewish commonwealth in Palestine. This program, accepted by the overwhelming majority of Zionists and indeed backed by the great majority of Jews, became the watchword of Jewish demands for the postwar period.

Palestine Arabs countered with the organization of a new Arab Higher Committee in November 1945, backed by the Arab League. Para-military groups sprang up among them too.

The United States Congress passed resolutions favoring Jewish aspirations in Palestine (December 1945), and President Truman called upon Britain to open Palestine to 100,000 Jewish displaced persons from Europe. An Anglo-American inquiry committee was sent to Europe and Palestine; it held hearings also in Washington and in Arab capitals. Its report suggested the immediate entry of the 100,000 and the establishment of a state that would be neither Jewish nor Arab. The British Labor government (whose members and party had been known as stanch pro-Zionists for many years and had been committed to a pro-Jewish policy on Palestine during their election campaign) ignored these suggestions.

In February 1946 Jamal Husayni, exiled leader of the ex-Mufti's party, was readmitted to Palestine. In August the ex-Mufti left France in a plane, arrived in Egypt, and was received by the King, who granted him asylum. Early in 1947 Fawzi Qawuqji, "commander" of the Arab rebellion in 1936-39, returned from Germany to the East. Other exiles also flocked back. These strengthened the agitation among the Arabs, especially as now they could look to the Arab League.

The report of the inquiry commission was ignored by the British and resented by the Arabs, who opposed any immigration whatsoever and demanded that the White Paper of 1939 be carried out: i.e., that a Palestine national government be established. Since the Arabs constitute two thirds of the population, this necessarily would mean an Arab government, most probably headed by the ex-Mufti.

To the Jews, with such prospects for the national home, nothing was left but stubborn resistance. An attempt was made by both British and American experts to elaborate a plan based on the recommendations of the commission, and again the partition scheme came up. Among the Jews the idea also gained ground: they were anxious to secure as soon as possible a solution that would enable them to absorb substantial immigration and to secure international status for the national home of the Jewish people. These deliberations broke down.

In September 1946 the British government convened a conference on Palestine attended by representatives of the Arab states. It was suspended in October, and resumed in January 1947, only to end in an impasse. In December 1946 the 22nd Zionist Congress met in Basel and decided that only modifications in British policy would justify Jewish participation in the London conference. Since these were not forthcoming, the Jews did not attend the conference.

As President Truman gave expression again to his desire to see the resumption of substantial Jewish immigration to Palestine, a conflict arose between the British government and the United States, expressed especially in utterances of Foreign Secretary Ernest Bevin.

This course of affairs was reflected in new acts of violence in Palestine. The rising crescendo of terror and antiterrorist measures, and the growing bitterness of all concerned, turned the small country into a pathetic imbroglio of broken pledges and battered hopes.

Transjordan

On March 22, 1946, a treaty of independence was concluded between Transjordan and Great Britain in which the independence of Transjordan was promulgated. In an appendix military bases were granted to Great Britain. The emir Abdallah became the king of the Transjordan Hashimite Kingdom (May 25).

The King is pursuing a policy aiming at a Greater Syria and rapprochement with Turkey, which country he visited in 1947.

Iran

The war awakened and raised many apprehensions in Iran about the intentions of Germany and the U.S.S.R. These were intensified by the wave of German tourists and technicians. From the south came also a wave of pro-Axis Arabs escaping after the 'Iraqi revolt of 1941.

The German attack on the U.S.S.R. brought the Soviets and Britain together in Iran. On August 25-30, 1941, British forces from the south and Soviet forces from the north moved into Iran. On September 16 Riza Shah abdicated and his son Muhammad Riza Shah succeeded him. Four days later constitutional rule was re-established.

On January 29, 1942, an Anglo-Soviet-Iranian Treaty was concluded under which the leaders of the occupying forces were to "respect the territorial integrity, sovereignty and political independence of Iran." They also took over the defense of the country against aggression, while the Shah agreed to take steps necessary in wartime and authorized Great Britain and the U.S.S.R. to maintain forces, although this was not to be considered military occupation. These forces were to be withdrawn not later than six months after hostilities between the Axis and the Allies had been suspended. Vichy French and Japanese agents were ousted.

A tremendous transportation of supplies to the U.S.S.R. via Iran began from the Persian Gulf northward. In 1943 six thousand tons of supplies were sent daily from three ports on the Persian Gulf. But Iran suffered from scarcity and privations. Dr. Arthur Millspaugh was sent from the United States to assist Iran in her economic and financial administration.

But differences developed between Iran and the occupying powers on the one hand and among the Allied powers themselves on the other. The northern part of Iran was more and more isolated by the Russians; travelers and Iranian officials were barred from the north in 1943. In the wake of the Teheran conference the Allies issued a declaration on Iran: they were "at one with the Government of Iran in the desire for the maintenance of the independence, sovereignty and territorial integrity of Iran."

On September 9 Iran had declared war on the Axis powers. But the tensions of both national and international origin continued to plague the administration. Thus the United States had to protest the attacks on Dr. Millspaugh's financial mission (1944). The Soviets applied for oil concessions in the north, but the Iranian authorities tried to postpone any decision until after the war.

A vigorous Leftist movement (Tude) developed in the cities. In 1945 the importance of Iran from the point of view of military communications decreased after the Straits to the Black Sea and Russia's southern harbors became accessible to the Allies. But Iran loomed large in international affairs due to the movement that established an autonomous regime in Adharbayjan protected by the presence of Soviet forces.

In January 1946 Iran lodged a protest before the United Nations against the presence of Russian troops in Iran. In March this question was taken up. Russia demanded postponement of a Security Council examination but then stated that her troops would leave in six weeks. On April 4 Iran requested postponement of the case.

The new premier, Qawam as-Saltanah, known as a statesman in rather good standing with the Russians, went to Moscow in February, but apparently no agreement was achieved. He was ready to recognize the separate regime in Adharbayjan within the framework of Iran. By March 2 British troops had left Iran. The Majlis could not be convened because the Tude supporters prevented the attendance of a quorum.

Russians troops left by May 6. But negotiations conducted by the Adharbayjan regime with Teheran were not conclusive. When the new elections for the Majlis were announced, the government decided to send troops to the provinces in order to secure peaceful and free elections. The Adharbayjan regime refused to admit Iranian troops; fighting ensued. In mid-December, Tabriz, the capital, was seized by government troops and the local regime dissolved.

Chronological Table

106 Fall of the Nabatean kingdom
273 End of the Arab dynasty of Palmyra
529 The Ghassanid Harith V, patricius and phylarch of the Arabs
530 Abyssinians in South Arabia
ca. 250-602 The Lakhmids of Hirah
610 Arab victory over Persians at Dhu Qar
622 The Hijrah, Muhammad's migration to Medina, beginning of Islamic era
624 Muhammad's victory over the Meccans at Badr
625 His defeat at Mt. Uhud
627 The War of the Trench
628 Jewish colonies in Arabia crushed
629 Byzantine victory over a Muslim army at Mu'tah
630 Conquest of Mecca. Battle of Hunayn
632 The farewell pilgrimage. Death of the Prophet (June 8)
632-634 The caliph Abu Bakr. Revolts in Arabia put down
633 Conquest of southern Mesopotamia
634 Battle of Ajnadayn (?) against the Byzantines in Palestine
634-644 The caliph 'Umar
635 Conquest of Damascus. Persians defeated at Qadisiyah
636 Byzantines defeated on R. Yarmuk
637 Persians defeated at Jalula. The council of Jabiyah
639 Conquest of Egypt
640 Conquest of Persia
644 The caliph 'Uthman
647 Tripolitania conquered
649 Sea war opened against Byzantines by Mu'awiyah, Cyprus taken
651 Yezdegerd, last Sassanid, assassinated in Khorasan
653 'Uthman's Qur'an recension
656-661 Caliph 'Ali
656 Battle of the Camel
657 Battle of Siffin
658 Arbitration at Adhruh
661-750 The Umayyad dynasty
661-680 Mu'awiyah I
662-675 Ziyad ibn-Abihi, governor in 'Iraq
670 'Uqbah b. Nafi' conquers N. W. Africa

674-679 Constantinople besieged
680-683 Yazid I
680 Husayn's death at Kerbela
683-692 The pretender 'Abdallah b. az-Zubayr in Mecca
683 Fighting among the Arabs of Syria
684-685 Marwan I
685-705 'Abd-al-Malik
685-687 Mukhtar's revolt in 'Iraq
691 Mus'ab ibn-az-Zubayr killed in battle. 'Abd-al-Malik conquers 'Iraq
692 Hajjaj ibn-Yusuf captures Mecca
694-714 Hajjaj governor of 'Iraq
705-715 Walid I
711 Battle of Wadi Bakkah, conquest of Spain
711-712 Conquest of Sind and of Transoxania
715-717 Sulayman
717-720 'Umar II, reform of taxation
720-724 Yazid II
724-743 Hisham
732 Battle of Tours and Poitiers
741 Berber revolt. Hostilities with Byzantines in Asia Minor
743-744 Walid II
744-750 Marwan II, reorganized army
746 Rebellions of the Kalb in Syria and of the Kharijites in 'Iraq. Abu Muslim's propaganda on behalf of the 'Abbasids in Khorasan
748 Qahtabah defeats the Umayyad governor of Khorasan
749 All Persia seized by the 'Abbasids; their march into Kufah
750 Marwan's defeat on R. Zab, his death in Egypt
750-754 As-Saffah, extirpation of the Umayyads
754-775 Al-Mansur
756-788 The Umayyad 'Abd-ar-Rahman—emir of Cordova
762-763 'Alid rebellions in 'Iraq and in Medina. Foundation of Baghdad
767 Death of Abu Hanifah
775-785 Al-Mahdi, Persian influences on Arabic literature, struggle against Manicheans
778-780 Al-Muqanna' leads revolt in Khorasan
778 Charlemagne's campaign in Spain
785-786 Al-Hadi; the great mosque of Cordova erected
786-809 Harun ar-Rashid, flowering of Arabic literature
796-822 Hakam I in Spain, revolts in Cordova, city republic in Toledo
799 Ibn-Aghlab, hereditary governor in Africa
803 Fall of the Barmakids
809-813 Al-Amin
813-833 Al-Ma'mun. Efflorescence of Islamic scholarship and sciences. Mu'tazilah and the controversy on the creation of the Qur'an
817 Attempt at reconciliation with the 'Alids
819 Tahir as governor of Khorasan, the Samanids as his vassals
822-852 'Abd-ar-Rahman II of Cordova
831 Palermo seized by the Arabs

833-842 Al-Mu'tasim. Orthodox reaction. Turkish mercenaries
836 Samarra founded
837 The communist sect of Babak crushed in Persia
842-847 Al-Wathiq
847-861 Al-Mutawakkil
ca. 850 The Uigur kingdom in central Asia
852-886 Muhammad I in Cordova. Christian martyrs, rebellions of converts
861-862 Al-Muntasir
862-866 Al-Mu'tazz
866-869 Al-Muhtadi
869 'Ali ibn-Muhammad founds a kingdom of Negro slaves in Basra
868-906 Tulunids as hereditary governors of Egypt
869-892 Al-Mu'tamid; his brother al-Muwaffaq in charge of affairs
871-879 Ya'qub as-Saffar (the Coppersmith) rules Persia
876 Muwaffaq defeats Ya'qub at Dayr al-'Aqul
877 Ahmad ibn-Tulun occupies Syria
883 The state of Negro slaves destroyed
888-912 'Abdallah of Cordova against the rebels
890 First appearance of the Qarmatians in 'Iraq
892-902 Al-Mu'tadid
ca. 900 Rise of the Zaydites in South Arabia
902-908 Al-Muktafi, fights the Qarmatians
908-932 Al-Muqtadir, death of the rival caliph 'Abdallah ibn-al-Mu'tazz
909 Abu 'Abdallah defeats the last Aghlabid on behalf of the Fatimids
910 'Ubaydallah founds the Fatimid caliphate in al-Mahdiyah
912-961 'Abd-ar-Rahman III of Cordova, introduces Saqalibah troops
913-942 The Samanid Nasr II
923 Death of the historian Tabari
928 The Qarmatians in Mecca, the Black Stone of the Ka'bah carried away
929 'Abd-ar-Rahman of Cordova assumes title of caliph
932-934 Al-Qahir
932-940 Ar-Radi
932-967 The Buyid Mu'izz-ad-Dawlah as guardian of the caliph
936 Muhammad ibn-Ra'iq as amir al-umara
939 'Abd-ar-Rahman defeated by Ramiro of León at Simancas
940-943 Al-Muttaqi
943-946 Al-Mustakfi
944-967 The Hamdanid Sayf-ad-Dawlah in Aleppo fighting the Byzantines; al-Mutanabbi, the poet, and al-Farabi, the philosopher, at his court
951-961 The Samanid 'Abd-al-Malik. The Turk Alptigin in Ghaznah
961-976 Hakam I of Cordova
969 Jawhar conquers Egypt for the Fatimids. Cairo founded
976-997 Subuktigin of Ghaznah
996-1021 The Fatimid al-Hakim in Egypt. Rise of the Druze sect
998-1030 Mahmud of Ghaznah. Epos of Firdawsi (*d.* 1020)

1006 Mahmud defeats the Ilek khan of Turkestan
1023-1091 Abbadids of Seville
1027-1031 Hisham III, last Umayyad in Cordova
ca. 1030 Al-Biruni's description of India
1037 The Seljuqs Tughril Beg and Da'ud seize Khorasan
1055 Tughril Beg takes over from the last Buyid the control over the caliph al-Qa'im
1062 The Almoravid Yusuf ibn-Tashfin conquers Morocco
1063-1072 Tughril Beg's successor, Alp Arslan. Wars with the Byzantines [1071 Battle of Manzikert]
1072-1092 Seljuq sultan Malikshah; his wazir Nizam-al-Mulk; the theologian al-Ghazzali (*d.* 1111). 'Umar Khayyam, Hariri.
1072-1107 The Seljuq Sulayman in Asia Minor
1107-1300 His progeny in the Konya sultanate.
1083 Alfonso VI of Castile defeats al-Mu'tamid of Seville
1086 Yusuf ibn-Tashfin defeats the Spanish Christians near Zallaqah
1090 Yusuf deposes the petty dynasts during his second campaign in Spain
1099 Crusaders capture Jerusalem
1107-1130 Muhammad ibn-Tumart founds the Almohad regime
1132-1163 'Abd-al-Mu'min the Almohad; his successors, Yusuf (till 1184) and Ya'qub al-Mansur (–1199)
1137 Dissolution of the Seljuq power under the Atabegs
1140 Atsiz founds the dynasty of Khwarizm shahs
1145 End of the last Almoravid, Tashfin
1150 The Ghorids destroy Ghaznah
1154 Nur-ad-Din Zengi (1146-1173) captures Damascus
1171 Saladin (Salah-ad-Din) Ayyubi overthrows the Fatimids in Egypt
1174 He captures Damascus and Syria
1180-1225 An-Nasir, the last statesman on the 'Abbasid throne
1187 Saladin defeats the Franks at Hattin and captures Jerusalem
1193 Death of Saladin; division of his realm
1195 Al-Mansur, Almohad, defeats Castilians at Alarcos
1199-1220 Khwarizm shah Muhammad at the peak of his power
1203 Temuchin–Chingiz Khan (after 1206) founds the Mongol Empire
1218-1238 Sultan Kamil of Egypt
1220 Mongols conquer Khwarizm, Bukhara, Samarqand
1220-1231 The last Khwarizm shah Jalal-ad-Din Mangubirti
1225 Almohads abandon Spain; rise of the Marinids in Fez, Zijanids in Tlemsen, Hafsids of Tunis, ibn-Hud in Spain
1227 Death of Chingiz Khan. His empire divided under Ogotay, the Great Khan
1232-1492 Nasrids, Banu-l-Ahmar of Granada. Construction of Alhambra
1248 Louis IX of France at Damietta
1254-1517 Mamluk rule in Egypt
1256-1291 The Persian poet Sa'di
1258 Hulagu captures Baghdad; end of the 'Abbasid caliphate

1260 Mamluks defeat Mongols at 'Ayn Jalut
1273 Death of the Persian mystic Jalal-ad-Din ar-Rumi
1277 The Mamluk Baybars (1266-1277) defeats the Mongols at Albistan
1326 Orkhan, Osmanli chieftain, captures Brusa
1337 His attack repulsed by Byzantium
1357 Gallipoli conquered by Prince Suleyman
1362-1389 Murad I, conqueror of Adrianople
1369 Timur conquers Khorasan and Transoxania
1371 Serbs defeated on the Maritza, lose Macedonia
1385-1386 Turks in Nish and Sofia
1387 Turks defeated at Plochnik
1389 The Battle of Kossovo Polye. Death of the Persian poet Hafiz
1389-1402 Bayezid
1390 Philadelphia seized
1391-1393 Seljuq emirates submit to Osmanlis
1393 Bulgarians submit to Osmanlis
1400 Timur in Sivas
1402 Bayezid defeated and captured by Timur at Ankara; Seljuqs reinstated
1403-1421 The Osmanli Muhammad I fighting his brothers
1405 Death of Timur. His empire divided
1408 Kara Koyunlu victory over Miran Shah
1416 Victory of the Venetian fleet over the Turks near Gallipoli. Execution of the rebel Badr-ad-Din
1421-1451 Murad II
1430 Capture of Salonica
1443 An army of crusaders under John Hunyadi defeats the Turks at Jalowatz
1447-1452 The Timurid Ulugh Beg
1448 Murad repels Hunyadi on Kossovo Polye
1451-1481 Muhammad II
1453 Conquest of Constantinople
1456 Siege of Belgrade
1458 George Brancovich dies. Serbs subjugated
1461 Conquest of Peloponnesus and of Trebizond of the Comneni
1468 Subjugation of the Albanians
1469 The Timurid Abu Sa'id defeated by Uzun Hasan
1469-1506 The Timurid Husayn Baikara in Herat
1470 The Venetians lose Negroponte on Euboea; their alliance with Uzun Hasan
1473 Uzun Hasan defeated by Muhammad at Terjan
1475 The Genoese expelled from Caffa; the Crimean Tartars vassals of the Ottomans
1479 Peace with Venice
1481-1512 Bayezid II. His struggle with his brother Jem [who died in Naples, 1495]
1492 Fall of Granada and of the Moors in Spain
1497-1503 Construction of the Bayezid mosque in Constantinople

1499-1503 War with Venice
1502 The Safavid Isma'il of Ardabil introduces Shi'ism as state religion in Persia
1512-1520 Selim I Yavuz. Persecution of the Shi'ites
1514 Selim defeats Shah Isma'il at Chaldiran
1516 Selim defeats the Mamluk Qansuh al-Ghuri near Marj Dabiq
1517 Conquest of Egypt
1520-1566 Suleyman I the Great, Kanuni
1522 Conquest of Rhodes
1526 Louis of Hungary slain in the battle of Mohacs
1532 Siege of Güns. Andrea Doria on the shores of Morea
1534 Capture of Tabriz and Baghdad
1533-1546 Khayr-ad-Din Barbarossa kapudanpasha against the Spanish fleet
1543 Subjugation of Hungary
1544 Sa'di Sharifs in Morocco
1547 Piri Re'is takes Aden
1550 Construction of the Suleymaniye mosque in Constantinople
1551 Piri Re'is takes Masqat
1566 Suleyman dies near Szigeth
1566-1574 Selim II
1570 Conquest of Cyprus
1571 Don John of Austria sinks the Ottoman fleet at Lepanto
1574-1595 Murad III
1577-1585 War with Persia, seizure of Tiflis, Kars, and Tabriz
1578-1610 Ahmad I al-Mansur seizes Timbuktu
1586-1628 'Abbas the Great shah of Persia
1595-1603 Muhammad III
1599 Death of the court historian Sa'd-ad-Din
1600 Death of the ghazel poet Baqi
1603-1617 Ahmed I, revolt of the Druze prince Fakhr-ad-Din
1606 Peace of Sitvatorok
1617-1622 Mustafa I
1618-1622 Osman II
1623-1640 Murad IV
1633 Defeat of Fakhr-ad-Din
1638 Baghdad recaptured
1640-1648 Ibrahim
1645 War against Venice on Crete
1648-1687 Muhammad IV (Awji). Hajji Khalifah's cosmography
1651 Victory of the Venetian fleet at Paros, 1656 near the Straits
1656 Muhammad Köprülü grand wazir
1664 Filali rule in Morocco. Ottomans defeated at St. Gothard on the Raab
1665 French bombard Algiers and Tunis
1669 Venice cedes Crete to Turkey
1672 Poland cedes Podolia and the Ukraine
1673 Sobieski's victory at Choczim

1676 Sobieski's victory at Lwów and his defeat at Zuravna
1679 Death of the explorer Evliya Chelebi
1681 Turks cede Kiev to Russia
1683 Turks before Vienna
1686 Turks lose Hungary
1687 Turks defeated at Mohacs
1687-1691 Suleyman II
1688 Austrians take Belgrade
1689 Defeat at Nish. Mustafa Köprülü grand wazir
1690 Belgrade recaptured
1691 Mustafa Köprülü slain in the battle of Szalankemen
1691-1695 Ahmed II
1695-1703 Mustafa II
1696 Peter the Great takes Azov
1697 Turks defeated at Zenta on R. Theiss
1699 Peace of Karlowitz
1703-1730 Ahmed III
1711 Peter the Great defeated on R. Pruth
1714 Venice loses her last dependencies in Morea and in the Aegean
1716 Prince Eugene, victorious at Peterwardein, captures Temesvar
1718 Peace of Passarowitz
1722 The last Safavid deposed by the Afghan Mir Mahmud. Russian conquests in the Caucasus
1729-1730 The Afghans driven out of Persia by Nadir Kuli Khan
1730-1754 Mahmud I
1735-1739 Victorious war against Austria and Russia
1736-1747 Nadir Shah of Persia
1739 Nadir takes Delhi
1740 Muhammad ibn-'Abd-al-Wahhab in Dar'iyah (Arabia)
1750-1779 Karim Khan Zendi of Shiraz rules Persia
1754-1757 Osman III
1757-1774 Mustafa III
1757 Wahhabis take al-Hasa
1761 Treaty of friendship between the Turks and Frederick the Great
1770 War with Russia. Annihilation of the Turkish fleet at Cheshme
1773-1789 'Abd-al-Hamid I
1774 Peace of Kuchuk Kainarji. Austria occupies Bukovina
1779-1797 Agha Muhammad founds the dynasty of the Kajars
1783 Catherine subjugates the Crimean Tartars
1784 Convention of Ainali Kavak
1789 Napoleon in Egypt
1789-1807 Selim III, first attempt at reform after French pattern
1801 Wahhabis raid Kerbela
1803-1804 They capture Mecca and Medina
1804 Serb revolt under Karageorgios
1807 Treaty of Fath 'Ali Shah (1797-1834) with Napoleon against Russia
1807-1808 Mustafa IV

1808-1839 Mahmud II
1811 Muhammad 'Ali wipes out the Mamluks
1812 Bucharest peace with Russia. Tusun, son of Muhammad 'Ali, on his campaign against the Wahhabis, seizes Mecca and Medina
1818 Ibrahim, son of Muhammad 'Ali, crushes the Wahhabis
1821-1829 The Greek uprising
1826 Mahmud wipes out the Janizaries
1827 Triple alliance against Turkey. Naval battle of Navarin
1830 French occupy Algeria
1831-1832 Ibrahim conquers Syria. 'Abbas Mirza conquers Khorasan
1832 Ibrahim defeats the Turks near Konya
1833 Peace of Kütahya. Treaty with Russia signed at Hunkyar Iskelesi
1834-1848 Muhammad shah of Persia
1835 'Abd-al-Qadir defeats French at Macta. Moltke and von Berg in Turkish service
1836 Recapture of Tripolitania
1837 *Bash vekil* replaces grand wazir. Persians besiege Herat (defended by an Englishman)
1839 Turko-Egyptian war. Turkish defeat of Nasibin. Kabul and Kandahar occupied by the British. Aden occupied by the British
1839-1861 'Abd-al-Majid
1839 Return to the office of grand wazir. Reshid Pasha minister of foreign affairs.
1840 London conference to regulate Egyptian-Turkish relations
1842 Druze revolt. Reorganization of Lebanon. Dost Muhammad drives the British out of Afghanistan
1843 'Abd-al-Qadir crosses into Morocco. Muhammad b. 'Ali founds the order of Sanusiyah in Tripolitania
1844 Mirza 'Ali Muhammad, the Bab
1845 The marabut Bu Ma'za in Algeria. 'Abd-al-Qadir captured
1848 Muhammad 'Ali dies. 'Abbas (–1854) his successor
1848-1896 Nasir-ad-Din Shah
1849 Faysal, Wahhabi, drives last Egyptian governor out of Arabia
1849-1852 Controversy over the holy places in Palestine
1850 Bab's followers massacred
1852 Danilo, first secular ruler of Montenegro
1853 Outbreak of the Crimean War
1854 Turks defend Silistria. Russian defeat on R. Alma
1854-1863 'Ali Sa'id Pasha of Egypt
1855 Fall of Sevastopol. Shamil leads a revolt of Lezghians against Russia
1856 Hatti Humayun. Peace of Paris. Britain's war against Persia
1859 Ibrahim Shinasi, beginnings of modern Turkish literature
1860 Construction begun of the Suez canal. Persecution of Christians in Damascus
1861-1876 'Abd-al-'Aziz
1863-1880 Isma'il pasha of Egypt; in 1866 assumes the title khedive
1869 Suez canal completed

1870 Muhammad ibn-'Abdallah, mahdi in Sudan
1873 Constitutional status of Egypt redefined
1875 Introduction of mixed courts in Egypt
1873-1894 Sultan Hasan of Morocco
1875 Egyptians capture Harar in Ethiopia; are defeated by Emperor John. Isma'il sells his Suez shares to Britain. Turkish state bankruptcy. Revolt in Herzegovina
1876 Atrocities in Bulgaria. Midhat's conspiracy against Sultan 'Abd-al-'Aziz. Murad V
1876-1909 'Abd-al-Hamid II
1876 Serbia and Montenegro declare war. Midhat as grand wazir introduces the Turkish constitution
1877-1888 Russo-Turkish war. Battle for Plevna and the Shipka pass. Russians in Adrianople. Armistice of San Stefano. Cyprus ceded to Britain
1878 Berlin Congress
1880-1892 Tawfiq, khedive of Egypt
1881 French occupy Tunisia. 'Arabi defeated at Tell-al-Kabir. British occupy Egypt
1882 Mahdi drives Egyptians out of Sudan
1883 Mahdi occupies 'Ubayd
1885 Khartum attacked. Gordon killed. Death of the Mahdi. His Khalifah 'Abdallah Abu Bakr
1888 Mahdists defeat Ras Adal in Ethiopia, destroy Gondar, subjugate the Equatorial province
1889 Defeat the Abyssinians at Gallabat. Emperor John slain
1892 Rabih founds a kingdom on Lake Chad
1894 French capture Timbuktu
1894-1907 Sultan 'Abd-al-'Aziz of Morocco
1896 Kitchener defeats Mahdists at Umm Durman. Khalifah slain. Greek-Turkish war. Nasir-ad-Din assassinated
1896-1909 Shah Muzaffar-ad-Din
1900 Rabih's realm destroyed by the French
1904 Conference of Algeciras. Persian constitution
1906 The Dinshaway affair. Cromer's resignation
1907 Persia divided into Russian and British spheres of influence
1908 Revolution of the Young Turks
1909 Revolution in Persia. Muzaffar-ad-Din abdicates. Shah Ahmed. Second march on Istanbul
1909-1918 Sultan Muhammad V
1911-1912 Italy captures Tripolitania
1912 Balkan war. Loss of Adrianople and Salonica
1913 Enver recaptures Adrianople. Peace treaties of Constantinople and Athens (1914)
1914 November 1. Turkey in World War I with the Central Powers. Husayn Kamil, sultan of Egypt

1915 Attack on the Suez canal. Battle of the Straits. Early in December General Townshend encircled at Kut-al-'Amarah at the head of the Anglo-Indian forces landed in Basra in the autumn of 1914

1916 April 29. Townshend's capitulation. Russian advances in Caucasus and Persia

1917 March—British take Baghdad. December—conquest of Palestine. Fu'ad, Sultan of Egypt. Sultan Muhammad VI Wahid-ad-Din.

1918 Lawrence occupies Damascus (October). October 30—Armistice of Mudros. Rise of the Wafd movement in Egypt

	Turkey	Egypt	Syria Lebanon	Palestine	'Iraq	Arabia	North Africa	Persia
1919	Greeks in Smyrna (May 15) Mustafa Kemal in Anatolia (May 15) Erzerum congress (July 23) National Pact	Nationalist upheaval						
1920	Allies occupy Istanbul (March) National Assembly open at Ankara (April 23) San Remo Conference on mandates Peace of Sèvres	Milner Mission	French expel King Faysal					Riza Khan marches on Teheran
1921	Mustafa Kemal (Ghazi) defeats the Greeks on R. Sakarya Treaties with France and Russia	Zaghlul in the Seychelles			King Faysal (Aug. 23)		'Abd-el-Krim's revolt in the Rif of Morocco	
1922	Greeks driven out of Asia Minor Peace of Lausanne	Fu'ad as king (March 15)		Constitution promulgated				
1923	Republic (October 29) 'Abd-al-Majid as caliph	Constitution promulgated						
1924	Caliphate abolished (March 3)	Fu'ad dissolves parliament Zaghlul as premier				Ibn-Sa'ud captures Hijaz		

	Turkey	*Egypt*	*Syria Lebanon*	*Palestine*	*'Iraq*	*Arabia*	*North Africa*	*Persia*
1925	Kurdish rebellion Dervish orders abolished Western hat introduced		Rebellion		Mosul secured			Riza Khan Pehlevi, shah of Iran
1926	Conspiracy in Smyrna	Zaghlul premier again	Republic of Greater Lebanon			'Asir annexed to Hijaz All-Islam congress in Mecca	His defeat	
1927		Zaghlul's death Sarwat negotiates a treaty with Britain						
1928	Latin alphabet							
1929				Disturbances				Amanallah's abdication Transiranian railroad (1929-1938)
1930	Revolt in Menemen (Asia Minor) Joins the League of Nations Limitation on number of mosques							

1932					Joins the League of Nations Nestorians' revolt			
1933				Disturbances	Death of Faysal —Sept. 8 King Ghazi			
1934	Balkan Pact Treaty with Iran Family names introduced Mustafa Kemal Ataturk					War between Ibn-Sa'ud and Imam Yahya of Yemen Peace treaty of Taif		Cf. Turkey
1935	First women in National Assembly			Arab agitation against rising Jewish immigration				Women's emancipation University of Teheran
1936		Treaty with Great Britain Fu'ad's death (April 28) King Faruq		Royal Commission	*Coup d'état* Oct. 29			

	Turkey	*Egypt*	*Syria Lebanon*	*Palestine*	*'Iraq*	*Arabia*	*North Africa*	*Persia*
1937	Treaty with Syria about the Sanjaq of Alexandretta Treaty of Sa'dabad with 'Iraq Iran, Afghanistan	Cabinet of Muhammad Mahmud Pasha	Cf. Turkey	The Mufti escapes	Cf. Turkey			Treaty of Sa'dabad
1938	Ataturk's death (Oct. 11) Ismet Inonu, president	Parliament dissolved Decline of the Wafd		Royal Commission Report: partition scheme				
1939				February, London conference	King Ghazi killed in car accident (Feb. 4) Four-year-old King Faysal II British consul murdered in Mosul			

Bibliography*

REFERENCE WORKS

Encyclopaedia of Islam, London and Leyden, 1913-38.
Lane-Poole, St., *The Mohammadan Dynasties, Chronological and Genealogical Tables*, Westminster, 1894.
Zambaur, E. de, *Manuel de généalogie et de chronologie pour l'histoire de l'islam*, Hanover, 1927.

HISTORY OF STUDY

Barthold, V. (W.), *The Geographical and Historical Study of the East* (in Russian), St. Petersburg, 1911, Leningrad, 1925; [German tr. 1913].
Kiernan, R. H., *The Unveiling of Arabia*, London, 1937.
Becker, C. H., in his *Islamstudien* (see below).

LITERATURE

Brockelmann, C., *Geschichte der arabischen Literatur*, 5 vols., Weimar and Leyden, 1898-1942.
Browne, E. G., *A Literary History of Persia*, 4 vols., London, 1902.
Gibb, H. A. R., *Arabic Literature*, London, 1926.
Levy, R., *Persian Literature*, London, 1923.
Nicholson, R. A., *A Literary History of the Arabs*, London, 1907, 1914, 1930.

COLLECTED AND COLLECTIVE WORKS

Hurgronje, Chr. Snouck, *Verspreide Geschriften*, 6 vols., Bonn, 1923-27.
Becker, C. H., *Islamstudien*, 2 vols., Leipzig, 1924-32.
Nallino, C. A., *Raccolta di scritti editi e inediti*, 5 vols., Rome, 1939-44.
The Legacy of Islam, edited by the late Sir Thomas Arnold and Alfred Guillaume, Oxford, 1931, 1943.
The Arab Heritage, edited by N. A. Faris, Princeton, 1944.

THE ARABS. EXPANSION OF ISLAM

Weil, G., *Geschichte der Chalifen*, 3 vols., Mannheim, 1848-51.
Müller, A., *Der Islam im Morgen- und Abendland*, 2 vols., Berlin, 1885-87.

* See also bibliographical footnotes to the text.

Muir, W., *The Caliphate,* London, 1891; edited by T. M. Weir, Edinburgh, 1924.
Arnold, Th. W., *The Preaching of Islam,* London, 1896 . . . 1935.
Huart, Cl., *Histoire des Arabes,* 2 vols., Paris, 1912-13.
Gaudefroy-Demombynes, M., *Le Monde musulman* (*Histoire du monde,* VII, 1), Paris, 1931.
Hitti, Ph. K., *History of the Arabs,* London, 1937 . . . 1946.
Poliak, A. N., *History of the Arabs* (in Hebrew), Jerusalem, 1946.

Thomas, B., *The Arabs,* London, 1937.
Hitti, Ph. K., *The Arabs,* Princeton, 1943, 1946.

PRE-ISLAMIC ARABIA

Nöldeke, Th., *Geschichte der Perser unde Araber zur Zeit der Sasaniden,* Leyden, 1879.
O'Leary, D. L., *Arabia before Muhammad,* London, 1927.
Neilsen, D., ed., *Handbuch der altarabischen Altertumskunde,* Vol. I, Copenhagen, Leipzig, Paris, 1927.
Wellhausen, J., *Reste arabischen Heidentums,* 2nd. ed., Berlin, 1897.
Lammens, H., *Le Berceau de l'islam,* Vol. I, Rome, 1914.
Levi della Vida, G., in *The Arab Heritage,* edited by N. A. Faris, Princeton, 1944.
Lyall, Ch. J., *Ancient Arabian Poetry,* London 1930.

ARABIA—THE EARLY HISTORY OF ISLAM, SOURCES

Caetani, Leone, Principe di Teano, Duca di Sermoneta, *Annali dell' Islam,* 10 vols., Milan, 1905-26.
——, *Chronographia Islamica,* Fs. 1-4, Paris, 1912.
——, *Studi di storia orientale,* I, III, Milan, 1911-14.

THE PROPHET

Sprenger, A., *Das Leben und die Lehre des Mohammed,* 2nd ed., 3 vols., Berlin, 1869.
Margoliouth, D. S., *Mohammed and the Rise of Islam,* New York, 1905.
Muir, W., *The Life of Mohammad,* edited by T. H. Weir, Edinburgh, 1923.
Buhl, F., *Das Leben Muhammeds,* translated from the Danish by H. H. Schaeder, Leipzig, 1930.
Andrae, Tor, *Mohammed, the Man and His Faith* (tr.), New York, 1936.

THE ARAB EMPIRE

Vloten, G. van, *Recherches sur la domination arabe, le chiitisme et les croyances messianiques sous le califat des Omaiyades,* Amsterdam, 1894.
Wellhausen, J., *Das arabische Reich und sein Sturz,* Berlin, 1902; (tr.) *The Arab Kingdom and Its Fall,* Calcutta, 1927.
Lammens, H., *Etudes sur le siècle des Omayyades,* Beyrouth, 1930.

THE 'ABBASIDS

Goeje, M. J. de, *Mémoire sur les Carmathes du Bahrain et les Fatimides*, Leyden, 1886.
Vloten, G. van, *De Opkomst der Abbasiden in Chorasan*, Leyden, 1890.
Massignon, L., *La Passion d'al-Hosain ibn Mansour al-Hallaj*, 2 vols., Paris, 1922.
Bowen, H., *The Life and Times of Ali ibn Isa, "the Good Vizier,"* Cambridge, 1928.
Mez, A., *Die Renaissance des Islams*, Heidelberg, 1922; (tr.) *The Renaissance of Islam*, London, 1937.

PERSIA, AFGHANISTAN

Sykes, Sir P. M., *A History of Persia*, 2 vols., 1915 . . . 1930.
——, *A History of Afghanistan*, London, 1940.

ISLAM AND ISLAMIC CIVILIZATION

Kremer, A. von, *Geschichte der herrschenden Ideen des Islams*, Leipzig, 1868.
——, *Culturgeschichte des Islams unter den Chalifen*, 2 vols., Vienna, 1875-77. [Vol. I tr.: S. Khuda Buksh, *The Orient under the Caliphs*, Calcutta, 1920; four chapters from Vol. II tr. in S. Khuda Buksh, *Studies, Indian and Islamic*, London, 1927.]
——, *Culturgeschichtliche Streifzüge auf dem Gebiete des Islams*, Leipzig, 1873. [Tr. in S. Khuda Buksh, *Contributions to the History of Islamic Civilization*, Vol. I, Calcutta, 1905, 1929.]
Goldziher, I., *Die Zahiriten*, Leipzig, 1884.
——, *Muhammedanische Studien*, 2 vols., Halle, 1888-90.
——, *Vorlesungen über den Islam*, Heidelberg, 1910; 2nd ed. prepared by F. Babinger, 1925.
——, *Die Richtungen der islamischen Koranauslegung*, Leyden, 1926.
Macdonald, D. B., *Muslim Theology, Jurisprudence and Constitutional Theory*, New York, 1903.
——, *Religious Attitude and Life in Islam*, Chicago, 1909.
Margoliouth, D. S., *The Early Development of Mohammedanism*, London, 1914.
Wensinck, A. J., *The Moslem Creed*, Cambridge, 1932.
Lammens, H., *L'Islam;* (tr.) *Islam, Beliefs and Institutions*, London, 1929.
Masse, H., *Islam*, New York, 1938.
Guillaume, A., *The Traditions of Islam*, Oxford, 1924.
Nicholson, R. A., *The Mystics of Islam*, London, 1914.
——, *Studies in Islamic Mysticism*, Cambridge, 1921.
Arberry, A. J., *An Introduction to the History of Sufism*, London, 1943.
Levy, R., *An Introduction to the Sociology of Islam*, 2 vols., London, 1931-33.
Tritton, A. S., *The Caliphs and Their Non-Muslim Subjects*, Oxford, 1930.

Arnold, Th., *The Caliphate*, Oxford, 1924.
Barthold, W., *Mussulman Culture* (tr.), Calcutta, 1934.
Grunebaum, G. von, *Medieval Islam*, Chicago, 1946.
Mieli, A., *La Science arabe*, Leyden, 1938.
Browne, E. G., *Arabian Medicine*, Cambridge, 1921.
Boer, T. J. de, *The History of Philosophy in Islam*, London, 1903, 1933.
Horten, M., *Die Philosophie des Islam*, Munich, 1924.
Creswell, K. A. C., *Early Muhammadan Architecture*, 2 vols., Oxford, 1932-40.
Briggs, M., *Muhammadan Architecture in Egypt and Palestine*, Oxford, 1924.
Richmond, E. T., *Moslem Architecture*, London, 1926.
Diez, E., *Die Kunst der islamischen Völker*, Berlin, 1915.
——, and Gluck, H., *Die Kunst des Islam*, Berlin, 1925.
Kühnel, E., *Islamische Kleinkunst*, Berlin, 1925.
Marçais, G., *Manuel d'art musulman, L'Architecture*, 2 vols., Paris, 1926-27.
Migeon, G., *Manuel d'art musulman, Arts plastiques et industriels*, 2 vols., Paris, 1927.
Dimand, M. S., *A Handbook of Muhammadan Art*, New York, 1930, 1944.
Arnold, T. W., *Painting in Islam*, Oxford, 1928.
Pope, A. U., *A Survey of Persian Art*, London and New York, 1928-36.
Farmer, H. G., *A History of Arabian Music to the 13th Century*, London, 1929.

AFRICA, SPAIN

Fournel, L., *Les Berbers*, 2 vols., Paris, 1877-81.
Mercier, E., *Histoire de l'Afrique septentrionale*, 3 vols., Paris, 1888-91.
Faure-Biquet, G., *Histoire de l'Afrique septentrionale sous la domination musulmane (740 à 1835)*, Paris, 1905.
Meakin, Budget, *The Moorish Empire*, London, 1899.
Lane-Poole, St., *The Moors in Spain*, New York, 1899.
Cour, A., *L'Etablissement de la dynastie des cherifs au Maroc et leur rivalité avec les Turcs de la Régence d'Alger (1509-1830)*, Algiers, 1904.
Dozy, R., *Histoire des Musulmans d'Espagne jusqu'à la conquête de l'Andalousie par les Almoravides (711-1110)*, new edition prepared by E. Levi-Provençal, Leyden, 1932; [tr. *Spanish Islam*, London, 1913].
Levi-Provençal, E., *L'Espagne musulmane au Xe siècle, institutions et vie sociale*, Paris, 1932.
——, *La Civilisation arabe en Espagne*, Cairo, 1938.
Amari, M., *Storia degli Musulmani di Sicilia*, 3 vols., Florence, 1854-72; new edition by C. A. Nallino, Catania, 1933-39.

MEDIEVAL EGYPT

Wiet, G., *L'Egypte arabe de la conquête arabe à la conquête ottomane, 642-1517*, Paris, 1938 [G. Hanotaux, ed., *Histoire de la nation egyptienne*, Vol. IV].
Lane-Poole, St., *Egypt in the Middle Ages*, London, 1901, 1925.
Wüstenfeld, F., *Geschichte der Fatimidenchalifen*, Göttingen, 1881.
Becker, C. H., *Beiträge zur Geschichte Ägyptens unter dem Islam*, Strassburg, 1911-12.

THE CRUSADES

Stevenson, W. B., *The Crusaders in the East*, Cambridge, 1907.
Grousset, R., *Histoire des croisades et du régime franque à Jerusalem*, 3 vols., Paris, 1934-36.
Gaudefroy-Desmombynes, M., *La Syrie à l'époque des Mamlouks d'après les auteurs arabes*, Paris, 1923.
Atiya, A. S., *The Crusade in the Late Middle Ages*, London, 1938.
Cahen, C., *La Syrie du Nord à l'époque des croisades et la principauté franque d'Antioche*, Paris, 1940 (Inst. Français de Damas, Bibl. Orient., I).

SYRIA

Lammens, H., *La Syrie*, 2 vols., Beyrouth, 1921-38.

CENTRAL ASIA, TURKS, MONGOLS

Howorth, H. H., *History of the Mongols*, London, 1876-1927.
Barthold, W., *Turkestan down to the Time of the Mongol Invasion* [translated by H. A. R. Gibb in the E. J. W. Gibb Memorial Series, New Series, Vol. V] London, 1928.
——, (tr.) *12 Vorlesungen über die Geschichte der Türken Mittelasiens*, Berlin, 1935.
——, *Ulug Beg und seine Zeit*, Leipzig, 1935.
Blochet, E., *Introduction à l'histoire des Mongols* [Gibb Memorial Series, XII].
Cingis Han, Die Geschichte seines Lebens nach den chinesischen Reichannalen, von F. A. Krause [Heidelberger Akten der Portheim-Stiftung], 1935.
Vladimirtzow, B., *The Life of Chingis Khan*, London, 1930.
——, *Social Organization of the Mongols* (in Russian), Leningrad, 1934.
Grousset, R., *L'Empire des steppes*, Paris, 1938.
——, *L'Empire mongol*, Paris, 1941.
Gordlevsky, V., *The Seljuq State* (in Russian), Moscow, 1941.
Sanaullah, M. F., *The Decline of the Seljuqid Empire*, Calcutta, 1938.

THE OTTOMAN TURKS

Hammer-Purgstall, J. von, *Geschichte des osmanischen Reiches*, 10 vols., Pest, 1827-35; 2nd ed. in 4 vols., 1840; French ed., Paris, 1844.

Zinkeisen, J., *Geschichte des osmanischen Reiches in Europa*, 7 vols., Gotha, 1840-63.
Jorga, N., *Geschichte des osmanischen Reiches*, 5 vols., Gotha, 1908-15 (to be used with caution).
Lane-Poole, St., *The Story of Turkey*, New York, 1891.
Jonquière, de la, *Histoire de l'empire ottoman*, 2 vols., Paris, 1914.
Silberschmidt, M., *Beiträge zur Frage der Entstehung des türkischen Reiches nach venezianischen Quellen* (Beitrag zur Kulturgeschichte der Renaissance, herausgegeben von W. Götz), Leipzig, 1923.
Shay, M. L., *The Ottoman Empire from 1720 to 1734 as Revealed in Dispatches of the Venetian Baili*, Urbana, Ill., 1944.
Ranke, L. von, *Die Osmanen und die spanische Monarchie im 16. und 17. Jahrhundert* (Werke 35/36).
Übersberger, H., *Russlands Orientpolitik in den letzten zwei Jahrhunderten*, Stuttgart, 1913.
Rosen, G., *Geschichte der Türkei 1826-1856*, 2 vols., Leipzig, 1866-67.
Ranke, L. von, *Serbien und die Türkei im 19. Jahrhundert* (Werke 42/43).
Sax, C. von, *Geschichte des Machtverfalls der Türkei*, 2nd ed., Vienna, 1913.
Lybyer, A. H., *The Government of the Ottoman Empire in the Time of Suleiman the Magnificent*, Cambridge, Mass., 1913.
Merriman, R. B., *Suleiman the Magnificent*, Cambridge, Mass., 1944.
Miller, W., *The Ottoman Empire and Its Successors, 1801-1927*, Cambridge, 1923, 1936.
Hasluck, F. W., *Christianity and Islam under the Sultans*, 2 vols., Oxford, 1929.
Stripling, G. W. F., *The Ottoman Turks and the Arabs, 1511-1574*, Urbana, Ill., 1942.
Midhat, A. H., *The Life of Midhat Pasha*, London, 1903.
Marriot, J. A. R., *The Eastern Question*, Oxford, 1917, 1940.
Driault, E., *La Question d'Orient*, Paris, 1920.
Earle, E. M., *Turkey, the Great Powers and the Baghdad Railway*, London, 1923.
Puryear, V. J., *International Economics and Diplomacy in the Near East . . . 1834-1853*, Stanford, 1935.
——, *France and the Levant from the Bourbon Restoration to the Peace of Kutiah*, Berkeley, 1941.
Temperley, H. W. V., *England and the Near East: The Crimea*, London, 1936.
Birge, J. K., *The Bektashi Order of Dervishes*, London, 1937.
Castle, W. Th. F., *Grand Turk*, London, 1943.
Bailey, F. E., *British Policy and the Turkish Reform Movement . . . 1826-1853*, Cambridge, Mass., 1942.
Gordon, L., *American Relations with Turkey, 1830-1930*, Philadelphia, 1932.
Miller, B., *Beyond the Sublime Port*, New Haven, 1931.
Yalman, A. E., *Turkey in the World War*, New Haven, 1930.

——, *The Development of Modern Turkey as Measured by Its Press*, New York, 1914.
Sousa, N., *The Capitulory Regime of Turkey*, Baltimore, 1933.
Yücel, H. A., *Ein Gesamtüberblick über die türkische Literatur* (tr.), Istanbul, 1941.
Gibb, E. J. W., *A History of Ottoman Poetry*, London, 1900-09.
Dehérain, H., L'Egypte turque [in Hanotaux, *Histoire de la nation egyptienne*, Vol. V].
Longrigg, S., *Four Centuries of Modern Iraq*, Oxford, 1925.

Egypt in the Nineteenth Century

Lane, E. W., *The Manners and Customs of the Modern Egyptians*, London, 1836.
Sabry, M., *L'Empire egyptien sous Mehemed Ali et la question d'Orient, 1811-49*, Paris, 1930.
Cromer, Earl of, *Modern Egypt*, New York, 1909, 1911.
Douin, G., *Histoire du règne du khedive Ismail*, 3 vols., Rome, 1933-39.
Ghorbal, S., *The Beginnings of the Egyptian Question and the Rise of Mehemet Ali*, London, 1928.
Dodwell, H. H., *The Founder of Modern Egypt*, Cambridge, 1931.
Sammarco, A., *Histoire de l'Egypte moderne*, 3 vols., Paris, 1933-37.
Dicey, E., *The Story of the Khedivate*, New York, 1902.
Charles-Roux, F. J., *L'Egypte de 1801 à 1882* (Hanotaux, *Histoire . . .*, Vol. VI).
Hasenclever, I., *Geschichte Ägyptens im 19. Jahrhundert*, Halle, 1917.
Crouchley, A. E., *The Economic Development of Modern Egypt*, London, 1938.
Rothstein, Th., *Egypt's Ruin*, London, 1910.
Crabites, P., *The Spoilation of Suez*, London, 1943.

The Islamic Countries After 1914

Toynbee, A. J., ed., *Survey of International Affairs*, London, 1925—.
Oriente moderno, 1921—.
Kohn, H., *A History of Nationalism in the East*, London, 1929.
——, *Nationalism and Imperialism in the Hither East*, London, 1932.
——, *Western Civilization in the Near East*, New York, 1936.
Boveri, M., *Minaret and Pipe-Line*, London, 1939.
Woodsmall, R. F., *Moslem Women Enter a New World*, New York, 1936.
Monroe, E., *The Mediterranean in Politics*, London, 1938.
Cumming, H. H., *Franco-British Rivalry in the Post-War Near East*, London, 1938.
Giannini, A., *L'Ultima fase della questione orientale (1913-32)*, Rome, 1933.
——, *Documenti per la storia della pace orientale (1915-32)*, Rome, 1933.
——, *Le Constituzioni degli stati del Vicino Oriente*, Rome, 1931.
Howard, H. N., *The Partition of Turkey*, Norman, Okla., 1931.
Driault, E., *La Question d'Orient 1918-37*, Paris, 1938.

Ireland, Ph. W., ed., *The Near East, Problems and Prospects*, Chicago, 1942.

Davis, H. M., *Constitutions, Electoral Laws, Treaties of States in the Near and Middle East*, Durham, N. C., 1947.

Gibb, H. A. R., ed., *Whither Islam*, London, 1932.

——, *Modern Trends in Islam*, Chicago, 1947.

Bonne, A., *The Economic Development of the Middle East*, New York, 1945.

——, ed., *Statistical Handbook of Middle Eastern Countries*, 2nd ed., Jerusalem, 1945.

TURKEY, 1918–

Mears, E. G., *Modern Turkey*, New York, 1925.

Blaisdell, D. C., *European Financial Control in the Ottoman Empire*, New York, 1929.

Toynbee, A. J., and Kirkwood, K. P., *Turkey*, New York, 1927.

Mikush-Buchberg, D., *Mustafa Kemal* (tr.), New York, 1931.

Allen, H. E., *The Turkish Transformation*, Chicago, 1935.

Kral, A. von, *Kamal Ataturk's Land*, London, 1938.

Webster, D. E., *The Turkey of Ataturk*, Philadelephia, 1939.

Shotwell, J. T., and Deak, F., *Turkey at the Straits*, New York, 1940.

Parker, J., and Smith, Ch., *Modern Turkey*, London, 1942.

Ward, B., *Turkey*, Oxford, 1942.

Jackh, E., *The Rising Crescent*, New York, 1944.

Tobin, Ch. M., *Turkey, Key to the East*, New York, 1944.

Spies, O., *Türkische Prosaliteratur der Gegenwart*, Berlin, 1943.

EGYPT

Charles-Roux, F. J., and Dehérain, H., in Hanotaux, *Histoire . . .*, Vol. VII, 1941.

Lloyd, Lord, *Egypt since Cromer*, 2 vols., London, 1933-34.

Young, G., *Egypt*, London, 1927.

Isawi, Ch., *Egypt*, London, 1947.

L'Egypte indépendante (Centre d'Etudes de Politique Etrangère, Travaux des groupes d'études, Vol. VII), Paris, 1938.

Youssef Bey, Amin, *Independent Egypt*, London, 1940.

Cleland, W., *The Population Problem in Egypt*, Lancaster, Pa., 1936.

Mboria, L., *La Population de l'Egypte*, Cairo, 1938.

SUDAN

Dehérain, H., in Hanotaux, *Histoire de la nation egyptienne*, Vols. VI, VII.

Behrmann, R. A., *The Mahdi of Allah*, London, 1932.

Hogben, S. J., *The Muhammadan Emirates of Nigeria*, Oxford, 1929.

Macmichael, H. A., *A History of the Arabs in the Sudan*, London, 1922.

Dujarric, G., *L'Etat mahdiste du Soudan*, Paris, 1899.

——, *La Vie du sultan Rabah*, Paris, 1899.

THE ARABS

Antonius, G., *The Arab Awakening*, London, 1938, New York, 1946.
Rossi, E., *Documenti sull' origine e gli sviluppi della questione araba (1875-1944)*, Rome, 1944.
Topf, E., *Die Staatenbildung in den arabischen Teilen der Türkei seit dem Weltkriege*, Hamburg, 1929.
Jung, E., *La Revolte arabe*, 2 vols., Paris, 1924-25.
——, *L'Islam et l'Asie devant l'impérialisme*, Paris, 1927.
Jovelet, L., *L'Evolution sociale et politique des "pays arabes" (1930-33)* [*Revue des etudes islamiques*], Paris, 1933.
Hüber, R., *Arabisches Wirtschaftsleben*, Heidelberg, 1943.
Abramovich, Z., and Guelfat, I., *Arab Economics* (in Hebrew), Tel Aviv, 1944.

ARABIA

Hurgronje, Chr. Snouck, *Mekka in the Latter Part of the 19th Century* (tr.), London, 1931.
Jacob, H. F., *Kings of Arabia*, London, 1938.
Rihani, A., *Ibn Saud of Arabia*, London, 1928.
——, *Arabian Peak and Desert*, New York, 1938.
——, *Around the Coast of Arabia*, Boston, 1930.
Philby, H. St. John B., *Arabia of the Wahhabis*, London, 1928.
——, *Arabia*, London, 1930.
Williams, K., *Ibn Saud*, London, 1933.
Armstrong, H. C., *Lord of Arabia*, London, 1934.
Twitchell, K. S., *Saudi Arabia*, Princeton, 1947.
Scott, H., *In the High Yemen*, London, 1942.
Helfritz, H., *Land without Shade*, New York, 1936.
Ingrams, H., *Arabia and the Isles*, London, 1942.
Wilson, A. T., *The Persian Gulf*, London, 1928.
Thomas, B., *Arabia Felix*, Toronto, 1932.
Stark, F., *The Southern Gates of Arabia*, New York, 1936.
——, *Seen in the Hadramauth*, New York, 1938.
——, *Winter in Arabia*, London, 1940.

SYRIA

Hourani, A. K., *Syria and Lebanon*, Oxford, 1946.

'IRAQ

Main, E., *Iraq—from Mandate to Independence*, London, 1935.
Foster, H. A., *The Making of Modern Iraq*, Norman, Okla., 1935, 1946.
Ireland, Ph. W., *Iraq*, London, 1937.
Facts and Prospects in Iraq series, 1944-45.
Van Ess, J., *Meet the Arab*, New York, 1943.

PALESTINE

The Government of Palestine, *Survey of Palestine*, 2 vols., Jerusalem, 1946.

Royal Institute of International Affairs, Information Paper No. 20, *Great Britain and Palestine, 1915-1945*, New York, 1946.

Hanna, P. L., *British Policy in Palestine*, Washington, 1942.

Nathan, R., Gass, O., and Creamer, D., *Palestine, Problem and Promise*, Washington, D. C., 1946.

Shim'oni, J., *The Arabs of Palestine* (in Hebrew), Tel Aviv, 1947.

Revusky, A., *The Jews in Palestine*, New York, 1945.

Cohen, I., *The Zionist Movement*, New York, 1946.

Böhm, A., *Die zionistische Bewegung*, 2 vols., Berlin and Tel Aviv, 1935-37.

Palestine: A Study of Jewish, Arab and British Policies (Esco Foundation study), 2 vols., New Haven, 1947.

Cf. sections in G. Antonius, *The Arab Awakening*, and A. H. Hourani, *Syria and Lebanon*.

Jeffries, J. M. N., *Palestine, the Reality*, London, 1939.

Crossman, R., *Palestine Mission*, New York, 1947.

Crum, B. C., *Behind the Silken Curtain*, New York, 1947.

TRANSJORDAN

Konikoff, A., *Transjordan, Economic Survey*, 2nd ed., Jerusalem, 1946.

IRAN *(Persia), Afghanistan, Nineteenth and Twentieth Centuries*

Browne, E. G., *A Year amongst the Persians* (1887-88), London, 1893.

——, *The Persian Revolution of 1905-09*, Cambridge, 1910.

——, *A Brief Narrative of Recent Events in Persia*, London, 1909.

Ellwell-Sutton, L. P., *Modern Iran*, London, 1942.

Haas, W. S., *Iran*, New York, 1946.

Millspaugh, A. C., *Americans in Persia*, Washington, 1946.

Sheean, V., *The New Persia*, New York, 1927.

Nakhai, M., *L'Evolution politique de l'Iran*, Paris, 1938.

Fox, E. F., *Travels in Afghanistan*, New York, 1943.

Schwager, J., *Die Entwicklung Afghanistans als Staat*, (Abh. des Inst. für Politik an der Univ. Leipzig, Heft 24), Leipzig, 1932.

Trinkler, E., *Through the Heart of Afghanistan*, London, 1928.

Ikbal Ali Shah, *Modern Afghanistan*, London, 1939.

Angus, H., *Afghanistan*, London, 1906.

NORTH AFRICA

Knight, M. M., *Morocco as a French Economic Venture*, New York, 1937.

Mellor, F. H., *Morocco Awakens*, London, 1939.

Usborn, C. V., *The Conquest of Morocco*, London, 1936.

Pellegrin, A., *Histoire de la Tunisie*, Paris, 1938.

Worsfold, W. B., *France in Tunisia and Algeria.*
Alzoune, C., *L'Algérie*, Paris, 1940.
Brodrick, A. H., *North Africa*, New York, 1943.
Liebesny, H. S., *The Government of French North Africa*, Philadelphia, 1943.
Albertini, E., Marcais, A. Y., and Yver, G., *L'Afrique du Nord française dans l'histoire*, Paris, 1937.

WORLD WAR II AND AFTER

Baker, R. L., *Oil, Blood and Sand*, New York, 1942.
Michie, A., *Retreat to Victory*, New York, 1942.
Arberry, A. J., and Landau, R., eds., *Islam To-Day*, London, 1943.
Chair, S. de, *The Golden Carpet*, New York, 1945.
Stark, F., *The Arab Island*, New York, 1946.
Speiser, E., *The United States and the Near East*, Cambridge, Mass., 1947.
Visson, A., The Coming Struggle for Peace, New York, 1945.
Articles in:
Foreign Affairs, New York
International Affairs, London, Toronto
Round Table, London
The Middle East Journal, Washington, D. C., 1947–
Journal of the Royal Central Asian Society.

The *Cambridge Medieval History* and the *Cambridge Modern History* contain a number of chapters on the Islamic countries.

Islam in the framework of world history is discussed in:

Toynbee, J. A., *The Study of History*, Oxford, 1934–.
Halphen, L., *Les Barbares, des grandes invasions aux conquêtes turqes du XI siècle*, Paris, 1926 . . . 1940.
Pirenne, H., *Mohammed and Charlemagne* (tr.), New York, 1939.
Caetani, L., *La Funzione dell' Islam nell' evoluzione della civiltà*, Rome, 1912.
Becker, C. H., in his *Islamstudien;* ["The Origin and Character of Islamic Civilization" and "Islam as a Problem" translated in S. Khuda Buksh, *Contributions to the History of Islamic Civilization*, II, Calcutta, 1930].
Schaeder, H. H., "*Der Orient und die griechische Erbe,*" in *Die Antike*, 1928.
Allbright, W. F., "Islam and the Religious of the Ancient Orient," in *Journal of the Oriental Society*, 1940.
Levi della Vida, G., "Dominant Ideas in the Formation of Islamic Culture," in *Crozier Quarterly*, 1944.

*Index**

I. PERSONS, TRIBES, PEOPLES, SECTS

* The sounds a and e are easily interchangeable. For names beginning with K consult also under Q.

II. GEOGRAPHICAL